George Washington

This statue of George Washington, cast from bronze, is in Alexandria, Virginia. Located on the Potomac River, Alexandria lies a few miles south of the nation's capital, Washington, D.C. Find out more about George Washington at: www.harcourtschool.com

Reflections

The United States:

MAKING A NEW NATION

Orlando Austin New York San Diego Toronto London

Visit *The Learning Site!* www.harcourtschool.com

MAPQUEST®   TIME® FOR KIDS

HARCOURT SCHOOL PUBLISHERS 

Reflections

THE UNITED STATES: MAKING A NEW NATION

Senior Author

Dr. Priscilla H. Porter
Professor Emeritus
School of Education
California State University, Dominguez Hills
Center for History–Social Science Education
Carson, California

Series Authors

Dr. Michael J. Berson
Associate Professor
Social Science Education
University of South Florida
Tampa, Florida

Dr. Margaret Hill
History–Social Science Coordinator
San Bernardino County Superintendent of Schools
Director, Schools of California Online Resources for Education: History–Social Science
San Bernardino, California

Dr. Tyrone C. Howard
Assistant Professor
UCLA Graduate School of Education & Information Studies
University of California at Los Angeles
Los Angeles, California

Dr. Bruce E. Larson
Associate Professor
Social Science Education
Secondary Education
Woodring College of Education
Western Washington University
Bellingham, Washington

Dr. Julio Moreno
Assistant Professor
Department of History
University of San Francisco
San Francisco, California

Series Consultants

Martha Berner
Consulting Teacher
Cajon Valley Union School District
San Diego County, California

Dr. James Charkins
Professor of Economics
California State University
San Bernardino, California
Executive Director of California Council on Economic Education

Rhoda Coleman
K–12 Reading Consultant Lecturer
California State University, Dominguez Hills
Carson, California

Dr. Robert Kumamoto
Professor
History Department
San Jose State University
San Jose, California

Carlos Lossada
Co-Director Professional Development Specialist
UCLA History–Geography Project
University of California, Los Angeles
Regional Coordinator, California Geographic Alliance
Los Angeles, California

Dr. Tanis Thorne
Director of Native Studies
Lecturer in History
Department of History
University of California, Irvine
Irvine, California

Rebecca Valbuena
Los Angeles County Teacher of the Year—2004–05
Language Development Specialist
Stanton Elementary School
Glendora Unified School District
Glendora, California

Dr. Phillip VanFossen
Associate Professor, Social Studies Education
Associate Director, Purdue Center for Economic Education
Department of Curriculum
Purdue University
West Lafayette, Indiana

Grade-Level Author

Dr. Thelma Foote
Associate Professor of History and African American Studies
Department of History
University of California, Irvine
Irvine, California

Content Reviewers

Dr. Shalanda Dexter-Rodgers
Assistant Professor
Department of Ethnic Studies
University of California, San Diego
San Diego, California

Dr. Walter Fleming
Department Head and Associate Professor
Native American Studies
Montana State University
Bozeman, Montana

Dr. Robert Green, Jr.
Professor
School of Education
Clemson University
Clemson, South Carolina

Dr. John P. Kaminski
Director, Center for the Study of the American Constitution
Department of History
University of Wisconsin
Madison, Wisconsin

Dr. Thomas D. Mays
Assistant Professor
Department of History
Humboldt State University
Arcata, California

Dr. Marilyn J. Westerkamp
Professor
Department of History
University of California, Santa Cruz
Santa Cruz, California

Dr. Pearl Ponce
Assistant Professor
History Department
California State University, San Bernardino
San Bernardino, California

Dr. Jack Rakove
W.R. Coe Professor of History and American Studies
Department of History
Stanford University
Stanford, California

Dr. Eugene Volokh
Professor
UCLA School of Law
Los Angeles, California

Classroom Reviewers and Contributors

Elly Alvarado
Teacher
Baird Middle School
Fresno, California

Brian Arcuri
Teacher
Longfellow Elementary School
San Francisco, California

Pamela Brown
Teacher
Hearst Elementary School
San Diego, California

Michelle Ferrer
Teacher
John Muir Elementary School
Long Beach, California

Ken Johnson
Teacher
Pinewood Elementary School
Tujunga, California

Robin Sischo
Teacher
Bullard TALENT School
Fresno, California

Hiromi Somawang
Teacher
Baird Middle School
Fresno, California

Helen Tross
Teacher
Santa Ana Unified
School District Office
Santa Ana, California

Maps
researched and prepared by

Readers
written and designed by

Acknowledgments appear in the back of this book.

Printed in the United States of America

ISBN 0-15-338503-0

5 6 7 8 9 10 048 15 14 13 12 11 10 09 08 07

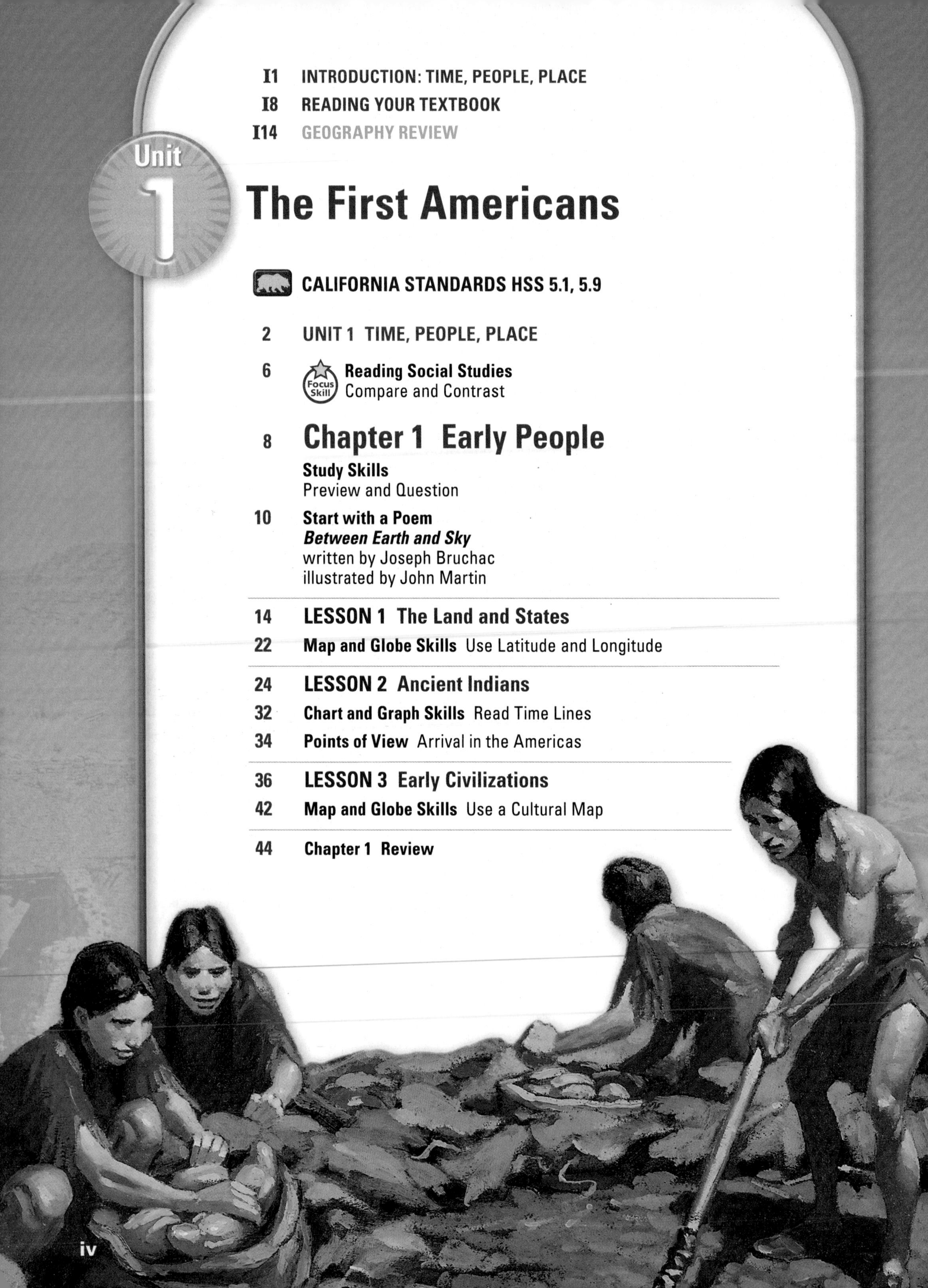

Unit 1

The First Americans

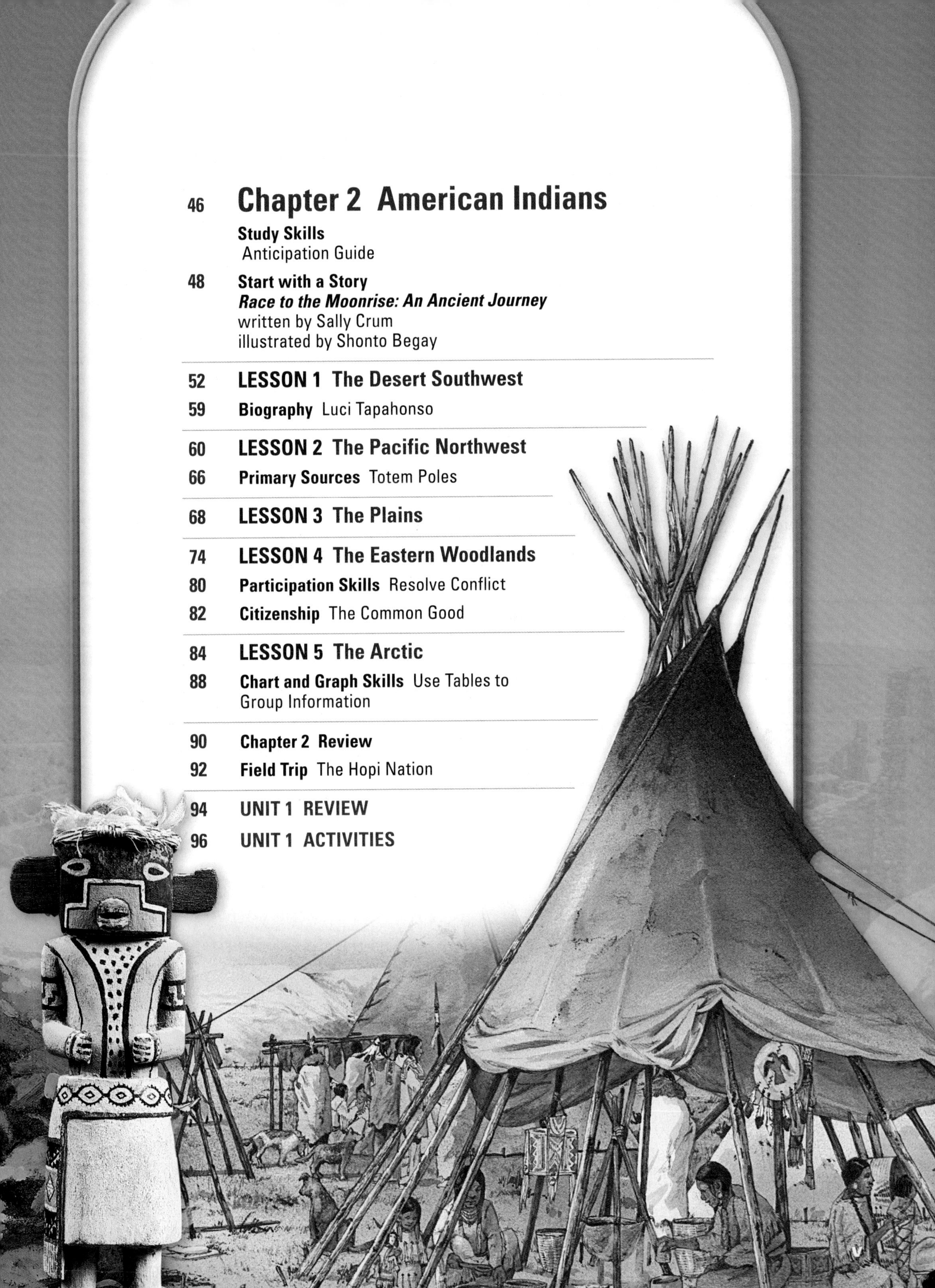

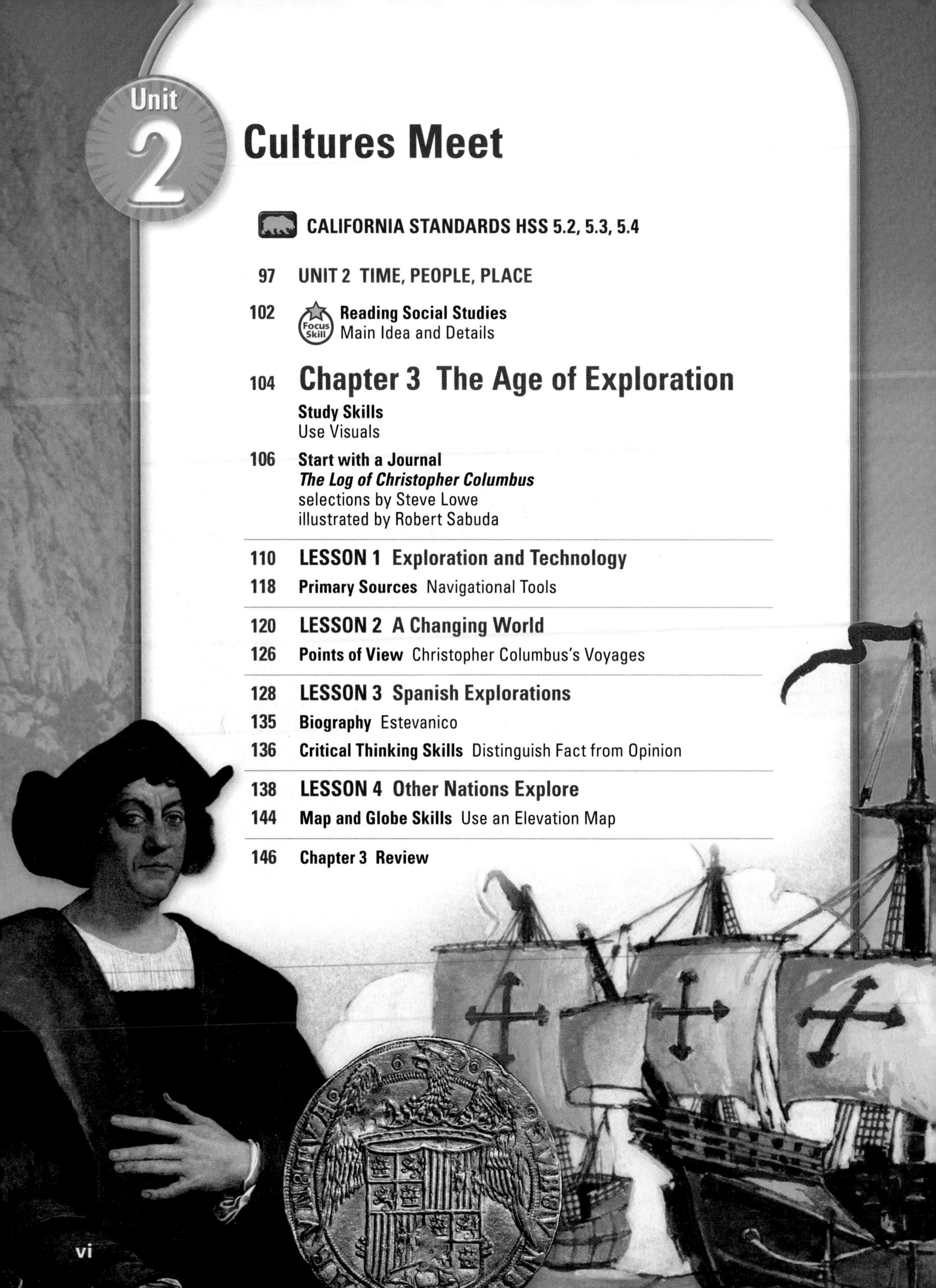

Unit 2

Cultures Meet

CALIFORNIA STANDARDS HSS 5.2, 5.3, 5.4

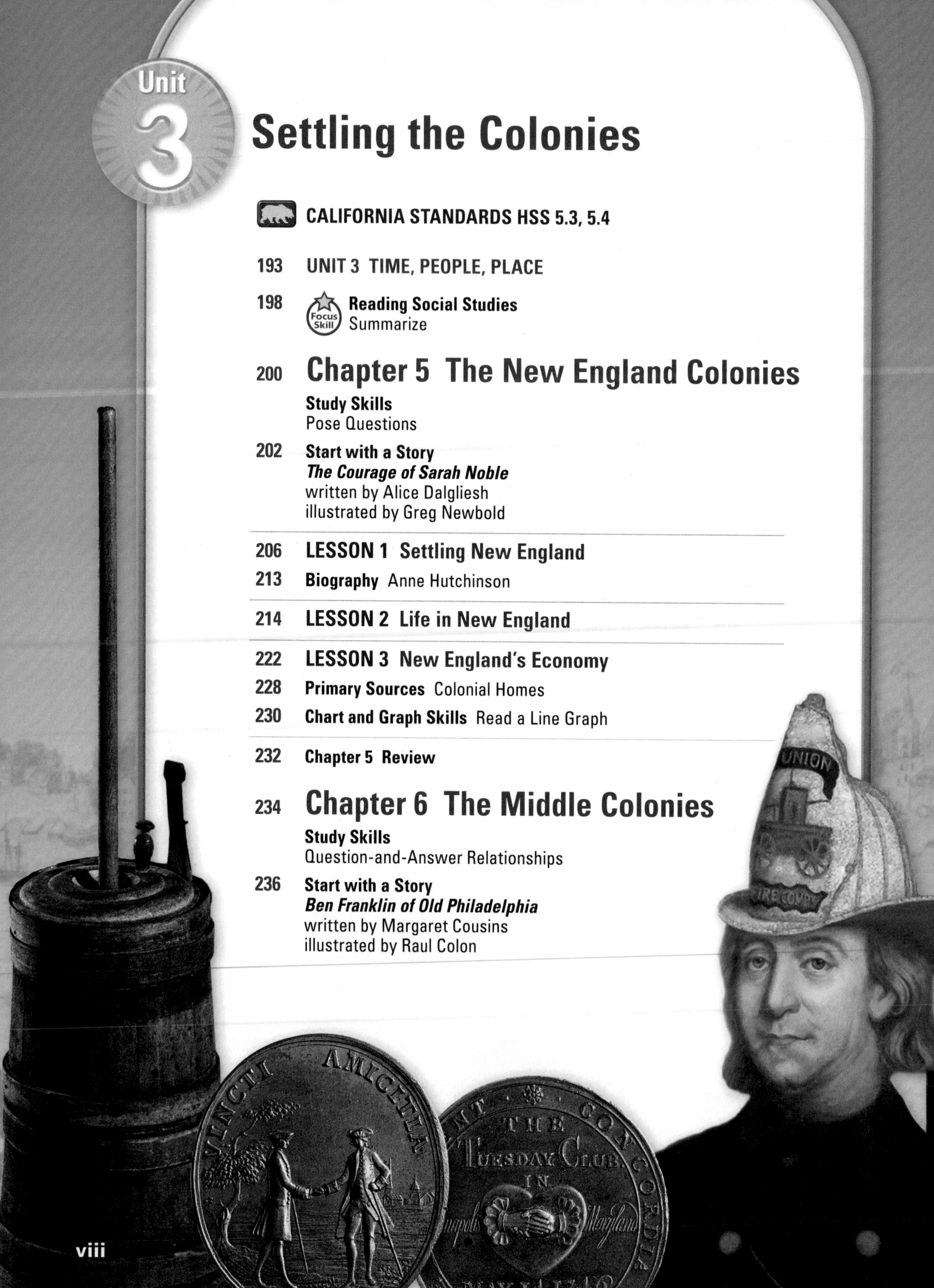

Unit 3

Settling the Colonies

CALIFORNIA STANDARDS HSS 5.3, 5.4

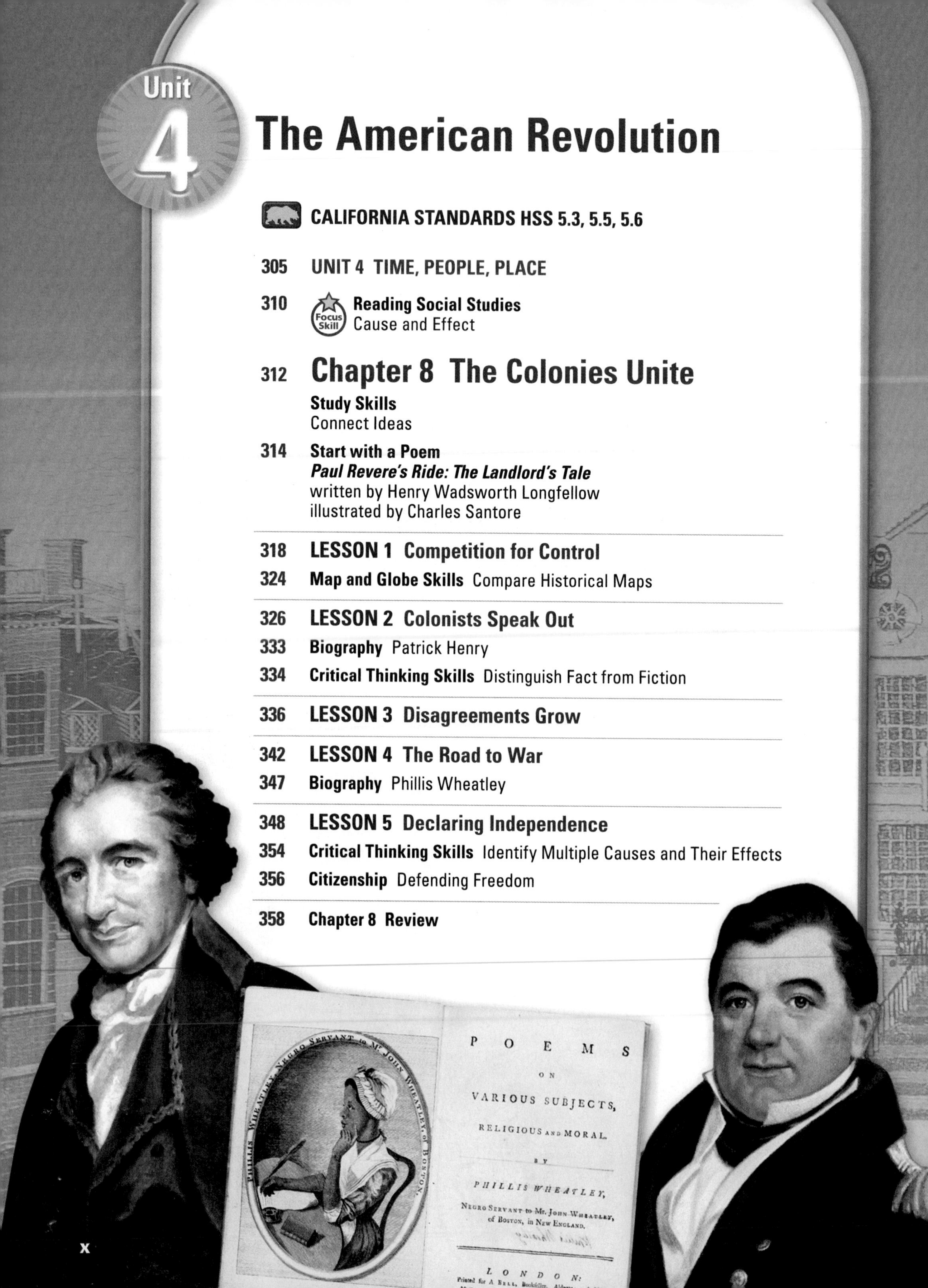

Unit 4 The American Revolution

CALIFORNIA STANDARDS HSS 5.3, 5.5, 5.6

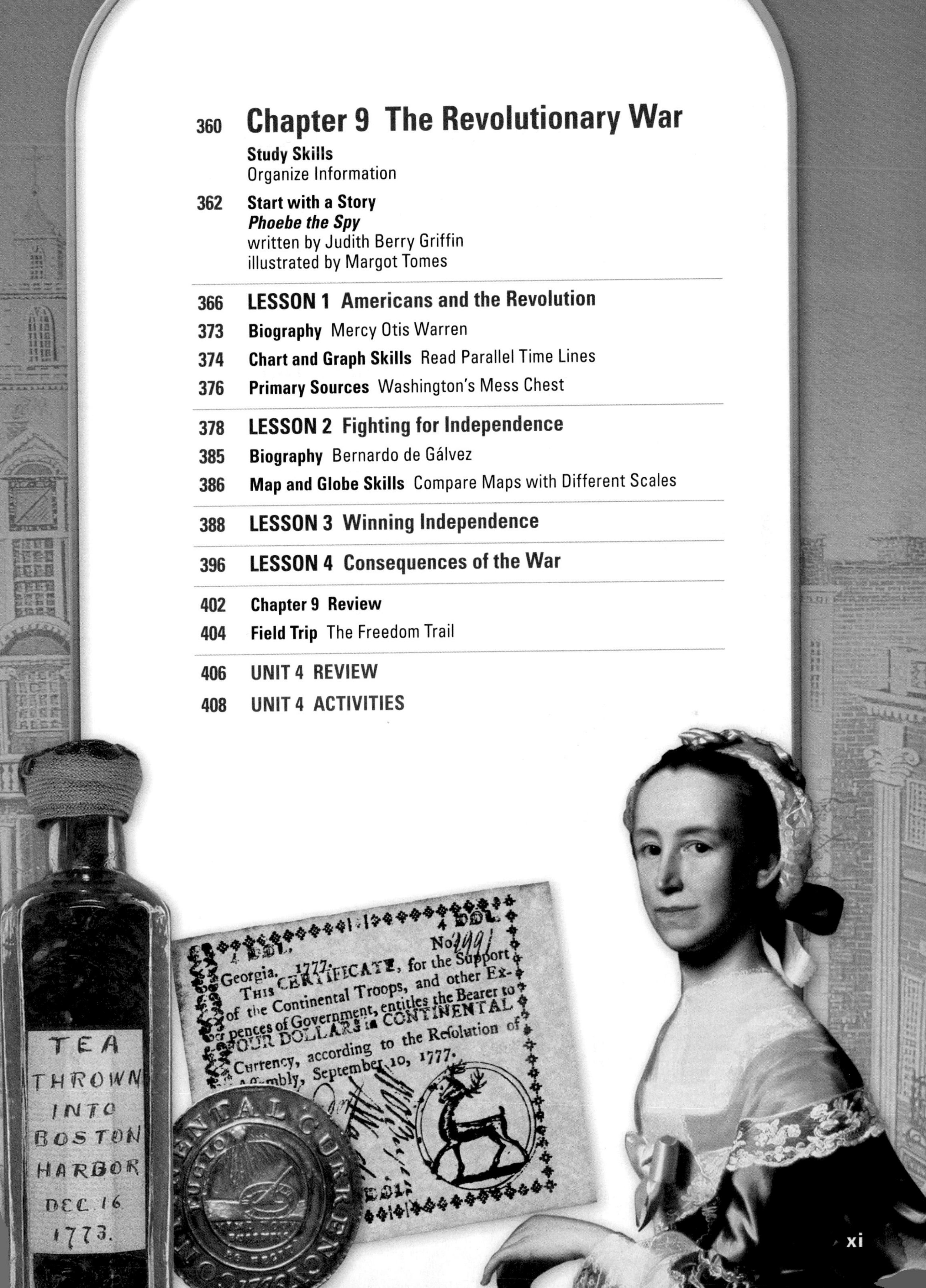
4 DOL.
No. 2991
Georgia, 1777.
THIS CERTIFICATE, for the Support of the Continental Troops, and other Expences of Government, entitles the Bearer to FOUR DOLLARS in CONTINENTAL Currency, according to the Resolution of Assembly, September 10, 1777.
TEA
THROWN
INTO
BOSTON
HARBOR
DEC. 16
1773.

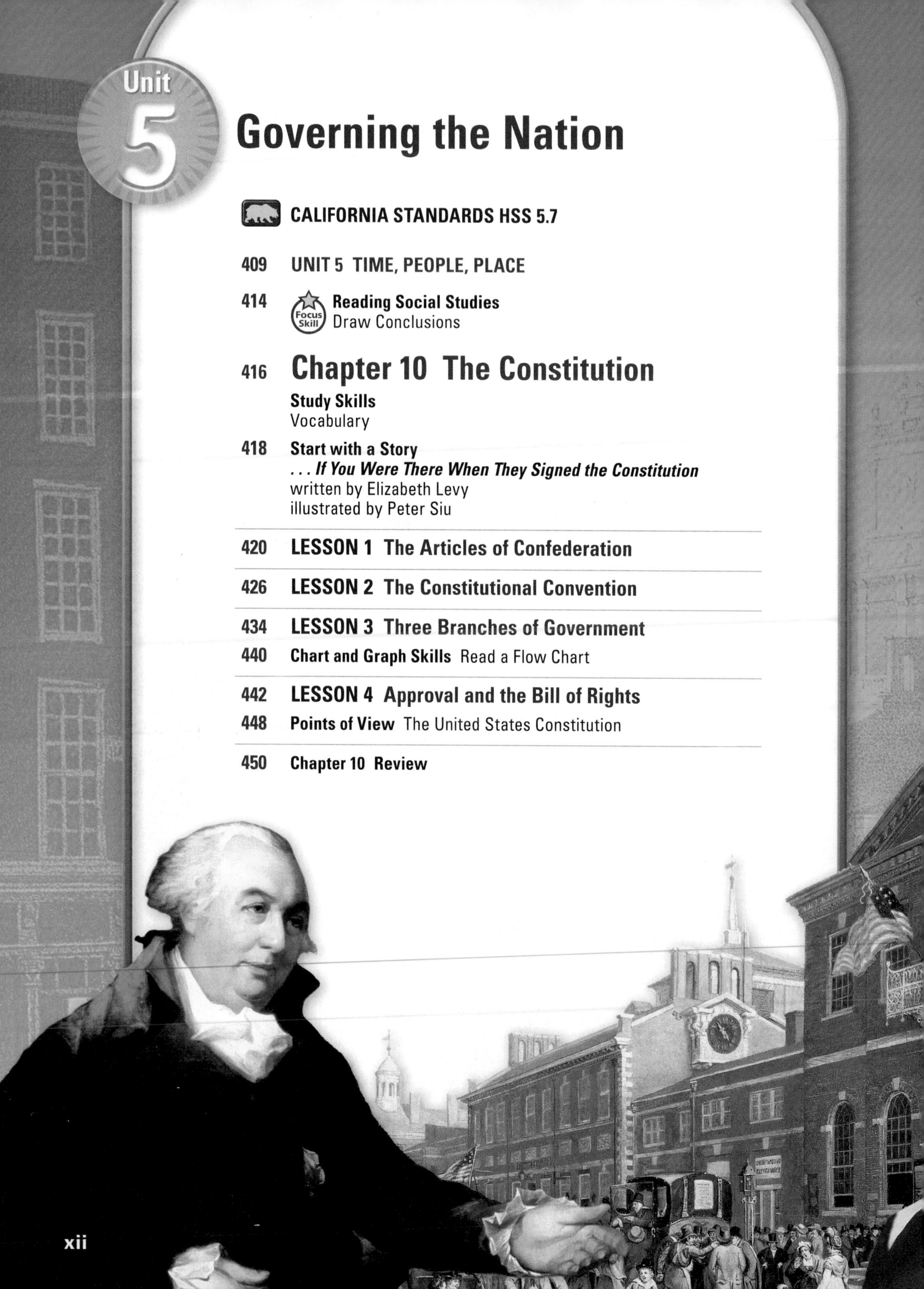

Unit 5

Governing the Nation

CALIFORNIA STANDARDS HSS 5.7

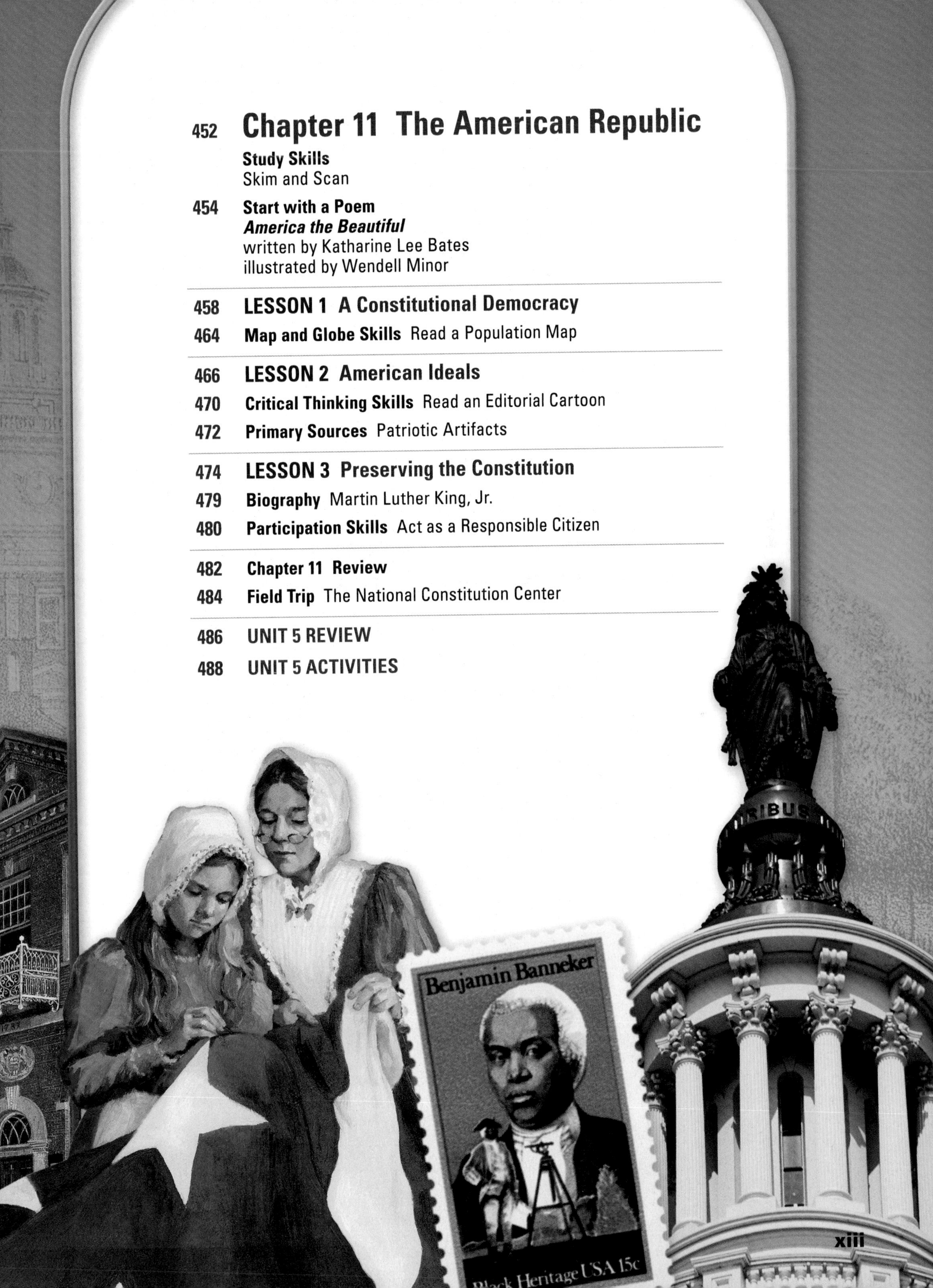

Benjamin Banneker
Black Heritage USA 15c

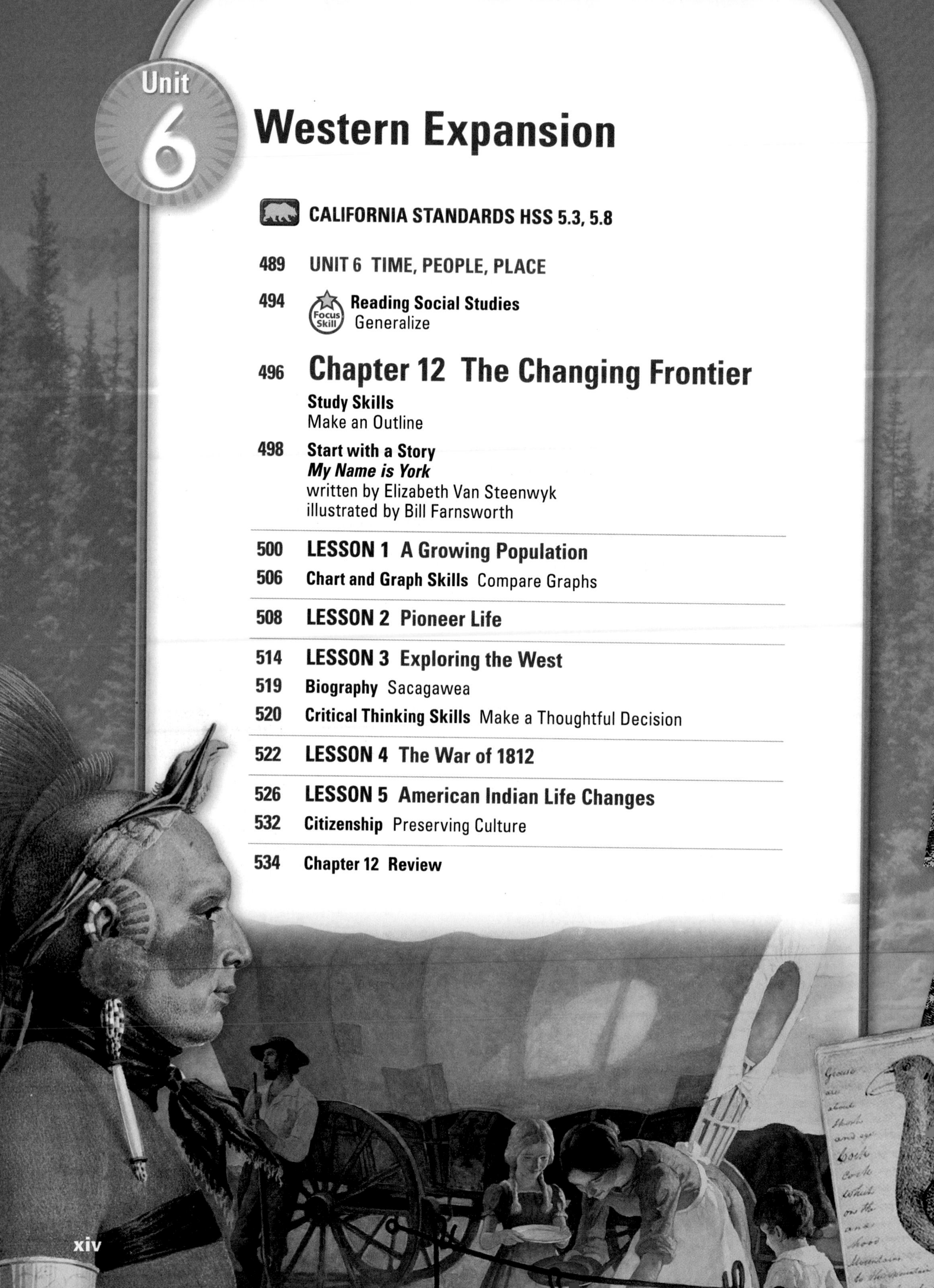

Unit 6

Western Expansion

CALIFORNIA STANDARDS HSS 5.3, 5.8

FOR YOUR REFERENCE

Features

Skills

CHART AND GRAPH SKILLS

CRITICAL THINKING SKILLS

MAP AND GLOBE SKILLS

PARTICIPATION SKILLS

READING SOCIAL STUDIES

STUDY SKILLS

Citizenship

Points of View

Literature and Music

Primary Sources

Documents

Biography

Geography

Cultural Heritage

Children in History

Field Trips

Visual Literacy

CHARTS, GRAPHS, AND DIAGRAMS

MAPS

Time Lines

A Closer Look

The Story Well Told

"The history of every country begins with the heart of a man or a woman."*

Willa Cather, *O Pioneers*

Have you ever wondered how the United States of America came to be and how its past continues to affect you today? This year you will find out. You will be studying the early history of the United States and its geography. You will read about what it was like to live during the **time** when important events in our nation took place. You will learn about some of the **people** who took part in those events and about the **place** where each event occurred. Read now the story of *The United States: Making a New Nation.*

*Willa Cather. *O Pioneers!* Buccaneer Books, Inc. 1993.

The United States:

MAKING A NEW NATION

The Story of The United States is about Time

Studying history helps you see how the present and the past are connected. It helps you identify both similarities and differences between the past and the present. It also helps you see how some things change over time and some things stay the same. As you learn to recognize these links, you will begin to think more like a historian—a person who studies the past.

Historians **research**, or investigate, the time in which events happened by looking for clues in the objects and documents that people left behind. They read diaries, journal entries, letters, newspaper articles, and other writings by people who experienced the events. They look at photographs, films, and artwork. They also listen to oral histories—stories told aloud by people who lived at the time. By examining such **evidence**, or proof, historians are better able to piece together the historical context for events—what the world was like at the time an event took place. The context helps them **interpret** the past and explain why events happened as they did.

To interpret the past accurately, historians must look closely at how events are connected to one another. They can better see such connections by studying the **chronology**, or time order, in which events happened. One way historians do this is by using time lines. A time line allows historians to place in chronological order key events from the period, or era, they are studying. A time line can also suggest how one event may have led to another.

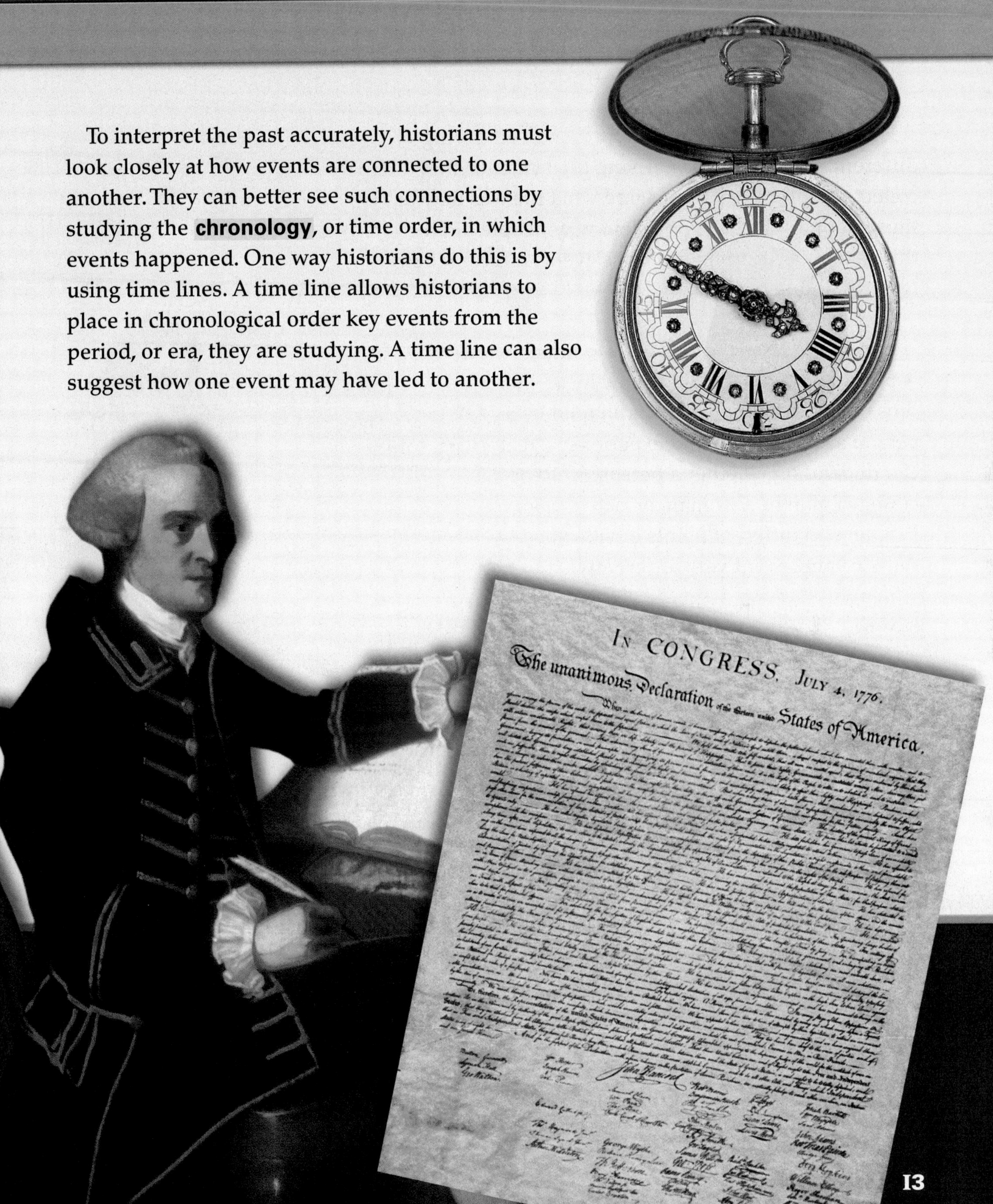

In CONGRESS. July 4, 1776.

The unanimous Declaration of the thirteen united States of America.

The Story of The United States is about People

Historians research the people who lived during different times in the past. Using the evidence they collect, historians try to imagine what life was like for those people. They try to explain why people did the things they did and how various events affected their feelings and beliefs.

Historians also study people's points of views. A person's **point of view** is how he or she sees things. A point of view is shaped by a person's background and experiences. It can depend on whether a person is old or young, a man or a woman, or rich or poor. People with different points of view may see the same event very differently.

People from the past can serve as role models for how to act—or how not to act—when troubling events occur. Historians identify key **character traits**, such as trustworthiness, respect, responsibility, fairness, compassion, and patriotism, that people from the past displayed. They look at how these character traits help make people good leaders, then and now.

The Story of The United States is about  Place

In addition to looking at the time in which events took place and the people who took part in them, historians must also consider the places in which those events occurred. Every place on Earth has features that set it apart from all other locations. Often, those features affected where events occurred. They may also have affected why the events unfolded as they did.

Maps can help historians to better understand the unique characteristics of a particular place. Maps show a place's location, but they can also tell historians about the land and the people who lived there—the routes people followed, where they settled, and how they used the land.

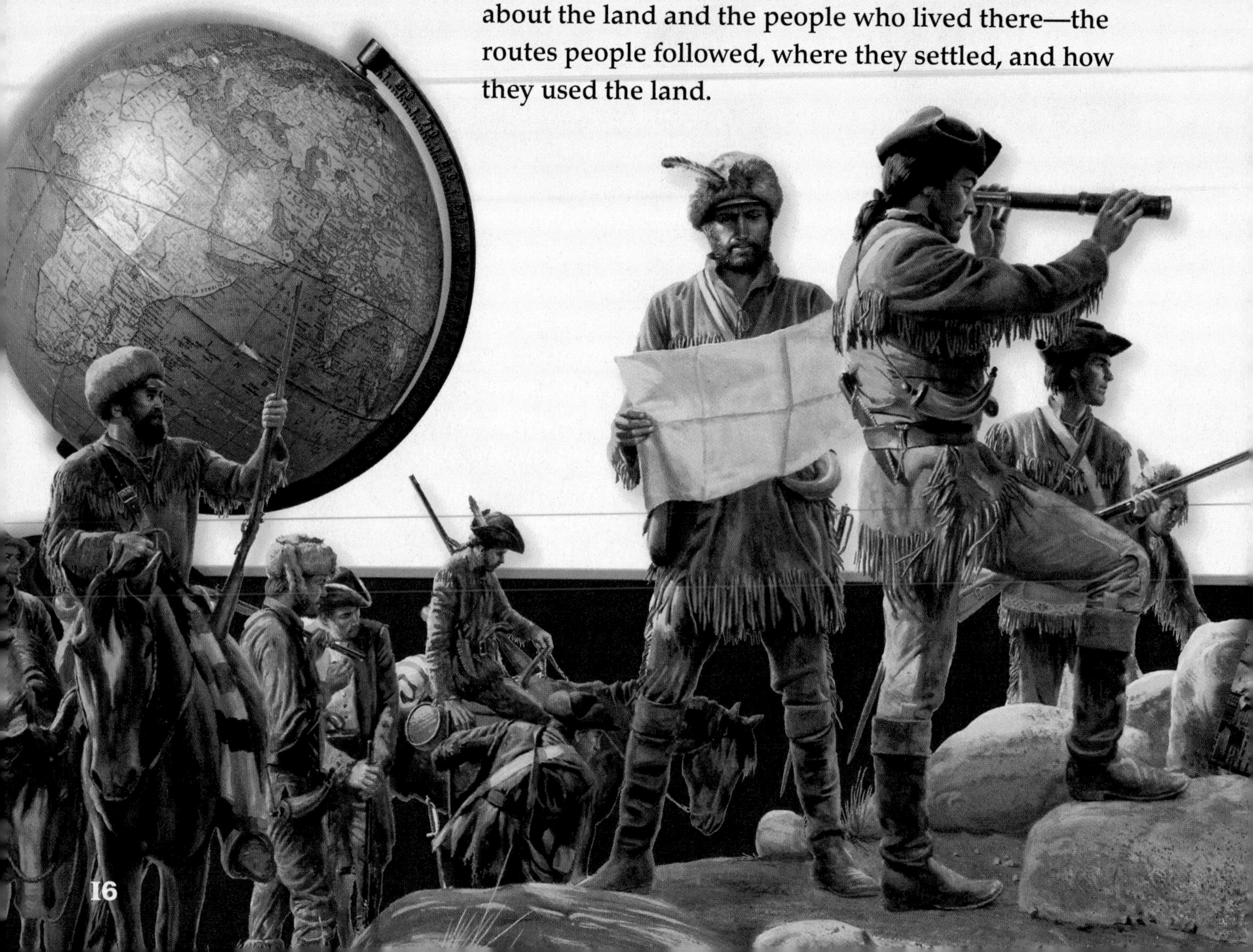

Maps, like other kinds of evidence, help historians more accurately write the story of the past. They are just one valuable tool that historians use to better understand how time, people, and place are connected.

Reading Your Textbook

GETTING STARTED

Unit Title

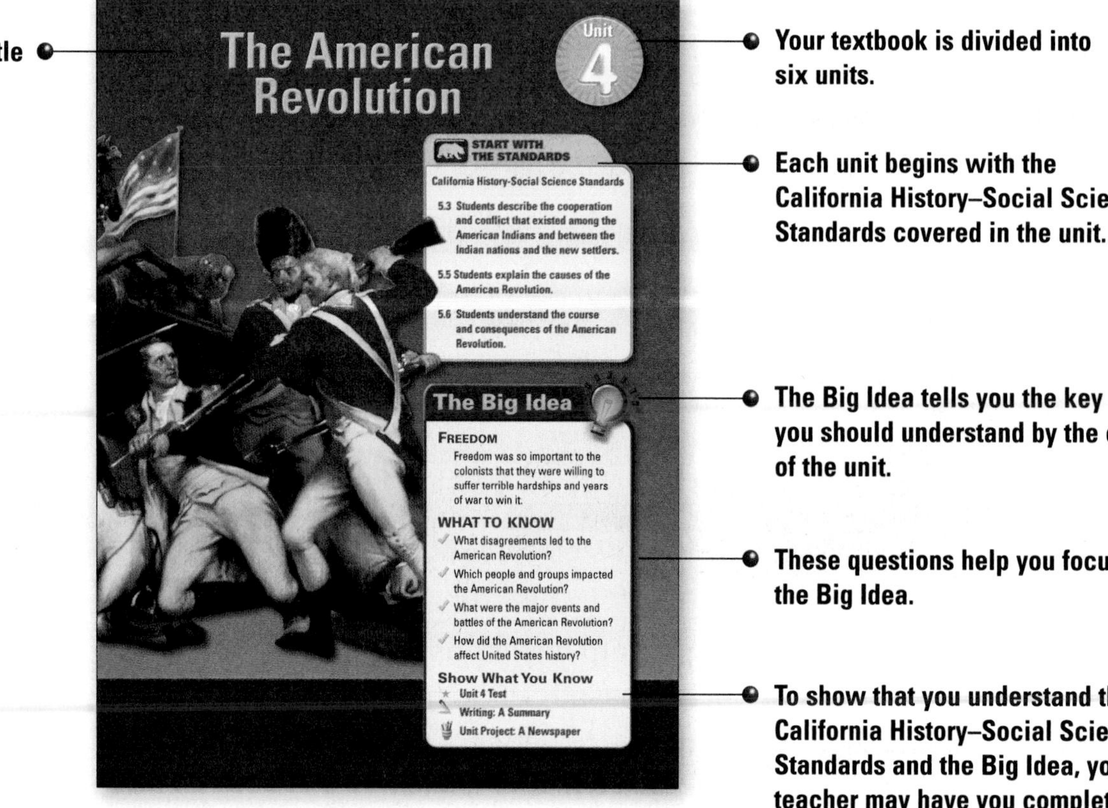

Your textbook is divided into six units.

Each unit begins with the California History–Social Science Standards covered in the unit.

The Big Idea tells you the key idea you should understand by the end of the unit.

These questions help you focus on the Big Idea.

To show that you understand the California History–Social Science Standards and the Big Idea, your teacher may have you complete one or more of these.

LOOKING AT TIME, PEOPLE, AND PLACE

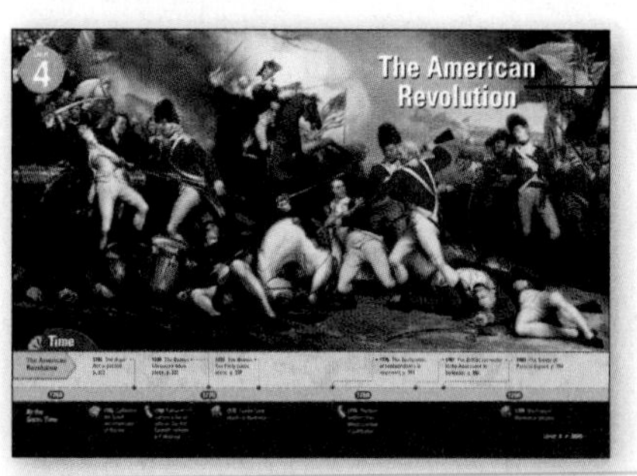

TIME pages identify important events and tell you when those events took place. You will read about these events in the unit.

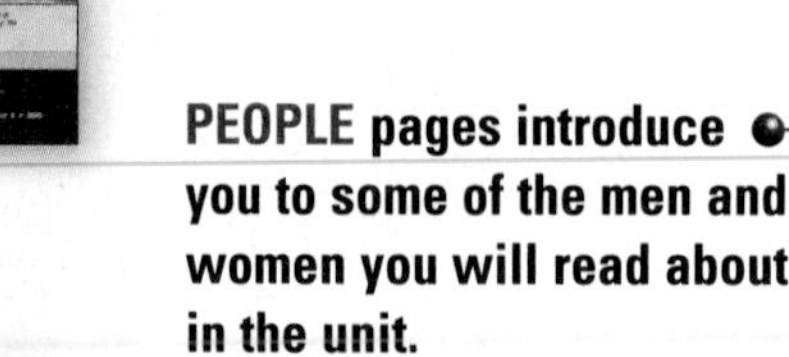

PEOPLE pages introduce you to some of the men and women you will read about in the unit.

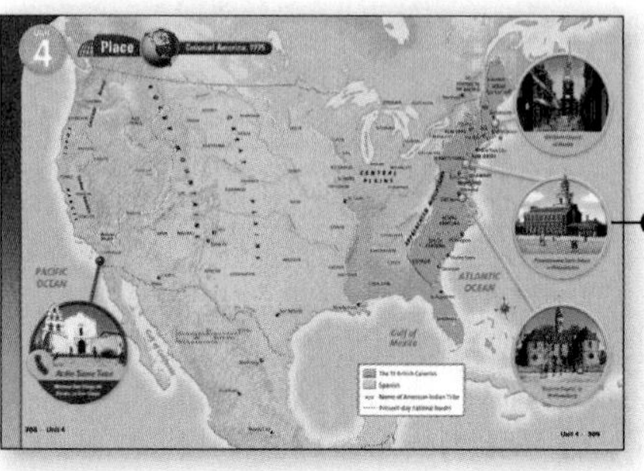

PLACE pages show where some of the events in the unit took place.

READING SOCIAL STUDIES

The Reading Social Studies Focus Skill will help you better understand the events you read about and make connections among them.

This statement describes the Focus Skill.

The Focus Skill is modeled for you, and you are asked to practice it.

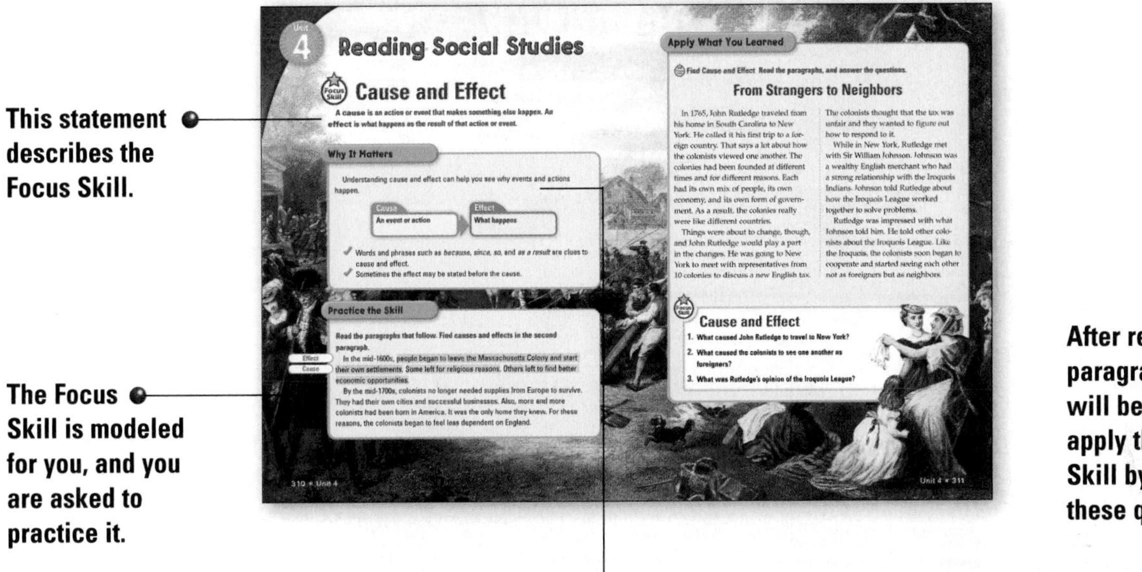

After reading some paragraphs, you will be asked to apply the Focus Skill by answering these questions.

This statement explains why this Focus Skill is important.

BEGINNING A CHAPTER

Each unit is divided into chapters, and each chapter is divided into lessons.

This Study Skill provides you with a strategy that you can use to remember and organize what you read.

Each chapter has a list of the California History–Social Science Standards covered in the chapter.

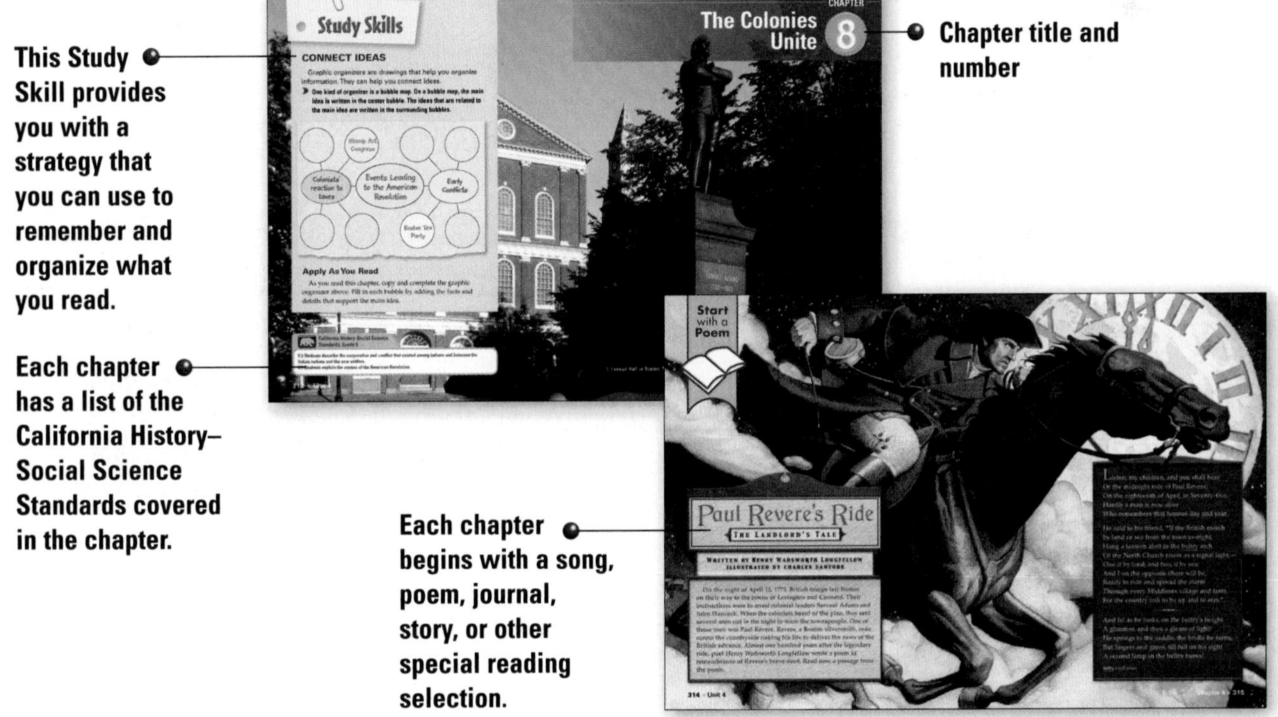

Chapter title and number

Each chapter begins with a song, poem, journal, story, or other special reading selection.

READING A LESSON

This question helps you focus on the lesson's main idea.

These statements tell you what you should be able to do at the end of the lesson.

Some of the people and places you will read about are listed.

Remember to apply the Reading Social Studies Focus Skill as you read the lesson.

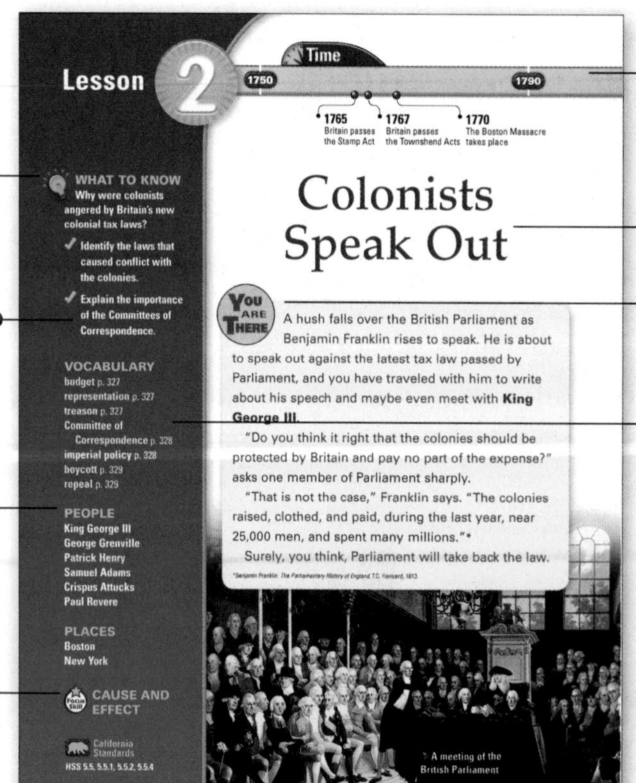

Lesson 2

Time

1750 — 1790

1765 Britain passes the Stamp Act

1767 Britain passes the Townshend Acts

1770 The Boston Massacre takes place

WHAT TO KNOW
Why were colonists angered by Britain's new colonial tax laws?

✓ Identify the laws that caused conflict with the colonies.

✓ Explain the importance of the Committees of Correspondence.

VOCABULARY
budget p. 327
representation p. 327
treason p. 327
Committee of Correspondence p. 328
imperial policy p. 328
boycott p. 329
repeal p. 329

PEOPLE
King George III
George Grenville
Patrick Henry
Samuel Adams
Crispus Attucks
Paul Revere

PLACES
Boston
New York

CAUSE AND EFFECT

California Standards
HSS 5.5, 5.5.1, 5.5.2, 5.5.4

326 ▪ Unit 4

Colonists Speak Out

YOU ARE THERE A hush falls over the British Parliament as Benjamin Franklin rises to speak. He is about to speak out against the latest tax law passed by Parliament, and you have traveled with him to write about his speech and maybe even meet with **King George III**.

"Do you think it right that the colonies should be protected by Britain and pay no part of the expense?" asks one member of Parliament sharply.

"That is not the case," Franklin says. "The colonies raised, clothed, and paid, during the last year, near 25,000 men, and spent many millions."*

Surely, you think, Parliament will take back the law.

*Benjamin Franklin. The Parliamentary History of England. T.C. Hansard, 1813.

A meeting of the British Parliament

A time line shows when some of the key events in the lesson took place.

Lesson title

You Are There puts you in the time when events in the lesson took place.

These are the new vocabulary terms you will learn in the lesson.

Some lessons have special features in which you can read about Citizenship, Children in History, Geography, Primary Sources, and Points of View.

PRIMARY SOURCES

Stamp Act Protest

Analyze Drawings
This 1765 drawing shows a group of colonists in New Hampshire protesting the Stamp Act.

1. The coffin represents the wish to see the Stamp Act die.
2. The figure made of straw represents a stamp tax collector.
3. This angry protestor prepares to throw a rock at the straw figure.

Why do you think the protesters placed the straw figure high on a pole?

The Stamp Act

After the French and Indian War ended, the British Parliament reviewed its **budget**, or plan for spending money. British leader **George Grenville** said that Parliament needed more money to pay off the costs of the war. He argued that the American colonists should pay higher taxes. Parliament agreed and passed the Sugar Act in April 1764.

Less than a year later, in March 1765, Parliament passed the Stamp Act. The Stamp Act placed a tax on paper documents in the colonies. Newspapers, legal documents, and even playing cards had to have a special stamp on them to show that the tax had been paid.

In the colonies, the reaction to the Stamp Act was quick and angry. Many colonists said that Parliament could not tax them because the colonists had no **representation**, or voice, in Parliament.

In 1765, delegates from nine colonies met in New York City in what became known as the Stamp Act Congress. James Otis of Massachusetts spoke out against the Stamp Act. The colonists began repeating the words—no taxation without representation.

That same year, **Patrick Henry** told his fellow members of the Virginia House of Burgesses that Parliament did not represent the colonies. Those who agreed with Parliament shouted "Treason! Treason!" By accusing Henry of **treason**, they were saying he was guilty of working against his own government. Still, the House of Burgesses voted not to pay the new taxes set by Parliament.

READING CHECK CAUSE AND EFFECT
What caused Parliament to pass new taxes?

Chapter 8 ▪ 327

Key people and places are boldfaced.

Vocabulary terms are highlighted in yellow.

Each short section concludes with a READING CHECK question, which helps you check whether you understand what you have read. Be sure that you can answer this question correctly before you continue reading the lesson.

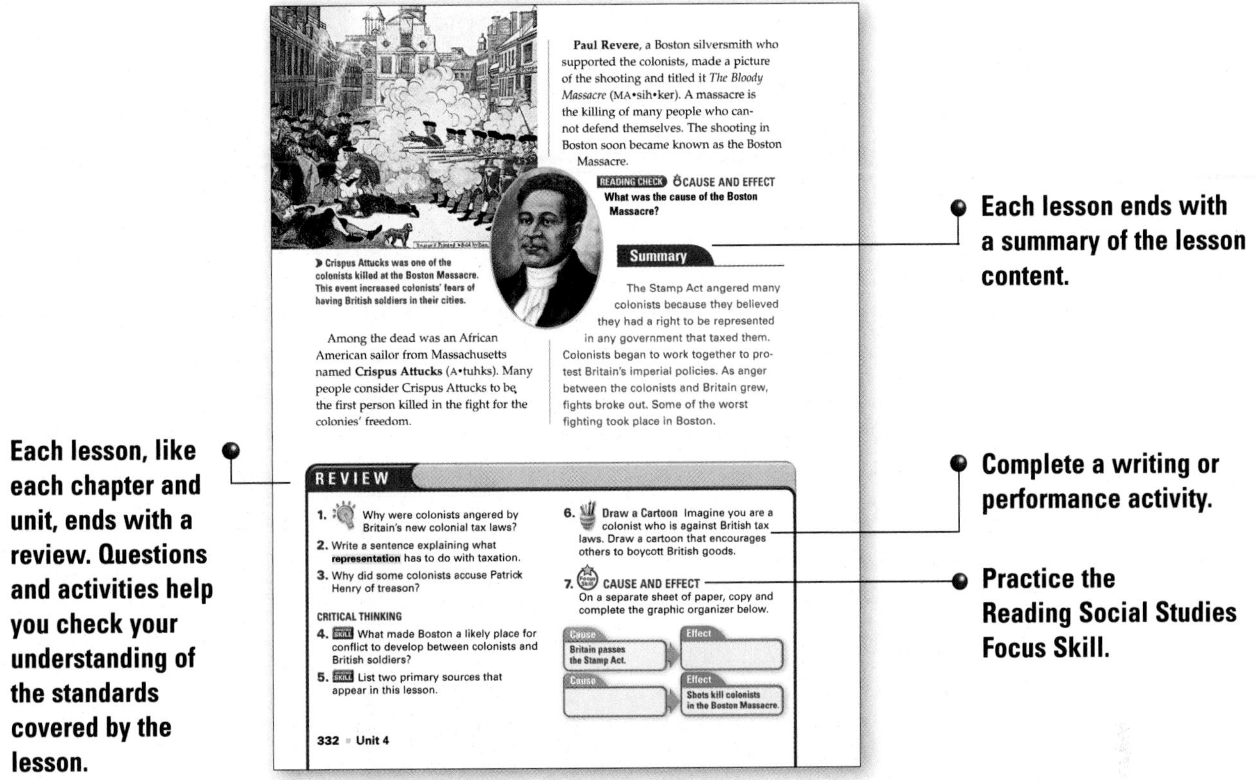

Paul Revere, a Boston silversmith who supported the colonists, made a picture of the shooting and titled it *The Bloody Massacre* (MA•sih•ker). A massacre is the killing of many people who cannot defend themselves. The shooting in Boston soon became known as the Boston Massacre.

READING CHECK CAUSE AND EFFECT
What was the cause of the Boston Massacre?

Crispus Attucks was one of the colonists killed at the Boston Massacre. This event increased colonists' fears of having British soldiers in their cities.

Among the dead was an African American sailor from Massachusetts named **Crispus Attucks** (A•tuhks). Many people consider Crispus Attucks to be the first person killed in the fight for the colonies' freedom.

Summary

The Stamp Act angered many colonists because they believed they had a right to be represented in any government that taxed them. Colonists began to work together to protest Britain's imperial policies. As anger between the colonists and Britain grew, fights broke out. Some of the worst fighting took place in Boston.

REVIEW

1. Why were colonists angered by Britain's new colonial tax laws?
2. Write a sentence explaining what **representation** has to do with taxation.
3. Why did some colonists accuse Patrick Henry of treason?

CRITICAL THINKING

4. SKILL What made Boston a likely place for conflict to develop between colonists and British soldiers?
5. SKILL List two primary sources that appear in this lesson.
6. Draw a Cartoon Imagine you are a colonist who is against British tax laws. Draw a cartoon that encourages others to boycott British goods.
7. CAUSE AND EFFECT On a separate sheet of paper, copy and complete the graphic organizer below.

Cause	Effect
Britain passes the Stamp Act.	
	Shots kill colonists in the Boston Massacre.

332 ■ Unit 4

Each lesson ends with a summary of the lesson content.

Each lesson, like each chapter and unit, ends with a review. Questions and activities help you check your understanding of the standards covered by the lesson.

Complete a writing or performance activity.

Practice the Reading Social Studies Focus Skill.

LEARNING SOCIAL STUDIES SKILLS

Your textbook has lessons that help you build your Participation Skills, Map and Globe Skills, Chart and Graph Skills, and Critical Thinking Skills.

This statement tells you why it is important to learn this skill.

You will be able to practice and apply the skill.

SPECIAL FEATURES

Biographies give in-depth background about some of the people who lived at the time.

Each biography focuses on a trait that the person showed.

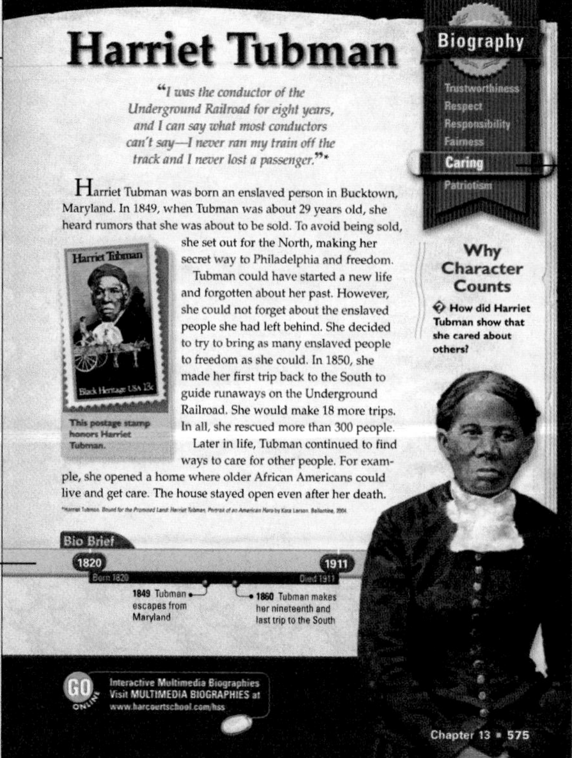
Harriet Tubman

Biography

Trustworthiness
Respect
Responsibility
Fairness
Caring
Patriotism

*"I was the conductor of the Underground Railroad for eight years, and I can say what most conductors can't say—I never ran my train off the track and I never lost a passenger."**

Harriet Tubman was born an enslaved person in Bucktown, Maryland. In 1849, when Tubman was about 29 years old, she heard rumors that she was about to be sold. To avoid being sold, she set out for the North, making her secret way to Philadelphia and freedom.

Tubman could have started a new life and forgotten about her past. However, she could not forget about the enslaved people she had left behind. She decided to try to bring as many enslaved people to freedom as she could. In 1850, she made her first trip back to the South to guide runaways on the Underground Railroad. She would make 18 more trips. In all, she rescued more than 300 people.

Later in life, Tubman continued to find ways to care for other people. For example, she opened a home where older African Americans could live and get care. The house stayed open even after her death.

This postage stamp honors Harriet Tubman.

Why Character Counts

How did Harriet Tubman show that she cared about others?

Bio Brief

1820 Born 1820

1911 Died 1911

1849 Tubman escapes from Maryland

1860 Tubman makes her nineteenth and last trip to the South

Interactive Multimedia Biographies
Visit MULTIMEDIA BIOGRAPHIES at
www.harcourtschool.com/hss

Chapter 13 ■ 575

A time line shows when the person was born and died and some key events in his or her life.

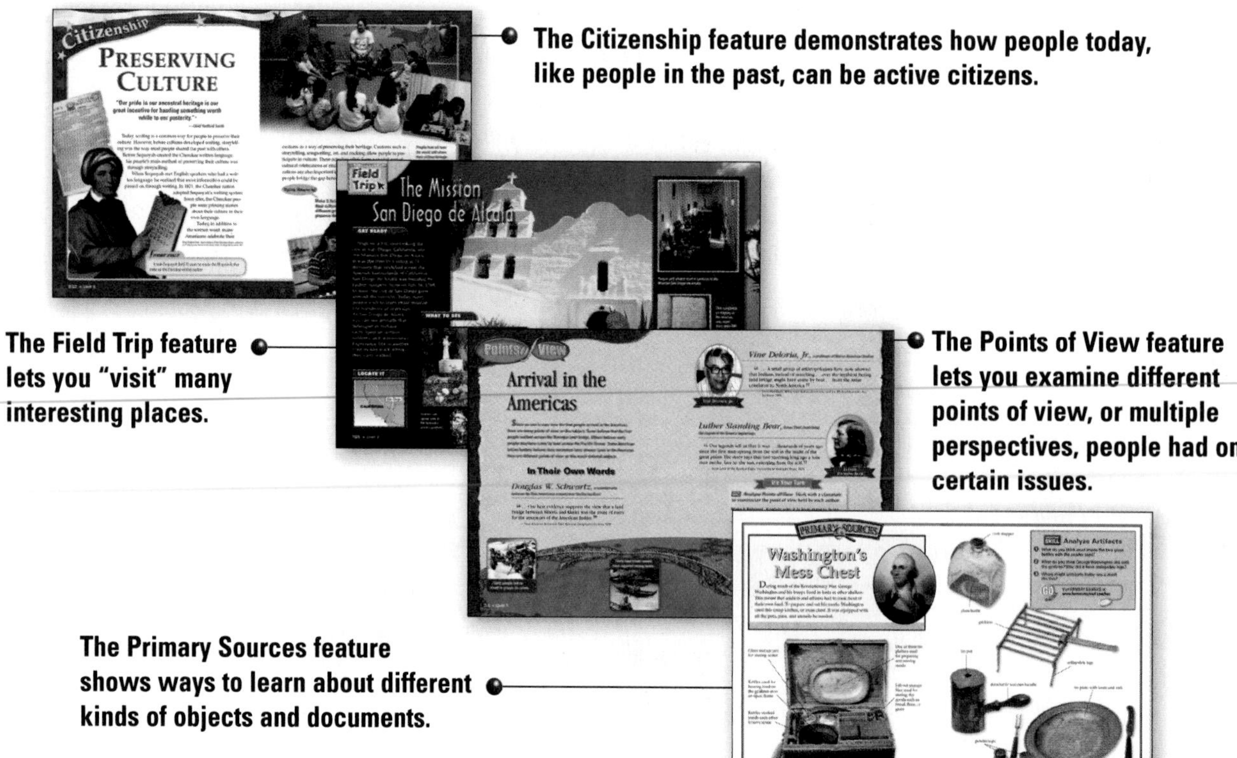

The Citizenship feature demonstrates how people today, like people in the past, can be active citizens.

The Field Trip feature lets you "visit" many interesting places.

The Points of View feature lets you examine different points of view, or multiple perspectives, people had on certain issues.

The Primary Sources feature shows ways to learn about different kinds of objects and documents.

FOR YOUR REFERENCE

At the back of your textbook, you will find different reference tools. You can use these tools to look up words and/or to find information about people, places, and other topics.

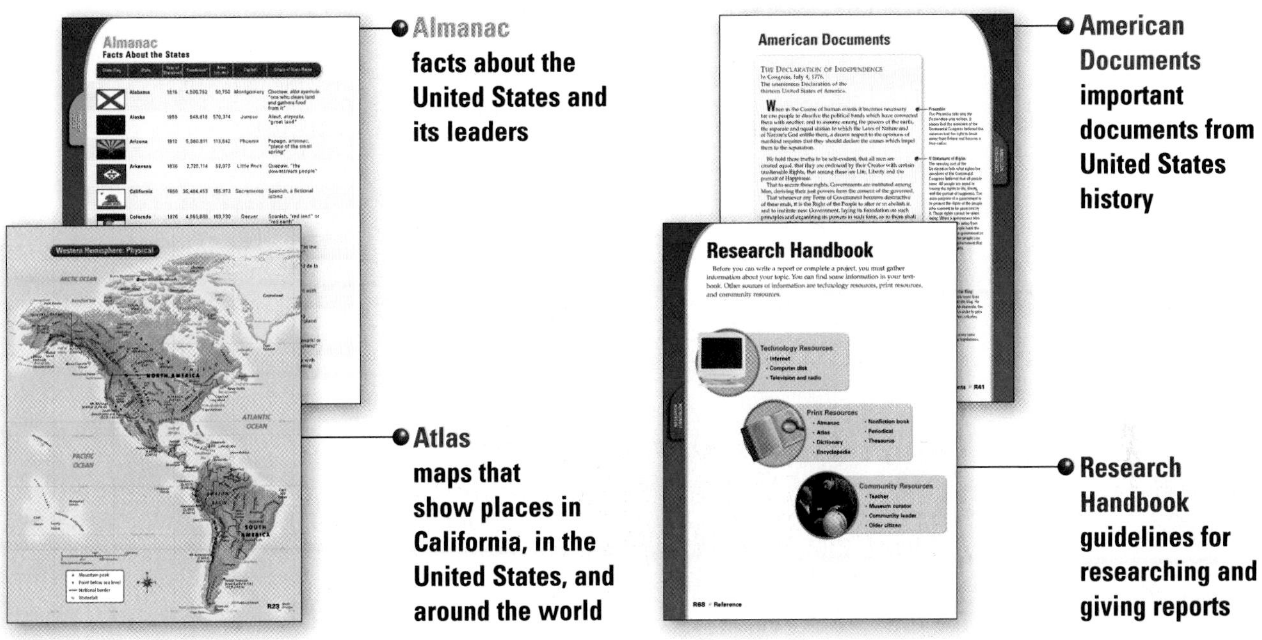

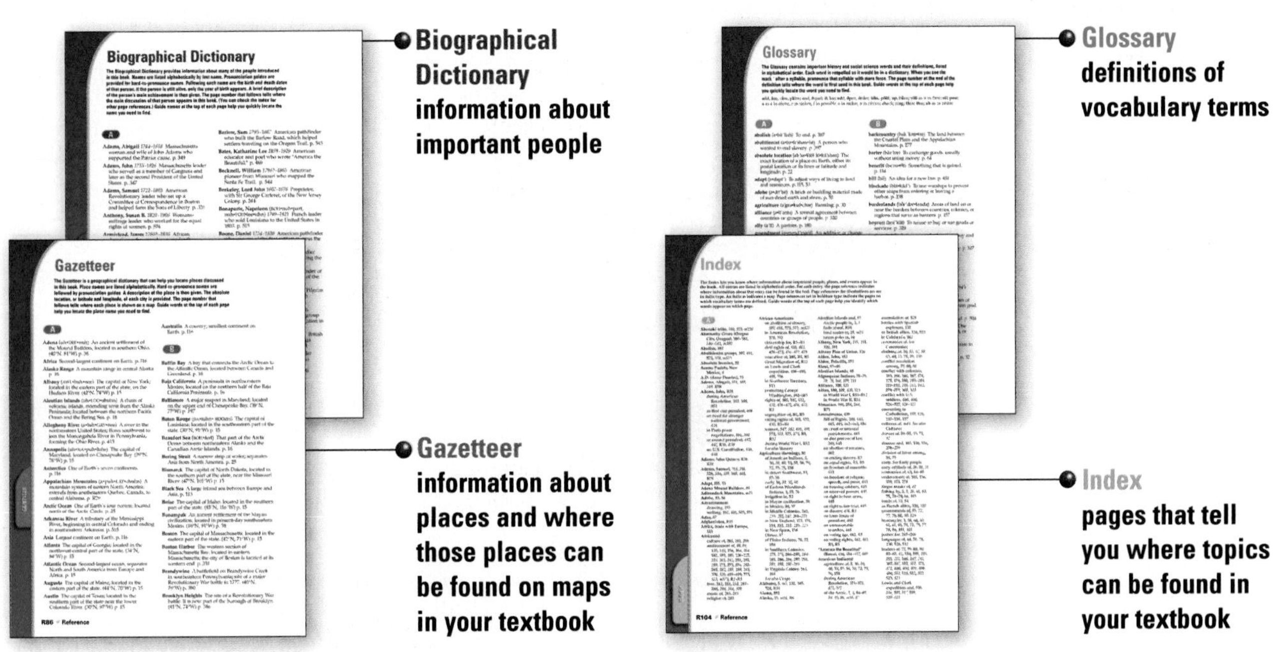

The Five Themes of Geography

Learning about places is an important part of history and geography—the study of Earth's surface and the way people use it. Geographers often think about five main themes, or topics, when they study Earth and its geography. Keeping these themes in mind as you read will help you think like a geographer.

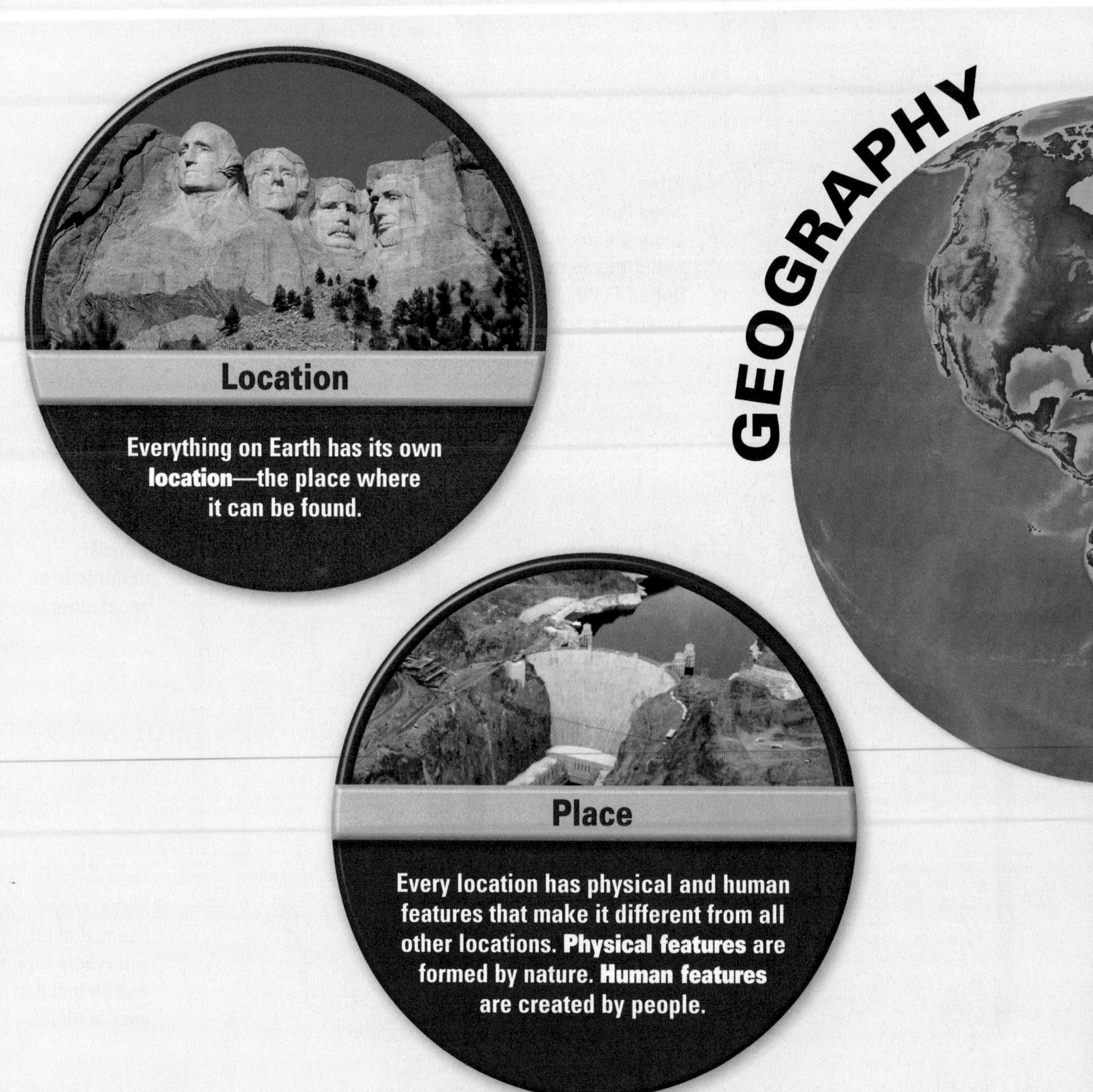

THEMES

Human-Environment Interactions

People and their surroundings interact, or affect each other. People's activities may **modify**, or change, the environment. The environment may affect people, requiring them to **adapt**, or adjust, to their surroundings.

Movement

Every day, people in different parts of our state and country and around the world exchange products and ideas.

Regions

Areas of Earth with main features that make them different from other areas are called regions. A **region** can be described by its physical features or its human features.

Looking at Earth

A distant view from space shows Earth's round shape. You probably have a globe in your classroom. A globe is also a sphere. It is a model of Earth that shows Earth's major bodies of water and its seven **continents**, or largest land masses. Earth's continents, from largest to smallest, are Asia, Africa, North America, South America, Antarctica, Europe, and Australia.

Because of its shape, you can see only one half of Earth at a time when you look at a globe. Halfway between the North Pole and the South Pole on a globe is a line called the **equator**.

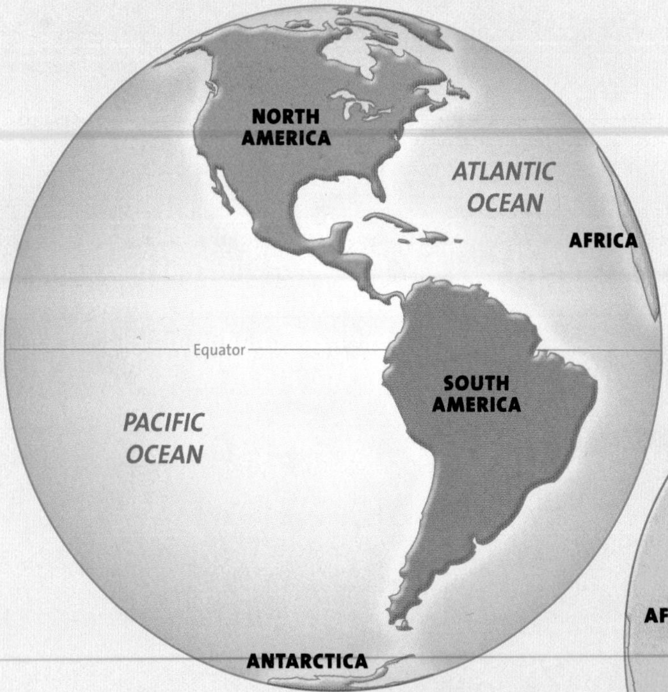

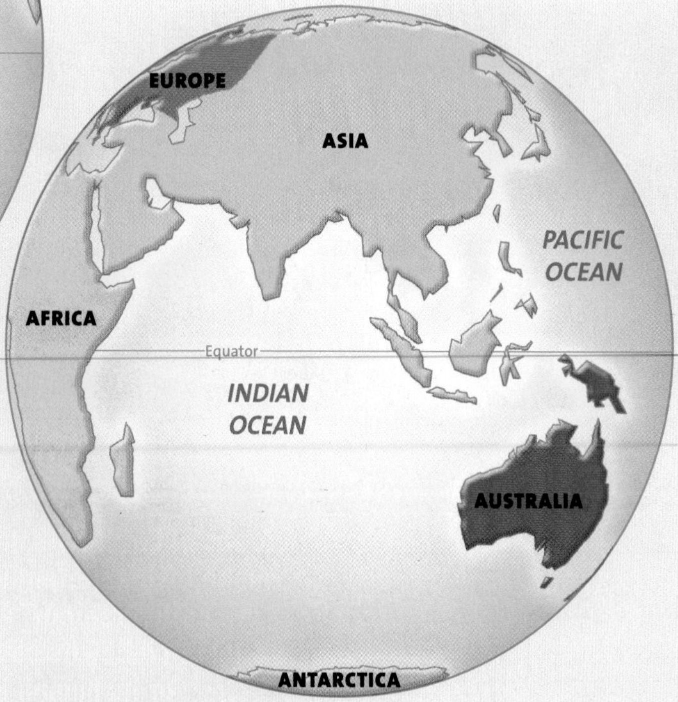

The equator divides Earth into two equal halves, or **hemispheres**. The Northern Hemisphere is north of the equator, and the Southern Hemisphere is south of it. Another line, the **prime meridian**, runs north and south, dividing Earth into the Western Hemisphere and the Eastern Hemisphere.

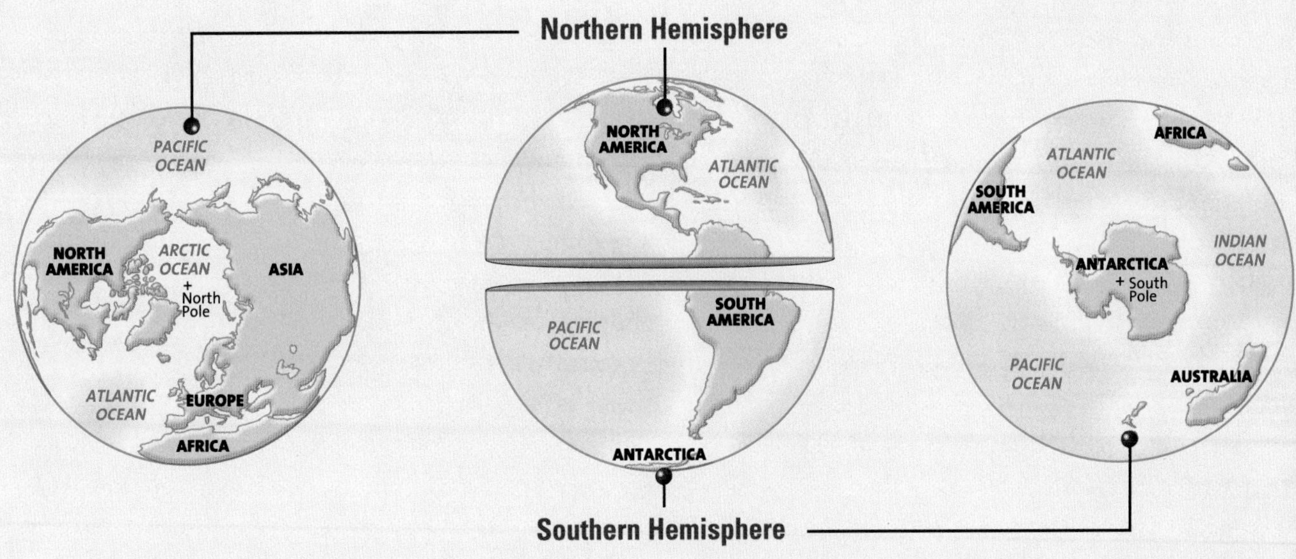

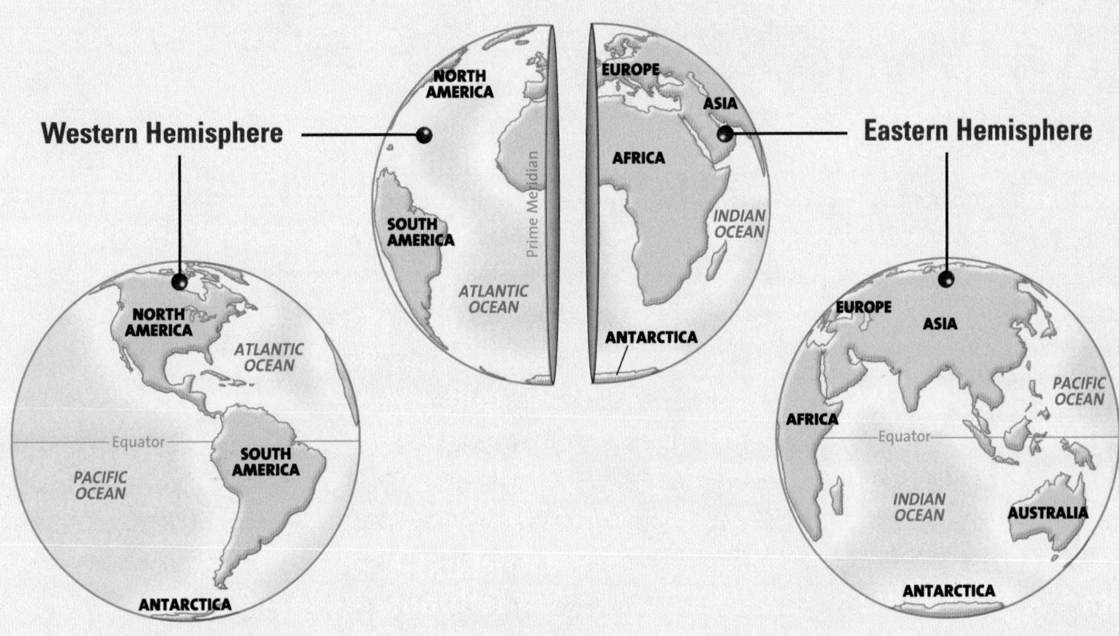

Geography Terms

1 **basin** bowl-shaped area of land surrounded by higher land

2 **bay** an inlet of the sea or some other body of water, usually smaller than a gulf

3 **bluff** high, steep face of rock or earth

4 **canyon** deep, narrow valley with steep sides

5 **cape** point of land that extends into water

6 **cataract** large waterfall

7 **channel** deepest part of a body of water

8 **cliff** high, steep face of rock or earth

9 **coast** land along a sea or ocean

10 **coastal plain** area of flat land along a sea or ocean

11 **delta** triangle-shaped area of land at the mouth of a river

12 **desert** dry land with few plants

13 **dune** hill of sand piled up by the wind

14 **fall line** area along which rivers form waterfalls or rapids as the rivers drop to lower land

15 **floodplain** flat land that is near the edges of a river and is formed by silt deposited by floods

16 **foothills** hilly area at the base of a mountain

17 **glacier** large ice mass that moves slowly down a mountain or across land

18 **gulf** part of a sea or ocean extending into the land, usually larger than a bay

19 **hill** land that rises above the land around it

20 **inlet** any area of water extending into the land from a larger body of water

21 **island** land that has water on all sides

22 **isthmus** narrow strip of land connecting two larger areas of land

23 **lagoon** body of shallow water

24 **lake** body of water with land on all sides

25 marsh lowland with moist soil and tall grasses

26 mesa flat-topped mountain with steep sides

27 mountain highest kind of land

28 mountain pass gap between mountains

29 mountain range row of mountains

30 mouth of river place where a river empties into another body of water

31 oasis area of water and fertile land in a desert

32 ocean body of salt water larger than a sea

33 peak top of a mountain

34 peninsula land that is almost completely surrounded by water

35 plain area of flat or gently rolling low land

36 plateau area of high, mostly flat land

37 reef ridge of sand, rock, or coral that lies at or near the surface of a sea or ocean

38 river large stream of water that flows across the

39 riverbank land along a river

40 savanna area of grassland and scattered trees

41 sea body of salt water smaller than an ocean

42 sea level the level of the surface of an ocean or a sea

43 slope side of a hill or mountain

44 source of river place where a river begins

45 strait narrow channel of water connecting two larger bodies of water

46 swamp area of low, wet land with trees

47 timberline line on a mountain above which it is too cold for trees to grow

48 tributary stream or river that flows into a larger stream or river

49 valley low land between hills or mountains

50 volcano opening in the earth, often raised, through which lava, rock, ashes, and gases are forced out

51 waterfall steep drop from a high place to a

Reading Maps

Maps can provide you with many kinds of information about Earth and the world around you. A map is a drawing that shows all or part of Earth on a flat surface.

To help you read maps more easily, mapmakers add certain features to most of their maps. These features usually include a title, a map legend, a compass rose, a locator, and a map scale.

Sometimes mapmakers need to show certain places on a map in greater detail, or they must show places that are located beyond the area shown on the map. Find Alaska

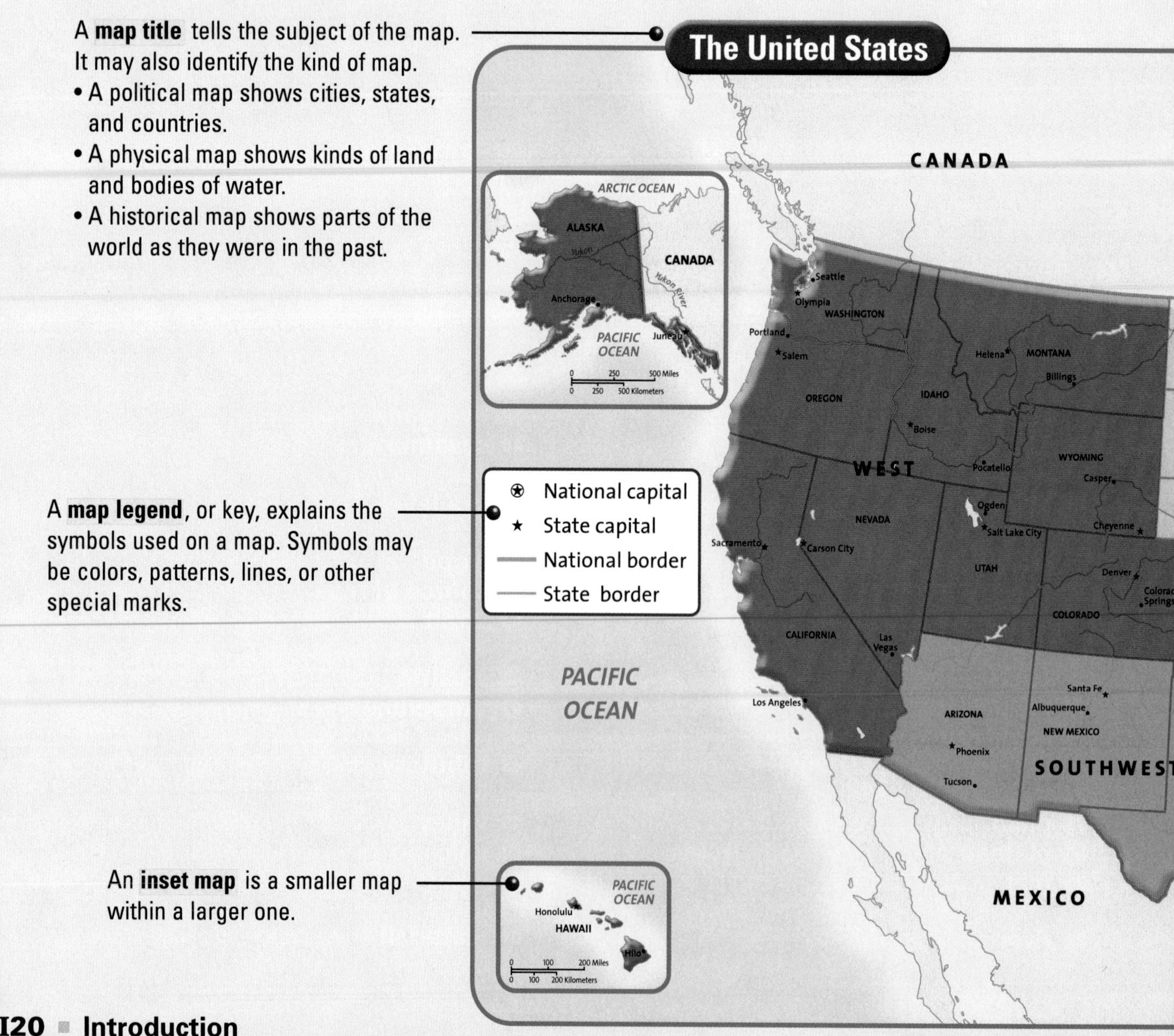

A **map title** tells the subject of the map. It may also identify the kind of map.
- A political map shows cities, states, and countries.
- A physical map shows kinds of land and bodies of water.
- A historical map shows parts of the world as they were in the past.

A **map legend**, or key, explains the symbols used on a map. Symbols may be colors, patterns, lines, or other special marks.

An **inset map** is a smaller map within a larger one.

and Hawaii on the map of the United States on pages R24–R25. The map there shows the location of those two states in relation to the location of the rest of the country.

Now find Alaska and Hawaii on the map below. To show this much detail for these states as well as the rest of the country, the map would have to be much larger. Instead, here Alaska and Hawaii are each shown in a separate inset map, or a smaller map within a larger map.

A **locator** is a small map or globe that shows where the place on the main map is located within a larger area.

A **map scale** compares a distance on the map to a distance in the real world. It helps you find the real distance between places on a map.

A **compass rose**, or direction marker, shows directions.

- The **cardinal directions** are north, south, east, and west.
- The **intermediate directions**, or directions between the cardinal directions, are northeast, northwest, southeast, and southwest.

Finding Locations

To help people find places on maps, mapmakers sometimes add lines that cross each other to form a pattern of squares called a **grid system**. Look at the map of the United States below. Around the grid are letters and numbers. The columns, which run up and down, have numbers. The rows, which run from left to right, have letters. Each square on the map can be identified by its letter and number. For example, the top row of squares on the map includes square A-1, square A-2, square A-3, and so on.

United States

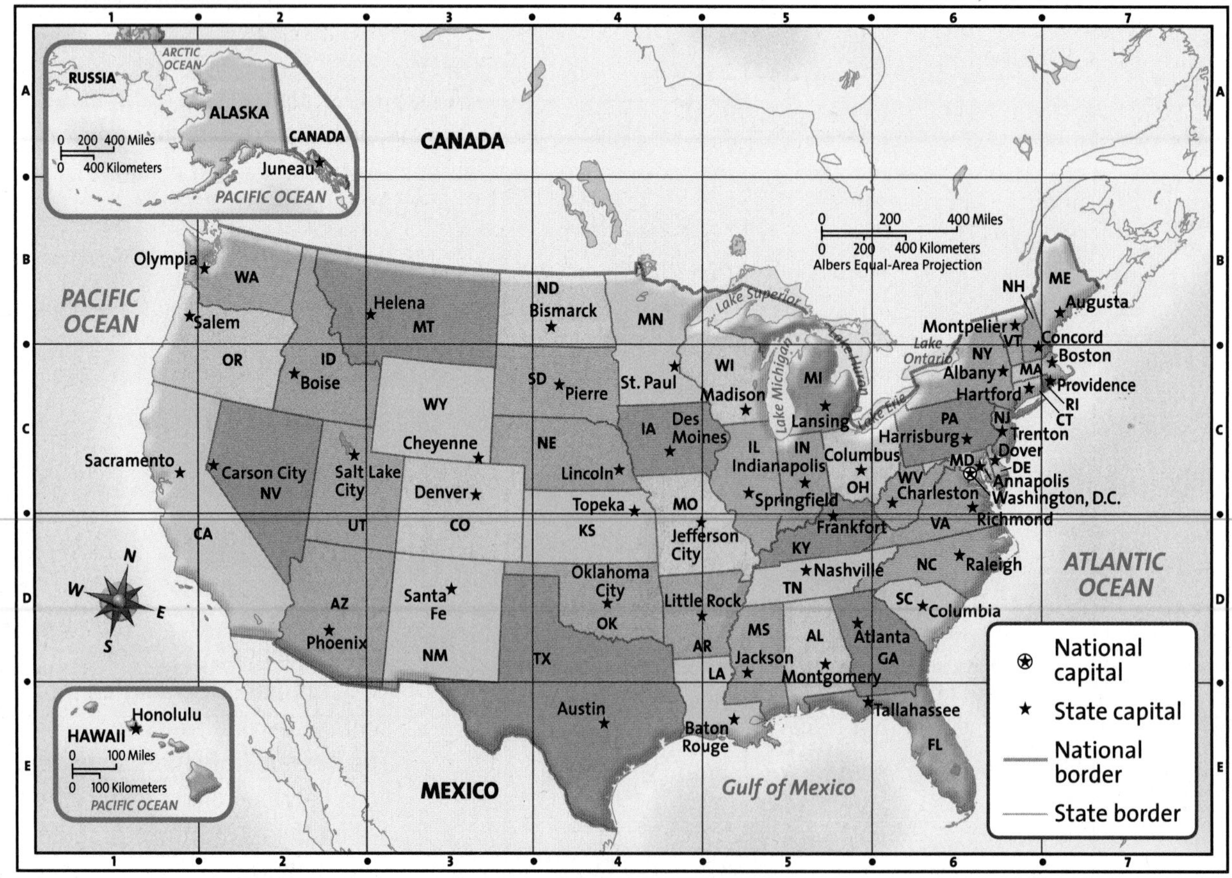

The First Americans

START WITH THE STANDARDS

California History-Social Science Standards

5.1 Students describe the major pre-Columbian settlements, including the cliff dwellers and pueblo people of the desert Southwest, the American Indians of the Pacific Northwest, the nomadic nations of the Great Plains, and the woodland peoples east of the Mississippi River.

5.9 Students know the location of the current 50 states and the names of their capitals

The Big Idea

Geography

People interact with their environment and are affected by it.

What to Know

- ✓ How does the geography and climate of the United States differ from region to region?
- ✓ What was the impact of early North American civilizations?
- ✓ How did geography and climate affect American Indian groups?

Show What You Know

- ★ Unit 1 Test
- Writing: A Report
- Unit Project: An American Indian Book

Time

The First Americans

About 12,000 years ago
Ancient Indians hunt large animals, p. 28

12,000 years ago

8,000 years ago

The First Americans

About 5,000 years ago
Ancient Indians begin farming, p. 30

About 1,000 years ago
The Navajo move to the desert Southwest, p. 56

About 800 years ago
More than 30,000 people live in Cahokia, p. 39

4,000 years ago

PRESENT

Unit 1

People

Desert Southwest People

- Lived in what is now Mexico, Texas, New Mexico, and Arizona
- Experts at making baskets and pottery
- Main crop was corn

Eastern Woodlands People

- Lived mostly in areas east of the Mississippi River in what is now the United States
- Used wood to make canoes, tools, and shelters
- Main crops were corn, beans, and squash

Pacific Northwest People

Plains People

Pacific Northwest People

- Lived in what is now Canada, Washington, and Oregon.
- Skilled whalers and fishers
- Traveled long distances to trade

Plains People

- Lived in a wide area from what is now Texas to Canada
- Main food source was buffalo

Arctic People

- Lived in an area that covered much of what is now Canada and Alaska
- Used kayaks for fishing
- Skilled seal hunters

Pueblo Bonito, in what is now New Mexico

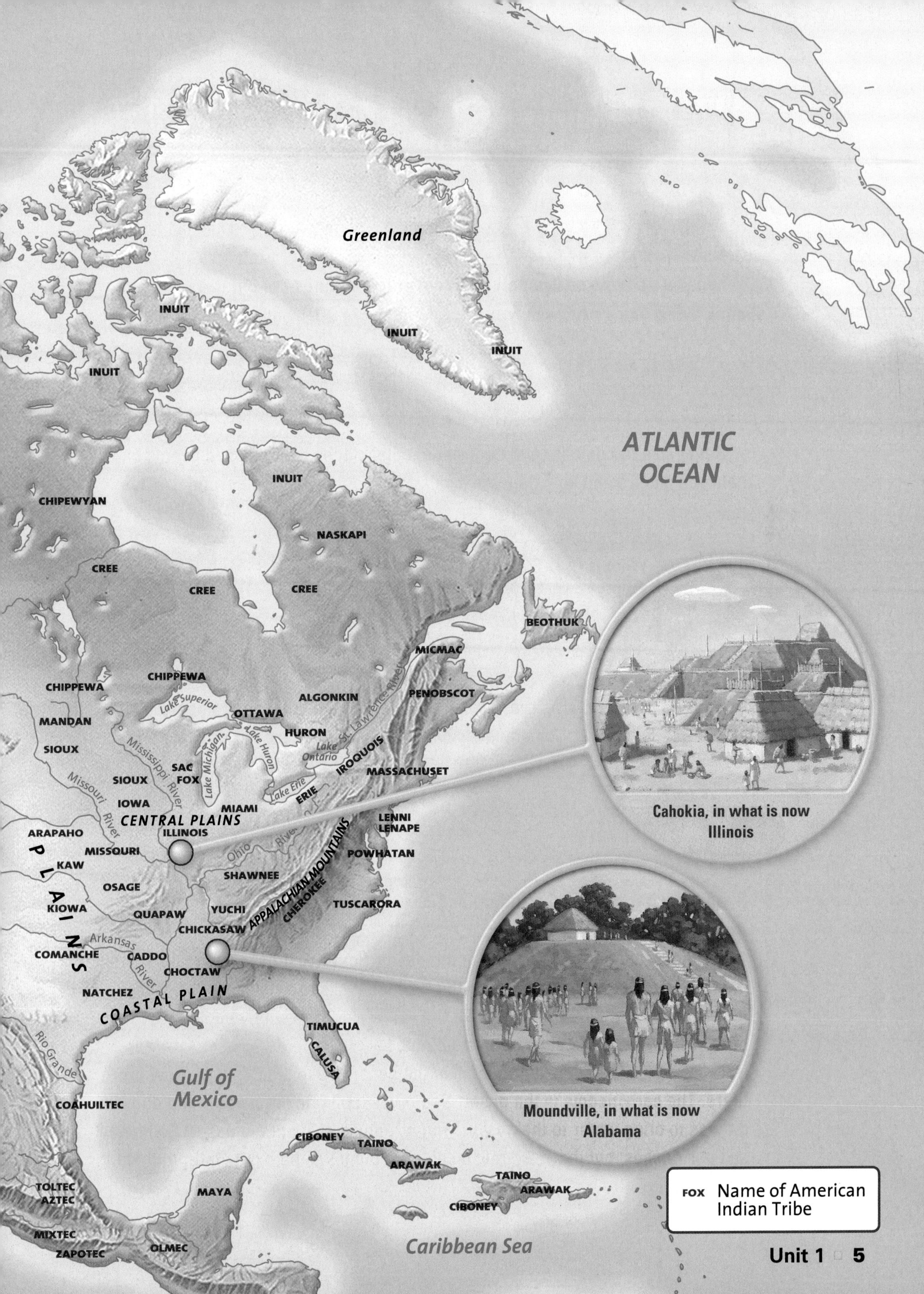

Cahokia, in what is now Illinois

Moundville, in what is now Alabama

Reading Social Studies

Compare and Contrast

When you compare, you tell how two or more things are alike, or similar. When you contrast, you tell how they are different.

Why It Matters

Being able to compare and contrast people, places, objects, and events can help you understand how they are similar and how they are different.

Topic 1	Similar	Topic 2
What is different	What is alike	What is different

- *Like, both, all, also, too, similar,* and *same* are words that compare.
- *But, instead, unlike, however, different,* and *differ* are words that contrast.

Practice the Skill

Read the paragraph, and compare and contrast early Americans and modern Americans.

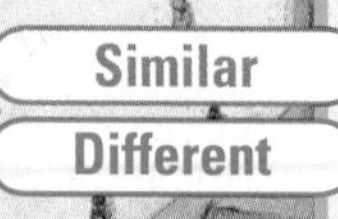

For thousands of years, people in the desert Southwest have lived with extreme heat. Early people built homes with thick adobe walls to help stay cool. Many modern homes in the region are built the same way. However, people today have air-conditioning, while early people did not.

The extreme heat and little rainfall in the desert make it difficult to grow crops there. The early people in the desert Southwest collected rainwater and dug ditches to bring water to their crops. Today, people living in the desert Southwest still use ditches, but they also rely on electric pumps to help get water to them.

Apply What You Learned

Compare and Contrast Read the paragraphs, and answer the questions.

Living History

It is amazing to think that Americans today have some things in common with early Americans. Much has changed in the thousands of years since people first settled the Americas. Yet in some ways, history lives on.

Long ago, beans and corn were important foods in many parts of the Americas. They are important foods today, too. In fact, they have been on dinner tables for thousands of years. Many early Americans also enjoyed popcorn, just as many people do today.

Many early Americans used canoes and kayaks to travel down rivers and across lakes. In fact, *canoe* and *kayak* both come from Indian words. Many people still use these same boats. Today, however, most people use them for enjoyment, instead of for transportation.

Some early American groups built large cities with hundreds of buildings. Before building a city, they would plan ahead and set aside places for shops, homes, and religious buildings. Today, city planners organize cities and neighborhoods in much the same way.

Focus Skill

Compare and Contrast

1. **How are foods today similar to the foods of early Americans?**
2. **How are the ways early Americans used kayaks and canoes different from the ways people use them today?**
3. **How is the way Americans today plan cities similar to the way early Americans planned cities? How is it different?**

Study Skills

PREVIEW AND QUESTION

Previewing a lesson to identify main ideas, and asking yourself questions about those ideas, can help you read to find important information.

- **To preview a lesson, read the lesson title and the section titles. Look at the pictures, and read their captions. Try to get an idea of the main topic and think of questions you have about the topic.**
- **Read to find the answers to your questions. Then recite, or say, the answers aloud. Finally, review what you have read.**

Early People				
Preview	Questions	Read	Recite	Review
Lesson 1 The United States can be divided in different ways.	How is the land in the United States divided?	✓	✓	✓
Lesson 2				

Apply As You Read

As you read this chapter, remember to preview each lesson. Use a chart like the one above to list the main topics and your questions.

California History-Social Science Standards, Grade 5

5.1 Students describe the major pre-Columbian settlements, including the cliff dwellers and pueblo people of the desert Southwest, the American Indians of the Pacific Northwest, the nomadic nations of the Great Plains, and the woodland peoples east of the Mississippi River.
5.9 Students know the location of the current 50 states and the names of their capitals.

CHAPTER

Early People

Acoma Pueblo in Acoma, New Mexico

Between Earth and Sky

by Joseph Bruchac
illustrated by John Martin

Many people use poems, songs, or stories to tell about important events and people in their past. Some of these stories are legends. A legend is a story handed down by a group of people over time. Some legends tell about brave or heroic people. Others try to explain the origins of animals, plants, and the physical features found in the world.

If we should travel
far to the South,
there in the land
of mountains and mist,
we might hear the story
of how Earth was first shaped.

Water Beetle came out
to see if it was ready,
but the ground was
still as wet as a swamp,
too soft for anyone to stand.

Great Buzzard said, "I will help dry the land."
He began to fly close above the new Earth.
Where his wings came down,
valleys were formed,
and where his wings lifted,
hills rose up through the mist.

So the many rolling valleys and hills
of that place called the Great Smokies
came into being there.
And so it is that the Cherokee people,
aware of how this land was given,
know that the Earth is a sacred gift
we all must respect and share.

Far from here
to the West is a desert land where
I'itoi, the Elder Brother,
looked out and then said to the people,
"In this place you will live
as long as you remember
all around you is sacred."

Though it seems to be empty and dry,
the desert is always filled with life.
Those tall cactuses that lift their arms
up into the sky are ancient people
who promised to always look over those
chosen to live in this sandy place.
The clouds in the sky are also alive.
They are ancient beings who care for the people.
They will answer with rain
when you ask for their help.

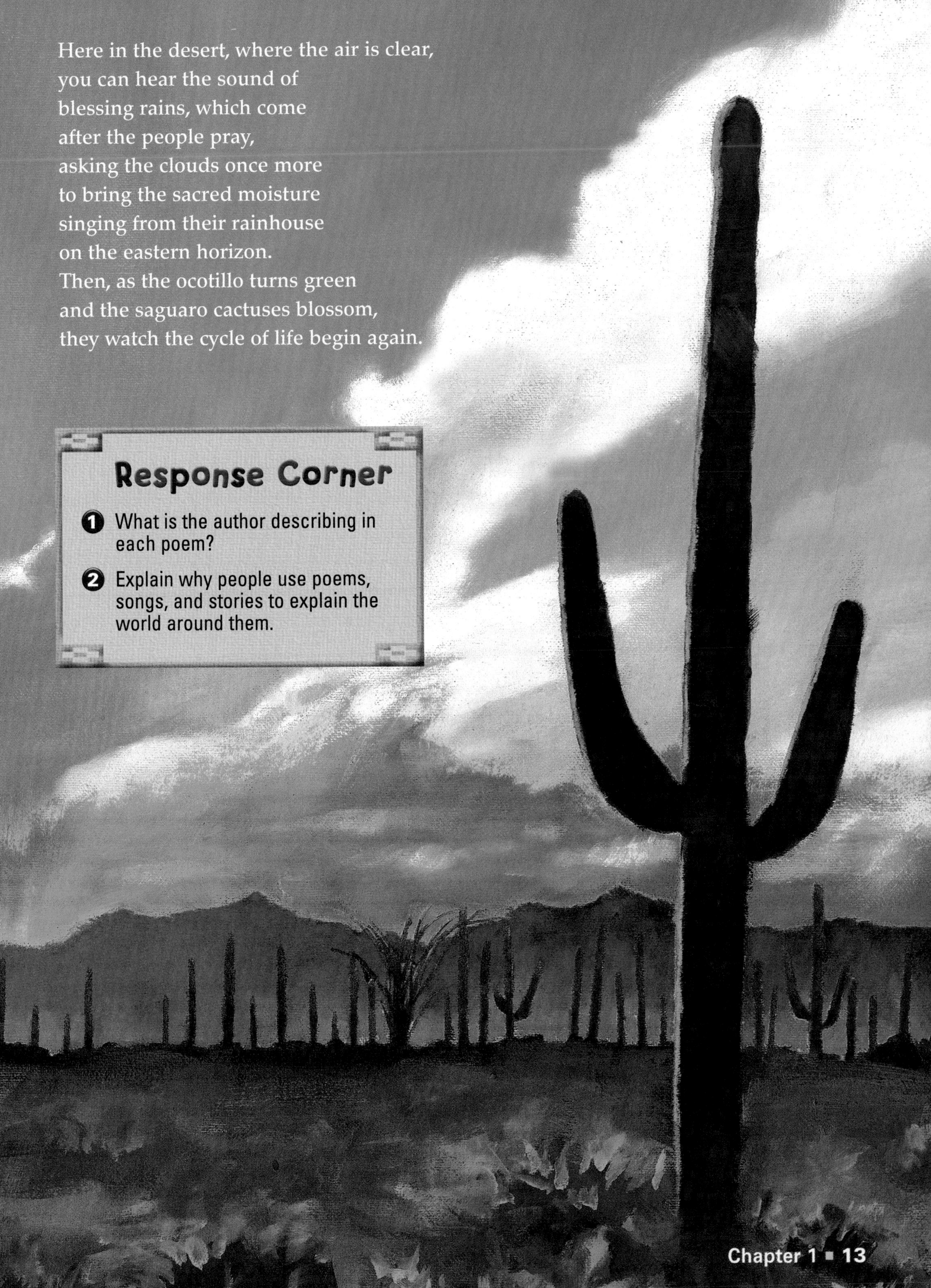

Here in the desert, where the air is clear,
you can hear the sound of
blessing rains, which come
after the people pray,
asking the clouds once more
to bring the sacred moisture
singing from their rainhouse
on the eastern horizon.
Then, as the ocotillo turns green
and the saguaro cactuses blossom,
they watch the cycle of life begin again.

Response Corner

1. What is the author describing in each poem?
2. Explain why people use poems, songs, and stories to explain the world around them.

Lesson 1

The Land and States

WHAT TO KNOW
How do the geography and climate differ as you travel across the 50 states?

- ✓ Identify and describe some of the major landforms and bodies of water in the United States.
- ✓ Learn the location of the 50 states and their capitals.

VOCABULARY
landform region p. 15
climate p. 16
environment p. 18

PEOPLE
Robert Louis Stevenson

PLACES
Coastal Plain
Appalachian Mountains
Interior Plains
Mississippi River
Great Lakes
Rocky Mountains
Great Basin
Sierra Nevada

COMPARE AND CONTRAST

HSS 5.1, 5.1.1, 5.9

YOU ARE THERE

Imagine that you could live anywhere on Earth. Would you choose to live near the ocean or near mountains? Would you rather live in a region where winters are long and snowy or where most days are sunny and warm?

No matter how you answer these questions, you can find all these different places in the same country. The United States is a large country made up of 50 states. You may know what the land and climate are like in one state, but you may wonder how they differ in other parts of the country.

The San Juan Mountains cover more than 12,000 square miles in southwestern Colorado.

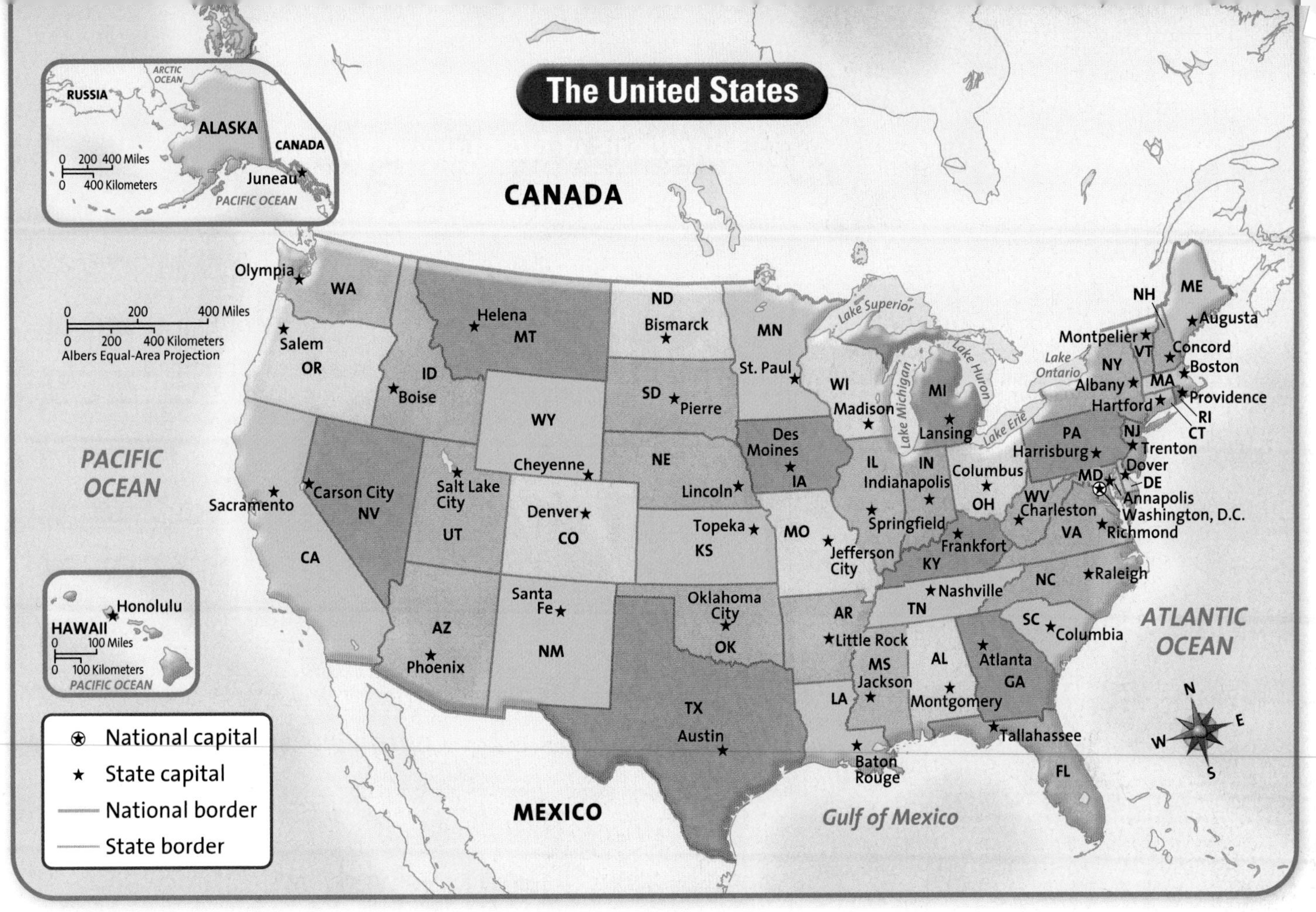

ANALYSIS SKILL **Analyze Maps** **You can use this map to learn the names of all the states and their capitals.**

Location **Which state capital is closest to Sacramento?**

A Nation of 50 States

The United States is a nation of incredible beauty that is made up of 50 states, each with its own capital. Of the 50 states, 2 are separated from the others. The island state of Hawaii lies far to the west in the Pacific Ocean. Alaska, the northernmost state, is separated from the states to the south by the country of Canada.

Because the United States is so large, geographers sometimes divide it into landform regions. A **landform region** has mainly one kind of landform—such as mountains, hills, plateaus, or plains—throughout. Each region is unique, or unlike the others, because of the shape of its landforms and the way they came to be. Dividing the country into landform regions makes it easier to compare and contrast different parts of the country.

READING CHECK **COMPARE AND CONTRAST**
How does the state of Hawaii differ from other states in the nation?

ANALYSIS SKILL Analyze Maps

Regions What mountain region lies to the east of the Mississippi River?

The Coastal Plain

In the late 1800s, a well-known writer named **Robert Louis Stevenson** traveled across the United States. Stevenson was living in Scotland when he received word that Fanny Osbourne, his sweetheart, was ill. Osbourne lived in the United States, and Stevenson decided to go there. He did not realize how much his trip across the United States would teach him about the nation's geography and climate. **Climate** is the kind of weather a place has over a long time.

On August 7, 1879, Stevenson left Scotland. He boarded a ship and spent ten stormy days crossing the Atlantic Ocean. As the ship neared New York City,

Stevenson looked out on a broad, tree-lined plain. This flat, low land along the Atlantic Ocean is part of a much larger region called the **Coastal Plain**.

The Coastal Plain begins along the coast of Massachusetts as a narrow strip of land no more than 10 miles wide. It gets much wider farther south, near Florida. From Florida, the Coastal Plain extends west along the Gulf of Mexico into Texas and the country of Mexico.

READING CHECK **COMPARE AND CONTRAST**
What is the difference between the Coastal Plain in Massachusetts and in Florida?

The Appalachians

Stevenson did not stay in New York City long. Osbourne lived on the Pacific Coast of the United States—in San Francisco, California. To reach California, Stevenson boarded a train for the long journey to the western coast.

When the train reached Pennsylvania, the land began to change. Instead of being flat, it was now filled with wide valleys and hills. This area of valleys and hills on the eastern side of the **Appalachian** (a•puh•LAY•chuhn) **Mountains** is called the Piedmont (PEED•mahnt). *Piedmont* means "at the base of a mountain." The Piedmont begins in New Jersey and extends as far south as Alabama.

The tree-covered Appalachian Mountains rise above the Piedmont. This 2,000-mile-long mountain range, or group of connected mountains, runs from southeastern Canada to central Alabama.

The Appalachian Mountains are the oldest mountains in North America. Over time, the mountains' peaks have been eroded, or worn down by rain and wind. The highest peaks in the Appalachians are about 7,000 feet tall.

A large part of the Appalachians is made up of a series of ridges and valleys that run next to each other. Among these ridges are the Great Smoky, Blue Ridge, Catskill, and White Mountains.

READING CHECK **COMPARE AND CONTRAST**
How is the Piedmont different from the Coastal Plain?

The Appalachian Mountains are more than 250 million years old.

The Interior Plains

West of the Appalachian Mountains, the land gets flat again. Here, in the center of the United States, Stevenson saw other plains, which we call the Interior Plains.

The **Interior Plains** stretch across the middle of the United States, from the Appalachian Mountains in the east to the Rocky Mountains in the west. Most of the land in the Interior Plains is flat, with many streams and rivers. In the middle of the country, these waters drain into the **Mississippi River**. Here, the mighty Mississippi is fed by large rivers such as the Arkansas, the Illinois, the Ohio, and the Missouri. Also in the Interior Plains are the five **Great Lakes**, which make up the world's largest group of freshwater lakes.

In the eastern part of the Interior Plains, often called the Central Plains, the land is mostly flat with numerous streams and rivers. During his journey across the Central Plains, Stevenson wrote that "the country was flat . . . but far from being dull. All through Ohio, Indiana, Illinois, and Iowa, . . . it was rich and various."*

When Stevenson's train stopped in the middle of Nebraska, he saw that the **environment**, or the surroundings in which people, plants, and animals live, was yet again different. This western part of the Interior Plains is called the Great Plains, and includes parts of 10 states.

In the Great Plains, the land becomes much flatter and the climate much drier. There are few rivers and almost no trees. To Stevenson, the land seemed to look the same for mile after mile. He wrote that a person "may walk five miles and see nothing; ten, and it is as though he had not moved."*

READING CHECK **COMPARE AND CONTRAST**
How do the Central Plains differ from the Great Plains?

*Robert Louis Stevenson. *From Scotland to Silverado.* Harvard University Press, 1966.

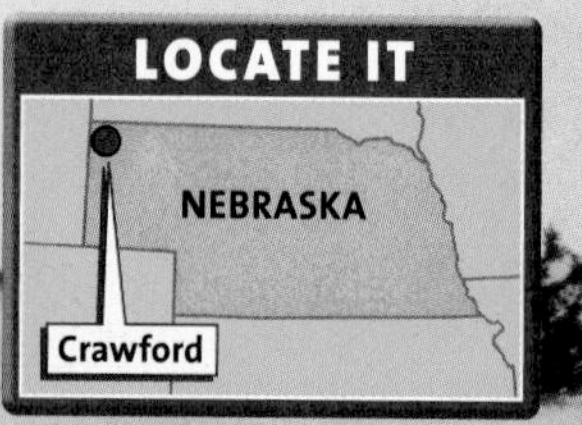

This field in Nebraska is part of miles and miles of flat land that make up the Great Plains.

The Rocky Mountains and Beyond

As Stevenson's train moved west, the flat Interior Plains gave way to the towering **Rocky Mountains**. The Rockies cover much of the western United States and are our country's largest and longest mountain range. They stretch from Mexico through Canada and into Alaska. Like the Appalachians, the Rockies are made up of smaller ranges.

The Rocky Mountains are much younger than the Appalachians. The peaks of the Rockies appear sharp and jagged because they have not been eroded for as long a time. More than 50 peaks in Colorado alone are higher than 14,000 feet. In the mountains, climate can vary as the land rises up. Because the Rockies are so high, many of the peaks are covered with snow all year long.

Stevenson's train moved slowly, taking two days to cross the Rocky Mountains. Then the environment changed once again. Now Stevenson looked out the window and saw only "desert scenes, fiery hot and deadly weary."*

Between the Rocky Mountains on the east and other mountains farther west is a large area of land that is mostly dry. It is sometimes called the Intermountain Region. *Intermountain* means "between the mountains." Part of this land is the **Great Basin**, which includes Nevada and parts of five neighboring states. A basin is low, bowl-shaped land with higher land all around it. At the southwestern edge of the Great Basin lies Death Valley, California. The lowest point in North America, part of Death Valley lies more than 250 feet below sea level.

READING CHECK **COMPARE AND CONTRAST**
How do the Rocky Mountains differ from the Appalachian Mountains?

*Robert Louis Stevenson. *From Scotland to Silverado.* Harvard University Press, 1966.

More Mountains and Valleys

Stevenson's train left the desert and headed west toward more mountains. Lying just inside California is the **Sierra Nevada** (see•AYR•uh nuh•VA•duh). *Sierra Nevada* is Spanish for "snowy mountain range." The eastern slope of the mountains is so steep that riders on Stevenson's train were pinned to their seats as the train climbed the mountains!

Other mountains lie north of the Sierra Nevada, in Washington and Oregon. These mountains make up the Cascade Range. West of the Sierra Nevada and the Cascade Range are three large, fertile valleys. The largest is the more than 400-mile-long Central Valley in California. The others are the Puget Sound Lowland in Washington and the Willamette (wuh•LA•muht) Valley in Oregon.

Along the Pacific Ocean in California, Oregon, and Washington are the Coast Ranges. These low mountains give the Pacific a rocky, rugged look. At many places these mountains drop sharply into the ocean. Unlike the Atlantic Coast, the Pacific Coast has very little flat land.

ANALYSIS SKILL Analyze Maps **Climate influences life in every area of the United States.**

Regions **In which climate region is your community located?**

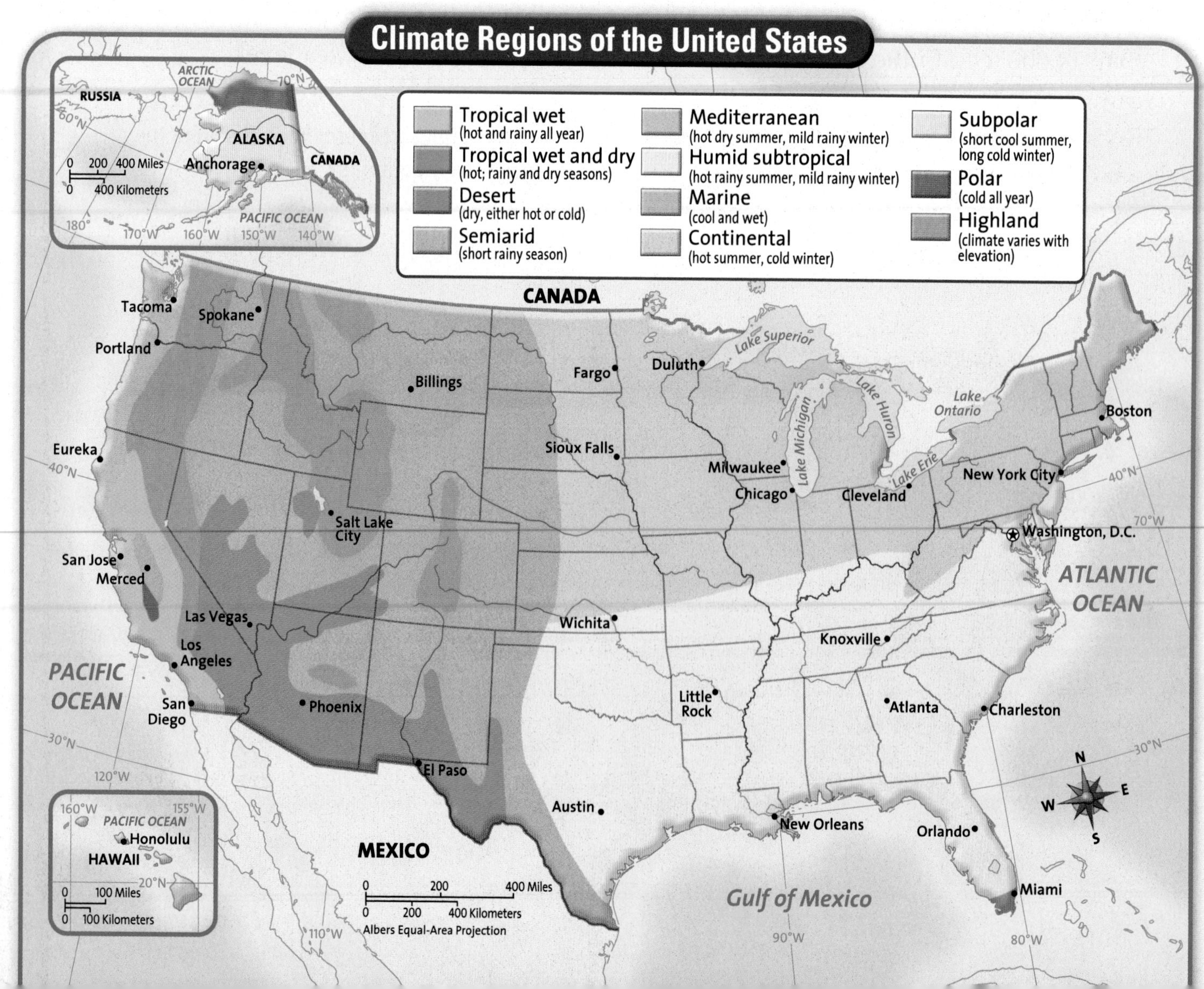

In Big Sur, California, steep cliffs have formed where the Coast Ranges meet the Pacific Ocean.

Stevenson arrived in San Francisco 24 days after he had left home. At long last, he met Osbourne, who had regained her health. He had traveled from one coast of the United States to the other. He had seen much of the country and many of its major landform regions. By taking a train across the United States, Stevenson had learned much about the country's diverse geography and climate.

READING CHECK COMPARE AND CONTRAST
How do the Coast Ranges differ from the Sierra Nevada?

Summary

The United States is made up of 50 states, each with its own capital. Because the country is so large, its geography and climate vary from one part of the country to another. Geographers sometimes divide the country into landform regions.

REVIEW

1. How do the geography and climate differ as you travel across the 50 states?
2. Write a sentence that includes the terms **landform region** and **environment**.
3. What two states are separated from the others?

CRITICAL THINKING

4. ANALYSIS SKILL Why do you think Robert Louis Stevenson wrote about the geography and climate of the United States during his trip?
5. **Make Flash Cards** Use notecards or take sheets of construction paper and cut them into 50 small cards. On one side of each card write the name of a state and on the other side write the name of its capital. Study the cards and then work with a classmate to quiz each other on state capital names.
6. Focus Skill **COMPARE AND CONTRAST** On a separate sheet of paper, copy and complete the graphic organizer below.

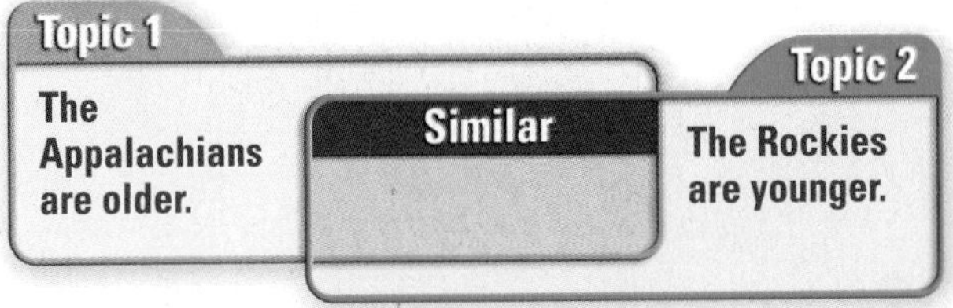

Use Latitude and Longitude

WHY IT MATTERS

The **relative location** of a place is where it is compared to other places on Earth. For example, the Coastal Plain is between the Piedmont and the Atlantic Ocean. But lines of latitude and lines of longitude help you describe the **absolute location**, or exact location, of any place on Earth.

WHAT YOU NEED TO KNOW

Mapmakers use a system of imaginary lines to form a grid system on maps and globes. The lines that run east and west are the **lines of latitude**. Lines of latitude are also called **parallels** (PAIR•uh•lelz). This is because they are parallel, or always the same distance from each other.

Lines of latitude are measured in degrees north and south of the equator, which is labeled 0°, or zero degrees. The parallels north of the equator are marked *N* for *north latitude*. The parallels south of the equator are marked *S* for *south latitude*.

The lines that run north and south on a map or globe are the **lines of longitude**, or **meridians**. Each meridian runs from the North Pole to the South Pole. Meridians meet at the poles.

The meridian marked 0° is called the prime meridian. Lines of longitude to the west of the prime meridian are marked *W* for *west longitude*. They are in the Western Hemisphere. The meridians to the east of the prime meridian are marked *E* for *east longitude*. They are in the Eastern Hemisphere.

Latitude and Longitude

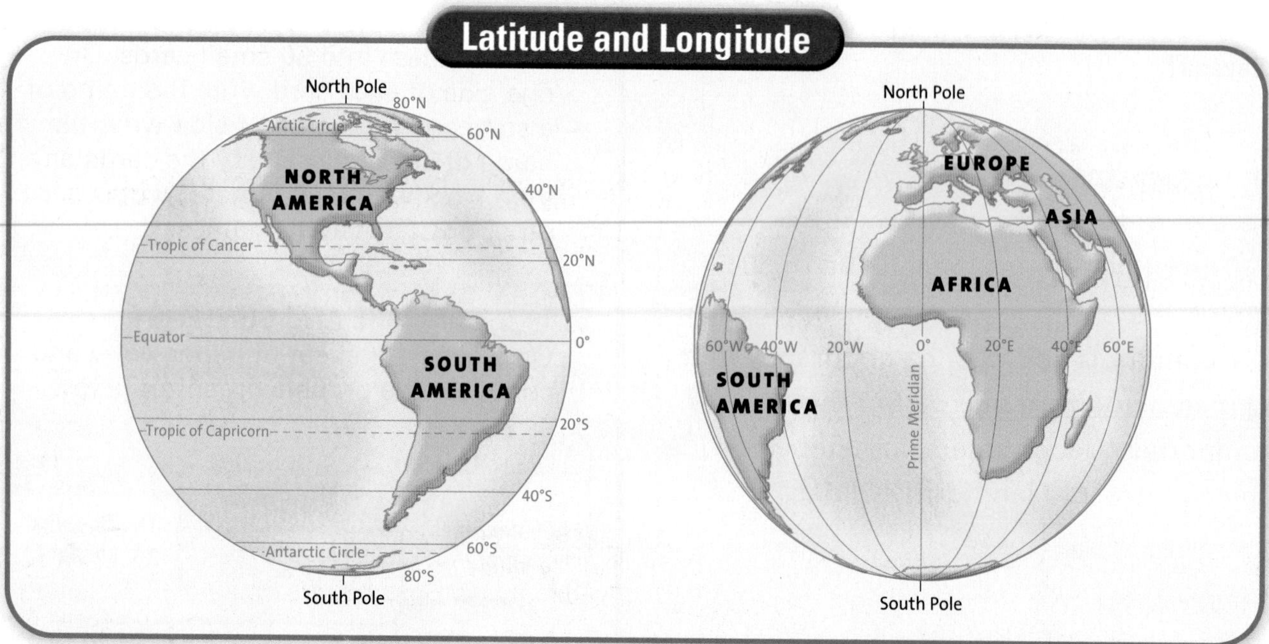

United States Latitude and Longitude

⊛ National capital
★ State capital

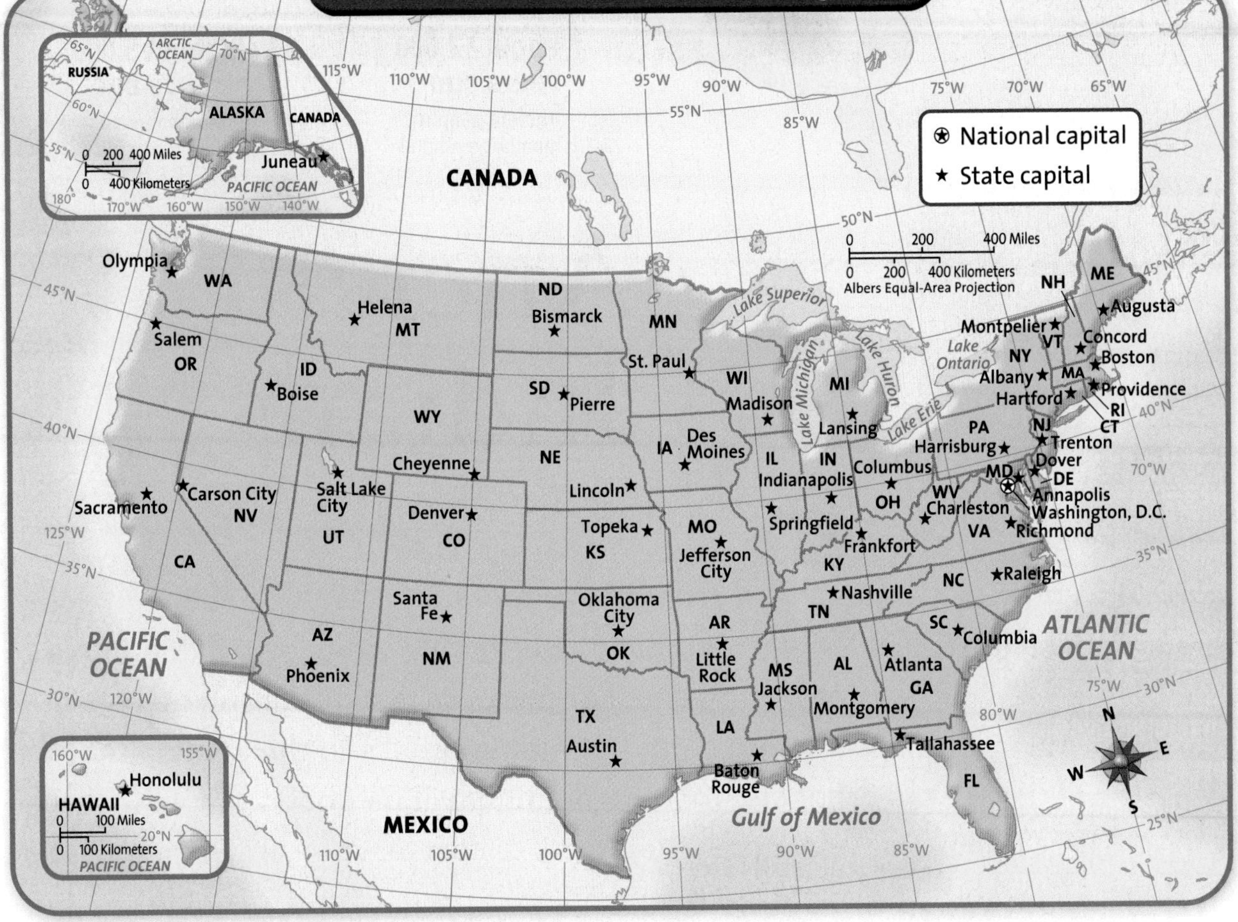

PRACTICE THE SKILL

The map above shows state capitals in the United States and uses lines of latitude and longitude to give absolute location.

On the left-hand side of the map, find 40°N. At the bottom, find 120°W. Use your fingers to trace these lines to the point where they cross. Carson City, Nevada, near the border of California, is not far from this point. So you can say that Carson City is near 40°N, 120°W.

Use the map to answer these questions.

1. Which state capital is nearest to 40°N, 105°W?
2. Which state capital is nearest to 30°N, 85°W?
3. Which state capital is farther north—Salem, Oregon, or Madison, Wisconsin?

APPLY WHAT YOU LEARNED

ANALYSIS SKILL Make It Relevant Use latitude and longitude to describe the location of your state's capital city. Write a short paragraph to describe how you found the capital's location.

Practice your map and globe skills with the **GeoSkills CD-ROM**.

Lesson 2

12,000 years ago — PRESENT

about 12,000 years ago
Ancient people hunt large animals

about 5,000 years ago
Ancient people begin farming in the Americas

WHAT TO KNOW
How did people first come to live in the Americas?

- ✓ Identify possible explanations of how people came to live in the Americas.
- ✓ Explain how early people in the Americas lived, hunted, and farmed.
- ✓ Understand how changes in the environment affected early peoples' lives.

VOCABULARY
ancestor p. 25
theory p. 25
migration p. 25
artifact p. 26
legend p. 27
generation p. 27
nomad p. 28
agriculture p. 30
culture p. 31

PLACES
Beringia
Clovis

HSS 5.1, 5.1.1

Ancient Indians

YOU ARE THERE The time is more than 10,000 years ago and you and your family are busy settling into a new campsite. For many days, your group has been tracking a herd of mammoths, and the adults are hopeful that the hunting will be good here. In the meantime, you work as fast as you can, gathering wild plants to help feed your group. The air is bitterly cold, but you keep warm by gathering the plants quickly. By tomorrow your group will join together in the first hunt, and you hope that it will be a great success.

The Land Bridge Story

The history of the United States begins with the first people in North America many thousands of years ago. They are the **ancestors**, or early family members, of present-day American Indians. How did these first people come to live in North America and South America?

After many years of study, scientists are still not sure of the answer. However, they do have several possible explanations, or theories. A **theory** is an idea based on study and research.

One theory is that there was once a "bridge" of dry land between the continents of Asia and North America. Scientists call this land bridge **Beringia** (buh•RIN•jee•uh). It was named for the Bering Strait, the narrow body of water that now separates Russia from Alaska.

Scientists who study Earth's past have found proof that thousands of years ago, there were several Ice Ages, or long periods of freezing cold. During the Ice Ages, huge, slow-moving sheets of ice called glaciers (GLAY•sherz) covered large parts of Earth.

Scientists think that so much of Earth's water was trapped in glaciers that the level of the oceans fell by as much as 350 feet. Because of this, the Earth had more dry land—including Beringia—than it does now.

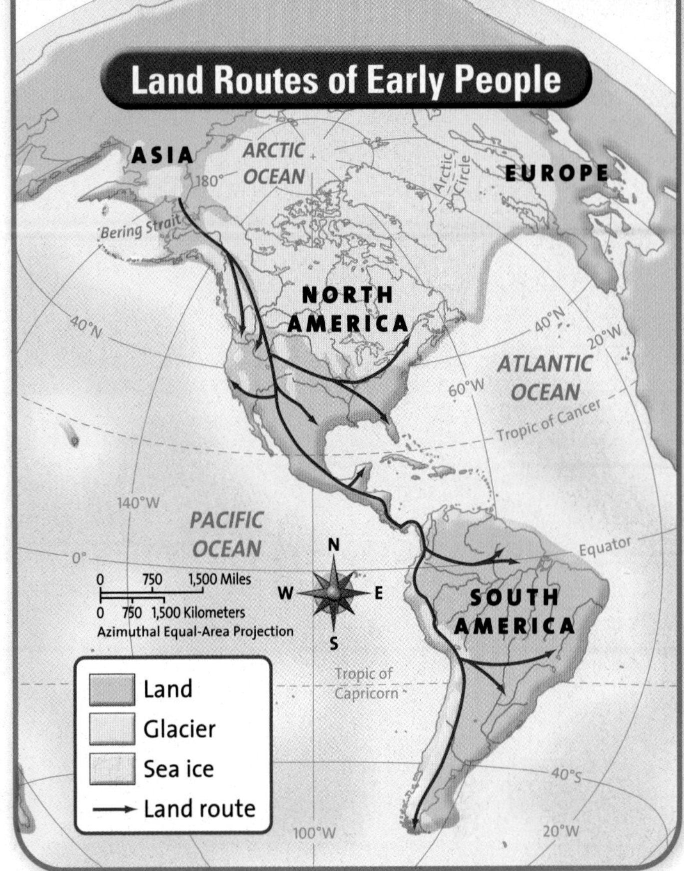

Analyze Maps

Movement About how many miles is it from Asia to the tip of South America?

Many scientists believe that thousands of years ago, groups of hunters and their families walked from Asia across the land bridge to North America. This **migration**, or movement of people, probably took place very slowly. Groups may have moved only a few miles in an entire lifetime. At that rate, they would have taken hundreds of years to just reach Alaska!

READING CHECK **COMPARE AND CONTRAST**
How did the geography and climate of the Ice Ages differ from those of today?

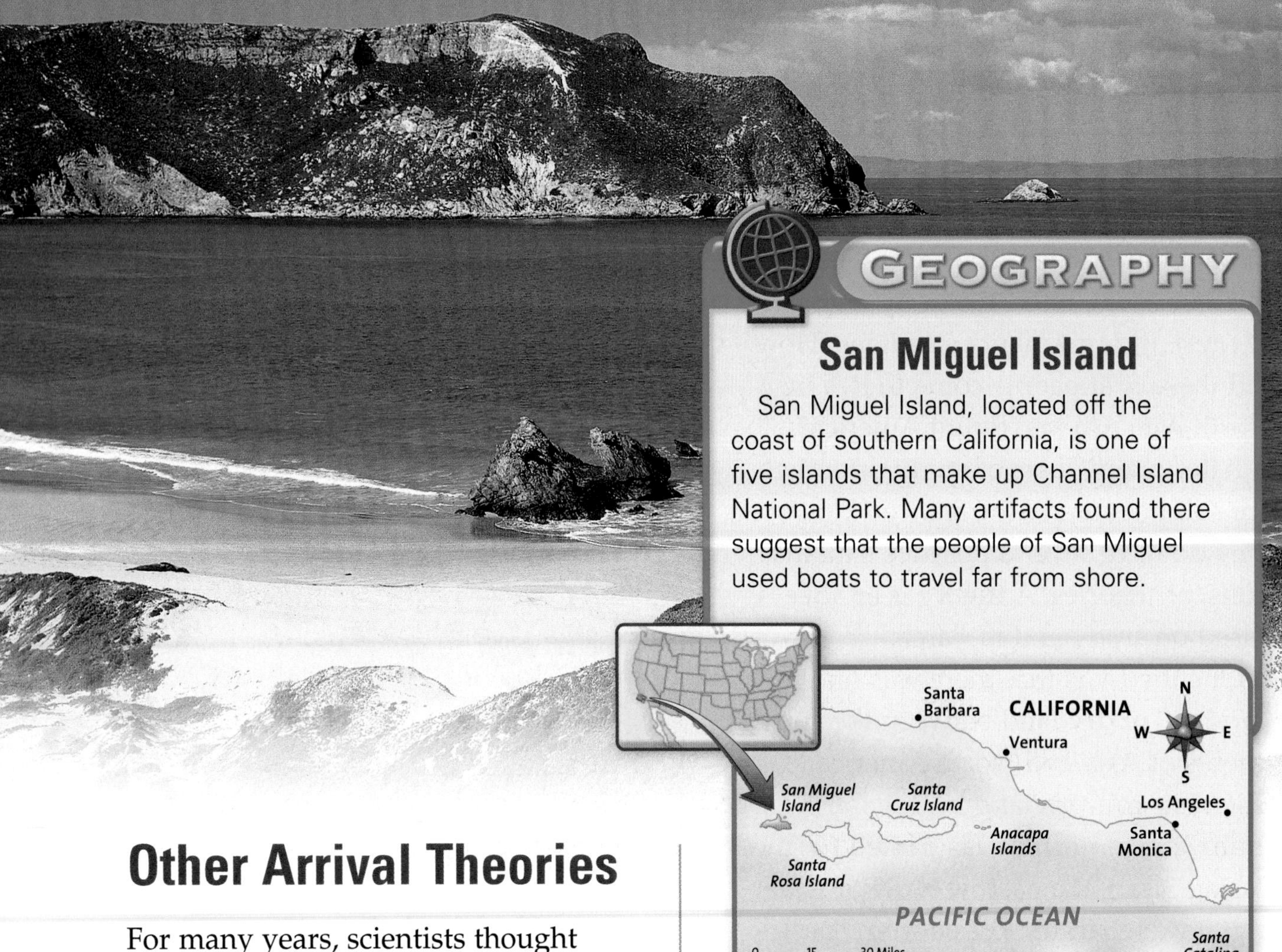

GEOGRAPHY

San Miguel Island

San Miguel Island, located off the coast of southern California, is one of five islands that make up Channel Island National Park. Many artifacts found there suggest that the people of San Miguel used boats to travel far from shore.

Other Arrival Theories

For many years, scientists thought that people arrived in the Americas about 12,000 years ago. Recently, however, archaeologists have found objects that may be more than 12,000 years old. Archaeologists (ar•kee•AH•luh•jists) are scientists who study the remaining traces of early people.

At Meadowcroft Rock Shelter, in Pennsylvania, some archaeologists have found stone tools that may have been made 14,000 years ago. Objects recently uncovered at Monte Verde (MOHN•tay VAIR•day), in Chile, may be 13,000 years old. These **artifacts**, or objects made by people, include huts, digging sticks, and even a child's footprint.

Some scientists disagree about the dates of certain artifacts, but most now think that people probably arrived in the Americas before 12,000 years ago. If so, those people may have crossed Beringia during another, earlier Ice Age.

Other discoveries hint that people may have come to the Americas in a different way. They may have traveled by boat. On San Miguel Island, about 25 miles off the coast of California, archaeologists have found artifacts that may date back 10,000 years. Archaeologists know that the people who made the artifacts used boats, because they lived on an island and ate deepwater fish caught far from shore. To catch these fish, they made hooks out of seashells.

READING CHECK **COMPARE AND CONTRAST**
How are the theories of migration to the Americas different?

Origin Stories

This sculpture represents the Iroquois Tree of Peace.

Ideas about the arrival of the first Americans also come from their descendants. In ancient times, most people passed on their history by memorizing stories. They told these **legends**, or stories handed down from the past, to their children and their grandchildren. As a result, generations of American Indians have learned these stories. A **generation** is the average time between the birth of parents and the birth of their children.

American Indian groups have all used legends to tell about their past. The stories that tell about their origins, or beginnings, are called origin stories.

Some American Indian origin stories explain how the world was made. For example, the Blackfoot tell a story of Old Man the Creator. According to the story, he made the animals and the plants and formed plains and mountains.

The Huron tell an origin story that begins with water covering Earth. According to the story, land was formed from a tiny bit of soil taken from the claws of a turtle. The turtle had picked up the soil from the bottom of the ocean. Because of this story and others like it, some American Indians use the name *Turtle Island* to describe the Americas.

No one knows exactly when the first Americans arrived. However, many American Indians believe that their people have always lived in the Americas.

READING CHECK SUMMARIZE
What is another source of ideas about the origin of early people in the Americas?

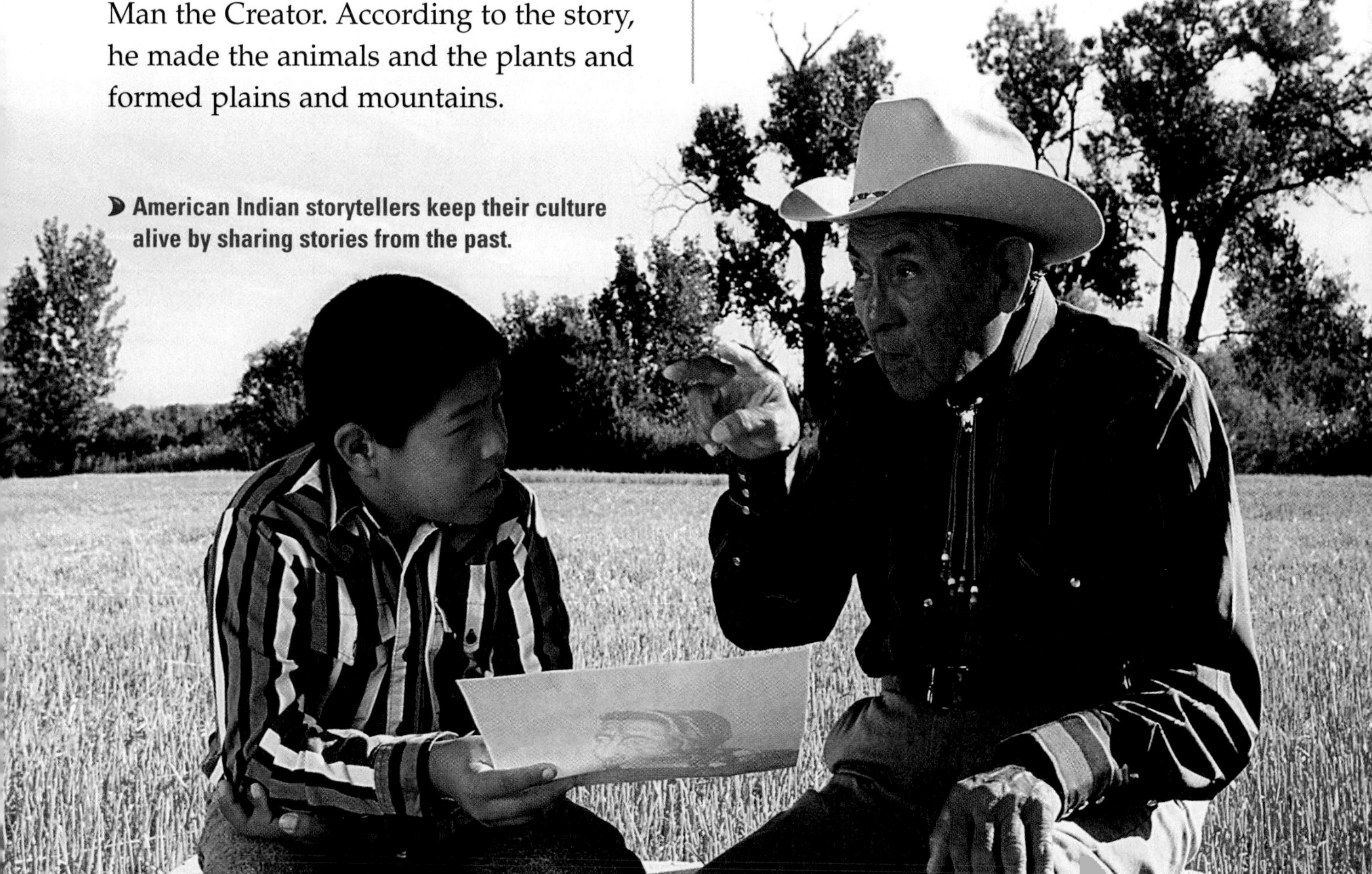

American Indian storytellers keep their culture alive by sharing stories from the past.

Early Ways of Life

No matter how the first people got to the Americas, they were most likely **nomads**, or people with no permanent homes. They lived in caves or in tents made of animal skins. They kept moving, following herds of animals that they could hunt. Archaeologists know this because they have found spear points near the bones of ancient animals.

After the last Ice Age ended, the climate of North America was cool and damp. The plants that grew then provided food for very large animals such as giant mastodons and woolly mammoths. These animals looked like huge, hairy elephants. They stood up to 14 feet tall, weighed as much as 10,000 pounds, and often had tusks up to 14 feet long.

The ancient Indians who hunted these giant animals ate the meat and used the fur, skins, and bones to make clothing, shelters, and tools. They also gathered wild foods, such as mushrooms. That is why scientists sometimes refer to these people as hunters and gatherers.

Compared to the huge animals they hunted, the ancient Indians were small and weak. They had to learn to work in groups to kill the animals. In time, they learned to sharpen stones into points and tie them to sturdy wooden sticks.

Various groups of ancient Indians invented different tools to help them hunt. Some made clubs and axes with stone blades. Later, other people invented a new kind of tool called the atlatl (AHT•lah•tuhl), which allowed hunters to throw their spears faster and farther.

In order to survive, the ancient Indians had to improve their tools. About the time the atlatl was invented, the ancient Indians came up with a new kind of spear point. Using a bone or a stone, they knocked off flakes, or small thin chips, from flint or other kinds of stone. They flaked the stone until the point was razor sharp. Then they hollowed out the point and fastened it tightly to a wooden spear. The spears were much better hunting weapons than earlier ones.

These deadly spear points are called Clovis points. They are named after the town of **Clovis**, New Mexico, where archaeologists first found them.

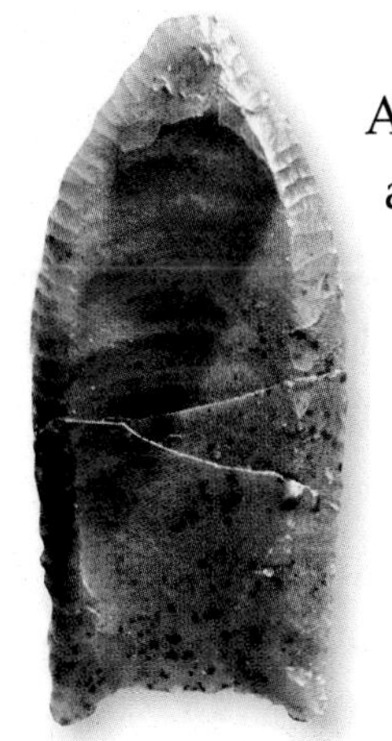

Clovis point

Slowly, the climate of North America changed, becoming warmer and drier. Most of the plants that the giant animals ate could no longer grow, which may be one reason these animals became extinct, or died out. About 10,000 years ago, most of them disappeared.

People had to find new sources of food, so they began to fish and to hunt smaller animals, such as deer and rabbits. The ancient Indians made new hunting tools, including the bow and arrow. They also began to eat a greater variety of plants.

READING CHECK **COMPARE AND CONTRAST**
How was life different for the ancient Indians after the giant animals became extinct?

Analyze Illustrations **Early people worked together to hunt large animals.**

1 Giant sloth
2 Woolly mammoth
3 Ancient armadillo
4 Ancient camels
5 Giant short-faced bear

Why were many people needed to hunt a woolly mammoth?

A New Way of Life

TIME **About 5,000 years ago**
PLACE **North America**

When the ancient Indians gathered more food than they could use right away, they found ways to store it. They used reeds, vines, and strips of wood to make baskets. Later, people learned to make storage containers out of other materials, such as clay.

Over time, some ancient Indians changed their lifeways, or ways of life, even more. They began to plant seeds and to grow food instead of only gathering it. This change was the beginning of **agriculture**, or farming, in the Americas.

Agriculture started at different times in different parts of the world. In the Americas, ancient Indians likely started farming about 5,000 years ago. Some of the earliest farmers lived in the Tehuacán (tay•wah•KAHN) Valley in central Mexico. In the fertile valley, they grew at least 12 kinds of maize (MAYZ), or corn, as well as avocados, squash, and beans. Maize was the most important crop for many people living in North America. It was grown all across the continent.

One way that farming changed the lives of many of the ancient Indian groups was by giving them a reason to stay in one place for longer periods of time. By about 5,000 years ago, some were building stronger homes and had started villages. Some groups also formed what are now called tribes. A tribe is a group of people who share the same language, land, and leaders.

Early people worked together to farm.

Many archaeologists believe that this sole of a shoe and these cave paintings (left) at Pedra Furada, Brazil, are proof that people arrived in the Americas earlier than previously thought.

The climate and natural resources of each area in which they settled affected how the groups lived. Over time, each group came to have its own culture. A **culture** is a way of life that sets a group apart from other groups. These unique cultures can sometimes be pieced together by scientists who study artifacts for clues about earlier lifeways.

READING CHECK GENERALIZE
How did farming change early peoples' lives?

Summary

There are many theories about how people got to the Americas. Climate changes forced early people to learn how to live in new environments. Once people began to farm, they also settled in villages. These early people developed different cultures based partly on where they lived.

REVIEW

1. How did people first come to live in the Americas?
2. How are the words **migration** and **nomad** related?
3. How did changes in the environment affect large animals?

CRITICAL THINKING

4. ANALYSIS SKILL How did the importance of the Bering Strait's relative location change as the land bridge disappeared?
5. ANALYSIS SKILL Did early people hunt giant animals before or after they started farming?
6. **Write a Paragraph** Describe how ancient Indians might have made tools for hunting.
7. Focus Skill **COMPARE AND CONTRAST** On a separate sheet of paper, copy and complete the graphic organizer below.

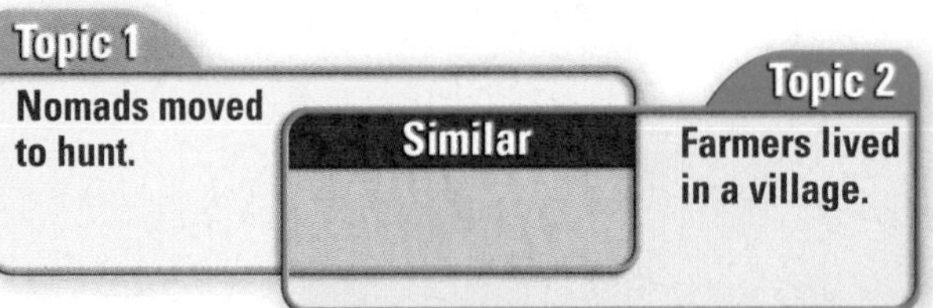

Read Time Lines

WHY IT MATTERS

An easy way to see relationships between events in history is to look at a **time line**. A time line is a diagram that shows events that took place during a certain period of time. Like a calendar, a time line can help you understand the order of events and the amounts of time between events.

WHAT YOU NEED TO KNOW

A time line looks like a ruler marked in dates instead of inches. Like inches marked on a ruler, there are dates on a time line that are equally spaced. However, not all time lines look the same or are read in the same way. Most time lines run horizontally, or across the page. But some run vertically, or down the page. Horizontal time lines, like the one shown below, are read from left to right. The earliest date is on the left end, and the most recent date is on the right end. The time line on page 33 is a vertical time line. It is read from top to bottom. The earliest date is at the top of the time line, and the most recent date is at the bottom.

Time lines can show events that took place during any period of time. Some time lines show events that took place over a **decade**, or a period of 10 years. Others show events that took place over a **century**, or a period of 100 years. Both a decade and a century are labeled on the horizontal time line below. Some time lines show events that took place over a **millennium**, or a period of a thousand years. A millennium is labeled on the vertical time line on page 33.

The vertical time line here shows dates from the ancient past to today. Notice the letters *B.C.* and *A.D.* in the middle of

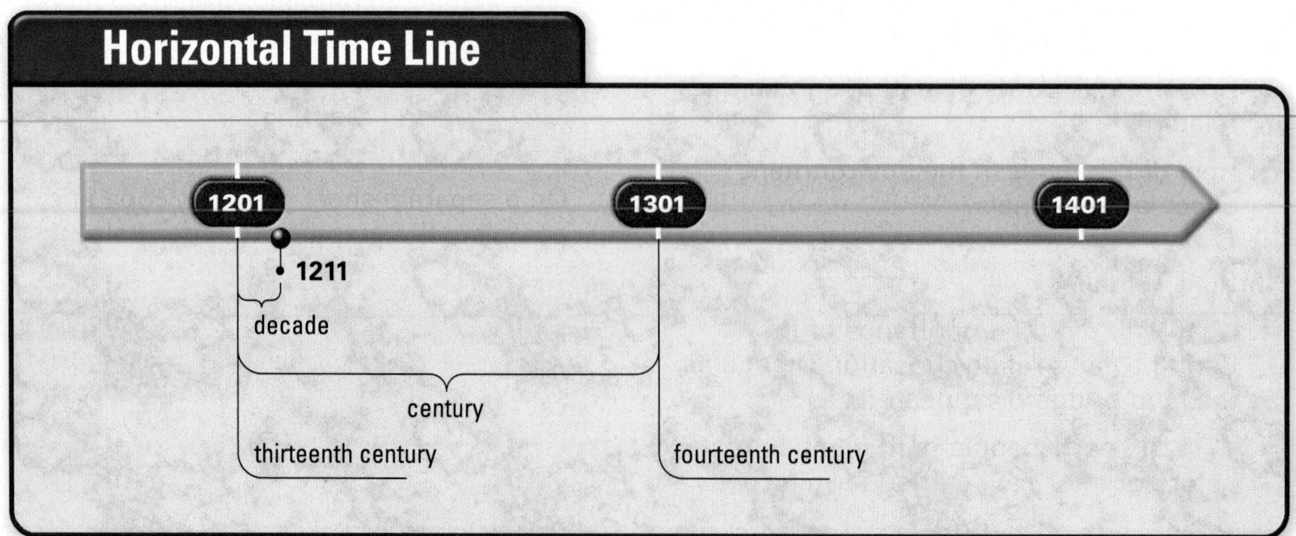

the time line. Many people today identify years by whether they took place before or after the birth of Jesus Christ. The years before are labeled *B.C.*, which stands for "before Christ." Years after the birth of Christ are labeled *A.D.* This stands for the Latin words *Anno Domini* which mean "in the year of the Lord."

An event that happened in 100 B.C. took place 100 years before the birth of Christ. An event that happened in A.D. 100 took place 100 years after the birth of Christ. Because every year in modern times is A.D., these letters are often not needed.

You may also see the letters *B.C.E.* or *C.E.* with dates. The abbreviation *B.C.E.* stands for "before the Common Era." It is sometimes used instead of *B.C.* The abbreviation *C.E.*, which stands for "Common Era," is sometimes used in place of *A.D.*

PRACTICE THE SKILL

Use the horizontal time line on page 32 to answer the following questions.

1. How many centuries are shown on this time line?
2. What was the first year of the thirteenth century?

Use the vertical time line on this page to answer these questions.

3. How many millenniums are shown on this time line?
4. Which year came earlier, 1000 B.C. or 500 B.C.?

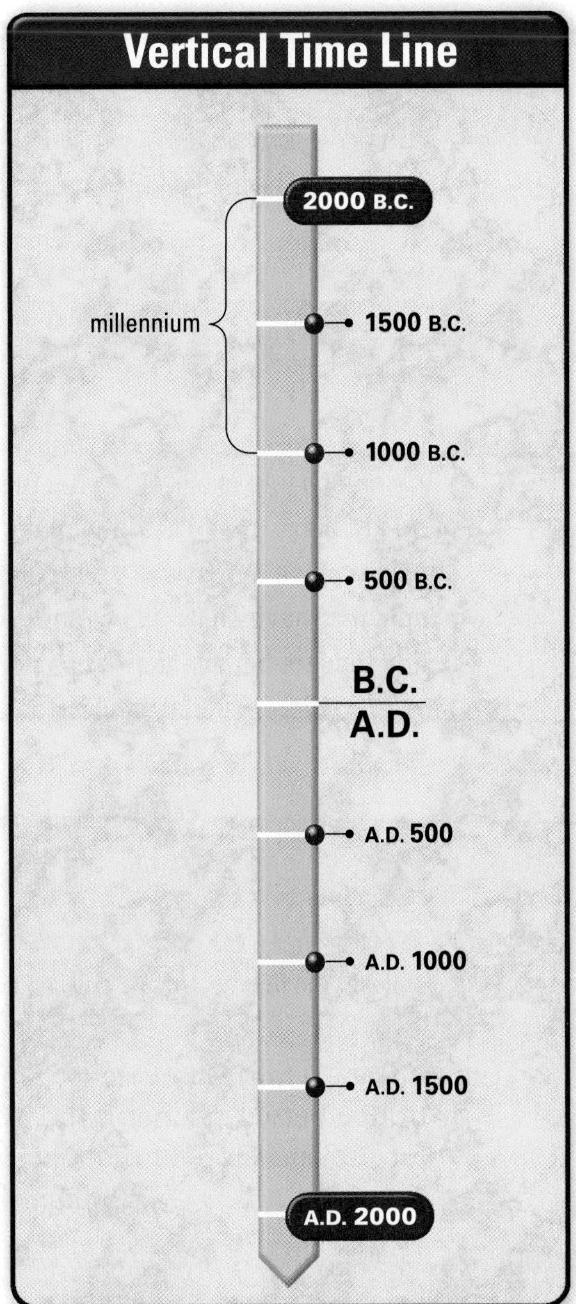

APPLY WHAT YOU LEARNED

ANALYSIS SKILL **Make It Relevant** Make a time line that shows the last 20 years in 5-year periods. Then mark on your time line important events that have taken place in your own life. Share your time line with other students.

Arrival in the Americas

Since no one is sure how the first people arrived in the Americas, there are many points of view on the subject. Some believe that the first people walked across the Beringia land bridge. Others believe early people may have come by boat across the Pacific Ocean. Some American Indian leaders believe their ancestors have always been in the Americas. Here are different points of view on this much-debated subject.

In Their Own Words

Douglas W. Schwartz, a scientist who believes the first Americans crossed over the Bering Strait

"... Our best evidence supports the view that a land bridge between Siberia and Alaska was the route of entry for the ancestors of the American Indian."

— from *Clues to America's Past.* National Geographic Society, 1976.

Early people had to travel in groups for safety.

Early boat travel would have required strong boats.

VINE DELORIA, JR.

Vine Deloria, Jr., a professor of Native American Studies

"... A small group of anthropologists have now allowed that Indians, instead of marching ... over the mythical Bering land bridge, might have come by boat ... from the Asian continent to North America."

— from *Red Earth, White Lies: Native Americans and the Myth of Scientific Fact.* Scribner, 1995.

Luther Standing Bear, Sioux Chief, describing the legend of the Sioux's beginnings

LUTHER STANDING BEAR

"Our legends tell us that it was ... thousands of years ago since the first man sprang from the soil in the midst of the great plains. The story says that one morning long ago a lone man awoke, face to the sun, emerging from the soil."

— from *Land of the Spotted Eagle.* University of Nebraska Press, 1978.

It's Your Turn

ANALYSIS SKILL **Analyze Points of View** Work with a classmate to summarize the point of view held by each author.

Make It Relevant Explain why it is important to learn about different points of view on a subject.

Some American Indian sites are more than 10,000 years old.

Lesson 3

Time

12,000 years ago — PRESENT

- **about 3,500 years ago** The Olmec civilization becomes powerful
- **about 1,700 years ago** The Mayan civilization becomes powerful

WHAT TO KNOW
In what ways did the people of the Americas create advanced civilizations?

- ✓ Explain how the location of early American civilizations affected the way that people lived.
- ✓ Describe achievements and customs of early American civilizations.

VOCABULARY
civilization p. 37
government p. 37
custom p. 37
tradition p. 38
hieroglyph p. 38
class p. 38
pueblo p. 40

PLACES
San Lorenzo
Cahokia
Moundville

COMPARE AND CONTRAST

California Standards
HSS 5.1, 5.1.1, 5.1.2, 5.1.3

Early Civilizations

YOU ARE THERE The crowd around you sits elbow to elbow, eagerly waiting for the game to begin. The sound of drums fills the air as the ballplayers march onto the field. Some of the ballplayers are wearing pads to protect themselves from injury. You can see why—the rubber ball they are using looks very hard. This ball game is played for honor. According to the rules of your people, the winning team will receive gifts, while the losing team will lose their lives.

➤ The Olmec ball game was one of the first team sports in history.

San Lorenzo (above) was once an important Olmec city. Artists there carved giant stone heads such as this one.

The Olmec

Once people began to have a more settled way of life, civilizations started to develop. A **civilization** is an advanced culture that usually has cities with well-developed kinds of learning, religion, and government. A **government** is a system for deciding what is best for a group of people. It protects members of the group, settles disagreements among them, and provides a way for the group to make rules and choose leaders.

The Olmec civilization was one of the earliest in the Americas. From about 1500 B.C. to A.D. 300, the Olmec ruled most of what is now southern Mexico. The area the Olmec lived in had a tropical climate with a rainy season and a dry season. The oldest Olmec city that archaeologists have discovered is **San Lorenzo**. Like many Olmec cities, it is located near a river. The location of some Olmec cities near rivers suggests that the Olmec used rivers to travel between cities and build a trade system. Olmec artifacts have been found in many areas of Mexico.

A strong trade system was just one achievement of the Olmec. They also developed a counting system and a calendar to keep track of the seasons. The Olmecs depended on the rainy season to water their crops.

No one is sure why the Olmec civilization fell from power, but it clearly had a great influence on other civilizations. Today, some historians call the culture of the Olmec the "mother culture" of the Americas, because many Olmec **customs**, or ways of doing things, were continued in later civilizations.

READING CHECK **COMPARE AND CONTRAST**
How was the Olmec civilization similar to our civilization today?

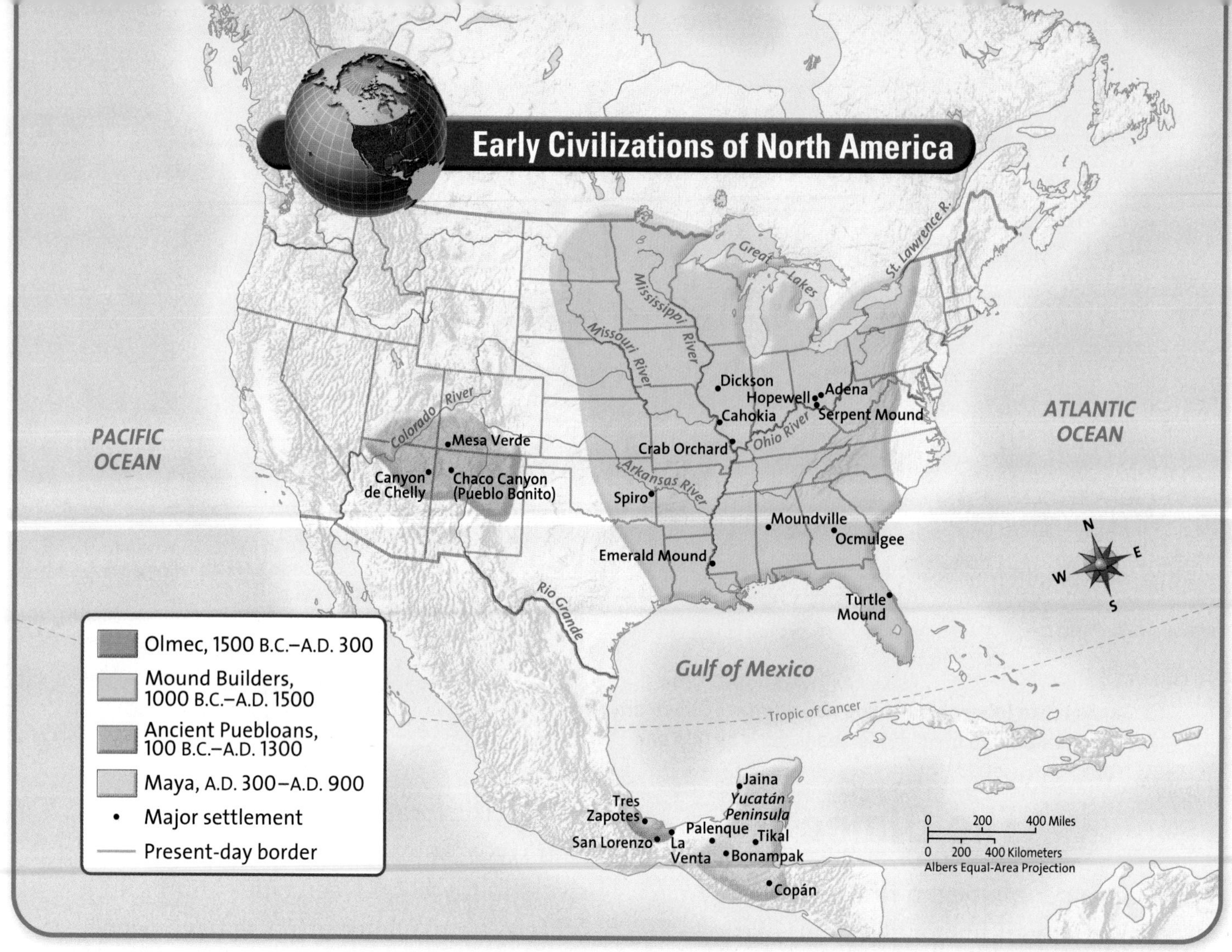

ANALYSIS SKILL Analyze Maps The Mayan and Olmec civilizations both developed in what is now Mexico.

Location Where was the Mayan civilization located?

The Maya

The Mayan civilization was influenced by Olmec traditions. A **tradition** is a way of life or an idea that has been handed down from the past. Between A.D. 300 and A.D. 900, the Maya ruled much of what is now southern Mexico, Guatemala, and northern Belize. The area the Maya lived in had a tropical climate that was hot and humid.

The Maya developed their own writing system, which allowed them to tell their history. Their writing system was based on **hieroglyphs** (HY•ruh•glifs), or picture symbols. They also used a counting system like the Olmec.

The Maya were divided into social classes. A **class** is a group of people in a society who have something in common. At the top of Mayan society were the religious leaders. Then came important families, traders, and farmers.

Scientists are not sure why the Mayan civilization fell. Some blame the fall on disease, while others think it was warfare. However, even after the Maya fell from power, their culture continued.

READING CHECK COMPARE AND CONTRAST
How were the Mayan and Olmec societies alike?

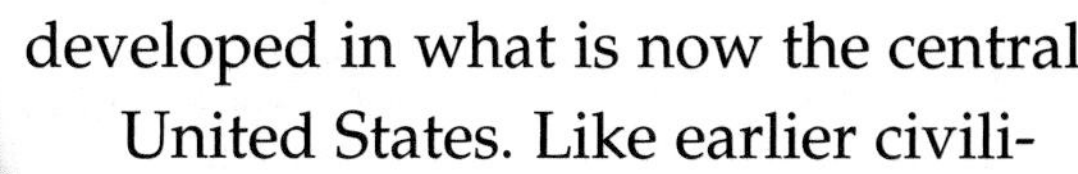

The Mound Builders

Archaeologists use the name *Mound Builders* to group together many American Indian tribes. What these groups had in common was that they all built mounds made of earth. However, their cultures, their locations, and even their reasons for building mounds differed.

The earliest Mound Builders were the Adena (uh•DEE•nuh). Their civilization was located in the Ohio River valley. It lasted from about 1000 B.C. to A.D. 200. The Adena mounds were used for burials. As more people were buried, the mounds got bigger and bigger. Some reached heights of 90 feet!

In about 300 B.C., another mound-building culture, called the Hopewell, developed in what is now the central United States. Like earlier civilizations, the Hopewell built a strong trade system. Its trade paths stretched from the Rocky Mountains to Lake Superior.

A shell head

The largest of the mound-building civilizations was the Mississippian. It developed in the Mississippi River valley in about A.D. 700. The largest Mississippian city was **Cahokia**, in present-day Illinois. By A.D. 1200, more than 30,000 people lived in Cahokia.

Moundville, in present-day Alabama was another large city. Religious leaders ruled the city and the surrounding area. People lived in this area from about A.D. 900 to A.D. 1500.

READING CHECK **MAIN IDEA AND DETAILS**
What was one way that American Indian groups used mounds?

This painting shows what a Mound Builders' settlement may have looked like.

The Ancient Puebloans

Look at the map of North America on page 38. Find the place in the Southwest where Utah, Colorado, Arizona, and New Mexico meet. This area is called the Four Corners. Some of the first people to settle this area are known as the Ancient Puebloans (PWEH•bloh•uhnz). The climate of the area they lived in was hot and very dry.

The Ancient Puebloans started to build their civilization in about A.D. 100. They lived in houses that had many floors and many rooms. These houses were often built against canyon walls or in caves. When the Spanish arrived in the Southwest more than 1,400 years later, they called this kind of home a **pueblo**, the Spanish word for "village."

Usually, there was no entrance on the first floor. Instead, people climbed ladders to the roof and entered from there. In case of enemy attack, they simply pulled up the ladders.

To feed themselves, the Ancient Puebloans grew maize, beans, and pumpkins. They farmed enough maize to enable them to store extra food in special storage rooms, for use in hard times.

The Ancient Puebloans also were expert basket makers. In fact, some of their baskets were so tightly woven that they were waterproof. These baskets were used for storage and sometimes for cooking food. A person could put corn mash in a basket and then drop into it a hot stone that cooked the mash.

The Ancient Puebloan culture thrived for about 1,000 years. At the culture's peak, the population may have been as high as 20,000.

Then people began to move away. Scientists think that a change in climate was part of the reason they left. Evidence shows that a terrible drought started in

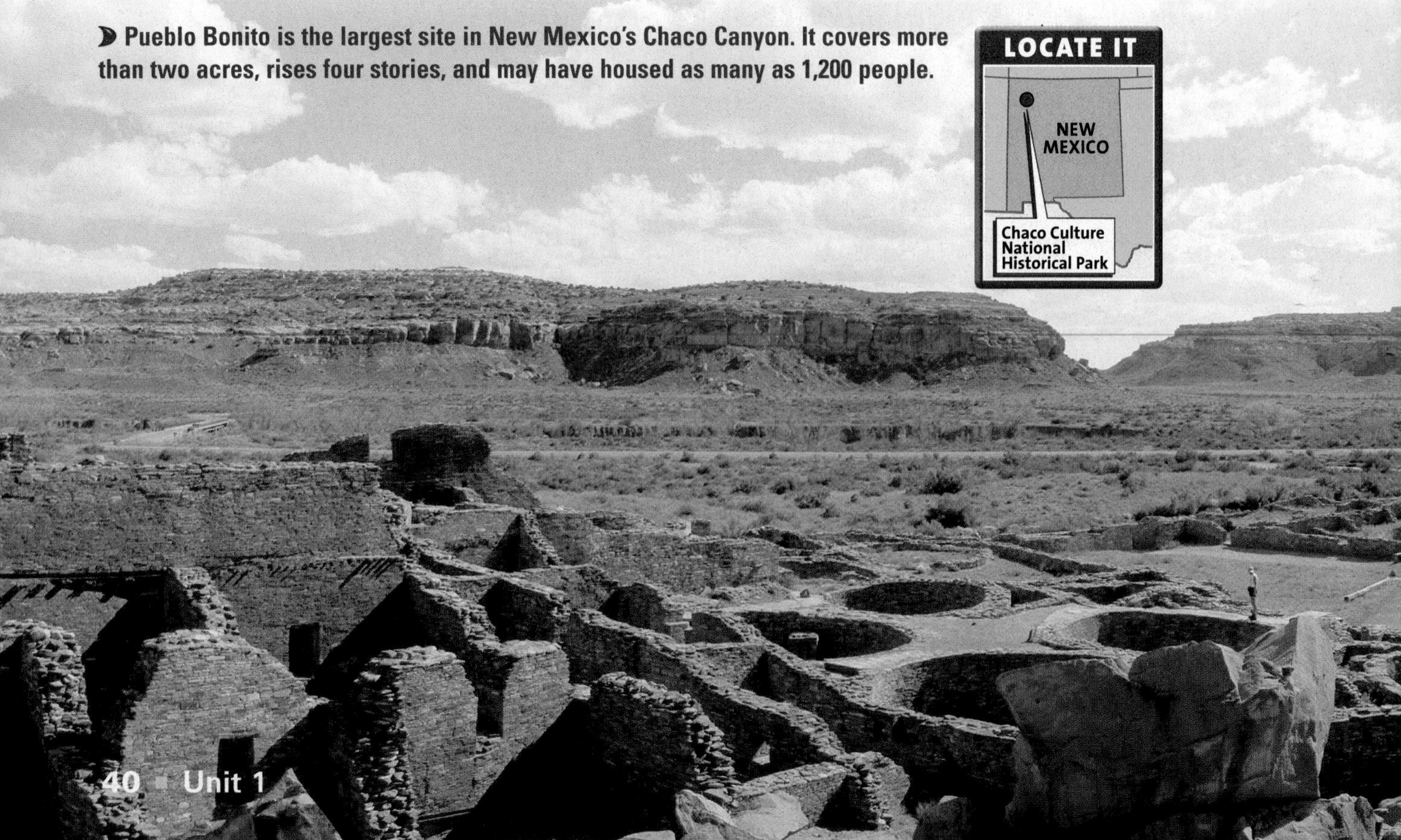

Pueblo Bonito is the largest site in New Mexico's Chaco Canyon. It covers more than two acres, rises four stories, and may have housed as many as 1,200 people.

At the area that is known today as Mesa Verde National Park in Colorado, early Americans carved stone villages into the canyon walls.

about A.D. 1276. Careful planning had helped the culture survive droughts before, but this drought lasted almost 25 years. It made the land completely dry. By A.D. 1300, the Ancient Puebloan civilization had disappeared from the Four Corners.

READING CHECK **COMPARE AND CONTRAST**
How was the climate of the area where the Ancient Puebloans lived different from the area where the Olmec lived?

Summary

The earliest civilizations in the Americas were influenced by the geography and climate of the areas in which the people lived. All of these civilizations developed different customs and traditions.

REVIEW

1. In what ways did the people of the Americas create advanced civilizations?
2. Write a description of a **pueblo**.
3. What did the Adena, Hopewell, and Mississippian cultures have in common?
4. What important form of communication helped the Maya record their history?

CRITICAL THINKING

5. ANALYSIS SKILL Why do you think some early civilizations were divided into classes?
6. **Draw a Plan** Imagine that you are designing a Mound Builder's city. Draw a building plan that includes mounds made of earth and other structures.
7. Focus Skill **COMPARE AND CONTRAST** On a separate sheet of paper, copy and complete the graphic organizer below.

Use a Cultural Map

WHY IT MATTERS

You already know that different kinds of maps can show different kinds of information. A cultural map is one that shows **cultural regions** of a place. Understanding cultural regions will help you know what the peoples who lived there had in common.

WHAT YOU NEED TO KNOW

On a cultural map, regions are usually identified by colors or symbols. The map on page 43 uses color to show North America's early cultural regions. In all, there are 11 colors, each representing a different cultural region.

Some American Indian dancers wore finger masks during certain ceremonies.

As you can tell from the map, each cultural region was home to several different American Indian groups. Each group was different from the other groups in the region. Yet the lifeways and traditions of all the groups in a region were affected by the same climate and landforms as well as the same animals and vegetation.

PRACTICE THE SKILL

Use the map on the next page to answer these questions.

1. Which cultural region includes most of the eastern United States?
2. Which cultural region includes most of present-day New Mexico and Arizona?
3. Which cultural region includes most of the central United States?

APPLY WHAT YOU LEARNED

ANALYSIS SKILL Partner with a classmate to play a guessing game. You and your partner should each choose an American Indian group shown on the cultural map. Then take turns asking each other questions about regions to try to figure out which group your partner chose.

Practice your map and globe skills with the **GeoSkills CD-ROM**.

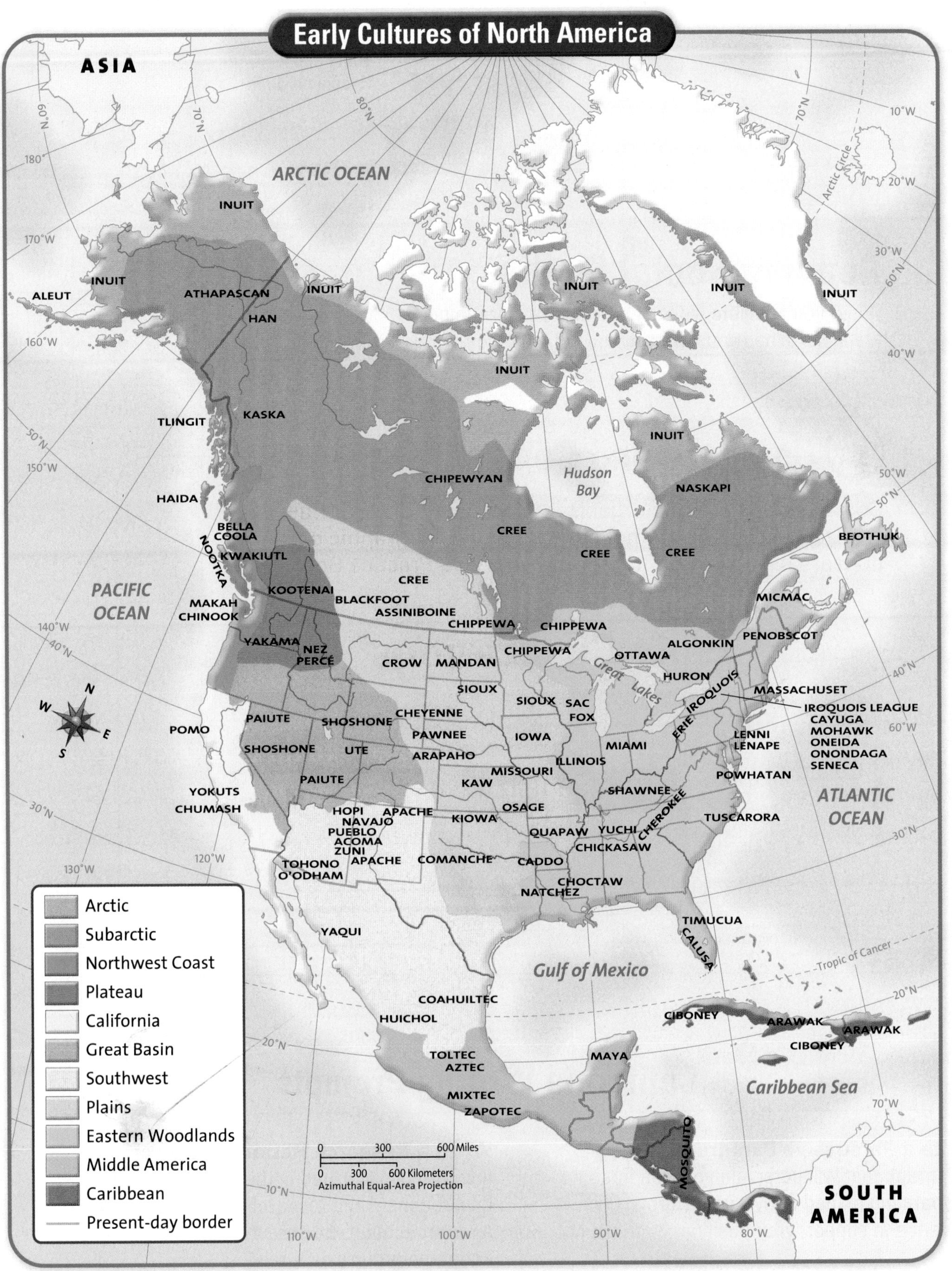

Map and Globe Skills

Time

about 12,000 years ago

about 12,000 years ago
People arrive in the Americas

Reading Social Studies

When you **compare**, you tell how two or more things are alike. When you **contrast**, you tell how they are different.

Compare and Contrast

Complete this graphic organizer to compare and contrast early civilizations in North America. A copy of this graphic organizer appears on page 12 of the Homework and Practice Book.

Early Civilizations

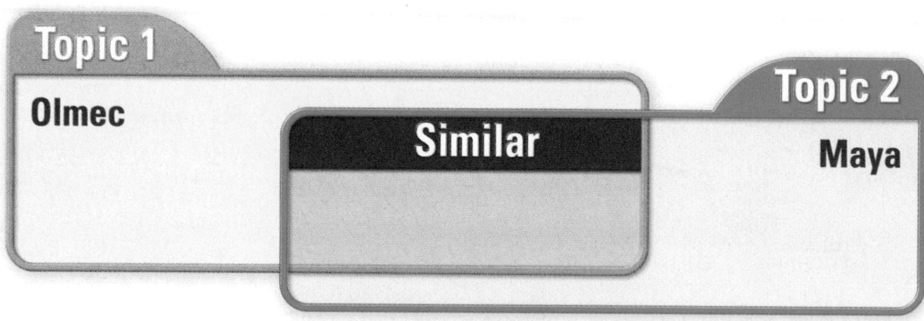

California Writing Prompts

Write a Persuasive Paragraph Write a paragraph that will persuade your readers that farming helped early villages grow. Give evidence to support your position.

Write a Research Report Choose one of the groups discussed in the lesson on Early Civilizations. Then research the group and write a report about it. Be sure to include information about the group's culture.

about 7,000 years ago

about 5,000 years ago
People begin farming in North America

about 3,500 years ago
The Olmec civilization is strong

about 3,000 years ago
Early Mound Builder groups develop

Use Vocabulary

Identify the term that correctly matches each definition.

1. an early family member
2. a story handed down from the past
3. the kind of weather a place has over a long time
4. a people's ways of doing things
5. picture symbols

climate, p. 16
ancestor, p. 25
legend, p. 27
custom, p. 37
hieroglyph, p. 38

Use the Time Line

Use the chapter summary time line above to answer these questions.

6. About how long ago did people in North America start farming?
7. About how many years passed between the time when the Olmec civilization was strong and the early Mound Builder groups developed?

Apply Skills

Use Latitude and Longitude

8. Use the map on page 23 to find out what state capital is located near 30°N, 85°W.

Recall Facts

Answer these questions.

9. What mountain range covers much of the eastern United States? the western United States?
10. What was Beringia?
11. What was one important achievement of the Olmecs?

Write the letter of the best choice.

12. From the Appalachian Mountains, which direction would you travel to reach the Great Plains?
    A east
    B west
    C north
    D south
13. Which statement best describes early people in North America?
    A They often hunted alone.
    B They lived in one place.
    C They hunted larger animals.
    D They built stone shelters.

Think Critically

14. ANALYSIS SKILL What physical features make the Intermountain Region a unique place?
15. ANALYSIS SKILL How is life in the Southwest today similar to the civilization of the Ancient Puebloans? How is it different?

Study Skills

ANTICIPATION GUIDE

An anticipation guide can help you anticipate, or predict, what you will learn as you read.

- **Read the lesson titles and section titles. These are clues to what you will read about.**
- **Read the Reading Check question at the end of each section.**
- **Predict what you will learn as you read.**

The Desert Southwest		
The Pueblo People		
Reading Check	Prediction	Correct?
In what ways were the Pueblo people like the Ancient Puebloans?	In this lesson, we will learn how the Pueblo people lived like the Ancient Puebloans.	✓
Pueblo Culture		
Reading Check	Prediction	Correct?

Apply As You Read

As you read the chapter, complete your own anticipation guide for each lesson. When you have finished reading, go back to see if your predictions were correct.

California History-Social Science Standards, Grade 5

5.1 Students describe the major pre-Columbian settlements, including the cliff dwellers and pueblo people of the desert Southwest, the American Indians of the Pacific Northwest, the nomadic nations of the Great Plains, and the woodland peoples east of the Mississippi River.

CHAPTER

American Indians

American Indian festival in Charlotte, North Carolina

Start with a Story

Race to the Moonrise

An Ancient Journey

Written by Sally Crum
Illustrated by Shonto Begay

Race to the Moonrise tells the story of Little Basket and her brother Long Legs, American Indian children living in the Southwest more than 800 years ago. One day, travelers appear in their village and ask Little Basket to go on a journey to save the villages to the north. Accompanied by her brother and her uncle, she must travel hundreds of miles to what is now Chimney Rock, Colorado, and present offerings to the gods. Read now as the two young travelers prepare for their very important journey.

Long Legs nervously rearranged his pack for the fourth time and thought about how nice it would be to carry real trade goods instead of rocks. He placed four balls of salt at the bottom of the pack. "Everyone likes salt in their rabbit stew," he mumbled. He put two small rubber balls on top of the salt. I've heard the people of the Far North don't play the ball court games but maybe we'll visit others who do on the way there, he thought.

Last night his mother had given him several small copper bells. Many years before her father was born, her great-grandfather had brought them from the Great City to the south. They were valuable. Long Legs carefully wrapped the bells in cotton cloth and tucked them between the rubber balls. Shell bracelets, pouches of corn and mesquite flour, and dried deer meat filled the rest of his pack.

Little Basket bounced toward him, carrying a stick birdcage with a red and green macaw in it. "I picked up Squawk at the aviary. You are taking him, aren't you?" she asked. The huge bird of the parrot family was calmly preening his long, scarlet tail feathers which almost touched the ground.

"Yes, he's more than a pet to me so I don't want to trade him. But we could trade lots of his feathers," said Long Legs. "I've taught him so many words, I consider him a friend."

aviary a place for keeping birds

preening dressing up; smoothing feathers

Squawk seemed disgusted. "Squawk good bird," he screeched.

Long Legs and Little Basket laughed. "We'll leave you enough feathers to keep you warm at night in the Far North," Long Legs told him.

"And I'll carry all the sunflower seeds you'll need to eat," added Little Basket.

Uncle and the three travelers from the Far North walked across the plaza to the children. Uncle looked upset. "We have a longer journey ahead than we thought," he said. "Our visitors have told me that Little Basket must take special offerings to present at Moonrise."

The youngest traveler looked at Long Legs. "Thunder Voice requires a beautiful bowl from the Mountain People, an ancient clay doll from the Canal People, white clam shells from the Salt Bay, a fine cotton cape from the Volcano People, and a painted mug from the Cliff Dwellers of the Far North People. He thinks the gods will surely talk to Little Basket if the trouble is taken to obtain these offerings."

Uncle turned to Long Legs and Little Basket. "We must leave soon and keep a steady pace. We will visit the Mountain People first but we can trade with them for only a day. We must then head west to the desert farms of the Canal People." . . .

Mother hugged Uncle and her children and with a brave smile said, "Every night I will look at the Traveler's Star and know it is shining over my dear ones, leading them in the right direction."

Little Basket's eyes filled with tears. Long Legs helped her with her pack and said cheerily, "We'll all be fine, Mother. And we may return with Father!"

The three visitors from the Far North ran ahead. They would travel straight north to home. As they moved farther away, the young one shouted back, "See you at the Moonrise Ceremony, Long Legs!" They were soon out of sight behind a low hill. . . .

The trail followed the river at the edge of the willows and cottonwood trees. It was just wide enough for the travelers to run single file. Thousands of years of foot travel had worn it deep into the desert soil. Uncle said the trail had been used

by the ancient hunters, before they learned to farm and even before the great trade routes were established. Long Legs could not imagine a world without farming or trading.

Over his shoulder, Long Legs took a last, quick look back toward his village. He caught the eye of Little Basket, who was running behind him, and flashed her a reassuring grin. He then turned his thoughts toward breathing easily. They would jog steadily much of the day. "Even if we keep up this pace," he muttered, "will we arrive in time for the Moonrise Ceremony at Finger Rocks?"

Response Corner

1. What special offerings was Little Basket required to present at the Moonrise Ceremony?
2. Imagine that you lived in the desert Southwest during the time of Little Basket and Long Legs. Write a story that describes your everyday life as a farmer or trader.

Lesson 1

The Desert Southwest

WHAT TO KNOW
How did the geography and climate of the desert Southwest affect the American Indians there?

✓ Describe how the Pueblo peoples adapted to their environment.

✓ Identify the importance of agriculture for the people of the desert Southwest.

VOCABULARY
adapt p. 53
adobe p. 53
staple p. 53
division of labor p. 54
surplus p. 54
ceremony p. 55
hogan p. 56

PEOPLE
Ancient Puebloans
Hopi
Zuni
Navajo

PLACES
Arizona
New Mexico

COMPARE AND CONTRAST

HSS 5.1, 5.1.1, 5.1.2, 5.1.3

YOU ARE THERE Darkness hides the flat-topped mesas and deep cliffs surrounding the valley where your people have made their home for centuries. As you stand on the top of your pueblo, you see the shapes of people gathering in a room below. Your brother calls for you to hurry. He has saved a spot for you next to the fire. You are excited because the storyteller is about to begin. Tonight, he will tell stories about your ancestors—the **Ancient Puebloans**.

FAST FACT
The Hopi grew 24 different kinds of corn, but blue and white were the most common.

The Pueblo People

The desert Southwest, with its mesas, deep canyons, steep cliffs, and rugged mountains, was a challenging place to live. Intense summer heat was usually followed by bitter winter cold.

Among the American Indians who were able to **adapt**, or adjust, their lifeways to the natural environment and its resources were the **Hopi** (HOH•pee) and the **Zuni** (ZOO•nee). The Hopi lived in what is today the state of **Arizona**. The Zuni lived farther east, in present-day **New Mexico**. In time, they and most other groups in the region became known as the Pueblo peoples. Like their Ancient Puebloan ancestors, they lived in pueblos built on mesas or on the sides of steep canyons.

The climate of the desert Southwest provided little rainfall so few trees grew. The Hopi and the Zuni used stones and mud to build their pueblos. Other groups built houses from **adobe**, sun-dried bricks made of clay mixed with straw. Some wood was used to build the roofs of the pueblos. The Pueblo people had to travel long distances into the mountains to find pine and juniper trees from which they could make beams for their roofs.

Even in their dry environment the Pueblo Indians were able to grow their **staple**, or main, foods of maize (corn), beans, and squash. They planted these crops at the bottoms of mesas, where they could catch rainwater. They found underground springs and built irrigation canals to water their crops. Irrigation is the use of canals, ditches, or pipes to move water to dry areas. The Pueblo also grew cotton, which was used to weave blankets and clothing.

READING CHECK **COMPARE AND CONTRAST**
In what ways were the Pueblo people like the Ancient Puebloans?

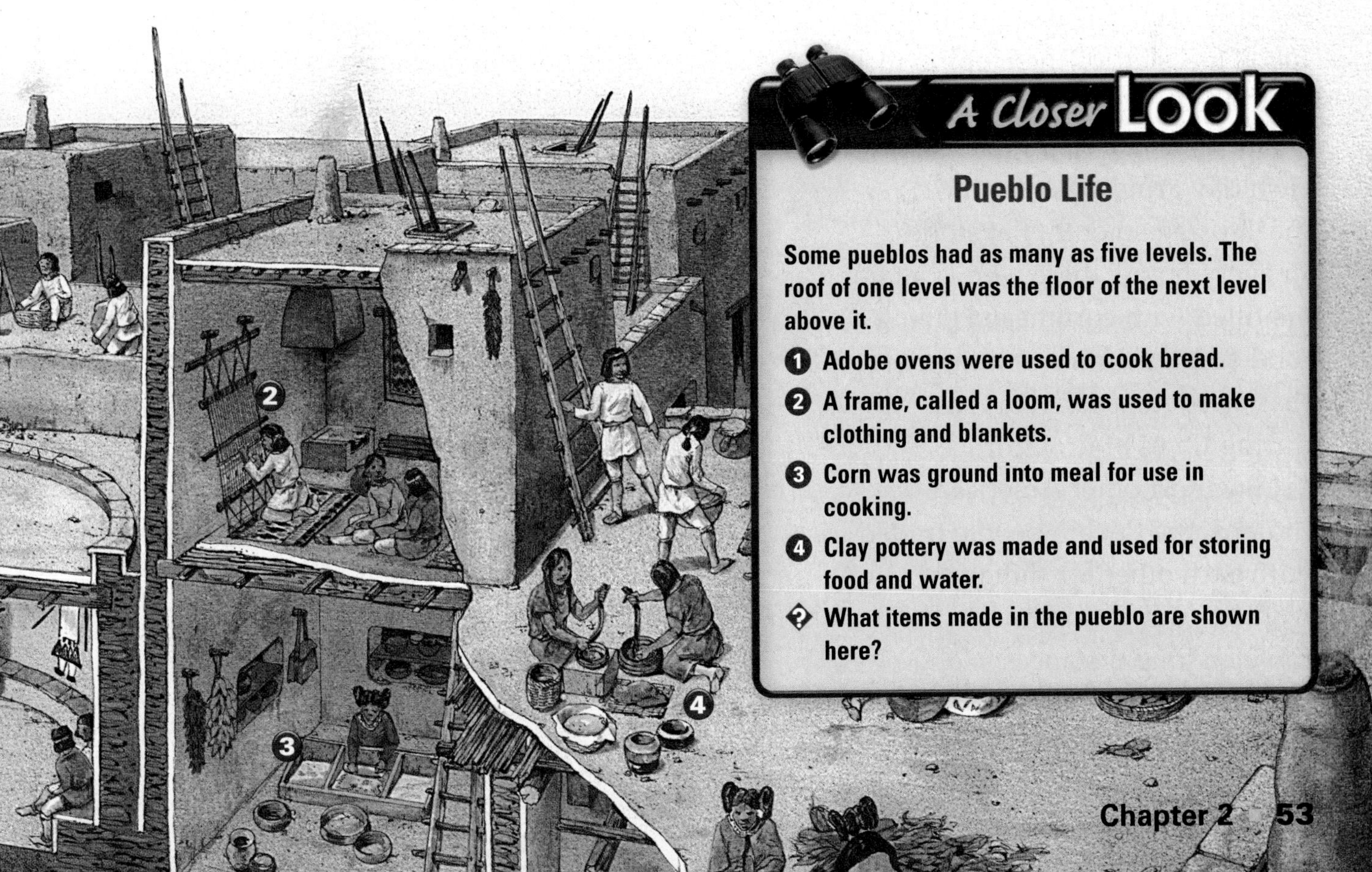

A Closer LOOK

Pueblo Life

Some pueblos had as many as five levels. The roof of one level was the floor of the next level above it.

1. **Adobe ovens were used to cook bread.**
2. **A frame, called a loom, was used to make clothing and blankets.**
3. **Corn was ground into meal for use in cooking.**
4. **Clay pottery was made and used for storing food and water.**

What items made in the pueblo are shown here?

Children IN HISTORY

Hopi Children

For hundreds of years, Hopi children have received little wooden kachina dolls. These dolls are not toys. Instead, they are learning tools. Each doll is decorated in a special way and represents an important human value, such as kindness, discipline, or respect for elders. Through the kachina dolls, children learn the importance of practicing these values in their own lives.

Make It Relevant Why do you think it might be important for children to learn respect for their elders?

Pueblo Culture

In Hopi society, jobs were divided among men and women. Men governed the villages, hunted, and tended crops, while women owned and cared for all property. Women cooked and cared for the children. This **division of labor** made it easier for the Hopi to meet their needs.

Hopi women spent hours each day grinding corn into meal, using smooth, flat stones. In every home, there were containers filled with cornmeal. Having a food **surplus**, or an amount more than needed, meant survival during times of drought.

Like most other American Indians, the Pueblo people traded with each other for things they wanted. They sometimes traveled long distances, along narrow paths, to trade their pottery and baskets with other tribes. These artifacts have been found as far north as present-day Colorado.

The Hopi often traded their pottery for copper bells, arrowheads, and shells. One of the most important trade items to the Hopi was salt, which they used to flavor and preserve their food. More importantly, they used salt to aid healing. When someone was injured, salt was placed on the wound to help it heal.

The Hopi, the Zuni, and other Pueblo people believed in gods of the sun, rain, and Earth. Spirits called kachinas (kuh•CHEE•nuhz) were an important part of the Hopi religion. The Hopi believed these spirits worked as messengers between people and the gods. They also believed that during special dances, the kachinas would enter the bodies of the dancers.

This doll is a Hopi lizard kachina.

Kachina dancers took part in many Hopi ceremonies. A **ceremony** is a series of actions performed during a special event, such as a religious service. Some ceremonies were held in underground rooms called kivas (KEE•vuhz).

Many Hopi ceremonies focused on matters such as weather and farming. The Hopi believed that a successful ceremony could help produce a good harvest. Hopi ceremonies usually lasted eight days, following a day of preparation. Other ceremonies could last even longer.

Just as in daily life, religion played an important role in the governments of the Pueblo Indians. Usually, a chief, who was also a religious leader, led the Hopi village. The chief made rules and enforced punishments.

Like the Hopi, the Zuni followed a religious form of government. The Council of High Priests controlled the Zuni government. These religious leaders ruled as a group. One member was in charge of ceremonies, while two other members enforced decisions regarding crime and carried out punishments.

READING CHECK **COMPARE AND CONTRAST**
How were men's jobs different from women's jobs in Hopi society?

This historic painting shows kachina dancers preparing for a ceremony.

The Navajo

Not all of the people who lived in the desert Southwest were Pueblo. Before moving to the region, peoples such as the **Navajo** (NA•vuh•hoh) lived mainly as nomads. They traveled in groups, hunting and gathering food. The Navajo began moving into the Southwest about A.D. 1025. They settled in the Four Corners area, where they still live.

Some of this land was also Hopi land. During a period of drought, some Hopi people came to live with the Navajo. In time, the Navajo began learning the Hopi customs. Eventually, they began growing food and making cotton clothing as the Hopi did. From the Hopi, they also learned how to farm in the desert.

The Navajo did not call themselves Navajo, which was a name given to them by the Pueblo peoples. Instead, the Navajo called themselves *Diné* (dee•NAY). In the Navajo language, *Diné* means "The People."

The homes of the Navajo were different from those of the Hopi and the Zuni. The Navajo built shelters called **hogans**. At first, the Navajo built hogans by covering a wooden frame with bark and mud, but later, they began to cover the wooden frame with adobe. Navajo hogans were often miles apart, rather than in villages as the shelters of Pueblo peoples were.

READING CHECK **COMPARE AND CONTRAST**
How were Navajo lifeways similar to and different from Pueblo lifeways?

These hogans (below) were built on Navajo land in Utah.

Two Navajo medicine people use colored sand to make a sandpainting inside a hogan.

Navajo Beliefs

The Navajo believed in gods they called the Holy People. Some gods, such as the Earth Mother, were kind, while others, such as the sun god, could cause crops to dry up. The Navajo believed they needed to honor the gods so that the gods would not use their power against the people.

Like the Pueblo Indians, the Navajo honored their gods in ceremonies. Navajo ceremonies were led by religious leaders and healers called medicine people. Medicine people called upon the gods to protect Navajo families, homes, and crops or to cure the sick. Medicine people memorized and sang songs or chants believed to have healing powers. Many of these songs and chants were hundreds of years old. They were often performed with music and lasted many hours.

In other healing ceremonies, medicine people might make sandpaintings, also called dry paintings, that were believed to help people. First, the medicine person created a pattern of symbols on the ground, using colored sand. Next, the sick person sat or lay down on the sandpainting.

After learning how to use cotton thread from the Hopi, the Navajo became well known for their skill as weavers. A Navajo woman shows her granddaughter how to weave.

Then, the medicine person held a ceremony that the Navajo believed would help the sick person feel healing powers. The painting was always rubbed away after the ceremony. Navajo religious beliefs led to art forms that are still practiced today.

READING CHECK **COMPARE AND CONTRAST**
How were Navajo beliefs like those of the Hopi?

Summary

The American Indians of the desert Southwest found ways to build successful communities in their dry, rocky environment. They divided work between men and women and their main crop was corn. Religion was an important part of their everyday lives.

REVIEW

1. How did the geography and climate of the desert Southwest affect the American Indians there?
2. Write a sentence about the Navajo, using the term **ceremony**.
3. Why was it important for the Hopi to store surplus food?

CRITICAL THINKING

4. ANALYSIS SKILL How did the location of the Pueblo peoples affect the kinds of shelters they built?
5. ANALYSIS SKILL How did the Hopi use kachinas to teach their children important values?
6. **Draw a Map** Draw a map of the United States and shade in the area where the American Indians of the desert Southwest lived.
7. Focus Skill **COMPARE AND CONTRAST** On a separate sheet of paper, copy and complete the graphic organizer below.

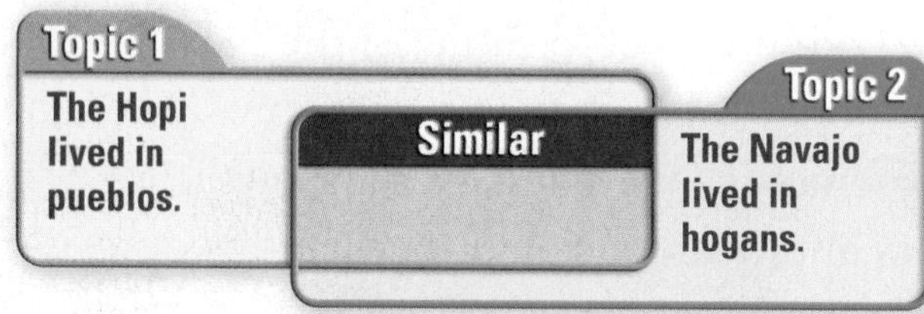

Luci Tapahonso

*“This is how we were raised.
We were raised with care and attention
because it has always been this way.
It has worked well for centuries.”**

Biography

Trustworthiness
Respect
Responsibility
Fairness
Caring
Patriotism

Luci Tapahonso is a Navajo poet who helps preserve Navajo culture through her writing. Tapahonso was born in Shiprock, New Mexico, and grew up in one of the largest American Indian communities in the country. She started writing poetry at the age of 9 and had her first book published in 1981.

Today, Tapahonso is a professor at the University of Arizona. She continues to write poetry and has read many of her poems on radio and television. She uses both the Navajo and English languages in her writings, which are often about the landscape of the Southwest and the history of her people.

Recently, Tapahonso was part of a group that helped plan and organize the National Museum of the American Indian in Washington, D.C. The museum, which covers ten thousand years of native history, opened in September 2004.

*Luci Tapahonso. *The Women Are Singing.* University of Arizona Press, 1993.

Why Character Counts

How does Luci Tapahonso work to keep the Navajo community strong?

Bio Brief

1953 — PRESENT

Born 1953

- **1953** Luci Tapahonso is born
- **1981** Tapahonso publishes her first collection of poems

GO ONLINE
Interactive Multimedia Biographies
Visit MULTIMEDIA BIOGRAPHIES at www.harcourtschool.com/hss

Lesson 2 The Pacific Northwest

WHAT TO KNOW
How did the geography and climate of the Pacific Northwest affect the American Indians there?

- Describe how the people of the Pacific Northwest met their needs and adapted to their environment.
- Describe the cultures of the American Indians of the Pacific Northwest.

VOCABULARY
harpoon p. 60
longhouse p. 62
clan p. 62
totem pole p. 63
economy p. 63
network p. 64
barter p. 64
potlatch p. 64

PEOPLE
Kwakiutl
Makah
Chinook

PLACES
Columbia River
The Dalles

COMPARE AND CONTRAST

HSS 5.1, 5.1.1, 5.1.2, 5.1.3

YOU ARE THERE Spring has finally come. For weeks, the tribe elders have been observing the sky's color, noting the wind's direction, and watching the stars' positions in the sky. Now they have decided that today is a good day to go hunting for a whale.

The whale hunters will take the village's biggest canoes. They carry with them their longest, heaviest **harpoons**—long spears with sharp shell points. If the hunt is successful, there will be singing and dancing to welcome the hunters home!

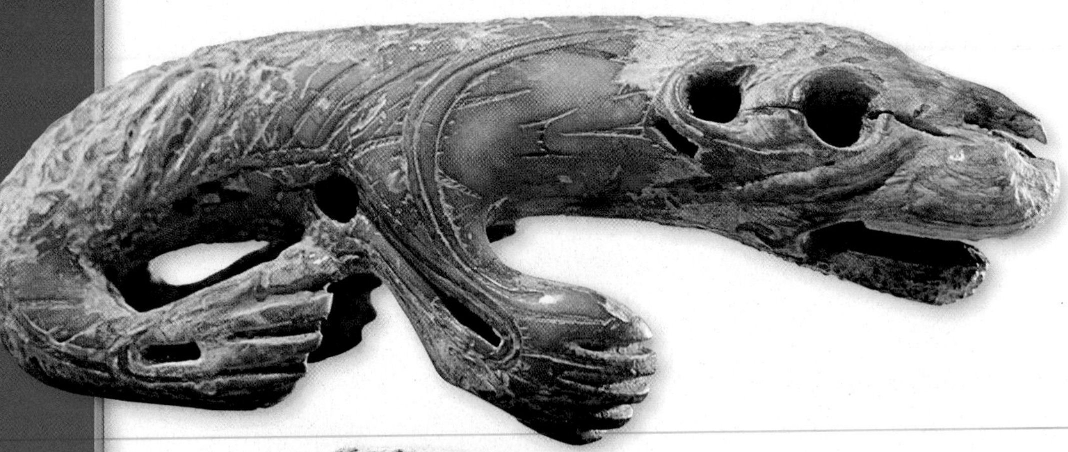

The whalebone artifact at the bottom may have been an art form or a tool, while the whalebone artifact at the top is the carved figure of a walrus.

During a whale hunt the chief harpooner showed his respect for the huge animal by singing a special song, promising to give the whale gifts if it allowed itself to be killed.

A Region of Plenty

The American Indians of the Pacific Northwest cultural region, also known as the Northwest Coast region, lived in a place that was very different from the desert Southwest. Nestled between the Pacific Ocean and rugged mountains to the east, the Pacific Northwest region included parts of what are now Oregon, Washington, and western Canada. Cool ocean winds brought heavy rains to the region, so forests grew tall and thick. These forests and the rivers that ran through them were filled with animals and fish.

Among the many groups who lived in the Pacific Northwest were the **Kwakiutl** (kwah•kee•YOO•tuhl), the **Makah** (mah•KAW), and the **Chinook** (shuh•NUK). Instead of farming, Indians in the Pacific Northwest met their needs by fishing and hunting and by gathering plants and nuts. Salmon was a staple food for most groups.

Whales were also an important resource. Whales supplied not only food but also fat, which could be melted into oil to burn in lamps. Most groups, including the Kwakiutl, captured only whales that became stranded on the shore. The Makah, however, built dugout canoes to hunt whales at sea. These boats—made from a large, hollowed-out log—were up to 6 feet wide and carried up to 60 people.

READING CHECK **COMPARE AND CONTRAST**
How were the whale-hunting methods of the Makah different from those of the Kwakiutl?

Resources and Trade

The enormous trees that grow in the forests of the Pacific Northwest provided the Makah and other groups with wood for boats as well as for houses and tools. The Makah built their villages near the Pacific Ocean, a common location for many Indians in the Pacific Northwest. The doors to the Makah's homes even faced the ocean.

The Makah built large wooden houses called **longhouses**. These rectangular homes were sometimes 60 feet long. Like the longhouses built by the Kwakiutl and other groups, Makah longhouses had a frame made of wooden poles. Planks, or wide boards, were used to cover the walls and floors.

The longhouses had slanted roofs that allowed rainwater to run off. Usually, they had no windows. When smoke collected from a cooking fire, planks could easily be removed from the roof to clear the air, because the planks were usually not permanently attached.

All the members of a **clan**, or extended family, lived in the same longhouse. This meant that grandparents, parents, aunts and uncles, and children often lived together. Each clan was headed by its oldest member. Older clan members passed down songs, dances, stories, and woodcarving skills to younger members.

Wood was so useful to the people of the Pacific Northwest that they made almost everything from it. Dishes, spoons, and other utensils were made of wood. So were ceremonial masks that were often used in storytelling.

A Closer LOOK

A Pacific Northwest Village

It is believed that many villages along the Northwest Coast had hundreds of inhabitants.

1. **Northwest Coast Indians used dugouts to fish for salmon and to hunt whales.**
2. **Salmon was dried on racks so that it could be kept for long periods of time.**
3. **Totem poles stood in front of many homes.**
4. **Baskets made with long, thin strips of wood were treasured trade items.**

? What activities are shown in this Pacific Northwest village?

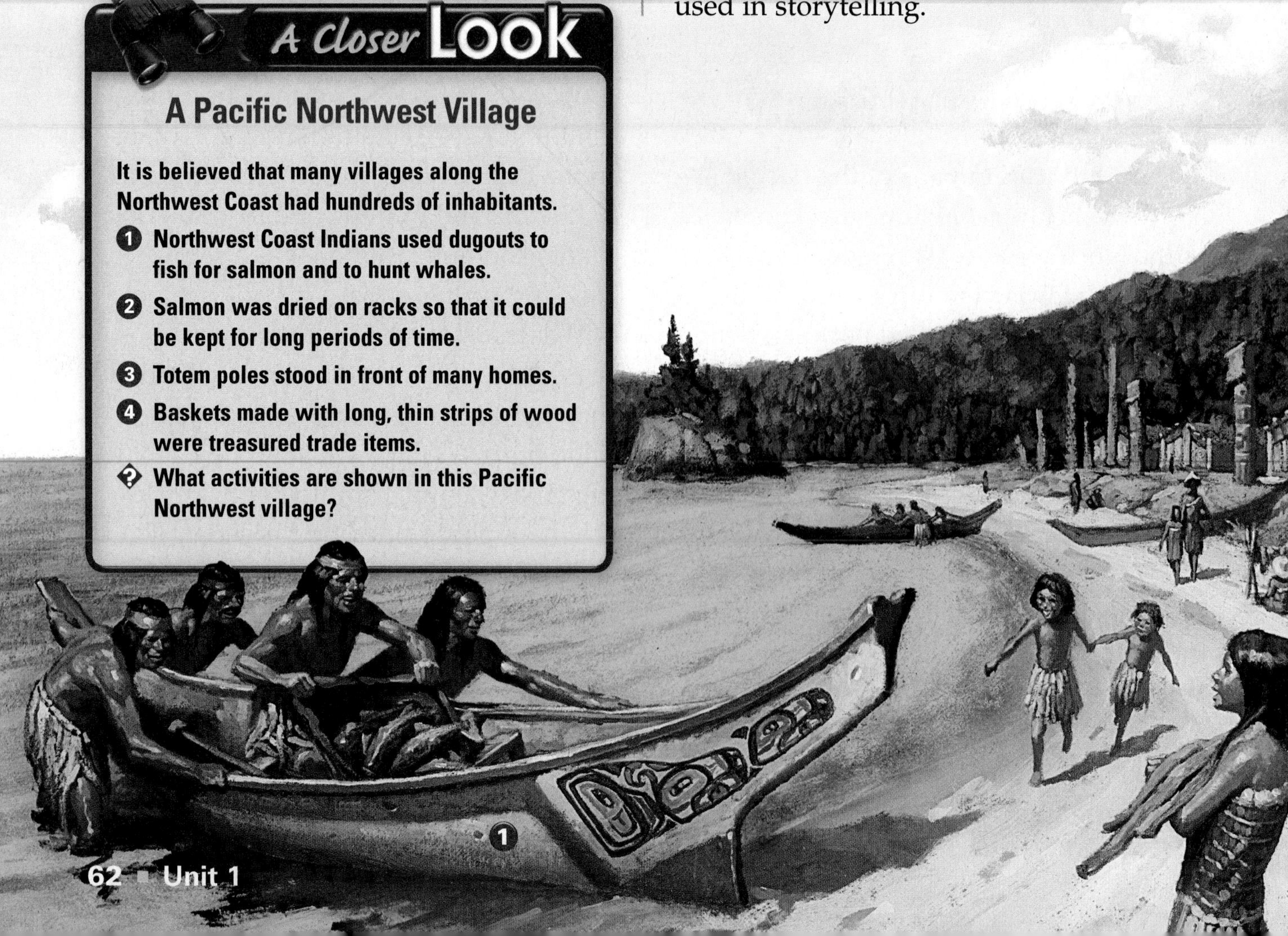

Among the wooden objects carved by Indians in the Pacific Northwest were **totem poles**, tall posts usually showing one or more characters. The characters represented different animals or spirits, and together they told a story.

Some totem poles stood guard at the front of houses. People entered those houses through a hole near the bottom of the totem pole. Other totem poles stood alone, away from the houses, often facing the sea. They were carved to mark graves or to welcome visitors.

Steep mountains and thick forests made overland travel difficult in the Pacific Northwest, but people could travel long distances on the region's waterways. Sometimes people used these water "highways" to fish or hunt or to travel for trade. Trading was a large part of this region's economy. An **economy** is the way the people of a state, region, or country use resources to meet their needs.

One of the greatest trading centers was located on the **Columbia River** at a place now called **The Dalles** (DALZ). People from dozens of tribes, some speaking very different languages, traveled hundreds of miles to trade there.

READING CHECK GENERALIZE
Why was wood important to the American Indians of the Pacific Northwest?

Trade and Wealth

The best-known traders among the Pacific Northwest Indians were the Chinook. The Chinook lived at the mouth of the Columbia River, which they controlled from the coast all the way to The Dalles—about 200 miles upriver.

The Chinook and other Pacific Northwest Indians were part of a large trade network. This **network** allowed goods and ideas to be passed from village to village over very long distances.

The Dalles was a center of the trade network because many groups gathered there, but the different languages they spoke made communication difficult. The Chinook were able to profit from trading at The Dalles because they developed a unique language for trade. It was made up of Chinook words as well as words borrowed from other Indian languages. This language allowed them to **barter**, or exchange goods, on behalf of two groups who were unable to trade with each other directly.

A plentiful supply of natural resources and a large trade network made many Pacific Northwest groups wealthy. One way they expressed their good fortune was through a celebration known as a **potlatch**. A potlatch was meant to show wealth. The word itself comes from a trade term that means "to give."

Historians think that the Kwakiutl, who lived along the coast of what is now Canada, helped develop the potlatch custom. They held potlatches to mark

The Columbia River (below) flows over 1,200 miles to its mouth at the Pacific Ocean. This great resource provided fish for many American Indian groups, including the Chinook of the Pacific Northwest.

major life events such as births, deaths, and marriages.

A Kwakiutl potlatch was a huge celebration, lasting up to ten days and including dancing, food, and speeches. The hosts of a potlatch gave expensive presents to their guests. Because of the great cost, clan members might spend years getting ready to hold a potlatch.

READING CHECK **CAUSE AND EFFECT**
What was the result of strong trade networks for the Indians of the Northwest Coast?

This painting of a potlatch shows a chief and his wife dressed to display their wealth.

Summary

The rich natural resources of the Pacific Northwest helped create a society focused on hunting and gathering and trade. Many people in this society became very wealthy. They displayed this wealth in expensive ceremonies.

REVIEW

1. How did the geography and climate of the Pacific Northwest affect the American Indians there?
2. Write a sentence explaining what the term **barter** has to do with the Chinook.
3. What was the purpose of a potlatch?

CRITICAL THINKING

4. **SKILL** How are a potlatch and a modern birthday celebration alike? How are they different?
5. **SKILL** How did the relative location of The Dalles affect the Chinooks' wealth?
6. **Draw a Chart** Draw a chart showing some of the many things the American Indians of the Pacific Northwest built using wood. Be sure to label each of the drawings on your chart.
7. **COMPARE AND CONTRAST** On a separate sheet of paper, copy and complete the graphic organizer below.

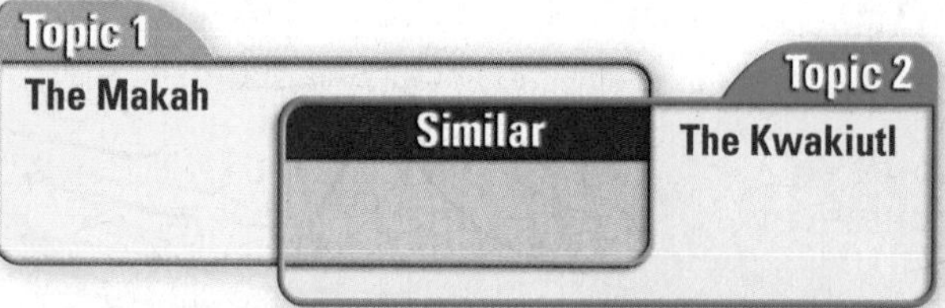

PRIMARY SOURCES

Totem Poles

Totem poles, also known as story poles, are an important part of American Indian culture in the Pacific Northwest. Totem poles are usually made from cedar trees and often have carvings of both animal and human figures. These figures often tell the story of a family or the family's ancestors. Today, totem pole carvers continue to create poles that show the history of the native people of the Pacific Northwest.

Some of the totem poles in Alaska's Sitka National Historic Park are more than 50 feet tall.

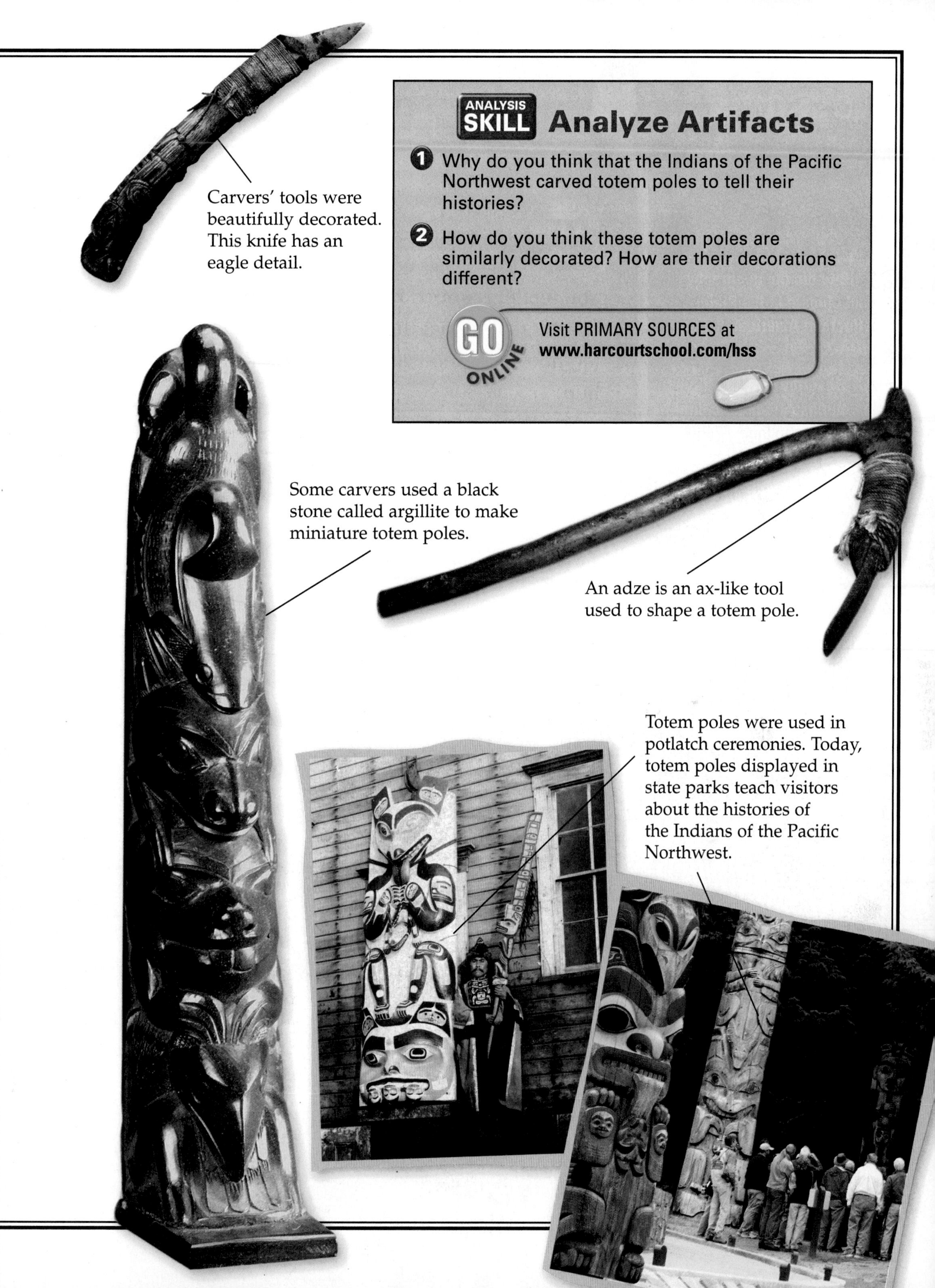

Carvers' tools were beautifully decorated. This knife has an eagle detail.

ANALYSIS SKILL **Analyze Artifacts**

1. Why do you think that the Indians of the Pacific Northwest carved totem poles to tell their histories?
2. How do you think these totem poles are similarly decorated? How are their decorations different?

GO ONLINE Visit PRIMARY SOURCES at **www.harcourtschool.com/hss**

Some carvers used a black stone called argillite to make miniature totem poles.

An adze is an ax-like tool used to shape a totem pole.

Totem poles were used in potlatch ceremonies. Today, totem poles displayed in state parks teach visitors about the histories of the Indians of the Pacific Northwest.

Lesson 3

The Plains

WHAT TO KNOW
How did the geography and climate of the Plains affect the American Indians there?

- ✓ **Describe how the Plains Indians adapted to their environment.**
- ✓ **Compare and contrast the ways of life of the people of the Plains.**

VOCABULARY
lodge p. 70
sod p. 70
tepee p. 71
travois p. 71
council p. 72

PEOPLE
Pawnee
Sioux
Cheyenne
Kiowa
Blackfoot

PLACES
Missouri River
Platte River

COMPARE AND CONTRAST

California Standards
HSS 5.1, 5.1.1, 5.1.2, 5.1.3

YOU ARE THERE The sound of thunder wakes you, and you quickly sit up. But this isn't ordinary thunder! You feel the ground rumbling beneath you. Only then do you realize that the sound you hear is the pounding hooves of thousands of buffalo fleeing your tribe's hunters.

You listen as your mother and grandmother talk about the hunt. Soon, there will be fresh meat to cook and dry. Grandmother has even promised to make you a new pair of moccasins from part of a buffalo hide.

FAST FACT

Hundreds of years ago, the buffalo herds on the Plains were so large that they sometimes blackened the horizon.

Life on the Plains

The Plains Indians lived on the Interior Plains between the Mississippi River and the Rocky Mountains. Among vast fields of green grasses, they hunted buffalo, or American bison. Buffalo were second only to water as the Plains Indians' most important natural resource. Millions of these animals once roamed the dry prairie land of North America.

Imagine a hunting party coming upon a herd of buffalo. Disguised in animal skins that cover their shoulders, the hunters slowly sneak up on some of the buffalo. A signal is given, all the hunters yell, and the frightened buffalo begin to run. The hunters drive the herd toward a steep cliff. Unable to stop, many of the animals fall over the side and are killed.

Buffalo were the main source of food for all the American Indian groups that lived on the Plains. The meat could be eaten raw or cooked, and it could be mixed with fat and berries to make pemmican, a dried meat that could be kept for months.

The buffalo also supplied the Plains Indians with materials to make clothing, tools, utensils, and shelters. The Indians used almost every part of the buffalo. They made blankets, clothing, and moccasins from the skins and carried water in bags made from the stomachs. They twisted the hair into cord, and they made needles and other tools from the bones and horns.

READING CHECK **COMPARE AND CONTRAST**
How did the Plains Indians use buffalo skins differently from buffalo bones and horns?

Analyze Diagrams **This chart shows only a few of the many uses the Plains Indians had for the buffalo.**

How did Plains Indians use the buffalo to become better hunters?

Farmers and Hunters

Although they all depended on the buffalo for most of their needs, different Plains Indians developed different ways of life. Their lifeways depended in part on where they lived.

Among the Plains Indians who lived mostly in the eastern part of the Plains, called the Central Plains, were the Mandan, **Pawnee**, Wichita (WICH•ih•taw), and smaller groups of the **Sioux** (SOO), who called themselves Nakota. These groups were both hunters and gatherers and farmers. They gathered plants and hunted deer, elk, and buffalo and farmed in the fertile valleys of the **Missouri River** and the **Platte River**. They grew mostly beans, corn, squash, and sunflowers, which they sometimes traded for other goods.

These Central Plains Indians lived in villages made up of large circular houses called **lodges**. Each lodge was home to several families, with sometimes as many as 60 people living in one lodge.

Each lodge was built of earth over a shallow pit. In the center was a shared fireplace under a hole in the roof for letting out smoke. Families could keep warm in the earth lodge during the cold winters. On the northern prairies, the lodges were covered by **sod**, a layer of soil held together by the roots of grasses. On the southern prairies, the lodges were covered with grasses or animal skins.

About twice a year, the villages emptied as men, women, and children took part in a great buffalo hunt. To reach the grasslands where the buffalo lived, the people walked from their villages in the river valleys, sometimes for several days.

READING CHECK **COMPARE AND CONTRAST**
How did types of lodges differ?

A Closer LOOK

Plains Life

The Plains Indians used their environment to obtain food and to make clothing and shelter.

1. **A travois made by using tepee poles served as a carrier that could be pulled by a dog.**
2. **The wooden poles used to build tepees were valuable because wood was scarce.**
3. **In hot weather, tepee flaps could be left open to let in cooling breezes.**
4. **Animal skins were stretched out and softened using a mixture of ashes and fat.**

What activities do you see in this illustration?

A Nomadic Society

Smoke rises from an early morning fire as a **Cheyenne** (shy•AN) woman prepares food. Wood is scarce, or in short supply, where she lives, so for fuel the woman burns dried buffalo droppings, called chips. She works quickly because her people are preparing to move.

The Cheyenne lived in the western part of the Interior Plains, called the Great Plains. They and other groups who lived there such as the **Kiowa** (KY•uh•wah), the Crow, and the Comanche (kuh•MAN•chee), were nomads who moved from place to place following herds of buffalo. They did not farm in the dry grasslands where they lived. The short grasses had such tough roots that a digging stick could not break the soil.

Since the Great Plains Indians had no permanent homes, they built shelters that were easy to move. One such shelter was a cone-shaped tent called a **tepee** (TEE•pee). To build a tepee, wooden poles were set in a circle and tied together at the top. Then the poles were covered with buffalo skins, leaving a hole at the top to let out the smoke from fires.

The Great Plains Indians also used their wooden poles to make a kind of carrier called a **travois** (truh•VOY). A travois was made of two poles tied together at one end and then fastened to a harness on a dog. Goods were carried on a buffalo skin tied between the poles.

READING CHECK COMPARE AND CONTRAST Why did the Great Plains Indians live as nomads instead of as farmers?

3

4

Plains Cultures

Like all American Indians, the Plains Indians had different customs and systems of government. The Lakota people, another branch of the Sioux, were seven nomadic groups, each of which made its own choices. Still, membership in the Lakota group guaranteed that the smaller groups would respect each other's hunting areas and would not fight each other.

The Cheyenne governed differently. They were ten groups that were independent of each other in many ways. However, each group sent its leaders to meet in a **council** of chiefs. All the groups of the Cheyenne had to follow the council's decisions.

Among the Plains Indians, every person in the group was equal. No one person was born more important than anyone else. Any man could become chief by proving himself a good hunter and a good leader of people. He became chief because his people chose and trusted him.

This cloth doll is an artifact of the Blackfoot.

Although they had different ways of governing themselves, many of the Plains Indians shared certain folklore traditions and religious beliefs. Among these was a belief in how they came to be. The **Blackfoot**, for example, believed that they were created by a spirit called Old Man. Old Man also made the animals and decided where they would live.

Among the Plains Indians who farmed, corn played an important role. Every year, they held ceremonies to celebrate and give thanks for the corn harvest.

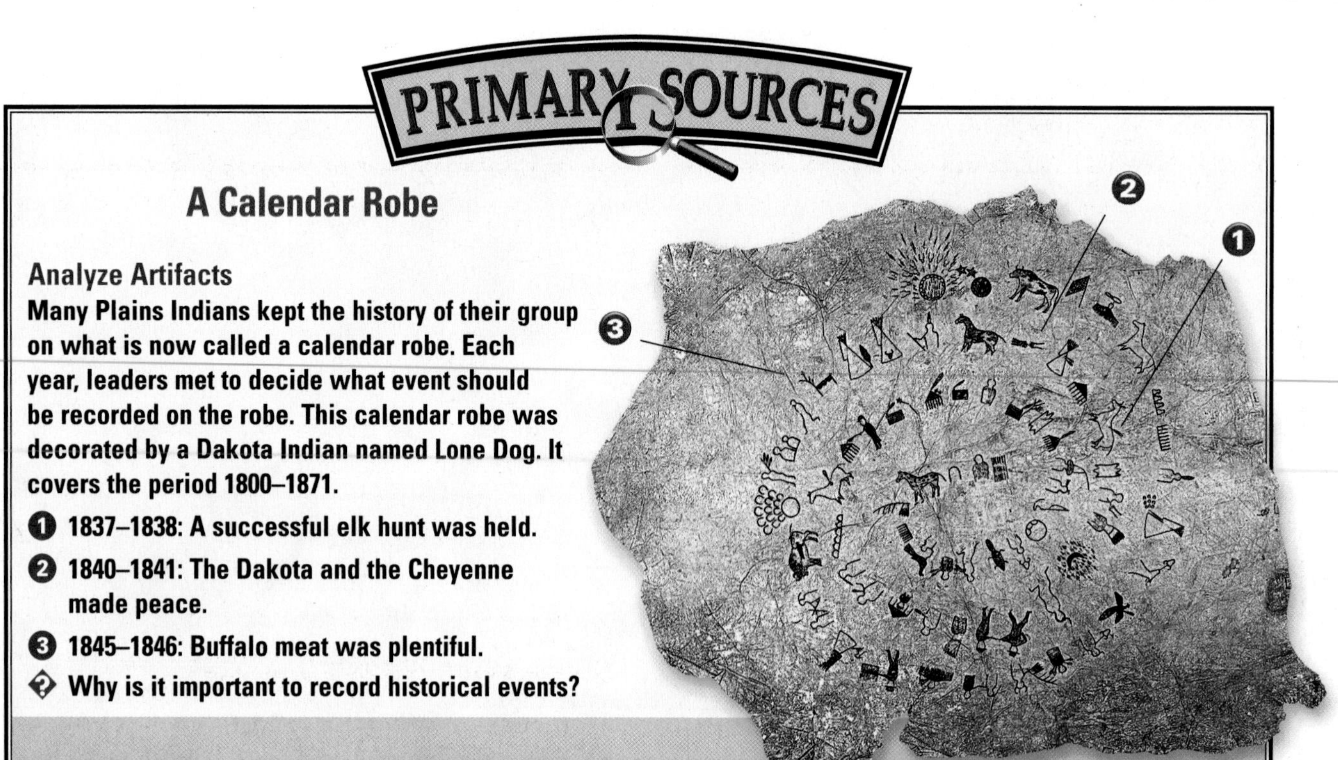

PRIMARY SOURCES

A Calendar Robe

Analyze Artifacts

Many Plains Indians kept the history of their group on what is now called a calendar robe. Each year, leaders met to decide what event should be recorded on the robe. This calendar robe was decorated by a Dakota Indian named Lone Dog. It covers the period 1800–1871.

1. **1837–1838: A successful elk hunt was held.**
2. **1840–1841: The Dakota and the Cheyenne made peace.**
3. **1845–1846: Buffalo meat was plentiful.**

Why is it important to record historical events?

Other ceremonies marked the beginning and end of buffalo hunts, the naming of a child, or the beginning of a marriage.

During the summer, many Plains Indians performed the Sun Dance ceremony, which they believed helped keep the buffalo strong. The Sun Dance also showed the Plains Indians' respect for nature. Different Plains groups gathered for the Sun Dance, which helped build a sense of unity.

READING CHECK **COMPARE AND CONTRAST**
How were the governments of the Lakota and the Cheyenne both alike and different?

Summary

The Plains Indians lived in a large region that stretched across the middle of North America. The Plains Indians were made up of many different groups. However, different groups lived in similar types of shelters, relied on the same sources of food, and shared certain religious beliefs.

Medicine people were important in the Blackfoot's religious ceremonies.

REVIEW

1. How did the geography and climate of the Plains affect the American Indians there?
2. Explain how **sod** is related to a Plains Indian **lodge**.
3. What was the purpose of a travois?
4. How could a person become chief of a Plains Indian group?

CRITICAL THINKING

5. ANALYSIS SKILL How did the Plains Indians use dogs? How are dogs used today?
6. **Draw a Building Plan** Give step-by-step instructions to build a tepee. Be sure to illustrate each step and include a list of materials, based on what you know about Plains Indians' tepees.
7. Focus Skill **COMPARE AND CONTRAST** On a separate sheet of paper, copy and complete the graphic organizer below.

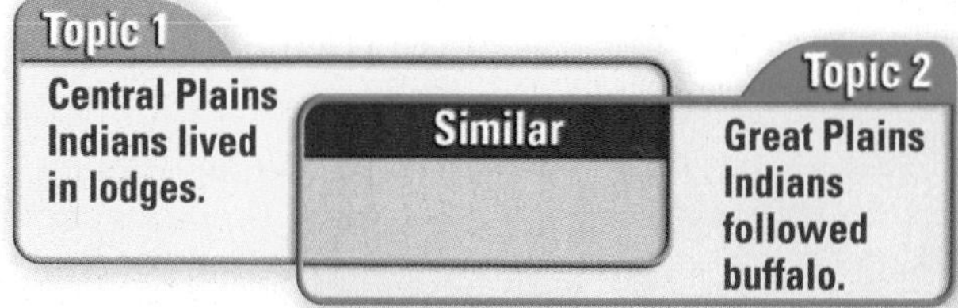

Lesson 4

The Eastern Woodlands

WHAT TO KNOW
How did the geography and climate of the Eastern Woodlands affect the American Indians there?

- ✓ **Describe how the Eastern Woodlands peoples adapted to their environment.**
- ✓ **Locate the Eastern Woodlands cultural region, and compare lifeways.**
- ✓ **Explain the Iroquois system of government.**

VOCABULARY
palisade p. 76
wampum p. 77
confederation p. 77
wigwam p. 78

PEOPLE
Iroquois
Hiawatha
Deganawida
Algonquian

PLACES
Great Lakes

Focus Skill **COMPARE AND CONTRAST**

California Standards
HSS 5.1, 5.1.1, 5.1.2, 5.1.3

YOU ARE THERE Imagine playing a ball game with other Iroquois children. Scooping up the ball in the small leather basket attached to the end of your stick, you run toward your opponent's goal, darting past the other players. You can hear your family's shouts of encouragement as you make your way across the long playing field. As you fling the ball toward the goal, your heart races with excitement. Your brave play will bring honor to you and your family. Score!

The Iroquois ball game was played using sticks of wood and a deerskin ball.

FAST FACT
Lacrosse as it is played today is closest to the game played by the Iroquois. Lacrosse uses sticks with nets on one end so that teammates can pass a ball to each other.

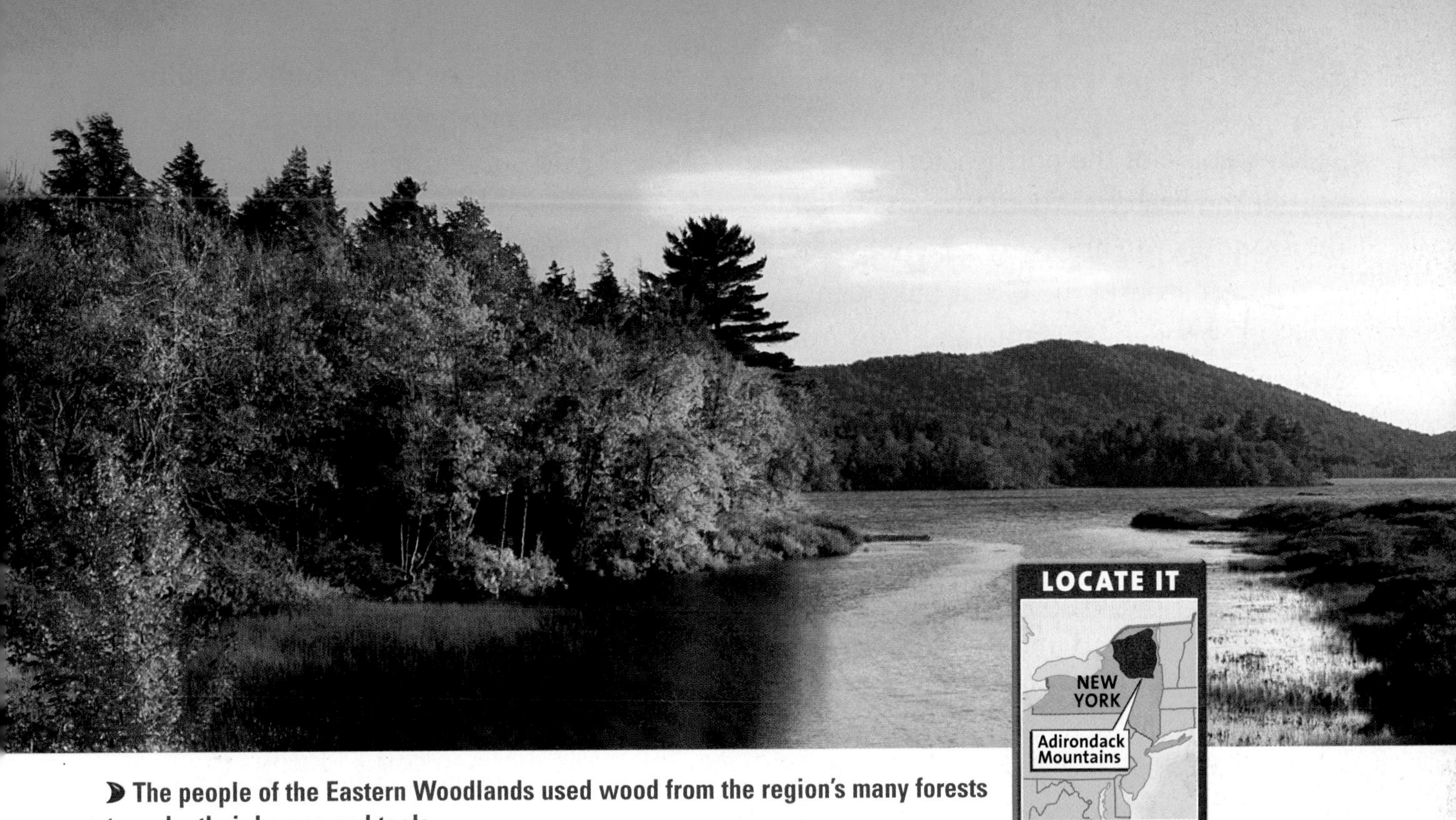

The people of the Eastern Woodlands used wood from the region's many forests to make their homes and tools.

Life in the Eastern Woodlands

The Eastern Woodlands cultural region stretched east of the Mississippi River, spreading across most of what is now the eastern half of the United States. The region's name came from the thick forests that once covered the region. Along the banks of rivers and streams flowing through the forests, the Eastern Woodlands people built their villages.

These people all shared the same important natural resource—trees. They used trees and tree bark to make canoes and shelters, and they carved tools and weapons from wood. Trees also provided the people with food, such as wild fruits.

The Eastern Woodlands people were farmers as well as hunters and gatherers. In the northeastern part of the Woodlands, where the soil was rocky, people did more hunting and gathering than farming. The men hunted animals for food and used antlers and bones to make tools. Using spears and nets, they fished in the region's many lakes and rivers. Meanwhile, the women prepared the food and used animal skins to make blankets, clothing, and moccasins.

In the southern areas, where the soil and climate were better for growing crops, the people raised corn, beans, squash, and other plants. Generally, the men cleared the land for planting and the women and children were responsible for planting, caring for, and harvesting crops.

READING CHECK COMPARE AND CONTRAST
How did life in the northeastern part of the Eastern Woodlands differ from life in the southern part?

The Iroquois

The people of the northeastern part of the Eastern Woodlands included the **Iroquois** (IR•uh•kwoy). They lived in the area around the **Great Lakes**, in what is now Pennsylvania and New York and the Lake Ontario region of Canada. Not all of the Iroquois people spoke the same language, but their languages were similar. They also had similar customs.

Like other Eastern Woodlands Indians, the Iroquois farmed and lived in villages. Most tribes built their villages along the banks of rivers or streams, for fresh water. These villages were often large and included several houses and a building for meetings and ceremonies. For protection against enemies, many Iroquois built **palisades**, or walls of tall wooden poles, around their villages.

Like the Makah, the Iroquois lived in longhouses. However, Iroquois longhouses had some differences. They were smaller, but could still fit up to 20 families. The frame of a longhouse was made by cutting poles from young trees, bending the poles, and then covering them with bark. Each longhouse was divided into sections, and each section was home to one or two families.

Near their villages, the Iroquois grew three main crops—corn, beans, and squash. The Iroquois called these the Three Sisters because all three were planted together in the same field. After a field was farmed for a few years, the soil became less fertile, so the Iroquois would then begin planting in another location.

Like many other American Indians, the Iroquois used wampum to make beaded designs that showed important decisions, events, or stories.

Wampum—strings of beads cut from seashells—was also traded and exchanged for goods.

Five of the largest Iroquois groups were the Mohawk, the Oneida (oh•NY•duh), the Onondaga (ah•nuhn•DAW•guh), the Cayuga (kay•YOO•guh), and the Seneca (SEH•nih•kuh). Known as the Five Nations, these peoples often battled each other over control of hunting areas. Even within a group, people sometimes fought to settle arguments.

A legend about one argument tells of an Iroquois warrior named **Hiawatha**, who it was said, saw his family killed by members of another group. By tradition, Hiawatha was expected to kill those who had killed his family. However, he wanted the fighting to stop.

Hiawatha left his village and met another Iroquois, named **Deganawida** (deh•gahn•uh•WEE•duh), who became known as the Peacemaker. In time, the two men persuaded the Five Nations to unite and work together as a group.

The group that was formed was called the Iroquois League. It acted as a **confederation**, a loose group of governments working together. Members from each of the five tribes were sent to speak for their group. They joined the Grand Council, which the league set up to settle disputes among the people peacefully.

READING CHECK **MAIN IDEA AND DETAILS**
What was the Iroquois League?

A Closer LOOK

An Iroquois Village

Iroquois villages were often located on top of steep-sided hills. The steep slopes helped protect Iroquois villages from enemies.

1. **Corn, beans, and squash were planted near Iroquois villages.**
2. **The Iroquois were skilled hunters, who made sharp arrowheads out of flint.**
3. **Iroquois women wove baskets using reeds.**
4. **The Iroquois used animal hides to make clothing.**

Why do you think it was common to have an open area at the center of Iroquois villages?

This drawing of Algonquian Indians was made by English settler John White in the early 1600s.

The Algonquians

Like the Iroquois, the **Algonquian** (al•GAHN•kwee•uhn) people are grouped together because they spoke similar languages. Most of the people who spoke Algonquian languages lived on the Coastal Plain near the Atlantic Ocean. Among them were the Delaware, the Wampanoag (wahm•puh•NOH•ag), and the Powhatan (pow•uh•TAN). Other Algonquian groups lived farther inland, around the Great Lakes. These people included the Ottawa (AH•tuh•wuh), the Chippewa (CHIH•puh•waw), and the Miami.

Most Algonquian people had anywhere from 1 to 20 villages. Some groups built longhouses similar to those of the Iroquois. Others built round, bark-covered shelters called **wigwams**. Apart from their shape, wigwams were made in much the same way as longhouses. The trunks of small trees were bent, tied together into a dome shape, and then covered with bark.

Like their Iroquois neighbors, the Algonquians hunted and gathered. Both groups farmed, but the Algonquians who lived near the coast did not rely on their crops for food as much as the Iroquois did. Fish was an important food source.

The Algonquians built birch-bark canoes to fish in the rivers and along the coast. They used animal bones and wood to make hooks and fishing traps.

The Algonquians made clothing mostly from deerskin, which kept them warm during the cold winters. Men wore shirts, leggings, and moccasins. They usually tied one or two eagle feathers to their hair. Women usually wore dresses. Both men's and women's clothing was decorated with feathers, shells, and porcupine quills.

Many Algonquian groups had leaders who governed more than one village. Some Algonquian people had two chiefs, one to rule during times of peace and the other to rule during times of war.

Among Algonquian groups, marriage ceremonies were very much alike. If a man wanted to marry a woman, he would take her a gift of meat from an animal he had hunted himself. This showed he was a good hunter. If the woman wanted to marry him, she would accept the gift of meat and cook it. This showed she was a good homemaker. When the couple shared the meal, they were considered married.

READING CHECK **COMPARE AND CONTRAST**
How did the diet of the Algonquians differ from that of the Iroquois?

▶ **Algonquians used beeswax to make dolls.**

Summary

The people of the Eastern Woodlands relied on trees for food, shelter, and transportation. The two main language groups of the Eastern Woodlands were the Iroquois and the Algonquians.

REVIEW

1. How did the geography and climate of the Eastern Woodlands affect the American Indians there?
2. How is the term **confederation** related to the Iroquois League?
3. Why was fish an important food source for the Algonquian peoples?

CRITICAL THINKING

4. ANALYSIS SKILL Why did American Indians in the same region often develop different ways of life? Explain.
5. ANALYSIS SKILL Why did the Iroquois groups choose to come together to form the Iroquois League?
6. **Give a Speech** Write and deliver a speech to try to persuade Iroquois leaders to join the Iroquois League. Be sure to include the benefits of working together.
7. Focus Skill **COMPARE AND CONTRAST** On a separate sheet of paper, copy and complete the graphic organizer below.

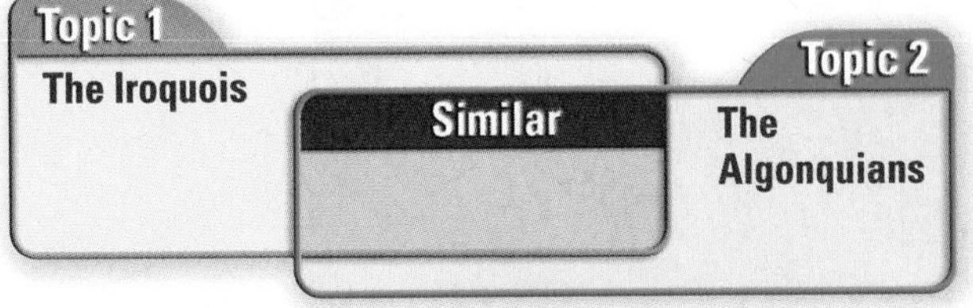

Resolve Conflict

WHY IT MATTERS

Hiawatha's goal was to find a way that the Five Nations could **resolve**, or settle, conflicts without turning to war. However, even before Hiawatha began his work, each tribe had its ways to settle disagreements.

For example, in the Mohawk tribe, if a member of one clan wronged a member of another clan, all the clans worked together to resolve the conflict. Because of their ability to resolve conflicts, the clans were able to stay part of one tribe.

Today, people must often resolve conflicts as they work together. A lot of times that means they have to compromise. To **compromise** is to give something up in order to get something else. Being able to compromise is important in resolving conflicts.

WHAT YOU NEED TO KNOW

Here are some steps you can follow to resolve a conflict through compromise.

Step 1 **Identify the problem.**

Step 2 **Tell your side of the story. Explain what you want to happen.**

Step 3 **Listen carefully as the other person tells his or her side of the story. Have that person explain what he or she wants to happen.**

Conflicts between American Indians were often resolved by a respected leader or chief.

Leaders in the United States government meet to resolve conflicts.

Step 4 **Discuss differences between the two versions.**

Step 5 **Together, hold a brainstorming session to think of possible compromises. Remember, you will each probably have to give up something in order to reach a compromise.**

Step 6 **Choose a compromise that seems as if it will work. For the compromise to be effective, both sides must agree.**

Step 7 **Try the compromise to which you both agreed. Plan to check later to make sure the compromise is still working.**

PRACTICE THE SKILL

Think of a conflict you recently faced. Determine whether the conflict was resolved. What did you give up to reach a compromise? What did you gain through the compromise?

APPLY WHAT YOU LEARNED

Make It Relevant With the help of your classmates, choose a conflict facing your class or your school. Form two groups, with each group taking one of the positions in the conflict. Then follow the steps listed to come to a compromise.

Citizenship

The Common Good

"Look and listen for the welfare of the whole people and have always in view not only the present but also the coming generations . . ."*

—from the Iroquois Constitution

To make sure their decisions were for the good of all, Iroquois leaders decided that they must all agree on any action to be taken.

For many years, the tribes of the Iroquois were not united. They often fought one another over land and resources. Then, in the 1500s, Hiawatha helped create peace among the different tribes.

According to legend, a spiritual leader named Deganawida came to Hiawatha and asked him to bring peace to the Iroquois. Hiawatha then spoke to all the Iroquois leaders in the hope of bringing the tribes together.

In time, Hiawatha was able to unite the Iroquois. The five tribes formed a confederation called

FAST FACT

The Song of Hiawatha, a poem written by Henry Wadsworth Longfellow in 1855, is one of the most famous poems in American history. Over the years, the poem has inspired many books and movies.

**The Iroquois Constitution: A Primary Source Investigation of the Law of the Iroquois* by Lesli J. Favor. Rosen Publishing Group, 2003.

People of all ages can volunteer. By voting, people can choose what they think will be good for their communities.

the Iroquois League. The Iroquois League was based on the idea that the tribes could work for a common good. This meant that they helped one another and thought about what was best for everyone. They also recognized those who worked for the good of the people and those who had a talent for teaching.

Today, many Americans continue to work for the common good by volunteering or by serving in the government. They help build shelters, feed the hungry, register voters, and count election ballots. They give countless hours of service to those in need. State and local communities often honor volunteers and teachers who give their time and effort to serve others.

Think About It!

Make It Relevant Why is it important for citizens to work together for the common good?

Volunteering to help feed the hungry is one way to work for the common good.

Lesson 5

The Arctic

WHAT TO KNOW
How did the geography and climate of the Arctic affect the American Indians there?

- ✓ Describe how the Aleut and the Inuit adapted to their environment.
- ✓ Analyze the customs and beliefs of the people of the Arctic.

VOCABULARY
kayak p. 86
igloo p. 86

PEOPLE
Aleut
Inuit

PLACES
Aleutian Islands

Focus Skill **COMPARE AND CONTRAST**

California Standards
HSS 5.1, 5.1.1, 5.1.2, 5.1.3

YOU ARE THERE You watch as your father begins to put together your home—not a home built of wood or stone, but one made entirely of ice. Your father cuts large blocks of ice from the ground and begins stacking them up. He shapes the blocks to fit them together snugly, without gaps between them.

After just a few hours, your home is complete, and you and your family enter. Your mother spreads a bearskin on the floor, and everyone gathers on it. You'll be warm tonight while cold winds blow all around your home of ice.

A Cold Land

The Arctic region near the North Pole has one of Earth's harshest climates. Because the region is so far north, the sun stays below the horizon for much of the winter, and it does not set for much of the summer. The land is mostly a flat and treeless plain of frozen ground. Summer temperatures seldom get warmer than 40°F, and winter temperatures usually average $^{-}25$°F.

Scientists think that the peoples of the Arctic region of the Americas arrived there after other peoples had moved farther south in the Americas. They believe that no one lived in the Arctic until 5,000 to 3,000 years ago.

Some of these Arctic peoples became known as the **Aleut** (a•lee•OOT) because they built their homes along the coast of the **Aleutian** (uh•LOO•shuhn) **Islands**. This chain of about 100 islands starts near what is now Alaska's southwestern tip and extends about 1,200 miles into the Pacific Ocean. The name *Alaska* comes from an Aleut word meaning "mainland."

A spear tip

Early Arctic people closely related to the Aleut were the **Inuit** (IH•nu•wuht), who lived in what is now Alaska and northern Canada. Since the Arctic region was too cold for farming, the Inuit had to hunt and gather their food and make their clothing and tools from the animals they hunted.

READING CHECK **COMPARE AND CONTRAST**
How was life different for the Arctic people than for people living farther south?

A Closer Look

An Inuit Family

The Inuit people learned the skills they needed to survive in their icy land.

1. **Igloos were made with blocks of ice that were cut with a long bone knife.**
2. **Sharpened bone tools were used to remove the skin from fish.**
3. **Bow drills were used to make holes or to cut through animal bones.**

Why do you think tools were so highly valued?

Arctic Ways of Life

To survive in the harsh environment, the Aleut and the Inuit developed their skills as hunters and fishers. With bows and arrows, they hunted such animals as arctic foxes, snowshoe hares, caribou, and polar bears. They also used harpoons and kayaks to hunt seals, walruses, and whales. A **kayak** (KY•ak) is a one-person canoe made of waterproof skins stretched over wood or bone.

Nothing in this cold, hard land was wasted. For example, the people caught seals not only for their meat but also for their skins, which were made into clothes and tents. Oil made from seal blubber, or fat, was used to light and heat houses. People also chewed the seal blubber to prevent hunger. Even the skeletons of animals were used, as people carved tools from the bones and tusks.

The Aleut lived together in large houses with beams made from whalebones and walls made of sod. It was customary for the Aleut to display their wealth. They did so through possessions such as shells and baskets.

The Inuit lived in different kinds of shelters. Some Inuit built **igloos**—homes made of ice—in which they lived during the winter months. A hole in the top of the igloo allowed smoke from cooking fires to escape. During the summer, the Inuit lived in tents made from animal skins. Other Inuit lived in tents or sod houses year-round.

Inuit groups were usually loosely formed bands of 60 to 300 people, with several families. The people hunted and traveled together, often sharing seal meat to survive. Like all Arctic people, the Inuit learned to make the most of the limited resources they had.

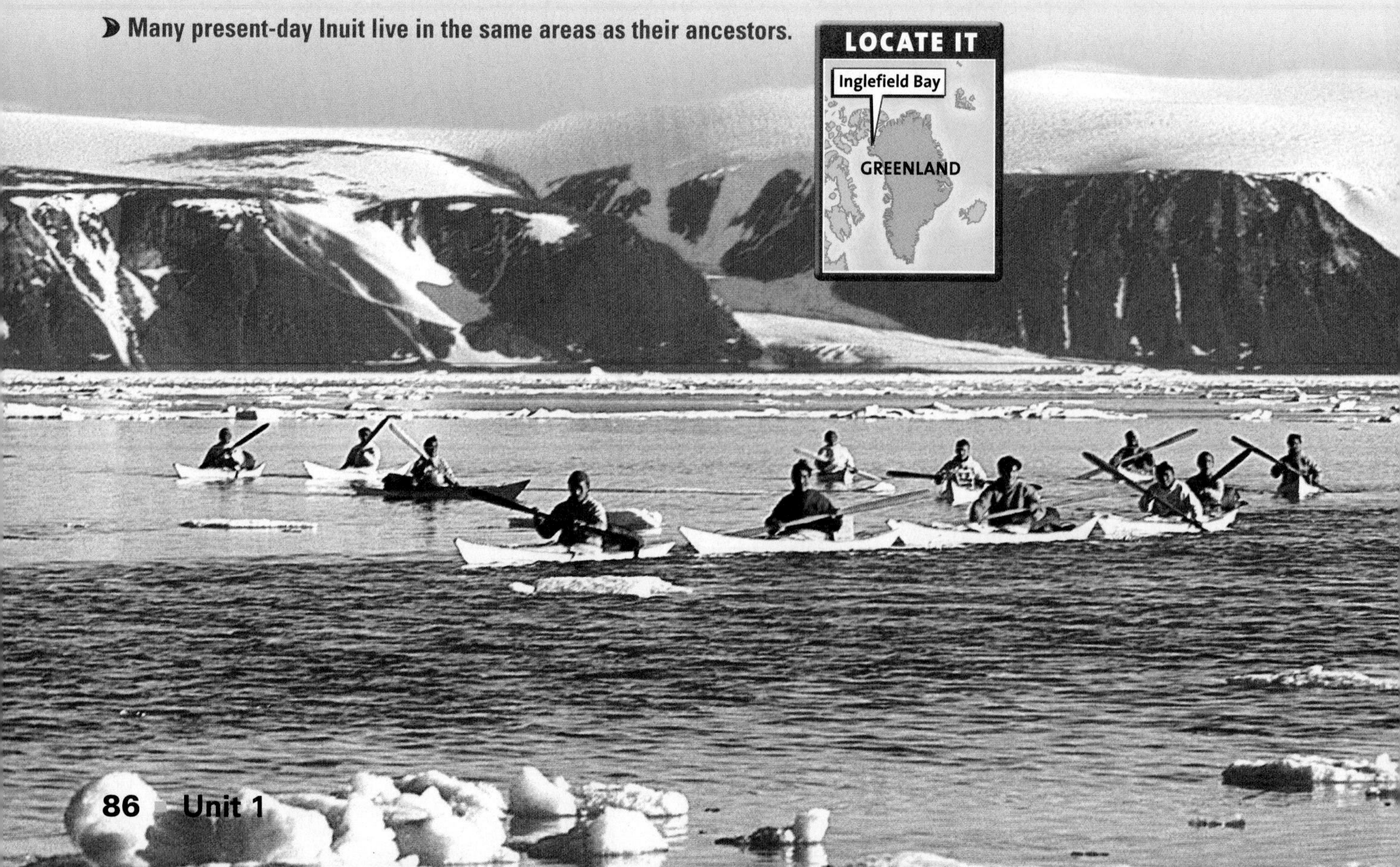

Many present-day Inuit live in the same areas as their ancestors.

The Inuit believe a person's name has the power to protect the person from harm. As a result, Inuit people often have many names, which are thought to act as guardian spirits. The Inuit believe that all things have a spirit and that a person's spirit is the source of his or her strength. Inuit names often come from words used to describe the environment, animals, or birds.

READING CHECK **COMPARE AND CONTRAST**
How did the shelters of the Aleut differ from those of the Inuit?

Summary

The cultures of the Aleut and the Inuit were shaped by the harsh environment in which they lived. They adapted to their difficult surroundings, and the members of each community worked together to survive.

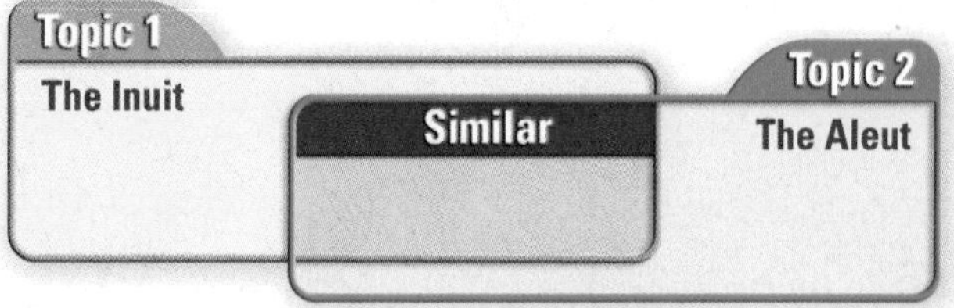

This ivory carving of two seals (left) was used to fasten a belt. An Inuit carver (above) continues his work.

REVIEW

1. How did the geography and climate of the Arctic affect the American Indians there?
2. Write a description of an **igloo**.
3. Why do you think Inuit groups had to share food to survive?

CRITICAL THINKING

4. SKILL How did the waters of the Arctic affect the peoples' ways of life?
5. SKILL How might limited resources affect the ways in which people live?
6. **Write a Poem** Write a poem about the life of an American Indian family living in the Arctic.
7. Focus Skill **COMPARE AND CONTRAST** On a separate sheet of paper, copy and complete the graphic organizer below.

Topic 1		Topic 2
The Inuit	Similar	The Aleut

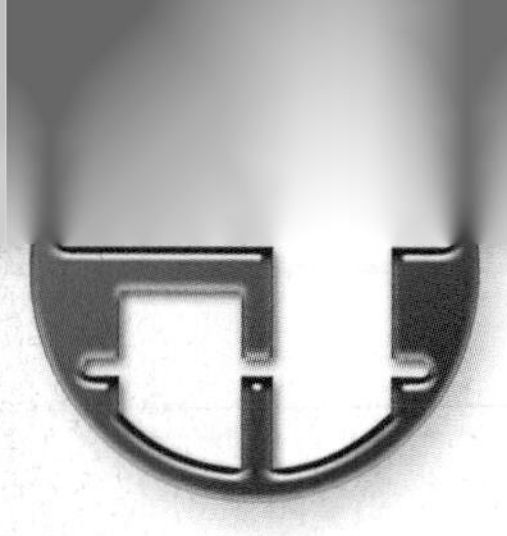

Use Tables to Group Information

WHY IT MATTERS

Information often is easier to find and to understand if facts are grouped together. Creating a table is an effective way to **classify**—that is, group together—kinds of information. Knowing how to create a table to classify information can make the information easier to locate and easier to learn.

WHAT YOU NEED TO KNOW

You have just finished reading about many different groups of American Indians. To make it easier to remember the names and locations of these tribes, you can put the information into a table.

Look at the two tables on page 89. The tables show the same facts. However, each table classifies them in a different way. Both identify the different groups, and both also identify the region in which each group lived. Table A classifies this information by region. Table B presents this information by group.

PRACTICE THE SKILL

Use the tables to answer these questions.

1. What groups lived in the desert Southwest? Which table did you use to find the answer?

This painting shows American Indians in what is now Canada.

Table A: Regions and their Groups	
REGION	**GROUP**
Desert Southwest	Hopi
	Zuni
	Navajo
Pacific Northwest	Makah
	Chinook
	Kwakiutl
Plains	Lakota
	Cheyenne
	Blackfoot
Eastern Woodlands	Mohawk
	Powhatan
	Seneca
Arctic	Aleut
	Inuit

Table B: Groups and their Regions	
GROUP	**REGION**
Aleut	Arctic
Blackfoot	Plains
Mohawk	Eastern Woodlands
Cheyenne	Plains
Chinook	Pacific Northwest
Hopi	Desert Southwest
Powhatan	Eastern Woodlands
Inuit	Arctic
Makah	Pacific Northwest
Lakota	Plains
Zuni	Desert Southwest
Kwakiutl	Pacific Northwest
Navajo	Desert Southwest

2. In what region did the Cheyenne live? Which table did you use to find the answer?
3. Which table makes it easier to find out how many groups lived in the Arctic?
4. If you wanted to know the region in which a particular group lived, which table would you use?

APPLY WHAT YOU LEARNED

In Chapter 1, Lesson 3, you read about other ancient peoples of the Americas—peoples such as the Olmec and the Adena. Make a two-column table. Use the table to group together the cultures and their locations, the way they are presented in that lesson. When you have finished, compare your table with the tables of your classmates. Did you all group information in the same way?

This Kiowa artifact is decorated with beads in the shapes of leaves.

Reading Social Studies

When you **compare**, you tell how two or more things are alike.
When you **contrast**, you tell how they are different.

Compare and Contrast

Complete this graphic organizer to compare and contrast the American Indians who lived in different regions of North America. A copy of this graphic organizer appears on page 24 of the Homework and Practice Book.

American Indians

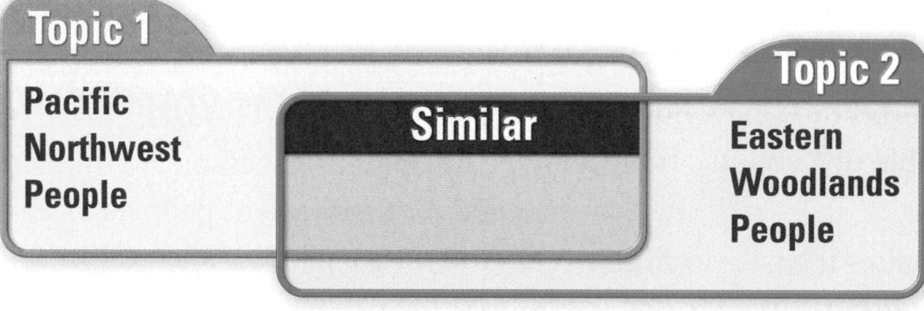

California Writing Prompts

Write a Persuasive Composition The tribes of the Iroquois League worked together to settle disputes. To discuss issues, each tribe sent someone to speak for its members at the Grand Council. Write a persuasive composition about the benefits of this type of government.

Write a Research Report Imagine that you are a scientist who is studying a Pueblo historical site. Write a research report describing the land of the desert Southwest and how the Pueblo people built their homes.

Use Vocabulary

Identify the term that correctly matches each definition.

surplus, p. 54
hogan, p. 56
harpoon, p. 60
clan, p. 62
barter, p. 64
council, p. 72
wigwam, p. 78
kayak, p. 86

1. an extended family
2. a group of leaders
3. a one-person canoe
4. an amount that is more than what is needed
5. a round shelter covered with bark
6. a wooden frame shelter covered with bark and mud
7. a long spear with a sharp point
8. to trade goods

Apply Skills

Resolve Conflict

9. Think of an issue that you and a friend disagree about. Make a list of the steps that you might follow to resolve the conflict. Include a compromise that could resolve the conflict.

Compare Tables

10. Look at the tables on page 89. Identify which groups lived in the Eastern Woodlands.

Recall Facts

Answer these questions.

11. How did the Pueblo Indians get water for their crops?
12. How did the Chinook language help trade among the Pacific Northwest Indians?
13. What did the phrase Three Sisters mean to the Iroquois?
14. What were three ways in which Arctic peoples used seals?

Write the letter of the best choice.

15. What did the people of the Great Plains most often use as fuel for their fires?
    A wood
    B sod
    C buffalo chips
    D whale oil
16. Which resource was the most important to the Eastern Woodlands people?
    A adobe
    B trees
    C whales
    D buffalo

Think Critically

17. ANALYSIS SKILL What caused many tribes in the desert Southwest to make their homes from adobe?
18. ANALYSIS SKILL What human and physical characteristics of the Arctic region made it a unique place for early people to live?

Field Trip

The Hopi Nation

GET READY

The Hopi Nation is made up of 12 villages. The villages are located at the tops and at the bases of three mesas in northeastern Arizona. Many Hopi still follow their traditional way of life. They perform Kachina ceremonies, produce traditional craft work, and farm the land as they have done for hundreds of years. On a visit to the Hopi Nation, you can learn about Hopi culture and see examples of how the Hopi keep their traditions alive.

LOCATE IT

ARIZONA

Hopi Nation

WHAT TO SEE

Visitors to the Hopi Nation may have the chance to see a Kachina ceremony. The Kachina dances express prayers for rain, health, and bountiful harvests.

Hopi artists create jewelry, baskets, and pottery. They use patterns and styles that have been passed down from generation to generation.

This young girl is dressed for the Butterfly Dance, which celebrates the harvest.

A VIRTUAL TOUR

GO ONLINE

Visit VIRTUAL TOURS at www.harcourtschool.com/hss

Review

THE BIG IDEA

Geography People interact with their environment and are affected by it.

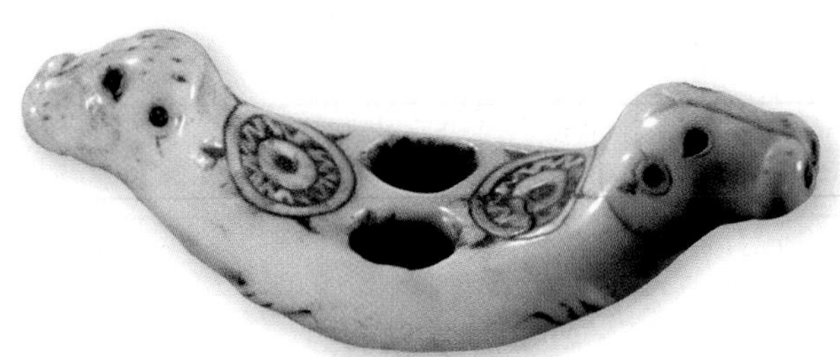

Summary

The First Americans

People have lived in North America and South America for many thousands of years. The land bridge theory is one idea about how the first people arrived. About 5,000 years ago, people started farming in the Americas. About 3,500 years ago, the Olmec built a powerful civilization.

American Indians were influenced by the geography and climate of the regions where they lived. People of the desert Southwest built homes and developed farming methods that were suited to a hot, dry region. In the Pacific Northwest, plentiful natural resources allowed people to thrive by hunting, gathering, and trading. Plains Indians had varied cultures. Some depended heavily on buffalo to meet their needs. Others combined hunting and farming.

Eastern Woodlands people used trees to make homes, canoes, and tools. American Indians of the Arctic region had to learn to adapt to a cold, harsh land. They hunted seals and whales.

Main Ideas and Vocabulary

Read the summary above. Then answer the questions that follow.

1. What is a theory?
   - **A** an object made by humans
   - **B** a story handed down from the past
   - **C** an idea based on study and research
   - **D** a person who has no permanent home
2. What was one challenge faced by people of the desert Southwest?
   - **A** thick forests
   - **B** a hot, dry climate
   - **C** long, cold winters
   - **D** frequent flooding
3. Which animal was most important to the Plains Indians?
   - **A** salmon
   - **B** whales
   - **C** buffalo
   - **D** woolly mammoths
4. What does it mean to adapt?
   - **A** to adjust
   - **B** to perform actions at a special event
   - **C** to exchange goods
   - **D** to make decisions with a group

Recall Facts

Answer these questions.

5. How is the location of Alaska different from that of the other states?
6. How did the lives of ancient people change when the climate became warmer?
7. Why is the Olmec culture sometimes called the "mother culture"?
8. What were three natural resources that were important to the people of the Pacific Northwest?
9. What were two materials that Plains Indians used to build their homes?

Write the letter of the best choice.

10. Which animals did the ancient Indians hunt during the last Ice Age?
    A woolly mammoths
    B deer
    C rabbits
    D fish
11. What was the main crop of the people of the desert Southwest?
    A rice
    B corn
    C wheat
    D barley
12. In which two regions did American Indians hunt whales?
    A the Plains and the Pacific Northwest
    B the Eastern Woodlands and the Plains
    C the Arctic and the Eastern Woodlands
    D the Pacific Northwest and the Arctic
13. What was wampum made from?
    A trees
    B deer
    C shells
    D stones

Think Critically

14. ANALYSIS SKILL How was the Iroquois League an example of cooperation between tribes?
15. ANALYSIS SKILL What are the physical characteristics of the Pacific Northwest? How did these characteristics make it a unique place for Indians to live?
16. ANALYSIS SKILL How does the environment of North America affect how people live today?

Apply Skills

ANALYSIS SKILL Use a Cultural Map

Use the cultural map below to answer the following questions.

17. Which Iroquois tribe held the most land?
18. Which tribe lived farthest west?
19. Which tribe controlled the least amount of land?
20. How did the locations of the tribes make working together so important?

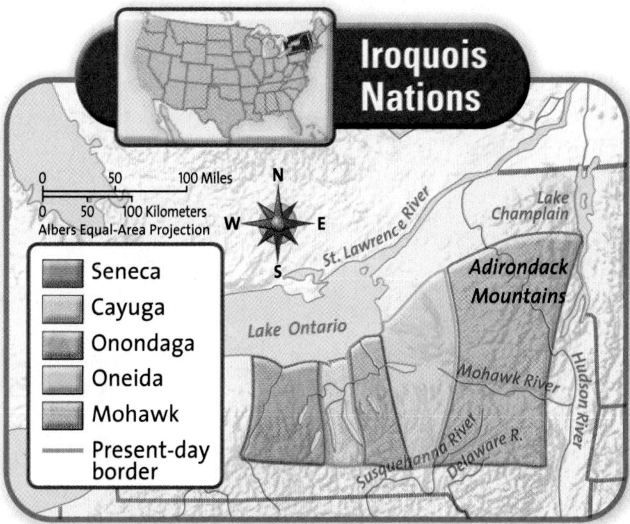

Unit 1

Activities

Read More

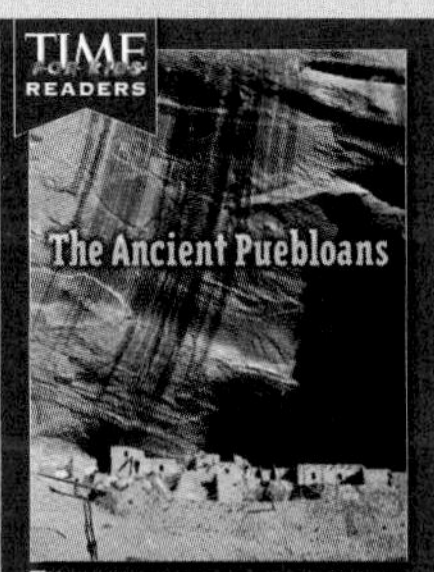

- *The Ancient Puebloans* by Shirley Frederick.

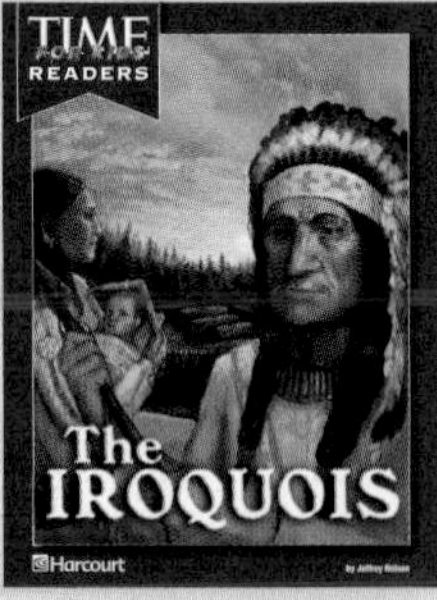

- *The Iroquois* by Jeffrey Nelson.

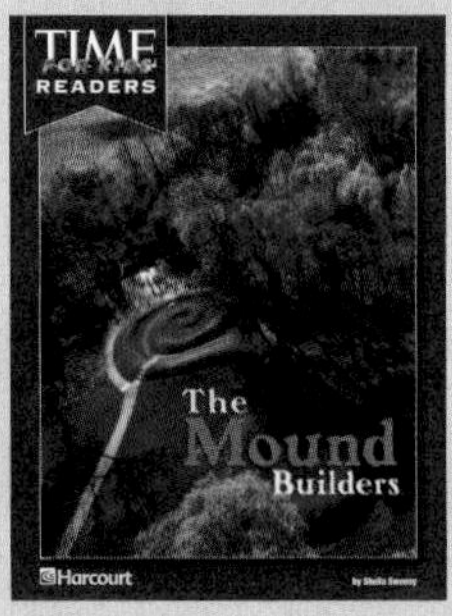

- *The Mound Builders* by Sheila Sweeny.

Show What You Know

Unit Writing Activity

Write a Report Choose two American Indian groups you have read about in this unit. Then write a report that compares and contrasts how their environments affected their ways of life. Tell about where their villages were located, the kinds of homes they built, the foods they ate, and how they made their clothing and tools. Provide facts, details, examples, and explanations in your report.

Unit Project

An American Indian Book Write and also illustrate a book about the American Indian groups discussed in this unit. Your book should include drawings, charts, poems, and maps that describe how each group's environment affected its way of life. When you have finished your book, make a cover that shows a map of North America with labels for each group and its region.

GO ONLINE Visit ACTIVITIES at **www.harcourtschool.com/hss**

Cultures Meet

Unit 2

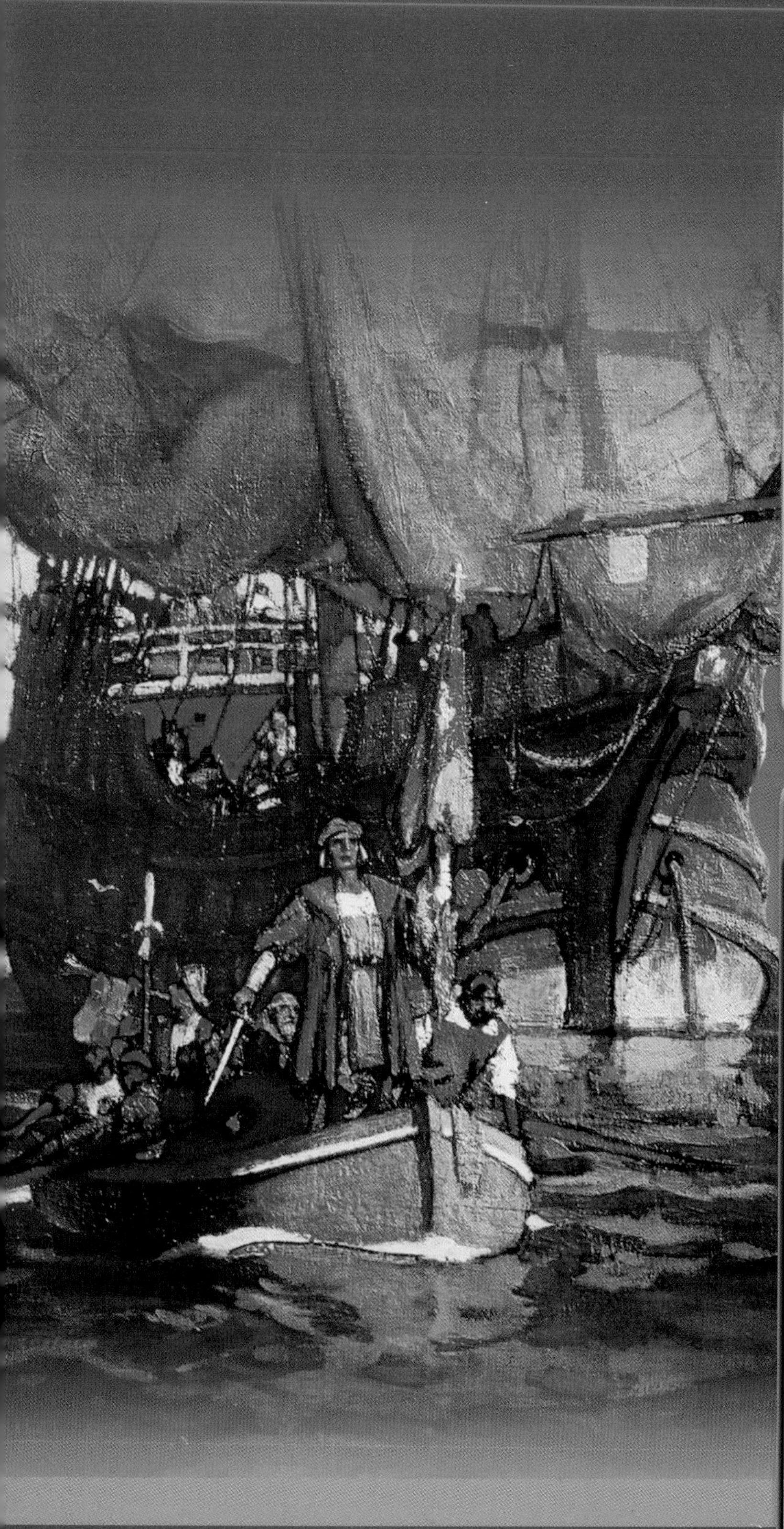

California History-Social Science Standards

5.2 Students trace the routes of early explorers and describe the early explorations of the Americas.

5.3 Students describe the cooperation and conflict that existed among the American Indians and between the Indian nations and the new settlers.

5.4 Students understand the political, religious, social, and economic institutions that evolved in the colonial era.

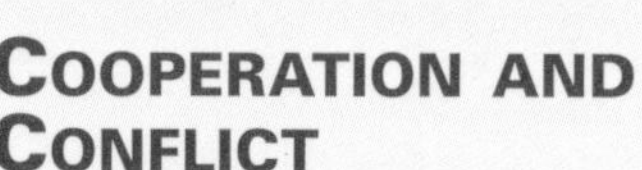

Cooperation and Conflict

Europeans came to the Americas to find riches, build settlements, and bring their religion to others.

What to Know

- ✓ Why did Europeans begin to explore different areas of the world?
- ✓ What explorers led key expeditions and what routes did they follow?
- ✓ How did European explorations impact American Indians?

Show What You Know

- ★ Unit 2 Test
- Writing: A Persuasive Advertisement
- Unit Project: A Museum of Exploration

Unit 2

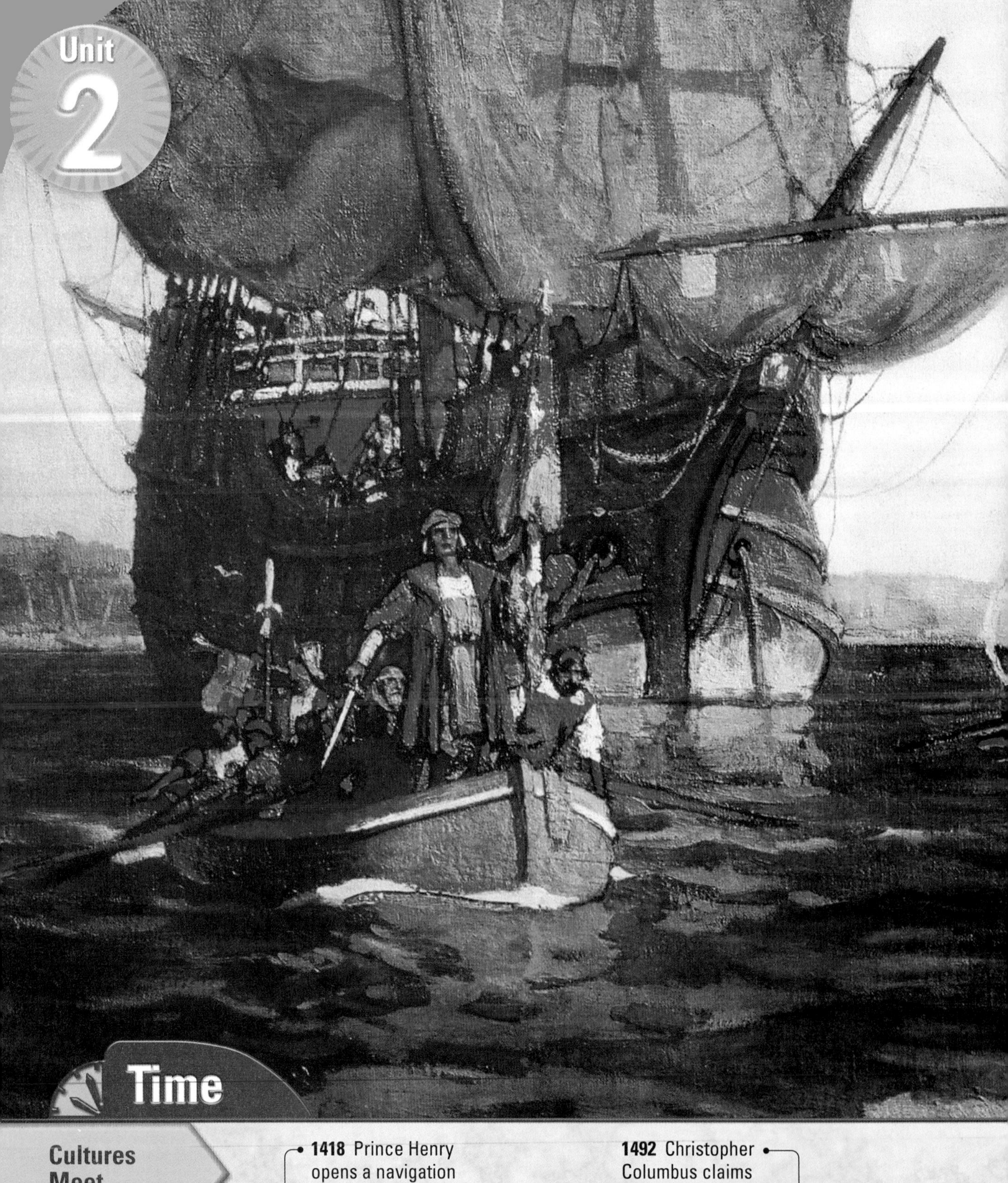

Time

Cultures Meet

1418 Prince Henry opens a navigation school in Portugal, p. 112

1492 Christopher Columbus claims land in the Americas for Spain, p. 116

1400

1450

1500

Cultures Meet

1610 Spain establishes a settlement at Santa Fe, p. 157

1620 English Pilgrims settle the Plymouth Colony, p. 170

1550

1600

1650

Christopher Columbus

1451–1506

- Italian sailor who explored the Americas for Spain
- Made four journeys to the Americas

Bartolomé de Las Casas

1484–1566

- Catholic priest who spoke out against the cruel treatment of American Indians
- Wrote a book called *Tears of the Indians*

People

1451–1506	Christopher Columbus
1484–1566	Bartolomé de Las Casas
1503?–1539	Estevanico
1510–1554	Francisco Vásquez de Coronado

Timeline: 1450 · 1500 · 1550

John Smith

1580–1631

- English sailor who traveled to many parts of the world
- Served as leader of the Jamestown settlement

Tisquantum (Squanto)

1585?–1622

- American Indian who lived near the Plymouth Colony
- Worked as an interpreter between the colonists and the Indians

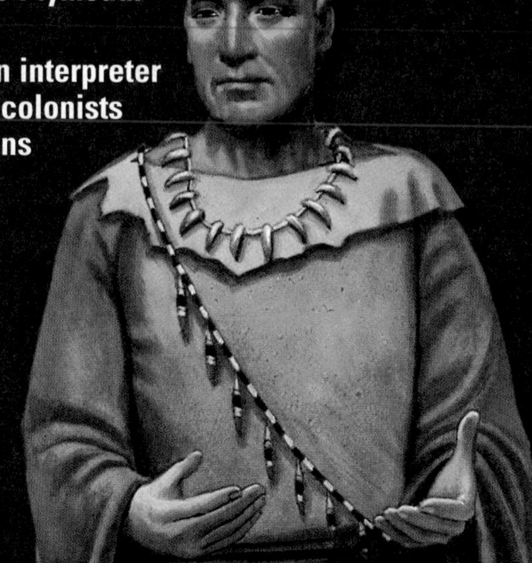

Estevanico

1503?–1539

- Enslaved African who took part in several Spanish explorations
- Learned to speak several American Indian languages

Francisco Vásquez de Coronado

1510–1554

- Spanish explorer
- Led an expedition in search of the Seven Cities of Gold

1600 1650 1700

1580 • John Smith 1631

1585? • Tisquantum (Squanto) 1622

1590 • William Bradford 1657

1595? • Pocahontas 1617

William Bradford

1590–1657

- English leader who led the Pilgrims to North America
- Served as governor of the Plymouth Colony

Pocahontas

1595?–1617

- Daughter of Chief Powhatan
- Married an English settler named John Rolfe

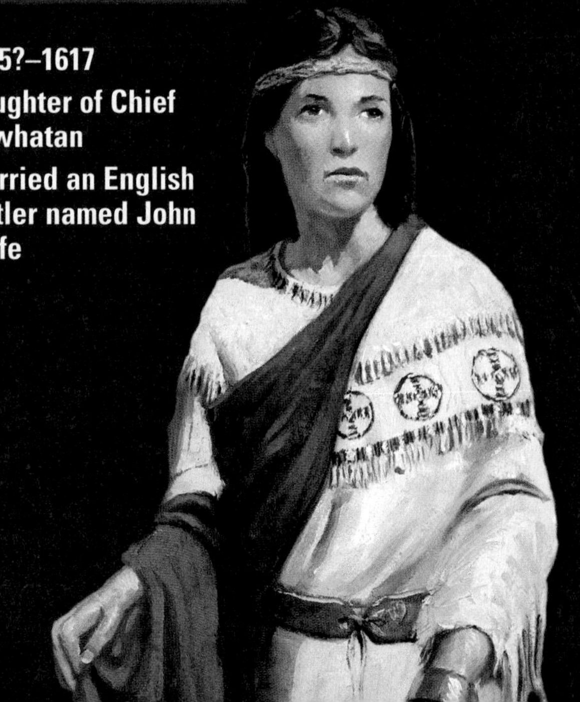

Unit 2

Place

North America, 1620

CHINOOK
YAKIMA
CASCADE RANGE
Columbia River
NEZ PERCE
ROCKY MOUNTAINS
Missouri River
MANDAN
CROW
GREAT PLAINS
SIOUX
SIOUX
COAST RANGES
Snake River
SHOSHONE
KLAMATH
CHEYENNE
MODOC
PAIUTE
SHOSHONE
Great Salt Lake
IOWA
POMO
SIERRA NEVADA
PAWNEE
MIWOK
SHOSHONE
ARAPAHO
UTE
Colorado River
KANSA
YOKUTS
PAIUTE
Arkansas River
CHUMASH
Mojave Desert
HOPI
NAVAJO
KIOWA
Santa Fe
CAHUILLA
APACHE
WICHITA
APACHE
COMANCHE
PACIFIC OCEAN
PIMA
APACHE
Rio Grande
CONCHO
TONKAWA
PIMA
Gulf of California
TOBOSO
Monterrey
Saltillo
TEPEHUAN
ZACATECA
Guadalajara
Mexico City

0 200 400 Miles
0 200 400 Kilometers
Albers Equal-Area Projection

At the Same Time

Chumash Indian cultural region

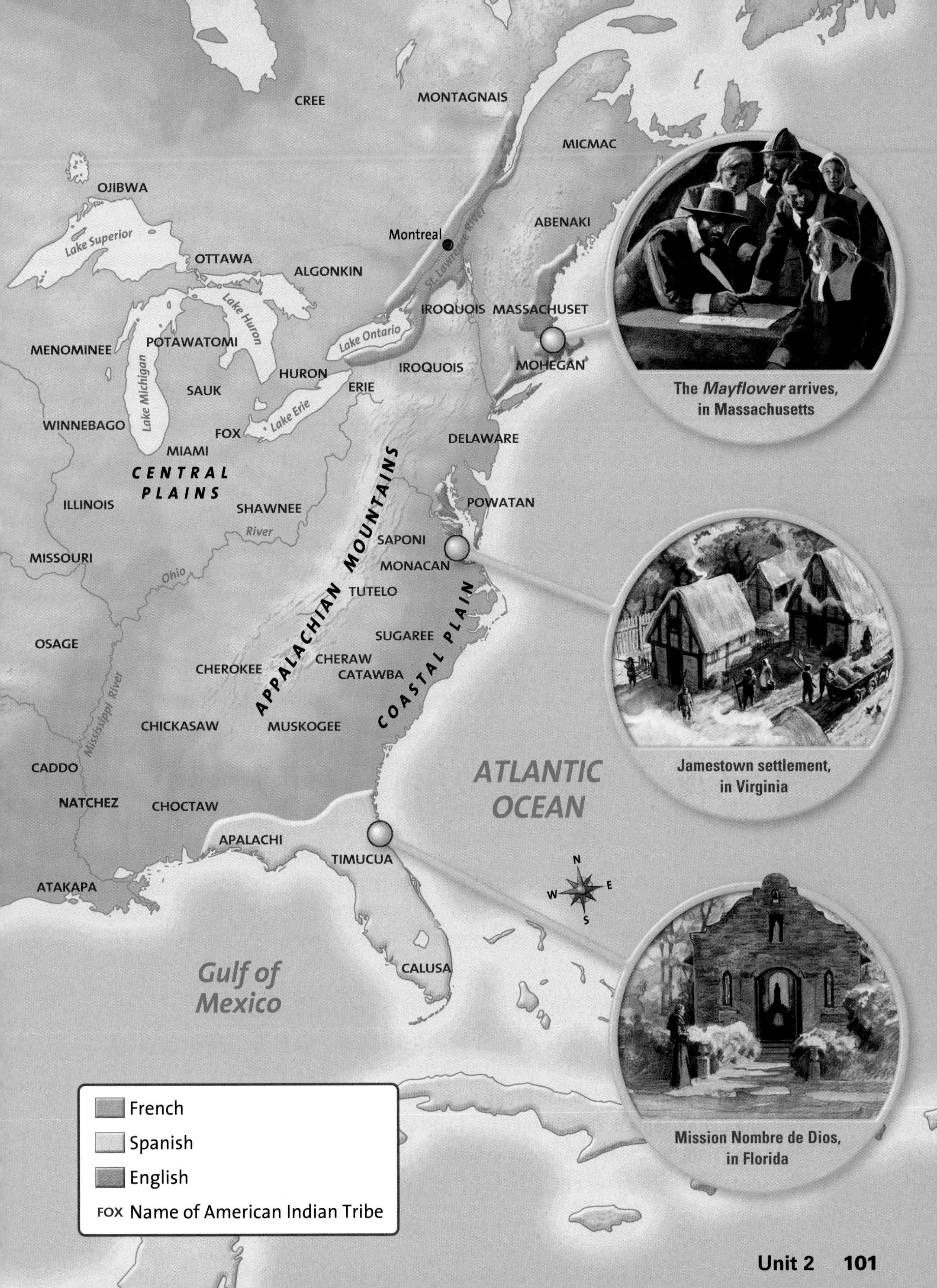

The *Mayflower* arrives, in Massachusetts

Jamestown settlement, in Virginia

Mission Nombre de Dios, in Florida

Unit 2

Reading Social Studies

Main Idea and Details

The main idea is the most important idea of a paragraph or passage. Details give more information about the main idea.

Why It Matters

When you identify and understand the main idea and details, you can better understand what you read.

Main Idea

The most important idea of a paragraph or passage

Details

Facts about the main idea	Facts about the main idea	Facts about the main idea

- ✓ The main idea is often given at the beginning of a piece of writing.
- ✓ In a long article, each paragraph has a main idea and details. The whole article also has a main idea and details.

Practice the Skill

Read the paragraphs, and identify details that support the main idea.

Main Idea
Details

The Taino were American Indians who lived on islands in the Caribbean Sea. They grew crops, fished, and hunted. They were peaceful people.

Another American Indian group that lived on islands in the Caribbean Sea was the Carib people. Like the Taino, the Carib also farmed, hunted, and fished. Unlike the Taino, the Carib were warlike. They were expert navigators who traveled long distances in large canoes.

Apply What You Learned

Main Idea and Details Read the paragraphs, and answer the questions.

Americans and Europeans Meet

The Taino were among the first Americans to meet European explorers. They were friendly and generous. Christopher Columbus wrote about them, "When you ask for something, they never say no. To the contrary, they offer to share with anyone."*

Taino men spent much of their time fishing. They went to sea in canoes, some of which were as big as ships. They used spears to catch big fish and nets to catch smaller ones. The men also hunted small animals.

The women grew manioc, a plant that they used to make flour for bread. They also grew sweet potatoes, corn, and cotton. Women used cotton to make hammocks. A hammock makes an ideal bed for sleeping outdoors in a hot climate because it is cool. It also keeps the sleeper off the ground and away from snakes.

Taino children played and gathered food. They ate sea grapes, birds' eggs, and even snails. Many children had pet dogs and parrots. They also played a ball game that was a little like soccer.

The Taino's lives were not completely carefree. Their life spans must have been short, because about half of all the Taino people were children. Also, the Taino had warlike neighbors, the Carib people, who lived on nearby islands.

Although the Taino welcomed the Europeans, the meeting turned out to be disastrous for them. The Europeans killed many Taino and made slaves of many more. Still more died of European diseases. Soon, the peaceful Taino had been wiped out.

Focus Skill

Main Idea and Details

1. **What is the main idea of the first paragraph?**
2. **What main point does the third paragraph make about how Taino women spent their time?**
3. **What details explain the idea that although the Taino were peaceful, they faced dangers?**

*Christopher Columbus. *The Four Voyages of Christopher Columbus*. Penguin Books, 1992.

Study Skills

USE VISUALS

Visuals can help you better understand and remember what you read.

- **Photographs, illustrations, diagrams, charts, and maps are different kinds of visuals.**
- **Visuals often show information that appears in the text, but they show it in a different way.**
- **Many visuals have titles, captions, or labels that help readers understand what is shown.**

✓	What kind of visual is shown?
✓	What does the visual show?
✓	How does the visual relate to the chapter, lesson, skill lesson, or feature you are reading?
✓	How does the visual help you better understand the subject of what you are reading?

Apply As You Read

As you read this chapter, use visuals and the visual checklist to help you gain new information from the text.

California History-Social Science Standards, Grade 5

5.2 Students trace the routes of early explorers and describe the early explorations of the Americas.
5.3 Students describe the cooperation and conflict that existed among the American Indians and between the Indian nations and the new settlers.

CHAPTER

The Age of Exploration

Replicas of Christopher Columbus's ships

Start with a Journal

The Log of Christopher Columbus

selections by Steve Lowe
illustrated by Robert Sabuda

In 1492 most Europeans thought the world was only as big as the continents of Europe, Asia, and Africa. No one knew what existed beyond the Atlantic Ocean. However, some people wanted to find out. The Italian explorer Christopher Columbus believed that if he traveled west, he could reach Asia. Facing the unknown, he and his crew set sail in hopes of finding a new trade route and riches. What they found was an entirely different land. During the journey, Columbus kept a record of daily events. Read now a few entries from his log.

Sunday September 9, 1492

This day we completely lost sight of land, and many men sighed and wept for fear they would not see it again for a long time. I comforted them with great promises of land and riches. To sustain their hope and dispel their fears of a long voyage, I decided to reckon fewer leagues than we actually made. I did this that they might not think themselves so great a distance from Spain as they really were.

Thursday October 11, 1492

About 10 o'clock at night, while standing on the sterncastle, I thought I saw a light to the west. It looked like a little wax candle bobbing up and down. . . . I am the first to admit that I was so eager to find land that I did not trust my own senses, so I called for Pedro Gutierrez, the representative of the King's household, and asked him to watch for the light. After a few moments, he too saw it.

Friday October 12, 1492

The moon, in its third quarter, rose in the east shortly before midnight. . . . Then, at two hours after midnight, the *Pinta* fired a cannon. . . . I hauled in all sails but the mainsail and lay-to till daylight. The land is about 6 miles to the west.

Friday October 12, 1492

At dawn . . . I went ashore in the ship's boat. I unfurled the royal banner. After a prayer of thanksgiving I ordered the captains of the *Pinta* and the *Niña* . . . to bear faith and witness that I was taking possession of this island for the King and Queen. . . . To this island I gave the name *San Salvador*. . . .

No sooner had we concluded the formalities of taking possession of the island than people began to come to the beach. . . . They are very well-built people. . . their eyes are large and very pretty. . . . Many of the natives paint their faces . . . others paint their whole bodies. . . . They are friendly. . . .

sterncastle a building or structure on a ship raised above the deck, at the rear of the ship

lay-to rested

Response Corner

1. Why do you think Columbus kept a private log of the miles the ships actually traveled?
2. Write a paragraph about how Columbus might have viewed the people he encountered.

Tuesday November 27, 1492

As I went along the river it was marvelous to see the forests and greenery, the very clear water, the birds, and the fine situation, and I almost did not want to leave the place. I told the men with me that, in order to make a report to the Sovereigns of the things they saw, a thousand tongues would not be sufficient to tell it, nor my hand to write it, for it looks like an enchanted land.

sovereigns the king and queen

Time

1400

1650

1450 Johannes Gutenberg develops a new printing press

1492 Christopher Columbus lands at San Salvador

Lesson 1

WHAT TO KNOW
Why did Europeans begin to look for a sea route to Asia?

- ✓ Explain the reasons for European exploration.
- ✓ Identify the technology that made ocean exploration possible.

VOCABULARY
technology p. 111
navigation p. 112
expedition p. 112
empire p. 113
entrepreneur p. 114
cost p. 114
benefit p. 114
Reconquista p. 115

PEOPLE
Marco Polo
Prince Henry
Christopher Columbus
King Ferdinand
Queen Isabella

PLACES
Portugal
Spain
San Salvador

MAIN IDEA AND DETAILS

California Standards
HSS 5.2, 5.2.1, 5.2.2

Exploration and Technology

You Are There

It is the winter of 1470 in your small village in Spain. Flames crackle in the fireplace as your father reads aloud from a book. The words describe a faraway land in Asia called Cathay. It is a place of amazing inventions and wealthy rulers.

An explorer named **Marco Polo** wrote these words long ago. Now, thanks to the spread of the printing press, many Europeans are reading Polo's book for the first time. As you listen, you dream of sailing to Asia and finding adventure and riches.

Marco Polo wrote about Asia in *The Travels of Marco Polo.*

Gutenberg's printing press used small metal pieces, each with a raised letter or number. Ink was spread over the pieces, and a large screw was turned to press them onto paper.

A Rush of New Ideas

In the 1400s, Europeans entered into a new age of learning, science, and art. Historians call this time of new ideas the Renaissance (REH•nuh•sahns), which means "rebirth." It began in Italy and then spread to Portugal, Spain, France, England, and other European countries.

Johannes Gutenberg helped with this spread of ideas by developing a printing press in the 1450s. Before this time, most books were hand-written. The new printing press made books faster.

One of the most popular books during the Renaissance was *The Travels of Marco Polo*. Written almost 200 years earlier, this book described Marco Polo's voyage to Cathay, as China was then called. Europeans were amazed when they read about Chinese inventions, such as gunpowder and the compass—a tool for finding directions.

European merchants were interested in the great wealth Marco Polo described. They wanted to buy and then resell Asian goods such as silks and spices. Soon, traders from Europe began traveling the long, difficult land routes to Asia.

At the time, no Europeans had traveled to Asia by sea. They had no maps that showed the world accurately. Sailors also lacked the **technology**, the scientific knowledge and tools, needed for such a long trip. Sailors and scientists began working to solve these obstacles, or problems.

READING CHECK **MAIN IDEA AND DETAILS**
What obstacles prevented Europeans from sailing to Asia?

The World Awaits

Prince Henry of **Portugal** helped solve some of these problems by starting a school of navigation. **Navigation** is the science of planning and following a route. The aim of his school was to improve ships, maps, and navigational technology.

At the school, sailors learned how to sail a new kind of ship, the caravel. Compared to other ships, the caravel was more seaworthy. This long, narrow ship could carry more cargo, sail quickly over long distances, and could move in any direction.

Mapmakers at Prince Henry's school read the journals of early explorers. They found descriptions of bodies of water and land shapes and used these details to draw up new, more accurate maps.

Cultural Heritage

Asian Technology

Chinese ideas and inventions changed the lives of Europeans. For example, gunpowder was unknown to Europe until contact was made with China. The Chinese used gunpowder in fireworks and rockets. In Europe, gunpowder led to the making of new weapons.

Some historians believe that the compass was also a Chinese invention that was passed on to Europeans. Compasses helped sailors tell in which direction they were sailing.

Tools such as this compass made sailing easier.

To keep their ships on the right course, sailors used navigational tools. Prince Henry hired scientists to improve two of these tools—the compass and the astrolabe. Sailors used the compass to help them make a rough estimate of their longitude, or their distance east or west of a location. They used the astrolabe to calculate the positions of the sun, moon, and stars. This information helped sailors to determine latitude, or their distance north or south of the equator.

All these and other developments made ocean exploration possible. In search of a sea route to Asia, dozens of Portuguese ships made **expeditions**, or trips taken with the goal of exploring. Prince Henry believed that the most direct sea route to Asia from Europe would be to sail south around Africa and then east across the Indian Ocean. Eventually, the Portuguese did find this route.

Europeans had known about Asia through trade and Marco Polo's writings. Traders had long been using the Silk Road—a series of land routes between China and Italy. At this time, Europeans referred to all of Asia as "the Indies."

Europeans also traveled to Africa. They traded with merchants in North African cities such as Gao (GOW), Timbuktu (tim•buhk•TOO), and Jenné (jeh•NAY). These cities were the centers of rich empires. An **empire** is a collection of lands ruled by the nation that conquered them.

Since the rest of the continents lie much farther away from Europe, Europeans did not even suspect that these continents existed. Nor did they know that people there had built large civilizations. In South America, the Inca Empire ruled over as many as 12 million people. In Central America, the Aztec Empire covered 80,000 square miles of present-day Mexico. As many as 5 million people lived under the rule of the Aztecs. In North America, there were American Indians from the Pacific coast to the Atlantic coast.

READING CHECK MAIN IDEA AND DETAILS
What were the aims of Prince Henry's school of navigation?

Caravels were smaller, lighter, and faster than other ships of the time.

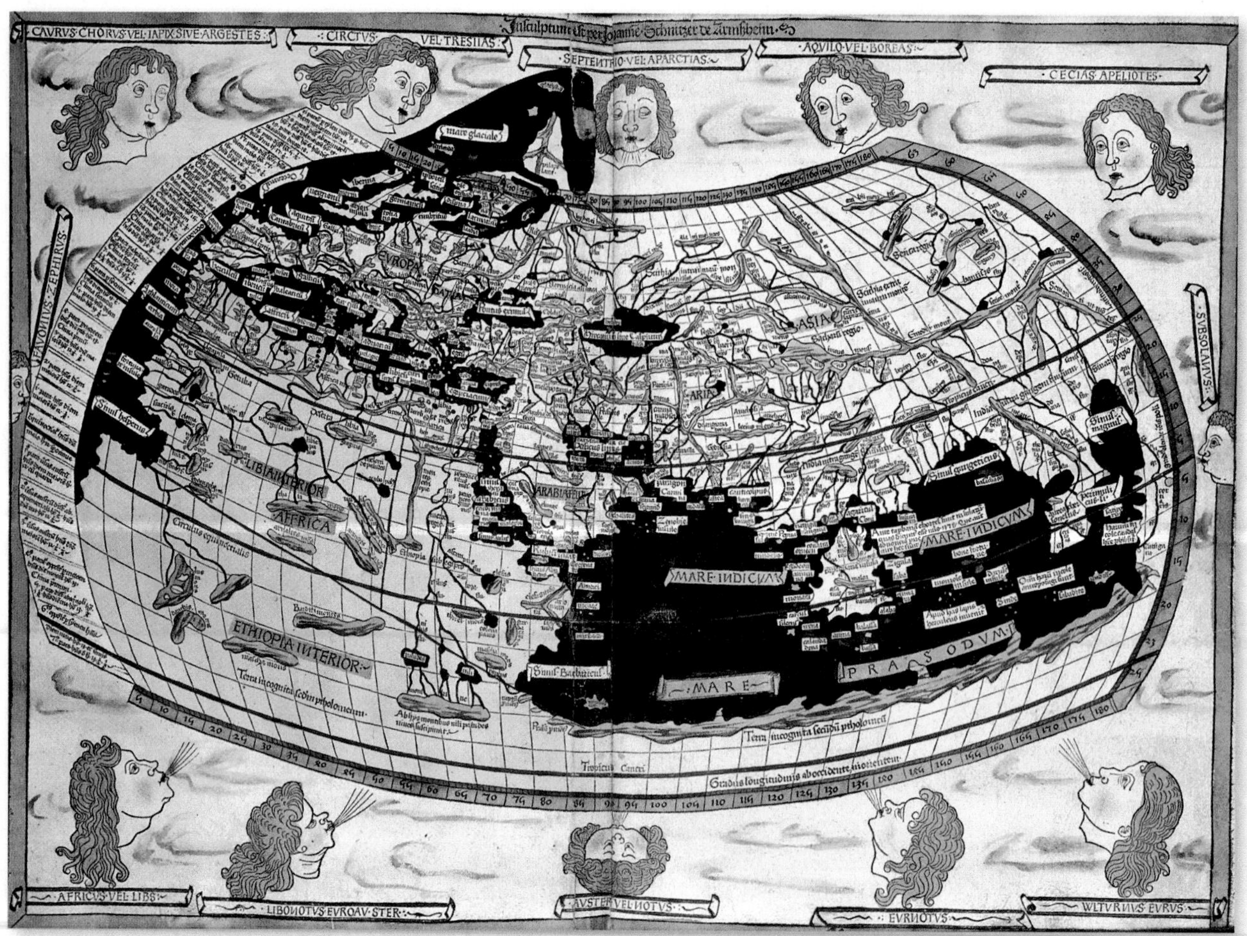

The information for this world map came from Ptolemy (TAH•luh•mee), a Greek astronomer who lived in the A.D. 100s. Republished in 1482, the map shows only Europe, Africa, and Asia.

The Business of Exploring

In many European countries, most sailors thought the only way to reach Asia was to sail east. However, some people thought Asia could be reached by sailing west across the Atlantic. One of them was an Italian sailor who had already sailed along the coasts of Europe and Africa. The sailor's name was **Christopher Columbus**. He believed that sailing west across the Ocean Sea, as the Atlantic Ocean was then known, was a more direct route to Asia than sailing around Africa. But he could not prove it until he had the money for a ship, a crew, and supplies.

Explorers had to be **entrepreneurs** (ahn•truh•pruh•NERZ) as well as sailors. They organized and ran their expeditions like an entrepreneur sets up and manages a business. Often, explorers had to persuade others that the **cost**, or effort made to gain something, of an expedition was worth the risk. Ships and supplies were expensive, and there were many risks. For example, a ship could be lost at sea or fail to find anything of value.

However, the **benefit**, or reward gained, was the chance of finding riches worth many times the cost. This would more than repay the expenses paid by the trip's supporters.

Finding a ruler to pay for Columbus's trip would not be easy. His idea of sailing west seemed risky. No one knew how far west Asia was. The first person Columbus asked for money was King John II of Portugal, Prince Henry's nephew. The king was not interested in Columbus's idea and turned him down. By sailing around Africa, the Portuguese had already found a sea route to Asia from Europe.

Three years later, in 1485, Columbus asked **Spain's** monarchs, **King Ferdinand** and **Queen Isabella**, to support his plan. Ferdinand and Isabella were Catholic, and at the time, they were focused on fighting a war to push all Muslim people out of Spain. This movement to make Spain all Catholic was called the **Reconquista** (ray•kohn•KEES•tah). Under the Reconquista, Muslims had to stop following their Islamic religion and become Catholic or leave the country. By 1492, Ferdinand and Isabella had claimed all of the land the Muslims once held in Spain. They had also forced many thousands of Jews to leave Spain.

When Spain was united under one religion, Columbus again asked Ferdinand and Isabella to support his voyage. He promised the monarchs great wealth and new lands. Columbus also said that he would take the Catholic religion to the people of Asia. The king and queen agreed to support his plan.

READING CHECK **MAIN IDEA AND DETAILS**
How did Columbus persuade the king and queen of Spain to support his expedition?

This painting shows Christopher Columbus asking King Ferdinand and Queen Isabella of Spain to support his expedition.

Two Worlds Meet

TIME 1492

PLACE San Salvador

On August 3, 1492, Columbus and a crew of 90 sailors sailed from Spain on three ships—the *Niña* (NEEN•yuh), the *Pinta* (PEEN•tuh), and the *Santa María*. More than two months later, he and his crew were still at sea, facing many obstacles, or hardships. Often, fierce storms battered their ships. When there was no wind to fill the sails, they sometimes drifted for days. The sailors grew restless and homesick.

Eventually, they began to notice a change in the weather. Then they saw birds flying south. Columbus changed course, hoping to follow the birds to land.

The night of October 11, 1492, was a good night for sailing. A strong wind pushed the ships from behind. The moon was behind them, too, shining like a lantern on the sea in front of them. In the early morning hours of October 12, the sailors finally saw their goal—land!

All three ships anchored off an island that Columbus named **San Salvador**. He claimed the island and other islands he visited for Spain. Columbus believed he had reached Asia and was now in the Indies, so he called the people he met on the island *Indians*.

The people Columbus met were members of the Taino (TY•noh) tribe. The Tainos welcomed Columbus and his men, but the Europeans were disappointed not to find any Asian silk or spices. Columbus did collect a few gold items and some of the islands' animals and plants. Before leaving for Spain, he also took several Tainos.

Children IN HISTORY

Diego Bermúdez

Some of the sailors on Columbus's expedition were as young as 12. That was the age of Diego Bermúdez when he sailed on the *Santa María* in 1492. Diego was a page, which was the lowest rank on a ship. Pages did the jobs that most sailors did not want to do, like cooking, cleaning, and keeping track of the time. Diego kept track of the time by using an hourglass. It was actually a half hourglass. Every 30 minutes, when the sand had all fallen to the bottom of the glass, Diego rang a bell and yelled out a short prayer. This let everyone know what time it was.

Make It Relevant What jobs do you have to do at home or at school?

When Columbus and his men returned to Spain, they were treated like heroes. They had crossed the Atlantic Ocean and returned home. When King Ferdinand and Queen Isabella saw the gold, animals, plants, and people from the Indies, they paid for another expedition. The Spanish rulers made it clear that the reasons for this second expedition were to find more riches, start settlements in the Indies, and convert the Indians to the Catholic religion.

READING CHECK **MAIN IDEA AND DETAILS**
What obstacles did Columbus and his crew face?

Summary

In the 1400s, stories of riches in Asia made sailors eager to explore. New ships and tools made exploration possible. While most explorers looked eastward for a route to Asia, Columbus sailed west and reached land across the Atlantic Ocean.

REVIEW

1. Why did Europeans begin to look for a sea route to Asia?
2. Explain how **technology** helped improve **navigation**.
3. What did Columbus find on his 1492 voyage?

CRITICAL THINKING

4. ANALYSIS SKILL What were the advantages and disadvantages of sailing west to Asia?
5. Why did Columbus need to think like an entrepreneur?
6. **Draw a Chart** Imagine that you are a ruler who has been asked to give money for an expedition. Draw a chart that lists the costs and the benefits of supporting an expedition.
7. Focus Skill **MAIN IDEA AND DETAILS** On a separate sheet of paper, copy and complete the graphic organizer below.

Main Idea

Europeans faced obstacles in finding a sea route to Asia.

Details

PRIMARY SOURCES

Navigational Tools

Navigational tools allowed sailors to explore far-away lands and still find their way back home. With most of these tools, sailors used the sun, moon, and stars to determine location. In the 1400s, European navigators used the astrolabe to measure latitude. The compass was also used, but it was not always reliable. By the 1700s, more accurate tools were developed, including the sextant and the chronometer.

This compass has a map showing towns and cities in northern Europe.

A chronometer kept very accurate time and was used to measure the positions of certain stars based on the time.

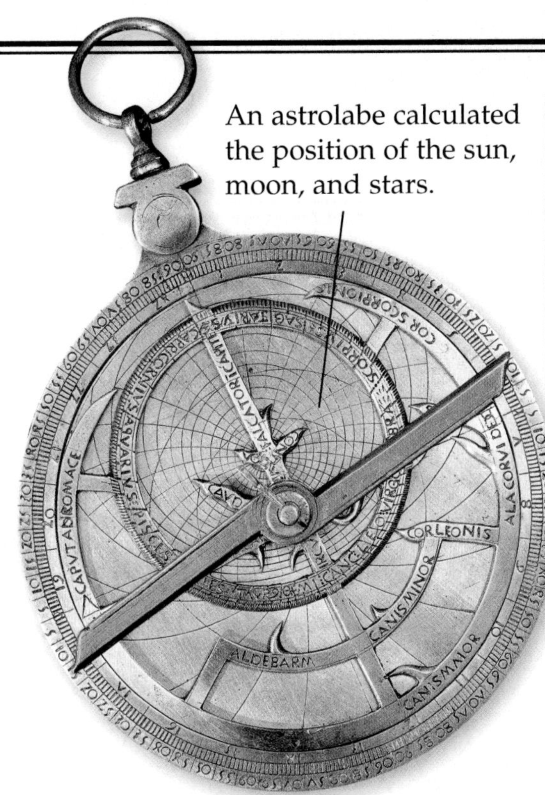

An astrolabe calculated the position of the sun, moon, and stars.

ANALYSIS SKILL **Analyze Artifacts**

1. Which tool do you think was the most effective for navigation? Explain your answer.
2. How do you think sextants were used?
3. Which of these tools do you think sailors use today?

GO ONLINE Visit PRIMARY SOURCES at **www.harcourtschool.com/hss**

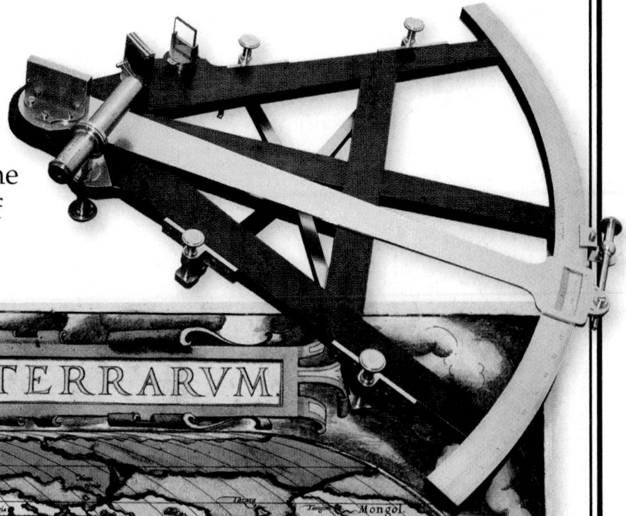

Sextants (right) were used to determine the altitude, or the height above the horizon, of the sun or stars. This map of the world was created by Abraham Ortelius in 1574.

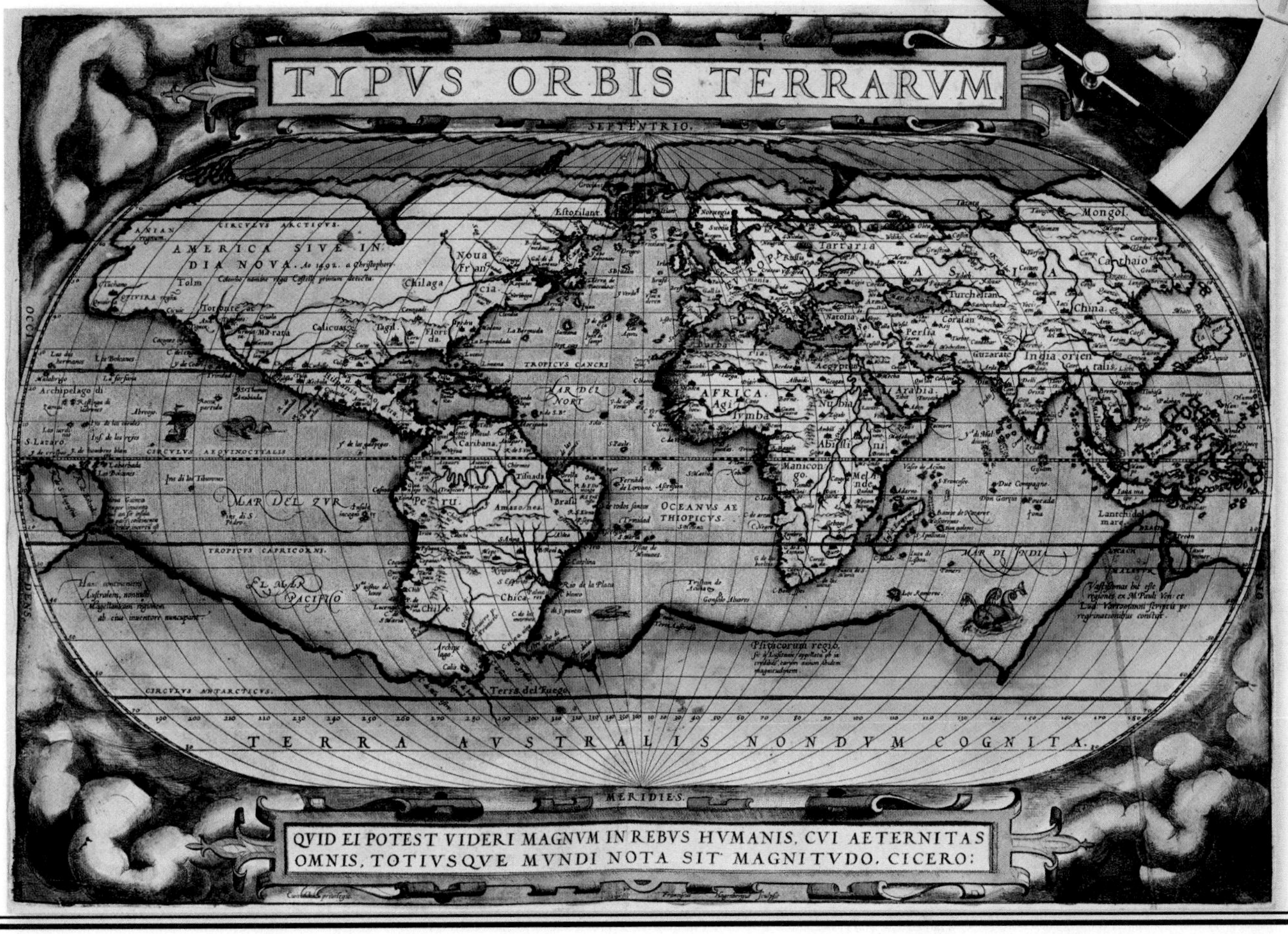
TYPVS ORBIS TERRARVM
SEPTENTRIO.
AMERICA SIVE INDIA NOVA
AFRICA
MAR DEL ZVR
OCEANVS AETHIOPICVS
TERRA AVSTRALIS NONDVM COGNITA.
MERIDIES.
QVID EI POTEST VIDERI MAGNVM IN REBVS HVMANIS, CVI AETERNITAS OMNIS, TOTIVSQVE MVNDI NOTA SIT MAGNITVDO. CICERO:

Lesson 2

Time

1400 — 1650

1497 Caboto reaches Newfoundland

1513 Balboa sights the Pacific Ocean

1522 The Magellan expedition completes a voyage around the world

WHAT TO KNOW
Why did Europeans explore the Americas, and what did they find?

- ✓ Describe the aims, obstacles, and accomplishments of early explorers.
- ✓ Trace the routes of the explorers and identify the areas they claimed.

VOCABULARY
isthmus p. 123
treaty p. 125

PEOPLE
Giovanni Caboto
Amerigo Vespucci
Vasco Núñez de Balboa
Ferdinand Magellan

PLACES
England
Newfoundland
Philippine Islands

MAIN IDEA AND DETAILS

California Standards
HSS 5.2, 5.2.2, 5.2.3, 5.2.4

A Changing World

YOU ARE THERE It is June 1497, and you have been at sea for more than a month. You signed up for this journey in England after hearing about Columbus's successful expeditions. However, now you are beginning to have second thoughts. Fog surrounds your ship, and almost everyone on board looks worried. "This cold air chills me to the bone," says a crew member. You squint to try to see through the fog, but it is no use. Whatever is out there remains a mystery.

➤ Caboto plants the English flag on what is now Canada.

Caboto sailed to present-day Newfoundland.

Caboto's Expedition

After his first voyage, Columbus returned to the Indies three times. He never found riches, but he did prove the possibility of sailing across the Atlantic. Soon after Columbus's return, most European monarchs wanted to send their own ships to the Indies. They were determined to claim new lands, expand their power, and discover riches.

In **England**, King Henry VII heard of Columbus's success for Spain. The king paid an Italian sailor named **Giovanni Caboto** (kah•BOH•toh), whom the English called John Cabot, to lead an expedition. King Henry's aim was for Caboto's expedition to help England compete for land and wealth.

In May 1497, Caboto and a crew of 18 sailed west on a course far north of Columbus's original route. After a long, slow journey, they reached land on June 24. After stepping ashore, Caboto claimed the land for England. He then sailed south along the coast for some distance before returning to England. Years later, Caboto's son Sebastian described the place: "It is a very sterile [lonely] land. There are in it many white bears, and very large stags like horses. . . ."*

When Caboto returned to England, he said he had found China. Caboto, like Columbus, thought he had been to Asia. Many people today believe Caboto actually reached the coast of present-day **Newfoundland**, now a part of Canada.

READING CHECK **MAIN IDEA AND DETAILS**
What was the aim of King Henry VII when he paid for Caboto's expedition?

*Sebastian Cabot, 1544 map notes. *North American Exploration* by Michael Golay and John S. Bowman. John Wiley & Sons, Inc., 2003.

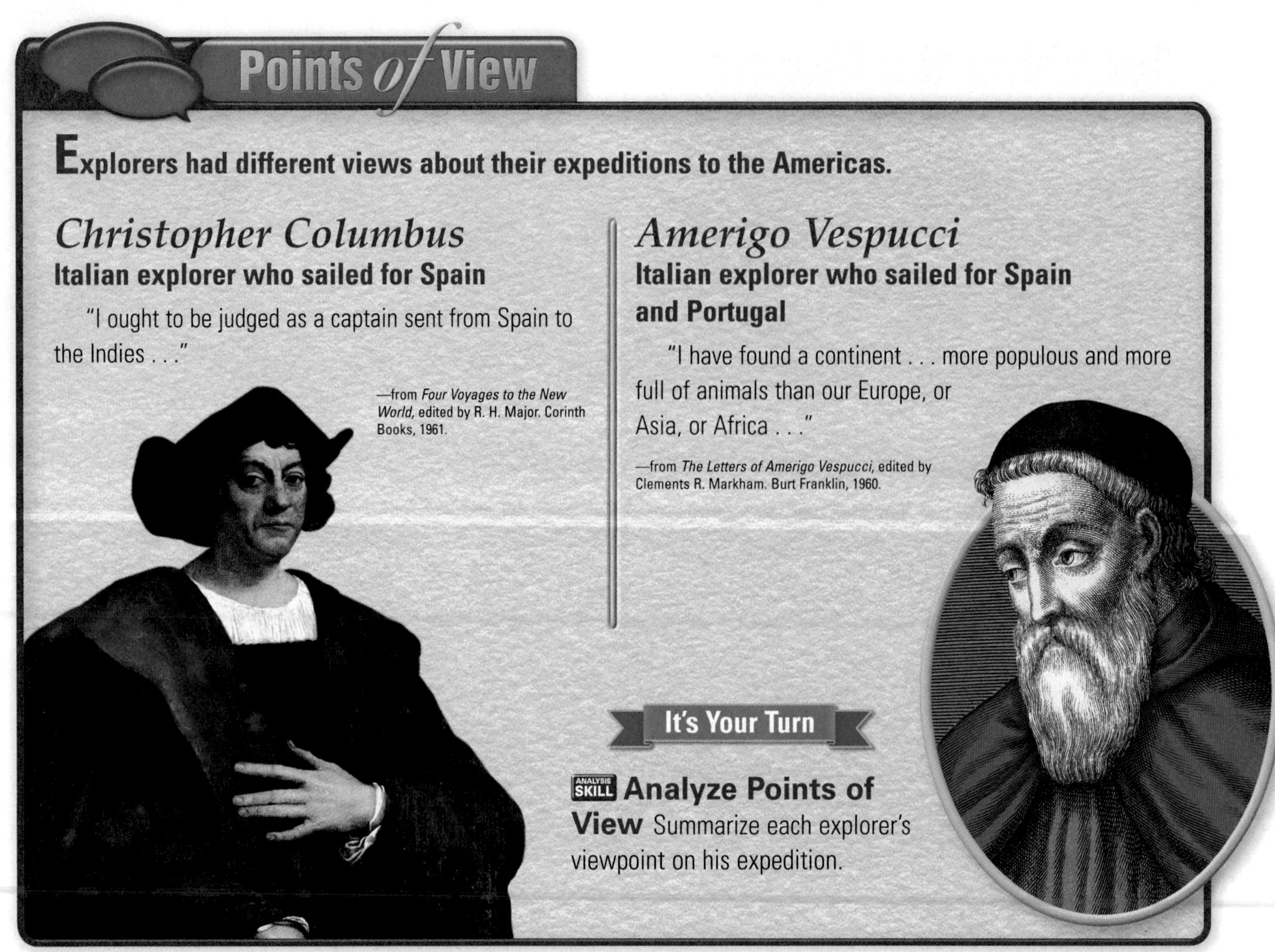

A New Map of the World

Not everyone believed that Columbus and Caboto had found Asia. **Amerigo Vespucci** (veh•SPOO•chee) of Italy aimed to find out for himself. In 1499, he sailed to a place just south of where Columbus had landed. Two years later, Vespucci sailed on an expedition down the coast of South America.

Vespucci looked for signs that he had reached Asia, but he could find none. In the areas he explored he did not find any large cities or wealthy rulers. Also, the places he saw did not fit Marco Polo's descriptions of Asia. Vespucci began to think that maybe Earth was larger than most people thought. If so, that would mean Asia was farther away from Europe than Columbus believed.

Vespucci came to realize that he, Columbus, and Caboto had found a continent previously unknown to Europeans. In 1507, a German map-maker named Martin Waldseemüller (VAHLT•zay•mool•er) published a world map that included this continent. He named it for Amerigo Vespucci, calling it America. The land on this new map stood for the present-day continent of South America. Later, the use of the word *America* was also applied to the land known today as the continent of North America.

READING CHECK **MAIN IDEA AND DETAILS**
What was Vespucci's main accomplishment?

Reaching the Pacific

After Vespucci's voyages, other explorers sailed around the mysterious "new" lands, but none could find China. It seemed more and more likely that Vespucci had been right. Still, Europeans could not be sure they were *not* in Asia. They wondered what these lands could be if they were not a part of Asia.

The Spanish explorer **Vasco Núñez de Balboa** (NOON•yays day bahl•BOH•uh) answered that question. Balboa was one of the first Europeans to settle in the Americas. He had set up a farm on the island of Hispaniola (ees•pah•NYOH•lah), but he was not a good farmer and soon owed money to many people. Instead of paying them, he escaped from Hispaniola by hiding in a barrel on a ship bound for what is now Colombia. There, he met the survivors of a failed Spanish settlement and helped them settle in what is now the country of Panama.

While searching for gold in the region, Balboa met a group of Indians who told him about a vast ocean to the west. In 1513, Balboa and some other explorers hiked west across the Isthmus of Panama, which connects the continents of North America and South America. An **isthmus** is a strip of land that connects two large land areas. Eventually, Balboa's group reached a huge ocean known today as the Pacific Ocean.

READING CHECK **CAUSE AND EFFECT**
What caused Balboa to search for an ocean west of the Americas?

Balboa was 38 years old when he journeyed to the Pacific Ocean.

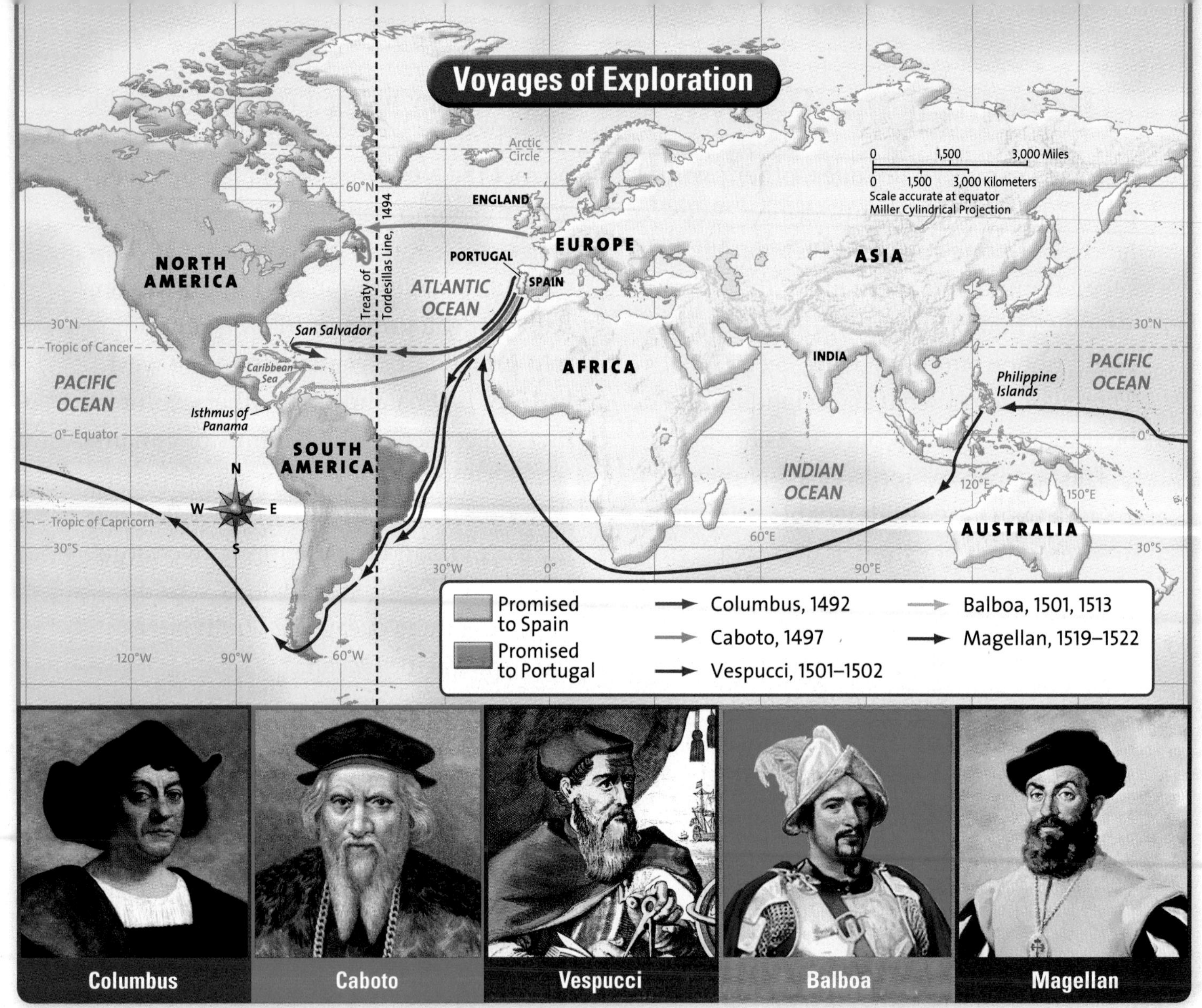

ANALYSIS SKILL Analyze Maps

Movement Which explorer sailed across the Pacific Ocean?

A New View of the World

With the aim of finding a western route to Asia, the Portuguese explorer **Ferdinand Magellan** (muh•JEH•luhn) also proved Vespucci was right. In 1519, Magellan left Spain with five ships and about 250 sailors. They sailed to present-day Brazil. After passing through a waterway at the tip of South America, the sailors found themselves in the same ocean that Balboa had seen. Magellan named it the *Pacific*, which means "peaceful," because its waters seemed still compared with those of the Atlantic.

Magellan expected to cross the Pacific in a few days, but it took more than three months. Many sailors died of hunger and illness. Magellan himself was killed in a battle in the **Philippine Islands**, 500 miles off the coast of southeastern Asia. Despite the obstacles, one ship made it back to Spain in 1522. The sailors onboard were the first to travel around the world.

As more expeditions were organized, more lands were claimed. Often, the same land was claimed by more than one country. The Catholic rulers of Spain and Portugal asked Catholic Church leaders to settle such a case. In 1493, Church leaders drew a line on a map through the Atlantic Ocean. Portugal was promised the land to the east of the line, and Spain was promised the land to the west.

In 1494, Spain and Portugal signed the Treaty of Tordesillas. A **treaty** is an agreement between countries. In this treaty, Spain and Portugal agreed to move the dividing line farther west. This change gave Portugal the land that would become part of the country of Brazil.

READING CHECK **MAIN IDEA AND DETAILS**
What did Magellan's expedition accomplish?

Summary

After Columbus's voyages, rulers were eager to pay for trips across the Atlantic. Explorers such as Caboto, Vespucci, Balboa, and Magellan explored many different areas. Spain and Portugal divided the Americas between themselves.

One side of this gold coin shows King Ferdinand and Queen Isabella (left).

REVIEW

1. Why did Europeans explore the Americas, and what did they find?
2. Use the term **treaty** to explain how Spain and Portugal divided lands in the Americas.
3. What two oceans did explorers cross when they sailed west from Europe to Asia?

CRITICAL THINKING

4. ANALYSIS SKILL How did the relative location of what is now Brazil affect Portugal's claims in the Americas?
5. ANALYSIS SKILL What were the causes of European expeditions across the Atlantic Ocean?
6. **Make an Explorers Table** Make a table that lists the name of each explorer in this lesson and the area that person explored. Then use your table and the map on page 124 to trace their routes and describe the distances they traveled.
7. Focus Skill **MAIN IDEA AND DETAILS**
On a separate sheet of paper, copy and complete the graphic organizer below.

Main Idea

Details

Vespucci sails to South America.	Balboa reaches the Pacific Ocean.	Magellan sails west to Asia.

Christopher Columbus's Voyages

There is no question that the four voyages of Columbus changed the world. However, the exact impact and meaning of these historical events are debated even today. Some see Columbus as a heroic figure—a man of courage, curiosity, and daring. Others see him as one who brought great hardship to people who meant him no harm. Here are different points of view in this ongoing debate.

On Columbus's first voyage he traveled about 4,100 miles before reaching the island he named San Salvador.

In Their Own Words

RUSSELL MEANS

Russell Means, an American Indian leader, writing about Columbus's treatment of Indians

"Columbus' arrival was a disaster from the beginning . . . he immediately began the enslavement . . . of the Indian peoples of the Caribbean islands."

— from an article in the *Denver Post.* October 12, 1991.

Robert S. McElvaine, a teacher and author, writing about Columbus's voyages

"The major long-term significance of Columbus' voyage is that it led to the mixing of the people of the world on an unprecedented scale and set in motion the process of making what would become the United States the most ethnically diverse society the world has known."

— from an article in the *Los Angeles Times.* October 12, 1992.

ROBERT S. MCELVAINE

KATHLEEN DEAGAN

Kathleen Deagan, a teacher and author, writing about the effect of Columbus's voyages on the Indians

"Regardless of how many Taínos were living in Hispaniola when Columbus arrived, the stunning reduction in their numbers was the most shocking immediate repercussion [effect] of European contact."

— from *Columbus's Outpost Among the Taínos.* Yale University Press, 2002.

It's Your Turn

ANALYSIS SKILL **Analyze Points of View** Work with a classmate to summarize the point of view held by each writer. Decide how each writer views Columbus's voyages.

Make It Relevant Why do you think people have different points of view on Christopher Columbus and his voyages?

Lesson 3

1400 — 1650

- **1513** Ponce de León reaches Florida
- **1521** Cortés destroys the Aztec capital
- **1539** De Soto begins his exploration of Florida

WHAT TO KNOW
Why did the Spanish explore and conquer large areas of the Americas?

- ✓ Describe the aims, obstacles, and accomplishments of Spanish explorers.
- ✓ Trace the routes of Spanish explorers and identify their claims.

VOCABULARY
grant p. 129
conquistador p. 129
reform p. 133
Reformation p. 133
Counter-Reformation p. 133
missionary p. 133

PEOPLE
Juan Ponce de León
Hernando Cortés
Estevanico
Francisco Coronado
Hernando de Soto
Martin Luther

PLACES
Florida
Mexico City
New Spain

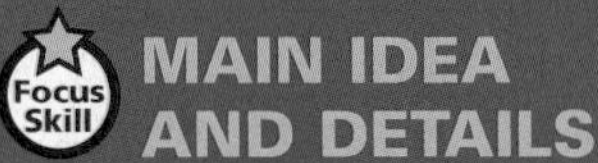
MAIN IDEA AND DETAILS

California Standards
HSS 5.2, 5.2.1, 5.2.2, 5.2.3

Spanish Explorations

YOU ARE THERE You trudge through the thick forest, waving the flies away from your face. The air is hot and humid, and your heavy armor seems to be getting even heavier with each step. Your commander has announced that he is seeking a "fountain of youth." The idea seems foolish to you, but you know it would be unwise to argue. As you near a clearing, a soldier in front orders everyone to stop. Your group has just come face to face with a group of American Indians.

Spanish explorer Juan Ponce de León led the first European expedition to Florida.

GEOGRAPHY

The Gulf Stream

Ponce de León became one of the first explorers to experience the Gulf Stream, one of the strongest ocean currents in the world. A current is a faster-flowing part of a body of water. The Gulf Stream starts in the Gulf of Mexico and flows through the Straits of Florida. It then travels north in the Atlantic Ocean. Spanish treasure ships returning from North America followed the Gulf Stream to get back to Europe faster.

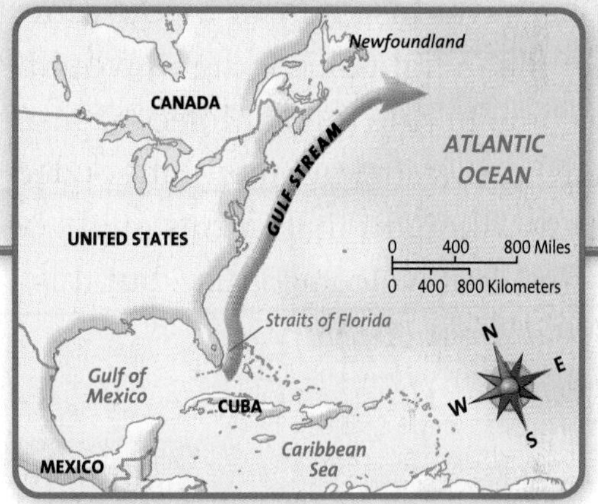

Juan Ponce de León

TIME 1513

PLACE Florida

Once Spain had claimed land in the Americas, more Spanish explorers and soldiers soon sailed there. Some wanted to find adventure and riches. Others wanted to win national glory and to convert the American Indians to Christianity. To encourage the explorers, the monarch of Spain offered large sums of money, called **grants**, to those who would lead expeditions. These Spanish explorers and soldiers became known as **conquistadors** (kahn•KEES•tah•dawrz), or "conquerors."

Juan Ponce de León (POHN•say day lay•OHN) had sailed with Columbus on his second voyage and later helped conquer Puerto Rico. From the Indians who lived there, he had heard about an island to the north called Bimini (BIH•muh•nee). He also may have heard that the island had a so-called Fountain of Youth, which supposedly made old people young again.

In 1513, Ponce de León set out to find Bimini. Instead, he landed in what is now the state of **Florida**. He named the land *La Florida*, Spanish for "flowery," and claimed it for Spain. Though Ponce de León never found the Fountain of Youth, he was the first Spanish explorer to set foot on land that became part of the United States.

READING CHECK **MAIN IDEA AND DETAILS**
What was Ponce de León searching for when he reached Florida?

Early Conquistadors

In 1519, Spain sent **Hernando Cortés** to find gold in the land of the Aztecs. Cortés landed in what is now Mexico with about 650 soldiers. Cortés and his men marched west from the coast toward the Aztec capital, Tenochtitlán (tay•nohch•teet•LAHN). Along the way, they met Indians who disliked the Aztecs' harsh rule. The Indians gave food to the Spanish and even agreed to help them fight the Aztecs. Malintzin, an Indian woman who spoke the Aztec language, translated for the Spanish.

Cortés was also helped by the Aztecs' belief that a light-skinned god would one day come to rule them. Motecuhzoma (moh•tay•kwah•SOH•mah), the Aztec emperor, thought that Cortés might be this god and welcomed him, but this peace did not last very long.

Cortés took Motecuhzoma prisoner, and fighting broke out between the Spaniards and the Aztecs. The Aztecs were fierce fighters, but they did not have horses or guns like the Spanish. Many Aztecs also died from diseases accidentally brought over by the soldiers. By 1521, Cortés had conquered the Aztecs. On the ruins of Tenochtitlán, the Spanish built **Mexico City**, which became a major center in Spain's new empire in the Americas.

After Cortés found wealth among the Aztecs, the Spanish looked elsewhere for more riches. The Spanish leaders in Mexico City heard an American Indian story about cities made of gold. To see whether the story was true, they sent a priest named Marcos de Niza (day NEE•sah) on an expedition. De Niza brought an African slave, named **Estevanico** (es•tay•vahn•EE•koh), who was familiar with the Southwest. During

Spanish Conquistador and Aztec Warrior

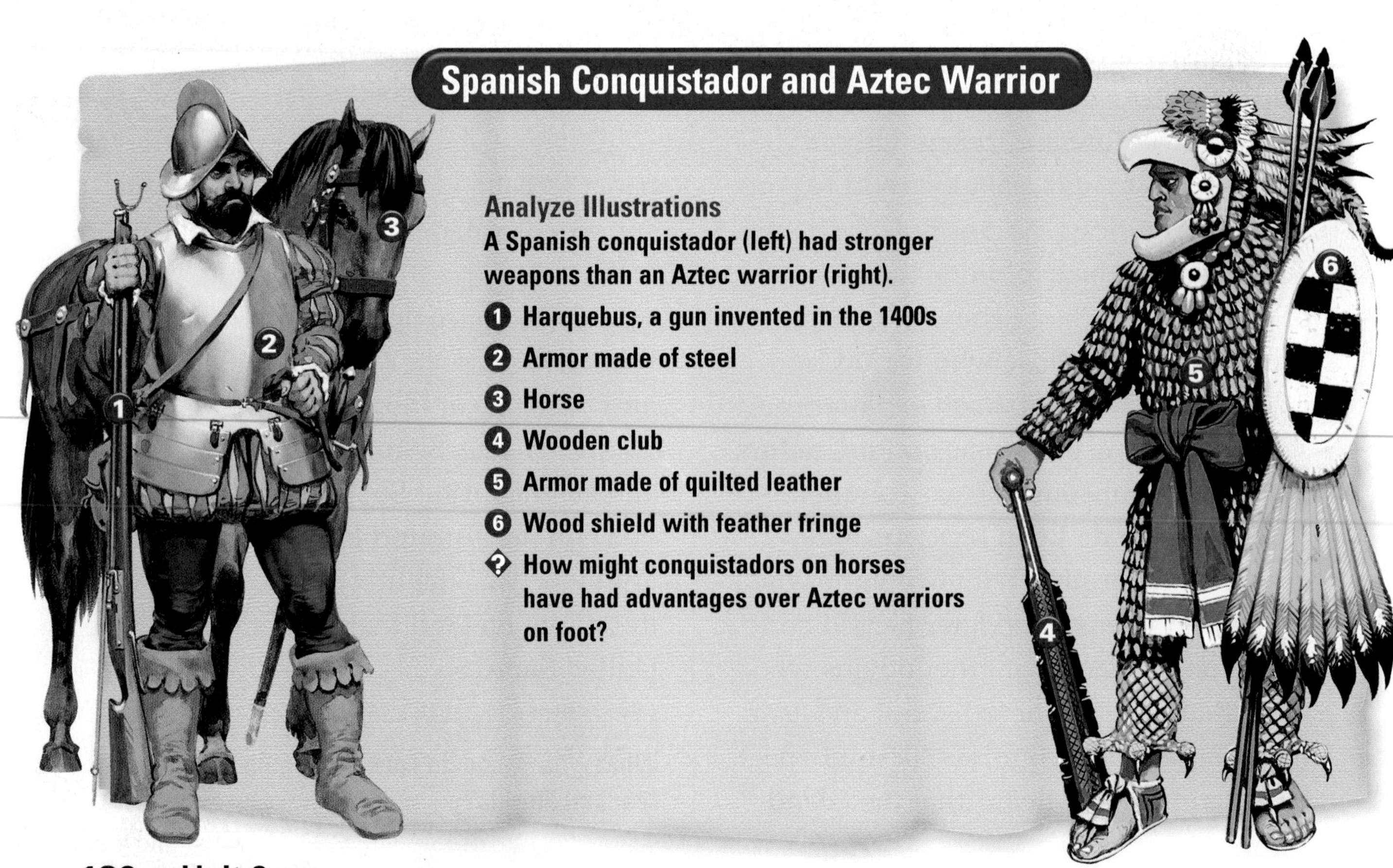

Analyze Illustrations

A Spanish conquistador (left) had stronger weapons than an Aztec warrior (right).

1. **Harquebus, a gun invented in the 1400s**
2. **Armor made of steel**
3. **Horse**
4. **Wooden club**
5. **Armor made of quilted leather**
6. **Wood shield with feather fringe**

? How might conquistadors on horses have had advantages over Aztec warriors on foot?

ANALYSIS SKILL Analyze Maps

Movement Which conquistador traveled through part of what is now the southwestern area of the United States?

the expedition, Estevanico was killed by Zuni Indians. De Niza, however, returned and said he had seen a golden city.

After hearing Marcos de Niza's story, **Francisco Vásquez de Coronado** (kawr•oh•NAH•doh) set out in 1540 with about 300 Spaniards, several Africans, and more than 1,000 American Indians to find the mysterious cities. Coronado and his men explored lands in what is now the southwestern United States. In all their travels, they did not find any gold. Coronado arrived back in Mexico City with no riches, but he had claimed lands for Spain. The Spanish lands in what are today Mexico, the southwestern United States, and Florida came to be known as **New Spain**.

READING CHECK MAIN IDEA AND DETAILS
What was the aim of Coronado's expedition?

De Soto in the Southeast

Spanish conquistador **Hernando de Soto** (day SOH•toh) helped conquer the Inca Empire in Peru, and his success there made him rich. He believed Florida might have rich empires like the Inca. De Soto wanted the wealth and glory that would come from defeating those empires.

In 1539, de Soto and 600 men sailed from Cuba and landed near Tampa Bay. They then traveled through every state that is now part of the southeastern United States. On their journey, they became the first Europeans to see the Mississippi River.

De Soto and his soldiers met many American Indians during this expedition, and these encounters often ended in brutal battles. One of the worst took place in Alabama. There, the Spanish fought the Mobile tribe. A Spanish soldier who witnessed the battle wrote later that the number of Indians killed may have been as high as 11,000. The Spanish lost many of their supplies during the fighting. Afterward, many of de Soto's men either starved to death or ran away.

In 1542, de Soto died of a fever. The soldiers buried him in the Mississippi River and made their way to Mexico. When the expedition ended in September 1543, only about 300 survived out of the 600 men who started the journey.

Although de Soto and his soldiers found no gold, they claimed much land for Spain. By this time, Spanish claims covered much of the southern half of what is now the United States.

READING CHECK **MAIN IDEA AND DETAILS**
What part of what is now the United States did de Soto explore and claim?

In addition to soldiers, Hernando de Soto's expedition included a diverse group of priests, farmers, and Indian scouts.

Missionaries to America

While the conquistadors were exploring the Americas, many changes were sweeping through Europe. Some people began to question the power of the Catholic Church. At the time, the Church forced people to obey its rules and to pay taxes. It even had its own court, which could punish people for disagreeing with Church rules and teachings.

A German priest named **Martin Luther** began to call openly for **reforms**, or changes, in the Catholic Church. This period of reforms is called the **Reformation**. Luther was forced out of the Church, but he gained many supporters. Those who protested the actions of Catholic leaders became known as Protestants. They began new churches, including the Lutheran Church.

The Catholic Church made some changes, but it also tried to keep its power through efforts that are called the **Counter-Reformation**. The Church banned books that went against its teachings, and it used its court to punish people who protested Catholic rules and beliefs.

During the Counter-Reformation, the Catholic Church concentrated on spreading its power to the Americas. Church leaders wanted to gain new followers and share in the wealth of the lands claimed by European countries. To help accomplish this, the Church sent religious teachers, or **missionaries**, to convert the American Indians to the Catholic religion.

Shortly after arriving in the Americas, missionaries held ceremonies for large numbers of American Indians to make

Saint Ignatius founded the Jesuits, a Catholic group whose main activity became missionary work.

them Catholic. It was not until later that the missionaries actually began teaching them about Catholic beliefs. Some missionaries forced the American Indians to accept Christianity and to work for them. Others helped them by providing food and health care. While many American Indians did keep their traditional religions, others were forced to change how they lived and worshipped.

READING CHECK **MAIN IDEA AND DETAILS**
What was the main result of the Counter-Reformation in the Americas?

Summary

Spanish conquistadors such as Juan Ponce de León, Hernando Cortés, Francisco Coronado, and Hernando de Soto explored and claimed large areas of the Americas for Spain. Missionaries brought Catholic beliefs to the American Indians.

REVIEW

1. Why did the Spanish explore and conquer large areas of the Americas?
2. Describe the effects of the **Counter-Reformation** on the Americas.
3. What lands made up the Spanish empire in the Americas known as New Spain?

CRITICAL THINKING

4. ANALYSIS SKILL What were some effects of Spanish exploration of the Americas?
5. ANALYSIS SKILL Why do you think the Spanish built Mexico City on the site of the Aztec capital?
6. **Write a Travelogue** Imagine that you are traveling with one of the explorers discussed in this lesson. Write a travelogue describing what you have seen and the people you have met.
7. Focus Skill **MAIN IDEA AND DETAILS** On a separate sheet of paper, copy and complete the graphic organizer below.

Main Idea

The Spanish had aims for exploring and settling in the Americas.

Details

Estevanico

Estevanico was not a Spaniard. He was an African who had been sold into slavery. He never led an expedition, but he may have walked across more of North America than any other explorer of his time.

Estevanico and his owner survived a disastrous Spanish expedition to Florida. Later, a Spanish commander in Mexico City chose Estevanico and another man to look for the Seven Cities of Gold. The commander must have trusted Estevanico's ability to survive in the wilderness. He also trusted Estevanico to return and to give a true report of what he had found.

Estevanico saw much of North America.

Estevanico was not an explorer by choice. As a slave, he had to go where his owner sent him. But he had much freedom in the wilderness. He had learned from other explorers how to use plants to cure some illnesses, and many Indians respected him as a medicine man. Estevanico did not survive his journey to find the Seven Cities of Gold. Still, his name is remembered today, along with those of the many other explorers who traveled through North America.

Why Character Counts

How did Estevanico's actions show that he was trustworthy?

1503 — Born 1503?

1539 — Died 1539

1528 Estevanico joins the Narváez expedition

1539 Estevanico is killed on an expedition to find the Seven Cities of Gold

Distinguish Fact from Opinion

WHY IT MATTERS

Recognizing fact and opinion helps you understand what you read. A **fact** is a statement that can be proved or checked. A fact is true for everyone. An **opinion** is a statement that tells what a person feels or believes. An opinion is held by one person or one group.

WHAT YOU NEED TO KNOW

Here are some ways in which you can check to see whether a statement is a fact:

- See whether the statement is true in your own experience and in other people's experiences. *On a sunny day, the sky is blue.* You know that this is a fact because you and others have seen the sky as it looks this way.
- Check trusted sources of information, such as an encyclopedia, an atlas, or another source.

Opinions cannot be proved or checked. An opinion may seem true to the person who holds it, but other people may have different opinions. Here is an example:

- Fact: It is snowing.
- Opinion: The weather is terrible.
- Opinion: The weather is beautiful.

Some statements contain clues that they are opinions. The words *I believe, I feel,*

Many historians believe that members of Francisco Coronado's expedition were the first Europeans to see the Grand Canyon and the Colorado River.

or *in my opinion* often begin an opinion statement. Words such as *best, worst, wonderful,* and *terrible* are often clues to opinion statements.

Writers often combine facts and opinions. Readers must pay close attention to notice the difference. Think about this sentence: *We went to Yellowstone National Park, the most beautiful place in the West.* The first part of the sentence is a fact, but the second part is an opinion.

Not every statement is either a fact or an opinion. For example, the statement *Los Angeles is in Canada* is not a fact because it is not true.

PRACTICE THE SKILL

Now read these sentences from Coronado's report to the leader who sent him on his expedition. Decide whether each sentence states an opinion, a fact, or both. If a sentence contains both a fact and an opinion, tell which part is which.

1. "The food which they eat in this country is corn, of which they have a great abundance."
2. "They make the best corn cakes I have ever seen anywhere, and this is what everybody normally eats."
3. "They have the very best arrangement and machinery for grinding that was ever seen."
4. "They have very good salt in crystals, which they bring from a lake a day's journey distant from here."*

APPLY WHAT YOU LEARNED

Write three facts that you have learned in this chapter. Then write three opinions about what you learned.

*Coronado's Report to Viceroy Mendoza, 1540. *History of Hawikuh* by Frederick W. Lodge. Ward Ritchie Press, 1937.

Lesson 4

1400 — 1650

1524 Verrazano searches for the Northwest Passage

1534 Cartier begins to explore the St. Lawrence River

1610 Hudson explores Hudson Bay

WHAT TO KNOW
Why did Europeans explore North America, and what did they find?

- ✓ Describe the aims, obstacles, and accomplishments of European explorers.
- ✓ Trace the routes of early explorers and identify the areas they claimed in what is now the United States.

VOCABULARY
Northwest Passage p. 139
mutiny p. 143

PEOPLE
Giovanni da Verrazano
Jacques Cartier
Henry Hudson

PLACES
Newfoundland
St. Lawrence River
Holland
Hudson Bay

MAIN IDEA AND DETAILS

California Standards
HSS 5.2, 5.2.1, 5.2.2, 5.2.3

Other Nations Explore

YOU ARE THERE

"Verrazano (ver•uh•ZAH•noh) will find it!" your father says as he slaps the dinner table with delight. It is 1524, and your family lives in Paris, France. "His aim is to get across America to Asia, and he will make it. The French will control the world's richest trade route, and we'll all be rich!"

"Yes, if Verrazano finds the Northwest Passage," your mother says, cutting a slice of bread. "But he faces many obstacles, and his voyage is very dangerous."

As you listen to them talk, your head is filled with questions. What is the Northwest Passage? Why has Verrazano gone to America, and what will he find?

➤ **Giovanni da Verrazano**

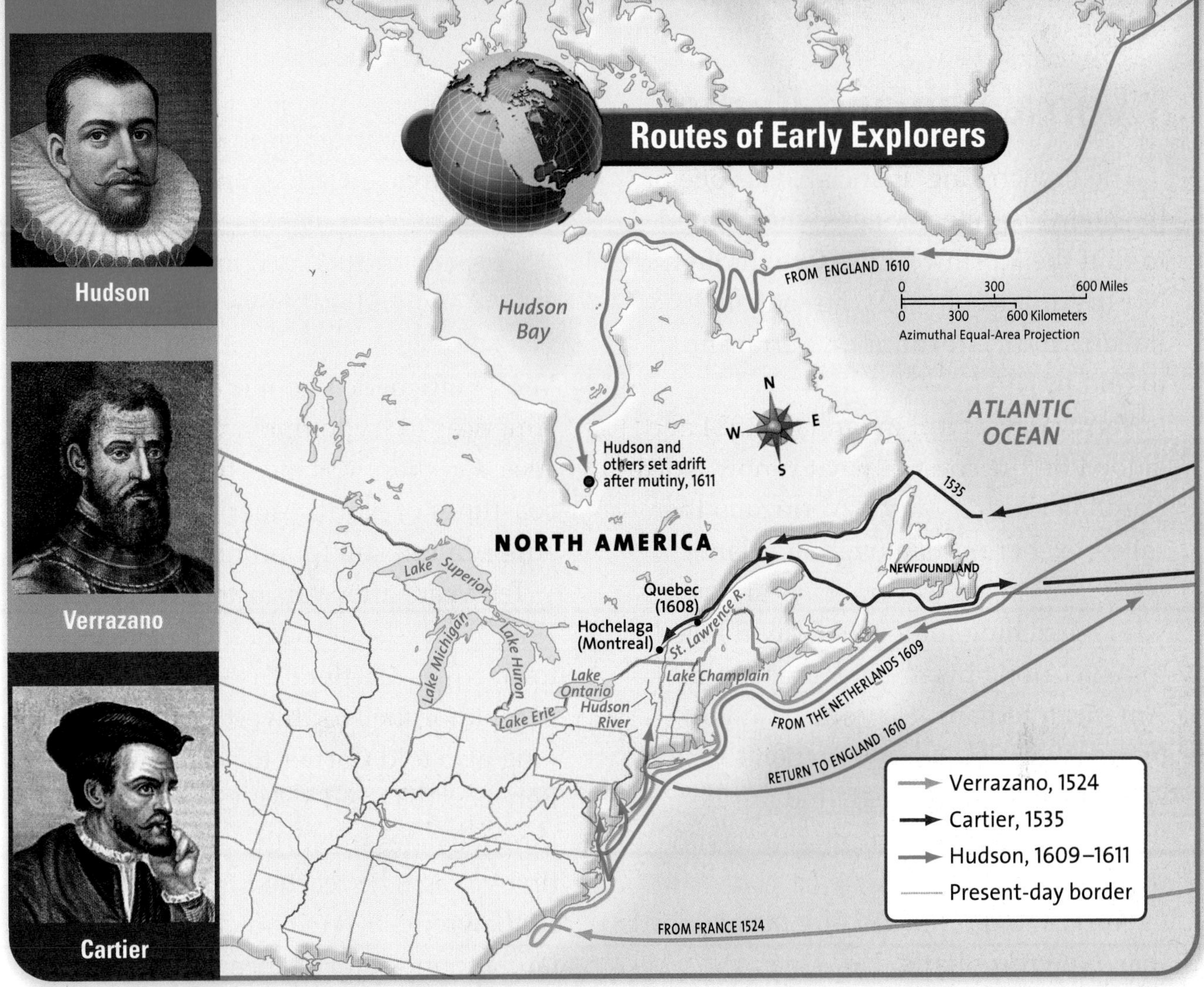

Analyze Maps

- **Place** Which waterways did Hudson explore?
- **Movement** What places did Cartier pass through?

The Northwest Passage

In the early 1500s, Spain became a vast and extremely rich empire. Spanish ships returned with treasure chests full of gold and silver from conquests in Mexico and South America. Expeditions were adding huge sections of the Americas to Spain's land claims. The rulers of other European countries believed that if they could find a shortcut to the riches of Asia, they might gain wealth and power, too.

The route followed by Magellan's expedition around South America to Asia was long and dangerous. Many thought that Asia might be reached more easily by sailing through or around North America. This belief led explorers to search for a route they called the **Northwest Passage**. The first country to find this waterway between Europe and Asia would control a valuable new trade route. The search for the Northwest Passage began in the 1500s and lasted for hundreds of years.

READING CHECK MAIN IDEA AND DETAILS
Why did European explorers want to find the Northwest Passage?

Verrazano and Cartier

The French king, Francis I, was one of the many European rulers who wanted to find the Northwest Passage through North America. In 1524, he sent an Italian sailor, **Giovanni da Verrazano**, to find it.

Verrazano set sail in January 1524 and landed on the coast of what is now North Carolina in early March. Verrazano then sailed farther north along the Atlantic coast, sailing into several bays and rivers while searching for a waterway that led to Asia. Along his route, Verrazano met American Indians. He wrote that the Narragansett Indians were friendly, but when he met the Abenaki Indians he found it difficult to communicate with them.

Verrazano did not sail any farther north than **Newfoundland**. He wrote:

> **"My intention [aim] on this voyage was to reach Cathay and the extreme eastern coast of Asia, but I did not expect to find such an obstacle of new land as I have found."***

Verrazano made two more voyages to the Americas to try to find a water route to Asia. On these voyages, he searched the coastlines of North America and South America but still found no passage.

Ten years after Verrazano's expedition, King Francis sent the French navigator **Jacques Cartier** (ZHAHK kar•TYAY) to look for the Northwest Passage. The king also told Cartier to search for gold. Between 1534 and 1541, Cartier made three voyages to North America. On his first voyage, he reached the mouth of the **St. Lawrence River** and claimed all the land around it for France.

*Giovanni da Verrazano to Francis I, *North American Exploration* by Michael Golay and John S. Bowman. John Wiley & Sons, Inc., 2003.

Jacques Cartier reported seeing many beavers and otters along the Saint Lawrence River. This interested traders in Europe, where furs could be sold for high prices.

On Cartier's second voyage, he traveled up the St. Lawrence River. During the trip, he wrote that he saw "fish in appearance like horses."* These were not fish, but actually walruses. The expedition inland went as far as what is now Montreal. Instead of the Pacific, however, Cartier reached river rapids. No boat could pass the fast-moving water, and he had to turn back.

In 1541, Cartier visited the St. Lawrence River again but was never able to find the Northwest Passage. In search of gold, he sailed up the river past what is now Quebec, but he found nothing and returned to France. However, the expeditions that Cartier made added to European knowledge of North America.

READING CHECK **MAIN IDEA AND DETAILS**
What were the aims of Cartier's expeditions?

*Jacques Cartier. *The Voyage of Jacques Cartier* edited by Henry P. Biggar. University of Toronto Press, 1993.

FAST FACT

When Cartier left North America to return to France, he took a supply of corn that was given to him by the Iroquois. Many Europeans had never seen corn before.

Exploring North America

1520 | 1570 | 1620

1524 Giovanni da Verrazano explores what is now New York Bay

1535 Jacques Cartier explores what is now Canada

1609 Henry Hudson meets with American Indians in what is now New York

ANALYSIS SKILL **Analyze Time Lines** **It took several hundred years for Europeans to explore all of North America.**

❓ Did Cartier explore what is now Canada before or after Hudson explored New York?

Hudson's Voyages

By the 1600s, exploration was big business. No longer were kings and queens the only ones trying to increase their wealth and power by paying for these expeditions. European trading companies also began sending explorers to look for the Northwest Passage. Their aim was to establish trade routes so that they could buy and then resell Asian goods.

An English explorer named **Henry Hudson** made four voyages in search of the Northwest Passage. A company in England paid for his first two expeditions. In 1608, on his first voyage, Hudson reached an island east of Greenland. He then sailed farther north through the Artic Ocean but failed to find the Northwest Passage.

For his third voyage, Hudson was hired by the Dutch East India Company to find the Northwest Passage. On this expedition, he sailed to the Hudson River in what is today New York. Hudson spent a month exploring the river, which he named for himself. He claimed the whole Hudson River valley for the Dutch rulers in **Holland**.

An English company paid for Hudson's final voyage in 1610. He sailed along the northern coast of North America to the bay that also carries his name, **Hudson Bay**. Hudson claimed the land around the bay for England. He spent three months exploring the huge bay, located in east central Canada, north of present-day Ontario and Quebec.

By November, Hudson's ship was frozen in the ice, and after a cold winter and much suffering, his crew **mutinied**, or rebelled. They set Hudson and eight others adrift in a small boat. The men were never seen again.

READING CHECK **MAIN IDEA AND DETAILS**
Hudson claimed land for what two countries?

Summary

Explorers of North America hoped to find both riches and the Northwest Passage to Asia. Cartier and Hudson claimed lands for the countries that sent them. However, the Northwest Passage was not found.

Hudson lands on the coast of North America.

REVIEW

1.  Why did Europeans explore North America, and what did they find?
2. Use the word **mutiny** to describe the last voyage of Henry Hudson.
3. Why did Cartier and Hudson explore so far to the north?
4. Why did some trading companies send explorers to North America?

CRITICAL THINKING

5. ANALYSIS SKILL What were the costs and benefits of Hudson's expeditions?

6. **Draw a Picture** Research what the flags of Spain, England, France, and Holland looked like in 1600. Draw each flag and label it.

7. Focus Skill **MAIN IDEA AND DETAILS** On a separate sheet of paper, copy and complete the graphic organizer below.

Main Idea

Details

Explorers did not know American Indian languages.	Cartier's boat could not pass rapids.	Hudson's crew mutinied.

Use an Elevation Map

WHY IT MATTERS

Different maps provide different kinds of information. If you want to know how high or how low the land is, you need to use an elevation (eh•luh•VAY•shuhn) map. **Elevation** is the height of the land in relation to sea level. Elevation was important for early explorers to consider. Changes in elevation can affect the amount of time, food, or rest required to complete an expedition.

WHAT YOU NEED TO KNOW

The elevation of land is measured from sea level, usually in feet or meters. The elevation of land at sea level is 0 feet. Find sea level on Drawing A. The lines on this drawing of a mountain are contour lines. A **contour line** connects all points of equal elevation. Find the contour line for 1,640 feet on Drawing A. This line connects all the points on the mountain that are 1,640 feet above sea level.

Drawing B shows the mountain as you would see it from above. On the steeper side of the mountain, the contour lines are closer together. On the less-steep side, the lines are farther apart.

On Drawing C, color is added between the contour lines. A key is used instead of labels on the drawing. The key shows that every place in green is between sea level and 655 feet. The border between green and yellow on the map is a contour line for 655 feet. The borders between the other colors are also contour lines.

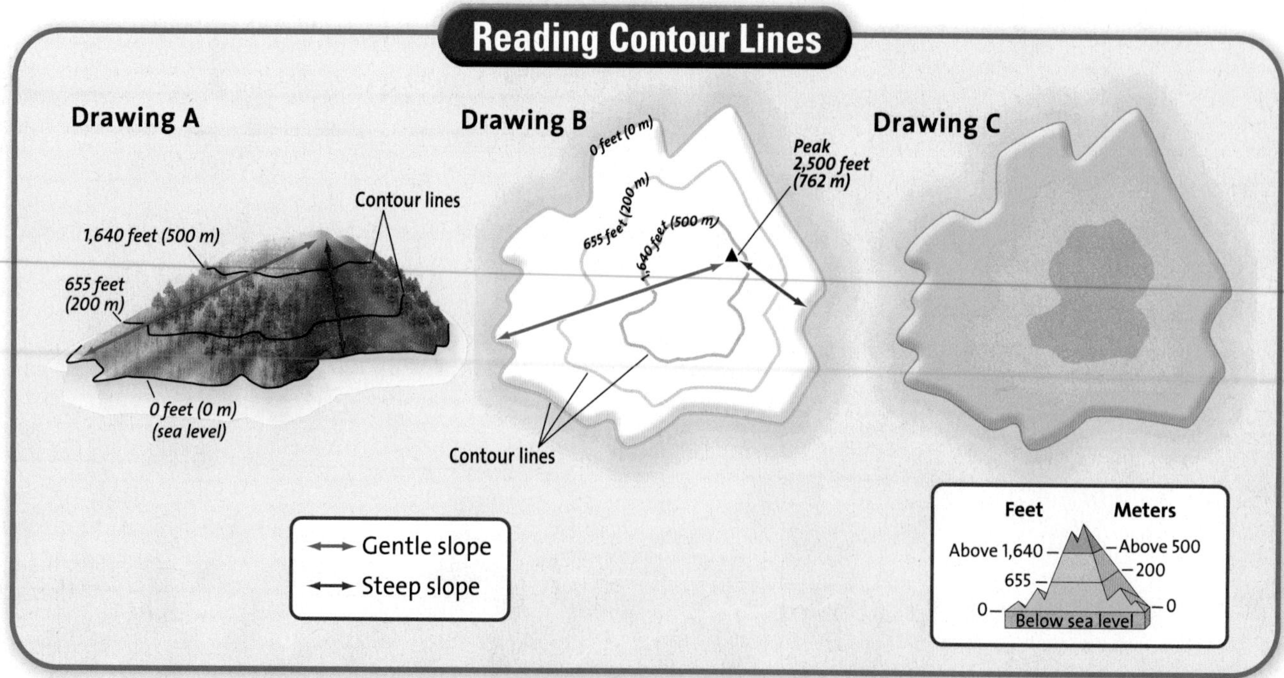

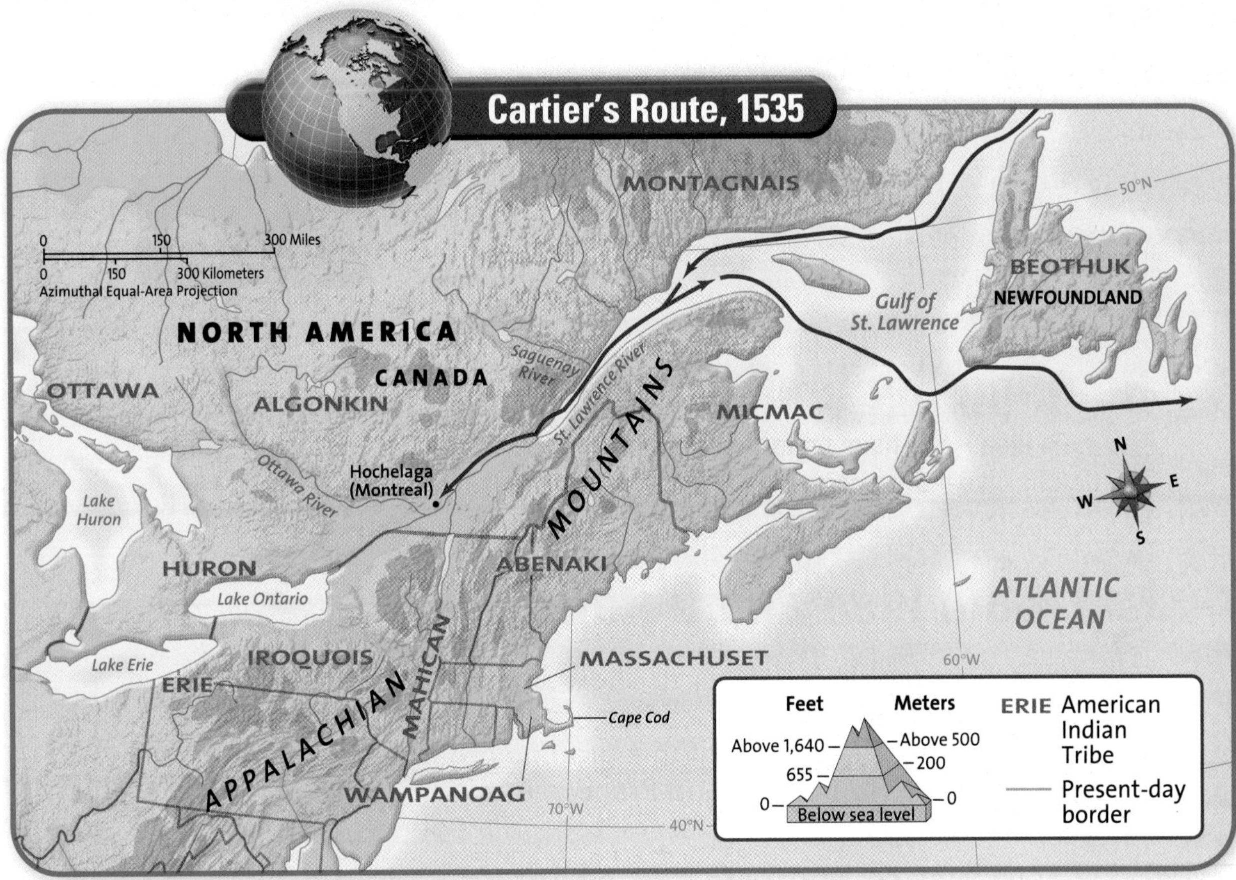

Most elevation maps use only a few important contour lines, with colors added between the lines. Look at the elevation map of North America on this page. Notice that this map does not show exact elevations. Instead, the key shows the range of elevation that each color stands for. On this map, green is used for land in the range between sea level and 655 feet.

PRACTICE THE SKILL

Use the map to answer the following questions.

1. What is the elevation of the land where Montreal is located?
2. What change in elevation would Cartier have seen if he traveled north from Montreal?
3. What range of elevations is shown by the color yellow?

APPLY WHAT YOU LEARNED

ANALYSIS SKILL Imagine that you have been asked to retrace Cartier's expedition and to keep a record of your experiences. Using the map above, describe changes in elevation along the way. How might these changes affect the progress of the expedition?

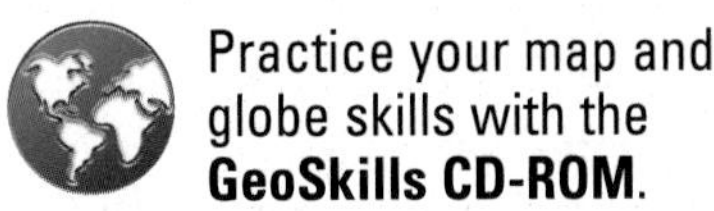

Chapter 3 Review

1492
Columbus lands at San Salvador

1513
Balboa sights the Pacific Ocean

Reading Social Studies

The **main idea** is the most important thought in a text.
The **details** give more information that supports the main idea.

Main Idea and Details

Complete this graphic organizer to show that you understand the main idea and supporting details about European explorations of the Americas. A copy of this graphic organizer appears on page 34 of the Homework and Practice Book.

The Age of Exploration

Main Idea

Europeans explored and claimed lands in the Americas.

Details

California Writing Prompts

Write a Persuasive Letter Imagine that you are an explorer who wants to go on an expedition. Write a letter to persuade a king or queen to pay for your expedition. Be sure to describe the benefits your expedition will deliver.

Write a Report Write a report about the Northwest Passage. Explain what it was and why Europeans hoped to find it. Also describe some explorers who searched for it.

1600 1700

1539
De Soto begins exploring the Southeast

1610
Hudson explores the Atlantic coast

Use Vocabulary

Identify the term that correctly matches each definition.

expedition, p. 112
entrepreneur, p. 114
treaty, p. 125
grant, p. 129
mutiny, p. 143

1. a sum of money or other payment given for a specific purpose
2. a trip taken with the goal of exploring
3. an agreement between two or more nations
4. a rebellion against the leader of one's group
5. a person who sets up and runs a business

Use the Time Line

Use the chapter summary time line above to answer these questions.

6. How many years after Columbus reached San Salvador did Balboa see the Pacific?
7. Did Hudson's expedition take place before or after de Soto's?

Apply Skills

Distinguish Fact from Opinion

8. Choose one of the explorers you read about in this chapter. Write two statements to express your opinions about that explorer. Then write two facts to support each opinion.

Recall Facts

Answer these questions.

9. What kinds of new technology enabled Europeans to explore the world?
10. What was the main goal of the earliest explorers who reached the Americas?
11. What European nations had claimed land in North America by 1610?
12. What part of North America did the French explore?

Write the letter of the best choice.

13. What was Coronado searching for in the Southwest?
    A the Northern Passage
    B the Seven Cities of Gold
    C the Fountain of Youth
    D the Indies
14. Which European explorer named Florida?
    A Christopher Columbus
    B Juan Ponce de León
    C Giovanni da Verrazano
    D Amerigo Vespucci

Think Critically

15. ANALYSIS SKILL How did the Spanish Reconquista affect Columbus's expedition?
16. ANALYSIS SKILL What were some of the costs and benefits of Coronado's expedition?

Study Skills

USE A K-W-L CHART

A K-W-L chart can help you focus on what you already know about a topic and what you want to learn about it.

- **Use the K column to list what you know about a topic.**
- **Use the W column to list what you want to learn about the topic.**
- **Use the L column to list what you have learned about the topic from your reading.**

Building the First Colonies		
K-What I Know	W-What I Want to Learn	L-What I Learned
• People from Spain built settlements in North America. • ________	• How did they build settlements? • What challenges did the settlers face? • ________	• ________ • ________ • ________

Apply As You Read

Complete your own K-W-L chart as you read this chapter.

California History-Social Science Standards, Grade 5

5.2 Students trace the routes of early explorers and describe the early explorations of the Americas.
5.3 Students describe the cooperation and conflict that existed among the American Indians and between the Indian nations and the new settlers.
5.4 Students understand the political, religious, social, and economic institutions that evolved in the colonial era.

CHAPTER

Building the First Colonies 4

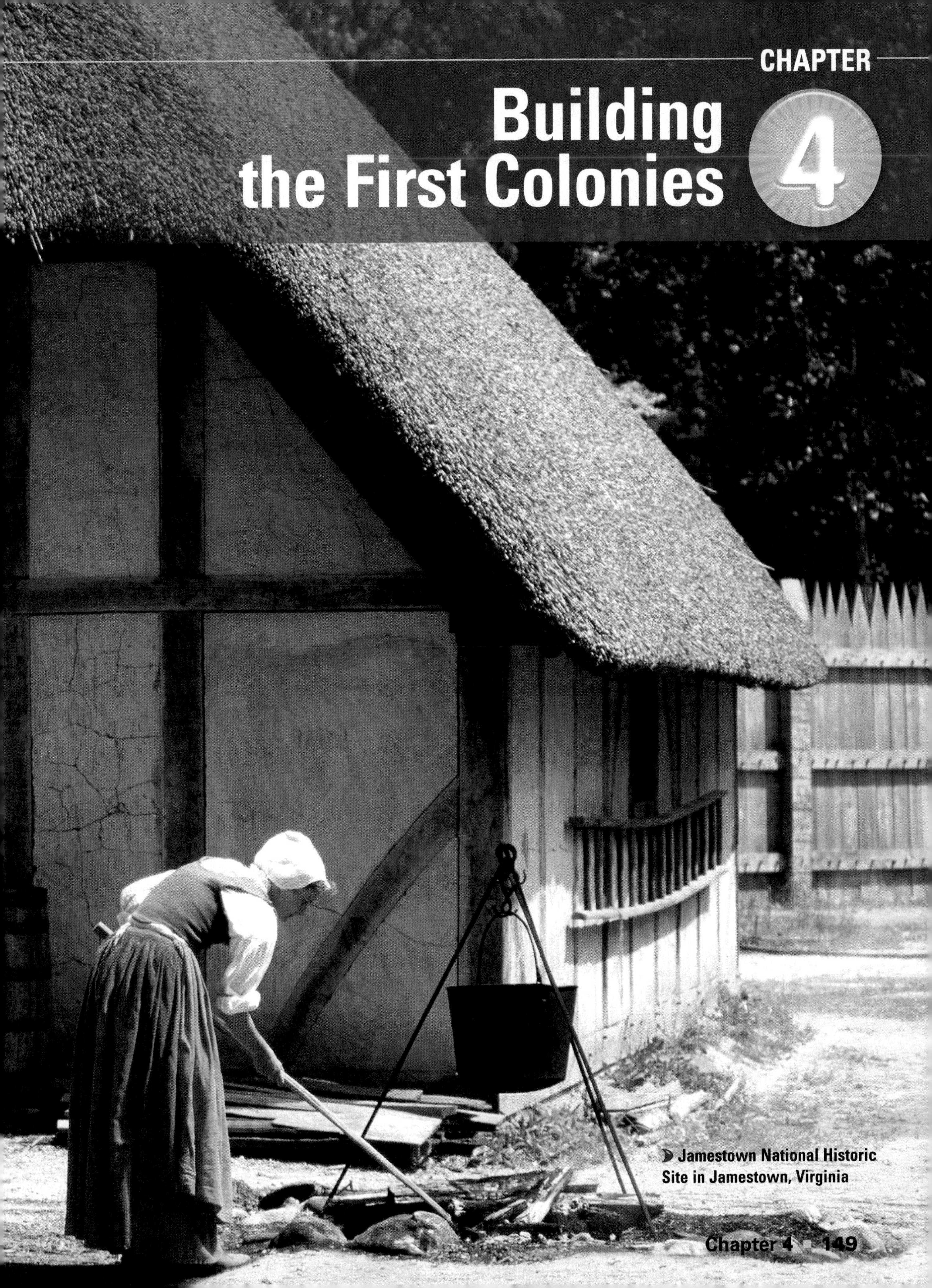

Jamestown National Historic Site in Jamestown, Virginia

Stranded at Plimoth Plantation 1626

written and illustrated by Gary Bowen

On October 12, 1626, a ship bound for the Jamestown settlement set sail from England. On November 6, the ship crashed along the New England coast near Plimoth Plantation, known today as Plymouth, Massachusetts. Rescued by the colonists, the ship's passengers remained stranded there. The following is a fictional journal of a 13-year-old passenger, Christopher Sears. After being rescued, Sears stays with the family of William Brewster, a Pilgrim church leader. Also living with the Brewsters was another boy, Richard More. Read now about Christopher's experiences at Plimoth Plantation.

November 24, 1626

His worship the Governor [William Bradford] met at the fort this afternoon with all of us who crossed on the *Sparrowhawk*. He told us that 21 other ships have arrived in Plimoth in six years, and said it may be months before another anchors again. We are to earn our board by working for the families with whom we reside. Our labors are to be reported weekly to Captain Sibsey or Master Fells.

I am happy that Richard lives and works here, too. When he was six years old, he came over on the *Mayflower* with two

brothers and a sister who did not survive their first year here. Richard says they had been told their mother and father died, but he does not remember their illnesses or any funeral service. He says his parents did not like each other.

My knee aches and I am cold because my garments are not warm enough for this climate.

December 23, 1626

Governor Bradford talked with me today and showed me the notes that he has been keeping since he arrived in 1620. He commended me for recording my experiences here and said that I am participating in a "great event, which is the founding of God's community."

His Worship suggested that I make larger woodcuts and consider using color. The physician gave me these mixtures.

December 30, 1626

I was measured for new woolen breeches as my old ones are too small. The Mistress plans to sew them from fabric that once was her skirt. She will re-dye the cloth with agrimony roots and nutshells because all textiles are imported and are difficult to come by here.

It is surprising that I have seen no spinning wheels or looms in Plimoth since they are so common in England.

January 23, 1627

Master Brewster will include me in his tutoring of Richard, Oceanus Hopkins (who was born aboard the *Mayflower*), and Peregrine White, who Master Brewster says is the first Anglo-Saxon born in New England.

We had cold eel pie in a <u>coffin</u> for dinner.

February 3, 1627

I am happy that my schooling continues.

Each evening Master Brewster works with me on herb lore, farming, reading, and scriptures. He says the Plimoth people are more learned than in most English villages, as all parents must educate their children, even if that requires tutoring in another home.

March 3, 1627

I was with a group of men organized by the Governor, cutting timbers in the forest.

Indians approached us, wanting to trade some furs, three turkeys, and a deer for grain. His Worship agreed to the barter, and the Indians will receive a bushel of corn.

April 5, 1627

I carried in 24 buckets of springwater to heat. Each member of the Brewster household had a bath today. It felt good to wash.

Love [the Brewster's son] cautioned me that it is unhealthy to have more than three or four baths a year because, if done

<u>**coffin**</u> a pastry crust

too often, all the body's natural protection against disease is washed away.

Tomorrow we will be fishing for herring, which is plentiful this month and next.

June 1, 1627

Because Master Brewster predicts rainy weather is coming, we worked doubly hard to sow our seeds for peas, beans, wheat, rye, barley, and turkey corn. Not all families have planted their crops yet.

Mistress Priscilla Alden gave birth to baby John. Master John Alden, her husband, was very pleased.

Love prepared mussels again.

July 1, 1627

The weather has been hot and dry and our garden has suffered. Richard and I carried buckets of water to give the crops a drink.

Since there is no rain in sight, we plan to cut a field of grain tomorrow. After it is turned over to dry thoroughly in the sun, we will stack the barley in the shape of cones.

I boiled seawater to replenish the Brewsters' salt supply.

Love says I am growing like a weed!

August 18, 1627

Today when we returned from the Indian settlement, I learned that two barks had arrived from Jamestown to transport the *Sparrowhawk* passengers to Virginia. For me it was not a welcome sight.

Response Corner

1. How did people at Plimoth Plantation get goods that they needed?
2. Compare Christopher Sears's daily activities with your own. Write a paragraph about how they are alike and how they are different.

Lesson 1

1400 — 1650

1535 New Spain is formed

1565 St. Augustine is built

The Spanish Colonies

WHAT TO KNOW
Why did Spain set up colonies in North America?

- ✔ Locate the lands in North America claimed by Spain.
- ✔ Describe relations between Spanish settlers and American Indians.

VOCABULARY
colony p. 155
plantation p. 156
slavery p. 156
borderlands p. 157
presidio p. 157
mission p. 157
hacienda p. 158

PEOPLE
King Philip II
Bartolomé de Las Casas
Pedro Menéndez de Avilés

PLACES
New Spain
Mexico City
St. Augustine
Santa Fe

MAIN IDEA AND DETAILS

California Standards

HSS 5.3, 5.3.1, 5.3.2, 5.3.3, 5.3.4, 5.4, 5.4.6

YOU ARE THERE

"When the king is angry, the whole palace shakes!" your sister whispers.

"Shhh! We're supposed to be working in the kitchen," you answer quietly. The two of you hide in a hallway and listen.

"Those who ignore my claims will be sorry," **King Philip II** thunders. "I need sailors and settlers. We will make North America ours once and for all! Send for one of my captains."

You're sure that the king will deal with those who dare to trespass on Spanish land.

Battles over Claims

By the 1500s, several European nations, including Spain, had sent explorers to claim land in the Americas. Often an explorer would put up a cross at the place where he came ashore. The cross was a sign that the land had been claimed. However, after claiming the land, the expedition moved on, leaving no one to protect the claim.

Most explorers would just step onto a beach and claim all the land for hundreds of miles around. They often claimed land they knew nothing about. Because European countries were competing with each other to win control of as much of the Americas as possible, more than one country often claimed the same land. American Indians also lived in most places the explorers claimed. Usually, no one paid attention to anyone else's rights or claims.

Spain had already claimed large parts of both North America and South America, but the Spanish learned that claiming land was not the same as controlling it. Over time, Spain realized that it needed to protect its claims in the Americas.

After establishing **New Spain** in 1535, Spain formed colonies to protect its lands and govern the people there. A **colony** is a land ruled by another country. Spain set up colonies in North America and Central America and on many islands in the Caribbean Sea. Most of New Spain's colonies were governed by Spanish leaders in **Mexico City**, the capital of New Spain.

READING CHECK **MAIN IDEA AND DETAILS**
How did Spain compete for control of land in the Americas?

Spain protected its claims to land in North America by building forts.

New Spain

At first, very few Spanish people settled in New Spain. After the discovery of gold and silver, though, many colonists came, hoping to get rich. Others came to start large farms, called **plantations**. By 1550, there were about 100,000 Spanish colonists spread across the Americas.

The Spanish needed many workers to grow crops, and mine gold and silver, so they forced the American Indians they had conquered into slavery. **Slavery** is the practice of holding people against their will and making them carry out orders. Many thousands of Indians died from hunger and overwork as slaves. Thousands more died from diseases that settlers unknowingly brought from Europe, such as measles, influenza, and smallpox. These diseases sometimes killed whole tribes.

Some colonists became concerned with how the Indians were being treated. One such colonist was **Bartolomé de Las Casas** (bar•toh•loh•MAY day lahs KAH•sahs). Las Casas was a landowner who freed his slaves and later became a priest. He spoke out in favor of better treatment of the Indians because he said the Indians had a complex civilization, and the Indians had souls like other humans.

As more Indians died, the colonists looked for other workers. They began to bring Africans to work as slaves in many areas of New Spain. Soon enslaved Africans were working under the same terrible conditions under which the Indians had worked.

READING CHECK **MAIN IDEA AND DETAILS**
How did Spanish settlements affect the lives of American Indians?

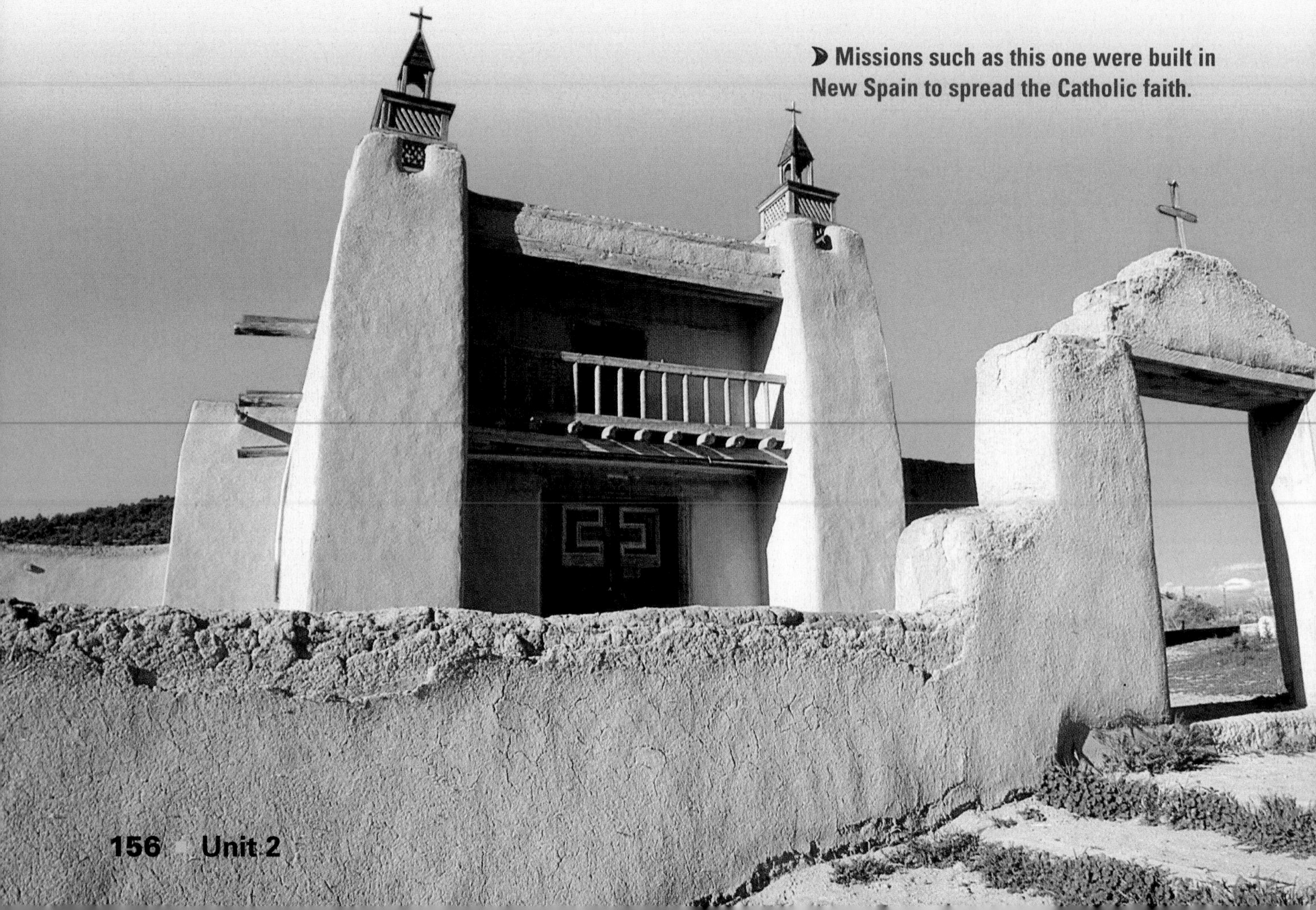

Missions such as this one were built in New Spain to spread the Catholic faith.

ANALYSIS SKILL Analyze Maps **Over time, New Spain's missions and borders spread northward. El Camino Real (el kah•MEE•noh ray•AHL), or "The Royal Road," connected many settlements to Mexico City.**

Location **Which mission site was farthest north?**

Settling the Borderlands

Spain also wanted to protect its lands north of Mexico City. These lands on the edge of Spain's claims were called **borderlands**. The borderlands stretched across what are today northern Mexico and the southern United States from Florida to California.

Spanish soldiers led the way, building **presidios** (pray•SEE•dee•ohz), or forts, in the borderlands. In 1565, **Pedro Menéndez de Avilés** (may•NAYN•days day ah•vee•LAYS) and 1,500 soldiers, sailors, and settlers sailed from Spain. They reached the area that is now **St. Augustine**, Florida. There they built the first permanent, or long-lasting, European settlement in what is now the United States.

Spanish gold coin

Spain's main aim in settling the borderlands was to protect its empire. However, the Spanish king also sent missionaries to convert the American Indians to Christianity.

The missionaries built religious settlements called **missions** in much of the southern half of North America. Spanish missionaries also helped settle **Santa Fe**, the capital of the New Mexico colony. In such places, missionaries and Indians lived side by side.

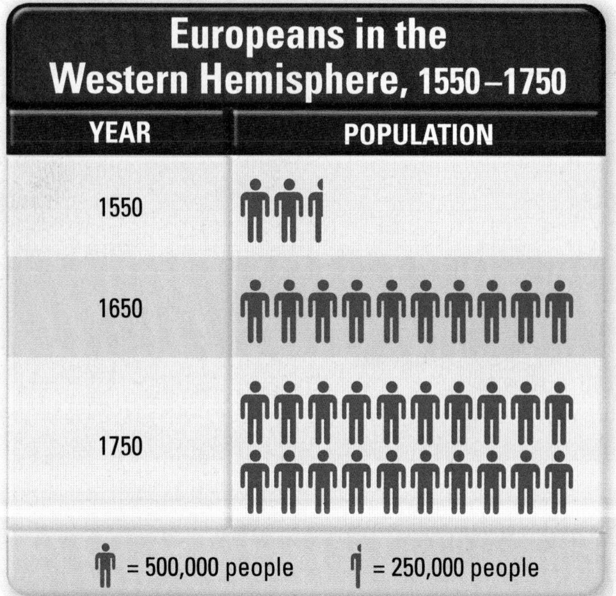

Analyze Graphs

How many Europeans lived in the Western Hemisphere in 1550?

At first, some American Indians chose to stay at the missions, where they learned new ways of living and working. However, many Indians were forced to work on mission farms and ranches. Some fought back, destroying churches and other mission buildings.

Some settlers in the borderlands of northern Mexico built large estates called **haciendas** (ah•see•EN•dahs), where they raised cattle and sheep. The Spanish—and the animals they brought with them—changed life for many Indian groups. Horses, long extinct in the Americas, once again roamed the land. The Plains Indians learned to tame horses for use in hunting and in war. The Navajo learned to raise sheep and to use their wool to make clothing and blankets.

READING CHECK **MAIN IDEA AND DETAILS**
How did new animals change Indian life?

Summary

In the 1500s, explorers often ignored one another's claims to lands. The Spanish acted to protect their claims by setting up settlements. Spain needed workers, so they made slaves of Africans and American Indians.

REVIEW

1. Why did Spain set up colonies in North America?
2. Write a sentence using the terms **hacienda** and **presidio** to describe life on the borderlands.
3. What role did religion play in Spanish settlements?

CRITICAL THINKING

4. ANALYSIS SKILL What were some of the costs and benefits of building colonies?
5. ANALYSIS SKILL What were some of the effects of building missions?
6. **Build a Model** Make a clay model of a Spanish presidio. Make sure your model has different areas showing where people lived and worked.
7. Focus Skill **MAIN IDEA AND DETAILS** On a separate sheet of paper, copy and complete this graphic organizer.

Main Idea

The Spanish built different kinds of settlements for different reasons.

Details

Bartolomé de Las Casas

Biography

Trustworthiness
Respect
Responsibility
Fairness
Caring
Patriotism

*"For all the peoples of the world are . . . rational beings. All possess understanding. . . ."**

Bartolomé de Las Casas was one of the first Europeans to work to improve the treatment of American Indians. When he arrived on the island of Hispaniola in 1502, Las Casas started a plantation and used American Indian enslaved workers, but he came to believe that enslaving the Indians was wrong.

In 1509, he freed his slaves and began to work for better treatment of Indians. Three years later he became a priest and began writing letters and essays questioning the treatment of the Indians as slaves.

Las Casas spoke out so strongly that the King of Spain, Charles I, agreed to pass laws to protect the Indians. Thanks to Las Casas' writings, in 1550 the king ruled that the Spanish could no longer enslave the Indians. This order, however, was not always carried out. Las Casas continued to work for better treatment of the Indians until his death in 1566.

Las Casas spoke to King Charles I on behalf of the Indians.

*Bartolomé de Las Casas. *Bartolomé de Las Casas in History: Toward an Understanding of the Man and His Work* by Juan Friede and Benjamin Keen. Northern Illinois University Press, 1971.

Why Character Counts

In what ways did Bartolomé de Las Casas take responsibility for the treatment of American Indians?

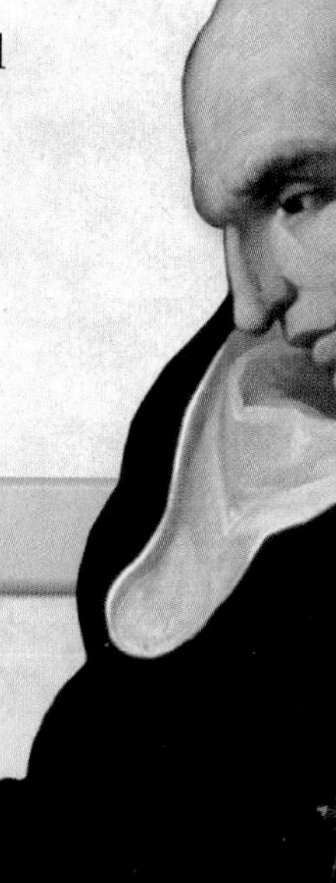

Bio Brief

1484 — Born 1484

1566 — Died 1566

1512 Las Casas becomes a priest

1550 Las Casas publishes *In Defense of the Indians*

GO ONLINE **Interactive Multimedia Biographies** Visit MULTIMEDIA BIOGRAPHIES at www.harcourtschool.com/hss

Lesson 2

1400 — 1650

1585 The first colonists arrive at Roanoke

1607 The Jamestown settlement is started

1619 The first Africans arrive in Virginia

The Virginia Colony

WHAT TO KNOW
Why did English settlers come to North America, and where did they settle first?

- ✓ **Learn how the Virginia Colony was settled.**
- ✓ **Describe the relations between the settlers and American Indians.**

VOCABULARY

raw material p. 161
stock p. 162
cash crop p. 164
indentured servant p. 164
legislature p. 165
represent p. 165
established church p. 165
royal colony p. 166
governor p. 166

PEOPLE

Queen Elizabeth I
John Smith
Pocahontas
John Rolfe

PLACES

Roanoke Island
Jamestown

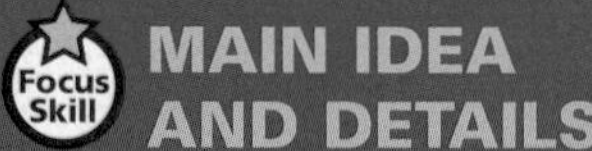

MAIN IDEA AND DETAILS

California Standards
HSS 5.3, 5.3.1, 5.3.3, 5.4, 5.4.1, 5.4.2, 5.4.3, 5.4.5, 5.4.6, 5.4.7

YOU ARE THERE

"We're getting off here!" your friend shouts. The year is 1587. You and 116 other settlers are on ships anchored off **Roanoke Island**, off the coast of present-day North Carolina.

Earlier, English settlers had built homes and a fort on Roanoke, but they didn't like the island. They all went home to England. "Maybe we'll be able to use the houses they built," you say as you gaze at your new home. Still, you do not have a good feeling about this place.

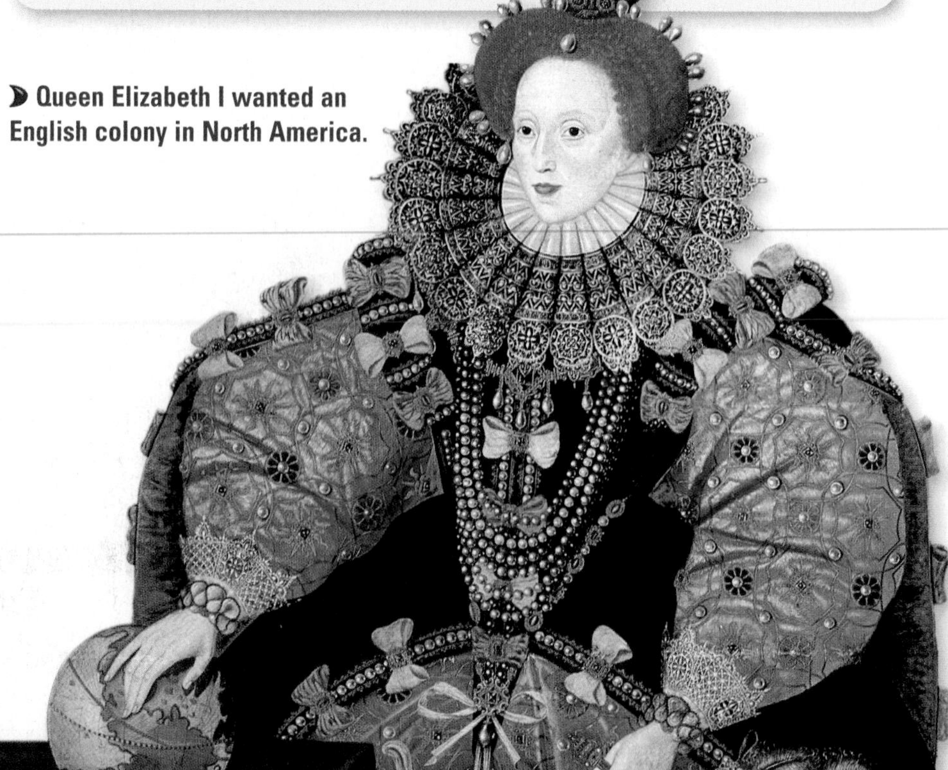

Queen Elizabeth I wanted an English colony in North America.

When John White returned to Roanoke Island, he found that the settlers were gone and that the word *Croatoan* had been carved into a post.

The Lost Colony

England saw that Spain had become wealthy as a result of its colonies in the Americas. Wanting to share in that wealth, **Queen Elizabeth I** of England encouraged her sea captains to attack Spanish treasure ships. The captured treasures increased England's wealth, and it became a powerful country.

Like many of its European neighbors, England wanted to set up colonies around the world. English leaders knew they would benefit from the lumber and other raw materials the colonies could provide. A **raw material** is a resource that can be used to make a product.

In 1584, Queen Elizabeth I told Walter Raleigh (RAW•lee) to set up a colony in North America. A year later, Raleigh sent about 100 colonists to Roanoke Island, in an area he named Virginia. The first colonists did not stay long. They ran low on food, and when another English ship arrived, all the settlers left.

John White led another group of settlers, who arrived at Roanoke Island in 1587. These settlers also ran low on food, and they faced attacks by American Indians. White went back to England to get food and supplies, but by the time he returned—three years later—all the settlers were gone!

What happened to the settlers remains a mystery. Some historians think they went to live with Indians on Croatoan Island, because the word *Croatoan* was found carved on a post. Others believe that the settlers were killed in a battle with Indians. Roanoke became known as the Lost Colony.

READING CHECK **MAIN IDEA AND DETAILS**
What were some of the reasons England wanted to start colonies in North America?

Jamestown

TIME 1607

PLACE Jamestown, Virginia

Even though both of the settlements at Roanoke Island had failed, some English merchants wanted to start a new colony in Virginia. With the permission of King James I, these merchants set up the Virginia Company.

The Virginia Company was owned by many people, each of whom had given money to set up the company. In return, each owner had received **stock**, or a share of ownership, in the company. The owners hoped the company would make a profit, because if it did, each owner would make money.

In 1607, three ships sent by the Virginia Company sailed into the deep bay now called Chesapeake Bay. The ships carried 105 colonists, all of whom were men. The first women colonists did not arrive until 1619. The new settlers sailed up a river they named the James River, in honor of their king. They chose a spot along the shore and began to build a settlement they called **Jamestown**.

Jamestown's location turned out to be a poor choice for a settlement. The land was low and swampy. Swamps meant mosquitoes, and mosquitoes could carry deadly diseases.

Many of the colonists were not used to farmwork, and they did not know how to hunt and fish in this unfamiliar land. They had come to Virginia to get rich, and they were so busy looking for gold

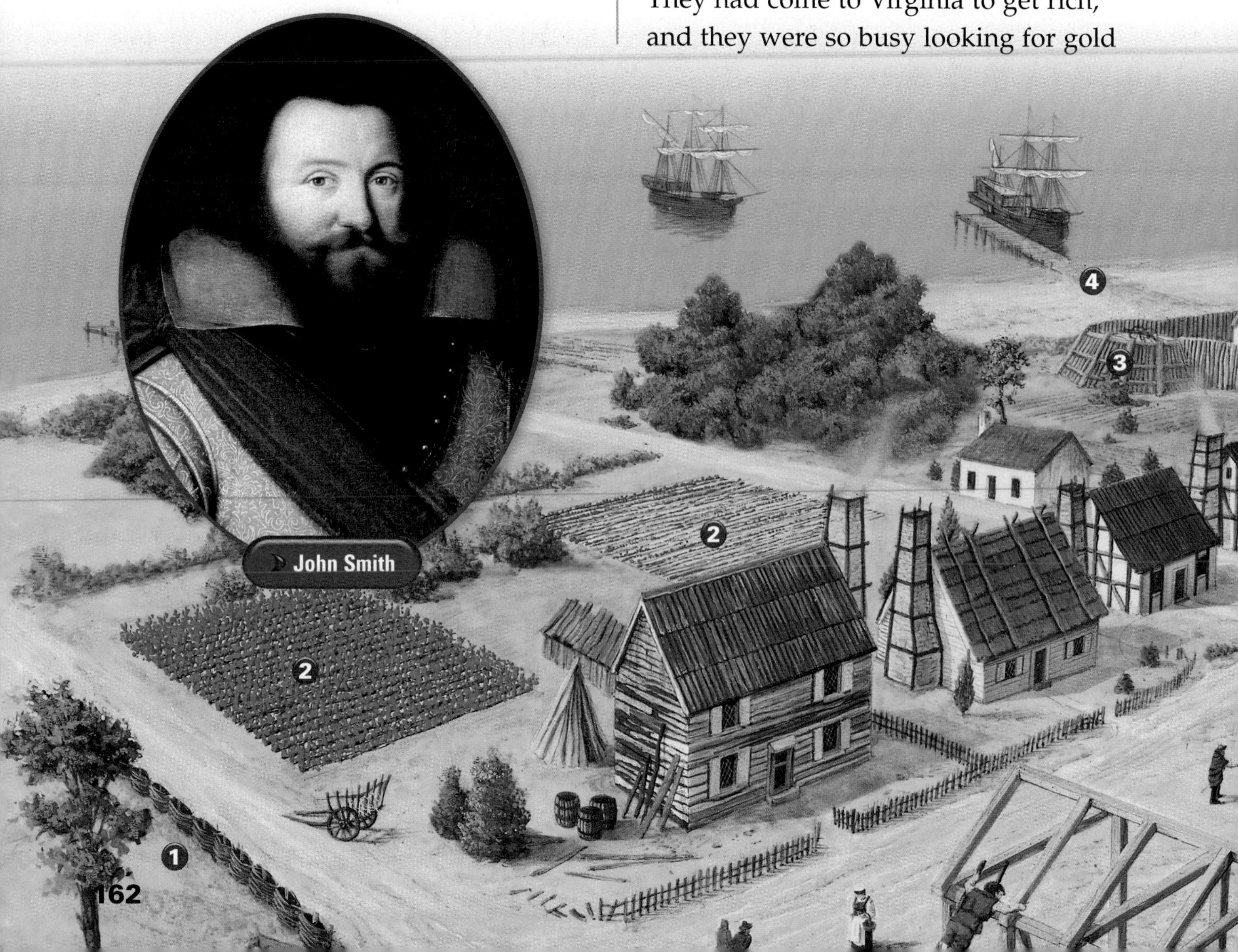

John Smith

that no one bothered to plant or gather food. When the food they had brought ran out, there was little to eat. During their first winter, more than half the colonists died.

Jamestown might have become another Roanoke if it had not been for Captain **John Smith**, a soldier, explorer, and writer. When he became leader of Jamestown, he made an important rule for the colonists—anyone who did not work did not eat. The colonists were soon busy planting gardens, building shelters, and putting up palisades to protect Jamestown from Indian attacks.

During this time, more than 30 tribes of Eastern Woodlands Indians lived in Virginia. Most belonged to the Powhatan (POW•uh•tan) Confederacy, whose members were united under one main chief. When the colonists heard this, they gave the name *Powhatan* to all the tribes as well as to the chief.

From the start, there were conflicts between the Powhatan and the colonists. The colonists often stole Powhatan crops. These thefts led to fighting, during which both sides would capture people.

One day, while exploring, Captain Smith was captured. A legend says that Chief Powhatan ordered Smith to be killed, but the chief's daughter **Pocahontas** (poh•kuh•HAHN•tuhs) saved his life. Historians do not know if this story is true, but there was a short-lived peace between the colonists and the Powhatan Confederacy. During this time, both groups cooperated by trading goods.

READING CHECK **MAIN IDEA AND DETAILS**
How did John Smith contribute to the survival of the Jamestown settlement?

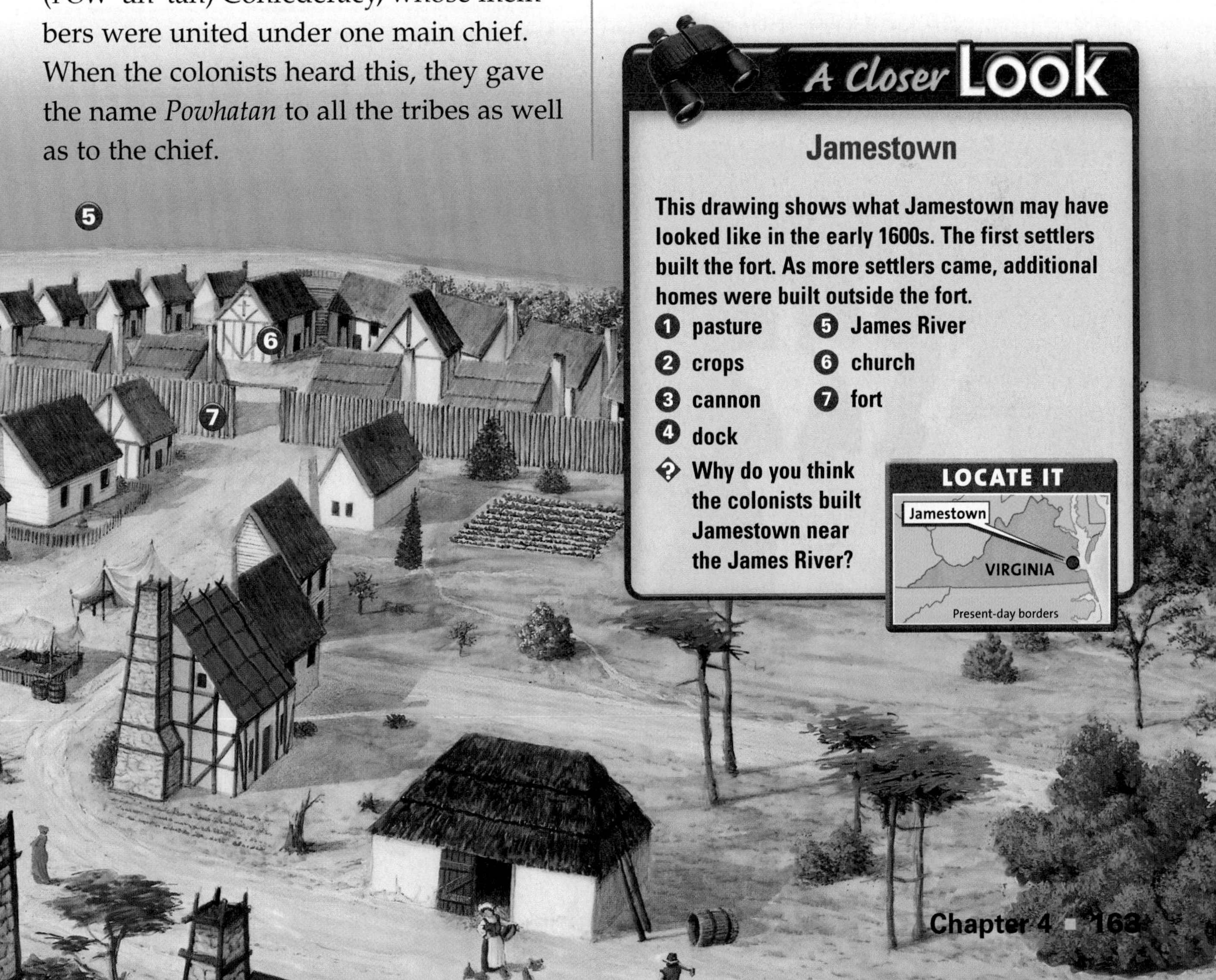

A Closer LOOK

Jamestown

This drawing shows what Jamestown may have looked like in the early 1600s. The first settlers built the fort. As more settlers came, additional homes were built outside the fort.

1. pasture
2. crops
3. cannon
4. dock
5. James River
6. church
7. fort

Why do you think the colonists built Jamestown near the James River?

LOCATE IT

Growth and Change

Because living conditions at Jamestown continued to be a problem, many people died in the colony's early years. However, more colonists arrived every year, so the population grew. In time, the colonists even found a way to make a profit. It was not gold that made Jamestown successful, but a crop called tobacco.

A Jamestown leader named **John Rolfe** experimented with growing different kinds of tobacco. By 1613, Rolfe had found a West Indian tobacco that proved to be very popular in England. The colonists at Jamestown were soon growing tobacco as a **cash crop**—a crop that people grow to sell. The Virginia Company made a lot of money selling its tobacco all over Europe.

Farmers grew tobacco on plantations that spread out around Jamestown. Growing tobacco required many workers, so the Virginia Company offered to pay for people's passages, or trips, to Virginia. In exchange, the people agreed to work without pay for a certain length of time, usually four to seven years. After that time, these **indentured servants** were given their freedom.

In 1619, the first Africans arrived in Jamestown. Historians do not know for sure whether these workers were treated as indentured servants or as slaves. In time, however, Virginia's economy came to rely more on enslaved workers, and more Africans were brought to the colony and forced to work as slaves.

READING CHECK **MAIN IDEA AND DETAILS**
Why was slavery introduced into Virginia?

Dutch traders sold the first Africans to Jamestown colonists in 1619.

CITIZENSHIP

Democratic Institutions

The House of Burgesses helped establish the belief that people could govern themselves.

In the early 1600s, the people of England had a king, but they also had elected leaders. The elected leaders made the laws in a lawmaking group called Parliament. The Virginia House of Burgesses was modeled after the English Parliament. Members of the House of Burgesses met once a year to make laws for the Virginia Colony and to decide on taxes. Electing a legislature to make decisions for the people continues to be an important right that Americans have today.

The Virginia House of Burgesses

Early Government

By 1619, the Virginia Colony had more than 1,000 colonists. With so many people, the colony needed laws to keep order. The Virginia Company said the colonists could have the same rights as people living in England. As a result, the colonists chose to set up a **legislature**, or a lawmaking branch of government.

Virginia's legislature, called the House of Burgesses (BER•juhs•iz), first met in 1619. It was the first representative assembly in the English colonies. Now colonists could elect members to **represent**, or speak for, them in the government. Only men who owned property could become members and vote in the House of Burgesses. Women, indentured servants, and slaves were not allowed to hold office, or even to vote.

The House of Burgesses passed several laws for Virginia. One law said that everyone had to go to church on Sundays. In Virginia, religion and government were not separate. Virginia had an **established church**, or a church supported by the government. In Virginia, this was the Church of England, also called the Anglican Church. Laws and taxes supported the Church of England.

READING CHECK **MAIN IDEA AND DETAILS**
What is an established church?

This engraving shows Chief Powhatan.

The Powhatan Wars

As more colonists arrived in Virginia, they continued to spread out onto Powhatan lands. The Powhatans had already lost much of their land. In 1622, the Powhatans attacked and killed more than 340 colonists in order to defend their land. The colonists fought back in a series of wars, pushing the Powhatans back and taking over their remaining lands.

The bloody Powhatan Wars and the debts of the Virginia Company led King James I to take over Virginia, making it a **royal colony**. This meant that the king owned the colony. To help run the colony, the king picked a **governor** who shared power with the House of Burgesses.

READING CHECK **MAIN IDEA AND DETAILS**
What led to the Powhatan Wars?

Summary

Starting in the 1580s, England set up colonies in North America. The Virginia Colony developed slowly. As the colony grew, slavery was introduced and the Powhatan Wars were fought.

REVIEW

1. Why did English settlers come to North America, and where did they settle first?
2. Use the term **royal colony** in a sentence about Virginia.
3. What was the job of the House of Burgesses?

CRITICAL THINKING

4. ANALYSIS SKILL How did the relative location of Jamestown make life difficult for the English settlers?
5. How do you think the Africans who were brought to Virginia felt?
6. **Write a Persuasive Letter** Write a letter to persuade people to settle in the Virginia Colony. Be sure to describe the benefits of living in Virginia.
7. Focus Skill **MAIN IDEA AND DETAILS** On a separate sheet of paper, copy and complete this graphic organizer.

Main Idea

Details

The population of Virginia grew.	People wanted laws to keep order.	The Virginia Company gave some colonists rights.

Pocahontas

The name Pocahontas means "playful one" in the Algonquian language. Pocahontas was the daughter of the powerful Chief Powhatan. She was about 12 years old when the first English settlers arrived at Jamestown. In 1607, Powhatan Indians captured John Smith and took him to Chief Powhatan. Smith believed that he was going to be killed, but Pocahontas kept him from being harmed. This famous event may have been just acted out as a ceremony, but no one is sure.

This painting shows Pocahontas supposedly saving John Smith's life.

For a time, Pocahontas's friendship with the settlers helped ease conflicts between her people and the English. Once, she convinced the settlers to release several Powhatan warriors they had captured.

However, this time of cooperation between the English and the Powhatan did not last long. In 1613, an English settler kidnapped her, hoping that her father would pay a ransom. While she was held by the English, Pocahontas fell in love with another settler, John Rolfe, and they were married in 1614. In 1616, Pocahontas, Rolfe, and their baby son Thomas went to England. Later, Pocahontas became sick and died on the way home to Virginia. She was only 22 when she died, but the story of her life is still told in books and art.

Why Character Counts

How did Pocahontas's actions show she cared for others?

Bio Brief

1595 — Born 1595?

1617 — Died 1617

1607 Pocahontas meets English settlers

1614 Pocahontas marries John Rolfe

Interactive Multimedia Biographies
Visit MULTIMEDIA BIOGRAPHIES at www.harcourtschool.com/hss

Compare Primary and Secondary Sources

WHY IT MATTERS

To know what really happened in the past, you need to find proof. You can do this by studying and comparing two kinds of sources—primary sources and secondary sources.

WHAT YOU NEED TO KNOW

Primary sources are the records and artifacts made by people who saw or took part in an event. These people may have written down their thoughts in a journal, or they may have told their story in a letter or a poem. They may have made a speech, produced a film, taken a photograph, or painted a picture. Primary sources may also be objects or official documents that give information about the time in which they were made or written. A primary source gives people of today a direct link to a past event.

A **secondary source** is not a direct link to an event. It is a record of the event made by someone who was not there at the time. If someone who only heard or read about an event writes a magazine article, a newspaper story, or a book, that is a secondary source.

This title page of John Smith's book (A), John White's drawing of an Algonquian Indian (B), and coins found at Jamestown (C) are primary sources.

Sometimes a source can be either primary or secondary, depending on how the event is reported. Newspapers are a good example. A newspaper article written by a reporter who saw an event is a primary source. A newspaper article written by a reporter who heard about the event from an eyewitness is a secondary source. Oral histories, textbooks, and online resources can also be either primary or secondary sources.

PRACTICE THE SKILL

Look at these photographs of objects and printed materials that give information about the Virginia Colony. Use them to answer these questions.

1. How are items B and E alike and different?
2. What kind of information might be found in item A but not in item F?
3. Why might secondary sources D and F also be considered primary sources?

APPLY WHAT YOU LEARNED

ANALYSIS SKILL Look through your textbook for examples of primary and secondary sources. Explain to a classmate what makes each source you selected a primary or a secondary source.

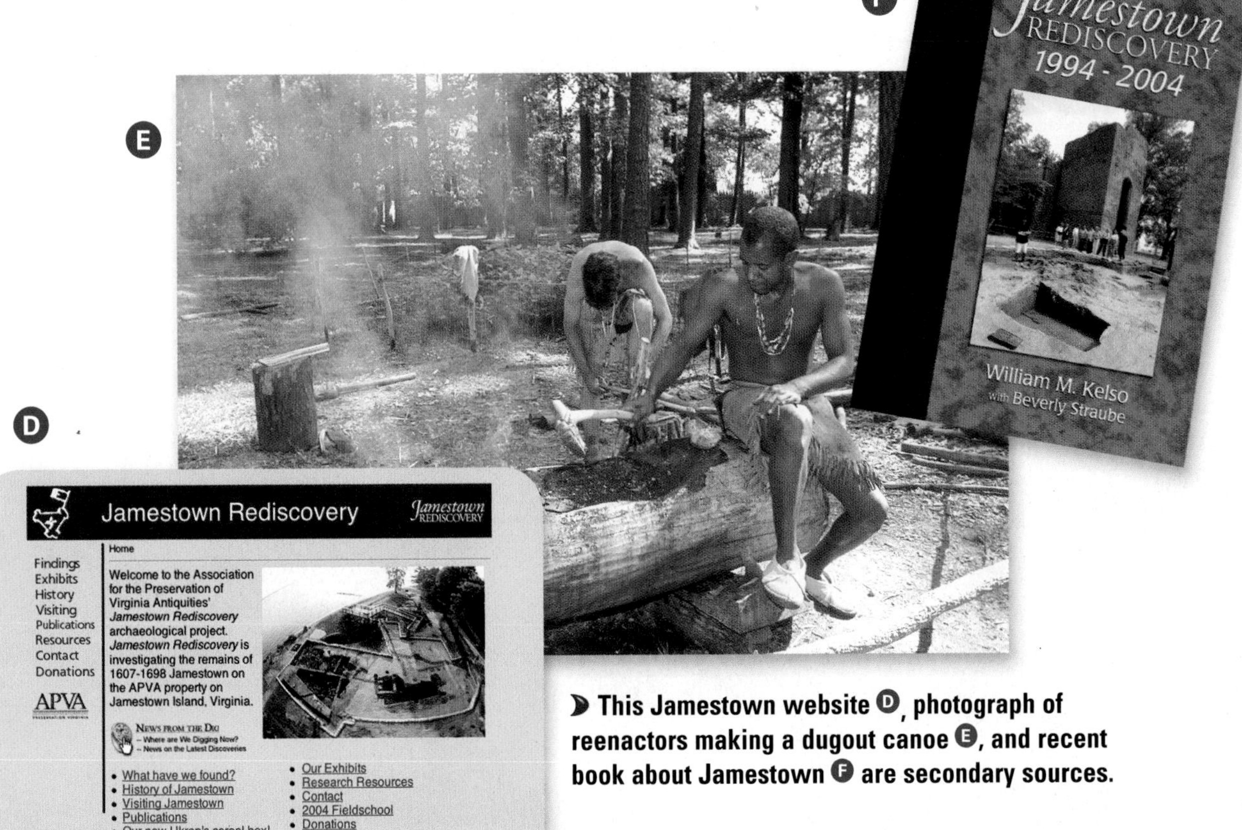

This Jamestown website D, photograph of reenactors making a dugout canoe E, and recent book about Jamestown F are secondary sources.

Lesson 3

Time

1400 — 1650

1620 The *Mayflower* sails to Plymouth

1621 Pilgrims and Wampanoag celebrate the first Thanksgiving

The Plymouth Colony

WHAT TO KNOW
Why did the English settle in New England?

- ✓ Learn how people lived in the Plymouth Colony.
- ✓ Describe the cooperation and conflict between English settlers and American Indians.
- ✓ Explain how English settlers developed ways to govern themselves.

VOCABULARY
pilgrim p. 171
compact p. 172
self-government p. 172
majority rule p. 172

PEOPLE
King Henry VIII
William Bradford
Samoset
Tisquantum

PLACES
Plymouth

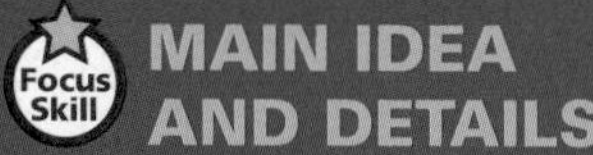

MAIN IDEA AND DETAILS

California Standards
HSS 5.3, 5.3.2, 5.3.3, 5.3.5, 5.4, 5.4.2, 5.4.3, 5.4.5

YOU ARE THERE

You are deep in the cargo hold of a ship. You have barely enough light to see, and the air is so stale that you wish you didn't have to breathe. The ship is rising and falling with the waves, but you're getting used to that. Your mother brings you your dinner—dry bread, cold dried meat, and an onion.

You've been living like this for two months, below deck on the *Mayflower*. North America will have to be a wonderful place, you think, to make this awful trip worthwhile.

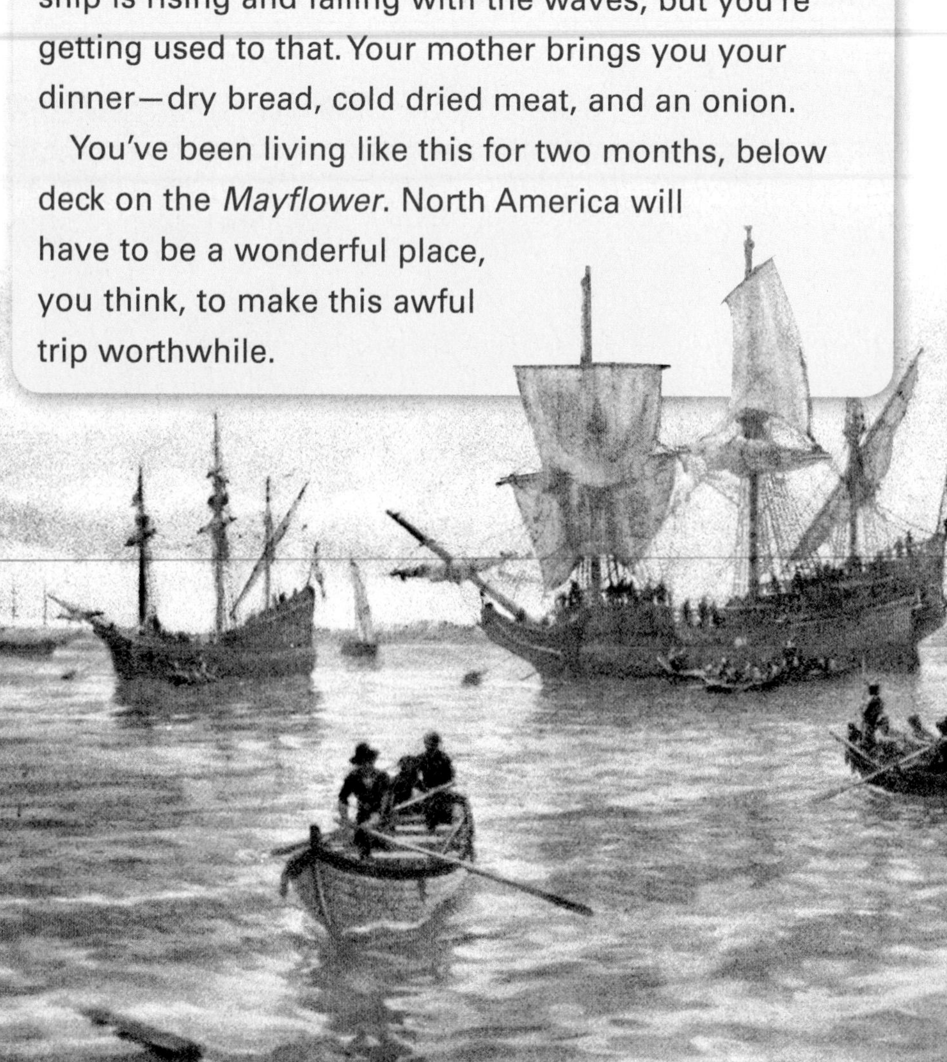

The Pilgrims' Journey

John Smith left Jamestown and in 1614 explored north along the Atlantic coast. He made a map of the northern area he explored, named the region New England, and wrote a book called *A Description of New England*. Today, the region includes six states—Connecticut, Rhode Island, Massachusetts, New Hampshire, Vermont, and Maine.

Many people in England read Smith's book. It made them think about building new communities in the region he described. Some people wanted to move there to make money, and others wanted to move there for religious reasons.

Years earlier, **King Henry VIII** had banned the Catholic Church in England and replaced it with the Church of England. Everyone in England had to belong to the Church of England, and those who chose not to were punished.

Hoping to follow their own religious beliefs, one group of English people had moved to the Netherlands. They were known as Separatists because they had left, or separated from, the Church of England. In time, they came to be known as Pilgrims. A **pilgrim** is a person who makes a journey for religious reasons.

The Pilgrims had religious freedom in the Netherlands, but they did not like the Dutch ways. They wanted to build their own society and to worship as they pleased. In North America, the Pilgrims would get their chance.

The Virginia Company agreed to pay the Pilgrims' passage to North America. In return, the Pilgrims would repay the company with lumber and furs from their new home. They left England in 1620, on a ship called the *Mayflower*.

READING CHECK
MAIN IDEA AND DETAILS Why did the Pilgrims want to go to North America?

In this painting, Pilgrims board rowboats to make their way toward the *Mayflower*.

Women were not given the chance to sign the Mayflower Compact because at this time in history, women had fewer rights than men had.

The Mayflower Compact

The *Mayflower* was headed for Virginia, but things did not go as planned because storms blew the ship off course. The *Mayflower* landed at Cape Cod, in what is now Massachusetts.

The settlers arrived in a place with no government. To keep order, all the men aboard the *Mayflower* signed a **compact**, or agreement. This document became known as the Mayflower Compact. The signers agreed that fair laws would be made for the good of the colony, and they promised to obey these laws. This meant that they would govern themselves.

At a time when monarchs ruled, **self-government** was a very new idea. The Mayflower Compact gave everyone who signed it the right to share in making laws, but women were not allowed to sign so they could not help make laws. It also included the idea of **majority rule**. If more than half the people agreed to a law or a decision, everyone had to follow it.

The settlers took several weeks to find a place for their colony. They chose a site on a harbor. Fresh water and good land for growing crops were nearby. John Smith had named the place **Plymouth**.

William Bradford, a leader of the Pilgrims, wrote,

> **"Being thus arrived in a good harbor and brought safe to land, they fell upon their knees and blessed the God of heaven."***

READING CHECK **MAIN IDEA AND DETAILS**
Why was the Mayflower Compact important?

* William Bradford. *Of Plymouth Plantation 1620–1647*. Modern Library, 1981.

Building a Colony

Although the settlers tried to make wise decisions, the first winter was very hard. It was cold and long, and by spring, 50 of the 102 settlers who had reached Cape Cod had died.

In the spring, the survivors got a very welcome surprise when an Abenaki Indian named **Samoset** arrived, saying, "Welcome, Englishmen." Samoset had learned English from sailors who fished along the Atlantic coast.

Several days later, Samoset returned to Plymouth with **Tisquantum**, or Squanto, as the English called him. He was a Wampanoag (wahm•puh•NOH•ag) Indian who spoke English quite well. Years before, Tisquantum had been taken and sold as a slave in Spain. After he escaped, he spent several years in England before at last returning to his homeland.

Tisquantum stayed with the Plymouth colonists, showing them where to fish and how to plant squash, pumpkins, and corn. Because food was scarce, the Pilgrims were glad to live in peace with the Wampanoag. Both groups benefited from their cooperation. The colonists and the Indians both had valuable items that the other group wanted.

Tisquantum helped the colonists trade for furs from neighboring Indian tribes. The Indians were able to trade furs for items such as metal goods and cloth. Metal goods were especially valuable to the Indians because the metal could be reshaped and used to make tools or jewelry.

READING CHECK **MAIN IDEA AND DETAILS**
How did Tisquantum help the Pilgrims?

People can visit this re-creation of the Plymouth settlement to see how colonists lived.

Cultural Heritage

Thanksgiving Day

In the fall of 1621, the Pilgrims gathered their first harvest. William Bradford, governor of the Plymouth Colony, decided they should have a celebration to "rejoice together" and to give thanks to God. Since this festival would come at the same time as the Indian celebration of the autumn harvest, he invited the neighboring Wampanoag Indians to join the Pilgrims for the three-day festival.

The Plymouth festival is what many people today think of as the first Thanksgiving. Thanksgiving became a national holiday in the United States in 1863. That year, President Abraham Lincoln declared the last Thursday in November as Thanksgiving Day.

This painting gives an artist's view of the first Thanksgiving.

Plymouth Grows

When the Plymouth colonists first arrived, there was very little food available. To help, the colony's leaders decided that the harvest would be divided equally among the families. Then, in 1623, the leaders decided to divide the land among the colonists. The result was that the people worked harder.

The Plymouth colonists began to prosper from their farming, as well as from fishing and fur trading. As new colonists arrived, earlier colonists had extra goods ready to trade. However, the population of Plymouth remained low during its first ten years. By 1630, there were only about 300 colonists.

After 1630, other English colonists began to settle in different areas of New England, and life there began to change. Many of the new colonists were not friendly toward the Indians and settled on more of their lands. Some colonists did not see a need to cooperate with the Indians. As conflicts between the Indians and the colonists increased, trade between the two groups ended.

This made life more difficult for the colonists and the Indians. Over time, the way the groups felt about one another changed. William Bradford, one of Plymouth's early governors, had once helped make peace with local Indians, but he later supported a war to push many Indians out of New England. Such actions also caused problems between Indian tribes. As the amount of available land decreased, tribes often fought with each other for control of hunting grounds.

READING CHECK **MAIN IDEA AND DETAILS**
How did the relationship between the Indians and the colonists change?

Summary

The Pilgrims left Europe to find religious freedom. When they arrived in Plymouth, the settlers wrote the Mayflower Compact to set up self-government. Early on, American Indians helped the colonists, but later the two sides stopped cooperating.

This American Indian woman demonstrates native lifeways at the Plymouth Plantation historical site.

REVIEW

1. Why did the English settle in New England?
2. Write a sentence about the Plymouth Colony using the terms **compact** and **self-government**.
3. Why were women not allowed to help make laws in the Plymouth Colony?

CRITICAL THINKING

4. ANALYSIS SKILL Do you think the ideas of the Mayflower Compact are still important to people today? Why or why not?
5. ANALYSIS SKILL Is the Mayflower Compact a primary source? Why or why not?
6. **Write a Speech** Write a speech from the point of view of an American Indian speaking to the Pilgrims.
7. Focus Skill **MAIN IDEA AND DETAILS**
On a separate sheet of paper, copy and complete this graphic organizer.

Main Idea

The Virginia Company agreed to pay for the Pilgrims' passage to North America.

Details

Lesson 4

Time

1400 — 1650

1608 Champlain founds Quebec

1626 The Dutch set up New Amsterdam

WHAT TO KNOW
Why did the French and the Dutch set up colonies?

- ✓ Describe how European nations struggled for control of North America.
- ✓ Describe the relations between French and Dutch settlers and American Indians.

VOCABULARY
internecine p. 180
ally p. 180
proprietary colony p. 182

PEOPLE
Samuel de Champlain
Peter Minuit
Jacques Marquette
Louis Joliet
La Salle

PLACES
Quebec
New Netherland
New Amsterdam
New Sweden
New Orleans

MAIN IDEA AND DETAILS

California Standards

HSS 5.2, 5.2.2, 5.2.3, 5.3, 5.3.1, 5.3.2, 5.3.4, 5.3.5, 5.4.1, 5.4.2, 5.4.5

The French and the Dutch

You Are There The year is 1608, and you're traveling with your father on a trading mission. Your people, the Huron, have started trading furs with the French, and your father wants you to learn how to bargain with the newcomers.

When you arrive at the trading place, you sit quietly and watch. The men use hand signals to communicate, and when a trade is agreed on, they nod their heads. Your father has brought several furs, so you expect to take many new things back home. You just hope you'll be able to carry them all!

New France

While Spain and England were building colonies in North America, France was claiming more land in what are today Canada and the northeastern United States. French claims to this region, which became known as New France, began with Jacques Cartier. He explored the St. Lawrence River in the early 1500s and began an important trading partnership with the Huron Indians.

French merchants wanted the wealth that came from the fur trade. The French king wanted to increase his country's power. He encouraged merchants to start colonies in North America.

Eventually, a group of merchants hired **Samuel de Champlain** (sham•PLAYN) to find a place to build a settlement. In 1608, Champlain founded **Quebec** along the St. Lawrence River. Quebec was the first French settlement in North America, but by 1625 its population had grown to only about 60 people.

Starting in the 1630s, French Catholic missionaries began arriving in New France. These missionaries often lived with Indian tribes to learn their language. The aim of the missionaries was to convert the Indians to the Catholic religion.

Some French fur traders also lived with Indian tribes and learned their language and ways of life. Since these traders spent much of their time traveling with the Indians they did not build many permanent settlements.

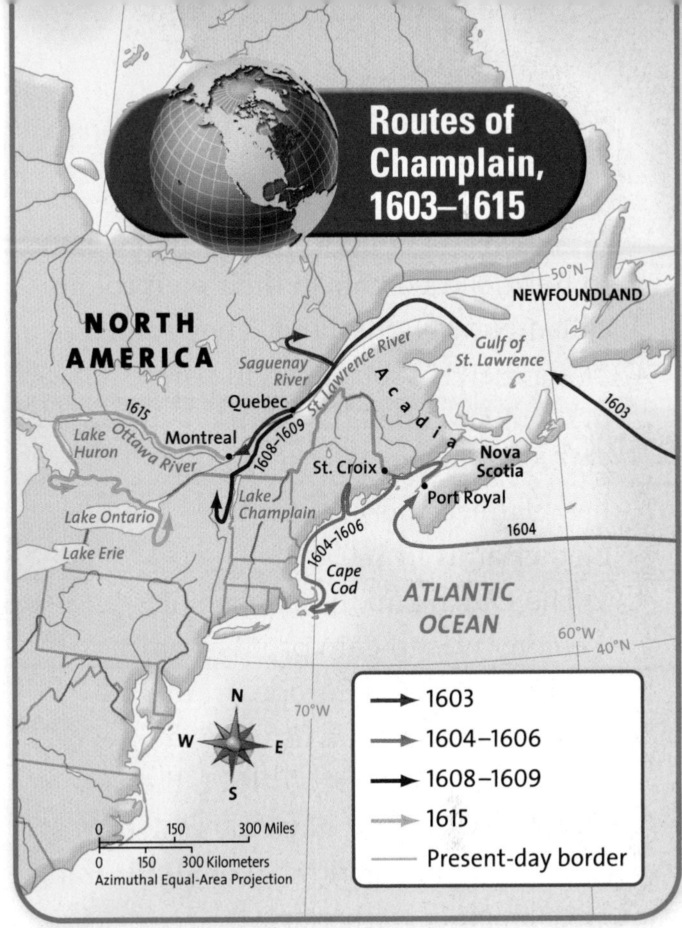

ANALYSIS SKILL Analyze Maps

Movement **About how far did Champlain travel to reach Lake Huron from Montreal?**

Unlike Spain's and England's colonies, New France grew slowly. Most French people were not interested in settling in North America. In the 1600s, the French built only two major settlements in all of North America—Quebec and Montreal.

READING CHECK MAIN IDEA AND DETAILS **Why did New France grow slowly?**

This statue of Samuel de Champlain stands in Canada.

H. MAC-CARTHY SCULP.

New Netherland

Not long after the English started colonies in North America, the Dutch began to build settlements in their own colony, called **New Netherland**. They settled along the Hudson River, in parts of what are today New York and New Jersey. Henry Hudson had claimed this area for the Netherlands in 1609.

Dutch West India Company seal

The Dutch aim in establishing a colony was to gain profits from the sale of furs to Europe. At this time in history, fur hats were in style all over Europe. In 1621, the Dutch government gave the Dutch West India Company control over all fur trade areas in New Netherland.

By 1626, **Peter Minuit** (MIN•yuh•wuht) was governor of New Netherland. During his time as governor, the Dutch bought Manhattan Island from the Indians who were living there. As in other places, the Indians' ideas about land were different from those of the new settlers. The Indians believed that the land was for all people to use. They thought the Dutch were paying them only for the use of the resources on the land, not for the land itself.

In 1626, the Dutch began laying out a town on the south end of Manhattan Island. They called the settlement **New Amsterdam**, after the city of Amsterdam in the Netherlands. New Amsterdam was built next to a harbor where the Hudson River flows into the Atlantic Ocean. This location was good for trade. Traders sailed down the Hudson to New Amsterdam to unload their furs and to get supplies. Ships waited in the harbor to carry the furs to Europe.

By the 1630s, New Amsterdam had about 200 people and 30 houses. It also had a countinghouse, where workers could keep track of furs and money, and warehouses for storing food and furs. For protection, the colonists built a fort with high walls made of stone.

In 1638, Swedish settlers founded the colony of **New Sweden** to the south of New Netherland. New Sweden included parts of present-day Pennsylvania, New Jersey, and Delaware. When the Swedes began building settlements, the Dutch worried these new settlers would enter the fur trade. Dutch colonists and the Algonquian Indians had established a strong fur trading relationship, but this relationship would soon face trouble.

By the late 1630s, conflicts with Indians had grown because the settlers had cleared more land for farms. The colonists and the Indians attacked each other's farms and villages. The colonists then sent out an army that destroyed Indian villages all over New Netherland.

In 1645, after many colonists and Indians had been killed, the two sides signed a peace treaty. By then, the Algonquian population of New Netherland had been nearly wiped out.

READING CHECK **MAIN IDEA AND DETAILS**
How did conflicts with the Dutch affect the Indians in New Netherland?

A Closer LOOK

New Amsterdam, 1640s

New Amsterdam continued to grow. By 1643, more than 400 people lived there.

1. **Ships arrived at the public dock on the East River.**
2. **The center of New Amsterdam grew up around the fort. The marketplace, the church, and the windmill were there.**
3. **Streets were made from paths that farmers used to travel to and from the town center.**

? How do you think New Amsterdam's relative location affected its economy?

Exploring New France

As English and Dutch colonists moved into parts of New France, fighting over the fur trade began among the settlers. Indian tribes also experienced **internecine** (in•ter•NEH•seen) conflicts, or fighting between groups. Both the Huron and Iroquois Indians wanted to control lands in present-day Canada. The Huron were **allies**, or partners, with the French, while the Iroquois were partners with the Dutch and the English. Fierce fighting between these groups nearly destroyed the Huron population and the French fur trade.

The new French king, Louis XIV, did not want to lose France's North American lands, so he made New France a royal colony. He sent Count de Frontenac (FRAHN•tuh•nak) to explore the western part of New France. He knew that there was a large river west of Quebec that Indians called *Mississippi*, meaning "Father of Waters." He hoped the Mississippi would prove to be the Northwest Passage.

In 1673, a small group, led by Catholic missionary **Jacques Marquette** (mahr•KET) and fur trader **Louis Joliet** (zhohl•YAY), set out to find the Mississippi. With help from Indians, they did find the Mississippi. However, because the river kept taking them south, they knew it was not the Northwest Passage. They floated down the river to the present-day state of Mississippi. There, they met some Indians who told them that Europeans lived farther south. Fearing the Europeans might be Spanish soldiers, the French turned back.

Later, French explorer René-Robert Cavelier (ka•vuhl•YAY), known as Sieur de la Salle, or "Sir" La Salle, set out to find the mouth of the Mississippi River. In 1682, **La Salle** led an expedition that traveled south from the Illinois River. During the difficult trip, a member of the expedition wrote that, after running out of food, they were "living only on potatoes and alligators."*

After two months, the explorers reached the mouth of the Mississippi at the Gulf of Mexico. La Salle claimed the entire Mississippi River valley for France and named the region Louisiana in honor of King Louis XIV.

In 1684, La Salle tried to start a settlement near the mouth of the Mississippi River, but hardships led to disagreements among the settlers. Three years later La Salle was killed, and the settlement failed.

READING CHECK **MAIN IDEA AND DETAILS How did French explorers advance the king's aims?**

*from a member of the LaSalle expedition in *North American Exploration* by Michael Golay and John S. Bowman. Wiley and Sons, Inc., 2003.

Huron Indian statue

Exploring The Mississippi

American Indians and the French often cooperated at trading posts. French traders exchanged blankets and cooking pots for furs and animal skins.

Marquette and Joliet on the banks of the Mississippi, 1673

Champlain settles Quebec, 1608.

La Salle claims the valley of the Mississippi in 1682.

A Colony and a Capital

The French king then sent another expedition to Louisiana. Pierre Le Moyne (luh•MWAHN) and his brother Jean-Baptiste (ZHAHN ba•TEEST) reached the northern coast of the Gulf of Mexico in 1699. Soon after, they found the mouth of the Mississippi River. The members of the expedition built a settlement along the river, and in time, more settlers came, but they experienced many of the same hardships that La Salle had faced.

In 1712, the French king made Louisiana a **proprietary colony** (pruh•PRY•uh•ter•ee). This meant that he gave the whole colony to one person, who would own it. In 1717, John Law, a Scottish banker, became Louisiana's owner. Law formed a company to build plantations and towns and he brought in thousands of new settlers. In 1722, **New Orleans**, one of the colony's first towns became Louisiana's capital.

Despite Law's efforts, however, the colony still needed more workers. Many plantation owners began to bring in enslaved Africans to do the work. The French government soon passed laws that restricted where Africans in Louisiana could live and what kind of work they could do.

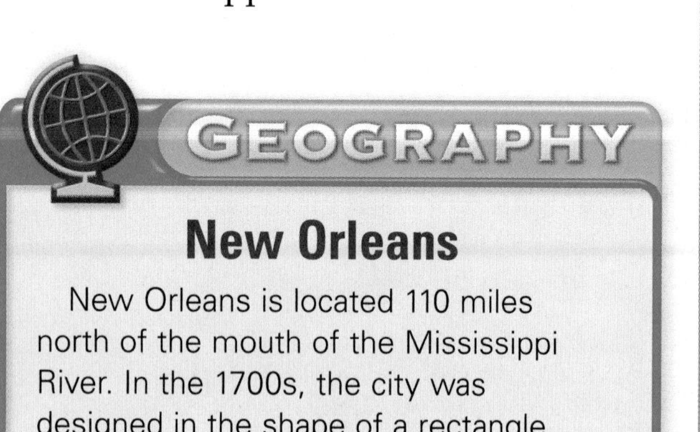

New Orleans

New Orleans is located 110 miles north of the mouth of the Mississippi River. In the 1700s, the city was designed in the shape of a rectangle made up of 44 blocks. At first, the city had more houses than people to fill them. Next to the river was the town's center, a large, open square surrounded by government and religious buildings. The Catholic Church had a large role in the development of New Orleans. The city also had a colorful social life and people from all over the world.

Like the rest of New France, Louisiana failed to attract enough people for it to prosper. By 1763, there were only 80,000 French colonists living in New France, an area stretching from Canada to Louisiana. By the same year, in a much smaller area, there were more than 1,500,000 English colonists in North America.

READING CHECK **MAIN IDEA AND DETAILS**
Why was it hard for the French to control land in North America?

Summary

The French and Dutch both began building settlements in North America in the 1600s. Both groups wanted to control the fur trade, and this often led to fighting between the settlers and Indians. The French and Dutch had trouble bringing settlers to North America, so the population of their colonies remained low.

Colonial Systems in North America

	SPANISH COLONIES	ENGLISH COLONIES	FRENCH COLONIES
Location	Central America and southern North America	Atlantic Coast of North America	Northeastern North America and Mississippi River valley
Government	Ruled by leaders loyal to the Spanish monarch	Ruled by leaders loyal to the English monarch and colonial assemblies	Ruled by leaders loyal to the French monarch
Religion	Only Catholics allowed to settle	Most early settlers were Protestant	Most settlers were Catholic
Economy	Mostly gold and silver mining	Farming, fishing, and trading	Mostly fur trading

Analyze Tables

How was English colonial government different from that of Spain and France?

REVIEW

1. Why did the French and the Dutch set up colonies?
2. Write definitions of the terms **ally** and **proprietary colony**.
3. How was New Amsterdam's location an advantage?

CRITICAL THINKING

4. Why do you think some American Indian tribes made partnerships with settlers?
5. ANALYSIS SKILL Put the following settlements in order from earliest to latest: New Amsterdam, New Orleans, Quebec.
6. **Draw an Advertisement** Using what you have learned, draw an advertisement telling people why they should settle in New France or New Netherland.
7. Focus Skill **MAIN IDEA AND DETAILS** On a separate sheet of paper, copy and complete the graphic organizer.

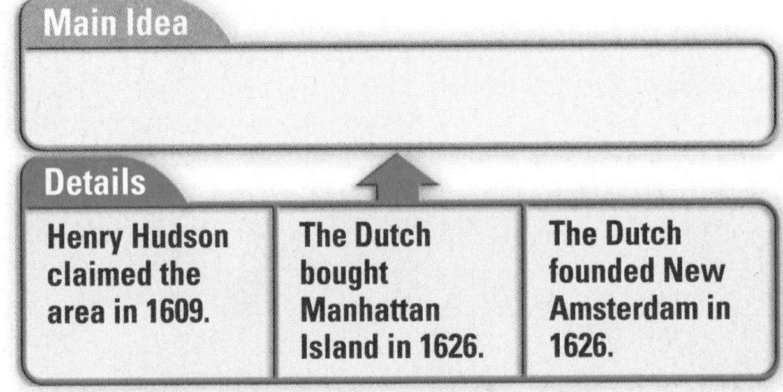

Read a Historical Map

WHY IT MATTERS

By the middle of the 1600s, many European nations had claimed land in North America. The historical map on page 185 shows the areas claimed by these nations. A historical map gives information about a place at a certain time in history.

WHAT YOU NEED TO KNOW

Colors are important map symbols. Sometimes colors help you tell water from land on a map. Colors on a map can also show you the areas claimed by different cities, states, or countries.

PRACTICE THE SKILL

Use the map on page 185 to answer these questions.

1. What color is used to show the land claimed by the English? by the French? by the Spanish? by the Dutch? by the Swedish?
2. What country claimed most of the land along the Atlantic coast?
3. What country claimed most of the land in the West?
4. What country claimed the least amount of land?

APPLY WHAT YOU LEARNED

ANALYSIS SKILL Write a paragraph that describes what this historical map shows and how it is shown. Then explain why historical maps are useful.

Practice your map and globe skills with the **GeoSkills CD-ROM**.

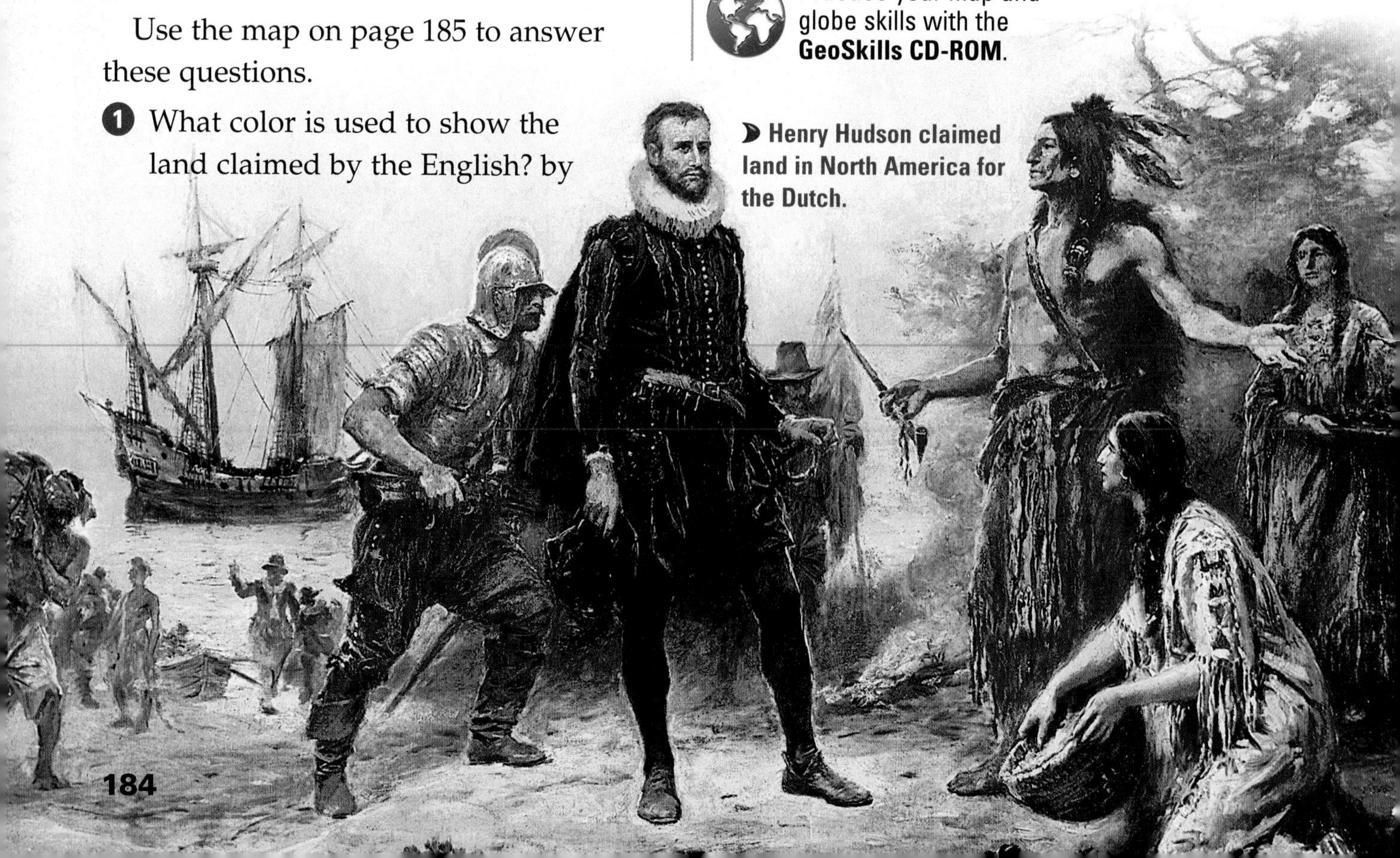

Henry Hudson claimed land in North America for the Dutch.

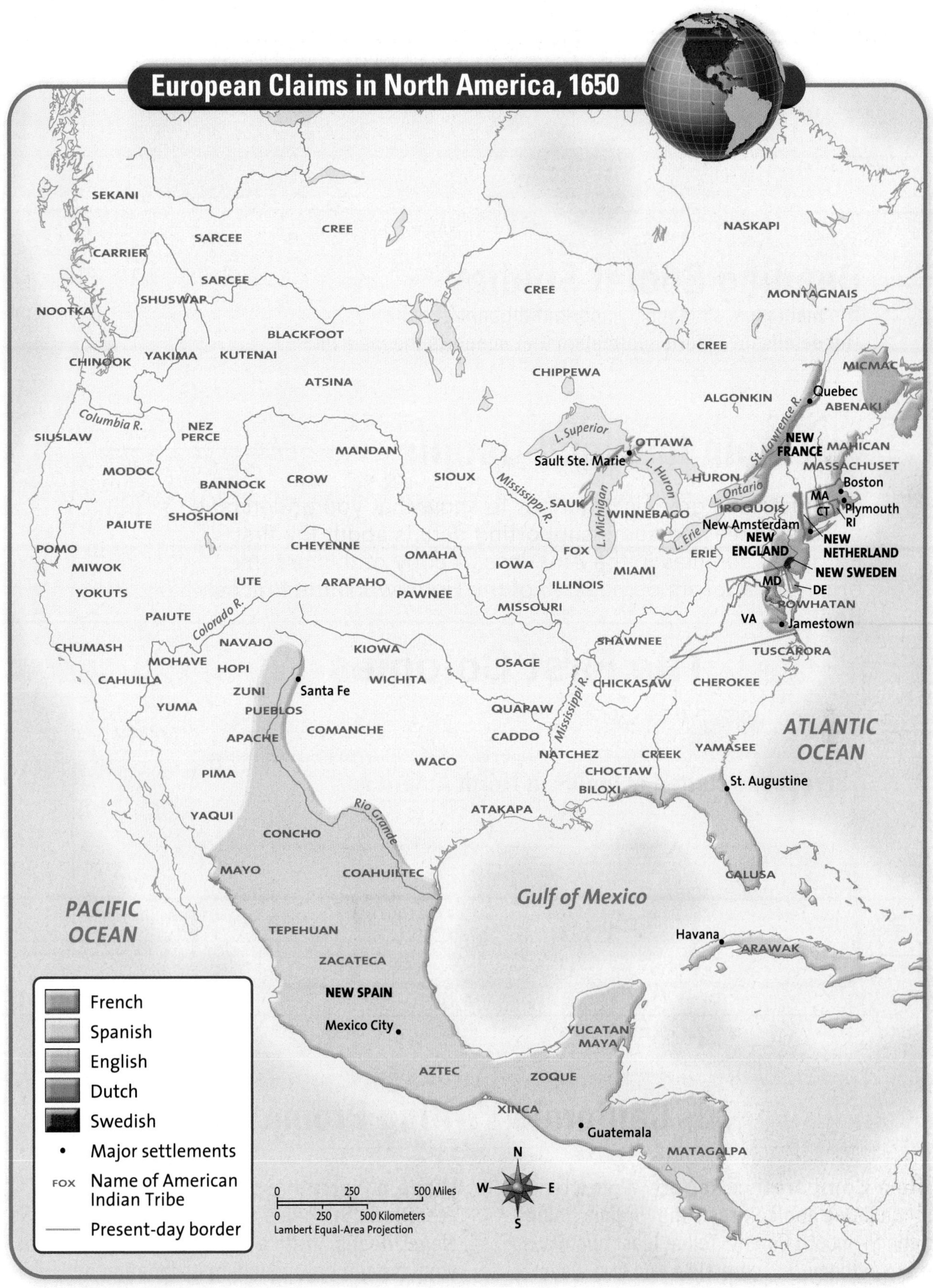
European Claims in North America, 1650
SEKANI
SARCEE
CREE
NASKAPI
CARRIER
SARCEE
SHUSWAP
NOOTKA
CREE
MONTAGNAIS
BLACKFOOT
CREE
CHINOOK
YAKIMA
KUTENAI
CHIPPEWA
MICMAC
ATSINA
Quebec
ALGONKIN
ABENAKI
Columbia R.
NEZ PERCE
L. Superior
SIUSLAW
St. Lawrence R.
NEW FRANCE
OTTAWA
MAHICAN
MANDAN
Sault Ste. Marie
MASSACHUSET
MODOC
L. Huron
HURON
Boston
BANNOCK
CROW
SIOUX
Mississippi R.
L. Ontario
MA
Plymouth
CT
SAUK
L. Michigan
IROQUOIS
RI
SHOSHONI
WINNEBAGO
New Amsterdam
PAIUTE
NEW ENGLAND
NEW NETHERLAND
L. Erie
POMO
CHEYENNE
OMAHA
FOX
ERIE
MIWOK
IOWA
MIAMI
NEW SWEDEN
UTE
ARAPAHO
MD
YOKUTS
ILLINOIS
DE
PAWNEE
POWHATAN
MISSOURI
PAIUTE
Colorado R.
VA
Jamestown
NAVAJO
SHAWNEE
CHUMASH
KIOWA
TUSCARORA
MOHAVE
HOPI
OSAGE
CAHUILLA
Santa Fe
WICHITA
CHICKASAW
CHEROKEE
ZUNI
Mississippi R.
YUMA
PUEBLOS
QUAPAW
COMANCHE
ATLANTIC OCEAN
APACHE
CADDO
NATCHEZ
CREEK
YAMASEE
WACO
PIMA
CHOCTAW
St. Augustine
BILOXI
ATAKAPA
Rio Grande
YAQUI
CONCHO
MAYO
COAHUILTEC
CALUSA
PACIFIC OCEAN
Gulf of Mexico
TEPEHUAN
Havana
ARAWAK
ZACATECA
NEW SPAIN
Mexico City
YUCATAN MAYA
AZTEC
ZOQUE
XINCA
Guatemala
MATAGALPA
French
Spanish
English
Dutch
Swedish
Major settlements
FOX Name of American Indian Tribe
Present-day border
0 250 500 Miles
0 250 500 Kilometers
Lambert Equal-Area Projection
N
W
E
S

Time

1400 — 1500

1535 New Spain is formed

Reading Social Studies

The **main idea** is the most important thought in a text.
The **details** give more information that supports the main idea.

Focus Skill Main Idea and Details

Complete this graphic organizer to show that you understand the main idea and some supporting details about the first European colonies in the Americas. A copy of this graphic organizer appears on page 46 of the Homework and Practice Book.

The First Colonies

Main Idea

Europeans started colonies in North America.

Details

California Writing Prompts

Write a Comparative Report Write a report that compares and contrasts the Virginia Colony and the Plymouth Colony. Tell at least two ways that the settlements were alike and two ways that they were different.

Write a Narrative Imagine that you are a reporter in St. Augustine, New Amsterdam, or New Orleans. Write a short story that describes your chosen city, including its location and why it was founded.

1600

1700

1607
The settlement of Jamestown is founded

1620
The *Mayflower* sails to Plymouth

1684
La Salle claims Louisiana for France

Use Vocabulary

Write a sentence to explain how each pair of terms is related.

1. **plantation** (p. 156), **slavery** (p. 156)
2. **raw material** (p. 161), **cash crop** (p. 164)
3. **legislature** (p. 165), **represent** (p. 165)
4. **royal colony** (p. 166), **proprietary colony** (p. 182)
5. **internecine** (p. 180), **ally** (p. 180)

Use the Time Line

Use the chapter summary time line above to answer these questions.

6. When was New Spain formed?
7. How many years after the English founded Jamestown did the *Mayflower* sail to Plymouth?

Apply Skills

Compare Primary and Secondary Sources

8. Look at pages 178 and 179. Identify the primary source and the secondary source. Explain your choices.

ANALYSIS SKILL **Read a Historical Map**

9. Use the map on page 185 to identify which European nation claimed most of the land along the Rio Grande by 1650.

Recall Facts

Answer these questions.

10. Why did Spain build missions in the borderlands of New Spain?
11. Who settled the Plymouth Colony, and what was their reason for doing so?
12. Why did some colonists enslave American Indians and Africans?

Write the letter of the best choice.

13. What cash crop helped the Virginia Colony grow and prosper?
    A cotton
    B rice
    C tobacco
    D sugarcane
14. What was the main reason French and Dutch settlers started colonies in North America?
    A They wanted religious freedom.
    B They wanted to gain profits from the sale of furs to Europe.
    C They wanted to set up plantations.
    D They wanted to govern themselves.

Think Critically

15. ANALYSIS SKILL What are two examples of cooperation and two examples of conflict between early European colonists and American Indians?
16. ANALYSIS SKILL How did the relative location of the Plymouth Colony affect trade with England?

The Mission San Diego de Alcalá

GET READY

Mission San Diego de Alcalá, in San Diego, California, was the first in a string of 21 missions that stretched across the Spanish borderlands of California. San Diego de Alcalá was founded by Father Junípero Serra on July 16, 1769. In time, the city of San Diego grew around the mission. Today, many people visit to learn about mission life hundreds of years ago. At San Diego de Alcalá, you can see artifacts that belonged to Indians, early Spanish settlers, soldiers, and missionaries. Experience life in another time as you walk where they once walked.

LOCATE IT

WHAT TO SEE

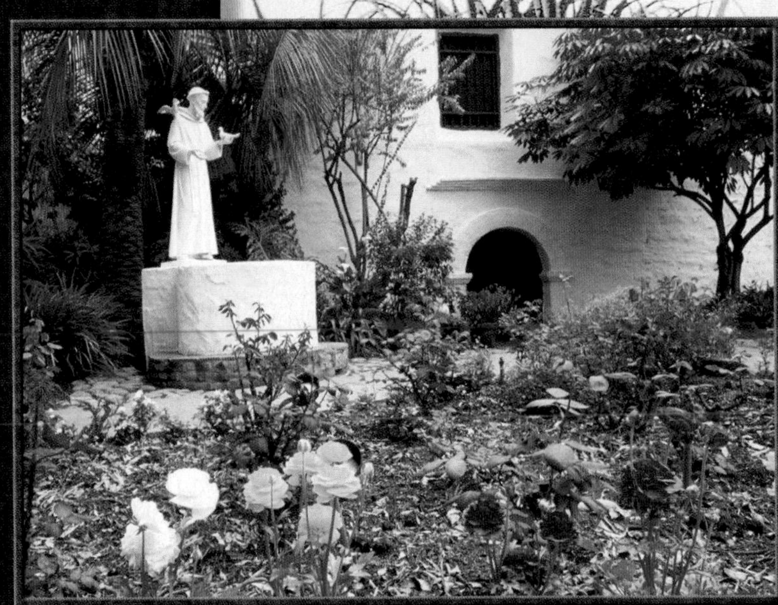

Visitors can spend time in the mission's scenic gardens.

People still attend church services at the Mission San Diego de Alcalá.

This songbook, on display at the mission, was used more than 200 years ago.

A statue of Father Junípero Serra stands on the mission grounds.

A VIRTUAL TOUR

GO ONLINE Visit VIRTUAL TOURS at **www.harcourtschool.com/hss**

Unit 2

Review

 THE BIG IDEA

Coooperation and Conflict Europeans came to the Americas to find riches, build settlements, and bring their religion to others.

Summary

Cultures Meet

In the late 1400s, new technology allowed Europeans to begin exploring the world. Many hoped to find a sea route to Asia for trade. These explorations led people to the Americas. European countries soon sent more explorers to claim and settle those new lands.

As a result of these expeditions, Spain formed New Spain from lands claimed in North America, including what are now Mexico and much of the southwestern United States. England claimed much of the Atlantic Coast and built settlements in present-day Virginia and Massachusetts. The Dutch founded the colony of New Netherland in present-day New York and New Jersey. France claimed much of what is now Canada and the entire Mississippi River valley, to form New France.

By 1700, much of North America was divided among these European nations, despite the fact that American Indians already lived there. Some colonists and Indians formed peaceful relations and exchanged goods and ideas, but many more fought over the land and resources.

Main Ideas and Vocabulary

Read the summary above. Then answer the questions that follow.

1. What is an expedition?
   A a ship designed for long voyages
   B a trip taken with the goal of exploring
   C a method of finding and following a route
   D an agreement between two nations

2. What were Europeans searching for when they first reached the Americas?
   A more land for farming and ranching
   B furs and lumber to sell in Europe
   C a sea route to Asia
   D religious freedom

3. What is a colony?
   A a group of people who make laws
   B a person who conquers other people
   C a share in the ownership of something
   D a land that is ruled by another country

4. Which European country explored and claimed what is now Canada?
   A England
   B France
   C the Netherlands
   D Spain

Recall Facts

Answer these questions.

5. Who was the first explorer to claim land in the Americas for Spain?
6. What were Verrazano and Cartier searching for when they explored the Americas?
7. What was England's first permanent settlement in North America?
8. What was the Mayflower Compact?
9. Who claimed for France all of the Mississippi River valley?

Write the letter of the best choice.

10. Which tools helped sailors determine their latitude and longitude?
    - **A** the compass and the caravel
    - **B** the hourglass and the astrolabe
    - **C** the compass and the astrolabe
    - **D** the telescope and the caravel
11. Which region of North America did Francisco Vásquez de Coronado claim for Spain?
    - **A** the Northeast
    - **B** the Northwest
    - **C** the Southeast
    - **D** the Southwest
12. Which of these settlements was founded first?
    - **A** Jamestown
    - **B** New Amsterdam
    - **C** New Orleans
    - **D** St. Augustine
13. With which settlers did Indians mainly fight in the Powhatan Wars?
    - **A** Dutch
    - **B** English
    - **C** French
    - **D** Spanish

Think Critically

14. ANALYSIS SKILL What were some of the costs and possible benefits of expeditions?
15. ANALYSIS SKILL What role did religion play in the exploration and settlement of North America?

Apply Skills

ANALYSIS SKILL **Use a Historical Map**

Use the historical map below to answer the following questions.

16. Which nation claimed most of the land along the Atlantic coast?
17. Which American Indian groups lived in areas claimed by France?

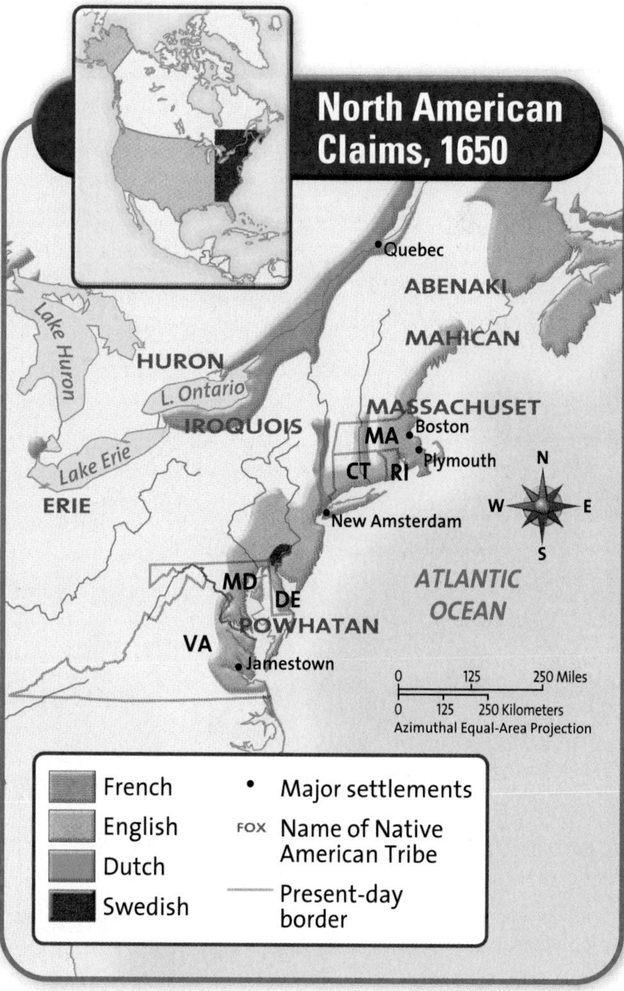

Unit 2

Activities

Read More

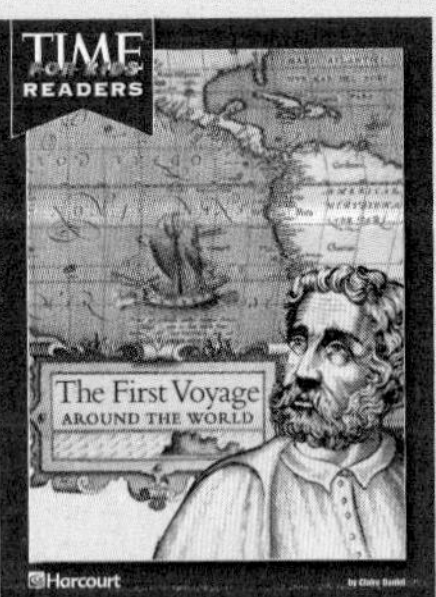

■ *The First Voyage Around the World* by Claire Daniel.

■ *Cabeza de Vaca* by Scott Cameron.

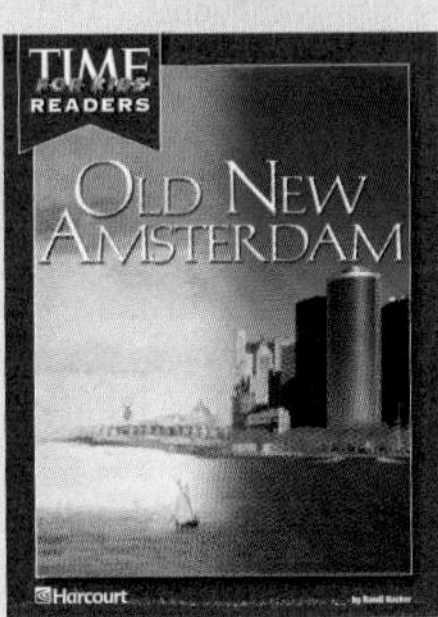

■ *Old New Amsterdam* by Randi Hacker.

Show What You Know

Unit Writing Activity

Write a Persuasive Advertisement Imagine that you are living in the 1600s, in a country that has started a colony in North America. Your job is to persuade settlers to come to the new colony. Write an advertisement describing its location, why it was founded, and what life is like there. Organize your ideas and support your position with relevant evidence.

Unit Project

A Museum of Exploration Build a museum exhibit about the exploration and early colonization of North America. Decide which people, places, and events to include in your museum and how you will present them. Prepare brief reports, journal entries, drawings, maps, and models for your museum.

Visit ACTIVITIES at
www.harcourtschool.com/hss

Settling the Colonies

START WITH THE STANDARDS

California History-Social Science Standards

5.3 Students describe the cooperation and conflict that existed among the American Indians and between the Indian nations and the new settlers.

5.4 Students understand the political, religious, social, and economic institutions that evolved in the colonial era.

The Big Idea

Commonality and Diversity

The 13 English colonies were founded in different regions of North America and for different reasons.

What to Know

- Why did different people come to the English colonies and where did they settle?
- How did new colonies impact American Indian groups?
- What kinds of governments, economies, and new ideas developed in the colonies?

Show What You Know

- ★ Unit 3 Test
- Writing: A Narrative

Unit 3

Time

Settling the Colonies

1619 The first Africans arrive in the Virginia Colony, p. 283

1632 Lord Baltimore founds the Maryland Colony, p. 273

1600

1650

Settling the Colonies

1681 William Penn founds the Pennsylvania Colony, p. 245

1733 James Oglethorpe founds the Georgia Colony, p. 276

1700

1750

John Winthrop

1588–1649

- English Puritan leader
- Served as governor of the Massachusetts Colony

Anne Hutchinson

1591–1643

- Puritan settler who began preaching in her home
- Forced to leave Massachusetts because of her beliefs

1550 | 1600 | 1650

- 1588 • John Winthrop 1649
- 1591 • Anne Hutchinson 1643
- 1638? • Metacomet
- 1644 • William Penn

Benjamin Franklin

1706–1790

- Pennsylvania leader and famous inventor
- Published Poor Richard's Almanac

George Whitefield

1714–1770

- English minister who helped lead the Great Awakening
- Popular throughout England and the 13 Colonies

Metacomet

1638?–1676

- Known to the English as King Philip
- Led the Wampanoag Indians in King Philip's War

William Penn

1644–1718

- English Quaker who founded the Pennsylvania Colony
- Encouraged fair and peaceful relations with American Indians

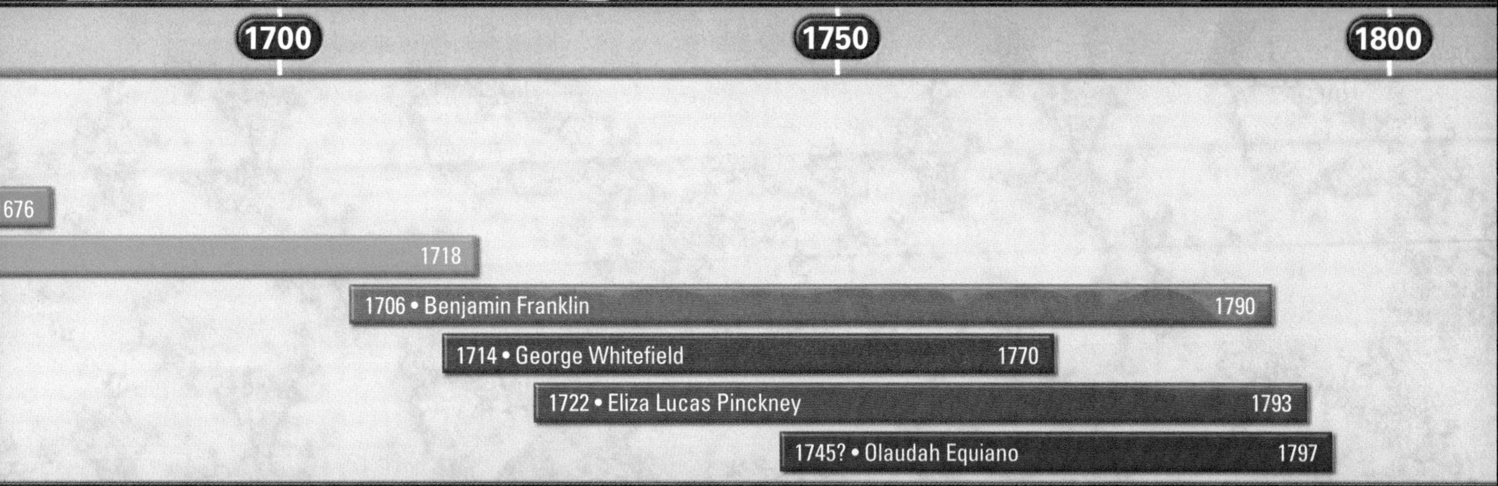

1700 1750 1800

676

1718

1706 • Benjamin Franklin 1790

1714 • George Whitefield 1770

1722 • Eliza Lucas Pinckney 1793

1745? • Olaudah Equiano 1797

Eliza Lucas Pinckney

1722–1793

- Daughter of a South Carolina plantation owner
- Experimented with crops such as indigo and silk

Olaudah Equiano

1745?–1797

- Enslaved African who later purchased his freedom
- Spoke out against slavery in his writings and speeches

Unit 3

Place

The Thirteen English Colonies

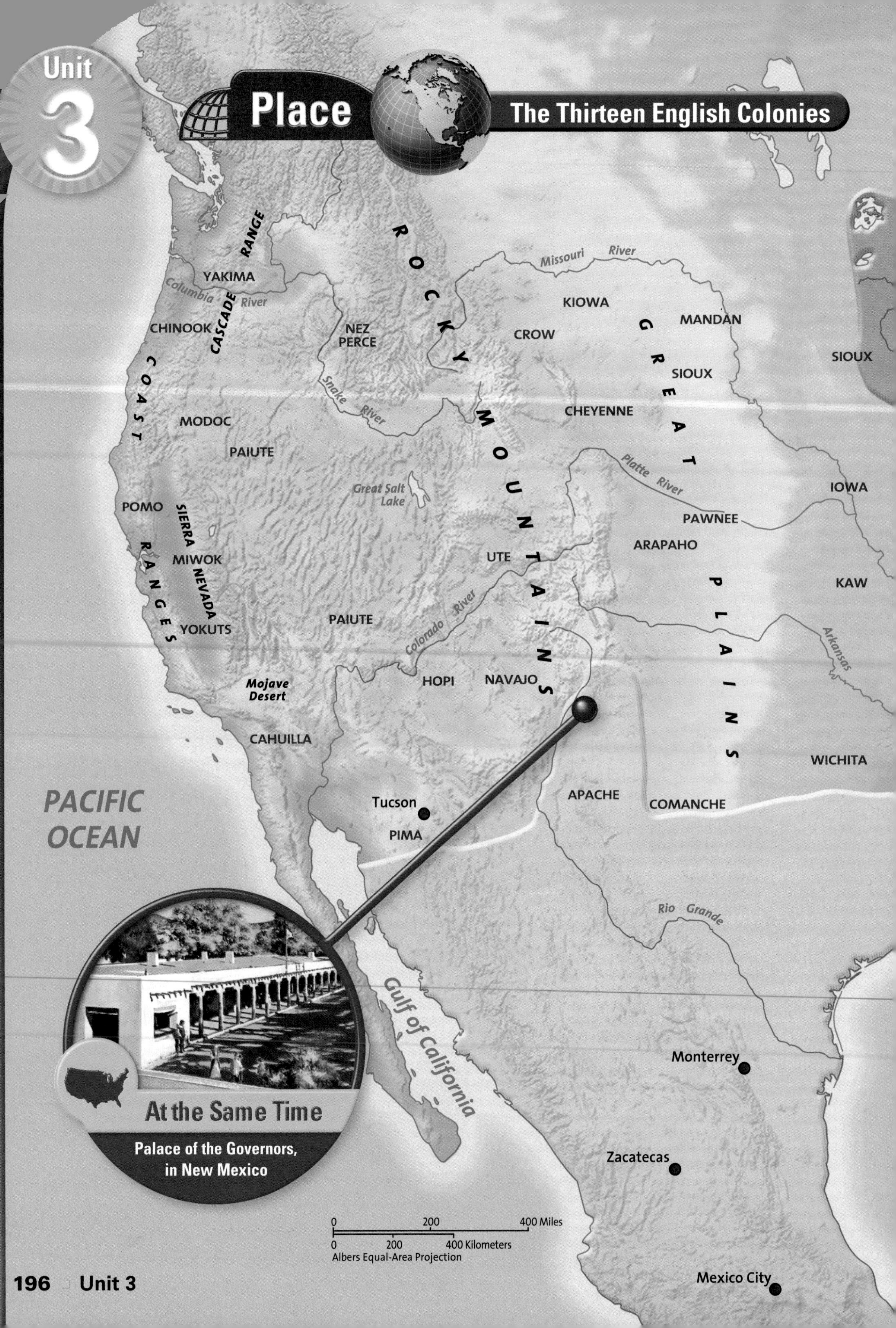

At the Same Time

Palace of the Governors, in New Mexico

Mystic Seaport, in Connecticut

New York Harbor, in New York City

Westover Plantation, in Virginia

Reading Social Studies

Summarize

When you **summarize**, you state in your own words a shortened version of what you read.

Why It Matters

Summarizing can help you understand and remember the most important information of a paragraph or passage.

Key Fact		Summary
Important idea from the reading	→	A shortened version of what you read
Key Fact		
Important idea from the reading	→	

- ✓ A summary includes only the most important ideas from what you read.
- ✓ Always use your own words when you summarize.

Practice the Skill

Read the paragraphs. Then write a summary for the second paragraph.

Facts

Summary

Settlers came to North America from different European countries, but Spain set up the first permanent settlement to be started by Europeans in what is now the United States. In 1565, Spanish colonists founded St. Augustine, in Florida. (In 1565, Spain founded St. Augustine, the first permanent European settlement in what is now the United States.)

Most settlers who came to North America in the 1600s were English. One reason for this was that England had more people than it could feed. Poor people and orphans were sometimes sent to America—sometimes against their will.

Apply What You Learned

 **Summarize Read the paragraphs, and answer the questions.**

Young Colonists

Many children came to North America from England without their families. Some of them were orphans. Others were the children of poor families. In England, many parents could not earn enough money to feed their children. Children fled to cities to beg for food. England had a law that said poor children had to be taken in and cared for, but there were usually more children than there were people to care for them.

In the Virginia Colony, tobacco plantations needed lots of workers. The owners of the Virginia Company saw an opportunity to put English children to work. They asked English leaders to allow the company to take children to the Virginia Colony as indentured servants. As indentured servants, the children were required to work for the company for a certain period of time, usually seven years. After they completed their service, they would be given some basic supplies, some food, and their freedom.

Many children, however, did not survive long enough to be granted their freedom. The climate and living conditions in North America were very different from those in England. Sickness killed many indentured servants within the first two years of service.

Indentured service, though, was often the only option for many poor children and adults. If they could survive their period of service, they would earn a fresh start in a new land.

Summarize

1. **Why did many orphans and poor children become indentured servants?**
2. **Why did the Virginia Company want to bring children to the Virginia Colony?**
3. **How would you describe life for young colonists in North America?**

Study Skills

POSE QUESTIONS

Posing, or asking, questions as you read can help you improve your understanding.

- **Think of questions that might be answered by reading. For example, you may ask how events are related.**
- **Use the questions to guide your reading. Look for answers as you read.**

Questions	Answers
In what ways were the settlers in Massachusetts like those who settled at Plymouth?	Like the settlers at Plymouth, the settlers at Massachusetts wanted to live by their Christian ideas.
Why did people settle in areas near the colony of Massachusetts?	

Apply As You Read

Before you read the chapter, write a list of questions. Look for the answers as you read. Be sure to look also for the answer to complete the chart above.

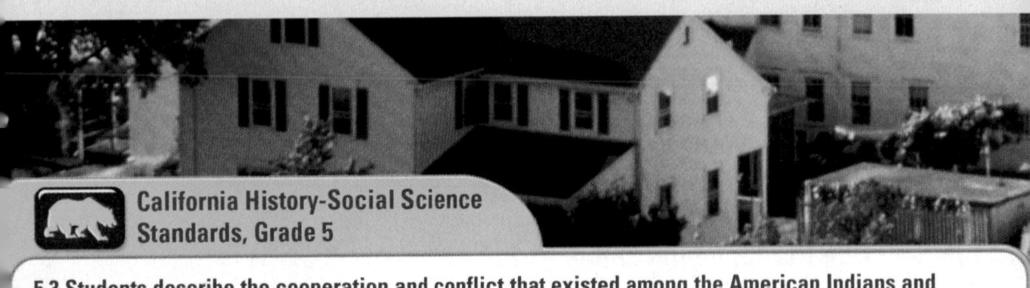

California History-Social Science Standards, Grade 5

5.3 Students describe the cooperation and conflict that existed among the American Indians and between the Indian nations and the new settlers.
5.4 Students understand the political, religious, social, and economic institutions that evolved in the colonial era.

CHAPTER

The New England Colonies

5

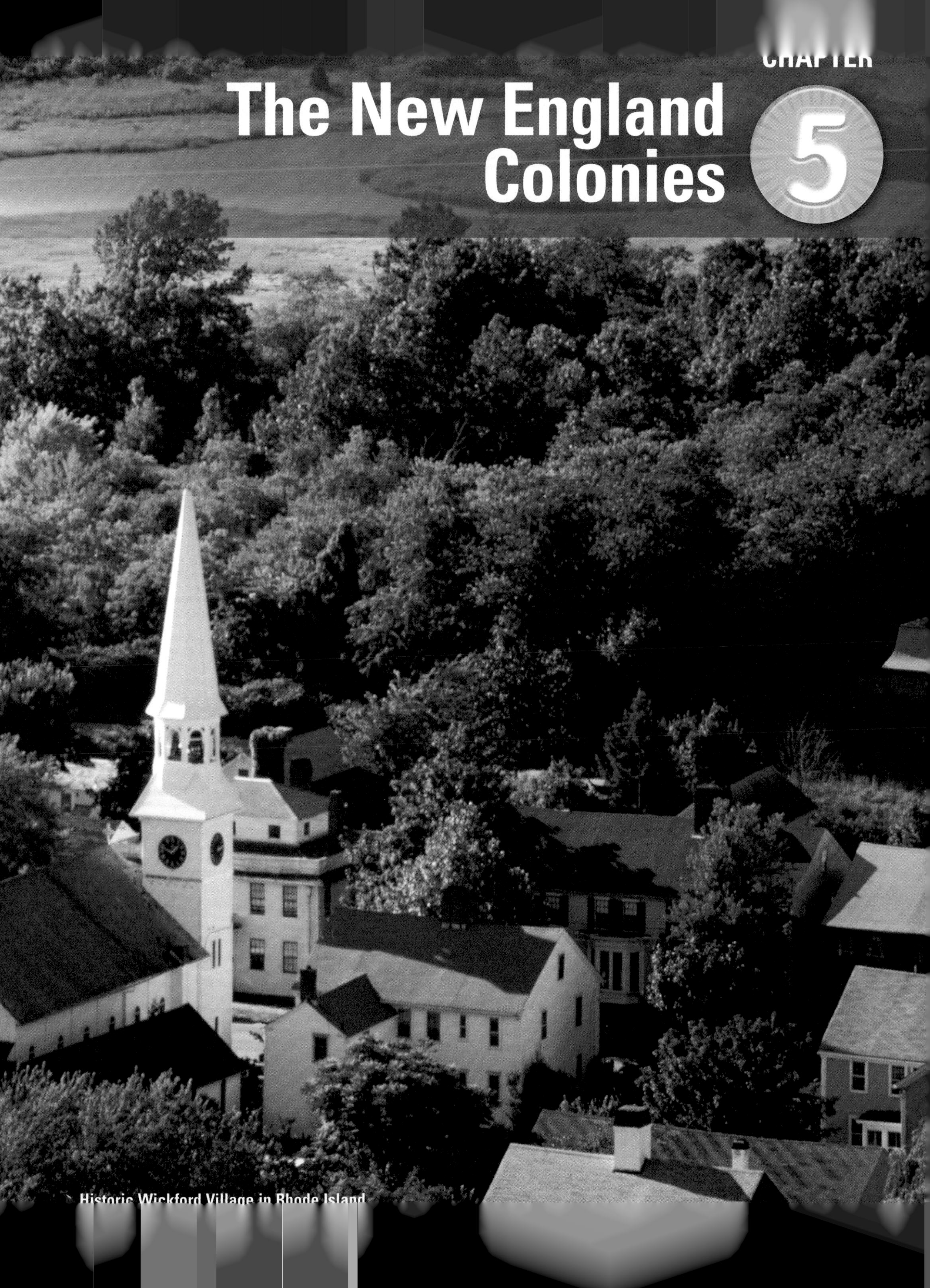

Historic Wickford Village in Rhode Island

Start with a Story

The Courage of Sarah Noble

written by Alice Dalgliesh
illustrated by Greg Newbold

In 1707, eight-year-old Sarah Noble lived in Westfield, Massachusetts, with her mother, father, and seven brothers and sisters. When her father, John, decided to move the family to Connecticut, Sarah offered to go with him to cook while he built a new home for their family.

At her new home, Sarah befriended Tall John and his family, American Indians who lived nearby. When Sarah's father traveled back to Massachusetts to get the rest of his family, Tall John's family cared for Sarah. Read now about Sarah's experiences in the Indian village.

October days were warm and sunny. The Indian women spread the corn out to dry. At night Sarah helped them to cover it carefully, so the heavy dew would not wet it.

There were many things to do. Tall John's wife taught Sarah how to weave a basket. And because Sarah's clothes were stiff and heavy, the Indian woman made her clothes of deerskin, such as the Indians wore when the days grew colder. She also made a pair of deerskin moccasins. Sarah's feet felt light and free; she walked softly as the Indian children did.

Often she thought of her family. Were they on the way? Would Hannah and Margaret be afraid of wolves? Stephen would not be. And the baby was too young to know about the danger . . .

There was nothing, she thought, to be afraid of here with Tall John and his family. But there *was*.

The pleasant, quiet days came to an end, and all at once Sarah felt that there was fear and disturbance in the air.

disturbance disorder, trouble

More Indians kept watch on Guarding Hill. The Indians from the North must be coming.

So Sarah scarcely knew whether to sleep at night. Suppose . . . Suppose . . . But tired from long days in the sun she slept at last, always with a fold of her cloak caught in her hand. And before she slept she said to herself:

Keep up your courage, Sarah Noble. Keep up your courage.

Once in the night she wakened and listened. Tall John had told her, partly in words and partly by signs, that all along the Great River there were hills like Guarding Hill, where men kept watch. If the Indians from the North were coming, the word would be passed from hill to hill by calling—and the villages would be ready.

Sarah listened and listened. Once she seemed to hear a long, low wailing.

Was this the signal? Were the Indians coming down from the North?

wailing a sad cry

She waited for the village to waken, but everything was still. In the darkness she could hear the even sleep-breathing of Tall John and his wife, of Small John and Mary.

"Why, it's nothing but a wolf!" said Sarah. Soon her heart beat quietly and she, too, was breathing evenly in sleep.

In the morning Tall John told her that there had been fear—but the danger had passed. The river villages would not be raided.

So forgetting all her fears of the night before, Sarah played with the other children. It was such a charming game they played in the warm sunshine. Taking off all their moccasins they placed them in a row, then hid a pebble in one. Sarah was pleased when it came her turn to guess—and she guessed right. The pebble was in her own shoe! In the middle of the game she turned suddenly, feeling that someone was watching her.

And it was her father! John Noble stood there, saying not a word. His eyes crinkled up at the corners the way they did when he was amused, and he said, "Sarah! I had thought you were one of the Indian children!"

"Father!" said Sarah, and ran to him. "Has my mother come?"

"We are all here, now," said her father. "I have come to take you home. But, daughter, I think it would be well to put on your own clothes, or your mother will surely not know you!"

So Sarah put on her clothes, piece by stiff piece. She now thought of buttons as tiresome, and as for petticoats . . . The moccasins she kept on, for her feet refused to go into those heavy leather shoes. When she was ready to leave, she saw Tall John looking sadly at her.

"You go . . . Sarah . . . " he said.

"I must," said Sarah. "My mother is here."

Tall John said nothing, but swung Sarah up on his shoulder, as he had done many times before.

Response Corner

1. Why did Sarah become frightened?
2. How were the clothes given to her by the Indians different from her old clothes?
3. Do you think Sarah liked living in her new environment? Write a paragraph explaining why or why not.

petticoat a skirt usually worn under other clothing

Lesson 1

Time

1600 — 1750

1630 The Massachusetts Colony is founded

1636 Roger Williams founds Providence

1675 King Philip's War begins

Settling New England

WHAT TO KNOW
Why did people start colonies in New England?

- ✓ Describe the location of the New England Colonies.
- ✓ Identify the people who founded colonies in New England.
- ✓ Examine relations between American Indians and settlers.

VOCABULARY

charter p. 207
dissent p. 208
expel p. 208
consent p. 209
sedition p. 209
frontier p. 212

PEOPLE

John Winthrop
Roger Williams
Anne Hutchinson

PLACES

Massachusetts
Rhode Island
Connecticut
New Hampshire

SUMMARIZE

HSS 5.3, 5.3.2, 5.3.3, 5.4, 5.4.1, 5.4.2, 5.4.3, 5.4.7

YOU ARE THERE

You walk outside your small village and look out at the sea. Ten years ago, you and your family traveled here from England to build a religious community. At first, you were sad to leave England, but you have learned to adjust to your new life. Your experiences have taught you that life in this colony requires hard work and a strong spirit. Recently, you have heard that new settlers from England will soon arrive. You hope they are prepared for all the challenges they will face.

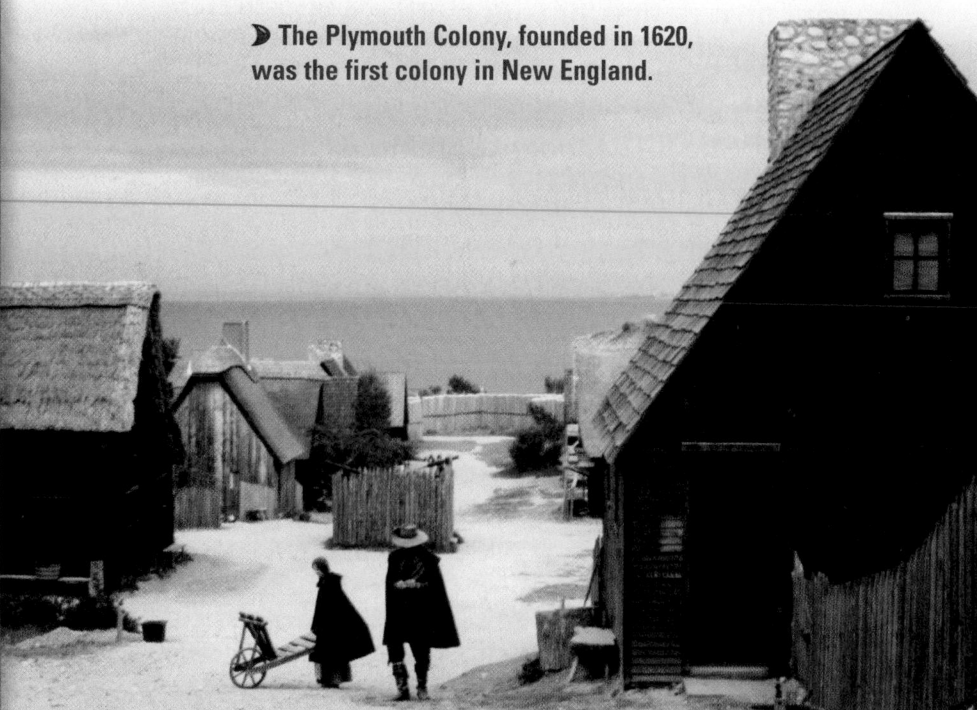

▶ The Plymouth Colony, founded in 1620, was the first colony in New England.

From 1630 to 1643, more than 20,000 Puritans left Europe to settle in New England.

A City on a Hill

In 1628, a small group of settlers arrived in North America with a **charter** from the king of England. This official paper gave them approval to start a colony in New England. With their charter, they built a village called Salem on a bay they called Massachusetts Bay.

Like the Pilgrims, these settlers came to New England to practice their religious beliefs and to start farms and businesses. Unlike the Pilgrims, however, they did not want to break away from the Church of England. They wanted to change the church to make it more "pure." For this reason, they were called Puritans.

In 1630, **John Winthrop** led the second group of Puritans to settle the **Massachusetts Bay Colony**. He hoped the colony would be seen by others as an example of Christian living. In a sermon, he said,

> **"... We shall be as a city upon a hill. The eyes of all people are upon us. ..."***

Winthrop's group of Puritans chose to build their "city upon a hill" to the south of Salem, near the mouth of the Charles River. They named their settlement Boston, after a town in England. Most early settlements in New England were built along the Atlantic coast to make it easier for colonists to get supplies from English trading ships.

John Winthrop

READING CHECK **SUMMARIZE**
Why did the Puritans found the Massachusetts Bay Colony?

*John Winthrop. *Pilgrims and Puritans: 1620–1676*, by Christopher Collier and James Collier. Benchmark Books, 1998.

New Ideas, New Settlements

In 1630, John Winthrop was elected governor of the Massachusetts Colony. He and the other Puritan leaders kept strict control over life in the colony in an effort to create the perfect society. They did not welcome people whose beliefs differed from their own, because they thought that **dissent**, or disagreement, might hurt their colony.

Some colonists did disagree with the Puritan leaders. One of those colonists was a minister in Salem named **Roger Williams**. He and his followers believed that their church should be separate from the colonial government and the strict rule of the Church of England. They also believed that Puritan leaders should not punish people for having different beliefs.

Williams disagreed with Puritan leaders over the treatment of the Indians, too. He argued that the settlers ought to live in peace with the Indians. Before long, Winthrop and the other Puritan leaders decided to punish Williams for his dissent. They held a court trial and found him guilty of spreading "new and dangerous opinions."* In 1635, the leaders voted to **expel** Williams, which meant he had to leave Massachusetts.

*Records of the court of assistants of the Colony of Massachusetts Bay, 1630–1692. AMS Press, 1928.

After Roger Williams was expelled from Massachusetts, the Narragansett Indians gave him shelter.

Anne Hutchinson's weekly meetings were seen as a challenge to the authority of the men who led the Puritan church.

Williams and his family moved south of Salem to what is now called Narragansett (nar•uh•GAN•suht) Bay. For a short time, they lived near the coast with the Narragansett Indians. Many of Williams's followers soon joined him there. In 1636, Williams bought land from the Narragansett and founded a settlement that he called Providence.

Williams organized a settlement based on the **consent**, or agreement, of the people and a spirit of cooperation with the Indians. The new settlement gave its people the freedom to follow any religion they chose.

The leaders of the Massachusetts Bay Colony faced another challenge to their authority, or power, from a colonist named **Anne Hutchinson**. Hutchinson questioned the teachings of the Puritan ministers and started holding popular religious meetings at her home.

Hutchinson's actions angered many Puritan leaders. In 1637, they brought her to trial on charges of **sedition** (sih•DIH•shuhn), or speaking in ways that caused others to work against the government. Hutchinson was found guilty and expelled from the colony.

With her family and several followers, Hutchinson left to start a settlement on an island near Providence. That settlement later joined Williams's settlement under the charter that formed the colony of **Rhode Island** in 1647.

READING CHECK **SUMMARIZE**
Why did Roger Williams wish to start a new settlement?

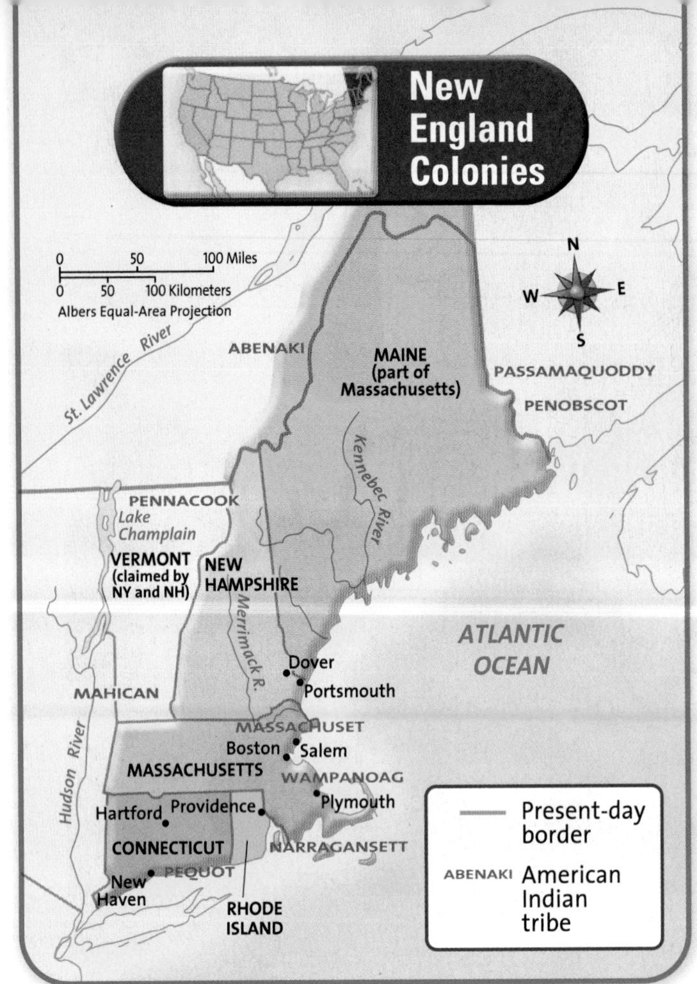

ANALYSIS SKILL Analyze Maps

Regions Which of the New England Colonies had the smallest amount of land?

New England Grows

Other settlers moved away from Massachusetts to find better farmland. They left the poor, rocky soil of coastal New England for the fertile Connecticut (kuh•NEH•tih• kuht) River valley to the west.

Most early Connecticut settlers came to find good farmland, but many also came because of their religious beliefs. One such settler was a Puritan minister named Thomas Hooker. He left Massachusetts because he disagreed with the way its leaders ruled. Hooker and his followers founded the settlement of Hartford. In 1636, Hartford and other nearby settlements became part of the colony of **Connecticut**.

In 1639, the leaders of the Connecticut Colony wrote the Fundamental Orders, a plan of government. These orders allowed voters to elect their leaders. However, the only people who could vote were white men who owned land.

Other colonists looking for economic opportunities moved north of Massachusetts. In 1623, a Scottish settler named David Thomson set out with a group to establish a fishing settlement near the mouth of a river. In 1679, this settlement, later known as Portsmouth, joined with others in the area to form the colony of **New Hampshire**.

READING CHECK CAUSE AND EFFECT
What caused farmers to settle in the Connecticut River valley?

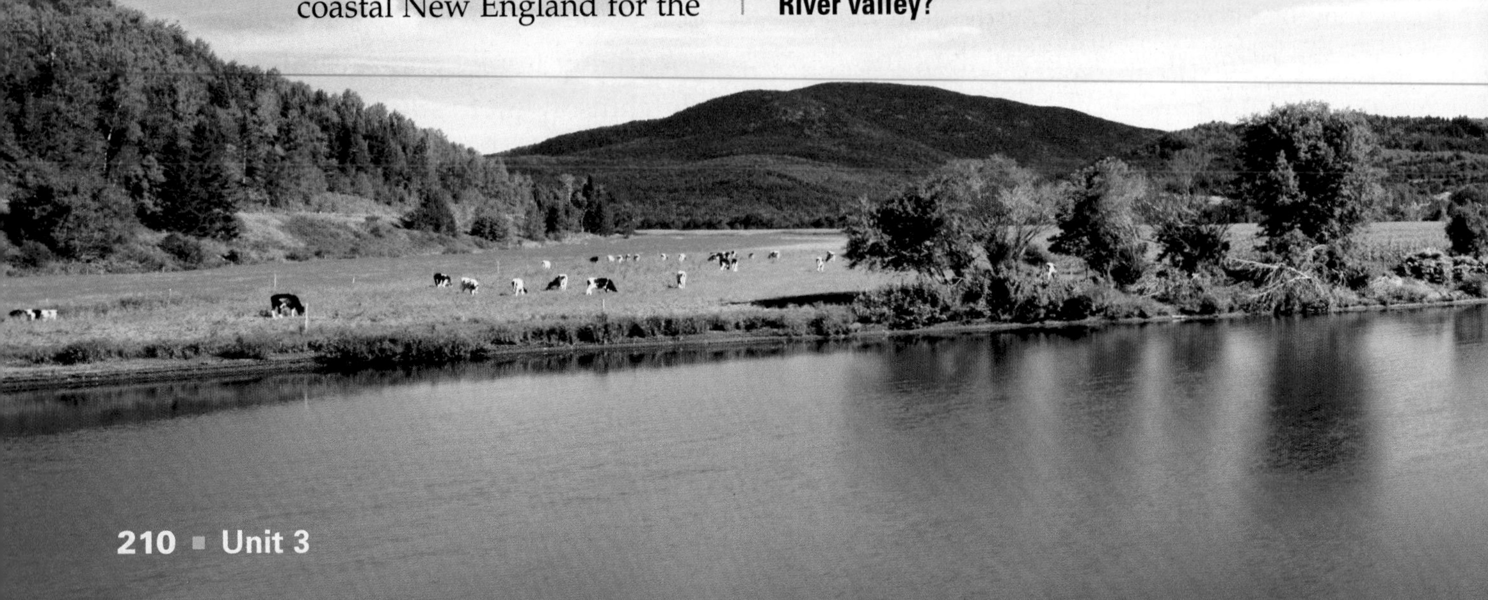

Growth Brings Conflict

As the colonists spread across New England, they settled where American Indians already lived and hunted. In the Connecticut River valley, fighting broke out between the colonists and the Pequot (PEE•kwaht) Indians. The Pequot wanted to stop the colonists from taking over their lands. With the help of the Narragansett and soldiers from Massachusetts, the Connecticut settlers defeated the Pequot in the 1630s. The conflict became known as the Pequot War.

The settlers and the Indians had different ideas about land ownership. The Mohegan (moh•HEE•guhn), Narragansett, Wampanoag (wahm•puh•NOH•ag), and other tribes believed that no one could own land. When they "sold" land to settlers, they thought they were agreeing to share it. The English, however, expected the Indians to leave the land.

Metacomet, known to the English as King Philip, was the leader of the Wampanoag Indians. When more English settlers began moving onto Indian lands, Metacomet decided that the Indians had to unite against the colonists. He said,

Metacomet

"I am resolved not to see the day when I have no country."*

In 1675, harsh feelings between the colonists and the Indians led to an all-out war. The colonists named it King Philip's War. The war began when a group of Indians attacked the town of Swansea in Rhode Island. In return, the settlers destroyed a nearby Indian village.

Over the next year, King Philip's War spread as far north as present-day Maine and as far south as Connecticut. In the end, both sides suffered terrible losses. Among the colonists, 1 of every 16 men died in battle. At least 3,000 American Indians, including Metacomet, died.

*Metacomet. *The Rhode Island Colony* by Dennis Fradin. Children's Press, 1989.

The Connecticut River flows through present-day New Hampshire, Vermont, Massachusetts, and Connecticut.

Cultural Heritage

American Indian Place Names

Most of New England's native people belonged to the Algonquian language group. Many place names in New England reflect this Algonquian heritage. The name *Massachusetts*, for example, means "at the big hill" in the Algonquian language. The name *Connecticut* comes from the Mohegan Indian word *quinnituqut*, meaning "at the long tidal river." Other places in the region, such as Narragansett Bay, were named for the tribes that lived there.

Some tribes were nearly wiped out, and most were forced to give up their lands.

Settlers soon moved onto those lands. Some began settling in western Connecticut, while others moved into present-day Vermont, northern New Hampshire, and Maine. The **frontier**, or the lands beyond the areas already settled by colonists, was being pushed west, too. By 1700, more than 90,000 colonists lived in New England.

READING CHECK **SUMMARIZE**
What were the two major effects of King Philip's War?

Summary

English settlers came to New England and built colonies along the Atlantic coast. Many lived by their religious beliefs. Over time, more settlers arrived, forcing American Indians to leave their lands.

The Niantic Indians, along with several other groups, did not take part in King Philip's War.

REVIEW

1. Why did people start colonies in New England?
2. Use the term **dissent** in a sentence about Roger Williams.
3. How did the physical features of New England affect colonists' decisions about where to settle?

CRITICAL THINKING

4. Why do you think the leaders of the Massachusetts Bay Colony forced out colonists who disagreed with their rule?
5. ANALYSIS SKILL In what ways did the actions of John Winthrop, Roger Williams, Anne Hutchinson, and Thomas Hooker show the importance of religious belief in early New England government?
6. **Draw a Map** Make a map that shows the location of the New England colonies. Your map should also list the date each colony was established and the person or group that founded it.
7. Focus Skill **SUMMARIZE**
On a separate sheet of paper, copy and complete this graphic organizer.

Key Fact
Metacomet asked Indians to unite.

Key Fact
Indians and settlers disagreed about land ownership.

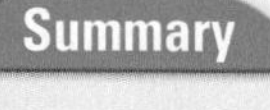

Summary

Anne Hutchinson

Biography

Trustworthiness
Respect
Responsibility
Fairness
Caring
Patriotism

*"You condemn me for speaking what in my conscience I know to be truth."**

Anne Hutchinson spoke those words at her trial in 1637, shocking the other colonists in her Puritan community. By defending her right to have her own religious beliefs, she was challenging the authority of the colony's leaders.

Hutchinson was born Anne Marbury in England in 1591. As a child, she looked up to her father, a church official who spoke out against the Church of England. At the age of 21, Anne Marbury married William Hutchinson, with whom she raised 15 children. In 1634, the Hutchinson family moved to Massachusetts.

At her new home in Boston, Hutchinson shared her beliefs at prayer meetings. She said that people did not need to follow church laws in order to please God. The colony's leaders said she had broken the law, so they put her on trial and voted to expel her from Massachusetts.

In 1638, with her family and followers, Hutchinson settled in what later became the Rhode Island Colony. After her husband died, she moved her family to what is now New York, where she was killed in an Indian raid in 1643. Anne Hutchinson's struggle for religious freedom set an example for others in her time.

*Anne Hutchinson. *Anne Hutchinson, Guilty or Not? A Closer Look at Her Trials* by Jean Cameron. Peter Lang Publishing, 1994.

Why Character Counts

In what ways did Anne Hutchinson struggle to be treated fairly?

Bio Brief

1591 — Born 1591

1643 — Died 1643

1634 Hutchinson moves to Boston and starts holding religious meetings

1637 Hutchinson is put on trial and expelled from Massachusetts

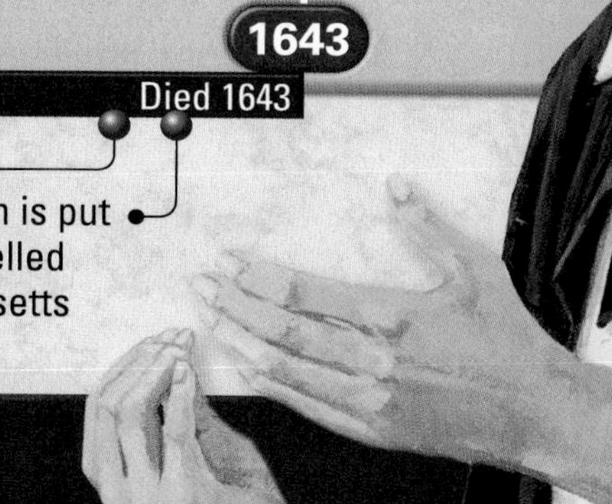

Interactive Multimedia Biographies
Visit MULTIMEDIA BIOGRAPHIES at www.harcourtschool.com/hss

Lesson 2

Time

1600 — 1750

1636 Harvard College is founded

1647 Massachusetts passes the first public school law

Life in New England

WHAT TO KNOW
How did the Puritans' religious beliefs affect life and government in the New England Colonies?

- ✓ Describe the religious beliefs and practices of the Puritans.
- ✓ Analyze the importance of town meetings and self-government in the English colonies.
- ✓ Describe how towns in New England were organized.

VOCABULARY

common p. 216
town meeting p. 217
public office p. 217

PLACES

Harvard University

Focus Skill **SUMMARIZE**

California Standards
HSS 5.4, 5.4.2, 5.4.3, 5.4.5, 5.4.7

YOU ARE THERE You sit beside your mother on a hard wooden bench in church. Across the aisle, your father and the Puritan men and boys listen quietly to the sermon. The church is cold this morning, but a box of heated coals warms your feet. You watch the sand run down the hourglass on the minister's pulpit. His sermon has already lasted three hours! You try hard to stay awake, because if someone catches you napping, you'll be punished. You wish the Puritans were not so strict about behavior in church.

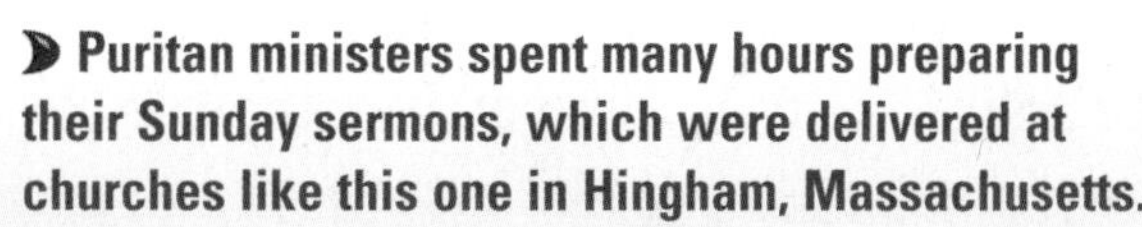

Puritan ministers spent many hours preparing their Sunday sermons, which were delivered at churches like this one in Hingham, Massachusetts.

FAST FACT

The first book printed in the English colonies was a prayer book printed in Boston in 1630.

Early New England colonists often carried their weapons with them wherever they went, including church.

A Religious Life

The Puritans based every part of their lives on their Christian religious beliefs. Before taking any action, they thought about the Bible's laws. They also considered how they might be judged by God and by their community. Their religious beliefs determined how the Puritans lived, worked, and spent their free time.

On Sundays, every person in a Puritan town had to attend church services. Puritan churches had no paintings, statues, or bells. The Puritans believed in simple religious practice. They thought that praying and reading the Bible were the best ways to worship God.

A Puritan church service lasted for most of the day, with a break for a meal at noon. People sat on hard wooden benches and could not nap. A person who fell asleep or did not behave properly was punished in front of everyone else.

The Puritans harshly punished people who missed church or who spoke out in dissent. The usual punishment for such behavior was several hours in the town stocks. In the stocks, a person's head, hands, and feet were locked uncomfortably into a wooden frame. Anyone who passed by could scold the person.

The Puritans lived by strict rules. For example, they discouraged stage plays and card games. They believed that such activities wasted time and dishonored God. Instead, they focused on working hard.

READING CHECK **SUMMARIZE**
How did the religious beliefs of the Puritans affect their daily lives?

A New England Town

Most people in colonial New England lived in small towns. The small size of a Puritan town made people feel that they belonged to a community. It also made it easier for them to help one another. People relied on their community for support. To be united, they lived, worked, and worshipped close together.

At the center of each town was the **common**. This was a parklike area shared by all the townspeople and used for grazing cattle, sheep, and other livestock. The colonists built their houses along the sides of the common.

Over time, the people added other buildings around the common. Larger towns in New England usually had an inn for travelers. In nearly every town, a school was built close to the common. Most towns also had a general store, a sawmill, and a blacksmith shop.

To meet their economic wants, people in most small towns in the colonies depended on a system of barter. Instead of using money, people traded with each other for goods and services. Some colonists specialized in a certain type of work. As a result, colonists depended on one another as they bartered for things. For example, a blacksmith might make

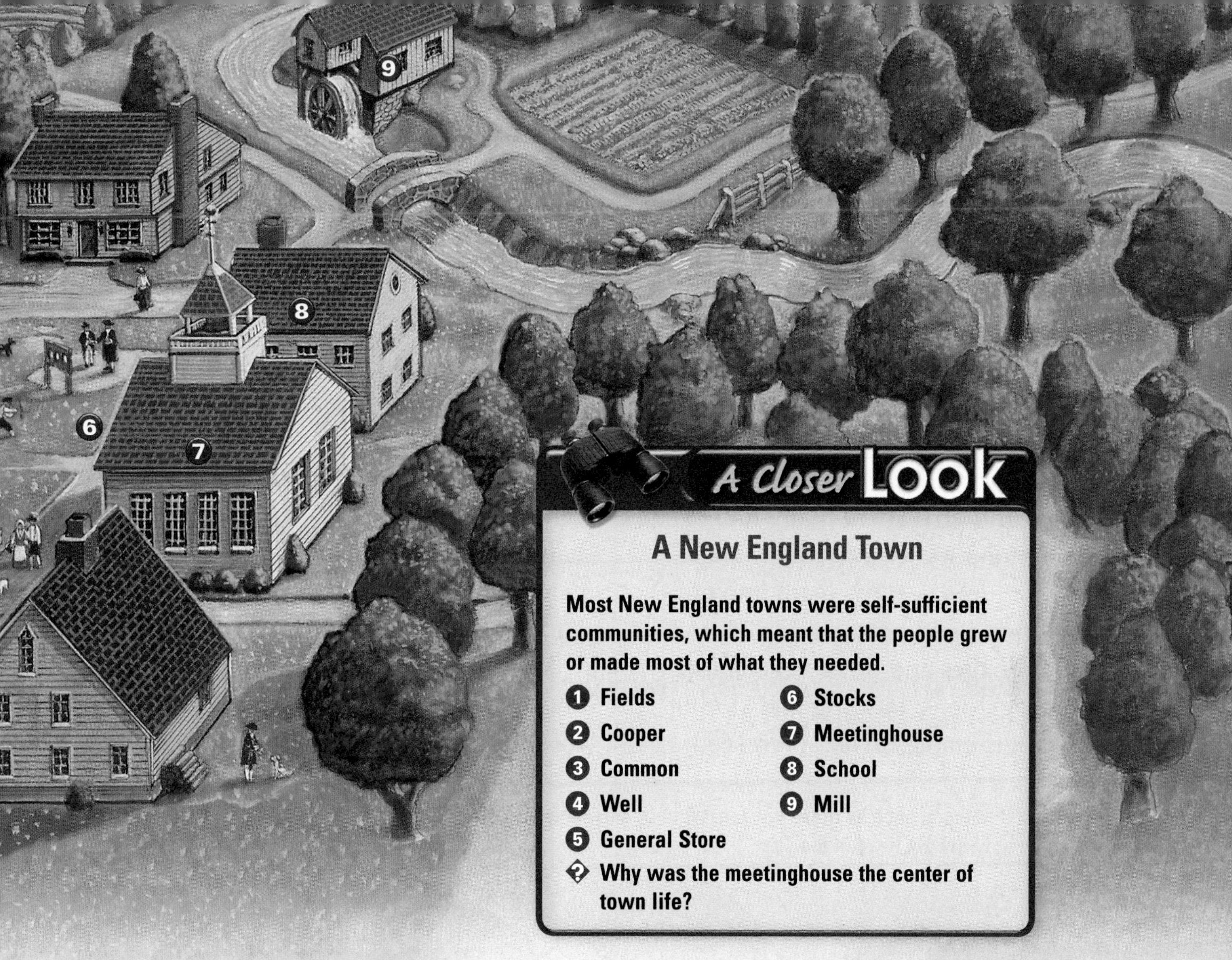

A Closer LOOK

A New England Town

Most New England towns were self-sufficient communities, which meant that the people grew or made most of what they needed.

1. Fields
2. Cooper
3. Common
4. Well
5. General Store
6. Stocks
7. Meetinghouse
8. School
9. Mill

Why was the meetinghouse the center of town life?

iron tools for his neighbor, the cooper. In exchange, the cooper might make barrels for the blacksmith.

Another building that stood near the common was the town's church, or meetinghouse. It was the center of town life, because all religious services were held there. The meetinghouse was also where the Puritans took care of all town government. Everyone in the town could attend a **town meeting**, but only male church members were allowed to vote. By the end of the 1600s, though, any man who owned property could vote. However, women, indentured servants, and slaves were not allowed to vote.

Every year, towns across New England held special town meetings at which voters elected people to **public offices**, or jobs for the community. These jobs included constable, town crier, grave digger, and fence viewer.

The constable's job was to maintain order and keep the peace. The town crier walked around town calling out important news for everyone to hear. The fence viewer made sure that all the fences around the crops were kept in good condition.

READING CHECK **DRAW CONCLUSIONS**
Why were town meetings important to New England colonists?

Home Life

The main room of a Puritan home had a large fireplace in which a fire was always kept burning. All cooking was done there. Most food was roasted over the fire or simmered in large iron kettles hung over the fire. Kettles were also used to heat water for cooking and washing. Baking was done in a small oven inside the fireplace.

Women and girls spent many hours preparing food for their families. They also used churns to turn cream into butter. They dried and preserved fruits and pickled cabbages and other vegetables from their gardens. Pickling and storing fruits and vegetables in jars preserved the food so that it would last through the cold, hard winter.

Women and girls also made the simple clothing worn by most colonists. As fabric was limited, even pieces of worn-out clothing were used to make new clothing and patchwork quilts to put on beds. Nothing useful went to waste.

Women and girls made many other items that their families used every day. They used animal fat to make soap and candles, and they used pig bristles, or hair, to make brushes. Women also took care of the children. Most Puritan families had seven or more children.

Men and boys hunted for food, furs, and hides. They cut firewood and made most of their own tools from wood.

Historical reenactors, such as these women, work at museums and living history sites to show how people lived in the past.

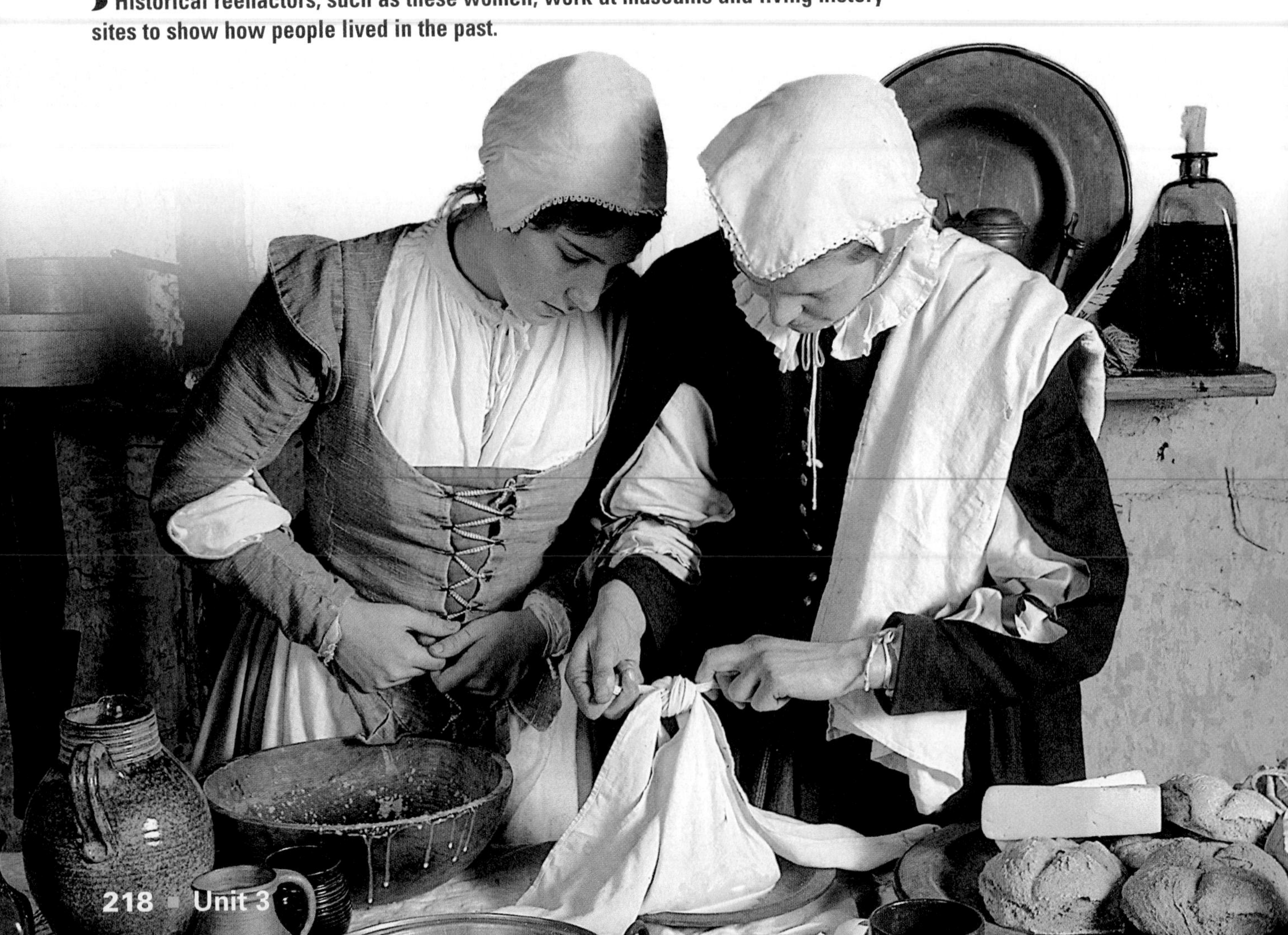

CITIZENSHIP

Democratic Values

The United States has a long tradition of representative government.

In New England town meetings, voters elected leaders for the whole colony. Each town in Massachusetts helped choose the governor. Voters also elected two people from their town to represent them in the colonial government. The governor, his assistants, and an assembly of town representatives formed the General Court, which passed laws and made decisions for the colony. Most New England colonies had similar forms of government. However, their charters all said they had to be loyal to the English government.

The men also took turns patrolling the borders of the town.

Most men and boys spent their days working in the fields outside the town. After clearing trees and rocks from the land, they plowed the soil and planted crops. The colonists grew corn, wheat, rye, and barley. Among the rows of corn, farmers also grew pumpkins and squash. They had learned some of their farming methods from the Wampanoag Indians.

Each autumn, all the people in town worked together to harvest the crops. They sent some of these crops to England in exchange for things such as paper, lead, and paint. They also sent crops to English colonies on the Caribbean Islands in exchange for sugar.

The Puritans raised cattle, hogs, and sheep as sources of food, leather, and wool. They made their own shoes from leather and wore warm clothing made from sheep's wool.

Life was difficult for the early Puritans, but they still found time for some leisure activities. Children usually had few toys, but they enjoyed playing games and sports. At night, families sat around the fire to read the Bible or other religious books. Often, the Puritans' leisure time combined play with work. For example, some children liked to fish and hunt, and others enjoyed sewing and quilt-making.

READING CHECK **SUMMARIZE**

How did women contribute to New England communities?

Schools

Schools were very important to the Puritans because they believed that every person should be able to read the Bible. At first, Puritan parents taught their children at home or sent them to home schools. Then, in 1647, Massachusetts passed a new law saying that every town with at least 50 families must have a school. All the other New England Colonies except Rhode Island passed similar laws. As a result, the New England Colonies had more schools than any of the other English colonies.

Puritan schools were among the first public schools in the English colonies. A typical school had only one room and one teacher. Most teachers were men, and many of them were very strict. Some often whipped students for bad behavior or even for a wrong answer!

The main subject taught in Puritan schools was reading, and many children used a schoolbook called the *New England Primer*. In colonial days, paper and ink were very expensive, so most students learned to read from a hornbook. This was a piece of paper showing the alphabet that was attached to a paddle-shaped frame. To protect it, the paper was covered with a thin, clear sheet of animal horn, sliced so thin that a person could see right through it.

Few Puritan children went to school for very long because their parents wanted them to help at home and on the farm. Many Puritans thought that learning how to read was enough education for most people.

Some boys, however, continued their education. They went to grammar schools, where they prepared to attend college. In 1636, the Puritans

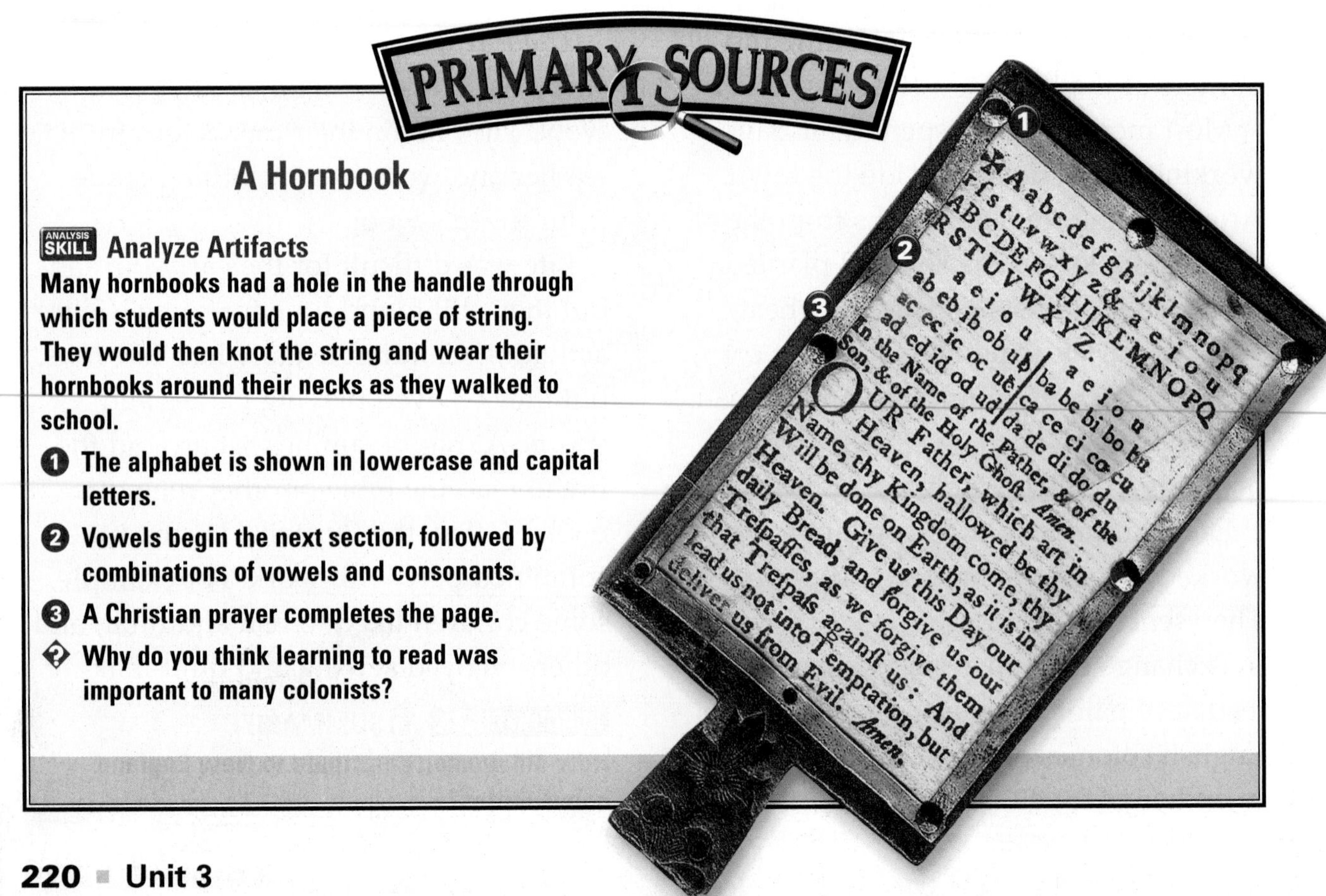

A Hornbook

ANALYSIS SKILL Analyze Artifacts

Many hornbooks had a hole in the handle through which students would place a piece of string. They would then knot the string and wear their hornbooks around their necks as they walked to school.

1. **The alphabet is shown in lowercase and capital letters.**
2. **Vowels begin the next section, followed by combinations of vowels and consonants.**
3. **A Christian prayer completes the page.**

? Why do you think learning to read was important to many colonists?

LOCATE IT

Cambridge

MASSACHUSETTS

Present-day borders

➤ This engraving shows Harvard College as it would have looked in 1725, nearly 100 years after it was founded.

founded Harvard College, now **Harvard University**, to train ministers. It was the first college in the English colonies, and in its first year it had only nine students. However, like the colonies, it would grow steadily through the 1600s and 1700s.

READING CHECK **SUMMARIZE**
Why was education important for the Puritans?

Summary

The Puritan way of life was based on religion. Religious beliefs also influenced Puritan laws and government. New England colonists believed in the importance of education, so most towns had schools.

REVIEW

1. How did the Puritans' religious beliefs affect life and government in the New England Colonies?
2. Write a sentence describing what a **town meeting** might have been like.
3. In what ways did New England colonists practice self-government?
4. How were the people of the New England Colonies able to get the goods and services they needed?

CRITICAL THINKING

5. ANALYSIS SKILL **Make It Relevant** How was an early New England town like your town? How was it different?
6. **Write a Narrative** Write a story about going to school in colonial New England. Your story should describe what a school looked like, the books students used, how the school was organized, and how teachers taught.
7. Focus Skill **SUMMARIZE**
On a separate sheet of paper, copy and complete this graphic organizer.

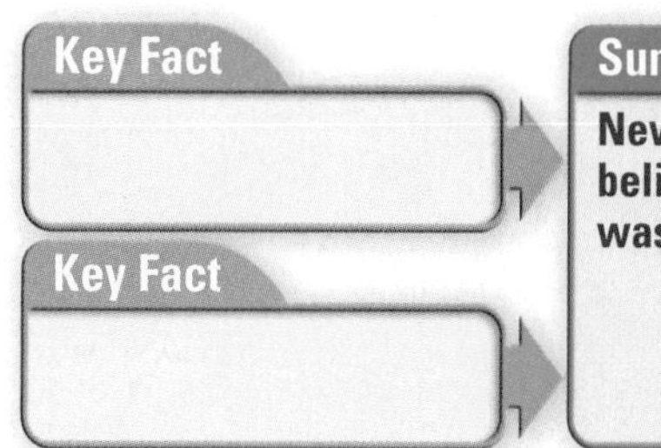

Lesson 3

Time

1600 — 1750

1700s Triangle trade routes are established

1750 Boston's population reaches more than 15,000

WHAT TO KNOW
How did New England's economy depend on the region's natural resources?

- ✓ Explain how a free-market economy developed in the colonies.
- ✓ Describe the triangular trade routes and how they affected the slave trade.

VOCABULARY

free market p. 223
industry p. 224
naval stores p. 224
export p. 226
import p. 226
triangular trade route p. 226
Middle Passage p. 226

SUMMARIZE

HSS 5.4, 5.4.1, 5.4.5, 5.4.6

New England's Economy

YOU ARE THERE You have been digging rows for planting all morning. Your back is aching, but there is still more to be done. Your mother walks up next to you and wipes the sweat from her forehead. She smiles and says, "In a few weeks this garden will give us extra vegetables for you and your brothers and sisters." Your stomach grumbles as you look down at the dirt and wonder why gardens can't grow faster.

➤ Most New England families had vegetable gardens.

Most New England farms had a variety of animals, such as cows, horses, chickens, and goats.

New England Farming

By 1750, several New England towns had become busy cities. Boston, one of the largest cities in the English colonies, had more than 15,000 people. Most people in New England, however, still lived in small towns surrounded by farmland.

At first, New England farmers struggled to grow crops in the region's hard, rocky soil. Before they could plant anything, they had to clear rocks and trees from the land. New England's long winters also made growing crops difficult.

Over time, farmers found ways to adapt to their environment. Many began raising herds of dairy cows and sheep. In time, colonists began to produce a surplus of farm goods, which they sold or traded for goods at local shops.

Farmers traded or sold larger surpluses of livestock, grain, wool, fruit, and firewood in port cities. At the docks, farmers bargained with merchants over prices or items to trade. The merchants then shipped the farm goods to England or to other colonies. There the goods were sold for more than the merchants had paid. Many merchants became wealthy from the steady trade with England.

This system of bargaining between farmers and merchants was part of the **free-market** economic system in the colonies. Colonists had the freedom to choose the goods and services they bought and produced. People were free to compete in business and to set different prices for goods and services.

READING CHECK **SUMMARIZE**
What did farmers do with their surplus goods?

Because colonists made so many things out of wood, carpenters were always busy. This reenactor is shaving a wooden board using the same kinds of tools colonists would have used.

Logging and Shipbuilding

The lumber industry made up a large part of the colonists' free-market economy. An **industry** is all the businesses that make one kind of product or provide one kind of service. In the vast forests of New England, especially in what are today New Hampshire and Maine, loggers cut down trees and sent them to sawmills to be made into lumber. Other colonists used their skills and knowledge, or human capital, to build houses, barns, and churches. Much of the lumber, though, was sent to markets in England, where there were fewer trees.

The forests of New England provided the raw materials to make ships, too. Logs cut in forests were floated down rivers to coastal towns. There, workers used the logs to produce **naval stores**, products used to build and repair ships. With boards of oak, shipbuilders crafted the ships' hulls. To make the masts, they used tall pines. Pine also provided turpentine and pitch to make tar, a coating that seals wood and makes ships watertight.

Europeans valued the strong ships built in New England. By the late 1700s, nearly one-third of all English ships had been built in the region. One reason was the low cost of building ships there. In Europe, wood was not as plentiful so it cost more to build ships there than in New England.

The shipbuilding industry contributed greatly to the growth and prosperity of coastal towns and cities. Several New England cities—including Boston and Portsmouth—became major shipbuilding centers.

READING CHECK **SUMMARIZE**

In what ways did the colonists use the forests in New England?

Fishing and Whaling

Many coastal towns in the New England Colonies prospered because of good fishing in the ocean waters. Fishers made a living by catching fish such as cod, herring, and mackerel.

There were so many fish that New Englanders could catch more than they needed. They dried their surplus fish and packed them in barrels. These were loaded onto ships and sent to markets in other English colonies or in Europe.

Thousands of whales, too, swam in the cold Atlantic waters. New England whalers hunted for whales along the coast. After they captured and killed a whale, they towed it to shore. The whalers then cut up and boiled the whale's blubber, or fat, to obtain oil, which was used in lamps.

So many whalers hunted close to shore that the number of whales started to decline. As a result, the whalers began sailing farther out into the ocean. As the years passed, whaling trips became longer and longer. Some whaling ships left their home ports and did not return for months or even years.

READING CHECK **SUMMARIZE**
Why did fishing and whaling become important industries in colonial New England?

New Bedford, Massachusetts

The first English colonists in what is now New Bedford, Massachusetts, settled there in 1634. The settlement was a quiet fishing town until the 1700s, when New England's whaling industry expanded greatly. New Bedford quickly became one of the busiest ports in the region. At its peak, New Bedford had a fleet of 329 whaling ships.

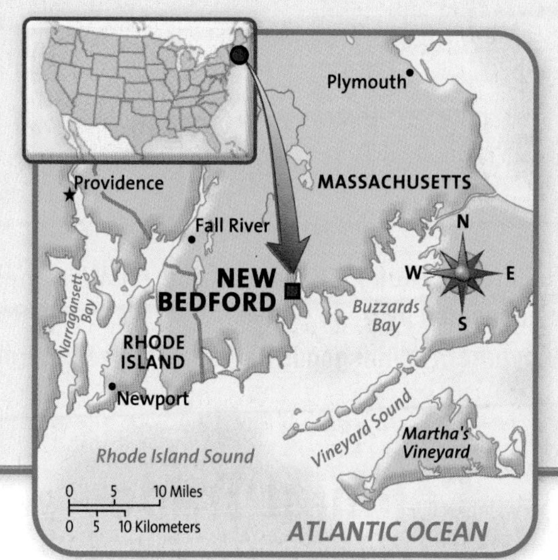

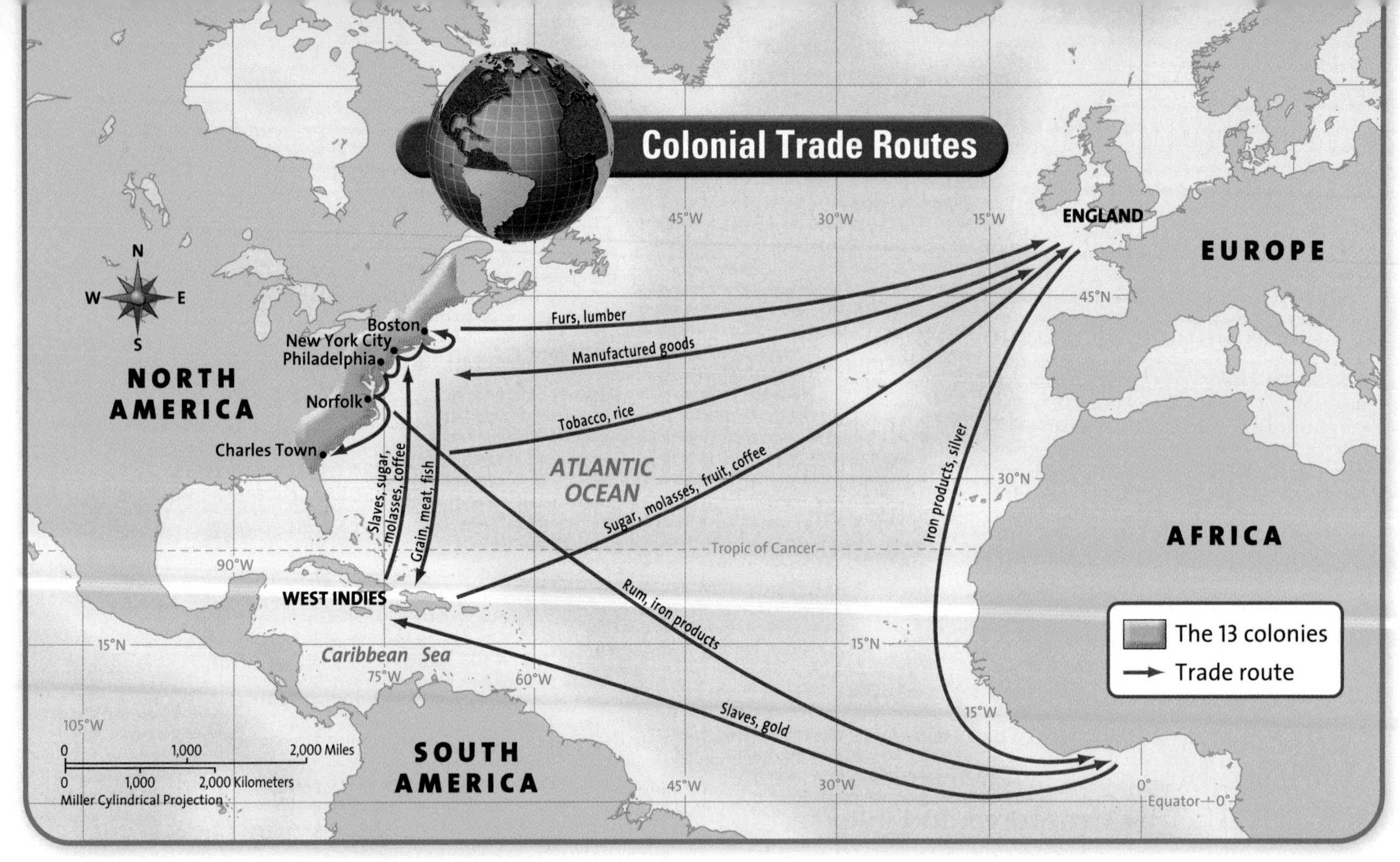

Analyze Maps England, Africa, the West Indies, and the English colonies were connected by trade routes.

Movement What goods did the colonies get from England?

Colonial Trade

As a result of the many ships built in New England, trading became the center of the region's economy. The English government set up strict rules for trade. The government insisted that the colonists send their **exports**, or products leaving a country, only to England or to other English colonies. The government expected the colonists to buy only English-made **imports**, or goods brought into a country.

Trading ships leaving New England carried furs, lumber, grain, whale oil, and dried fish to England. The ships then returned to New England with tea, spices, and wine, as well as English-made goods, such as cloth, shoes, and paper.

Some colonial trading ships made even longer ocean voyages. They followed what became known as the **triangular trade routes**. These routes connected England, the English colonies, and Africa. On a map, the routes formed triangles across the Atlantic Ocean.

Trading ships carried goods from England and raw materials from the English colonies and the West Indies. The ships also carried people who were captured from Central and Western Africa to become slaves. These people were sold as enslaved workers in the English colonies. During this time, millions of enslaved Africans were forced to travel across the Atlantic Ocean from Africa to the West Indies. This long ocean journey was called the **Middle Passage**.

Africans held in slave ships had almost no room to move. This model (above) shows the inside of a slave ship.

The Africans suffered terribly on the slave ships. Many of them died during the Middle Passage. Their long voyage in overcrowded ships was part of a large and cruel slave-trade business. During the 1700s, some people in the colonies became alarmed by the cruelty of the slave trade. Over time, some New England colonists began to form groups that tried to end slavery.

READING CHECK **SUMMARIZE**
What were the triangular trade routes?

Summary

By the 1700s, many industries made up New England's free-market economy. Many were based on the region's natural resources. Some colonists grew crops, cut lumber, or caught fish. Others used those resources to make products. Merchants made their living by trading. Trade routes connected the English colonies, England, and Africa. Enslaved Africans had to endure the Middle Passage.

REVIEW

1. How did New England's economy depend on the region's natural resources?
2. Use the terms **import** and **export** in a sentence about trade.
3. What was the Middle Passage?

CRITICAL THINKING

4. ANALYSIS SKILL How did the free-market economic system affect life in New England?
5. ANALYSIS SKILL How did the relative location of New England towns help the whaling industry there? How did that change with time?
6. **Write a List of Questions** Imagine that you are a colonist trying to decide what type of work you would like to do. Write a list of questions that you might ask a farmer, merchant, shipbuilder, and whaler.
7. Focus Skill **SUMMARIZE** Copy and complete this graphic organizer on a separate sheet of paper.

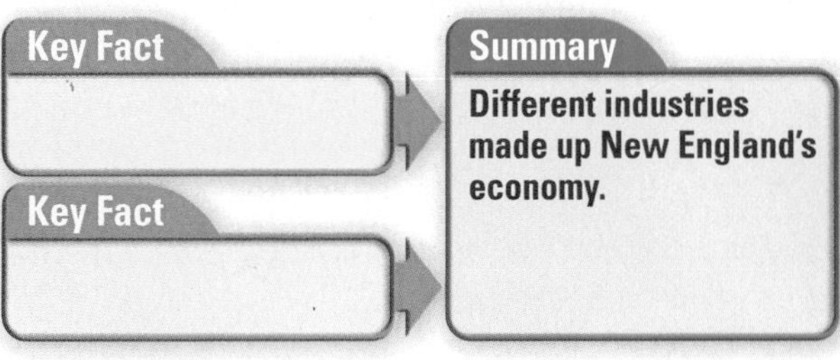

PRIMARY SOURCES

Colonial Homes

Most early colonial homes were simple buildings with only one or two rooms. As a result, most colonists did not have many tools or much furniture. They took care of the things they had because goods were difficult to replace. Most of the objects found in colonial homes were handmade. Colonists made many of their own tools, but more fancy items were often made in England or other European countries. This doll (right) is the kind of expensive item that only a few colonists could have afforded.

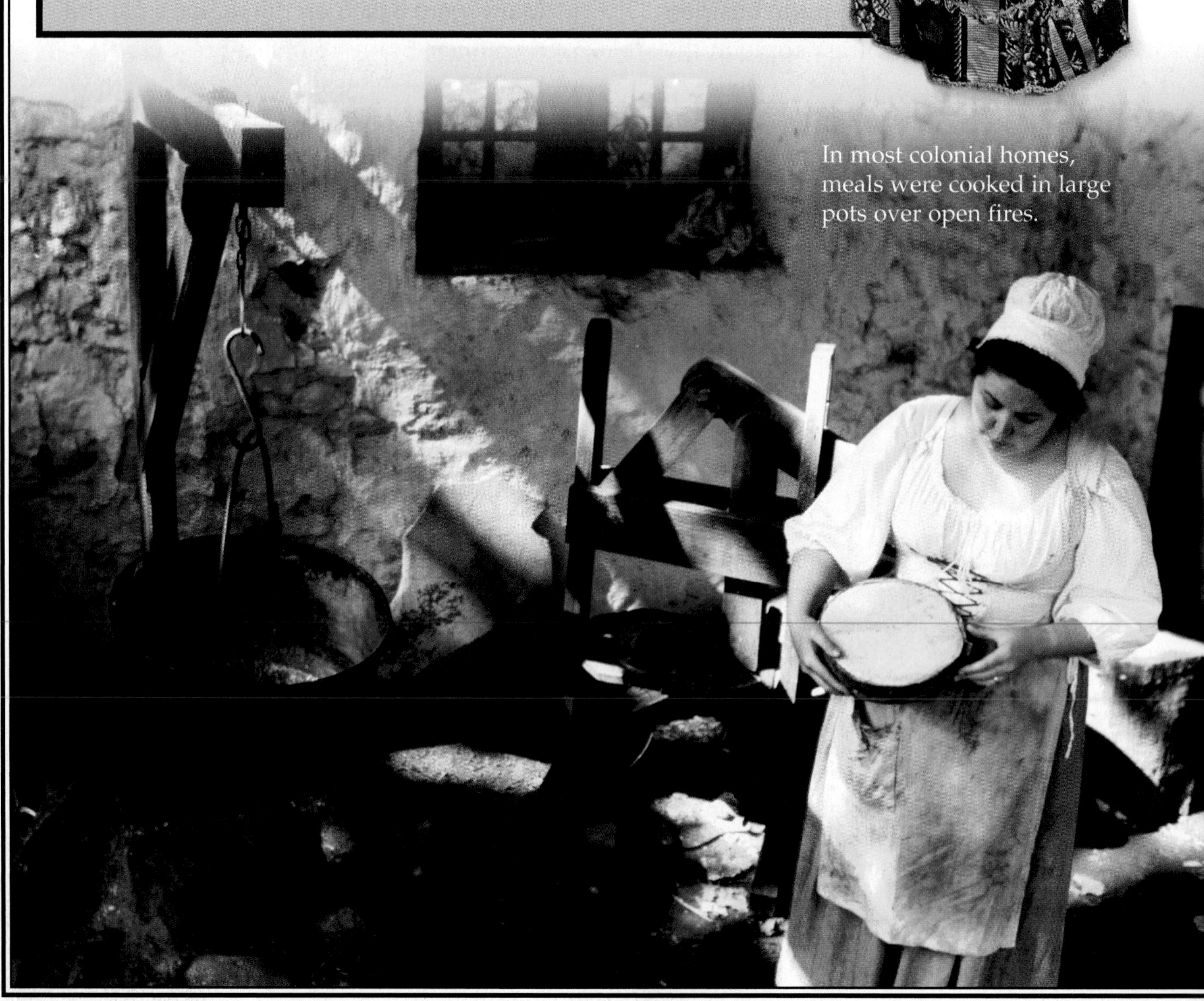

In most colonial homes, meals were cooked in large pots over open fires.

ANALYSIS SKILL Analyze Artifacts

1. What items do you think were made in the colonies? What items do you think came from Europe?
2. How are the decorations on the plate and the bridal chest similar?

GO ONLINE Visit PRIMARY SOURCES at **www.harcourtschool.com/hss**

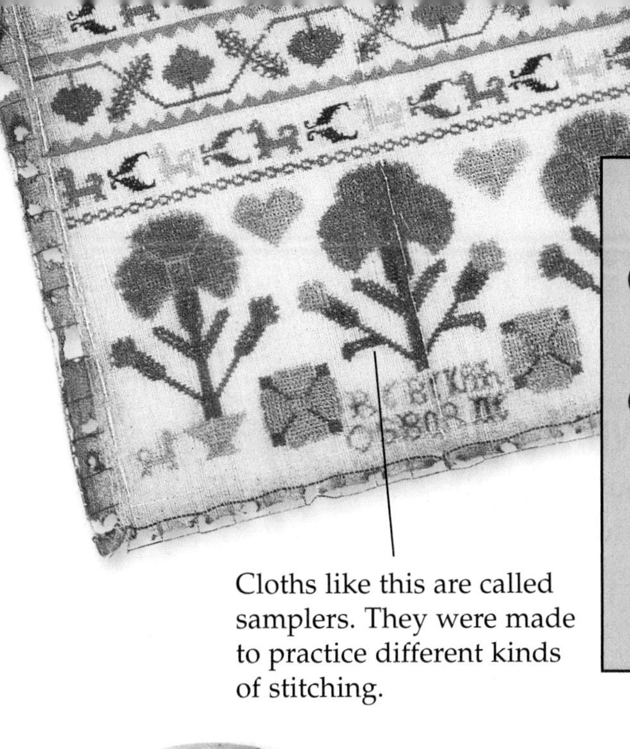

Cloths like this are called samplers. They were made to practice different kinds of stitching.

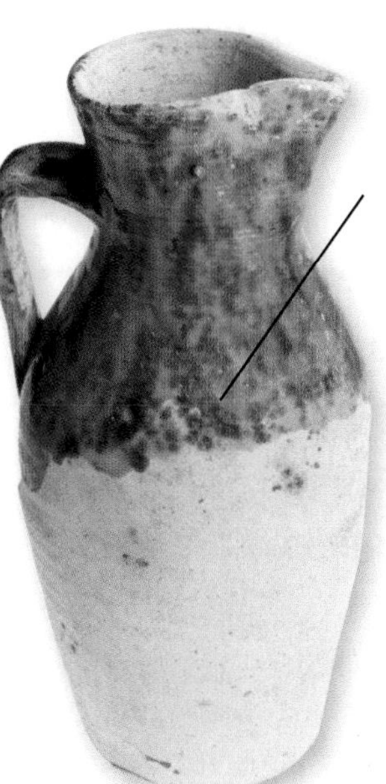

Clay pitchers were found in many colonists' homes.

This plate would have been used for display, not as tableware.

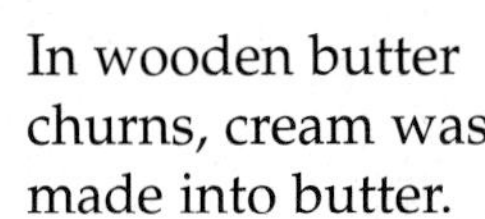

In wooden butter churns, cream was made into butter.

Blankets, quilts, and bed sheets were often stored in wooden bridal chests.

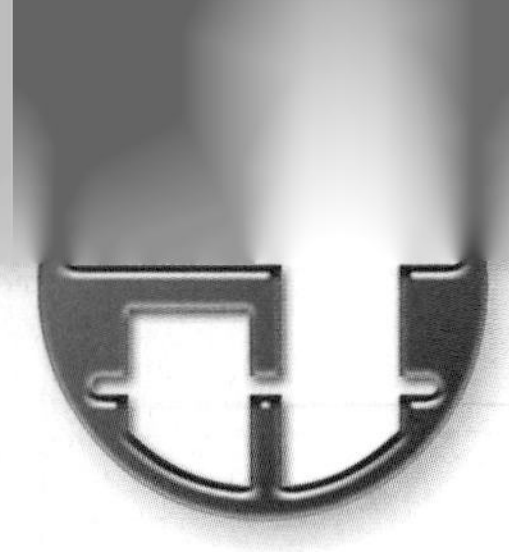

Read a Line Graph

WHY IT MATTERS

The first colonists arrived in New England in 1620. From then on, the population of the New England Colonies grew. Between 1650 and 1700, it increased rapidly.

The numbers that represent populations are often very large. When you read these numbers, it can be difficult to understand their meaning. Putting the numbers on a line graph helps you see the population changes that the numbers represent. A **line graph** is a graph that uses a line to show changes over time.

WHAT YOU NEED TO KNOW

You can use these steps to read information shown on a line graph.

Step 1 **Read the title of the graph. It tells you what information the graph shows.**

Step 2 **Read the labels along the bottom and side of the graph. They tell the kinds of information the graph gives.**

Step 3 **Use the dots on the graph and the numbers along its bottom and side to find exact data.**

Step 4 **Follow the line on the graph from left to right to see how the data change over time.**

The average age for marriage in colonial New England was twenty-three years old.

These reenactors show how an early New England family might have lived.

PRACTICE THE SKILL

Use the line graph on this page to answer these questions.

1. What information does this graph show? How do you know?
2. What kinds of information do the numbers along the bottom and the left-hand side of the graph give?
3. In which of the years was the population lowest? When was it highest? About how many people lived in New England during each of those years?
4. What was the population of the New England Colonies in 1670?

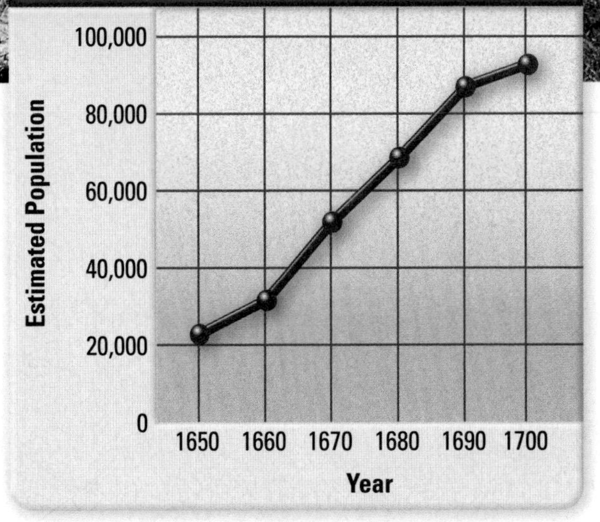

APPLY WHAT YOU LEARNED

Write a paragraph that explains what a reader can learn from the line graph on this page. Include the important information shown in the graph. Then decide whether you think a reader would learn more from the paragraph or from the graph. Explain your choice.

Chapter 5 Review

1630
English Puritans sail to Massachusetts

1635
Roger Williams is expelled from Massachusetts

Reading Social Studies

When you **summarize**, you tell a shortened version of what you have just read.

Focus Skill Summarize

Complete this graphic organizer to show that you can summarize the role of religion in the New England Colonies. A copy of this graphic organizer appears on page 56 of the Homework and Practice Book.

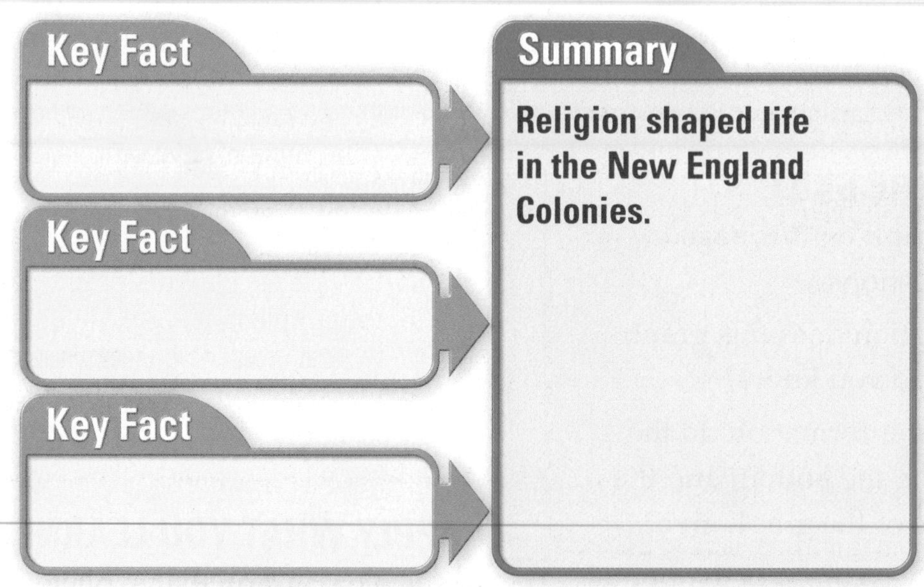

California Writing Prompts

Write a Narrative Imagine that you are about to sail to New England in 1630. Think about how you feel about leaving your home for an unknown place. Write a story that describes the setting and the conflicts you feel.

Write a Persuasive Letter Imagine that it is 1650 and you are part of a group that wants to start a colony in North America. Write a letter to persuade a company to pay for ships and supplies for your colony.

1675
King Philip's War begins

1750
Several New England towns become busy cities

Use Vocabulary

Identify the term that correctly matches each definition.

consent, p. 209
common, p. 216
industry, p. 224
naval stores, p. 224
imports, p. 226

1. agreement
2. products brought into a country
3. all the businesses that make one kind of product
4. a parklike area at the center of a town
5. products used to build and repair ships

Use the Time Line

Use the chapter summary time line above to answer these questions.

6. When did King Philip's War begin?
7. How many years after Puritans sailed to Massachusetts was Roger Williams expelled?

Apply Skills

Read a Line Graph

8. Study the line graph on page 231. About how much did the population of the New England Colonies grow between 1660 and 1670? Explain how you got your answer.

Recall Facts

Answer these questions.

9. What religious group made up the majority of New England's early settlers?
10. What were four important industries in the New England Colonies?

Write the letter of the best choice.

11. How did New England colonists practice self-government?
    A They attended town meetings.
    B They let the English government make all important decisions.
    C They allowed Spain to rule them.
    D They banned slavery.
12. Why did most early colonists settle in New England?
    A to trade for furs with American Indians
    B to start plantations
    C to start gold and silver mines
    D to live according to their religious beliefs

Think Critically

13. ANALYSIS SKILL What were some of the effects of the Puritans settling New England?
14. ANALYSIS SKILL List the names of all the New England Colonies in the order in which they were founded.

Study Skills

QUESTION-AND-ANSWER RELATIONSHIPS

By knowing that different types of questions need different types of answers, you will know how to write proper responses.

- **Questions with the words *who, what, where, when,* and *how* require you to use details in your answers.**
- **Questions that ask you to look at links between topics require that you make connections in your answers.**

Questions About Details	Questions About Connections
Question: Who was William Penn?	Question: How was William Penn's colony different from Massachusetts?
Answer: Quaker and founder of Pennsylvania	Answer: Pennsylvania had people of many different religions. Massachusetts had mostly people of one religion.
Question: What was the Great Awakening?	Question: What was the effect of the Great Awakening?
Answer:	Answer:

Apply As You Read

As you read, write down any questions you have about the people, places, or ideas discussed in this chapter.

California History-Social Science Standards, Grade 5

5.3 Students describe the cooperation and conflict that existed among the American Indians and between the Indian nations and the new settlers.
5.4 Students understand the political, religious, social, and economic institutions that evolved in the colonial era.

CHAPTER

The Middle Colonies

Pennsbury Manor in Morrisville, Pennsylvania

Start with a Story

BEN FRANKLIN of OLD PHILADELPHIA

WRITTEN BY MARGARET COUSINS
ILLUSTRATED BY RAUL COLON

Before Benjamin Franklin was an inventor, a printer, and one of the nation's greatest leaders, he was a son of a Boston soap-maker. By the age of 10, he was working with his father. Ben had little interest in soapmaking, but he did enjoy books. His father noticed this and arranged for Ben to work with his half brother James, a printer. In the print shop, Ben helped write pamphlets, set type, and even sell newspapers on the street.

After three years working for James, Ben decided to leave Boston. He traveled through New York and New Jersey, looking for work, but he didn't have much luck. Nearly penniless and in need of a job, Ben arrived in one of the most exciting cities in all of the American colonies—Philadelphia. After his arrival, Ben found work with another printer. Read now about Ben's first days in Philadelphia.

Ben Franklin worked at many things and he was a good business-man, but he always thought of him-self as a printer. He had come to Philadelphia to be a printer and no other kind of work entered his head.

After giving away his two extra rolls to an old lady and a boy who looked hungrier than he was, he followed the well-dressed crowds in the Philadelphia streets. It turned out that the crowd was going to the Quaker Meeting House.

Ben went in and sat down to think, but he fell fast asleep. He didn't wake up until somebody tapped him on the shoulder and told him church was over. Deciding that he had better catch up with his sleep before looking for work, he rented a room and slept for a long time. Then he hunted up Andrew Bradford, who was William Bradford's son.

"I just hired a hand," Mr. Bradford said, and this made Ben very sad. It seemed to him he was always just missing the boat.

"Maybe Samuel Keimer could use you," Mr. Bradford said, looking Ben over and liking what he saw.

They went to see Mr. Keimer, another printer.

"Neighbor," said Mr. Bradford to Samuel Keimer, "I have brought to see you a young man of your business; perhaps you may want such a one."

Mr. Keimer fingered his long beard and looked at Ben, whose looks had now been considerably improved by washing and clean clothes. He finally decided to give the boy a job, and Ben at last began to earn real wages.

During that first winter in Philadelphia, Benjamin had a wonderful time. He was a free man, with money jingling in his pockets. His father wasn't telling him what to do, and his brother wasn't bullying him . . .

At that time Philadelphia was the largest town in the American colonies—bigger than Boston and New York put together—and its people were the best educated and the richest. While it was not much like a big city, as we think of big cities today, it was the "city" of the colonies. Though Boston was a huddle of weathered gray houses, rising above the blue harbor, Philadelphia was a town of bright colors. Most of the shop fronts were painted red, blue, green, or yellow, and the big swinging signs in front of them were brilliant with paint and gilt. The carriages that bounced over the muddy, rutted streets were also bright with paint.

The people of Philadelphia wore bright colors and had a taste for fine clothes, although some of the Quakers still wore gray from head to foot. However, the rich Quakers followed the fashion and wore silks, satins, and velvets in all colors of the rainbow, along with wigs and jewelry. The ladies dressed in elaborate clothes, too, and with their high hairdos, they looked very pretty.

Philadelphians loved to have company and parties; they enjoyed getting together to talk and sing

and eat. People had fewer places of amusement to visit in those days, so they stayed at home and did a lot of talking. Conversation was important.

Ben Franklin loved to talk, too, and he read so many books that he had a good deal to talk about. In Philadelphia he met young people his own age who were interested in reading and in other things that he enjoyed. He began to make friends—something that was never very hard for Ben, and something that he continued to do until the end of his life.

His boss, Mr. Keimer, arranged for him to have room and board at the house of Mr. Read. This man was the father of Deborah Read, the girl who had laughed to see young Franklin carrying his puffy rolls down the street.

So began Ben's happy days in Philadelphia, the city that was to become his real hometown for the rest of his life, though he was to live all over the world.

Response Corner

1. Why did Ben Franklin travel to Philadelphia?
2. What made Philadelphia different from other colonial cities?
3. Why do you think Philadelphia would be an exciting place for young Ben Franklin?

Lesson 1

1600 — **1750**

1647 Peter Stuyvesant arrives in New Netherland

1664 England takes over New Netherland and renames it New York

1681 William Penn founds the colony of Pennsylvania

WHAT TO KNOW
Why did people from different places and backgrounds settle in the Middle Colonies?

- ✓ Identify the location of the Middle Colonies and the people who founded them.
- ✓ Describe how religion affected the Middle Colonies.

VOCABULARY
refuge p. 244
proprietor p. 245
trial by jury p. 245
justice p. 245

PEOPLE
King Charles II
Peter Stuyvesant
William Penn
Tamanend

PLACES
New York
New Jersey
Pennsylvania
Delaware

SUMMARIZE

California Standards

HSS 5.3, 5.3.1, 5.4, 5.4.1, 5.4.2, 5.4.3, 5.4.5, 5.4.6

Settling the Middle Colonies

YOU ARE THERE

The year is 1660 and **King Charles II** has asked you to study a map of the English colonies with him. The king is pleased with the colonies' performance. In the north, New England is producing plenty of lumber, and in the south Virginia's tobacco plantations are bringing him great wealth.

"The problem lies here right in the middle," says the king, "with that Dutch colony in the way!"

King Charles II

Fort Orange, built near where Albany, New York, now stands, began as a Dutch trading post.

The Breadbasket Colonies

While the Puritans were settling New England, other groups were setting up colonies to the south. This region, which included what are today New York, New Jersey, Delaware, and Pennsylvania, came to be known as the Middle Colonies. The region was given this name because of its relative location between the New England Colonies and southern settlements in Virginia.

When Europeans arrived in the Middle Colonies, they saw flat plains, rolling hills, grassy meadows, and thick forests. They discovered that when this land was cleared of trees and rocks, it was much better for farming than the land in New England. They also found that the climate was good for growing crops. The summers were long, and the amount of rain each year was just right for crops such as wheat, corn, and rye. The Middle Colonies produced so many crops used in making bread that they came to be called the "breadbasket" colonies.

In addition to fertile land, the region had several large harbors near the Atlantic Ocean. Settlers found that these harbors were connected to many of the region's deep rivers, such as the Hudson and Delaware Rivers. These rivers stretched far inland. Settlers knew these deep waterways would allow large ships to travel to inland settlements, making trade with the colonists there easier. All of the special features of this region attracted many different settlers.

READING CHECK **SUMMARIZE**
What attracted settlers to the Middle Colonies?

New Netherland Grows

This wooden box top has Dutch-style decorations.

The Dutch continued to control New Netherland—which included the Hudson Valley and surrounding lands. However, few people came to the colony because their country, the Netherlands, was wealthy and offered its citizens many freedoms. As a result, by 1640, only about 2,000 people lived in the colony—most of them in New Amsterdam. The colony was also troubled. Settlers had conflicts with American Indians and nearby English colonists over land.

The Dutch West India Company, which controlled the colony's trade, decided that a new leader was needed to raise their profits and bring order. In 1647, it sent **Peter Stuyvesant** (STY•vuh•suhnt), a former soldier, to govern the colony.

In the 1650s, Stuyvesant expanded New Netherland into what is now New Jersey. Then he pushed south into what is now Delaware, taking over the small colony of New Sweden in 1655. New Netherland now controlled more land, but it still did not have enough people to be successful.

To increase New Netherland's population, the Dutch West India Company allowed people from Belgium, Denmark, France, Italy, Spain, and Brazil to settle in the colony. Among these newcomers was one of the first groups of Jews to settle in North America.

Africans also lived in New Netherland. Most were captured and brought to the colony as slaves, the first arriving in 1626. Not all Africans in New Netherland were slaves; some were able to buy their freedom. Yet former slaves were not completely free. Each year, they had to pay their employers in money or goods in order to remain free.

The first slave auction in New Amsterdam was held in 1655.

READING CHECK **SUMMARIZE**

Why did few people from the Netherlands settle in New Netherland?

Peter Stuyvesant left New Netherland after the colony's surrender, but he later returned and lived in New York for the rest of his life.

The English Take Over

King Charles II wanted England to control the entire Atlantic coast of North America. He wanted to build more settlements, control the fur trade, and acquire more lands rich in natural resources. There was one thing that prevented the King from achieving this goal—the colony of New Netherland.

Both the English and the Dutch claimed ownership of lands in the Connecticut Valley as well as on Long Island. Charles II told his brother James, the Duke of York, he could have all of New Netherland if he could take the colony from the Dutch.

In 1664 the Duke of York sent four warships to take New Netherland. When the ships arrived off the coast of New Netherland, the English ordered Stuyvesant to surrender. They said if he did not, they would attack.

Stuyvesant wanted to battle the English. He tried to get the colonists to fight, but they refused. They knew they were outnumbered. The entire colony had less than 150 soldiers. Stuyvesant was forced to surrender and the English took control of New Netherland without firing a shot.

READING CHECK **SUMMARIZE**
Why did England want to control New Netherland?

Founding the Middle Colonies

1650 | 1675 | 1700

1664 The New York Colony is established

1664 The New Jersey Colony is established

1681 The Pennsylvania Colony is founded by William Penn

Analyze Time Lines **All of the Middle Colonies were founded in the 1600s.**

In what century was Pennsylvania founded?

New York and New Jersey

The Duke of York split the Dutch colony into two parts and named them **New York** and **New Jersey**. James kept New York for himself. The city of New Amsterdam became New York City. He gave New Jersey to two friends of his, John Berkeley and George Carteret.

The English treated the Dutch settlers fairly. They promised to protect their rights and property and allowed the colonists to elect some of their own leaders. Most Dutch settlers chose to stay.

At first, nearly all of the colonists lived in New York. To attract more settlers to New Jersey, Berkeley and Carteret offered to sell land at low prices. English people soon began arriving in New Jersey. Many of them were members of the Society of Friends, a religious group also known as the Quakers.

The Quakers believe that all people are equal. They refuse to fight in wars or to swear loyalty to any king or country. Others who did not share these beliefs often mistreated the Quakers. Thousands of Quakers were arrested in England and thrown into prison, and most were forced to leave the other English colonies.

In New Jersey, the Quakers hoped to find a **refuge**, or safe place, where they could live and worship as they pleased. In 1674, a group of Quakers bought Berkeley's share of New Jersey and founded the first Quaker settlement in North America.

READING CHECK **SUMMARIZE**

Why were the Quakers often mistreated by those who did not share their beliefs?

Pennsylvania and Delaware

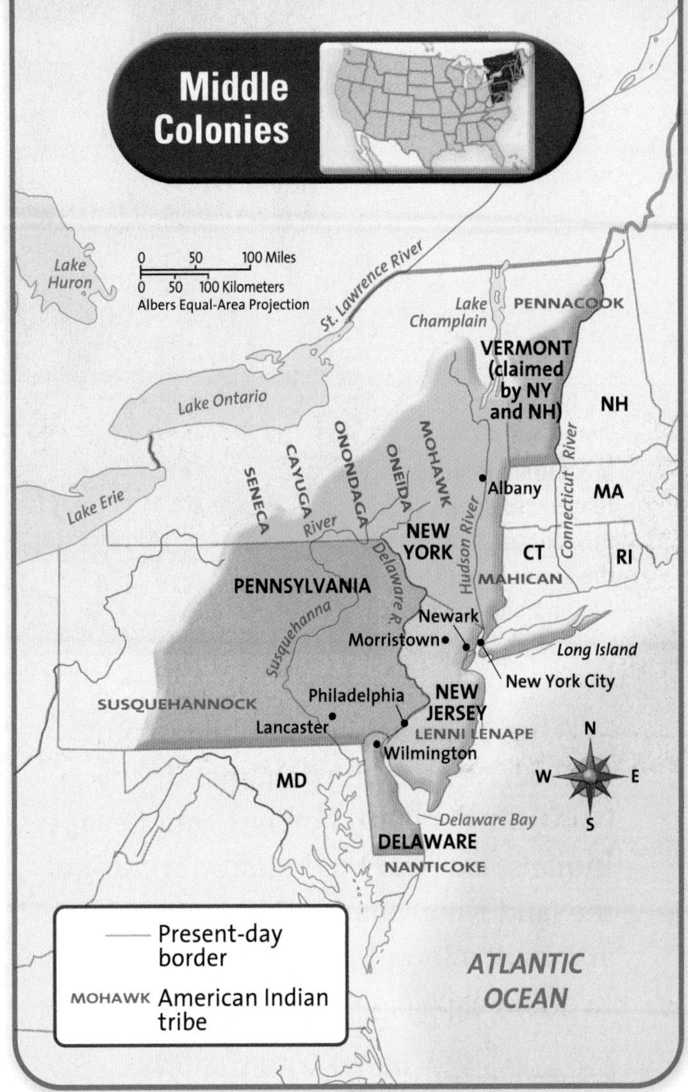

ANALYSIS SKILL **Analyze Maps**

Location What Pennsylvania city was on the Delaware River?

Starting in the 1680s, the Middle Colonies expanded. In 1681, King Charles II gave a charter to **William Penn**, an English Quaker. The charter made Penn the **proprietor**, or owner, of what is now **Pennsylvania**.

Penn was given the land because the king owed a large amount of money to Penn's father. The new colony was named Pennsylvania, which means "Penn's woods." Penn described the colony as a "Holy Experiment." He wanted all the people living in Pennsylvania—Quakers and non-Quakers—to live together peacefully.

In 1682, Penn wrote *The Frame of Government of Pennsylvania*. This plan of government set up a legislature called the General Assembly, which would make the laws for the colony. Penn's frame of government gave citizens of Pennsylvania freedom of speech, freedom of religion, and the right to a fair trial by jury. **Trial by jury** means that people accused of breaking laws have the right to have a group of fellow citizens decide their guilt or innocence.

Penn also became the owner of what is now **Delaware**. When colonists in Delaware asked for their own assembly, he granted it to them willingly. Penn also wanted American Indians to be treated with **justice**, or fairness. In a letter, he told local Lenni Lenape Indians his hopes for Pennsylvania:

> **"I desire to enjoy it with your love and consent, that we may always live together as neighbors and friends."***

▶ **William Penn**

*William Penn. *William Penn's Own Account of the Lenni Lenape*, edited by Albert Cook Myers. Middle Atlantic Press, 1970.

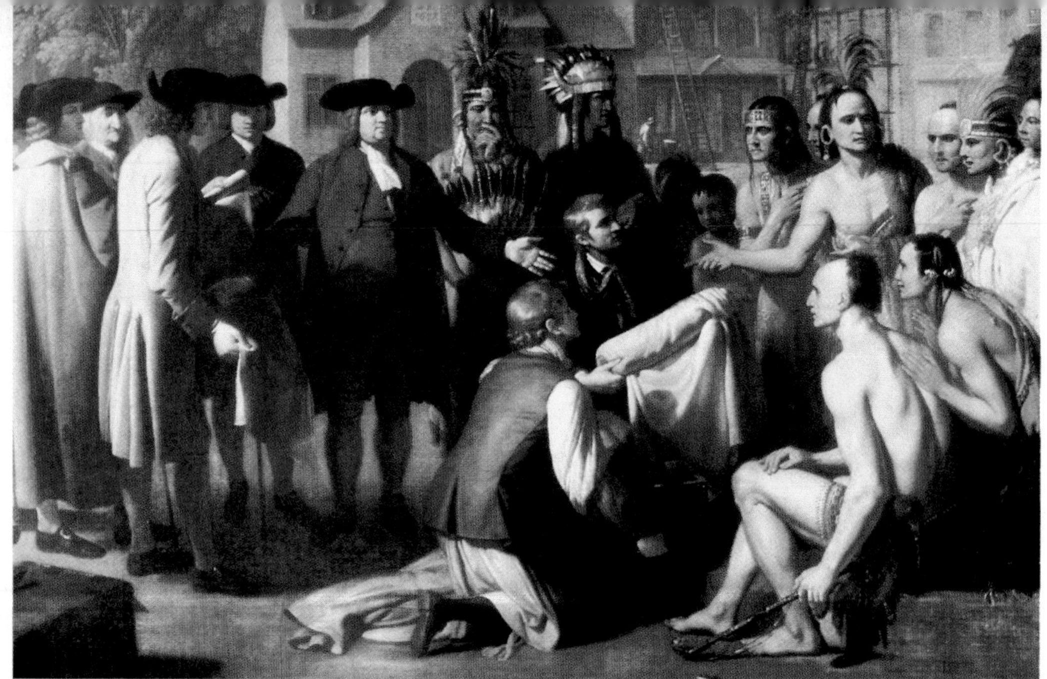

William Penn learned to speak the language of the Lenni Lenape Indians and tried to treat them fairly.

When Penn arrived in Philadelphia in 1682, he met with **Tamanend** (TAM•uh•nend) and other Lenni Lenape Indians. He paid the Indians for most of the land King Charles II had given him, and built a long-lasting peace with the Lenni Lenape.

READING CHECK DRAW CONCLUSIONS
How was Penn's treatment of the Indians related to Quaker beliefs?

Summary

The Middle Colonies were made up of the colonies of New York, New Jersey, Pennsylvania, and Delaware. People from many different places and backgrounds settled in the Middle Colonies. Some settlers came because of the rich land and others came to freely practice their own religion.

REVIEW

1. Why did people from different places and backgrounds settle in the Middle Colonies?
2. Use the term **trial by jury** in a sentence about the Pennsylvania Colony.
3. How does location explain why New York, New Jersey, Pennsylvania, and Delaware were called the Middle Colonies?

CRITICAL THINKING

4. ANALYSIS SKILL Why do you think William Penn wanted religious freedom in Pennsylvania?
5. **Make a Portrait** Draw a picture that shows a meeting between William Penn and American Indian leaders in Pennsylvania.
6. Focus Skill **SUMMARIZE**
On a separate sheet of paper, copy and complete this graphic organizer.

Key Fact	Summary
The Dutch controlled New Netherland.	
England wanted to expand.	

Tamanend

*"We will live in love with William Penn and his children as long as the creeks and rivers run."**

No one was surprised to hear Tamanend speak these kind words. He was a kind leader and was respected by all who knew him. Tamanend grew up along the Neshaminy Creek in the forests of what is now southeastern Pennsylvania. He belonged to the Lenni Lenape (LEH•nee LEH•nuh•pee) tribe, which the English called the Delaware. In his language, *Tamanend* means "affable," or friendly and easy to talk to. The name fit him well. One minister described Tamanend as having "every good and noble qualification that a human being can possess."**

Tamanend's wampum belt was meant to show cooperation between the Lenni Lenape and the English.

Tamanend met with Pennsylvania's colonial leaders five times over the years. In each meeting, he agreed to sell land. The colonists paid for the land with guns, clothing, tools, blankets, and other items. Tamanend divided these items equally among his tribe members. Not all colonial leaders were as fair as William Penn. Yet Tamanend always worked to honor the peace made between the Lenni Lenape and the people of Pennsylvania.

* Tamanend. *The Encyclopedia of Pennsylvania* by Frank H. Gille. Somerset Publishing, 1983.
** John Heckewelder. *History, Manners, and Customs of the Indian Nations.* Heritage Books, 1991.

Why Character Counts

In what ways did Tamanend earn the respect of his people and of William Penn?

Bio Brief

1628 — Born 1628?

1701 — Died 1701?

1683 Tamanend first meets with William Penn

1697 Tamanend attends his last meeting with Pennsylvania leaders

GO ONLINE **Interactive Multimedia Biographies**
Visit MULTIMEDIA BIOGRAPHIES at www.harcourtschool.com/hss

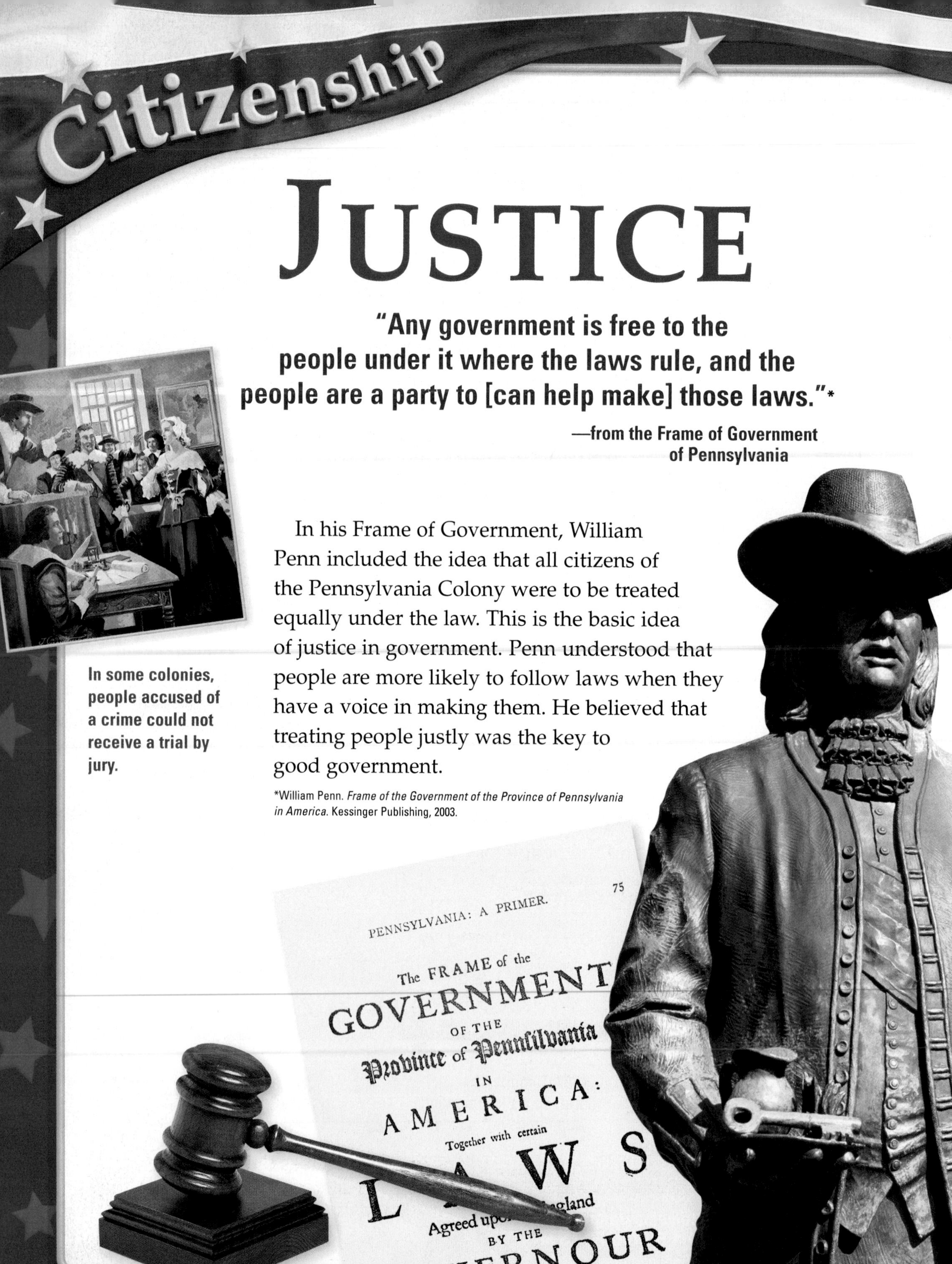

Citizenship

JUSTICE

"Any government is free to the people under it where the laws rule, and the people are a party to [can help make] those laws."*

—from the Frame of Government of Pennsylvania

In some colonies, people accused of a crime could not receive a trial by jury.

In his Frame of Government, William Penn included the idea that all citizens of the Pennsylvania Colony were to be treated equally under the law. This is the basic idea of justice in government. Penn understood that people are more likely to follow laws when they have a voice in making them. He believed that treating people justly was the key to good government.

*William Penn. *Frame of the Government of the Province of Pennsylvania in America.* Kessinger Publishing, 2003.

Lawyers, judges, and juries work to make sure that people receive fair trials.

One of the most important ways in which Penn guaranteed a fair government was to give citizens the right to a trial by jury. At that time, very few governments gave people this right. In a trial by jury, a group of citizens—rather than a single person, the judge—decides whether someone has broken the law. A trial by jury puts the power to make decisions in the hands of the people.

Today, equal justice is an important idea in American government. The Bill of Rights says that no citizen can "be deprived of life, liberty, or property, without due process of law." This means that all people in the United States have the right to equal treatment under the law.

The figure of Justice wears a blindfold because the law is supposed to treat all people equally.

Think About It!

Make It Relevant **The Bill of Rights guarantees United States citizens the right to a fair and public trial by jury. Why do you think it is important for trials to be public?**

Lesson 2

1682 William Penn arrives in Philadelphia

1730s The Great Awakening spreads through the colonies

Life in the Middle Colonies

WHAT TO KNOW
How did religious toleration help attract people of different cultures to the Middle Colonies?

- ✓ Understand the importance of religion to life in the Middle Colonies.
- ✓ Identify the significance and leaders of the Great Awakening.

VOCABULARY
diversity p. 251
immigrant p. 251
Great Awakening p. 252
religious toleration p. 252
militia p. 254

PEOPLE
George Whitefield
Jonathan Edwards
Benjamin Franklin

PLACES
Philadelphia
New York City

SUMMARIZE

California Standards
HSS 5.4, 5.4.2, 5.4.3, 5.4.4, 5.4.6

YOU ARE THERE It's a sunny day in 1699. You're hungry after a morning stroll around the city. You decide to stop for lunch at the White Lion Tavern, where English merchants gather to make deals and gossip.

While you wait for your food, you read the latest news in the papers. The Dutch wall is being torn down to make room for more houses. A new road, Wall Street, is being paved where the wall stood. You're not surprised to read that New York City has been called the fastest-growing town in the 13 colonies.

Many buildings in the New York Colony had Dutch-style architecture, a reminder of the colony's original founders.

Cultural Heritage

Festivals

The people who settled in the Middle Colonies brought their traditions with them when they came to North America. Today, people living in New York, New Jersey, Pennsylvania, and Delaware still celebrate their heritage in local festivals. Each year, people in New Jersey watch players compete in Scottish Highland Games. At the German Festival in Kutztown, Pennsylvania, people enjoy funnel cakes and soft pretzels. In Albany, New York, people wearing Dutch costumes begin the annual Tulip Festival by sweeping local streets. Taking part in these festivals helps people preserve the area's rich heritage.

A Mix of People

By 1700, more than 50,000 people lived in the Middle Colonies. They came from many places and backgrounds. One church minister described settlers of the Middle Colonies as a group of people thrown together from many parts of the world. Such **diversity** made the Middle Colonies an interesting place to live.

Who were the people of the Middle Colonies? At first, most were Dutch, French, Belgian, or Swedish. Then came the English Puritans and Quakers, as well as German, Irish, and Scottish settlers. Most Africans were brought to the Middle Colonies as enslaved people, but some Africans lived and worked as free persons.

The variety of people in the Middle Colonies could be seen in the city of **Philadelphia**. William Penn chose this city's name, which means "brotherly love" in Greek. Like all of Pennsylvania, Philadelphia was founded on the idea that people of diverse backgrounds could live peacefully together. The city covered a strip of land between the Schuylkill (SKOO•kuhl) and Delaware Rivers. Its busy port received many immigrants from different countries.

An **immigrant** is a person who comes into a country to make a new home there. Some immigrants left their original countries to escape war or to find religious freedom. Most immigrants wanted better economic opportunities, especially the chance to buy their own land. Many found more freedom and acceptance in the Middle Colonies than they had ever known.

READING CHECK **SUMMARIZE**

Why did immigrants come to the Middle Colonies?

The Great Awakening

In the 1720s, a new religious movement known as the **Great Awakening** began in the Middle Colonies. This movement changed the way that many people practiced their religion. It spread throughout the 13 colonies during the 1730s and 1740s.

Ministers such as **George Whitefield** and **Jonathan Edwards** gave speeches that marked a change in religious ideas and practices. They often talked about people having a direct relationship with God. Not only did these ministers preach new ideas, they practiced religion differently. They would travel long distances to give emotional speeches to people they had never met.

The Great Awakening helped bring people together, which led to greater **religious toleration**, or acceptance of religious differences. At the new revivals, or large prayer meetings, everyone was welcomed. Poor people could attend, and women played a large role in the movement. During the Great Awakening both free and enslaved Africans participated in religious gatherings. Such equal participation was rare at this time in history.

The Great Awakening was not popular with all people, and in time, differences split the movement, further increasing the diversity of religious beliefs. The number of church members in the colonies grew, as did the free exercise of religion.

READING CHECK **SUMMARIZE**
What was the Great Awakening?

Minister George Whitefield (right) used this movable field pulpit (below) for preaching outdoors.

Farmers in the Middle Colonies often hired free African Americans to help tend their farms.

Religion and Social Life

Unlike in the New England Colonies, many different religious groups lived in the Middle Colonies. Towns in these colonies often had more than one kind of church. A Presbyterian church, for example, might be only a block away from a Quaker meetinghouse. The first Jewish synagogue in the Middle Colonies was built in **New York City** in 1730.

Religion was a major part of social life in the Middle Colonies. After religious services, neighbors would talk and exchange news. Religion also affected the ways in which people viewed one another. Some colonists began to think that enslaving Africans was wrong. In 1688, Quakers in Germantown, Pennsylvania, became the first group to protest slavery in the English colonies.

The social life of colonists was as diverse as their religious beliefs. The colonists found many ways to have fun, depending on where they lived. In cities such as Philadelphia and New York City, there were dances, plays, concerts, and social clubs. Horse races were popular, as were bowling, sleigh rides, and ice-skating.

In the countryside, a barn raising was a big social event. A farm family would invite their neighbors to help them raise the frame for a new barn. Afterward, everyone enjoyed a big meal.

READING CHECK **SUMMARIZE**
How did the Middle Colonies differ from the New England Colonies?

Philadelphia Grows

As proprietor of the Pennsylvania Colony, William Penn planned not only its government but also its settlements. Penn designed Philadelphia, the colony's most important city, with wide streets and many public parks. Penn wanted the city to have plenty of space for people to work and to relax.

When Penn first visited Philadelphia in 1682 it had only ten houses. Fifty years later, it had more than 11,000 residents. Over time, Philadelphia became the largest and wealthiest city in all of the 13 colonies. By 1770 it had more than 28,000 people—a small population by today's city standards but very large for that time.

As Philadelphia grew, it became the home of many famous scientists and artists. The most famous Philadelphian was **Benjamin Franklin**, who helped improve the city in many ways. Franklin set up the first trained firefighting company in the 13 colonies and raised money to help build the city's first hospital. He set up a **militia**, or volunteer army, to protect the city and the rest of the colony. To educate others, he founded Pennsylvania's first college and first public library.

Benjamin Franklin earned his living as a printer. He printed the *Pennsylvania Gazette* newspaper. He also wrote and published *Poor Richard's Almanack*, a yearly book that had a calendar, weather forecasts, stories, jokes, and wise sayings. It was very popular and helped make Franklin a wealthy man.

Philadelphians wondered where Franklin found the time to do so much. He was a printer, a writer, a scientist, and an inventor. He also became a leader in the colony's government. It seems that Franklin followed his own almanac's advice: "Early to bed and early to rise, makes a man healthy, wealthy, and wise."*

READING CHECK **SUMMARIZE**

What were some of the ways in which Benjamin Franklin improved the city of Philadelphia?

*Benjamin Franklin. *Poor Richard's Almanack*. Peter Pauper Press, 1980.

Philadelphia was one of the most diverse cities in all of the colonies. The busy seaport made it a trade center that attracted merchants and skilled craftworkers.

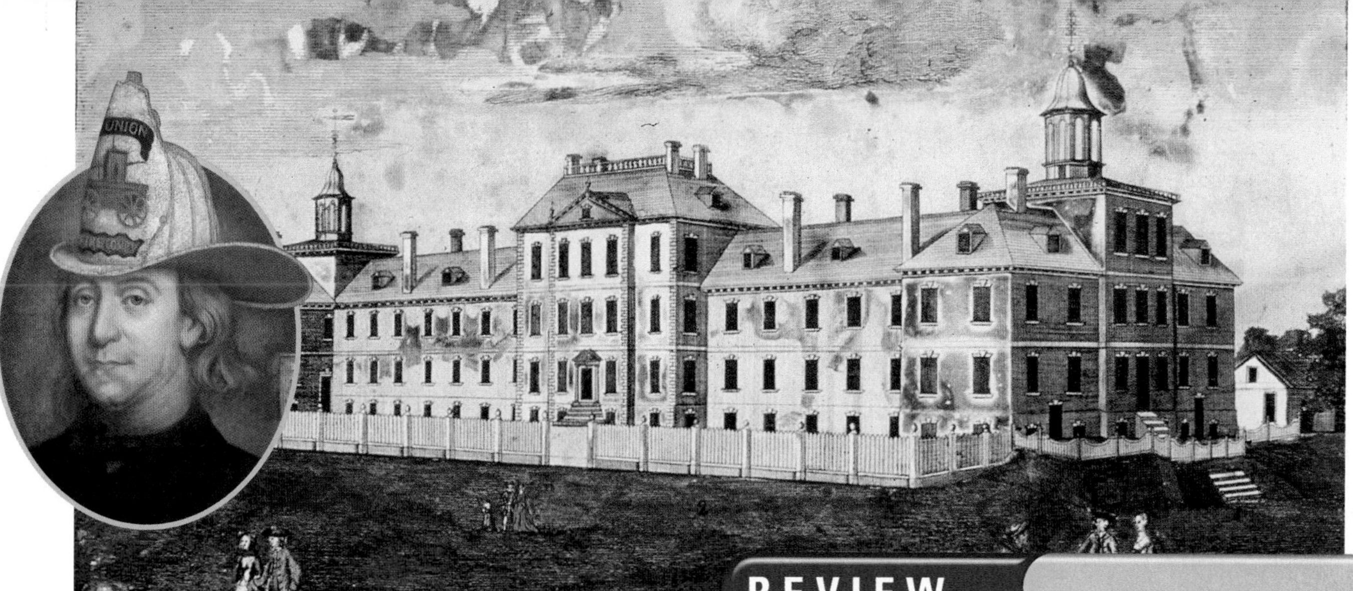

Benjamin Franklin (above left) helped establish a hospital (above right) and a fire company in Philadelphia.

Summary

The Middle Colonies were home to a mix of people, cultures, and religions. The Great Awakening added to the region's diversity. Philadelphia was the center of culture and the largest city in the Middle Colonies.

REVIEW

1. How did religious toleration help attract people of different cultures to the Middle Colonies?
2. Write a sentence about **diversity** in the Middle Colonies, using the term **immigrant**.
3. When did the Great Awakening take place, and who were some of its leaders?

CRITICAL THINKING

4. **Make It Relevant** If you lived in the Middle Colonies, would you want to live in a city or a farming community? Explain your choice.
5. ANALYSIS SKILL Why do you think the Great Awakening had such a strong effect on religious life in the colonies?
6. **Write a Narrative** Write a story about life in early Philadelphia. Be sure to describe the city's location, people, and businesses in your story.
7. Focus Skill **SUMMARIZE** On a separate sheet of paper, copy and complete this graphic organizer.

Key Fact	Summary
	Philadelphia attracted many diverse people.
Key Fact	

Lesson 3

1600 — 1750

1750
New York becomes the second-busiest port in the Middle Colonies

WHAT TO KNOW
How did geography affect the economy of the Middle Colonies?

- ✓ Explain why people chose to settle in the Middle Colonies.
- ✓ Understand the kinds of jobs and businesses that people had in the Middle Colonies.

VOCABULARY
prosperity p. 258
artisan p. 260
apprentice p. 260

PLACES
New York City
Hudson River
Philadelphia
Delaware River

SUMMARIZE

HSS 5.4, 5.4.1, 5.4.5

Busy Farms and Seaports

YOU ARE THERE

The year is 1700, and you live in England. Your friend Thomas eagerly reads a pamphlet that describes the new Pennsylvania Colony and its fine ports and productive farms.

"There is still a lot of land," Thomas says, "that anyone can purchase."

The land is cheap, and it's fertile. The summers are long enough that there are two harvests a year. "So, why are we still in England?" you ask.

Rich Farmlands

When settlers came to the Middle Colonies, they were amazed by the richness of the land and its abundant natural resources. Unlike New England, the Middle Colonies had lots of fertile soil. Since farming was how most people in the 13 colonies made their living, the Middle Colonies attracted many settlers.

Richard Frame used poetry to describe his feelings about the fertile land in the Middle Colonies. He wrote:

> **"The fields, most beautiful, yield such crops of wheat, And other things most excellent to eat."** *

Throughout the Middle Colonies wheat fields stretched as far as the eye could see. Although wheat, corn, and rye were the main crops, colonists also used the rich land for other things. Dairy cows thrived on the thick grasses, while hogs roamed the forests, growing fat on acorns and wild berries.

Farmers in the Middle Colonies usually traveled to market towns to sell or trade their livestock and crops. Every market town had a gristmill, which ground the farmers' grain into flour. Most towns also had a lumber mill. During visits to market towns, farm families shopped at the general store. There they purchased items they could not make or grow themselves, such as iron tools, shoes, paint, and buttons.

READING CHECK **SUMMARIZE**
How did geography affect the Middle Colonies' economy?

*Richard Frame. *Making Thirteen Colonies* by Joy Hakim. Oxford University Press, 1999.

Analyze Illustrations
Early gristmills used waterpower to run machines.

1 Farmers grow and harvest grain.
2 Farmers take the grain to the mill.
3 Millstones grind the grain into flour.
4 Flour is shipped to market.
How does the flour get to market?

Port Cities

The merchants who bought livestock and crops from farmers took these goods to port cities. These were the major centers of trade in the Middle Colonies, and the colonies' **prosperity**, or economic success, depended largely on the ports.

New York City was one of most important port cities in the Middle Colonies. The **Hudson River** helped make trade easier. Farmers, fur traders, and lumber workers in the countryside could float their goods down the river to New York City. Also, the port's deep harbor along the East River offered a good place for ships to dock.

Every year, the number of ships sailing into and out of New York City increased. When the English took over the city in 1664, about 35 ships used the port each year. By 1750, that number had grown to 600, making New York City the second-busiest port in the English colonies.

The busiest colonial port of the time was **Philadelphia**, which was built along the Delaware River, about 90 miles inland from the river's mouth. Farmers, merchants, and traders in Pennsylvania, New Jersey, and Delaware relied on the port of Philadelphia. Many shipped their goods down the **Delaware River** to the port. Those closer to the city moved their goods in wagons. From Philadelphia, the ships sailed down the river, into Delaware Bay, and across the Atlantic.

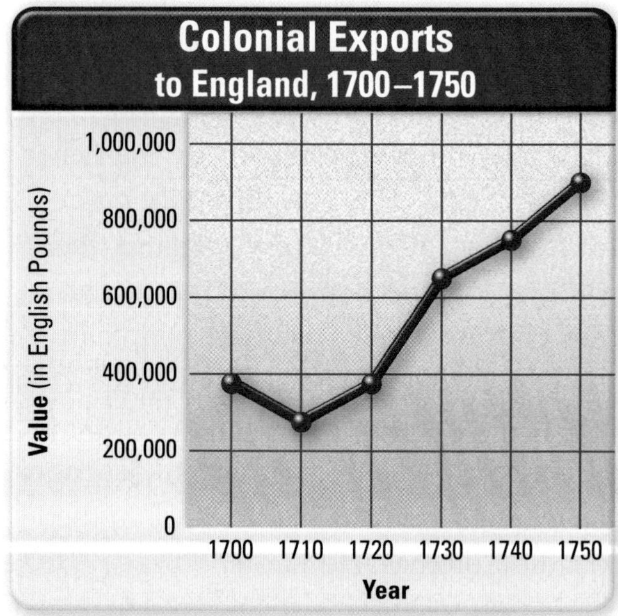

Analyze Graphs **The value of colonial exports is given in English money, or pounds.**

In what year did the colonies export the highest value of goods?

Watches, silver trays, and mugs were shipped from England to the colonies. Many of these goods entered the colonies through port cities, such as New York City (below).

Colonial port cities were exciting places. The bustling streets were full of sailors and, at times, even pirates. Busy workshops made ropes, sails, and barrels. Shipbuilders hammered ships together. Merchants argued over prices as dockworkers moved tons of goods. For many immigrants, their first view of North America was one of these fast-paced port cities.

As in New England, nearly all trade in the Middle Colonies was with England or with other English colonies. New England and the Middle Colonies exported many of the same kinds of goods, including furs, salted meat, and lumber. However, the Middle Colonies exported much more wheat and other grains. They also led all the other colonies in flour exports.

Most imports to the Middle Colonies came from England. Ships brought furniture, tea, gunpowder, medicines, and a variety of metals. Some ships also carried enslaved Africans. Most enslaved Africans in the Middle Colonies were craftworkers or servants.

READING CHECK **SUMMARIZE**

Why were New York City and Philadelphia good locations for ports?

Colonial Jobs

Immigrants arriving in the Middle Colonies could choose from a variety of jobs. In addition to farming and shipping, many colonists worked in skilled trades. Many of these **artisans**, or craftworkers, came to the colonies as indentured servants.

Most artisans used raw materials to make products. Blacksmiths used iron to create horseshoes and tools. Coopers made barrels out of wood. Carpenters and shipbuilders used wood to build houses and ships. Masons and bricklayers worked with stone and clay to pave streets and construct buildings.

Horseshoes were in high demand in the colonies.

Some workers depended on farm goods. These workers included bakers, butchers, flour millers, and soap makers. Dressmakers and tailors used wool, linen, and cotton to make clothing. Tanners turned animal skins into leather, which cobblers used to make and repair shoes.

None of these skills were taught in schools. Young people learned to do skilled jobs by becoming apprentices. An **apprentice** lived and worked with an artisan's family for several years, learning a skill in order to earn a living.

A few young colonists in wealthy families went to college to become lawyers, bankers, ministers, or leaders in the military or government. Still, most

Children in History

Apprentices

Hundreds of colonial boys, and some girls, became apprentices. Most started after the age of 10, but some were even younger. An apprentice usually worked seven years for an artisan, whom he called "master." In return for his work, the apprentice got a place to sleep and meals. He also learned a trade.

Benjamin Franklin became a printer's apprentice in Boston at the age of 12. Franklin never finished his apprenticeship. When he was 17 years old, he moved to Philadelphia and opened his own printing business.

Make It Relevant What kind of job would you choose if you were an apprentice?

▶ In colonial times, candle makers were called chandlers. Candles were made from tallow, which is animal fat.

professionals learned by doing, just as apprentices did. The professions were typically practiced by men.

Women and girls had fewer opportunities to work outside the home. However, they were still an important part of the Middle Colonies' growing economy. They often made the goods sold by artisan households.

READING CHECK **SUMMARIZE**
How did people learn to be artisans?

Summary

The fertile land, mild climate, wide rivers, and deep harbors of the Middle Colonies all led to economic success. The region's economy also depended on its many farmers, artisans, merchants, and sailors.

REVIEW

1. How did geography affect the economy of the Middle Colonies?
2. Use the term **artisan** to describe a job in the Middle Colonies.
3. What jobs did most enslaved Africans have in the Middle Colonies?

CRITICAL THINKING

4. ANALYSIS SKILL What was one effect of the English take over of New York City?
5. ANALYSIS SKILL What would be some of the costs and benefits of being an apprentice?
6. **Make a Chart** Make a two-column chart that lists colonial jobs and the products made by people who worked at these jobs.
7. Focus Skill **SUMMARIZE**
On a separate sheet of paper, copy and complete this graphic organizer.

Key Fact	Summary
The Middle Colonies had rich farmland.	
Many settlers came to the Middle Colonies.	

Make an Economic Choice

WHY IT MATTERS

Economic choices are decisions that may involve spending, saving, or earning money. For example, you might decide to earn more money by working in order to save up for something you want to buy.

People often save their money in banks, where they can earn interest on their money. **Interest** is the money a bank or a borrower pays for the use of money. People might also buy goods on credit, for which they pay a certain amount, plus interest, until the goods are paid for.

However you pay for what you want, you might have to give up the chance to buy something else, either now or in the future. This is called making a **trade-off**. When you give up something in order to buy something else, that is called an **opportunity cost**. Understanding trade-offs and opportunity costs will help you manage your resources and make thoughtful economic decisions.

WHAT YOU NEED TO KNOW

Some economic choices are difficult to make and require careful thinking. Here are some steps that you can follow to help you make those choices.

Step 1 **Identify your goal and the resources you have to meet it.**

Step 2 **Identify your alternatives.**

Step 3 **Discuss the advantages and disadvantages of each alternative.**

Step 4 **Choose and identify the opportunity cost of the choice.**

Establishing a print shop was not cheap. Printers had to buy equipment and supplies of paper, ink, and type.

This historical reenactor shows how coopers made barrels in colonial times.

Critical Thinking Skills

PRACTICE THE SKILL

You have read that most colonial apprentices worked for an artisan for seven years. After that time, apprentices became journeymen and earned wages. Most journeymen continued working for the same artisan for several more years. During this time, they saved money so they could start their own businesses.

Imagine that you are a journeyman and have just earned your first wages. You want to spend the money on new clothes, but you also want to buy newer and better tools. You do not have enough money to do both. You will have to make an economic choice.

1. What choice do you have to make, and why do you have to choose?
2. What is the trade-off for buying the clothes?
3. What is the opportunity cost of buying the tools?
4. What will you buy? Explain why.

APPLY WHAT YOU LEARNED

Make It Relevant Imagine that you want to buy a birthday present for a friend and a computer game for yourself. You do not have enough money for both. Explain to a partner the trade-offs and opportunity costs of your choices. Then explain your choice.

Time

1600

1650

1647
Peter Stuyvesant arrives in New Netherland

Reading Social Studies

When you **summarize**, you tell a shortened version of what you have just read.

Summarize

Complete this graphic organizer to show that you can summarize facts about the Middle Colonies. A copy of this graphic organizer appears on page 65 of the Homework and Practice Book.

The Middle Colonies

Key Fact	Summary
The Middle Colonies had long summers.	
The Middle Colonies had plenty of rain.	
The Middle Colonies had rich farmland.	

California Writing Prompts

Write a Research Report William Penn established good relations with American Indian tribes. Write a report with facts and details that explains how Penn accomplished this. Do more research, if needed.

Write a Persuasive Letter Imagine it is 1700 and you would like to work as an apprentice. Choose the type of work you would like to do, and then write a letter to a business owner to persuade that person to employ you.

1700

1750

1664
England takes over New Netherland and renames it New York

1681
William Penn founds Pennsylvania

1730s
The Great Awakening spreads through the colonies

Use Vocabulary

Identify the term that correctly matches each definition.

refuge, p. 244

proprietor, p. 245

militia, p. 254

artisan, p. 260

apprentice, p. 260

1. a volunteer army
2. an owner
3. a learner
4. a safe place
5. a craftworker

Use the Time Line

Use the chapter summary time line above to answer these questions.

6. When did William Penn found his colony?
7. How long did Peter Stuyvesant govern New Netherland before the English took over?

Apply Skills

Make Economic Choices

8. Review the information on pages 262–263. Then describe an economic choice you made and the trade-offs and opportunity costs of your choice.

Recall Facts

Answer these questions.

9. How did some enslaved people in New Netherland gain their freedom?
10. What were two effects of the Great Awakening?

Write the letter of the best choice.

11. What religious group did William Penn belong to?
   A Puritans
   B Catholics
   C Quakers
   D Anglicans
12. Which of the following was the most widely grown crop in the Middle Colonies?
   A tobacco
   B cotton
   C rice
   D wheat
13. How did Benjamin Franklin earn his living?
   A He was a fisher.
   B He was a printer.
   C He was a farmer.
   D He was a shipbuilder.

Think Critically

14. ANALYSIS SKILL What caused people of many different religious groups to settle in the Middle Colonies?
15. ANALYSIS SKILL In what way was the population of the Middle Colonies like the population of the United States today?

Study Skills

TAKE NOTES

Taking notes can help you remember what you have learned. These notes can also help you review for tests.

- **Write down important facts and ideas. You do not have to write in complete sentences.**
- **Organize notes in a way that will make them easy to reread later.**
- **One way to organize notes is in a chart. Write down the main ideas in one column and facts and details in another.**

The Southern Colonies	
Reading Notes	Class Notes
Lesson 1 • The first settlers arrived in Maryland in 1633. • ______	• Many Catholics came to Maryland because they could not freely practice their religion in England. • ______

Apply As You Read

As you read this chapter, use a two-column chart to take notes about each lesson.

California History-Social Science Standards, Grade 5

5.3 Students describe the cooperation and conflict that existed among the American Indians and between the Indian nations and the new settlers.
5.4 Students understand the political, religious, social, and economic institutions that evolved in the colonial era.

CHAPTER 7

The Southern Colonies

Frontier Culture Museum in Staunton, Virginia

Start with a Story

Molly Bannaky

written by Alice McGill illustrated by Chris K. Soentpiet

In 1683, young Molly Bannaky was working for a wealthy landowner in England. Every morning, she woke up at five o'clock to milk the landowner's cow. One morning, Molly spilled all the milk that was in her pail. For this mistake, she was taken to court for stealing. The court ruled that Molly had to leave the country and go to the American colonies.

For seven years, Molly worked as an indentured servant in the Maryland Colony. Afterward, she was given her freedom, and her life changed greatly. Read now about Molly's new life in the Maryland Colony.

After working for the planter for seven years, Molly was free to go. As the law required, the farmer gave her an ox hitched to a cart, a plow, two hoes, a bag of tobacco seeds, a bag of seed corn, clothing, and a gun. Acres and acres of fertile land stretched ahead of her. Just before sunset that same day, Molly left the road and went four miles into the wilderness, where she staked her claim.

That a lone woman should stake land was unheard of, but Molly's new neighbors saw the way she jutted out her chin. They helped her cart the tobacco to the warehouse to sell. But Molly soon realized that the farm was too much for her to manage alone.

One day Molly read a posted announcement that a ship would be landing soon. Because she needed help in working her land, she decided to watch the docking of this ship—a slave ship. She watched the men of Africa file by, one after the other. She saw the misery, anger, and shame on their faces as they were forced to mount the auction block. Then Molly noticed a tall, regal man who dared to look into the eyes of every bidder. Molly bought him and vowed to treat him well and set him free just as soon as her land was cleared.

Molly talked to this man, using her hands and arms to tell him of her homeland and of her years as an indentured servant. . . . He told her his name: Bannaky.

Molly and Bannaky grew to love each other. She signed his freedom papers, and a traveling minister performed their marriage rites . . . her neighbors came to accept this marriage and to respect Bannaky. In times of drought he shared his knowledge of irrigation and crop rotation, learned at an early age in his native country.

Years passed. Molly and Bannaky had four young daughters. . . . In time she had a grandson. . . . In her Bible, Molly wrote her new grandson's name: Benjamin Banneker. She taught this young boy to read and write. She told him about his grandfather, a prince who was the son of a king in Africa, and about her days as a dairymaid across the ocean in England.

When Benjamin Banneker grew up, he became a scientist and mathematician. He taught himself astronomy and land surveying. In 1791 and 1792, he worked with Andrew Ellicot, another surveyor, to plan the city of Washington D.C. Banneker became a famous author of his own almanac. In 1791 he sent a copy of his almanac to Thomas Jefferson. With it, he included a letter expressing his views on the injustice of slavery.

Response Corner

1. Why did Molly bring Bannaky to her farm?
2. Imagine that you have been sent to the Maryland Colony in 1683 to be an indentured servant. Write a brief description of what your daily life is like.

Lesson 1

Time

1600 — 1750

1632 Lord Baltimore founds the Maryland Colony

1712 The North Carolina and South Carolina Colonies are formed

1733 James Oglethorpe founds the Georgia Colony

WHAT TO KNOW
How did geography affect where people settled in the Southern Colonies?

- ✓ Describe the location and physical setting of the Southern Colonies.
- ✓ Explain why the Southern Colonies were founded.
- ✓ Discuss how slavery affected the Southern Colonies.

VOCABULARY
constitution p. 275
debtor p. 276
backcountry p. 277

PEOPLE
George Calvert
Cecilius Calvert
James Oglethorpe

PLACES
Maryland
Virginia
North Carolina
South Carolina
Georgia

SUMMARIZE

California Standards

HSS 5.3, 5.3.4, 5.4, 5.4.1, 5.4.2, 5.4.3, 5.4.6, 5.4.7

Settling the South

YOU ARE THERE The year is 1650 and you stand on a hillside looking down at the huge bay below. Two months ago, you boarded a ship in England to come to the **Maryland** Colony. The land looks very different from the crowded streets of London. Fields of crops stretch as far as you can see. You left London because you couldn't find a job there. Here, you'll be working for a wealthy landowner. From the looks of things, you'll be working a lot.

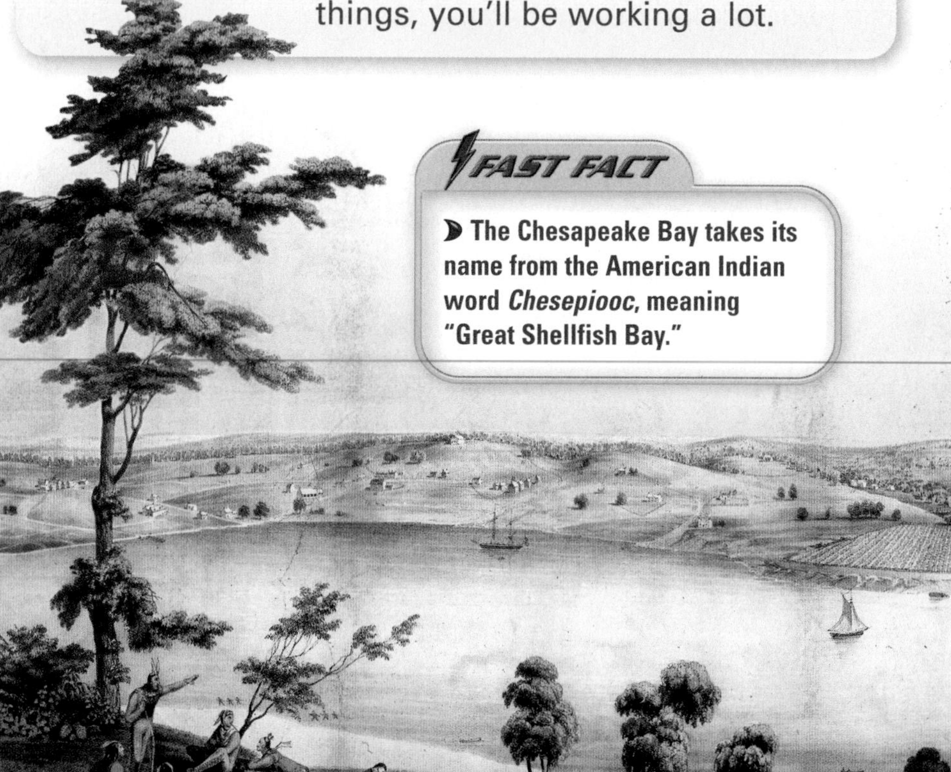

FAST FACT

The Chesapeake Bay takes its name from the American Indian word *Chesepiooc*, meaning "Great Shellfish Bay."

This painting shows an artist's view of the founding of Maryland. Why do you think people are shown carrying a cross?

Maryland

The Maryland Colony was founded by the Calverts, a family of wealthy English landowners. The Calverts, who were Catholic, wanted to build a colony in North America that not only made money, but also provided a refuge for Catholics. Like the Quakers who founded Pennsylvania, Catholics in England could not worship as they wished.

George Calvert, also called Lord Baltimore, had been a member of the Virginia Company. Calvert asked King Charles I to give him a charter for a new colony along the Chesapeake Bay, to the north of Virginia.

Calvert died before the charter was signed in 1632. His oldest son, **Cecilius Calvert**, became the new Lord Baltimore and the owner of the new colony. He called the colony Maryland.

Cecilius Calvert chose his brother, Leonard, to be Maryland's first governor. The Calvert brothers had learned from the unfortunate experiences at Jamestown, in the colony of Virginia, and they planned their colony carefully. There would be no "starving time" in Maryland.

In 1633, the Calverts sent the first colonists to Maryland. Most of these colonists arrived as indentured servants. The ships carrying them landed near the mouth of the Potomac River. There, the colonists founded their first settlement, now called St. Mary's City.

READING CHECK **SUMMARIZE**
What were the reasons for the founding of the Maryland Colony?

With the passage of the Toleration Act by Lord Baltimore, Maryland became known throughout the English colonies for its religious freedom.

Life in Maryland and Virginia

The Maryland Colony had much in common with its older neighbor, **Virginia**. The two colonies shared the same relative location next to the Chesapeake Bay and the Potomac River. They had the same mild climate, and tobacco grew in the fertile land along the Coastal Plain.

Some colonists in Maryland grew rich from huge tobacco plantations. However, most struggled on small farms. Many of Maryland's farmers had come to the colony as indentured servants. Maryland's government helped former servants by giving each of them land, clothes, tools, and barrels of corn.

In the early 1700s, more people lived in Virginia than in Maryland. In fact, Virginia had become the largest English colony in North America and, in 1699, moved its capital to Williamsburg.

Virginia and Maryland had similar governments. Both colonies had governors, and both elected representatives to assemblies. However, the king controlled the royal colony of Virginia, while the Calverts controlled the proprietary colony of Maryland.

Unlike Virginia, Maryland welcomed many different religions. In 1649, the Maryland assembly passed the Toleration Act, which allowed religious freedom in the colony to all Christians.

READING CHECK **COMPARE AND CONTRAST**
What physical features did Maryland and Virginia have in common?

The Carolina Colonies

As the populations of Maryland and Virginia grew, some colonists started building villages and farms farther south. In 1663, England's new king, Charles II, granted land for another colony called Carolina. The new colony stretched all the way from Virginia to Spanish Florida.

The charter divided Carolina among eight English leaders, called the Lords Proprietors. In 1669, these leaders wrote a **constitution**, or a written plan of government, for Carolina. The constitution allowed free, male colonists to elect some leaders and make some laws. Still, most of the power belonged to the proprietors and the king.

The Carolina Colony soon became hard to govern. It covered a huge area, and the colonists often ignored laws they disliked. In 1712, the colony was divided into two new colonies—**North Carolina** and **South Carolina**. In hilly North Carolina, farmers grew tobacco and corn. In contrast, farmers in South Carolina had problems growing tobacco in the flat, swampy land. When settlers from the West Indies arrived with their African slaves they started growing rice and the colony began to prosper. Rice soon became South Carolina's most important crop.

READING CHECK **SUMMARIZE**
Why was the Carolina Colony hard to govern?

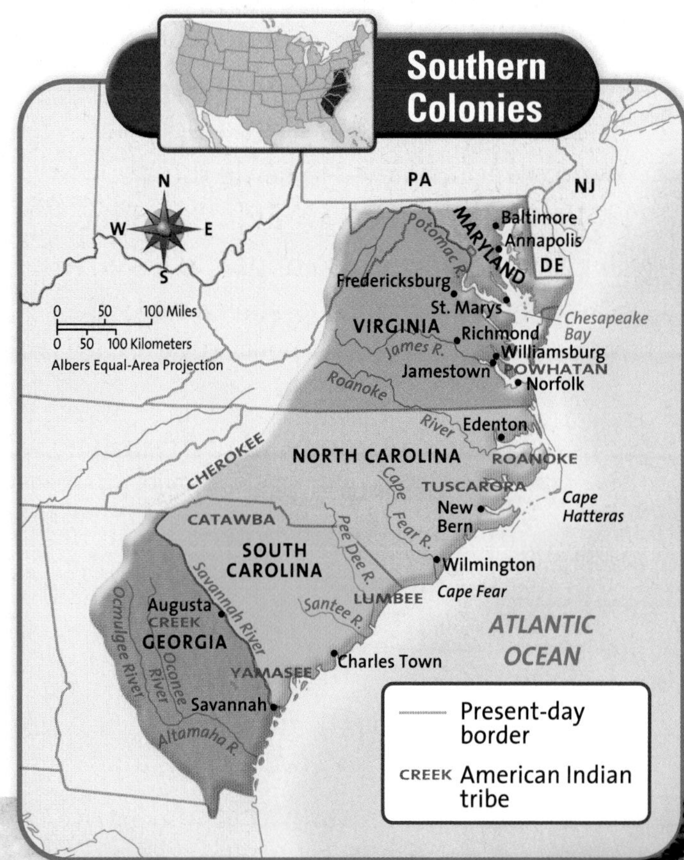

ANALYSIS SKILL **Analyze Maps** **Tobacco (below) was mostly grown in the upper South.**

Location **What was the southernmost city?**

Georgia

England, France, and Spain claimed the area to the south of South Carolina. By 1727, England's new ruler, King George II, knew that if he did not send colonists there, he might lose control of the area.

Then a wealthy English leader named **James Oglethorpe** had an idea. Why not send imprisoned English **debtors**—people who owed money—to settle the colony? The settlers would defend the land. Oglethorpe also hoped to give the debtors a chance to start a new life. He wrote,

> **"By such a Colony, many families, who would otherwise starve, will be provided for, and made masters of houses and lands."***

*James Oglethorpe. *Some Account of the Designs of the Trustees for Establishing the Colony of Georgia in America.* W. Q. Force, 1839.

James Oglethorpe

Oglethorpe's idea seemed like the perfect solution, and King George II gave Oglethorpe and his partners a charter. They named their colony **Georgia**, in honor of the king. In 1733, the first group of colonists arrived in Georgia and founded the settlement of Savannah.

Hoping to avoid conflicts, Oglethorpe did not allow trading with American Indians. He also limited the size of farms and did not allow slavery. As a result, Georgia had no plantations at first. However, the settlers were divided on the issue of slavery. By the 1740s, some settlers were illegally importing slaves to the colony. In 1751, Georgia's leaders decided to allow slavery. Over time, Georgia's successful economy was a result of plantations and the labor of enslaved Africans.

READING CHECK MAIN IDEA AND DETAILS
Why did James Oglethorpe found the Georgia Colony?

Heading West

In the early 1700s, most cities, towns, farms, and plantations in the 13 colonies were located near the coast, on the Coastal Plain. At that time, few colonists had settled in the Piedmont—the land between the Coastal Plain and the Appalachian Mountains. Settlers called this frontier region the **backcountry** because it was beyond, or "in back of," the area settled by Europeans.

The thick forests, hills, and lack of roads made travel to the backcountry difficult. However, by the mid-1700s, many settlers in the 13 colonies began to move to areas west of the Coastal Plain. From Pennsylvania, large numbers of German immigrants had begun moving into the backcountry of Virginia and the Carolinas. To get there, the settlers followed an earlier American Indian trail. As more people used the trail, it became wide enough for wagons to use. This widened trail eventually became known as the Great Wagon Road.

READING CHECK **SUMMARIZE**
Why was it difficult to reach the backcountry?

GEOGRAPHY

The Great Wagon Road

From Pennsylvania, the Great Wagon Road passed through the Shenandoah Valley of Virginia and along the eastern side of the Blue Ridge Mountains. The land there was hilly and travel on the road was difficult, but it was the only way to get wagons loaded with household goods to the backcountry. Thousands of people followed the old American Indian trail. Among them was Daniel Boone, who later became a well-known explorer.

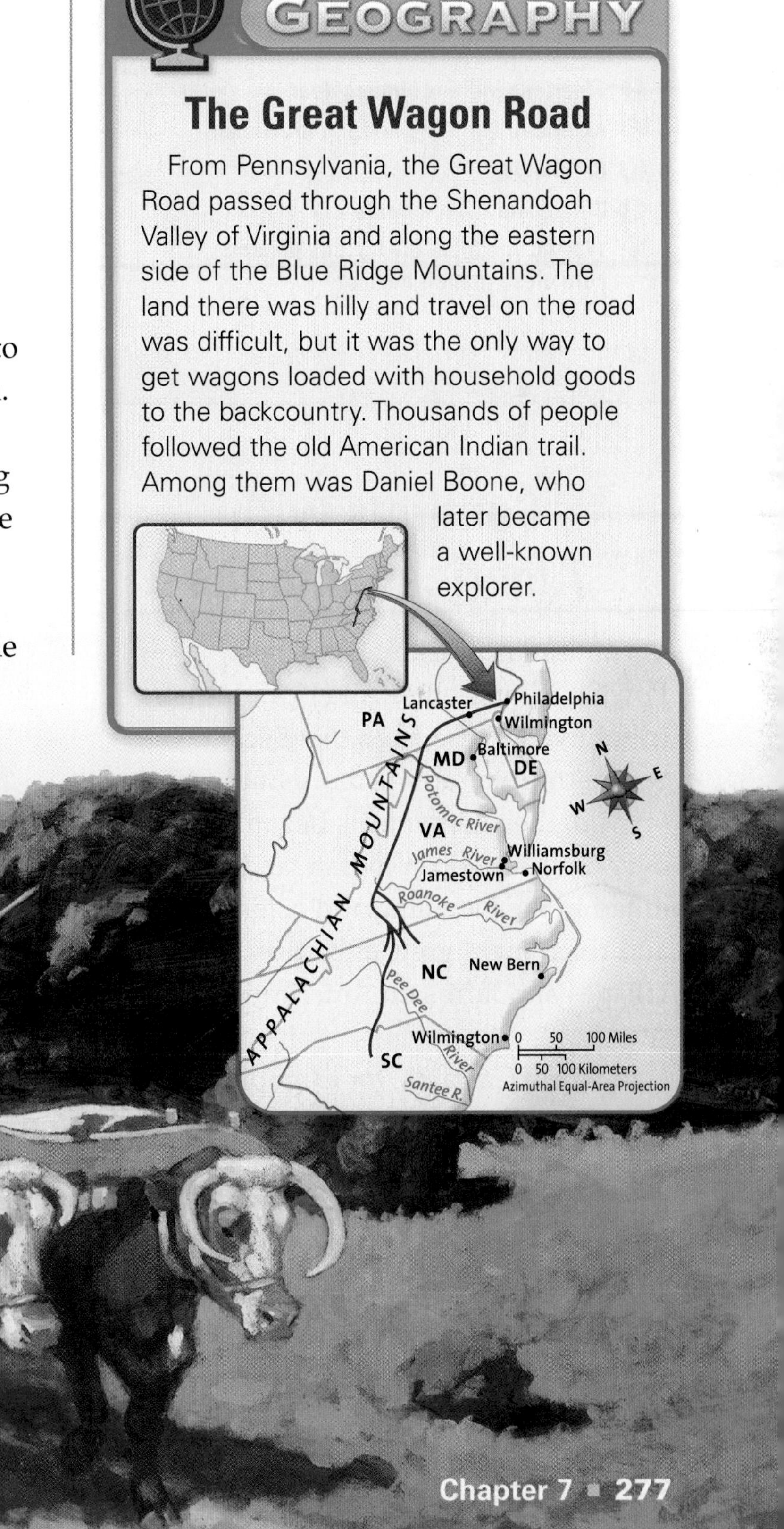

PRIMARY SOURCES

Secotan Village

ANALYSIS SKILL Analyze Drawings

The village of Secotan was an American Indian settlement near the Pamlico River in what is now North Carolina. This drawing of the village was made by John White, an early English colonist.

1. **American Indians hunting deer**
2. **American Indians gathering for a feast**
3. **Cornfields**
4. **Ceremonial dance circle**

? Why do you think the Indians planted corn close to their homes?

Conflicts with American Indians

Thousands of Cherokee, Creek, Powhatan, and other American Indian tribes lived in the areas that became the Southern Colonies. As more Europeans arrived, their settlements began to spill over onto American Indian lands. Just as it had in the New England colonies, anger and resentment grew as settlers built their villages and farms on American Indian sites.

In North Carolina, for example, German and Swiss settlers destroyed the Tuscarora village of Chattawka (chah•TAW•kah) in order to build the settlement of New Bern. Some colonists believed that the remaining American Indians were not treated fairly, either. During that time, one settler said that the other colonists had:

> **"cheated these Indians in trading, and would not allow them to hunt near their plantations, and . . . took away from them their game [animals], arms, and ammunition."***

In 1711, these and other land losses caused the Tuscarora to attack several settlements. The Indians hoped to frighten away the settlers, but their attacks led to the Tuscarora War. By 1713, when the war finally ended, 950 Tuscarora Indians had been either killed or captured and sold into slavery.

Settlers in the Southern Colonies kept pushing Indians away from their lands. Some Indians were captured and sent to the West Indies to work on sugarcane plantations. Others died while fighting the colonists over land or trade. Even peaceful Indian groups died in large

*Baron Christopher De Graffenreid. *North Carolina: The History of a Southern State.* Umi Research Press, 1973.

Town Creek Indian Mound was a center of religion and government for American Indians in the Pee Dee River valley in North Carolina.

numbers from European diseases such as smallpox and measles.

As their numbers decreased, several American Indian groups decided to move west to lands that European settlers had not yet reached. As they left, however, the settlers began to move still further inland.

READING CHECK **CAUSE AND EFFECT**
What effect did settlers have on American Indians in the Southern Colonies?

Summary

The Southern Colonies were made up of Virginia, Maryland, North Carolina, South Carolina, and Georgia. Some settlers came for land and others for religious reasons. Indentured servants and enslaved Africans were brought to the region as workers. Over time, conflicts grew between settlers and American Indians.

REVIEW

1. How did geography affect where people settled in the Southern Colonies?
2. Use the term **debtor** in a sentence about the founding of Georgia.
3. Which Southern Colony was founded as a refuge for Catholics, and who founded it?

CRITICAL THINKING

4. ANALYSIS SKILL How did the physical characteristics of the backcountry affect the movement of settlers?
5. ANALYSIS SKILL Identify one primary source and one secondary source in this lesson. Explain how you identified each.
6. **Make an Illustrated Time Line** Make a time line from 1600 to 1750. Then label the dates of important events in the settlement of the Southern Colonies. Draw pictures near those labels to illustrate what happened.
7. Focus Skill **SUMMARIZE**
On a separate sheet of paper, copy and complete the graphic organizer.

Key Fact	Summary
England wanted to protect its land claims.	
Oglethorpe started a colony for debtors.	

Read Circle Graphs

WHY IT MATTERS

You can learn about the population of the British colonies in many different ways. To compare the populations of different colonies, you might use a circle graph. A **circle graph** is a graph that shows data as parts of a whole.

This kind of graph is sometimes called a pie chart because it is round and divided into parts that are like pieces of a pie. You have probably seen such graphs in newspapers, on the Internet, on television, and in textbooks. To understand the information they contain, you need to know how to read a circle graph.

WHAT YOU NEED TO KNOW

The first circle graph on page 281 gives information about the population of the New England, Middle, and Southern Colonies in the middle of the 1700s. The second graph gives information about different ethnic groups living in those colonies. An **ethnic group** is a group of people from the same country, of the same race, or with a shared culture.

By 1750, more than 1 million people lived in the 13 colonies. Virginia had the largest population. Today, reenactors at Colonial Williamsburg show visitors what life was like in Virginia in the colonial era.

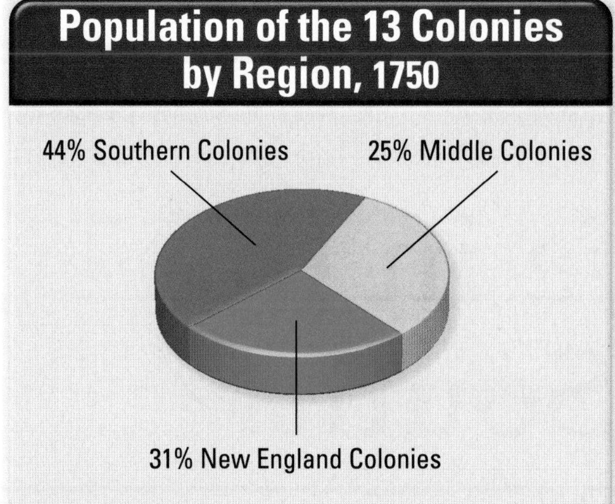

Population of the 13 Colonies by Ethnicity, 1750

51% English and Welsh
20% African
2% Other European
3% Dutch
4% Scottish
5% Irish
7% German
8% Scots-Irish

As on many circle graphs, the data on these graphs are given in percents, shown by the symbol %. A **percent** is one-hundredth of a total or a whole. For example, if you cut a pie into 100 equal pieces, those 100 pieces together are 100% of the pie, or the whole pie. Fifty pieces are one-half of the pie, or 50% of it. Ten pieces are one-tenth of the pie, or 10% of it. Each piece would be one one-hundredth, or 1%, of the whole pie.

PRACTICE THE SKILL

Use the circle graphs above to answer the following questions.

1. What percent of the total population lived in the Southern Colonies?
2. Which colonial region had the highest population? The lowest? How can you tell?
3. What percent of the total colonial population in 1750 was German?
4. Which ethnic group had the second-highest population in 1750?

APPLY WHAT YOU LEARNED

Make It Relevant Look through newspapers and magazines or on the Internet for an example of a circle graph. Write three questions that can be answered by reading that graph. Then trade circle graphs and questions with a partner, and answer the questions you receive.

This reenactor demonstrates the skills that workers needed in colonial times.

Lesson 2

Time

1600 — 1750

1619 First Africans arrive in Virginia

1750 About 200,000 slaves live in the Southern Colonies

Life in the South

WHAT TO KNOW
How did plantations affect life in the Southern Colonies?

- ✓ Describe how slavery influenced daily life in the Southern Colonies.
- ✓ Identify ways in which slaves tried to deal with the hardships of their lives.
- ✓ Describe what government was like in the Southern Colonies.
- ✓ Explain the role that religion played in Southern colonists' lives.

VOCABULARY
institutionalize p. 283
planter p. 284
overseer p. 284

PEOPLE
Anthony Johnson

PLACES
Spanish Florida
Fort Mose

Focus Skill **SUMMARIZE**

 California Standards
HSS 5.4, 5.4.3, 5.4.5, 5.4.6, 5.4.7

YOU ARE THERE The crowd that is gathered in the middle of the town's market square is looking at two people bound in shackles and standing on a platform. They were recently brought over from Africa on a slave ship and are about to be sold as slaves. You try to imagine how scared and heartbroken they must feel after having been taken so far away from their homes and families.

Iron shackles like these (above) were often used to bind the hands or feet of enslaved people.

Slavery and Society

The first Africans most likely arrived in Virginia in 1619. Within a few years, traders from Europe and the West Indies brought thousands of enslaved Africans to the colonies. These Africans had been taken from their homes, chained together in ships, and sent to colonial cities to be sold.

At first, Africans had been sold in the colonies as indentured servants. However, as the need for workers grew, assemblies began to pass laws making slavery legal. In time, slavery became **institutionalized** (in•stuh•TOO•shuh•nul•ized), or a part of life, in the colonies. By the mid-1700s, slavery was legal in all 13 colonies. These laws said that the children of enslaved people were also slaves. As a result, families were often split up and sold to different owners.

Many enslaved Africans ended up working on plantations in one of the Southern Colonies. By 1750, about 200,000 slaves lived in the region. The way slaves were treated varied with their owners. Slave owners were free to beat, whip, or insult slaves. Slaves had little hope of escape, and the law did not protect them.

Slaves were not allowed to speak out against slavery, but they did not accept the system. Slaves often did whatever they could to resist, or act against, slavery. They broke tools, pretended to be sick, or worked slowly. Such actions were dangerous, however, and slaves had to be careful to avoid punishment.

Enslaved Africans tried to deal with the hardships of their lives. They preserved their culture by telling stories about Africa and by singing African songs. By the late 1700s, the Christian religion also became a source of strength for some slaves.

READING CHECK SUMMARIZE
How did laws help institutionalize slavery?

One way enslaved Africans preserved their culture was through music. The gourd banjo (left) is an instrument that was developed in Africa. This portrait (right) shows an enslaved woman from South Carolina.

Plantation Life

Most slaves in the Southern Colonies lived and worked on plantations. Slave labor and cash crops such as tobacco and rice made some **planters**, or plantation owners, very rich. They became the richest people in the Southern Colonies.

Not all plantation owners were alike. A few started as poor indentured servants who slowly bought more land and slaves. Others were wealthy English settlers who had been granted huge pieces of land by the king or the royal governors.

The first plantations were built along rivers on the Coastal Plain. The rivers provided a way to ship cash crops to port cities. By 1750, settlers had moved farther west, and they had started large plantations there. As planters grew richer, the amount of land they owned also grew. Some plantations looked like small villages. The main building on a plantation was the planter's house, which was often two or three stories high. Slaves usually helped build these large homes.

In general, there were two kinds of slaves—field slaves and house slaves. Field slaves worked in the fields, raising crops such as tobacco, rice, and sugarcane. House slaves worked in the planter's home.

Many buildings surrounded the planter's home. Some were workshops, where slaves made nails, bricks, barrels, and other items used on the plantation. The kitchen was in a building by itself.

Wealthy plantation owners hired **overseers** to watch the field slaves as they worked. The overseer's house was

often near the planter's, but slave houses were usually far from the planter's house. A typical slave home was a one-room wooden building. Near their homes some slaves kept small gardens, which they tended after working the planter's land.

Most planters did not work in the fields, but they did have many responsibilities. Running a plantation was like managing a small town and a business at the same time. Planters had to provide food and housing for everyone on the plantation.

Besides taking care of the plantation, a planter's duties included public service, or working for the community. Planters often served as judges or as members of the colonial assembly. Some planters served as advisers to the governor.

A Closer LOOK

A Southern Plantation

Many plantations in the Southern Colonies were self-sufficient. Planters grew food, and skilled workers produced needed goods.

1. **fields**
2. **overseer's house**
3. **slave houses**
4. **hospital**
5. **kitchen**
6. **planter's house**

? How were plantations self-sufficient?

Because plantations were far apart, there were few schools. Instead, planters hired private tutors for their children. The tutors often lived and taught on the plantation. However, enslaved children were not allowed to receive an education.

READING CHECK **SUMMARIZE**
How were plantations like small villages?

Reenactors show how people on small farms prepared fields for planting.

Life on Small Farms

Much of the Southern economy depended on large plantations. However, most Southern colonists lived and worked on small farms. They planted and harvested their own crops.

Former indentured servants often became owners of small farms. Unlike planters, few became wealthy. Many families on small farms lived in one-story houses. Their children slept up in a loft, where goods were stored.

During the late 1600s, most families on small farms owned little furniture other than beds. By the middle of the 1700s, some farmers were a little better off. They were able to buy cushions for their hard wooden chairs. Some even bought glass mirrors and china plates.

People on small farms often lived far from each other. As a result, church services were both a religious and social event for people on small farms. Parents discussed news while children played together. Poor farm families looked forward to church days. Some families traveled for hours to reach the closest church.

People on small farms did not usually own slaves. Those who did rarely owned more than one or two. Slaves and owners lived and worked close together, but slaves still were not treated as equals. Some colonists thought slavery was wrong, but it continued because plantation owners claimed they depended on the work of enslaved Africans.

READING CHECK **SUMMARIZE**

How did most Southern colonists make their living?

Free Africans

Not all enslaved Africans in the Southern Colonies remained slaves. Some found ways to escape, and others were able to buy their freedom. However, it was difficult to escape from slavery.

Some free Africans were able to buy land and start their own farms. During the 1640s, a former slave named **Anthony Johnson** bought land in Virginia. Johnson soon became a wealthy tobacco planter. He even bought an enslaved African named Casor.

A few other free Africans were also wealthy enough to buy slaves. Most did not want to be a part of the system of slavery. However, some free Africans did buy enslaved relatives in order to free them.

Few slaves were lucky enough to be set free. Instead, they risked their lives to run away from their owners. Runaway slaves were often captured and returned to their owners. Those who were not captured often found help in **Spanish Florida** or from American Indian tribes.

As slaves escaped to Spanish Florida, the Seminole Indians provided food and shelter. Runaway slaves were given land on which to grow crops, and in return they agreed to give one-third of their crops to the Indians. These former slaves often dressed like Seminoles and learned the Seminole language. In time, they became known as the Black Seminoles.

Other free Africans in Spanish Florida started their own communities. In 1738, a new town for free Africans was settled.

Cultural Heritage

Fort Mose

In 1738, the Spanish governor of Florida set up the town of Fort Mose for free Africans. The governor hoped the settlement would help protect St. Augustine from English attacks. In many ways, the town of Fort Mose was like other Spanish towns. The African settlers of Fort Mose were loyal to Spain. They formed a military unit that fought beside Spanish soldiers and helped defend St. Augustine.

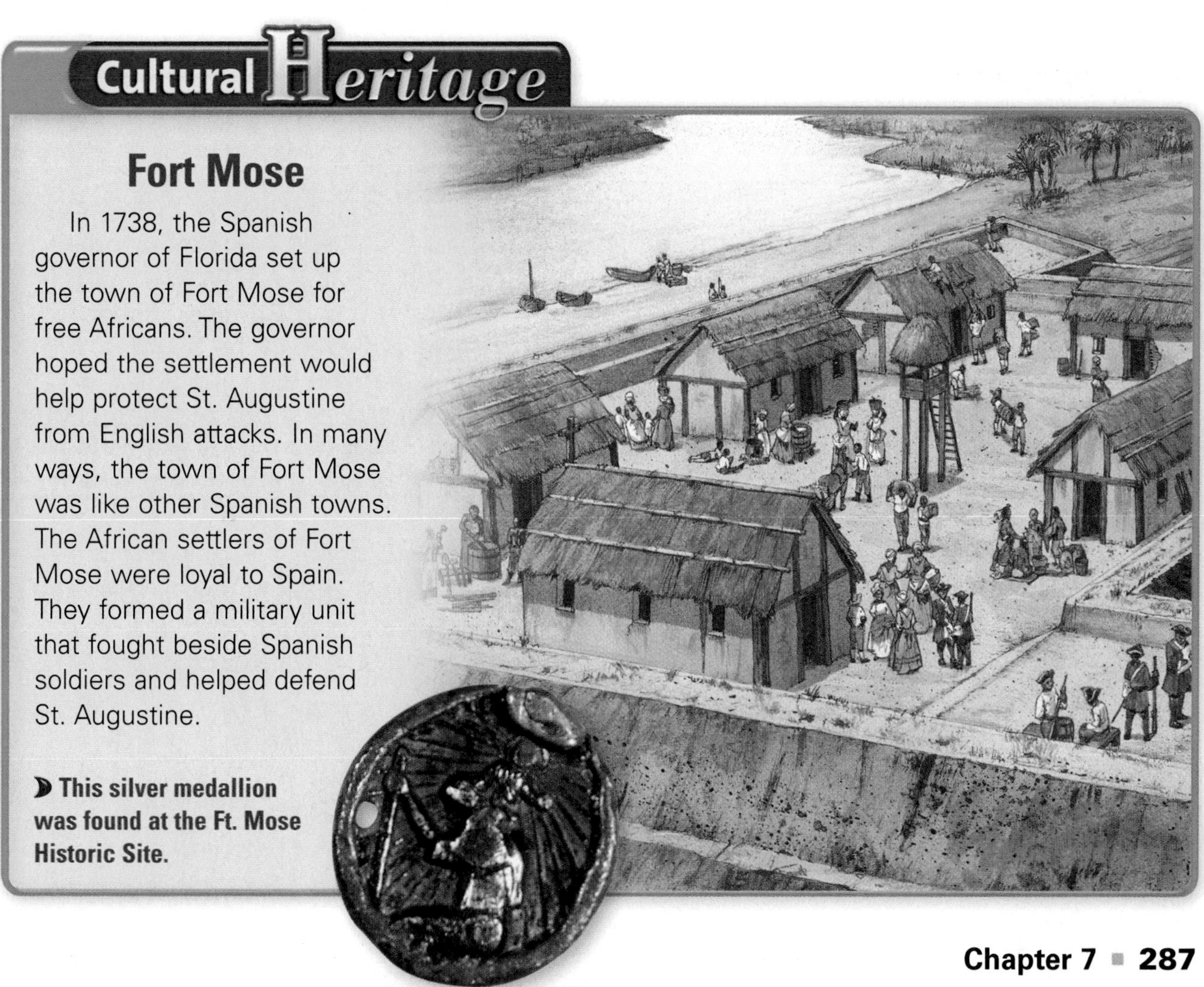

This silver medallion was found at the Ft. Mose Historic Site.

Enslaved Africans who ran away often had to journey hundreds of miles to reach safety.

Florida's governor decided to set up a town called **Fort Mose** (moh•SAY). This was the first settlement in North America for free Africans. While living in Spanish Florida, the people of Fort Mose were able to practice their African ways.

READING CHECK **SUMMARIZE**
How were some Africans in the Southern Colonies able to become free?

Summary

Life in the Southern Colonies was full of contrasts. Plantation owners were very rich, but they depended on the work of enslaved Africans. On small farms, many former indentured servants lived in poverty. Not all Africans were enslaved. Some bought their freedom or escaped.

REVIEW

1. How did plantations affect life in the Southern Colonies?
2. Describe the role of a **planter** and the role of an **overseer**.
3. How did enslaved people preserve their culture?

CRITICAL THINKING

4. How do you think enslaved people felt when their families were broken up?
5. ANALYSIS SKILL Why do you think more people in the colonies did not speak out against slavery?
6. **Draw a Scene** Choose a scene from daily life in the Southern Colonies that you read about in this lesson. Then draw a picture of that scene, and write a caption describing what it shows about life in a Southern Colony.
7. Focus Skill **SUMMARIZE** On a separate sheet of paper, complete this graphic organizer.

Key Fact	Summary
Plantations were self-sufficient.	
Enslaved people lived on plantations.	

Olaudah Equiano

*"When I looked around the ship and saw . . . black people of every description chained together, . . . I no longer doubted my own fate."**

Olaudah Equiano (OH•luh•dah ek•wee•AH•noh) was only 11 years old when he was taken away from his homeland on a slave ship. It was 1756. For the next ten years, he would be enslaved in the English colonies.

Olaudah Equiano was born in the African kingdom of Benin. He was the youngest of seven children, and his father was a leader in their village. One day, slave traders sneaked into the village and kidnapped Equiano and his sister. He never saw his family in Africa again.

The slave ship sailed to the West Indies, and Equiano was then sent to the Virginia Colony. There, he was sold to an English navy officer who took him on several journeys. Over time, Equiano was able to earn enough money from trading that he bought his freedom at the age of twenty-one.

Equiano later wrote a book about his life in Africa, his time as a slave, and his return to freedom. Equiano spent the rest of his life giving speeches around the world to try to end slavery.

*Olaudah Equiano. *The Interesting Narrative of the Life of Olaudah Equiano, or Gustavus Vassa, The African*, edited by Shelly Eversley. Modern Library, 2004.

Biography

Trustworthiness
Respect
Responsibility
Fairness
Caring
Patriotism

Why Character Counts

How did Equiano show he cared about enslaved people?

Bio Brief

1745 — Born 1745?

1797 — Died 1797

1756 Equiano is kidnapped and sold into slavery

1780 Equiano's autobiography is first published

Lesson 3

Time

1600 — 1750

1729 Baltimore, Maryland, is founded

1740s Charles Town exports 30 million pounds of rice per year

The Southern Economy

WHAT TO KNOW
How did people in the Southern Colonies use natural resources to earn a living?

- ✓ Understand how geography affected the economy of the Southern Colonies.
- ✓ Identify the major industries in the Southern Colonies.
- ✓ Explain how the Southern economy depended on slavery.

VOCABULARY
indigo p. 291
interdependence p. 292
broker p. 292

PEOPLE
Eliza Lucas Pinckney

PLACES
Charles Town
Baltimore
Wilmington

SUMMARIZE

HSS 5.4, 5.4.1, 5.4.5, 5.4.6

YOU ARE THERE It's so hot that your shirt sticks to your back. You and several other workers are loading hundreds of barrels of rice onto a ship in **Charles Town**, South Carolina. The huge ship arrived from England two days ago. Its tall mast casts a shadow across the entire dock. You stop for a moment to look up at the ship's sails. As you wipe the sweat from your forehead, you wish you were out at sea instead of stuck on this dock.

Charles Town, South Carolina, became the largest city in the Southern Colonies.

Children IN HISTORY

Eliza Lucas Pinckney

Eliza Lucas Pinckney moved to South Carolina with her parents in 1738. When she was 16 years old, her father had to return to the West Indies. Eliza started experimenting with indigo seeds her father had sent her. She worked so hard that she wrote, "I hardly allow myself time to sleep or eat." *

After three years, Eliza was able to grow an indigo plant that produced an excellent dye. She gave some of her seeds to neighbors and friends. Within a few years, South Carolina planters were selling 1 million pounds of indigo a year to clothmakers in Europe.

Make It Relevant Why is it important to work hard at whatever task you have?

*Eliza Lucas Pinckney. *The Letterbook of Eliza Lucas Pinckney*. University of South Carolina Press, 1997.

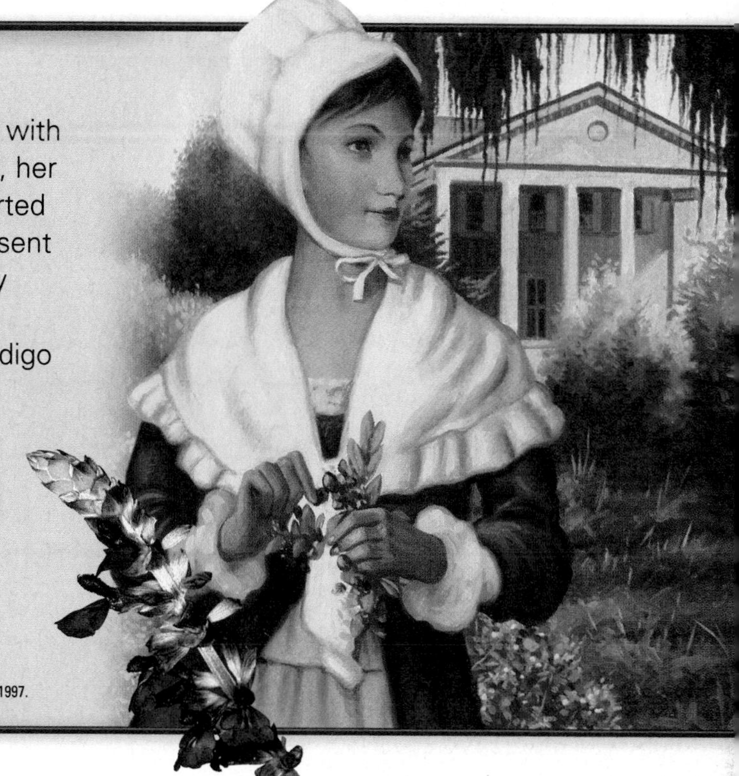

Cash Crops

Port cities like Charles Town were important to the economies of all the Southern Colonies. Plantations produced tons of cash crops each year, and those crops needed to be shipped to markets in England and the West Indies to be sold.

Plantations in different colonies grew different crops. In Maryland, Virginia, and northern North Carolina, tobacco was still the main cash crop. Growing tobacco required many workers and a lot of land. After about seven years, tobacco plants would use up all the nutrients in the soil. This meant that in order to grow more tobacco, farmers had to clear more land.

Tobacco plantations were not as successful farther south, in southern North Carolina, South Carolina, and Georgia. The climate there was too warm and wet for tobacco to grow well. With the labor of their slaves, many plantation owners and small farm owners began growing rice. In fact, rice became such an important cash crop in South Carolina that it was often called "Carolina gold."

On drier land, rice did not grow well. Here, landowners found they could grow indigo plants. From these plants, they made **indigo**, which is a blue dye that was used in the clothmaking process.

Indigo became an important cash crop after **Eliza Lucas Pinckney** experimented with the plant. Using seeds from the Caribbean, Pinckney spent several years growing different kinds of indigo. By the 1740s, planters across South Carolina had started growing indigo, too.

READING CHECK SUMMARIZE
What were some of the cash crops in the Southern Colonies?

The Economy Grows

Plantations were the most important part of the economy in the Southern Colonies. Planters owned much of the best land and most of the slaves. They also produced nearly all of the region's cash crops.

A Closer LOOK

Rice from Farm to Market

An enormous amount of labor was required to start a rice plantation. Most rice plantations were set up along tidal rivers and swamps. Slaves drained, cleared, and leveled swamps.

1. **After rice was planted, fields were flooded several times during the growing season. This helped the rice grow. When the water was drained from the field, workers tended to the plants.**
2. **Workers harvested the rice. They threshed, or separated, the rice grains from the plant.**
3. **When the rice was ready for market, brokers agreed to take the rice to England.**
4. **In England, a broker traded the rice for English goods.**

? Who do you think played the most important role in getting rice to market?

Although plantations were self-sufficient, their economies depended on others. Depending on others for goods or services is called **interdependence**. Owners of large plantations needed people to sell their crops. Most often, a broker did this. A **broker** is a person who is paid to buy and sell for someone else.

Planters sent their crops to England or the West Indies together with a list of things they wanted the broker to buy for them. The broker sold the crops overseas, bought what the planter wanted, and sent the goods back to the colonies.

As plantations grew larger and more productive, traders and merchants in the Southern port towns grew richer from exporting more cash crops. By the mid-1700s, some settlements along the southern Atlantic coast, such as Norfolk and Savannah, had grown into large towns and cities.

When ships carrying goods from England arrived, imported tea, coffee, furniture, and silverware were sold to planters and to people in the cities. Then the ships sailed back to England loaded with tobacco, rice, and indigo.

Relative location affected the success of both plantations and cities. The most successful plantations were often located near ports or deep rivers. Their location made it easier to ship crops to England and other markets. Likewise, cities located near rivers did well.

Charles Town, South Carolina, was built at the point where the Ashley and Cooper Rivers join and empty into a deep harbor. An early visitor to Charles Town wrote that the great number of ships would soon make it a busy town. He was right. By the 1740s, ships sailing from Charles Town carried about 30 million pounds of rice to England every year.

FAST FACT

The colonists had no standard money. They used coins and bills from Europe. Each colony also issued its own money, such as these coins.

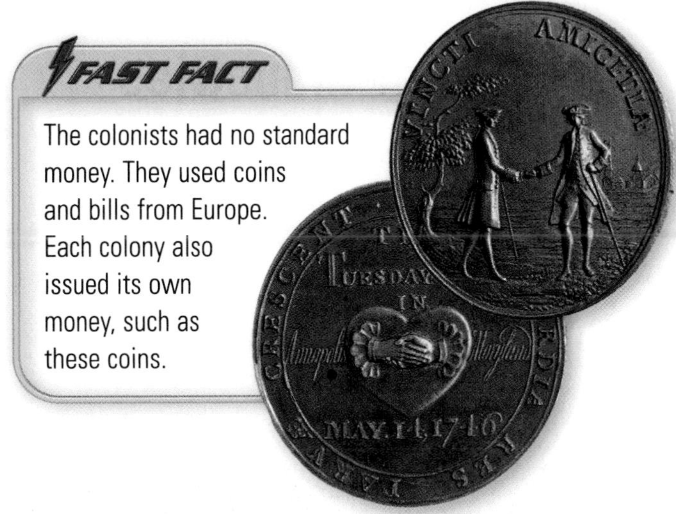

Baltimore, Maryland, was founded in 1729 on the Patapsco River, which flows into Chesapeake Bay. Baltimore prospered as the busy port exported increasing amounts of grain and tobacco produced in Maryland. As the demand for new ships grew, Baltimore also became a major center for shipbuilding.

READING CHECK **SUMMARIZE**
How did the relative location of Charles Town affect its growth?

Other Industries

Although agriculture and trade were the most important parts of the Southern Colonies' economy, the region did have other industries. Like farming, nearly all of these industries were based on the region's natural resources.

Thousands of deer, beavers, and other animals lived in the forests of the Southern Colonies. At first, the colonists traded with American Indians for furs to sell in Europe. Later, many settlers in the backcountry made a living as hunters and trappers. These settlers often lived beyond areas already settled by other colonists. They were also used to cooperating with the American Indians for profit.

The region's forests were important natural resources, too. The port city of **Wilmington**, North Carolina, became an important shipping center for forest products because of its location on the Cape Fear River. Wilmington was founded in the 1720s after colonists from South Carolina began moving north. They were looking for fertile soil to start new plantations. Instead, they found lots of trees. They brought in workers to cut down the trees and to build sawmills.

Colonists also found the trees useful for making naval stores. Southern pine trees provided tar, turpentine, and pitch needed to waterproof the wood and rope on ships. One colonial governor said in 1734, "There is more pitch and tar made in the two Carolinas than in all the other provinces on the Continent."*

Most of these naval stores were sent to England from Southern port cities such as Wilmington. However, some were kept for use in the Southern Colonies.

*Gabriel Johnston. *The Way We Lived in North Carolina.* University of North Carolina Press, 2003.

Baltimore's location near the Chesapeake Bay helped it become a busy port city.

Shipbuilding became a large industry in the colonies. In the late 1700s, Baltimore, Maryland's shipyards became well known for improving the way ships were built. Shipbuilders developed the Baltimore clipper. It was one of the world's fastest sailing ships.

READING CHECK **SUMMARIZE**
What were the other industries of the Southern economy based on?

Summary

The Southern Colonies had an interdependent economy. Enslaved Africans and other workers produced cash crops, furs, lumber, and naval stores. Then merchants and traders in port cities shipped these goods to England and to other colonies.

Southern Colony trappers and hunters often had to travel long distances.

REVIEW

1. How did people in the Southern Colonies use natural resources to earn a living?
2. What clues can you use to remember the meaning of the term **interdependence**?
3. What were the busiest port cities in the Southern Colonies? How do their locations help explain their growth?

CRITICAL THINKING

4. ANALYSIS SKILL Give one example of a primary source in this lesson. How do you know it is a primary source?
5. ANALYSIS SKILL How did the location of a farm in the Southern Colonies affect the kind of crops that were grown?
6. **Make a Table** Make a three-column table. List the Southern Colonies in the first column. In the second column, list major industries in each colony. Then make a third column that lists the goods produced.
7. Focus Skill **SUMMARIZE**
On a separate sheet of paper, complete this graphic organizer.

Key Fact	Summary
	Brokers were an important part of the Southern Colonies economy.

Key Fact

Read a Land Use and Products Map

WHY IT MATTERS

Colonists in North America depended on natural resources for their livelihood. Not all the colonies had the same resources, so they did not all make the same products. To find out about the resources and products in each colony, you can use a land use and products map. **Land use** is the way in which the land in a place is used.

WHAT YOU NEED TO KNOW

In the map on the next page, symbols stand for key resources found in the 13 colonies and for goods produced there. These goods were important not only because they were sold in the colonies but also because they were exported for sale in Europe. The map does not show every land use or product—just the most important ones.

PRACTICE THE SKILL

Use the land use and products map on page 297 to answer these questions.

1. What were the main crops produced in the Southern Colonies?
2. In which colonies was lumber an important product?
3. In which colonies were naval stores produced?
4. Based on this map, what generalizations can you make about the economy in each of the three colonial regions?

APPLY WHAT YOU LEARNED

ANALYSIS SKILL **Make It Relevant** Look through encyclopedias, atlases, and almanacs or on the Internet to find a land use and products map for your state. Then use the information on the map to write three sentences about the economy in your state.

Practice your map and globe skills with the **GeoSkills CD-ROM**.

Lumber (below) was sent to England for shipbuilding and naval stores. Tobacco (right) was cured, or hung up to dry, before it was packed in barrels and shipped.

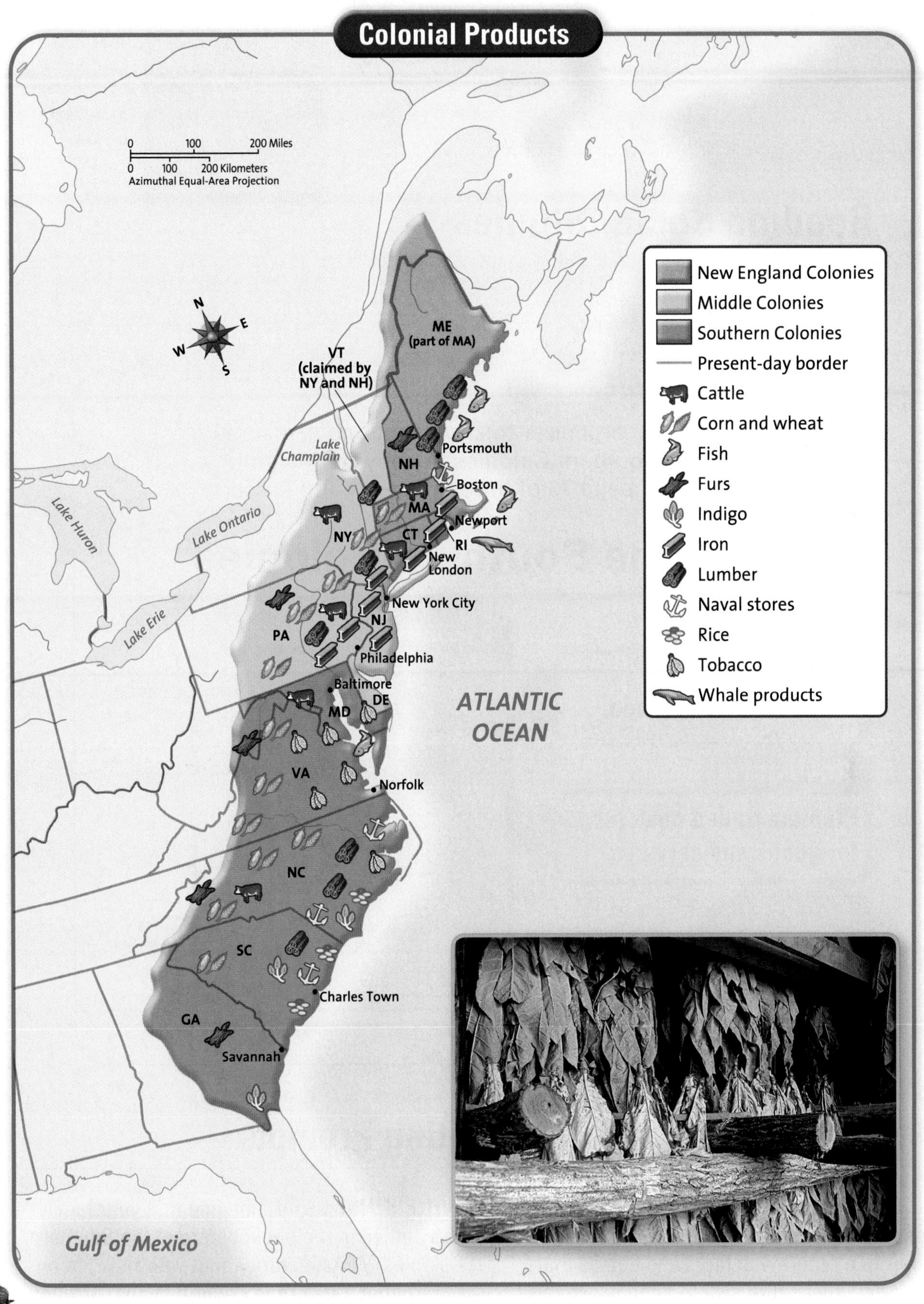

Colonial Products
0
100
200 Miles
0
100
200 Kilometers
Azimuthal Equal-Area Projection
N
E
S
W
New England Colonies
Middle Colonies
Southern Colonies
Present-day border
Cattle
Corn and wheat
Fish
Furs
Indigo
Iron
Lumber
Naval stores
Rice
Tobacco
Whale products
ME
(part of MA)
VT
(claimed by
NY and NH)
Lake
Champlain
Lake Huron
Lake Ontario
Lake Erie
NH
Portsmouth
Boston
MA
Newport
NY
CT
RI
New
London
New York City
NJ
PA
Philadelphia
Baltimore
DE
MD
VA
Norfolk
NC
SC
Charles Town
GA
Savannah
ATLANTIC
OCEAN
Gulf of Mexico

Time

1600

1650

1632
Lord Baltimore founds the Maryland Colony

Reading Social Studies

When you **summarize**, you tell a shortened version of what you have just read.

Summarize

Complete this graphic organizer to show that you can summarize facts about the Southern Colonies. A copy of this graphic organizer appears on page 76 of the Homework and Practice Book.

Life in the Southern Colonies

Key Fact	Summary
Planters grew cash crops such as tobacco.	
Planters traded cash crops for goods and services.	
Planters sold their cash crops in England.	

California Writing Prompts

Write a Report Enslaved Africans were able to preserve their culture under very hard conditions. Write a report with facts and details that explains how they were able to accomplish this.

Write a Narrative Imagine that your family has settled in the backcountry of the Southern Colonies. Write a story about your new life on the frontier. Be sure to describe your surroundings and any challenges you might face.

1700

1750

1712
The colonies of North Carolina and South Carolina are formed

1729
The city of Baltimore, Maryland, is founded

1733
James Oglethorpe establishes Georgia, the last of the 13 colonies

Use Vocabulary

Identify the term that correctly matches each definition.

constitution, p. 275
debtor, p. 276
institutionalize, p. 283
indigo, p. 291
broker, p. 292

1. to make a regular part of life
2. a person who buys and sells for another person
3. a written plan of government
4. a person who owes money
5. a blue dye

Use the Time Line

Use the chapter summary time line above to answer these questions.

6. In what year was Carolina divided into two colonies?
7. When was the last of the 13 colonies founded?

Apply Skills

Read a Circle Graph

8. Look at the circle graph showing ethnicity on page 281. What percent of the colonial population was African?

Recall Facts

Answer these questions.

9. What religious group did the Calvert family belong to?
10. How did enslaved people act against slavery?
11. Why were there few schools in the Southern Colonies?
12. Why was Fort Mose important?

Write the letter of the best choice.

13. What was the main cash crop in Virginia, Maryland, and North Carolina?
    - **A** rice
    - **B** tobacco
    - **C** indigo
    - **D** wheat
14. Which city was an important shipbuilding center?
    - **A** Jamestown, Virginia
    - **B** Baltimore, Maryland
    - **C** New Bern, North Carolina
    - **D** Savannah, Georgia

Think Critically

15. ANALYSIS SKILL Why were southern waterways important?
16. ANALYSIS SKILL How did the relative location of South Carolina affect the kind of crops grown there?

Field Trip

Colonial Williamsburg

GET READY

Colonial Williamsburg is the restored and rebuilt capital of eighteenth-century Virginia. The town is a living-history museum where you can experience the sights, sounds, and smells of colonial life. You can talk with people in historical costumes who stroll the streets or tend their shops. Guides bring history to life by portraying actual citizens who lived in Williamsburg in the 1700s. In Colonial Williamsburg, history is more than just names and dates. It is the story of people just like you who lived in another time.

LOCATE IT

VIRGINIA
Colonial Williamsburg

WHAT TO SEE

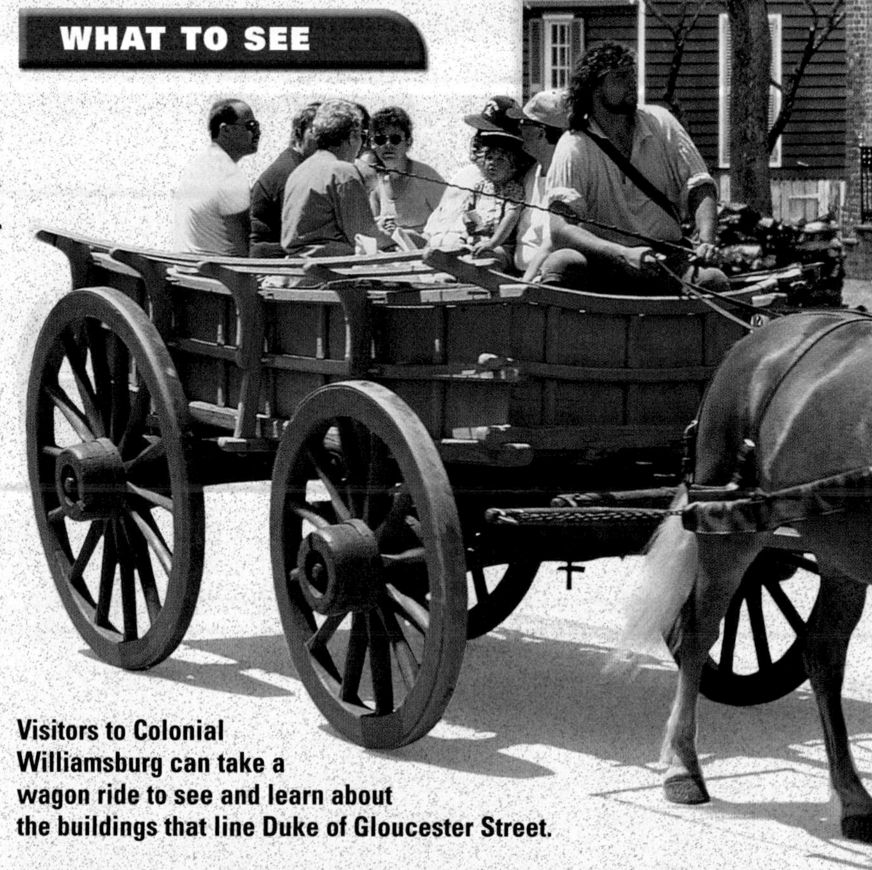

Visitors to Colonial Williamsburg can take a wagon ride to see and learn about the buildings that line Duke of Gloucester Street.

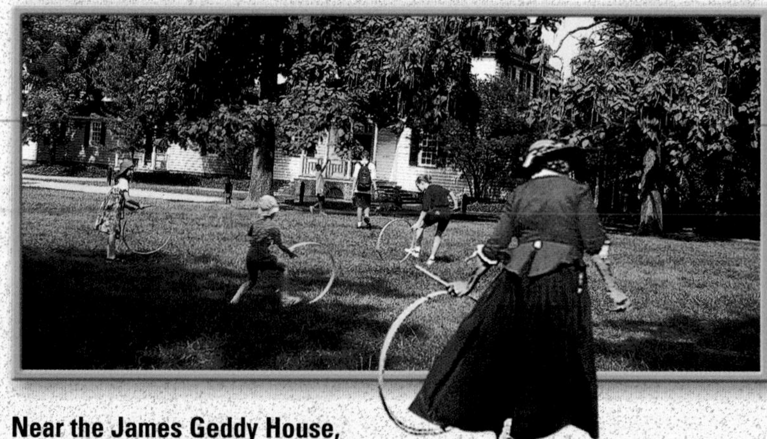

Near the James Geddy House, you can take turns at hoop-rolling, stilt-walking, ninepins, and other colonial children's games.

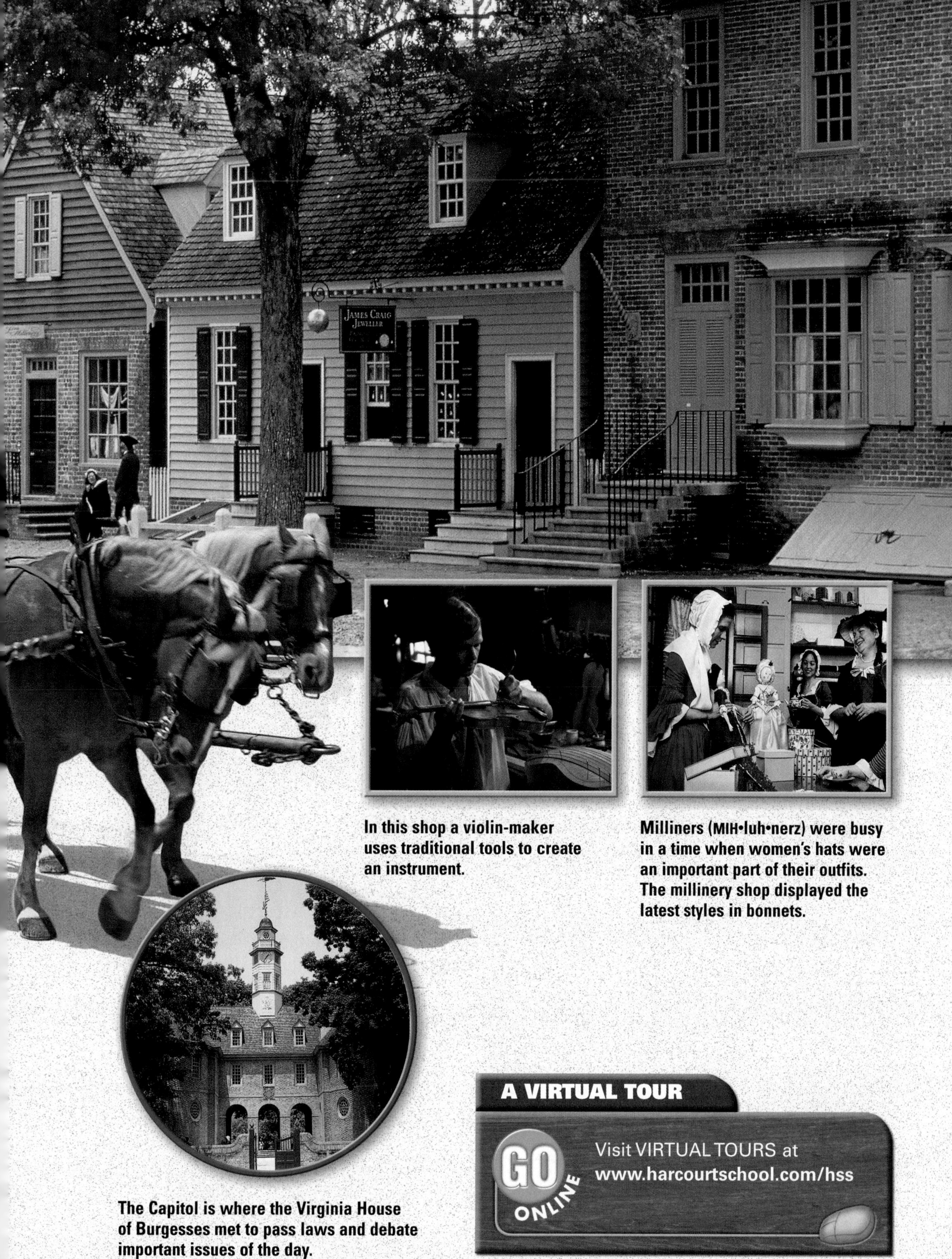

In this shop a violin-maker uses traditional tools to create an instrument.

Milliners (MIH•luh•nerz) were busy in a time when women's hats were an important part of their outfits. The millinery shop displayed the latest styles in bonnets.

The Capitol is where the Virginia House of Burgesses met to pass laws and debate important issues of the day.

A VIRTUAL TOUR

GO ONLINE

Visit VIRTUAL TOURS at www.harcourtschool.com/hss

Review

THE BIG IDEA

Commonality and Diversity The 13 English colonies were founded in different regions of North America and for different reasons.

Summary

Settling the Colonies

Thousands of English Puritans arrived in New England in the 1630s. Their religious beliefs shaped their lives. At town meetings, men who owned land elected public officials. These meetings taught the colonists to govern themselves.

The Middle Colonies—New York, New Jersey, Pennsylvania, and Delaware—were south of New England. People from many parts of the world settled there. Fertile land, a mild climate, rivers, and ports helped make the region prosperous.

Maryland, Virginia, North Carolina, South Carolina, and Georgia made up the Southern Colonies. Many enslaved Africans lived in this region. Most settlers owned small farms. A few lived on plantations and owned slaves. Southerners grew cash crops. Like other colonists, they sold these exports to England.

Early settlers often cooperated with American Indians, but growing settlements led to conflicts. Many Indians were killed, and others moved west.

Main Ideas and Vocabulary

Read the summary above. Then answer the questions that follow.

1. What did New England colonists do at town meetings?
   - **A** elected public officials
   - **B** raised barns
   - **C** built schools
   - **D** met with American Indians

2. What does the word prosperous mean?
   - **A** poor
   - **B** crowded
   - **C** successful
   - **D** fair

3. Where did most enslaved Africans live in North America?
   - **A** in the New England Colonies
   - **B** in the Middle Colonies
   - **C** in Spanish Florida
   - **D** in the Southern Colonies

4. What is an export?
   - **A** a product only made in New England
   - **B** a product stolen from another country
   - **C** a product that is never sold
   - **D** a product sold to another country

Recall Facts

Answer these questions.

5. What leader helped found the colony of Massachusetts?
6. What were four products that New England settlers exported?
7. Who were the Quakers?
8. What two ministers helped lead the Great Awakening?
9. In what ways did enslaved Africans respond to their condition?

Write the letter of the best choice.

10. Which region was called the "breadbasket colonies"?
    A New England
    B the Middle Colonies
    C the Southern Colonies
    D the backcountry
11. Which type of material do blacksmiths work with?
    A iron
    B wood
    C seeds
    D wax
12. Who established the Georgia Colony?
    A William Penn
    B John Winthrop
    C King George II
    D James Oglethorpe
13. Which statement best describes relations between settlers and American Indians in the Southern Colonies?
    A The Indians frightened away most of the settlers.
    B Both groups lived peacefully side by side.
    C The settlers pushed the Indians away from their lands.
    D The Indians cheated the new settlers in trade.

Think Critically

14. ANALYSIS SKILL Explain two reasons that farming was easier in the Middle Colonies than in New England.
15. ANALYSIS SKILL Describe the role that religion played in the founding of Maryland and Pennsylvania.

Apply Skills

Read a Land Use and Resources Map

Use the map below to answer the following questions.

16. What colony produced furs?
17. What colony produced mostly iron?
18. Which two colonies raised cattle?

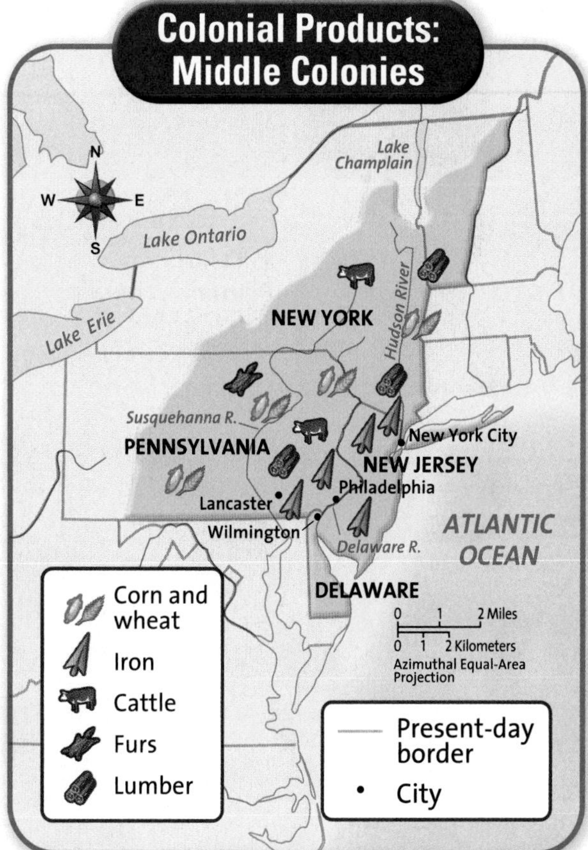

Unit 3

Activities

Read More

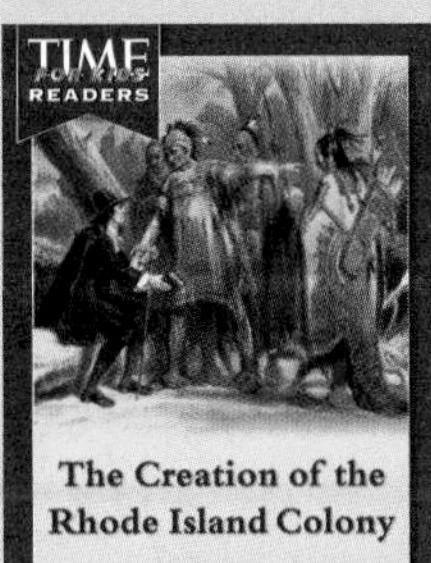

■ ***The Creation of the Rhode Island Colony*** **by Randi Hacker.**

■ ***William Penn: Founder of Pennsylvania*** **by Jeffrey Nelson.**

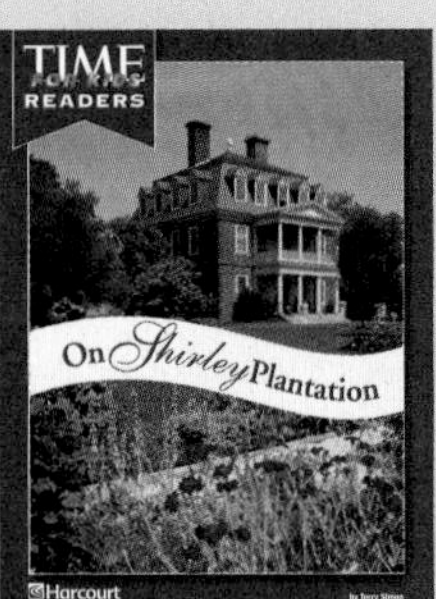

■ ***On Shirley Plantation*** **by Terry Simon.**

Show What You Know

Unit Writing Activity

Write a Narrative Imagine that you are a new settler in one of the colonies that you have read about. Write a story about what life is like in your colony. Tell about the role of religion, how your society is organized, how people govern themselves, and how colonists earn their livings. Make sure your narrative has a setting, or location, and a plot, or story.

Unit Project

A Colonial Fair Plan a display for a fair about daily life in the 13 English colonies. Focus on one New England, Middle, or Southern colony, and decide how you will show what life was like there. Your display should show the role of religion in your colony, how its society was organized, how the people governed themselves, and how they earned a living.

Visit ACTIVITIES at
www.harcourtschool.com/hss

The American Revolution

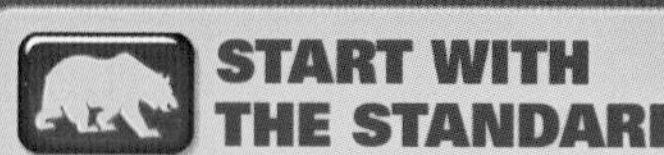

California History-Social Science Standards

5.3 Students describe the cooperation and conflict that existed among the American Indians and between the Indian nations and the new settlers.

5.5 Students explain the causes of the American Revolution.

5.6 Students understand the course and consequences of the American Revolution.

The Big Idea

FREEDOM

Freedom was so important to the colonists that they were willing to suffer terrible hardships and years of war to win it.

What to Know

- What disagreements led to the American Revolution?
- Which people and groups impacted the American Revolution?
- What were the major events and battles of the American Revolution?
- How did the American Revolution affect United States history?

Show What You Know

Unit 4

Time

The American Revolution

1765 The Stamp Act is passed, p. 327

1770 The Boston Massacre takes place, p. 331

1773 The Boston Tea Party takes place, p. 337

1760

1770

At the Same Time

1762 Catherine the Great becomes ruler of Russia

1769 Father Junípero Serra sets up the first Spanish mission in California

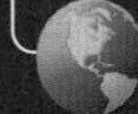

1770 James Cook explores Australia

The American Revolution

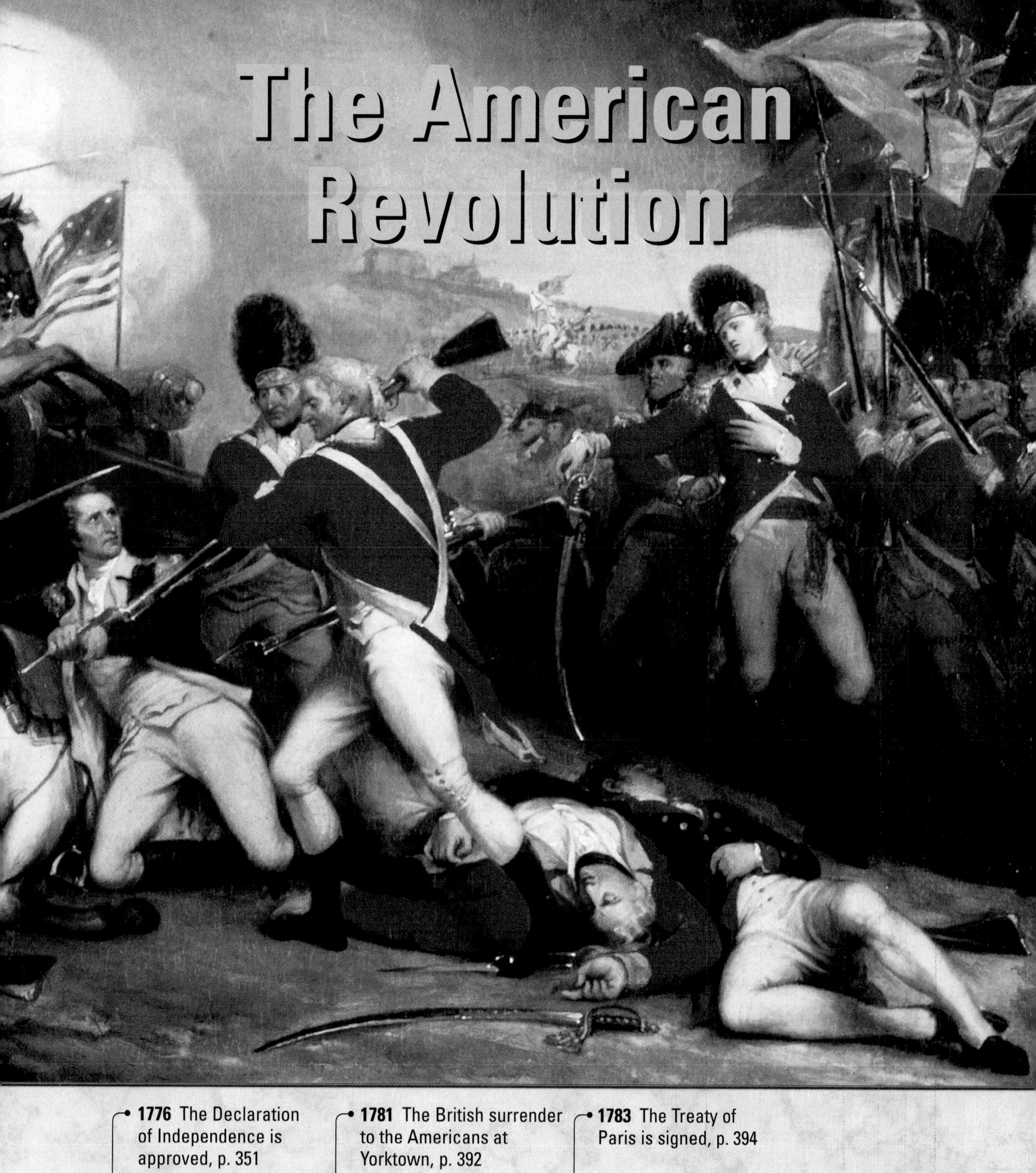

1776 The Declaration of Independence is approved, p. 351

1781 The British surrender to the Americans at Yorktown, p. 392

1783 The Treaty of Paris is signed, p. 394

1780

1790

Unit 4

People

Crispus Attucks

1725?–1770

- Killed by British soldiers at the Boston Massacre
- Often called the first person to be killed in the struggle for American freedom

Mercy Otis Warren

1728–1814

- Massachusetts patriot who wrote plays to protest British rule
- Wrote a history of the American Revolution

1725 — 1750 — 1775

- 1725? • Crispus Attucks — 1770
- 1728 • Mercy Otis Warren
- 1732 • George Washington
- 1736 • Patrick Henry
- 1742 • Thayendanegea
- 1743 • Thomas Jefferson
- 1746 • Bernardo de Gálvez — 1786
- 1754? • Mary Ludwig Hayes McCauley

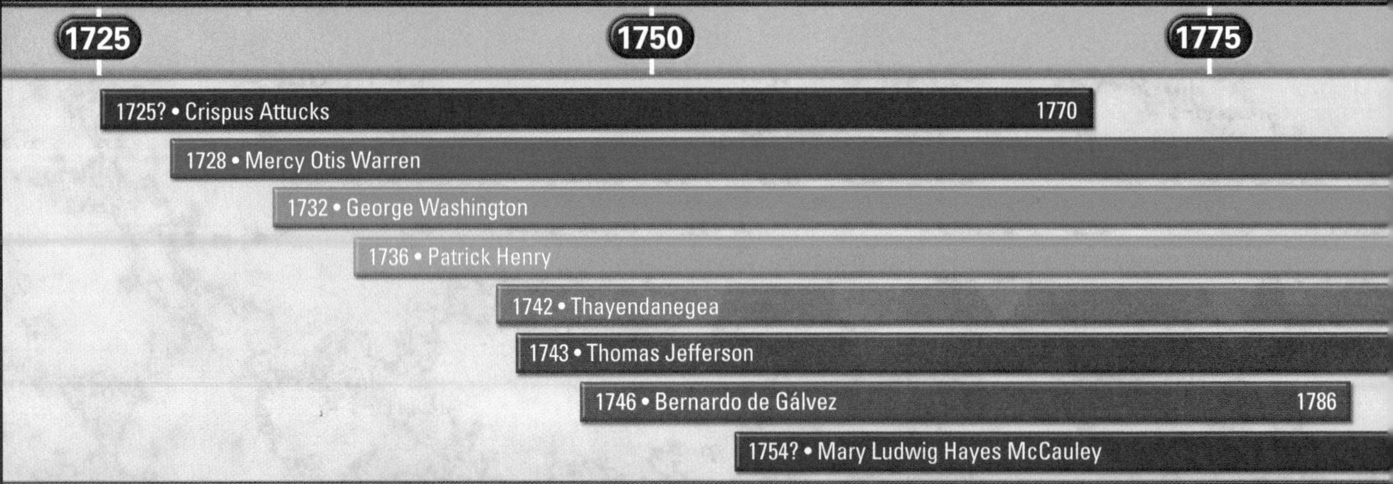

Thayendanegea

1742–1807

- Mohawk Indian leader who later took the name Joseph Brant
- Helped the British during the American Revolution

Thomas Jefferson

1743–1826

- Chief writer of the Declaration of Independence
- Served as the third President of the United States

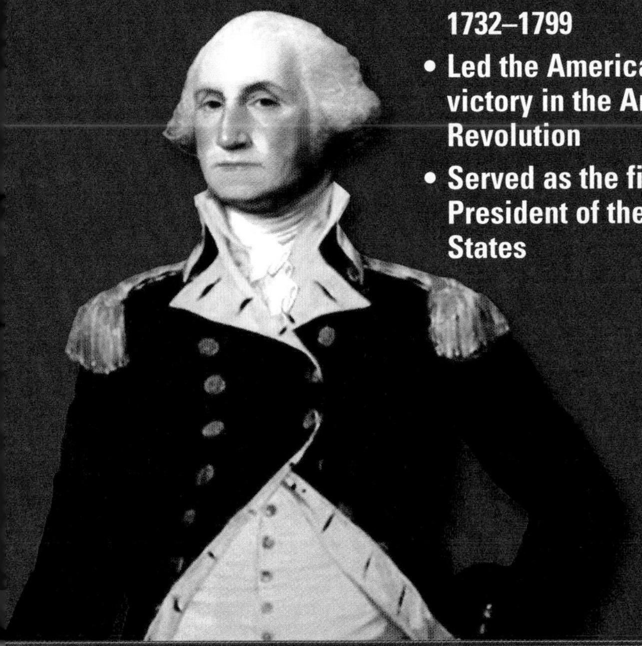

George Washington

1732–1799

- Led the Americans to victory in the American Revolution
- Served as the first President of the United States

Patrick Henry

1736–1799

- A member of the Virginia House of Burgesses
- Spoke out against British rule and taxes

1800 1825 1850

1814

1799

1799

1807

1826

1832

Bernardo de Gálvez

1746–1786

- Governor of Spanish Louisiana
- Helped the Americans during the Revolutionary War

Mary Ludwig Hays McCauley

1754?–1832

- Earned the nickname Molly Pitcher by carrying water to troops during the Battle of Monmouth
- Fired cannons during the battle after her husband was wounded

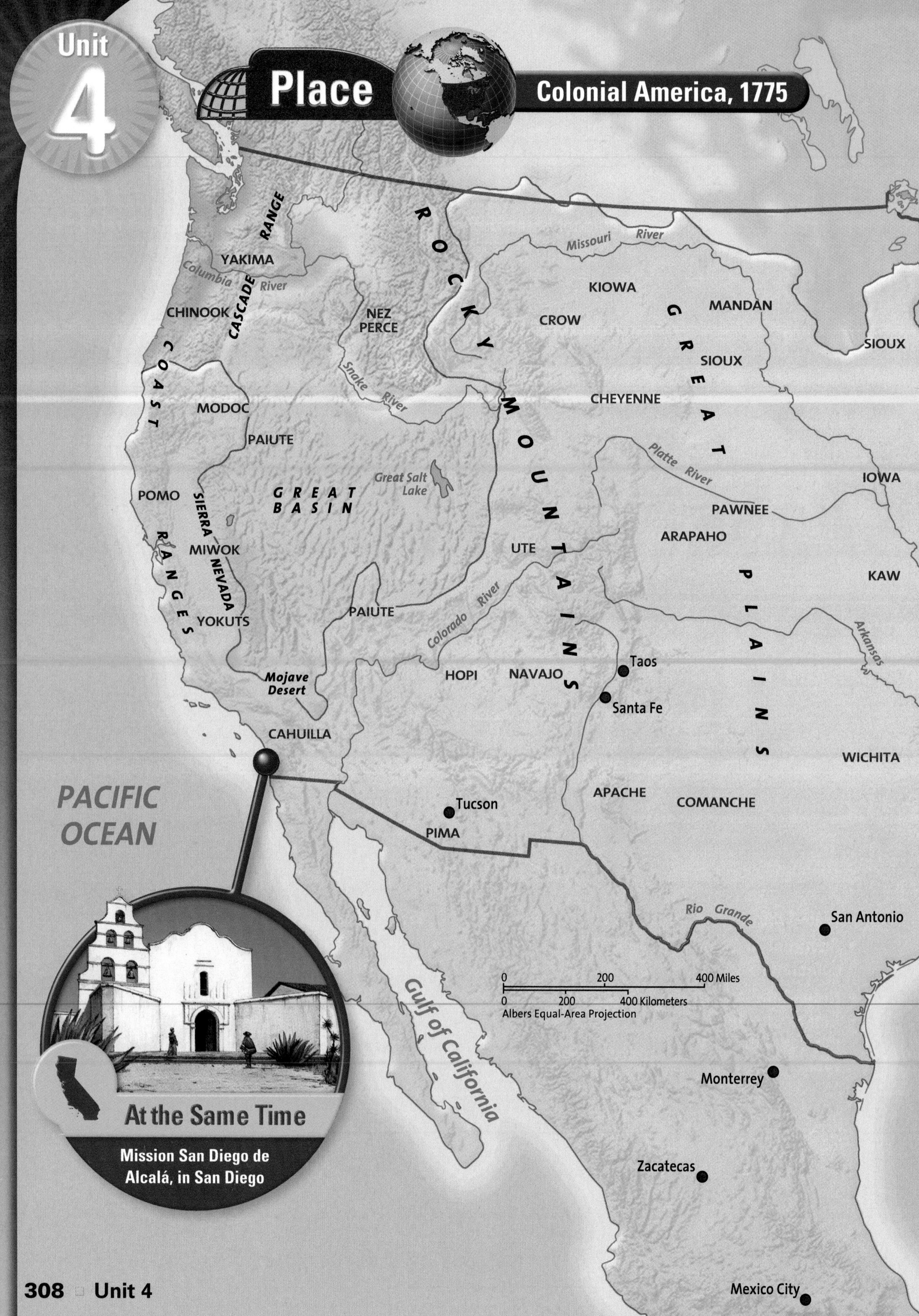

Mission San Diego de Alcalá, in San Diego

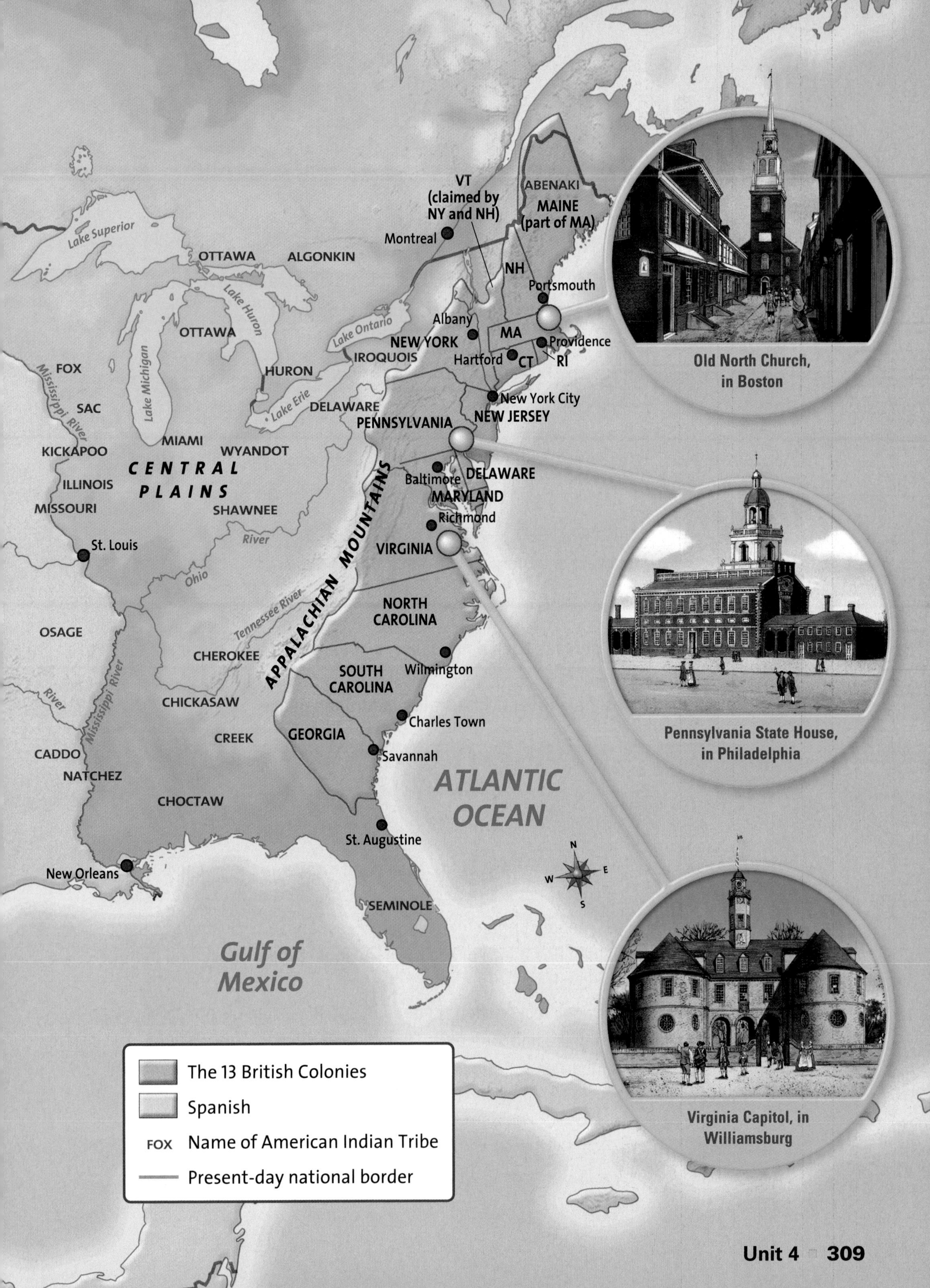

Old North Church, in Boston

Pennsylvania State House, in Philadelphia

Virginia Capitol, in Williamsburg

Reading Social Studies

Focus Skill: Cause and Effect

A **cause** is an action or event that makes something else happen. An **effect** is what happens as the result of that action or event.

Why It Matters

Understanding cause and effect can help you see why events and actions happen.

Cause		Effect
An event or action	→	What happens

- ✓ Words and phrases such as *because, since, so,* and *as a result* are clues to cause and effect.
- ✓ Sometimes the effect may be stated before the cause.

Practice the Skill

Read the paragraphs that follow. Find causes and effects in the second paragraph.

In the mid-1600s, people began to leave the Massachusetts Colony and start their own settlements. Some left for religious reasons. Others left to find better economic opportunities.

Cause — Effect

By the mid-1700s, colonists no longer needed supplies from Europe to survive. They had their own cities and successful businesses. Also, more and more colonists had been born in America. It was the only home they knew. For these reasons, the colonists began to feel less dependent on England.

Apply What You Learned

Find Cause and Effect **Read the paragraphs, and answer the questions.**

From Strangers to Neighbors

In 1765, John Rutledge traveled from his home in South Carolina to New York. He called it his first trip to a foreign country. That says a lot about how the colonists viewed one another. The colonies had been founded at different times and for different reasons. Each had its own mix of people, its own economy, and its own form of government. As a result, the colonies really were like different countries.

Things were about to change, though, and John Rutledge would play a part in the changes. He was going to New York to meet with representatives from 10 colonies to discuss a new English tax. The colonists thought that the tax was unfair and they wanted to figure out how to respond to it.

While in New York, Rutledge met with Sir William Johnson. Johnson was a wealthy English merchant who had a strong relationship with the Iroquois Indians. Johnson told Rutledge about how the Iroquois League worked together to solve problems.

Rutledge was impressed with what Johnson told him. He told other colonists about the Iroquois League. Like the Iroquois, the colonists soon began to cooperate and started seeing each other not as foreigners but as neighbors.

Focus Skill

Cause and Effect

1. **What caused John Rutledge to travel to New York?**
2. **What caused the colonists to see one another as foreigners?**
3. **What was Rutledge's opinion of the Iroquois League?**

Study Skills

CONNECT IDEAS

Graphic organizers are drawings that help you organize information. They can help you connect ideas.

- **One kind of organizer is a bubble map. On a bubble map, the main idea is written in the center bubble. The ideas that are related to the main idea are written in the surrounding bubbles.**

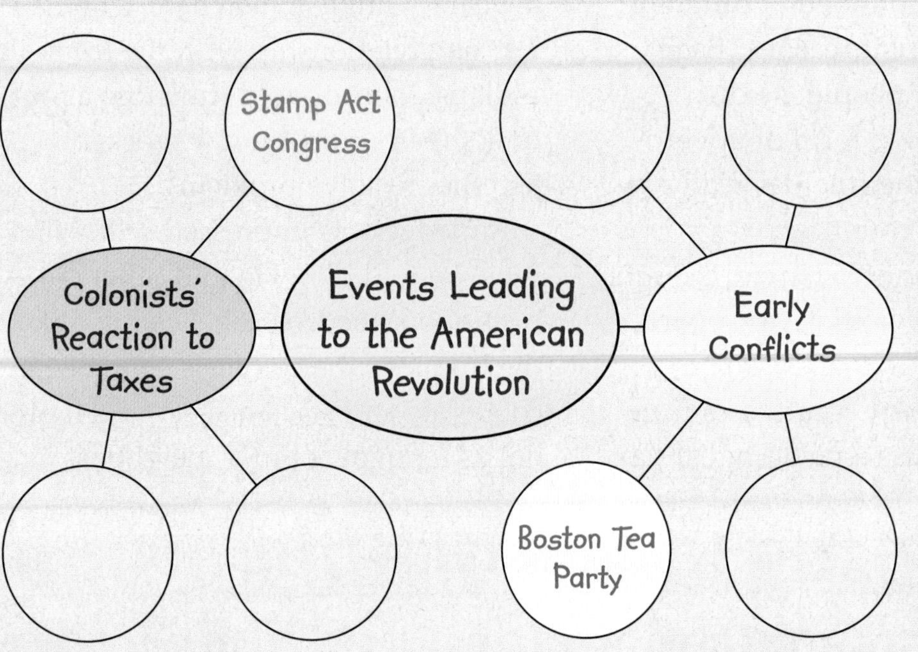

Apply As You Read

As you read this chapter, copy and complete the graphic organizer above. Fill in each bubble by adding the facts and details that support the main idea.

California History-Social Science Standards, Grade 5

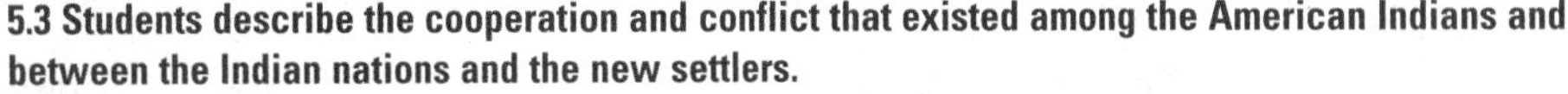

5.3 Students describe the cooperation and conflict that existed among the American Indians and between the Indian nations and the new settlers.
5.5 Students explain the causes of the American Revolution.
5.6 Students understand the course and consequences of the American Revolution.

The Colonies Unite

Faneuil Hall in Boston, Massachusetts

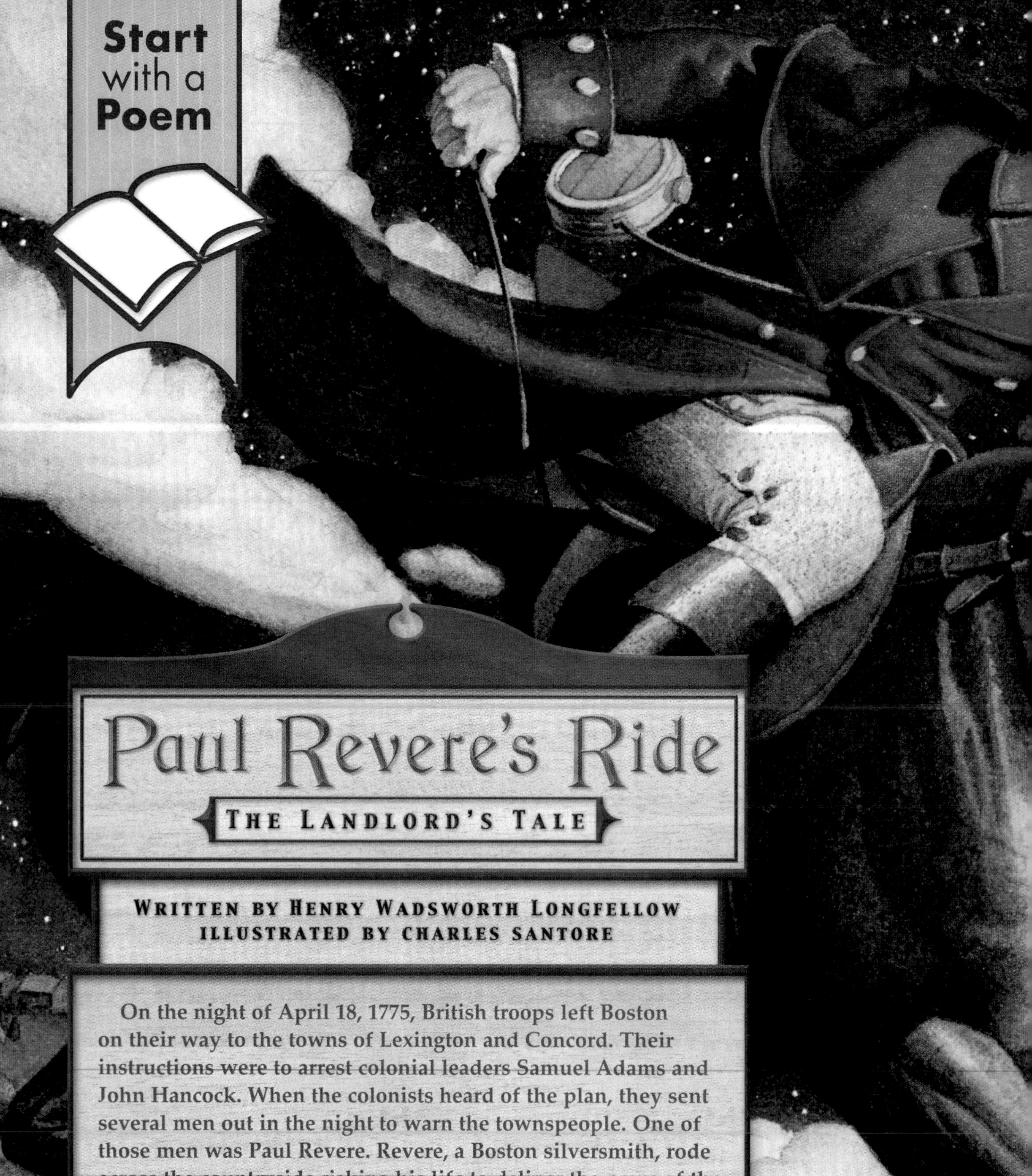

Paul Revere's Ride

The Landlord's Tale

Written by Henry Wadsworth Longfellow
Illustrated by Charles Santore

On the night of April 18, 1775, British troops left Boston on their way to the towns of Lexington and Concord. Their instructions were to arrest colonial leaders Samuel Adams and John Hancock. When the colonists heard of the plan, they sent several men out in the night to warn the townspeople. One of those men was Paul Revere. Revere, a Boston silversmith, rode across the countryside risking his life to deliver the news of the British advance. Almost one hundred years after the legendary ride, poet Henry Wadsworth Longfellow wrote a poem in remembrance of Revere's brave deed. Read now a passage from the poem.

Listen, my children, and you shall hear
Of the midnight ride of Paul Revere,
On the eighteenth of April, in Seventy-five;
Hardly a man is now alive
Who remembers that famous day and year.

He said to his friend, "If the British march
by land or sea from the town to-night,
Hang a lantern aloft in the belfry arch
Of the North Church tower as a signal light,—
One if by land, and two, if by sea;
And I on the opposite shore will be,
Ready to ride and spread the alarm
Through every Middlesex village and farm,
For the country folk to be up and to arm."...

And lo! as he looks, on the belfry's height
A glimmer, and then a gleam of light!
He springs to the saddle, the bridle he turns,
But lingers and gazes, till full on his sight
A second lamp in the belfry burns!

belfry a bell tower

A hurry of hoofs in a village street,
A shape in the moonlight, a bulk in the dark,
And beneath, from the pebbles, in passing, a spark
Struck out by a steed flying fearless and fleet;

That was all! And yet, through the gloom and the light,
The fate of a nation was riding that night;
And the spark struck out by that steed, in his flight,
Kindled the land into flame with its heat. . . .

You know the rest. In the books you have read
How the British Regulars fired and fled,—
How the farmers gave them ball for ball,
From behind each fence and farm-yard wall,
Chasing the red-coats down the lane,
Then crossing the fields to emerge again
Under the trees at the turn of the road,
And only pausing to fire and load.

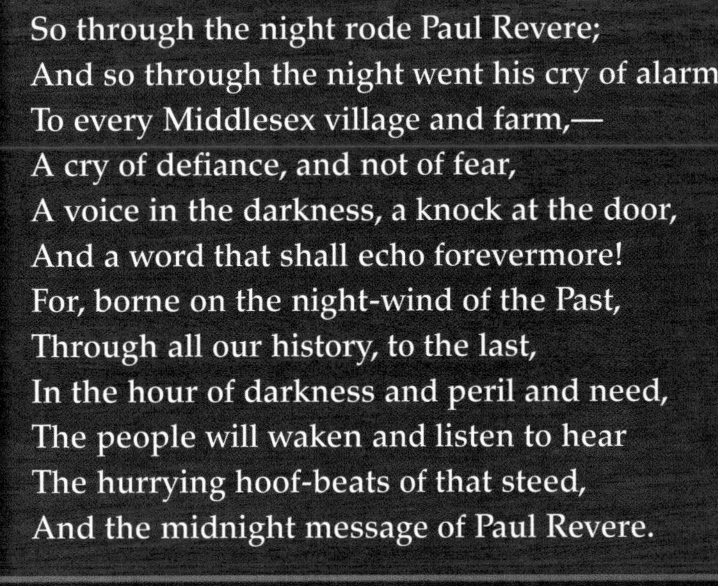

So through the night rode Paul Revere;
And so through the night went his cry of alarm
To every Middlesex village and farm,—
A cry of defiance, and not of fear,
A voice in the darkness, a knock at the door,
And a word that shall echo forevermore!
For, borne on the night-wind of the Past,
Through all our history, to the last,
In the hour of darkness and peril and need,
The people will waken and listen to hear
The hurrying hoof-beats of that steed,
And the midnight message of Paul Revere.

Response Corner

1. What does the author mean when he says, "And the spark struck out by that steed, in his flight, Kindled the land into flame with its heat"?
2. Write a poem about a famous event during the American Revolution or an American who lived during that time.

Lesson 1

1750 — 1790

1754 The Battle of Fort Necessity

1763 The French and Indian War ends

1764 Britain passes the Sugar Act

Competition for Control

WHAT TO KNOW
What events caused the French and Indian War?

- ✓ Describe the fight for control of North America.
- ✓ Describe how alliances between American Indians and colonists affected the French and Indian War.
- ✓ Explain the new laws passed after the French and Indian War.

VOCABULARY
alliance p. 320
delegate p. 320
Parliament p. 321
proclamation p. 322

PEOPLE
George Washington
Benjamin Franklin
William Pitt
King George III

PLACES
Fort Necessity
Albany

CAUSE AND EFFECT

California Standards
HSS 5.3, 5.3.1, 5.3.2, 5.3.3, 5.5, 5.5.1, 5.5.4

YOU ARE THERE It's bright and sunny outside **Fort Necessity**, but you're not interested in the weather. The Pennsylvania woods around you look dark and dangerous. Any minute now, your small fort may be attacked. You're scared, but you will fight to keep this land from becoming a French colony.

Listening carefully, you hear a twig crack in the woods. "Did you hear that?" you ask the soldier standing next to you.

There's a shout as one of the other soldiers in your group runs into sight. His uniform is torn and dirty. "It's the French!" he yells. "We're surrounded!"

A replica of the original Fort Necessity can be seen at Fort Necessity National Battlefield near Farmington, Pennsylvania.

Conflicting Claims

By the mid-1700s, Spain, France, and Britain, as England became known, were trying to keep control of their lands in North America. For the most part, Spain claimed southwestern lands. France claimed lands to the north and in the middle of what is now the United States. Most of the land that Britain claimed was along the Atlantic coast or in what is now Canada.

Both Britain and France claimed the Ohio Valley—a region that stretches about 1,000 miles along the Ohio River from the Appalachians to the Mississippi River. To the French, the Ohio Valley was an important link between France's lands in Canada and Louisiana. The British saw it as an area for trade and growth.

By about 1750, the French sent soldiers to the Ohio Valley to drive out British traders. They also began building forts near the eastern end of the valley. The British viewed this as an act of war.

READING CHECK **CAUSE AND EFFECT**
What caused the British and the French to compete for the Ohio Valley?

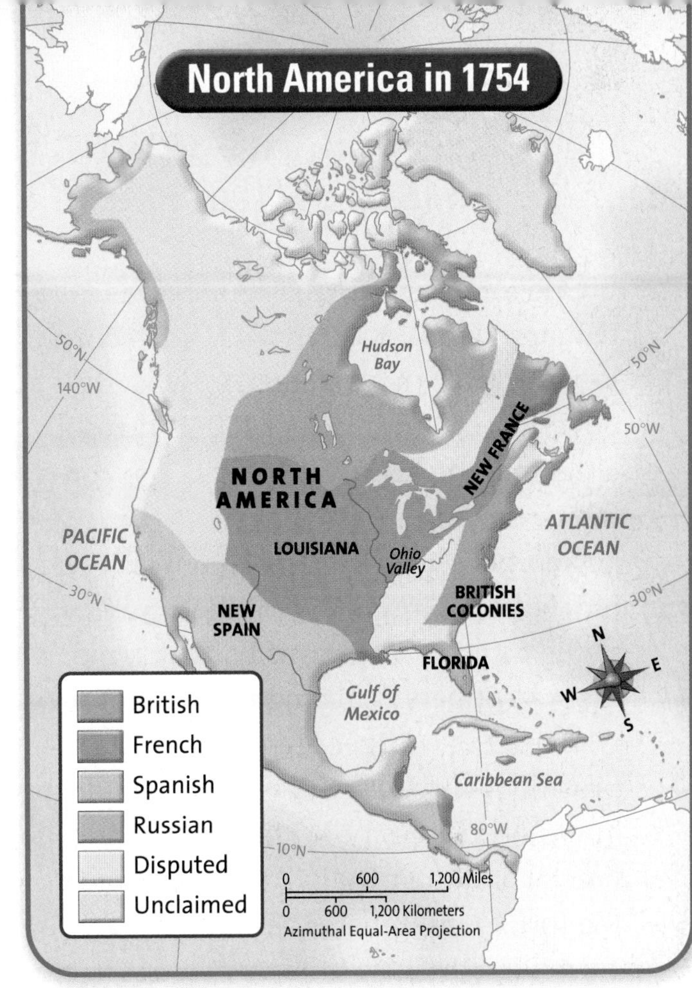

ANALYSIS SKILL Analyze Maps

Regions **Which two groups of Europeans claimed land east and west of the Ohio Valley?**

The French and Indian War Begins

One fort that the French built was Fort Duquesne (doo•KAYN), where Pittsburgh, Pennsylvania, now stands. In 1754, the governor of Virginia sent 150 British soldiers into the Ohio Valley to regain control of the area.

George Washington, then only 21 years old, led the Virginians. On their way to the fort, the Virginians battled some French soldiers. Washington thought they were part of a larger French force, so to protect themselves, the Virginians quickly built Fort Necessity. Within days, the French and their Indian allies attacked the fort. Outnumbered, the Virginians surrendered. This battle turned out to be the start of the French and Indian War.

By the mid-1700s, both France and Britain had formed alliances with many of the American Indian tribes in the Ohio Valley. An **alliance** is a formal agreement among groups or individuals. Once fighting broke out, the French and the British asked their Indian allies for help.

In 1754, colonial leaders met at **Albany**, New York, to discuss the war. Seven colonies sent **delegates**, or representatives. **Benjamin Franklin**, from Pennsylvania, proposed what became known as the Albany Plan of Union. He said that the colonies should join together under one government in order to fight the French. Franklin's plan was rejected because the colonies were not yet willing to work together.

READING CHECK **CAUSE AND EFFECT**
What caused the Albany Plan of Union to be rejected?

At the start of the war, the British had not yet adapted to fighting in the woods. Their red uniform jackets made them easy targets.

The British Road to Victory

As the French and Indian War continued, the colonists knew they needed more help if they were to win the war. So **Parliament**, the lawmaking body of the British government, sent an army to the colonies to help fight the French and their Indian allies. General Edward Braddock commanded the British.

In April 1755, Braddock and more than 1,800 British and colonial troops marched to attack the French at Fort Duquesne. Braddock invited George Washington along as an adviser. Washington later described how the soldiers looked in their bright, colorful uniforms—British red and colonial blue—marching off against a deep green forest.

The British soldiers had been trained to fight in open fields. They were surprised to find that the French fought like their Indian allies, from behind trees and large rocks. As a result, the early battles did not go well for the British, and Braddock was killed in the fighting. To win the war, British leader **William Pitt** sent more troops and supplies to the colonies.

Beginning in 1758, the war turned in Britain's favor. British soldiers captured several French forts, including Fort Duquesne. British troops and ships slowly circled around New France, defeating the French at Quebec and then at Montreal.

In the closing months of the war, which had spread to Europe, Spain joined France in the fight against the British. Britain had a stronger navy, however, and it defeated the Spanish forces in 1762. To make up for Spain's losses in the war, France gave Spain most of its lands west of the Mississippi River.

The French and Indian War ended in 1763, when the French and the British signed the Treaty of Paris. It gave Britain most of Canada, all French lands east of the Mississippi River, and Spanish Florida. The French lost nearly all their lands in North America.

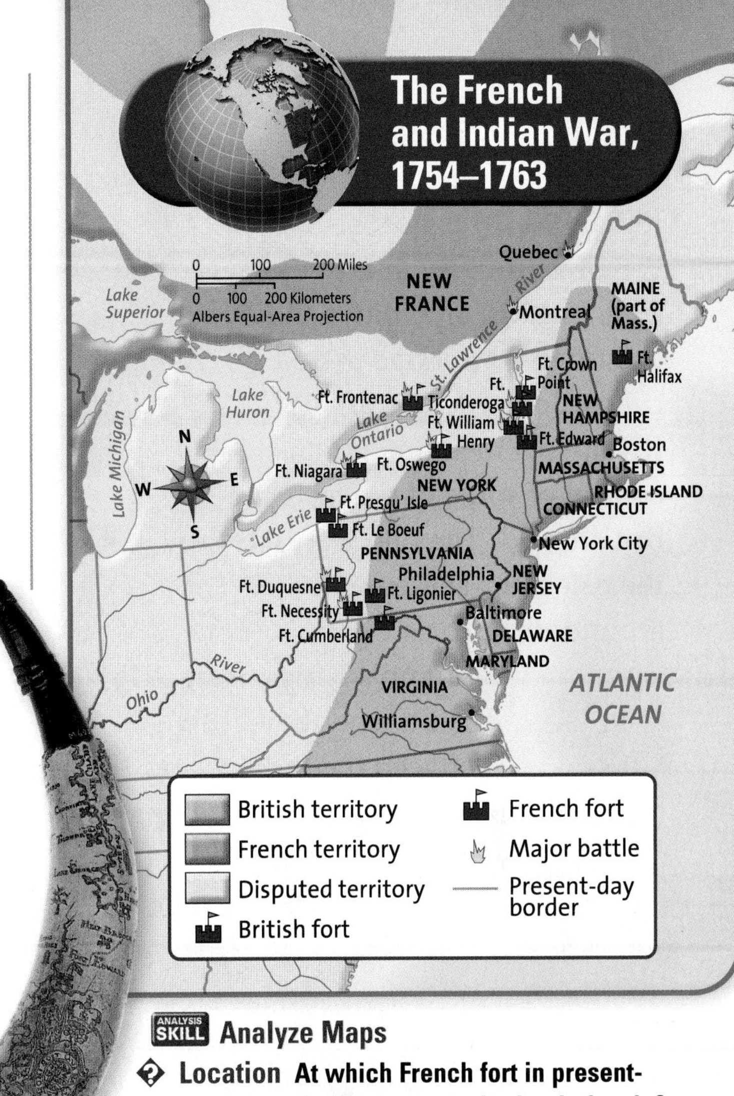

ANALYSIS SKILL Analyze Maps

Location At which French fort in present-day Pennsylvania was a major battle fought?

READING CHECK CAUSE AND EFFECT
What was the effect of the Treaty of Paris?

More Troubles

The end of the French and Indian War was not the end of Britain's troubles in the colonies. In 1763, an Ottawa Indian chief named Pontiac united tribes along the Mississippi River. Together, the Indians took control of some of the forts the British held. They hoped to destroy the colonists' settlements around those forts.

Chief Pontiac

Britain's **King George III** tried to end the fighting between the Indians and colonists by making a **proclamation**, or public announcement. The Proclamation of 1763 said that all lands west of the Appalachian Mountains belonged to the Indians. White settlers already in those lands were ordered to leave.

Most colonists ignored the Proclamation of 1763, and thousands more moved west. As a result, fighting between the Indians and the settlers continued. One British leader did not like the way settlers moved into Indian lands. He predicted that more people would move into the western areas of New York and start a war with the Indians there.

The Proclamation of 1763 upset many colonists. They believed they had fought the war to keep the French from blocking their settlement of the western frontier. The colonists did not like the British government telling them to stay out of those lands.

Colonists were also angered by new taxes passed by Parliament. The British thought the colonists should help pay for the cost of defending the colonies. In 1764, Parliament passed the Sugar Act to raise money for Britain. This act taxed the sugar and molasses brought into the colonies from the West Indies.

The Sugar Act mostly affected the shipping business of the New England Colonies. Many merchants objected to the tax. Still, the British government continued taxing goods in the colonies. Soon it would pass even more new taxes.

READING CHECK DRAWING CONCLUSIONS
How did colonists feel about British rule after the Proclamation of 1763?

➤ Many British leaders blamed Pontiac's rebellion on frontier settlers. These settlers often built and lived in log cabins.

Summary

Conflicting claims to North American land led to the French and Indian War. Britain defeated France in the war. After the war, Britain issued the Proclamation of 1763, but most colonists ignored it and kept moving west.

REVIEW

1. What events caused the French and Indian War?
2. Use the term **alliance** in a sentence about the French and Indian War.
3. How did colonists react to the Proclamation of 1763?

CRITICAL THINKING

4. ANALYSIS SKILL Why do you think the French soldiers chose to fight in the same way as their Indian allies?
5. ANALYSIS SKILL What was the main effect of Britain winning the French and Indian War?
6. **Write a Newspaper Story** Imagine you are a news reporter in 1763. Write a story describing colonists' concerns about the Proclamation of 1763.
7. Focus Skill **CAUSE AND EFFECT** On a separate sheet of paper, copy and complete the graphic organizer below.

Cause	Effect
	The French attack troops at Fort Necessity.
The British thought colonists should help pay for the war.	

Compare Historical Maps

WHY IT MATTERS

The Treaty of Paris that officially ended the French and Indian War changed the map of North America. You can learn about the changes by comparing the historical maps on page 325. A historical map shows information about a place at a certain time in history. Knowing how to compare historical maps can help you learn how a place and its borders changed over time.

WHAT YOU NEED TO KNOW

Follow these steps to compare the historical maps on page 325.

Step 1 **Study the map key for each map. Notice the colors on both maps. These colors show you which areas were claimed by Britain, France, Spain, and Russia.**

Step 2 **Look at Map B to find a pattern of stripes that mapmakers call hatch lines. Hatch lines may show land identified in two ways. The hatch lines on Map B show areas of British land reserved for American Indians.**

Step 3 **Study Map B to find the thick blue line. This line identifies the border created by the Proclamation Line of 1763.**

Flags over North America

Spain

These flags were flown over different parts of North America in the mid-1700s.

Russia

Britain

France

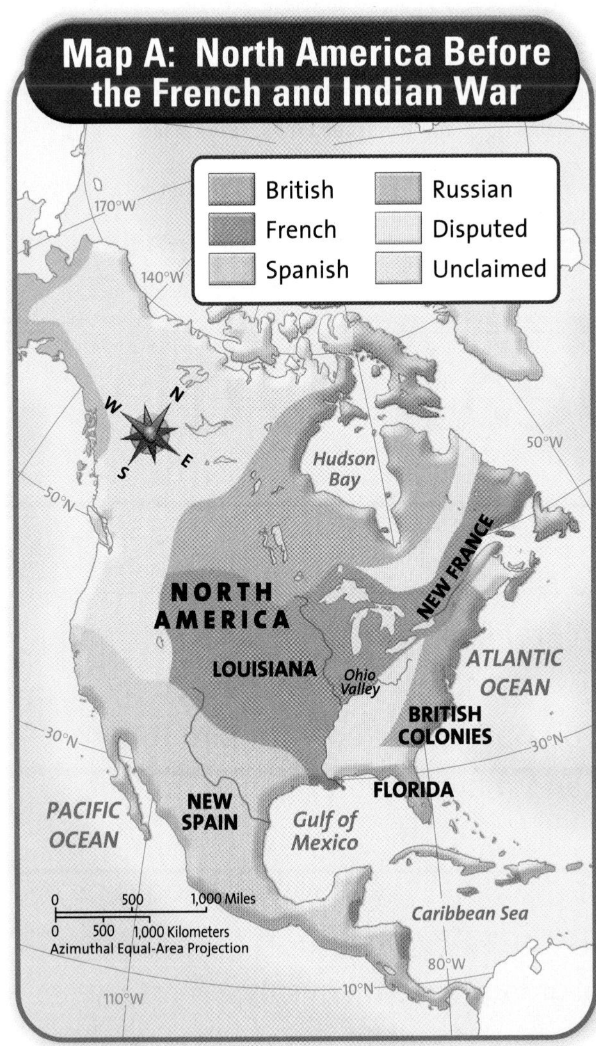

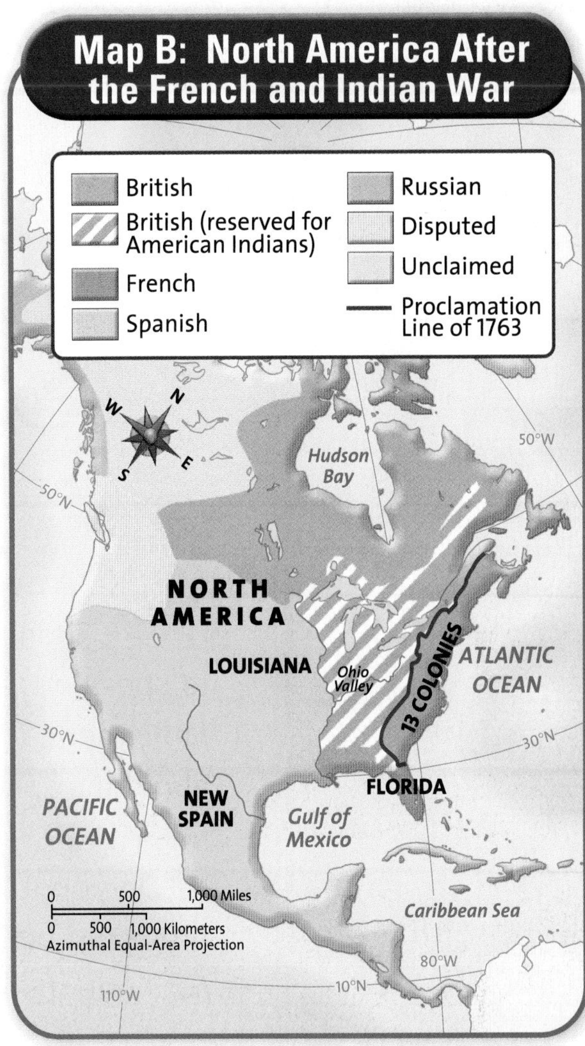

PRACTICE THE SKILL

Use Maps A and B to answer these questions.

1. Which country claimed Florida before the French and Indian War? after the war?
2. Why is the border created by the Proclamation Line of 1763 shown only on Map B?
3. Did Spain gain or lose land as a result of the French and Indian War?
4. Why does Map A have much more purple than Map B?

APPLY WHAT YOU LEARNED

ANALYSIS SKILL Study the maps on this page. Then use the information on the maps to write a summary of changes caused by the French and Indian War. Share your summary with a classmate.

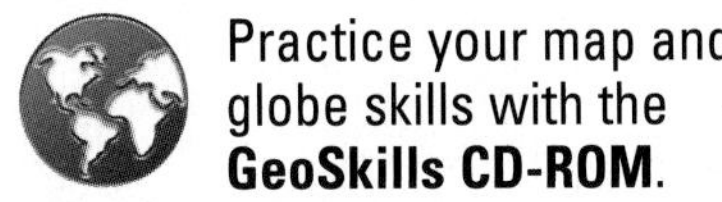
Practice your map and globe skills with the **GeoSkills CD-ROM**.

Lesson 2

1750 — 1790

1765 Britain passes the Stamp Act

1767 Britain passes the Townshend Acts

1770 The Boston Massacre takes place

Colonists Speak Out

WHAT TO KNOW
Why were colonists angered by Britain's new colonial tax laws?

- ✓ Identify the laws that caused conflict with the colonies.
- ✓ Explain the importance of the Committees of Correspondence.

VOCABULARY
budget p. 327
representation p. 327
treason p. 327
Committee of Correspondence p. 328
imperial policy p. 328
boycott p. 329
repeal p. 329

PEOPLE
King George III
George Grenville
Patrick Henry
Samuel Adams
Crispus Attucks
Paul Revere

PLACES
Boston
New York

CAUSE AND EFFECT

HSS 5.5, 5.5.1, 5.5.2, 5.5.4

YOU ARE THERE

A hush falls over the British Parliament as Benjamin Franklin rises to speak. He is about to speak out against the latest tax law passed by Parliament, and you have traveled with him to write about his speech and maybe even meet with **King George III**.

"Do you think it right that the colonies should be protected by Britain and pay no part of the expense?" asks one member of Parliament sharply.

"That is not the case," Franklin says. "The colonies raised, clothed, and paid, during the last year, near 25,000 men, and spent many millions."*

Surely, you think, Parliament will take back the law.

*Benjamin Franklin. *The Parliamentary History of England.* T.C. Hansard, 1813.

A meeting of the British Parliament

Stamp Act Protest

Analyze Drawings
This 1765 drawing shows a group of colonists in New Hampshire protesting the Stamp Act.

1. **The coffin represents the wish to see the Stamp Act die.**
2. **The figure made of straw represents a stamp tax collector.**
3. **This angry protester prepares to throw a rock at the straw figure.**

Why do you think the protesters placed the straw figure high on a pole?

The Stamp Act

After the French and Indian War ended, the British Parliament reviewed its **budget**, or plan for spending money. British leader **George Grenville** said that Parliament needed more money to pay off the costs of the war. He argued that the American colonists should pay higher taxes. Parliament agreed and passed the Sugar Act in April 1764.

Less than a year later, in March 1765, Parliament passed the Stamp Act. The Stamp Act placed a tax on paper documents in the colonies. Newspapers, legal documents, and even playing cards had to have a special stamp on them to show that the tax had been paid.

In the colonies, the reaction to the Stamp Act was quick and angry. Many colonists said that Parliament could not tax them because the colonists had no **representation**, or voice, in Parliament.

In 1765, delegates from nine colonies met in New York City in what became known as the Stamp Act Congress. James Otis of Massachusetts spoke out against the Stamp Act. The colonists began repeating the words—no taxation without representation.

That same year, **Patrick Henry** told his fellow members of the Virginia House of Burgesses that Parliament did not represent the colonies. Those who agreed with Parliament shouted "Treason! Treason!" By accusing Henry of **treason**, they were saying he was guilty of working against his own government. Still, the House of Burgesses voted not to pay the new taxes set by Parliament.

READING CHECK **CAUSE AND EFFECT**
What caused Parliament to pass new taxes?

Colonists Join Together

The Stamp Act Congress showed that colonists could work together, but to do so, they would need new ways to share information. News traveled slowly in those days. It could take weeks for people to find out about events in other colonies.

To speed information, the colonists formed **Committees of Correspondence**. Members of these committees started by corresponding with, or writing letters to, one another. Then, they used the mail to spread the news. In 1764, people in **Boston** formed a Committee of Correspondence in response to the Sugar Act. The next year, colonists in **New York** formed another committee. They wrote about important events, such as New York's protest of the Stamp Act.

In 1772, **Samuel Adams** asked leaders in Boston to begin a new Committee of Correspondence, and they agreed. The Boston committee began writing to other cities and towns, asking them to protest British **imperial policies**, the laws and orders issued by the British government.

Colonists soon spoke about the need for a Committee of Correspondence in every colony. Virginia formed a committee in 1773. The members wrote that all colonists should be "much disturbed by various rumors and reports of proceedings tending to deprive them of their . . . rights."* The Virginia colonists then asked other colonies to start their own Committees of Correspondence to gain support for their cause and share news and information.

**Virginia Resolutions Establishing a Committee of Correspondence, 1773.* Lillian Goldman Law Library, Yale University.

Delivering the Mail

Analyze Illustrations During the colonial era, delivering the mail took much longer than it does today.

About how long did it take mail to go from Boston to New York City? from Boston to Williamsburg?

Colonists wrote letters to express their points of view about British laws.

Working as a group, many colonists tried to force Britain to take back the Stamp Act. They decided not to buy goods that were taxed. More and more people in the colonies began to **boycott**, or refuse to buy, British goods.

Soon after the Stamp Act was passed, a group of colonists called the Sons of Liberty began working to stop it. This group took its name from a speech that was given in Parliament and that called the colonists "these sons of liberty."*

The Sons of Liberty captured several British officials who tried to collect the tax. They covered the officials in sticky tar and dumped feathers on them. People in Britain had used this practice, known as tarring and feathering, to scare away tax collectors.

Colonial teapot

Women played a role in resisting. They formed their own group, known as the Daughters of Liberty. In Rhode Island, members of the group began spinning and weaving cloth for sale in place of British cloth. The cloth was so popular that the women chose a large place to make it—the city courthouse!

By 1766, British merchants had lost a lot of money from the boycott. Sales of British goods fell by almost half in some colonies. More and more people in Britain spoke out against the Stamp Act. Soon after Benjamin Franklin spoke to Parliament, it voted to **repeal**, or take back, the act.

READING CHECK MAIN IDEA AND DETAILS
What did colonists want to accomplish by forming Committees of Correspondence?

*Isaac Barré. *Liberty: The American Revolution* by Thomas Fleming. Viking, 1997.

Colonists could gain support in distant cities by writing letters.

Children IN HISTORY

Supporting the Boycott

To support the boycott against British goods, sewing groups sprang up all over the colonies. Much of the spinning, weaving, and sewing was done by girls. Twelve-year-old Anna Green was part of a sewing group at her church in Boston. Each morning, as the minister read from the Bible, Anna worked away at the spinning wheel.

Fifteen-year-old Charity Clark spun wool at her home in New York City. In a letter to her cousin in Britain, she wrote, "Heroines may not distinguish themselves at the head of an Army, but freedom [will] also be won by a fighting army of [women] . . . armed with spinning wheels." *

Make It Relevant Would you have been willing to work in support of the boycott?

*Charity Clark. *We Were There, Too! Young People in U.S. History* by Philip Hoose. Melanie Kroupa Books, 2001.

The Townshend Acts

Soon more tax troubles began, as Parliament proposed new taxes for the colonies. In 1767, Parliament passed the Townshend Acts, which taxed imports such as glass, tea, paint, and paper brought into the colonies. The Townshend Acts also set up a new group of tax collectors. By passing the Townshend Acts, the British government showed it believed that Parliament still had the authority to make laws for the colonists.

The Daughters of Liberty asked people to stop drinking British tea, so some colonists drank tea made from local plants. Merchants in Boston would not import taxed goods. Some Boston colonists even refused to paint their houses because they did not want to pay the tax on paint.

Like the Stamp Act, the Townshend Acts were a failure for Britain. Sales of British goods in the colonies went down, and tax officers collected little money. In 1770, Parliament repealed all of the Townshend Acts except for the tax on tea. Still, many colonists resisted imperial policy by refusing to buy British tea.

As the colonies grew more rebellious, Parliament sent more soldiers to Boston and New York City. By 1770, about 9,000 British soldiers were in the colonies, and about 4,000 of them were stationed in Boston.

READING CHECK CAUSE AND EFFECT
What were some of the effects of the Townshend Acts?

The Boston Massacre

TIME **March 5, 1770**

PLACE **Boston, Massachusetts**

Having British soldiers in their cities angered many colonists. They made fun of the soldiers' bright red uniform jackets, calling them "lobsters" and "redcoats." Some of the soldiers became so angry that they destroyed colonial property.

The anger between the colonists and the British soldiers grew, and fights broke out more and more often. One of the worst fights took place in Boston on March 5, 1770, when a large crowd of angry colonists gathered near several British soldiers. The colonists shouted insults at the soldiers and began throwing rocks and snowballs at them.

As the crowd moved forward, the soldiers opened fire. Three colonists were killed on the spot, and two others died later.

GEOGRAPHY

Boston

Find the Old State House, also called the Town House, on the map of Boston shown below. Then look at the painting of Boston in 1770, which shows the Old State House in the middle. The Old State House was the headquarters of Britain's Custom House in Boston, where taxes on trade goods were paid and collected. The Boston Massacre took place just east of this building.

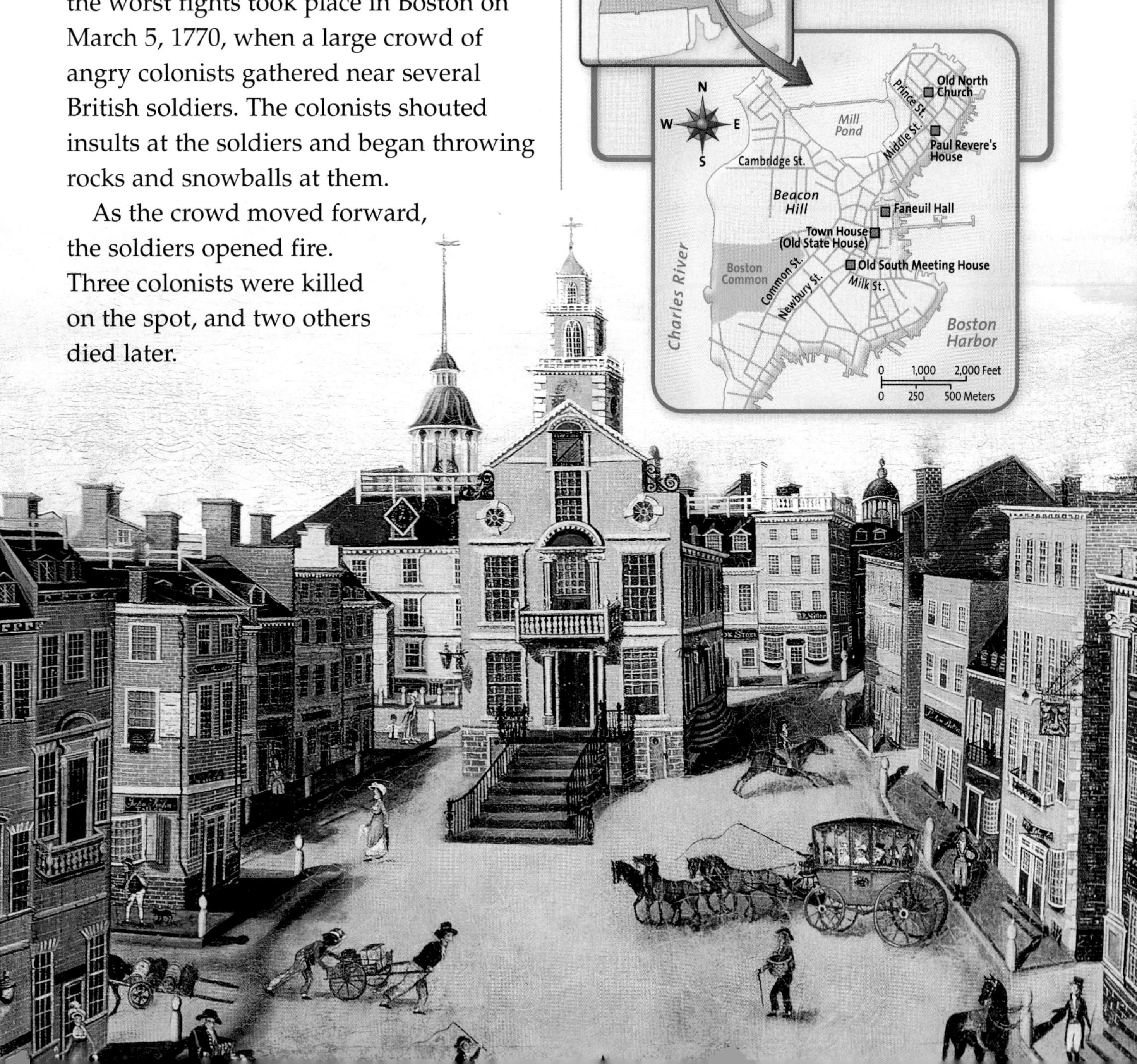

➤ **Crispus Attucks was one of the colonists killed at the Boston Massacre. This event increased colonists' fears of having British soldiers in their cities.**

Among the dead was an African American sailor from Massachusetts named **Crispus Attucks** (A•tuhks). Many people consider Crispus Attucks to be the first person killed in the fight for the colonies' freedom.

Paul Revere, a Boston silversmith who supported the colonists, made a picture of the shooting and titled it *The Bloody Massacre* (MA•sih•ker). A massacre is the killing of many people who cannot defend themselves. The shooting in Boston soon became known as the Boston Massacre.

READING CHECK **CAUSE AND EFFECT**
What was the cause of the Boston Massacre?

Summary

The Stamp Act angered many colonists because they believed they had a right to be represented in any government that taxed them. Colonists began to work together to protest Britain's imperial policies. As anger between the colonists and Britain grew, fights broke out. Some of the worst fighting took place in Boston.

REVIEW

1.  Why were colonists angered by Britain's new colonial tax laws?
2. Write a sentence explaining what **representation** has to do with taxation.
3. Why did some colonists accuse Patrick Henry of treason?

CRITICAL THINKING

4. ANALYSIS SKILL What made Boston a likely place for conflict to develop between colonists and British soldiers?
5. ANALYSIS SKILL List two primary sources that appear in this lesson.
6. **Draw a Cartoon** Imagine you are a colonist who is against British tax laws. Draw a cartoon that encourages others to boycott British goods.
7. Focus Skill **CAUSE AND EFFECT**
On a separate sheet of paper, copy and complete the graphic organizer below.

Cause	Effect
Britain passes the Stamp Act.	
	Shots kill colonists in the Boston Massacre.

Patrick Henry

Biography

Trustworthiness
Respect
Responsibility
Fairness
Caring
Patriotism

*"I know not what course others may take: but as for me, give me liberty or give me death!"**

These words rang out in the Virginia House of Burgesses on March 23, 1775. It was just six months after the First Continental Congress had sent its petition to Parliament. The speaker was Patrick Henry, a colonial leader. The purpose of his speech was to persuade Virginians to prepare for war against Britain.

Patrick Henry used his eyeglasses for reading.

Patrick Henry was born in Virginia in 1736. As a young man, Henry worked as a storekeeper and as a farmer. He later studied law and became a lawyer.

Over time, Patrick Henry became greatly admired for his skill as a public speaker. In 1765, he was elected to the Virginia House of Burgesses. Henry became an important voice among the colonists who opposed British rule. He encouraged them to work together and to think of themselves as Americans, not just colonists.

In 1776, Henry became the governor of Virginia. As governor, he worked hard to prepare Virginia for war. Unlike some leaders, Henry never held a high national office, but his words and speeches helped unite Americans everywhere.

*Patrick Henry. *Patrick Henry, Life, Correspondence, and Speeches* by William Wirt Henry. Charles Scribner's Sons, 1891.

Why Character Counts

How did Patrick Henry's words show his belief in liberty?

Bio Brief

1736 — Born 1736

1765 Henry is elected to the House of Burgesses

1775 Henry delivers his famous "liberty or death" speech

1799 — Died 1799

Interactive Multimedia Biographies
Visit **MULTIMEDIA BIOGRAPHIES** at
www.harcourtschool.com/hss

Distinguish Fact from Fiction

WHY IT MATTERS

If you are going to write a research paper or make a presentation in class, you need to know facts about history. So it is important to know if the historical accounts you are reading are true or made up. In other words, you need to be able to tell the difference between factual writing and fictional, or made-up, writing.

WHAT YOU NEED TO KNOW

One way to tell for sure if information is factual is to find the same information in a trusted reference source such as a dictionary or an encyclopedia or in a nonfiction book such as a textbook.

Other sources of facts are letters, diaries, and other documentary sources. **Documentary sources** are often produced at the time an event takes place, often by

It could not be proved in court that Captain Preston ordered his soldiers to fire on colonists at the Boston Massacre.

a person who experiences the event. However, documentary sources must be studied carefully. They can contain opinions or statements by the writer that may not be true.

Sometimes fiction writers base their stories on real people and events. But the writers add made-up details, such as words that the people did not say.

PRACTICE THE SKILL

Here are two descriptions of the Boston Massacre. The first description is from Ebenezer Bridgham, a witness to the events in Boston that day. His testimony was recorded in court. The second description tells what it was like to be at the Boston Massacre. This story is fiction, because no one present on that day recorded what happened.

In the fiction story, the writer is describing an actual event. However, she has made up details to make the story sound exciting. Read these two accounts, and answer the questions that follow.

> **"[The soldiers] stood with their [guns] before them, to defend themselves; and as soon as they had placed themselves, a party, about twelve in number, with sticks in their hands . . . immediately surrounded the soldiers, and struck upon their guns. . . . I saw the people near me on the left, strike the soldiers' guns, daring them to fire."***

> **"Those in front of the mob surged forward then, pushing against the soldiers. Again I heard Henry Knox's voice from somewhere close, pleading for sanity. But it was too late. The mob and the soldiers were pressing on each other, so close you couldn't tell one from the other. Shouts and curses filled the air. Then I heard the order ring through the night. 'Fire!'**
>
> **The world exploded in my ears. The sound echoed in my soul. I shut my eyes tight as muskets went off."****

1. How are the descriptions similar? How are they different?
2. Which description is a documentary source? Which is fictional? How are you able to tell?

APPLY WHAT YOU LEARNED

ANALYSIS SKILL Choose any statement in this lesson. Then check another nonfiction book to make sure the statement is a fact.

*Ebenezer Bridgham. *A History of the Boston Massacre* by Frederic Kidder. J. Munsell, 1870.

**Ann Rinaldi. *The Fifth of March: A Story of the Boston Massacre.* Gulliver Books, 1993.

Lesson 3

Time

1750 — 1790

1773 The Boston Tea Party

1775 The Battles of Lexington and Concord

Disagreements Grow

WHAT TO KNOW
What did colonists do when Parliament passed more tax laws?

- ✓ Explain why the colonists refused to accept the new laws passed by Parliament.
- ✓ Describe why fighting broke out at Lexington and Concord.

VOCABULARY
- **monopoly** p. 337
- **coerce** p. 338
- **blockade** p. 338
- **quarter** p. 338
- **congress** p. 339
- **petition** p. 339
- **Minutemen** p. 340
- **revolution** p. 341

PEOPLE
- Edmund Burke
- John Hancock
- Paul Revere

PLACES
- Philadelphia
- Lexington
- Concord

CAUSE AND EFFECT

California Standards
HSS 5.5, 5.5.1, 5.5.2, 5.5.4, 5.6, 5.6.1

YOU ARE THERE

The year is 1773. It's late at night, and you're supposed to be asleep. You hear your father leave the house, quietly closing the door. Tonight, he is going to a meeting with Samuel Adams. Your father said they plan to teach the British a lesson.

Angry shouts have been heard in the streets, and you're worried that your father may be hurt. He has promised to be careful, but all the same, you lie wide awake until you hear him come home again.

FAST FACT

After the Boston Tea Party, shown here, colonists sang a new song:

"Rally Mohawks!
Bring out your axes
and tell King George
we'll pay no taxes!"

—anonymous song

The Boston Tea Party

TIME **December 16, 1773**

PLACE **Boston, Massachusetts**

In 1773, Parliament passed the Tea Act, which gave Britain's East India Company a monopoly on tea. A **monopoly** is complete control of a good or service in an area, by either a person or a group. As a result of this monopoly, only the East India Company could legally sell tea to the colonies, and it could sell tea for less than colonial merchants could. This meant colonial merchants could not make money in the tea trade. The British government believed the colonists would choose to buy the cheaper tea—and pay the tax on it. Instead, many colonists decided to boycott tea.

Ships carrying thousands of pounds of tea set sail for the colonies. In November 1773, three of the ships arrived in Boston Harbor. Against the wishes of many colonists, the Massachusetts governor sided with the British by allowing the ships to dock. More than 1,000 colonists in Boston protested.

Many people think Samuel Adams planned what happened next. On the night of December 16, 1773, about 150 members of the Sons of Liberty dressed as Mohawk Indians and marched down to Boston Harbor.

At the harbor, hundreds of people had gathered on the docks to watch the event. When the Sons of Liberty arrived, they boarded the ships, broke open 342 chests of tea, and threw it all overboard. Their angry protest became known as the Boston Tea Party.

READING CHECK **CAUSE AND EFFECT** **What caused colonists to take part in the Boston Tea Party?**

The Coercive Acts

The Boston Tea Party greatly angered British leaders. In March 1774, Parliament passed a new set of laws to punish the Massachusetts colonists. The colonists called these laws the Coercive Acts because people were **coerced** (koh•ERST), or forced, to obey the laws.

One law closed the port of Boston until the colonists paid for the destroyed tea. To enforce this law, Parliament ordered the British navy to **blockade** Boston Harbor. British warships stopped other ships from entering or leaving the harbor.

To punish the colonists further, Britain stopped the Massachusetts legislature from making any laws. It put the colony under the control of British General Thomas Gage and banned all town meetings not approved by him. Britain also ordered the colonists to feed and house British soldiers. This order required colonists to **quarter** the soldiers even if they didn't want to.

Many colonists said the new laws were "intolerable." As a result, the laws also came to be known as the Intolerable Acts. The harshness of these laws led many colonists to feel that Britain was now their common enemy.

Not all British leaders agreed with these laws. In April 1774, **Edmund Burke** said to Parliament, "You will force them [to buy taxed goods]? Has seven years' struggle yet been able to force them?"* However, Parliament ignored Burke's request for cooperation.

READING CHECK **CAUSE AND EFFECT**
Why did Parliament pass the Coercive Acts?

*Edmund Burke. *The Writings and Speeches of Edmund Burke*, edited by Paul Langford. Oxford University Press, 1981.

CITIZENSHIP

Democratic Values

The right to privacy is one of our most valued rights in the United States today.

The English Bill of Rights guaranteed British citizens certain rights, including the right to privacy in one's own home. Soldiers and other government officials were not allowed to enter a home without the owner's permission or a warrant from a court of law. As more British soldiers were sent to North America, the British government needed more places for them to live. Some British soldiers took over colonists' homes and lived there without the owners' permission.

Many colonists were forced to take British soldiers into their homes.

SKILL **Analyze Time Lines**

Did the First Continental Congress meet before or after the Boston Tea Party?

The First Continental Congress

People in Britain worried about the unrest in the colonies. In June 1774, William Pitt, a member of Parliament, asked British leaders to be patient by saying, "[I] would advise the noble lords in office to adopt a more gentle mode [way] of governing America. . . ."*

In the colonies, many people feared that Britain might take stronger action to enforce its rule. In September 1774, representatives of the colonies met in **Philadelphia** to discuss how to respond to Britain. Because it was the first meeting of its kind on the North American continent, it was later called the First Continental Congress. A **congress** is a formal meeting of representatives.

The delegates decided to send a signed request to the king. This **petition** stated their basic rights as British citizens. It said that the colonists had the right to life and liberty, the right to assemble, or gather together, and the right to a trial by jury.

Congress set May 10, 1775, as the deadline for Parliament to respond. Also, Congress stopped most trade with Britain and asked the colonies to form militias.

READING CHECK **SUMMARIZE**
What did the petition sent by the First Continental Congress ask for?

*William Pitt. *William Pitt, Earl of Chatham* by Walford Davis Green. G. P. Putnam's Son, 1901.

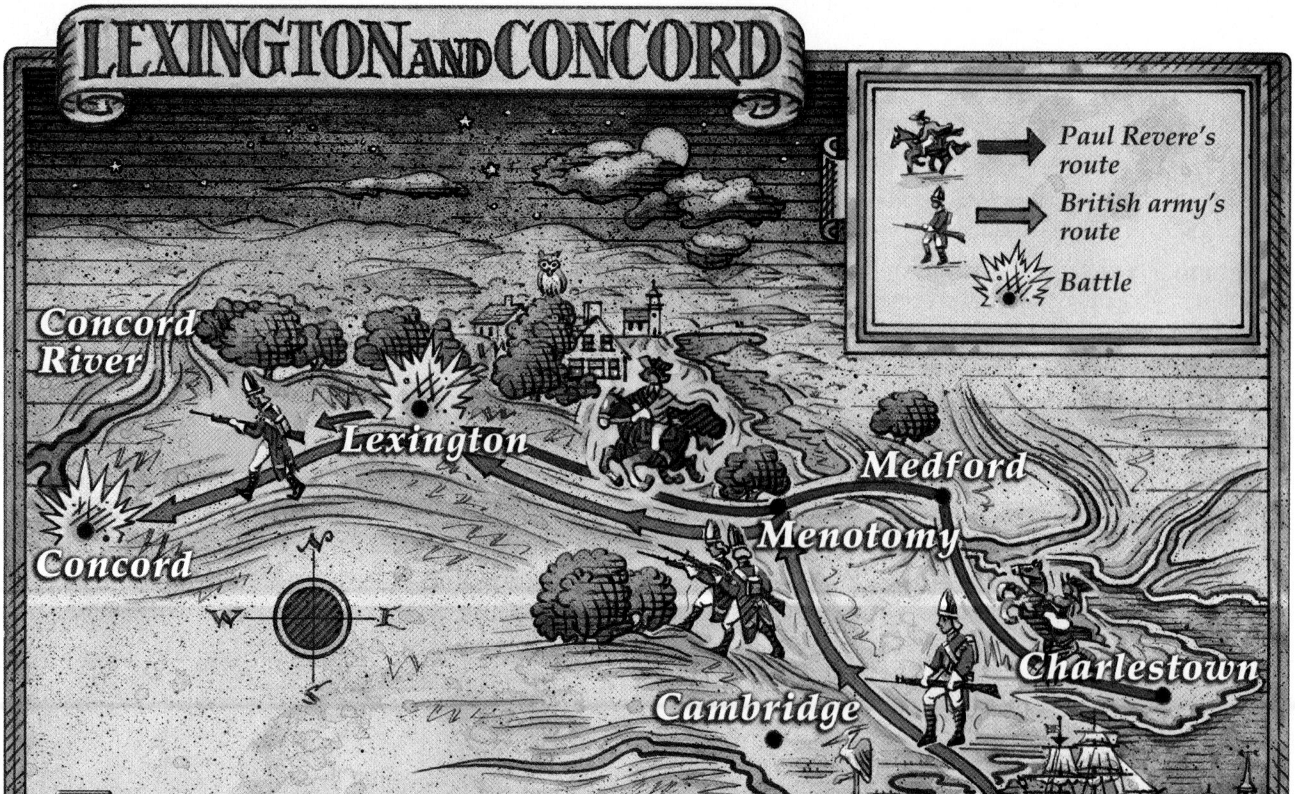

LEXINGTON AND CONCORD

Paul Revere's route
British army's route
Battle

Concord River
Lexington
Concord
Medford
Menotomy
Charlestown
Cambridge
Boston

ANALYSIS SKILL **Analyze Maps**

Place In which town did Revere's route begin?

Movement In which direction did Revere travel?

Lexington and Concord

TIME April 1775

PLACE Massachusetts

Colonists in Massachusetts quickly organized militia units. They were called **Minutemen** because they were said to be ready to fight at a minute's notice.

In April 1775, General Gage heard that Samuel Adams and **John Hancock**, two leaders of the Sons of Liberty, were meeting in **Lexington**. Gage also heard that the Minutemen were storing weapons in nearby **Concord**. He ordered more than 700 British soldiers to march to Lexington and Concord. They were to arrest Adams and Hancock and find the weapons.

The British wanted their march to Lexington to be a secret. However, **Paul Revere**, a member of the Sons of Liberty, found out about the plan and rode to Lexington to warn Adams and Hancock. When the British arrived in Lexington, the Minutemen were waiting for them. The leader of the Minutemen, John Parker, ordered his troops to "stand their ground." He shouted,

> **"Don't fire unless fired upon, but if they mean to have war, let it begin here."***

No one knows who fired first, but shots rang out. Eight Minutemen were killed, and several others were wounded. The British then marched to Concord, but the weapons they expected to find had been moved.

*Captain John Parker, April 1775. *Dictionary of American Quotations.* Penguin Reference, 1997.

➤ This statue of Paul Revere stands near the Old North Church in Boston. Two lanterns were hung in the church tower to signal British plans to cross the Charles River by boat.

As the British returned to Boston, the Minutemen fired at them from nearby woods and fields. By the time the British arrived in Boston, 73 had been killed and 174 wounded. Fewer than 100 colonists had been killed or wounded.

The poet Ralph Waldo Emerson later called the shots fired at Lexington and Concord "the shot heard round the world." The fighting marked the first step in creating the United States of America, and it was the beginning of a long, bitter war called the American Revolution. A **revolution** is a sudden, complete change of government.

READING CHECK **CAUSE AND EFFECT**
What caused the fighting at Lexington and Concord?

Summary

After the Boston Tea Party, Parliament passed laws to punish the colonists. The First Continental Congress sent the king a petition arguing for the rights of colonists. Battles at Lexington and Concord marked the start of war between Britain and the 13 colonies.

REVIEW

1. What did colonists do when Parliament passed more tax laws?
2. Use the term **petition** in a sentence about the First Continental Congress.
3. How did the Coercive Acts affect trade in Boston?
4. What was Paul Revere's role in the fighting at Lexington and Concord?

CRITICAL THINKING

5. ANALYSIS SKILL William Pitt's advice to Parliament asked for "a more gentle mode [way] of governing America." How do you think his idea could have solved Britain's problems with the colonies?
6. **Write a Poem** Write a poem about the events at the battles of Lexington and Concord. Use details from the lesson to describe the battle scenes.
7. Focus Skill **CAUSE AND EFFECT**
On a separate sheet of paper, copy and complete the graphic organizer below.

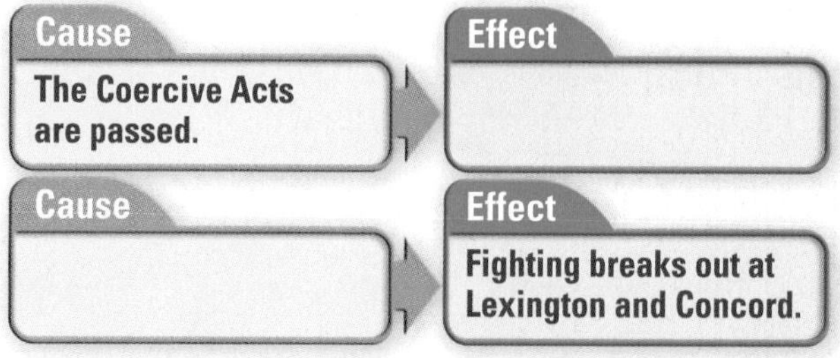

Lesson 4

1750 — 1790

1775 The Second Continental Congress meets

1775 The Battle of Bunker Hill

WHAT TO KNOW
How did the colonists prepare for war with Britain?

- ✓ Explain the significance of the Second Continental Congress.
- ✓ Understand the importance of the Battle of Bunker Hill.

VOCABULARY
commander in chief p. 343
earthwork p. 344
olive branch p. 345

PEOPLE
George Washington
John Dickinson
John Adams
King George III

PLACES
Breed's Hill

CAUSE AND EFFECT

California Standards
HSS 5.5, 5.5.2, 5.6, 5.6.1

The Road to War

YOU ARE THERE Today the Second Continental Congress is meeting in Philadelphia. You and many others are waiting in the street for news about the meeting, when several men walk by, talking hurriedly.

A woman nearby nudges your shoulder. "Look! That's **George Washington**," she whispers. "Some people say he'll lead us against the British."

You crane your neck, trying to see what Washington looks like. You wonder what kind of person would take on the powerful British army.

George Washington led the Continental Army during the Revolutionary War.

The assembly room at Independence Hall is where the Second Continental Congress met.

The Second Continental Congress

TIME 1775

PLACE Philadelphia, Pennsylvania

News of the fighting at Lexington and Concord spread quickly throughout the colonies. As a result, the Second Continental Congress was called to meet in Philadelphia on May 10, 1775. Colonial leaders gathered at the Pennsylvania State House to decide what the colonies should do. Only Georgia did not send representatives.

The delegates were divided in their views. Some called for war against the British. Others, such as **John Dickinson**, tried to persuade the group to avoid fighting. By June, however, Congress had agreed that the colonies should at least prepare for war.

The first step was to form an army. The Continental Army, as it came to be called, was the first united colonial army in the 13 colonies. It was made up of full-time soldiers, unlike the part-time militias that each colony already had.

George Washington was chosen to be the army's **commander in chief**, the leader of all the military forces. **John Adams**, a delegate from Massachusetts, suggested Washington partly because he had fought in the French and Indian War.

To supply the Continental Army, Congress asked each colony to contribute money to pay for guns, food, and uniforms. Congress also decided to print its own paper money, which came to be known as Continental currency. Congress paid the soldiers in bills called continentals.

READING CHECK **CAUSE AND EFFECT**
What caused Congress to form an army?

The Battle of Bunker Hill

By the time George Washington was chosen to lead the Continental Army, the first major battle of the Revolutionary War had already been fought. The Battle of Bunker Hill took place near Boston on June 17, 1775.

After sunset on June 16, colonial commanders Israel Putnam and William Prescott had arrived at **Breed's Hill**, across the Charles River from Boston. They ordered their soldiers to build **earthworks**, or walls made of earth and stone. When British General Thomas Gage learned of this the next morning, he sent General William Howe and 2,400 British soldiers to capture Breed's Hill. Shortly after noon, these soldiers began marching up the hill to the roll of drums. When the British drew close, the 1,600 colonists inside the earthworks let loose with a deadly hail of shooting. To save bullets, colonial commander Putnam said to his own soldiers,

> **"Don't fire until you see the whites of their eyes."***

Fighting on the hill was much fiercer than the British had expected. Twice they were forced back toward the river. One of the many soldiers who fought bravely at the earthworks was Peter Salem, a free African American. Salem wounded a British leader.

In Boston, thousands of people climbed to their rooftops to view the fighting

*Israel Putnam. *Liberty: The American Revolution* by Thomas Fleming. Viking, 1997.

across the river. They watched in horror as the nearby city of Charlestown was hit and set afire by cannons shooting from British ships in the harbor.

Back on Breed's Hill, the colonists were running out of ammunition and had to retreat from their earthworks. By early evening, the British had captured Breed's Hill. More than 1,000 British soldiers and about 350 colonists had been killed or wounded.

The battle at Breed's Hill was misnamed for nearby Bunker Hill. Although the colonists lost the battle, they had fought bravely. The British had learned that fighting the colonists would not be easy.

The Second Continental Congress, hoping to avoid more fighting, sent another petition to **King George III**. This petition, sent on July 5, 1775, came to be known as the Olive Branch Petition because it asked for peace. An **olive branch** is an ancient symbol of peace.

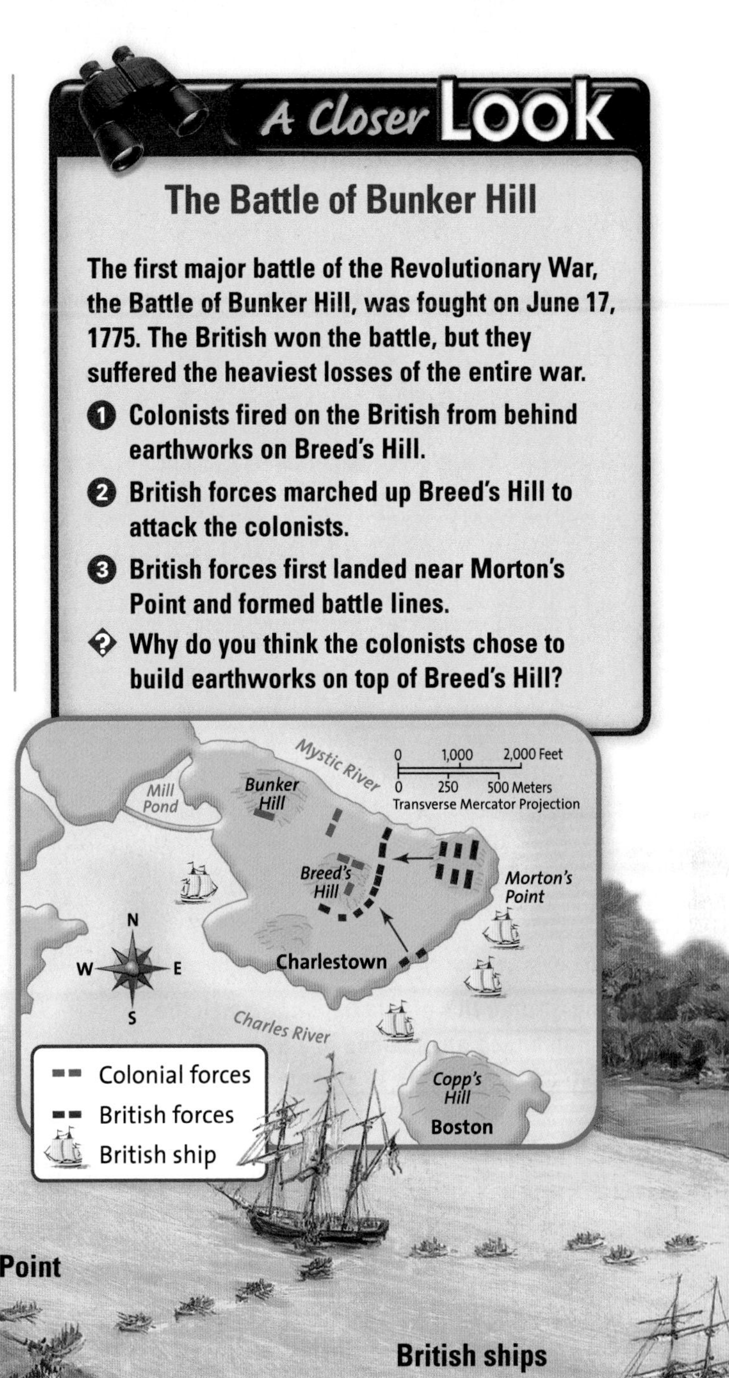

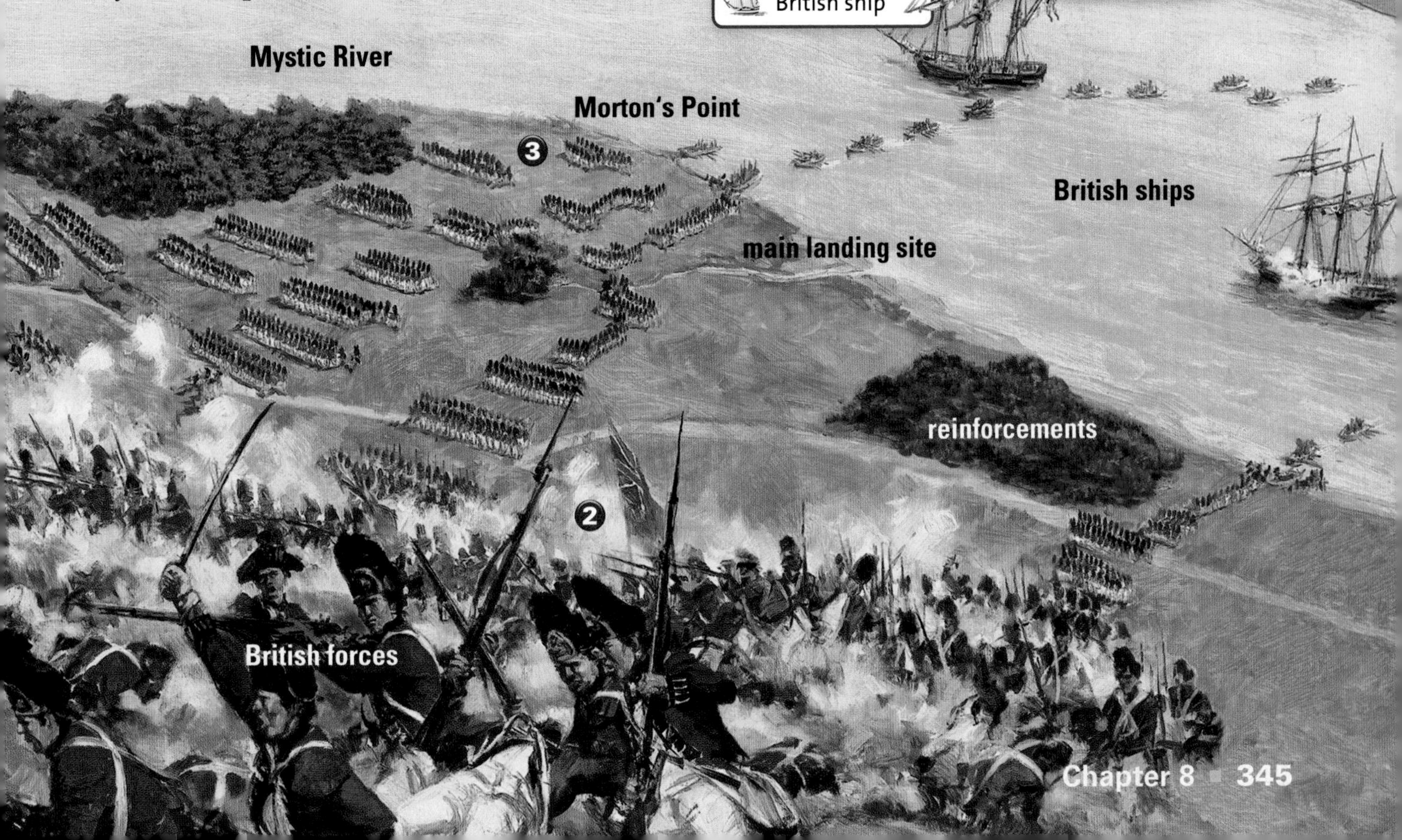

King George III's proclamation to crush the rebellion ended any chance of a peaceful resolution between the 13 colonies and Britain.

By the time the Olive Branch Petition reached London, it could do little good. The Battle of Bunker Hill had further angered British leaders, who advised King George III to get tougher with the colonists. On August 23, the king sent a proclamation promising to use every possible way to crush the rebellion. As a start, the king began to send more troops to the colonies.

READING CHECK **CAUSE AND EFFECT**
What caused the colonists to abandon Breed's Hill?

Summary

The Second Continental Congress formed the Continental Army and made George Washington the commander in chief. By that time, the first major battle of the Revolutionary War, the Battle of Bunker Hill, had been fought. The British prepared to fight the colonists.

REVIEW

1. How did the colonists prepare for war with Britain?
2. Use the term **earthwork** in a sentence about the Battle of Bunker Hill.
3. What did British leaders advise King George III to do after the Battle of Bunker Hill?

CRITICAL THINKING

4. Why was it necessary for the Second Continental Congress to print its own money?
5. ANALYSIS SKILL Why do you think the colonists were proud of the Battle of Bunker Hill, even though they lost?
6. **Conduct an Interview** Imagine you are a reporter who has been asked to interview General Washington. Write a list of questions you would ask and answers Washington might give.
7. Focus Skill **CAUSE AND EFFECT**
On a separate sheet of paper, copy and complete the graphic organizer below.

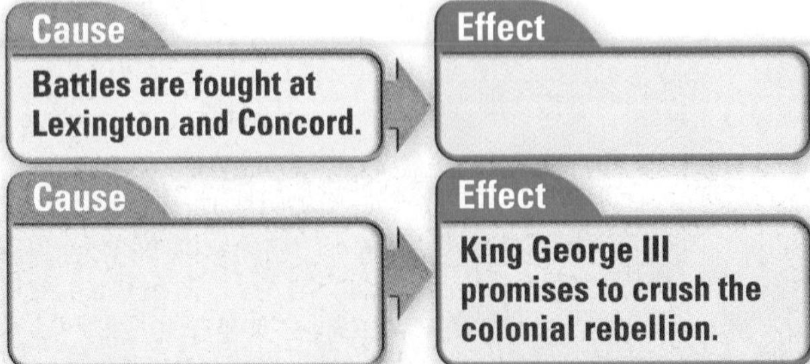

Phillis Wheatley

"A crown, a mansion, and a throne that shine,
*With gold unfading, WASHINGTON! be thine."**

Patriots are sometimes best able to express their feelings in poems, stories, or songs. Phillis Wheatley was such a patriot. Wheatley was not born in the 13 colonies, but she became a patriot in her new home. Wheatley was born in Africa and kidnapped by slave traders when she was about eight years old. She was sold to a Boston family named Wheatley, who gave her the name by which she is now known.

Phillis Wheatley's first book

One day, family members saw her trying to write on a wall with a piece of chalk. They later helped her learn to read and write. As a result, Wheatley began writing poetry as a teenager.

Wheatley's poetry was first published in 1770, and it became well known throughout the colonies and in England. She was the first African American woman in the colonies to have her work published. In 1775, Wheatley wrote a poem honoring George Washington for being named commander in chief of the Continental Army.

*Phillis Wheatley. *The Poems of Phillis Wheatley*, edited by Julian D. Mason. University of North Carolina Press, 1989.

Why Character Counts

How did Phillis Wheatley express her patriotism?

Bio Brief

1753 Born 1753?

1784 Died 1784

1761 Wheatley is taken to Boston

1770 Wheatley's poetry is first published

GO ONLINE **Interactive Multimedia Biographies Visit MULTIMEDIA BIOGRAPHIES at www.harcourtschool.com/hss**

Lesson 5

Time

1750 — 1790

1776 *Common Sense* is published

1776 The Declaration of Independence is issued

1777 The Articles of Confederation are written

Declaring Independence

WHAT TO KNOW
How did the 13 colonies cut their ties with Britain?

- ✓ Understand the people and events associated with the Declaration of Independence.
- ✓ Tell why the Declaration of Independence is important and identify its key political concepts.

VOCABULARY
independence p. 349
resolution p. 349
declaration p. 349
preamble p. 350
grievance p. 351
Articles of Confederation p. 352

PEOPLE
Thomas Paine
John Adams
Thomas Jefferson
John Hancock
John Dickinson

PLACES
Independence Hall

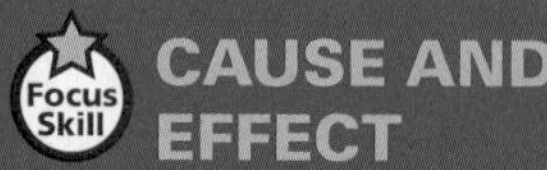
CAUSE AND EFFECT

California Standards
HSS 5.5, 5.5.2, 5.5.3, 5.5.4

YOU ARE THERE Your friend waves a pamphlet in your face. "This will change the course of history!" You notice that the pamphlet's title is *Common Sense*. Your friend says, "In here are all the reasons we should be our own country."

The year is 1776, and battles between the colonists and British soldiers have already taken place. However, many colonists still hope that they can avoid an all-out war with Britain. Your friend tells you, "*Common Sense* is going to make everyone want to be free of Britain."

In his pamphlet, or short book, titled *Common Sense*, Thomas Paine argued that the colonies should claim their independence.

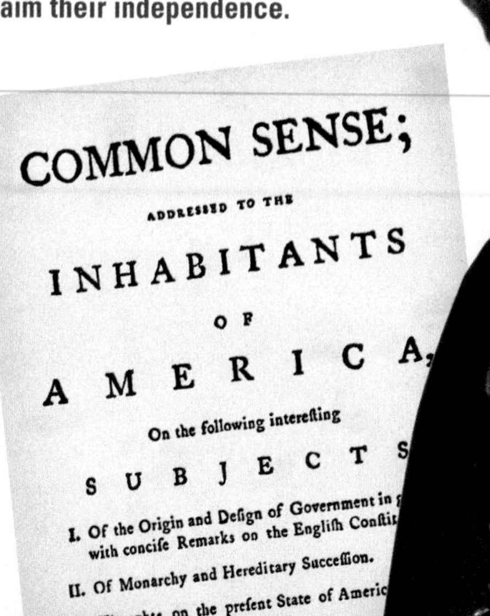
COMMON SENSE;
ADDRESSED TO THE
INHABITANTS
OF
AMERICA,
On the following interefting
SUBJECTS
I. Of the Origin and Defign of Government in g[illegible] with concife Remarks on the Englifh Conftit[illegible]
II. Of Monarchy and Hereditary Succeffion.
III. Thoughts on the prefent State of Americ[illegible]

Moving Toward Independence

More colonists were starting to think that their differences with Britain could not be settled. One person responsible for this change in thinking was **Thomas Paine**. In his pamphlet *Common Sense*, Paine wrote that the colonists should rule themselves.

From Georgia to New Hampshire, people were reading and talking about Paine's pamphlet. Many began to call for **independence**—the freedom to govern themselves. It was the only way, they said, to have liberty.

On June 7, 1776, Richard Henry Lee, of Virginia, slowly rose from his chair. He turned to his fellow delegates at the Second Continental Congress, in Philadelphia, and said that the 13 colonies no longer owed loyalty to the king. He called for a **resolution**, or a formal group statement, of independence: "Resolved: That these united colonies are, and of right ought to be, free and independent states."*

Congress debated the resolution and chose a committee to write a **declaration**, or official statement, about independence to be sent to the king. The committee included Benjamin Franklin of Pennsylvania, **John Adams** of Massachusetts, Robert R. Livingston of New York, **Thomas Jefferson** of Virginia, and Roger Sherman of Connecticut.

Jefferson, a 33-year-old lawyer who had studied government and law, used this knowledge to explain his ideas. The other members of the committee also added ideas, but Jefferson did most of the writing. Every evening for about 17 days, he wrote and rewrote the draft of the Declaration of Independence.

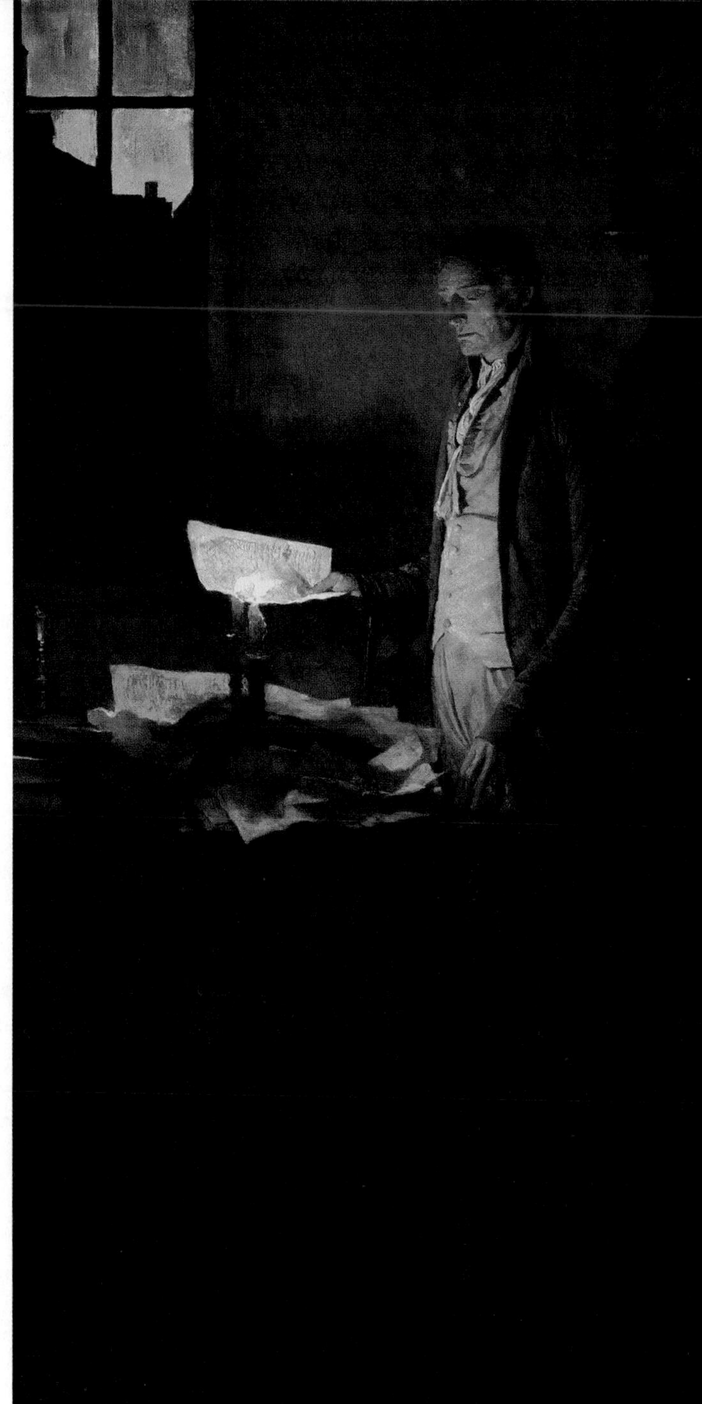

Thomas Jefferson's talents as a writer were well known to other members of the committee.

READING CHECK **CAUSE AND EFFECT**
What caused many people in the colonies to call for independence?

*The Continental Congress, June 7, 1776. Documents Illustrative of the Formation of the Union of the American States, Government Printing Office, 1827. House Document 398.

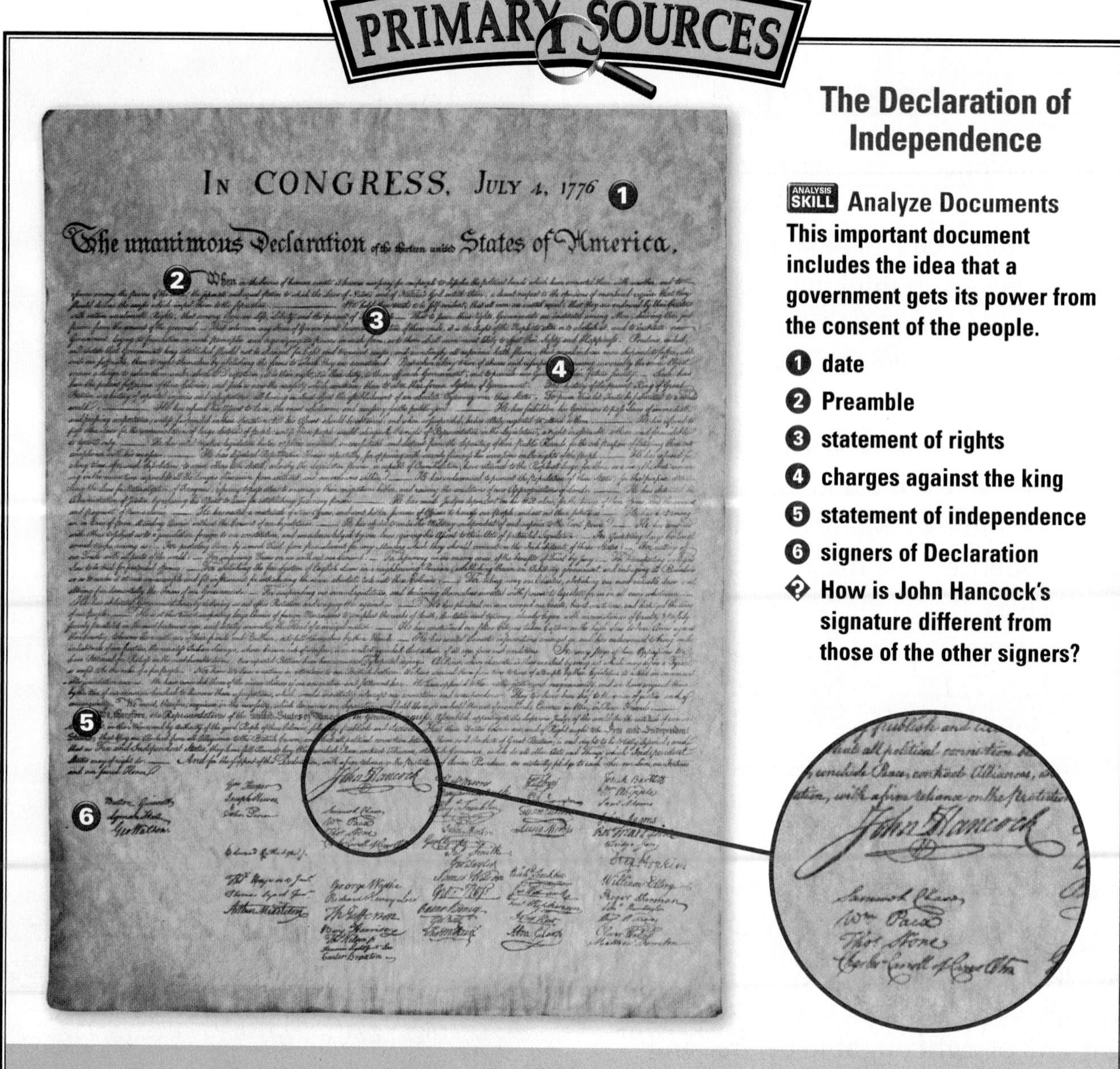

The Declaration of Independence

Analyze Documents This important document includes the idea that a government gets its power from the consent of the people.

1. date
2. Preamble
3. statement of rights
4. charges against the king
5. statement of independence
6. signers of Declaration

- How is John Hancock's signature different from those of the other signers?

The Declaration of Independence

Thomas Jefferson carefully planned the draft of the Declaration of Independence. The first part, called the **Preamble**, states why the Declaration was needed. Jefferson wrote that sometimes events leave a group of people no choice but to form a new nation.

The next part of the Declaration describes the colonists' main ideas about government. It argues for liberty and equality. Those political concepts were stated with some of the most famous words in United States history:

> **"We hold these truths to be self-evident, that all men are created equal, that they are endowed [provided] by their Creator with certain unalienable Rights, that among these are Life, Liberty, and the pursuit of Happiness."***

*from the *Declaration of Independence*.

The longest part of the Declaration lists the colonists' **grievances**, or complaints, against the British king and Parliament. Jefferson also listed the ways the colonists had tried to settle their differences with Britain peacefully. In the last part of the Declaration, Jefferson wrote that the colonies were free and independent states.

When he finished writing, Thomas Jefferson gave his draft to Congress. On June 28, it was read aloud to the delegates. For several days, it was discussed, and changes were made. Then, on July 2, the delegates voted to approve Richard Henry Lee's resolution to cut ties with Britain. The American colonies had now said that they were free and independent states.

On July 4, 1776, the Congress voted to accept the Declaration's final wording. Delegates from 12 colonies voted. New York had not yet given its delegates the power to vote.

On July 8, crowds gathered at the State House, today called **Independence Hall**. Bells rang out, and Colonel John Nixon announced the first public reading of the Declaration of Independence. Members of the Second Continental Congress also listened as Nixon read.

John Adams was so pleased by the people's joyful reaction to recent events that he wrote about them in a letter to Abigail Adams, his wife. He said that Independence Day should be celebrated "from this time forward evermore."*

READING CHECK **SUMMARIZE**
What important ideas did Thomas Jefferson express in the Declaration of Independence?

*John Adams. *The Book of Abigail and John*, edited by L. H. Butterfield. Harvard University Press, 1975.

Cultural Heritage

Independence Day

The Fourth of July, or Independence Day, is a national holiday. It is the birthday of the United States of America. The holiday was first celebrated on July 4, 1777, with fireworks and the ringing of the Liberty Bell. Although Independence Day had been celebrated for many years, it was not made an official holiday until 1941.

This famous painting of the signing of the Declaration of Independence shows the Second Continental Congress in what is today Independence Hall.

Forming a New Government

By August 2, a formal copy of the Declaration of Independence was ready to be signed by members of the Second Continental Congress. The first to sign it was **John Hancock**, the president of the Congress. He said that he wrote his name large enough so that King George III could read it without his glasses. The way he signed the document became so famous that the term *John Hancock* now means "a person's signature."

The work of the Second Continental Congress did not end with the final approval of the Declaration of Independence. With independence, a new government had to be formed. Congress quickly set up another committee. Its job was to develop a plan for how to unite the former 13 colonies into a new country.

John Dickinson, of Pennsylvania, was chosen to head the committee to write the plan of government. The committee decided that the new states—the former colonies—should form a confederation. This Confederation of the United States of America would bring the 13 independent states together into a firm league of friendship.

On July 12, 1776, Dickinson's report was presented to Congress. After debating the plan for more than a year, Congress finally approved it on November 15, 1777. The country's first plan of government was called the **Articles of Confederation**.

Under the Articles of Confederation, the voters of each state would elect leaders to their state legislatures. These state leaders would then choose representatives to a national legislature called the Congress of the Confederation. Each state, whether large or small, had one vote in the new Congress.

Until 1789, this Congress served as the government of the United States. The Congress made laws for the new nation and helped keep the states together during the Revolutionary War.

READING CHECK **CAUSE AND EFFECT What effect did the Articles of Confederation have on the new nation?**

Summary

Partly because of Thomas Paine's *Common Sense*, many colonists began to call for independence. Thomas Jefferson worked to write the Declaration of Independence. Later, Congress passed the Articles of Confederation, the country's first plan of government.

John Dickinson of Pennsylvania helped write the Articles of Confederation.

REVIEW

1. How did the 13 colonies cut their ties with Britain?
2. Use the words **preamble** and **grievance** in a sentence about the Declaration of Independence.
3. What are some of the ideas described in the Declaration of Independence?

CRITICAL THINKING

4. ANALYSIS SKILL Why do you think it was important for the colonies to take a united stand against Britain?
5. **Make It Relevant** How might your life be different if the Declaration of Independence had never been written?
6. **Write a Persuasive Letter** Imagine it is 1776. Write a letter to the editor of a local newspaper, telling why you support independence for the 13 colonies. Include evidence that supports your argument.
7. Focus Skill **CAUSE AND EFFECT** On a separate sheet of paper, copy and complete the graphic organizer below.

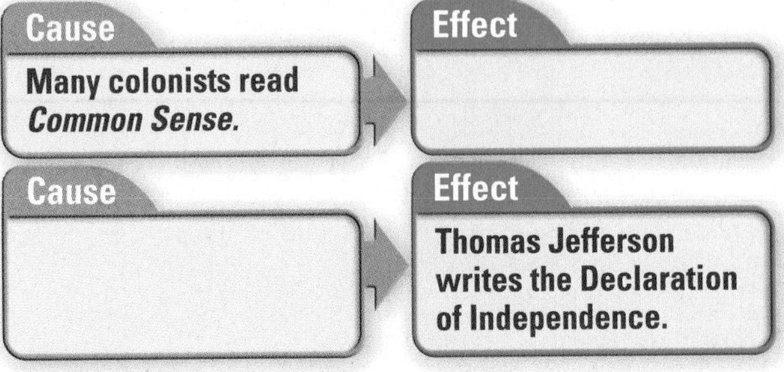

Identify Multiple Causes and Their Effects

WHY IT MATTERS

To recognize why things happen, it is important to understand causes and effects. A cause is an event or an action that makes something happen. An effect is what happens as a result of that event or action. Knowing about causes and effects can help you predict likely outcomes. Then you can make more thoughtful decisions.

WHAT YOU NEED TO KNOW

Sometimes events in history have more than one cause and more than one effect. You can use these steps to help you identify causes and their effects.

Step 1 **Look for the effects. Determine whether there is more than one effect.**

Step 2 **Look for the causes of the effects.**

Step 3 **Think about the connections between the causes and their effects.**

Minutemen first fought British troops at Lexington.

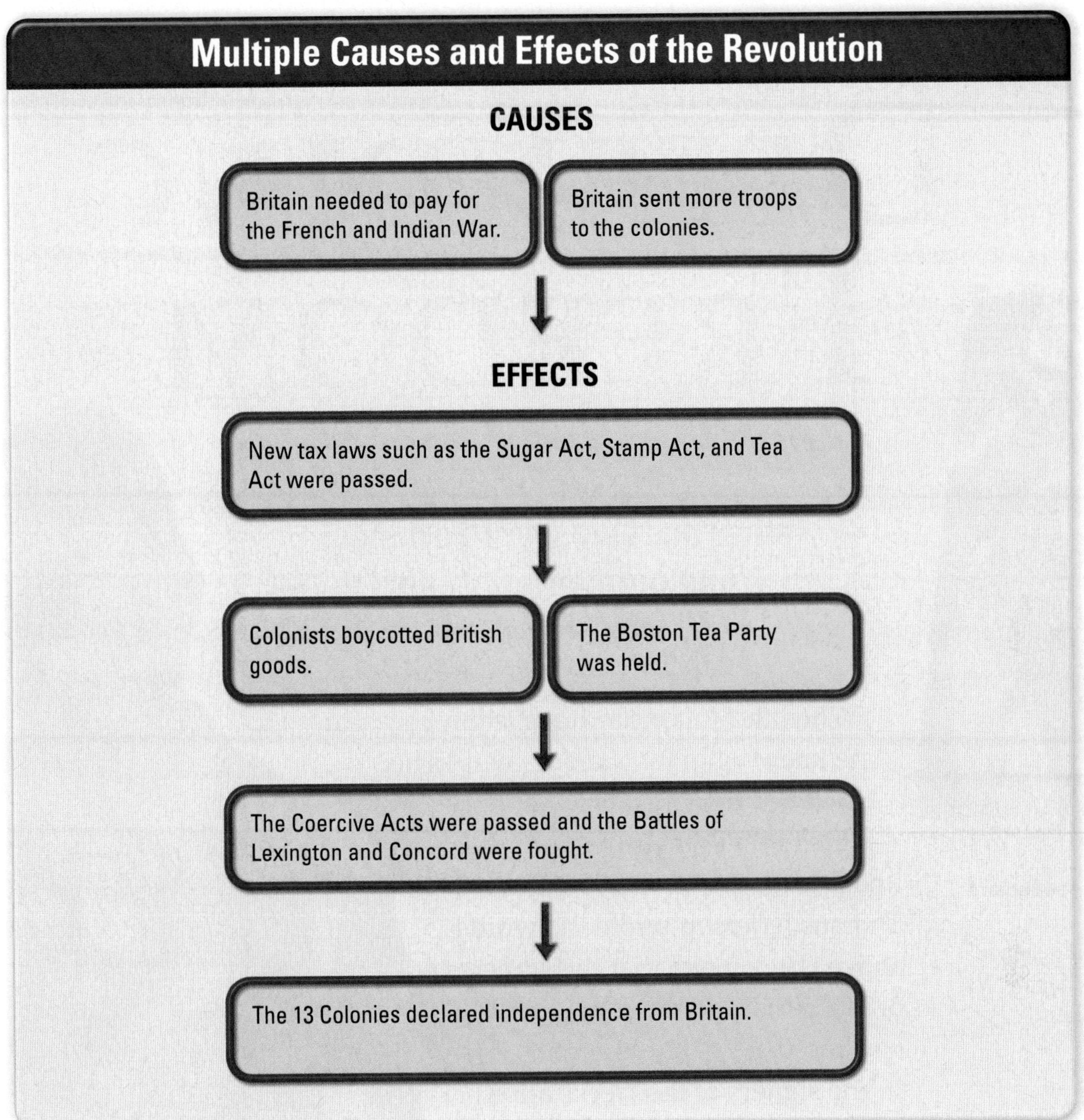

PRACTICE THE SKILL

The cause-and-effect chart above lists the causes and effects of British actions on the colonies. Use the chart to answer these questions.

1. What was the effect of Britain needing to pay for the French and Indian War?
2. What was one effect of new tax laws being passed?
3. In your opinion, did one cause have greater impact than the others? Why or why not?

APPLY WHAT YOU LEARNED

ANALYSIS SKILL Choose one of the lessons in this chapter. In that lesson, find at least one cause-and-effect relationship other than those shown in the chart. Then share your findings with a classmate.

Critical Thinking Skills

Citizenship

Defending Freedom

When the American Revolution began, no one knew what its outcome would be. However, the Patriots were determined to win their freedom. In the Declaration of Independence, Thomas Jefferson wrote the words above. They mean that the signers of the Declaration would defend one another, no matter what.

The signers of the Declaration were in terrible danger. If the colonies lost the war, the British would try them for treason.

These reenactors take part in a festival to honor Revolutionary War soldiers.

The signers of the Declaration of Independence were willing to risk their lives because they believed in freedom. During the war, five of the signers were captured by the British army. Twelve had their homes burned to the ground or taken by the enemy. Seventeen lost all their money, and nine lost their lives in the war. Others lost members of their families.

**The Declaration of Independence.* Bantam Classics, 1998.

Treason was a crime punishable by death. Benjamin Franklin tried to joke about this when it was his turn to sign the Declaration. "We must all hang together," he said, "or most assuredly we shall all hang separately."*

The signers were not the only Americans who risked all they had for freedom. Throughout the colonies, Patriots were willing to suffer terrible hardships and years of war to win their freedom. Thousands of them died in the struggle.

Since the United States won its independence, millions of others have served their nation or given their lives to keep our country free. The spirit of 1776 lives on today.

*Benjamin Franklin. *American Heritage Dictionary of American Quotation*, edited by Margaret Miner and Hugh Rawson. Penguin Reference, 1997.

Soldiers (above) help defend our country's freedom. The Tomb of the Unknowns (bottom left) honors soldiers who have given their lives in our country's wars.

Honoring our country's flag is one way that citizens can show their support of freedom.

Think About It!

Make It Relevant **Why is it important for citizens to continue to defend our country's freedom?**

Time

1750

1760

1754 The French and Indian War begins

1765 Parliament passes the Stamp Act

Reading Social Studies

A **cause** is an event or action that makes something happen. An **effect** is what happens as a result of that event or action.

Cause and Effect

Complete this graphic organizer to show that you understand the causes and effects of the American Revolution. A copy of this graphic organizer appears on page 88 of the Homework and Practice Book.

Uniting the Colonies

Cause	Effect
Britain needed money to pay for the French and Indian War.	
	Colonists staged the Boston Tea Party.
Britain passed the Intolerable Acts.	

California Writing Prompts

Write a Persuasive Letter Imagine that you are a colonial newspaper owner. Write a letter to persuade others that the colonists should separate from Britain. Support your position with evidence.

Write a Narrative Imagine you are a newspaper reporter who has just heard the first public reading of the Declaration of Independence. Write a narrative explaining the setting and the people's points of view on the Declaration.

1770 | 1780 | 1790

1775
Fighting breaks out at Lexington and Concord

1776
Declaration of Independence is signed

Use Vocabulary

Identify the term that correctly matches each definition.

representation, p. 327
treason, p. 327
boycott, p. 329
revolution, p. 341
independence, p. 349

1. to refuse to buy
2. the act of working against one's own government
3. a sudden change in people's lives or government
4. the act of speaking or acting for someone else
5. freedom to govern on one's own

Use the Time Line

Use the chapter summary time line above to answer these questions.

6. In what year did the French and Indian War start?
7. Did fighting in the colonies start before or after the Declaration of Independence was signed?

Apply Skills

Compare Historical Maps

8. Examine the maps on page 325. Then write a few sentences explaining how Britain's land claims in North America changed as a result of the French and Indian War.

Recall Facts

Answer these questions.

9. What was the purpose of the Proclamation of 1763?
10. Why did many colonists boycott British goods?
11. How did the Battle of Bunker Hill change Britain's view of the colonists?

Write the letter of the best choice.

12. Where did the Battles of Lexington and Concord take place?
    - **A** Massachusetts
    - **B** New York
    - **C** Pennsylvania
    - **D** Virginia
13. Who was chosen to be the commander in chief of the Continental Army?
    - **A** Samuel Adams
    - **B** Thomas Gage
    - **C** Thomas Jefferson
    - **D** George Washington

Think Critically

Think Critically

14. ANALYSIS SKILL What effects did the Committees of Correspondence have on communication between colonies?
15. ANALYSIS SKILL What were some of the benefits of the colonies declaring independence?

Study Skills

ORGANIZE INFORMATION

By organizing the information you read, you can better understand it. Graphic organizers can help you organize information.

- **Graphic organizers help you categorize, or group, information.**
- **Putting people, places, and events into categories makes it easier to find facts.**

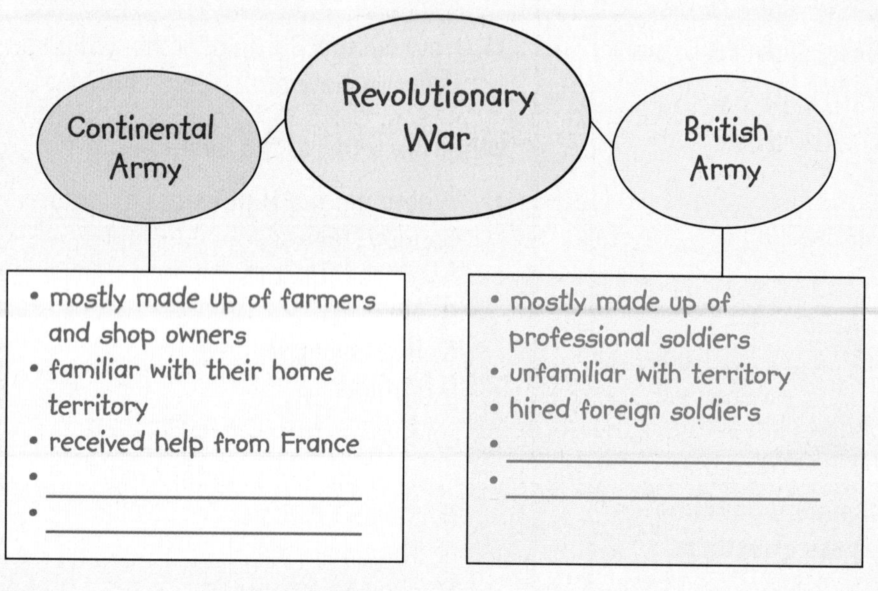

Apply As You Read

As you read the chapter, continue to add new facts and details to the organizer. You may also want to create additional organizers to categorize other important information that you read in the chapter.

California History-Social Science Standards, Grade 5

5.6 Students understand the course and consequences of the American Revolution.

CHAPTER

The Revolutionary War

Reenactors at Morristown National Historical Park in New Jersey

Start with a Story

Phoebe the Spy

by Judith Berry Griffin
illustrated by Margot Tomes

In 1776, Samuel Fraunces, an African American tavern owner in New York City, heard a rumor about a plan to kill General George Washington. To protect the general, Fraunces asked his daughter, Phoebe, to act as Washington's housekeeper. She was helped by a boy named Pompey. While she went about her work, Phoebe was to watch, listen, and guard the general from someone named "T." Read how Phoebe's bravery and quick thinking saved George Washington.

"I've come for my peas," he said softly.

"Oh! Mr. Hickey, sir!" she said. "You gave me such a start! I was—" She stopped and looked at him, even more startled. He looked ill? frightened? She couldn't tell which.

"Which is my plate, and which is General Washington's?" he said. "It wouldn't do for him to have more than me." He spoke quickly, without smiling this time.

"I never heard of such carryings on over a pile of peas!" Phoebe said. "This is the general's plate, and this is yours!" She turned away to fill Pompey's salt cellar and turned back just in time to see Hickey's hand move quickly away from General Washington's plate and slide into his pocket. Something winked for a second in the light—something shiny, like glass.

"What are you doing to General Washington's plate?" she said. "I told you yours is here!" She picked up the plate. Was it her imagination, or was there something grainy, like sugar, on the peas? Phoebe looked more closely, but as she looked, whatever it was seemed to have disappeared. An instant later she wasn't sure—had she seen anything at all? She thought of the window again and forgot about the peas. She had to serve General Washington.

salt celler a dish that holds salt

Leaving Hickey standing in the kitchen, Phoebe nervously entered the dining room, Pompey following with the salt. As she walked toward the general, Phoebe looked at every face around the table. Some of the guests were talking, some merely smiling. None seemed nervous or frightened. And then she noticed the empty chair. Who was missing? But even as she asked herself the question, she knew.

It was Mr. Green. Was he outside the house, with a gun, waiting? General Washington was sitting by the window, as she had feared. He sat back easily in his chair, listening to something General Gates was saying. The window was open! As she went past, Phoebe looked outside anxiously. There was not a sound, not a shadow, not a movement. The green grass was smooth and unruffled. Even the leaves in the trees beyond were still.

"Well, Phoebe!" General Washington exclaimed as she stopped beside his chair. "June peas! How did you get them so early in the season?"

"It wasn't me, sir," replied Phoebe, looking past him out the window. "It was your Mr. Hickey brought them in, fresh today. He says they're your favorite."

"And mine as well!" said General Gates. "Where is Mr. Thomas Hickey? I want to thank him!"

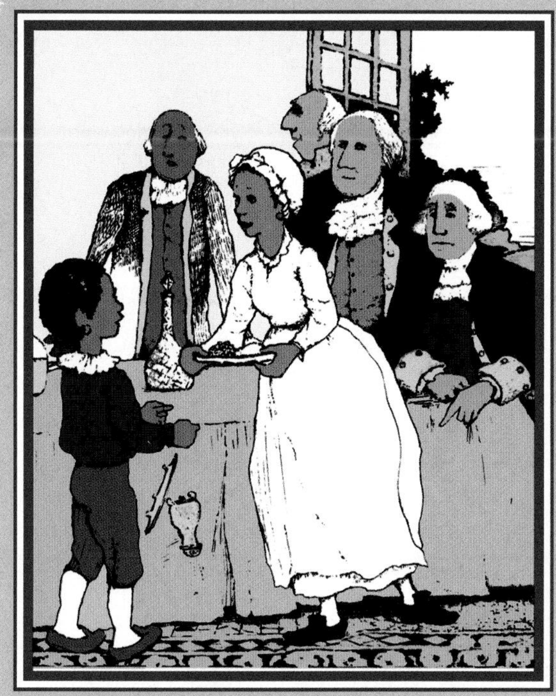

Phoebe started to put the plate down in front of General Washington. Then, in a flash, it came to her who she was looking for. Mr. Green was not hiding outside the window to shoot at the general. The person who was trying to kill him was here—in the kitchen! Phoebe stood like a stone, the plate still in her hands. She saw Hickey again—Thomas Hickey—laughing and teasing, bringing her candy and ribbons and seed for her chickens. And then bringing June peas for the general and sprinkling them with poison! T was for Thomas, member of General Washington's bodyguard!

Still holding the plate, she whirled around. Pompey was waiting behind her. "Run!" she screamed. "Run! Get my father!"

Everyone stopped talking. Pompey looked at her in amazement. "Y-your father?" he stammered. . . .

Everyone in the dining room sat frozen. All eyes were on Phoebe. "General Washington!" she cried. "Mr. Hickey has put poison in your dinner! I saw him!" There was a gasp from the table.

"What jest is this?" roared General Gates, getting up from his place and reaching for the plate. But before he could take it from her, Phoebe ran to the open window and threw the whole plate out into the yard.

Samuel and Phoebe Fraunces were free African Americans. Samuel owned the Queen's Head Tavern in New York City. The tavern, which still exists today, is located on Broad and Pearl Streets. It looks very much the way it did when Phoebe and her father lived there.

jest a joke

Response Corner

1. Who did Phoebe think was trying to harm General Washington?
2. Who was actually trying to harm General Washington, and how?
3. Imagine that you are a spy in charge of protecting General Washington. Write a journal entry describing how you saved Washington's life.

Lesson 1

Time

1750

1790

1776
British soldiers burn many areas in New Jersey

1777
Sybil Ludington warns American soldiers of a British attack

WHAT TO KNOW
How did the American Revolution affect people's lives?

- ✓ Describe the personal and economic impacts of the war.
- ✓ Explain the role of women during the war.
- ✓ Identify the roles of African Americans and American Indians during the war.

VOCABULARY
Patriot p. 367
Loyalist p. 367
neutral p. 367
inflation p. 368
profiteering p. 368
regiment p. 370

PEOPLE
Martha Washington
Deborah Sampson
Mercy Otis Warren
Abigail Adams
James Armistead
Chief Logan
Thayendanegea

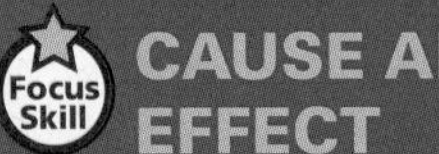

CAUSE AND EFFECT

California Standards
HSS 5.6, 5.6.1, 5.6.3, 5.6.4, 5.6.7

Americans and the Revolution

YOU ARE THERE

It is 1777. Hundreds of British soldiers are marching past your house in New Jersey. The rattle of their swords makes you shiver, as your mother pulls you and your little brother close. For three months, your father has been away fighting in the Continental Army. While he is gone, your mother has been running the family's printing business.

Outside, the last of the British soldiers are passing. Their coats make a line of red across the street. "Don't worry," you whisper to your brother. "We'll beat them all. You'll see."

▶ **This photograph shows historical reenactors dressed as British soldiers.**

FAST FACT

When a British soldier was hit by a bullet, his bright red uniform kept nearby soldiers from knowing he was bleeding. This helped prevent the other soldiers from getting scared and running away from the battle.

This painting detail shows British soldiers burning a family's home.

Personal Hardships

The approval of the Declaration of Independence showed that the colonial leaders had united against Britain. But the colonists themselves were not united. Many faced the difficult decision of whether to support independence or to remain loyal to the British king.

People in the colonies who supported independence called themselves **Patriots.** Those who remained loyal to the king called themselves **Loyalists**. Some colonists, however, chose to be **neutral**. They took neither side.

As people took sides, towns, friendships, and families were sometimes torn apart. One Patriot woman stayed in Boston while Loyalist members of her family moved away. She wrote, "When I seriously reflect that I have lost my father, mother, brother, and sisters . . . I am half distracted [in shock]. . . ."*

Colonists faced other personal hardships. Often their towns were robbed and destroyed by the British army. In 1776, for example, British soldiers burned many areas of New Jersey. They even stole beds from colonists' houses!

In some cases, the colonists destroyed their own possessions to keep the British from taking them. Some Patriot men and women burned their crops before the British army arrived. Their actions made sure that the British could not harvest the crops for food.

READING CHECK **CAUSE AND EFFECT**
What was the effect of the war on some colonial families?

*Lucy Knox. *Life and Correspondence of Henry Knox* by Francis S. Drake. S.G. Drake, 1979.

Analyze Graphs **Imports from Britain decreased as Congress printed more money (right) to pay for the war.**

By about how much did the amount of colonial imports decrease from 1775 to 1776?

Economic Hardships

Americans faced economic as well as personal hardships during the Revolutionary War. One problem was a shortage of imported goods. British ships set up blockades so that other ships could not unload goods at American ports.

As the shortage of goods grew worse, Americans faced severe wartime **inflation**, or an increase in the price of goods. Inflation meant that the colonists needed more money to buy goods and services. In just two months, the price of wheat and beef doubled!

Another cause of inflation was the falling value of Continental money. In order to pay for the war, the Second Continental Congress was printing more currency. By printing too much, however, the government caused its money to become less valuable.

Aside from inflation, another problem Congress had trying to finance, or pay for, the war was that it could not raise money through taxes. The states had to give permission before new tax laws could be passed.

To make matters worse, some farmers and shopkeepers began **profiteering**, or charging extra-high prices for their crops or goods. Laws were soon passed saying how much farmers could charge for food. These laws also made it illegal for people to hoard, or collect and hide, large amounts of goods and materials. Often, however, these laws were ignored.

READING CHECK **CAUSE AND EFFECT**
What effect did inflation have on the economy during the Revolutionary War?

Women and the War

As men left their homes to fight in the war, women took on new roles. Some women ran family farms or businesses. They worked as carpenters, blacksmiths, wagon drivers, and shipbuilders. Others formed groups to raise money for the war and collect clothing for the soldiers.

Some wives followed their husbands from battle to battle. In army camps, women cooked food and washed clothes. Some brought water to soldiers during battles. Every winter, **Martha Washington** traveled to be with her husband, George.

Some brave girls and women joined the men in battle. One night in 1777, 16-year-old Sybil Ludington rode on horseback to tell American soldiers of a British attack. **Deborah Sampson** dressed in men's clothes to fight, calling herself Robert Shirtliffe. Margaret Corbin was badly wounded after taking her husband's place in battle. Corbin became the first woman war veteran to be recognized by Congress.

Some women used their talents to support the Patriot cause. **Mercy Otis Warren** wrote patriotic poems and stories that often showed women heroes fighting for freedom. Later she wrote a history of the American Revolution, the first by a woman. **Abigail Adams** argued for freedom in letters she wrote to her husband, John. She also offered rooms in her home for children who had been made homeless by the war.

READING CHECK **SUMMARIZE**
What different roles did women play during the American Revolution?

Sybil Ludington

Martha Washington

Abigail Adams

James Armistead (right) spied on the British army. African Americans in the First Rhode Island Regiment (above) fought for the Patriots to gain their own freedom.

African Americans, Free and Enslaved

At the start of the war, one out of every five people in the 13 colonies was of African descent. Most lived as slaves in the Southern Colonies. African Americans everywhere in the colonies, however, recognized the promise of the Declaration of Independence. It had, after all, stated that "all men are created equal."

About 5,000 African Americans fought for the Continental Army. Many were promised their freedom as a reward for their service. This was the case for the soldiers in the First Rhode Island Regiment. A **regiment** is a large group of soldiers. The First Rhode Island Regiment fought bravely in several major battles during the war.

James Armistead, a Virginia slave, served as a spy for George Washington. The information that Armistead collected helped win an important battle at Yorktown. After the war, the Virginia government gave him his freedom.

Virginia's British governor also promised freedom to all slaves who fought for the British. He formed a regiment of more than 300 African Americans, who wore patches that said *Liberty to Slaves.*

Free African Americans were as quick to take sides. Peter Salem was among at least five African Americans who fought at the Battle of Concord. James Forten, a free African American from Philadelphia, was 14 years old when he joined the Continental Navy.

READING CHECK **CAUSE AND EFFECT**
Why did enslaved African Americans fight in the Revolutionary War?

People in the Western Lands

Despite the Proclamation of 1763, settlers had continued to move onto the land set aside for American Indians. Some Indian groups were angry about these settlers, but many depended on both the Americans and the British as trading partners.

When the Revolutionary War began, many American Indian groups chose to remain neutral. In 1775, one member of the Oneida tribe said, "We are unwilling to join either side."*

However, American Indian loyalties were soon divided. In the Revolutionary War, both the Americans and the British formed alliances with Indian groups.

Mingo **Chief Logan** chose to fight on the side of the British. In 1774, frontier settlers had killed his family. This caused Logan to fight against the Americans.

The Mohawk leader **Thayendanegea** (thay•en•da•NEG•ah), known as Joseph Brant, also fought for the British. The Mohawk members of the Iroquois League hoped to prevent more Americans from settling on their lands.

Other Indian nations of the league also allied with the British. However, the Oneida and Tuscarora nations decided to fight for the Americans. These opposing alliances led to the end of the league.

Like many American Indians, most settlers in the western lands remained neutral at first. After a while, however, their feelings began to change.

*Oneida warrior. *Liberty: The American Revolution* by Thomas Fleming. Viking, 1997.

The Mohawk leader Thayendanegea (center) and other Iroquois warriors (right) fought for the British. The king gave this medal (left) to the Iroquois as a symbol of friendship.

FAST FACT

About one-third of all Americans chose to remain neutral throughout the Revolutionary War.

At Johnson Hall in New York, the British met with their American Indian allies.

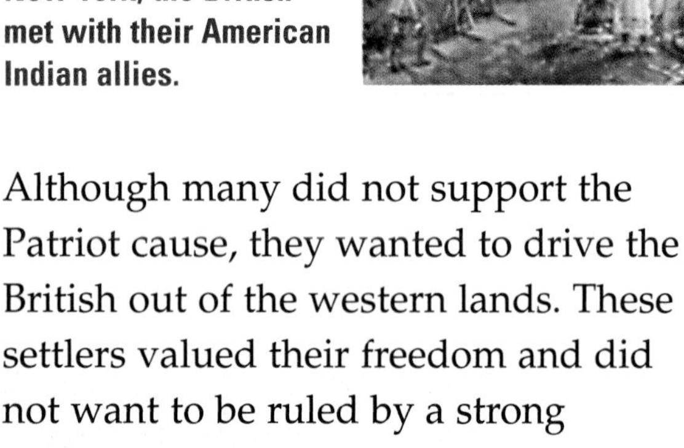

Although many did not support the Patriot cause, they wanted to drive the British out of the western lands. These settlers valued their freedom and did not want to be ruled by a strong government.

READING CHECK **CAUSE AND EFFECT**
What caused some American Indian groups to make alliances with the British?

Summary

During the Revolutionary War, Americans faced personal and economic hardships. Many women and African Americans contributed to the Patriot cause. At first, settlers in the western lands and American Indians were neutral, but later they joined the fighting.

REVIEW

1. How did the American Revolution affect people's lives?
2. Explain the difference between a **Loyalist** and a **Patriot**.
3. Why did Congress have problems financing the war?

CRITICAL THINKING

4. **Make It Relevant** Why do you think many people are willing to face hardships during war?
5. SKILL What were the costs and benefits of fighting in the war for American Indians?
6. **Write a Conversation** Write a conversation between a Patriot and a Loyalist. Make sure each speaker supports his or her position with evidence.
7. **CAUSE AND EFFECT** On a separate sheet of paper, copy and complete this graphic organizer.

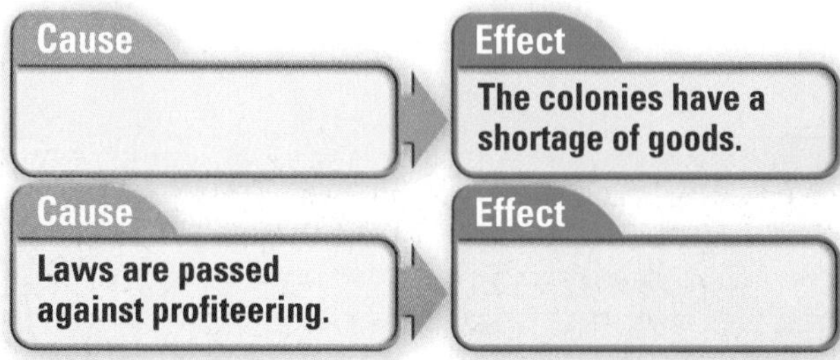

Mercy Otis Warren

*"Each fervent wish, I to my country lend, and thus subscribe, the patriot's faithful friend."**

As a girl growing up in Massachusetts, Mercy Otis Warren did not attend school, but she did take part in the history and literature lessons given to her brother. As an adult, she used this knowledge in writings that supported the American cause. Warren's brother and her husband were both involved in Massachusetts politics. She was also friends with John Adams, Martha Washington, and Thomas Jefferson.

Warren used her writing to express her political ideas. In 1773, she wrote a play that criticized the British governor of Massachusetts. The play warned that colonists would one day fight to win their independence.

Another of Warren's works was the pamphlet *Observations on the New Constitution*. In this pamphlet, published in 1788, she asked the new government to guarantee rights for women. Warren later wrote a book about the history of the American Revolution. Today, historians study her works to learn about the political leaders of her time.

* Mercy Otis Warren. *Plays and Poems of Mercy Otis Warren.* Scholars' Facsimiles and Reprint, 1980.

Biography

Trustworthiness
Respect
Responsibility
Fairness
Caring
Patriotism

Why Character Counts

How did Mercy Otis Warren's writings show her patriotism?

Bio Brief

1728 — Born 1728

1773 Warren's first play is published

1805 Warren writes a history of the American Revolution

1814 — Died 1814

Read Parallel Time Lines

WHY IT MATTERS

In the years leading up to the Revolutionary War, many events happened at about the same time. When groups of events happen at the same time in different places, showing them all on one time line can be difficult. Parallel time lines can help. **Parallel time lines** are two or more time lines that show events from the same period of time. Parallel time lines can also show events that happened in different places.

WHAT YOU NEED TO KNOW

The parallel time lines below and on page 375 show events that took place between 1770 and 1776. The bottom time line shows important events that happened in the colonies before the American Revolution. The top time line shows important events that took place in Britain during the same time. You can use these parallel time lines to compare events in the colonies with events in Britain.

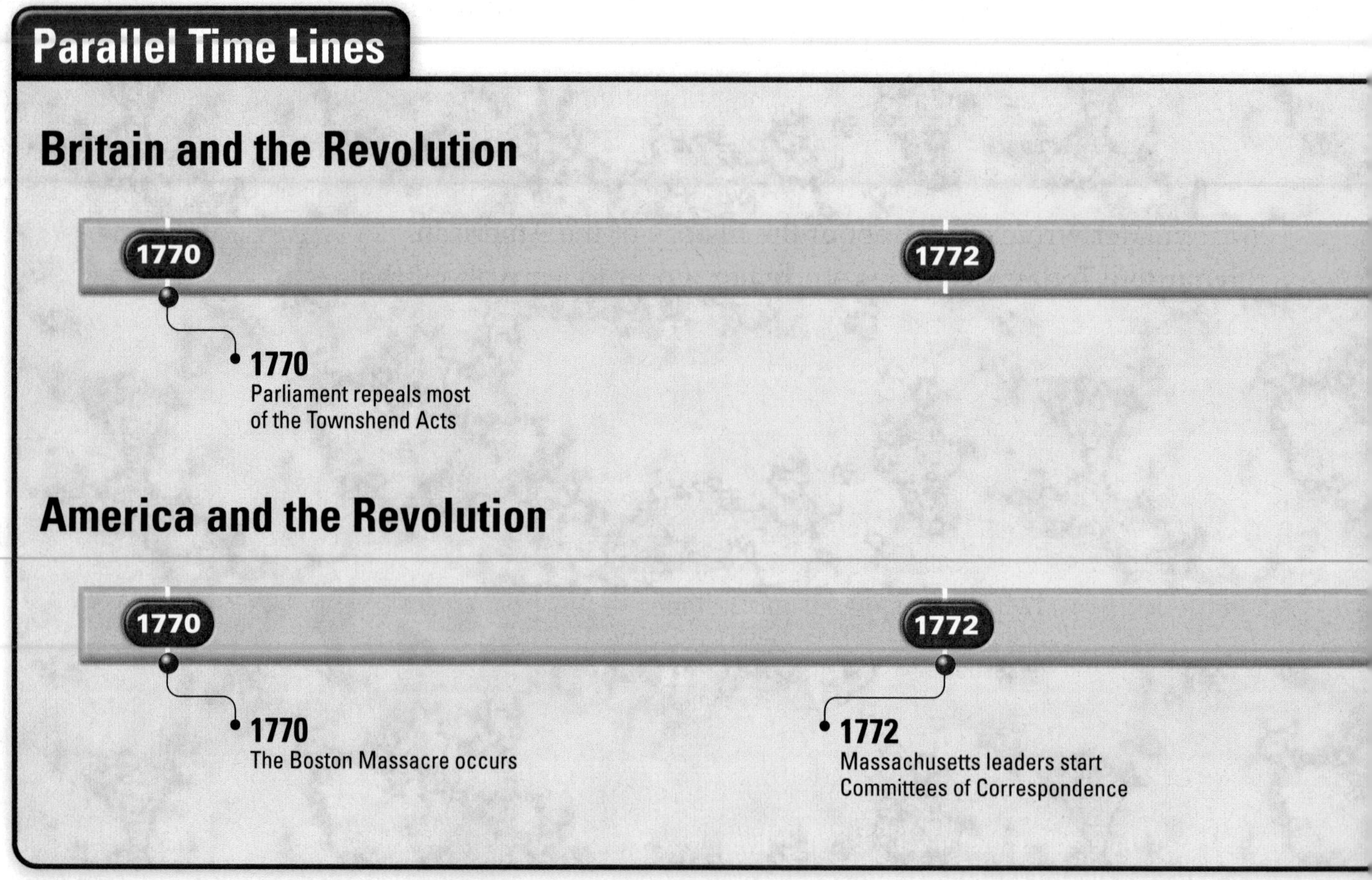

Parallel Time Lines

Britain and the Revolution

1770 1772

1770
Parliament repeals most of the Townshend Acts

America and the Revolution

1770 1772

1770
The Boston Massacre occurs

1772
Massachusetts leaders start Committees of Correspondence

PRACTICE THE SKILL

Use the parallel time lines below to answer these questions.

1. Which took place first—the Boston Massacre or the passage of the Coercive Acts?
2. Which time line shows the date the Declaration of Independence was approved?
3. Did the First Continental Congress meet before or after the repeal of the Townshend Acts?
4. What year did Massachusetts leaders start Committees of Correspondence?

APPLY WHAT YOU LEARNED

ANALYSIS SKILL Create parallel time lines of events that have happened in your own lifetime. Use one time line to show the important events that took place in your life, beginning with the year you were born and ending with the present year. Use the other time line to show important events that have happened in the United States during this same period of time.

Statue of the Patriot Tadeusz Kosciuszko

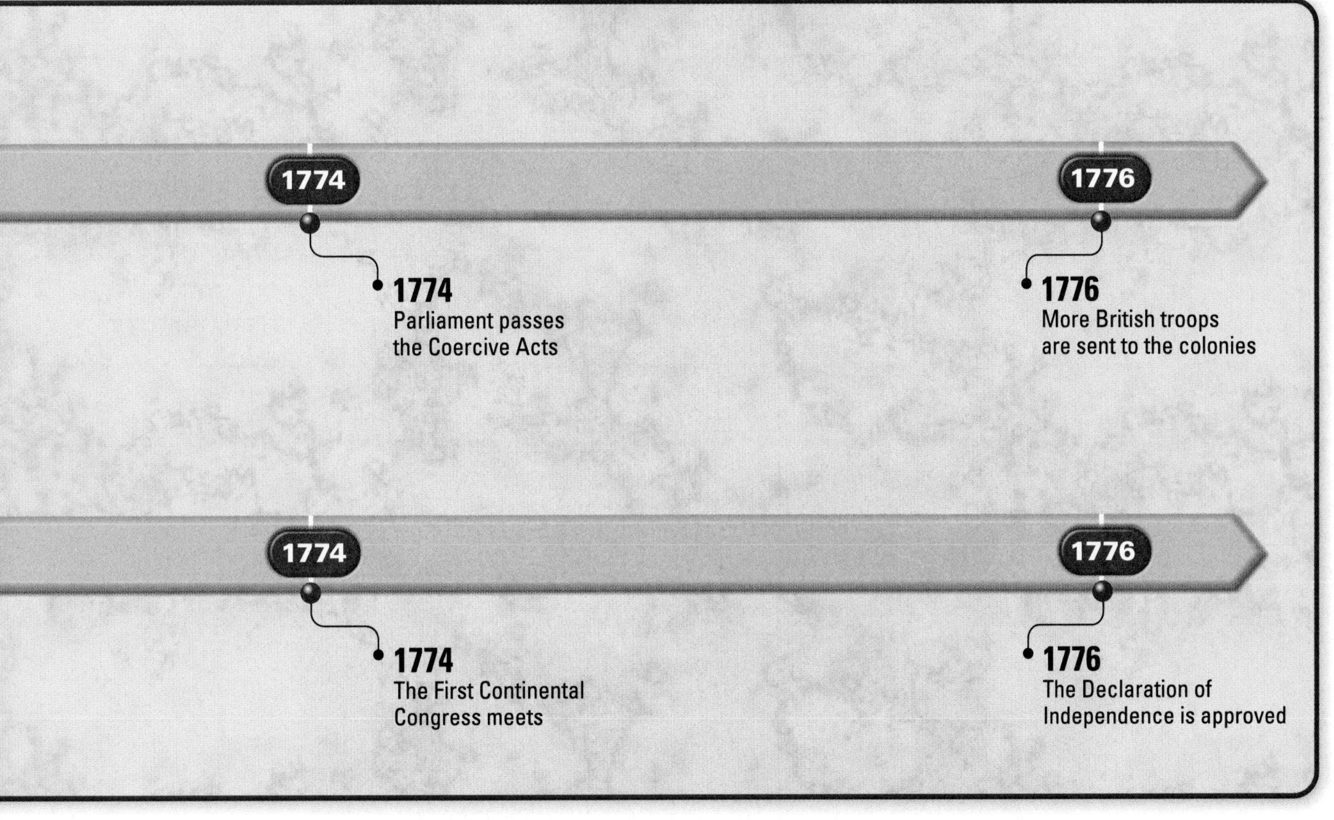

Chart and Graph Skills

PRIMARY SOURCES

Washington's Mess Chest

During much of the Revolutionary War, George Washington and his troops lived in tents or other shelters. This meant that soldiers and officers had to cook most of their own food. To prepare and eat his meals, Washington used this camp kitchen, or mess chest. It was equipped with all the pots, pans, and utensils he needed.

Glass storage jars for storing water

Kettles used for heating food on the gridiron over an open flame

Kettles stacked inside each other to save space

One of three tin platters used for preparing and serving meals

Lift-out storage bins used for storing dry goods such as bread, flour, or grain

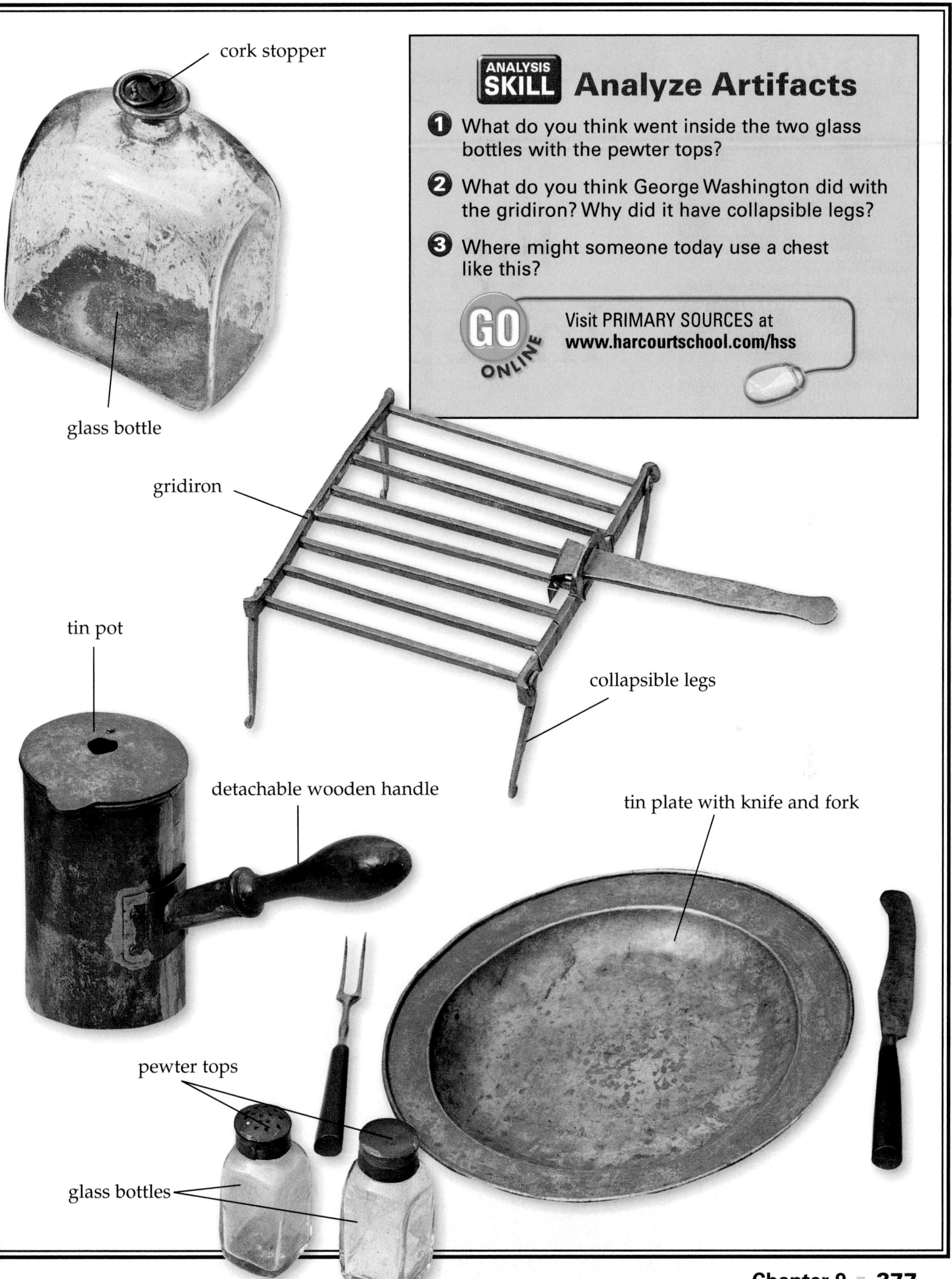

ANALYSIS SKILL

Analyze Artifacts

1. What do you think went inside the two glass bottles with the pewter tops?
2. What do you think George Washington did with the gridiron? Why did it have collapsible legs?
3. Where might someone today use a chest like this?

GO ONLINE Visit PRIMARY SOURCES at **www.harcourtschool.com/hss**

Lesson 2

Time

1750

1790

1776 The Battle of Trenton

1777 The Battle of Saratoga

WHAT TO KNOW

What were some of the important early events of the Revolutionary War?

- Identify the early battles, campaigns, and turning points.
- Examine the roles of American and British leaders.
- Describe how individuals and other nations contributed to the war's outcome.

VOCABULARY

enlist p. 379
mercenary p. 379
campaign p. 381
turning point p. 381
negotiate p. 383

PEOPLE

Marquis de Lafayette
Benedict Arnold
Friedrich von Steuben

PLACES

Trenton
Saratoga
Valley Forge

Focus Skill CAUSE AND EFFECT

California Standards

HSS 5.5.4, 5.6, 5.6.1, 5.6.2, 5.6.4

Fighting for Independence

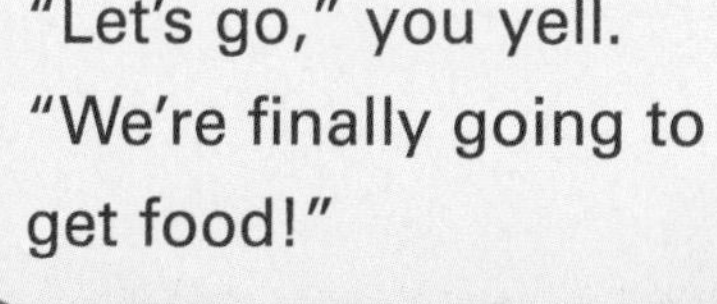

"The soldiers are starving," says the **Marquis de Lafayette** (mar•KEE duh lah•fee•ET). "They eat nothing but firecake made of flour and water." As you and the other soldiers listen, your stomach rumbles. It's been days since you've had anything but firecake to eat.

"Since Congress won't send help," General George Washington says, "I'll order the local farmers to sell us their crops."

The air outside is bitterly cold, but you don't care. "Let's go," you yell. "We're finally going to get food!"

The Marquis de Lafayette helped the Continental Army.

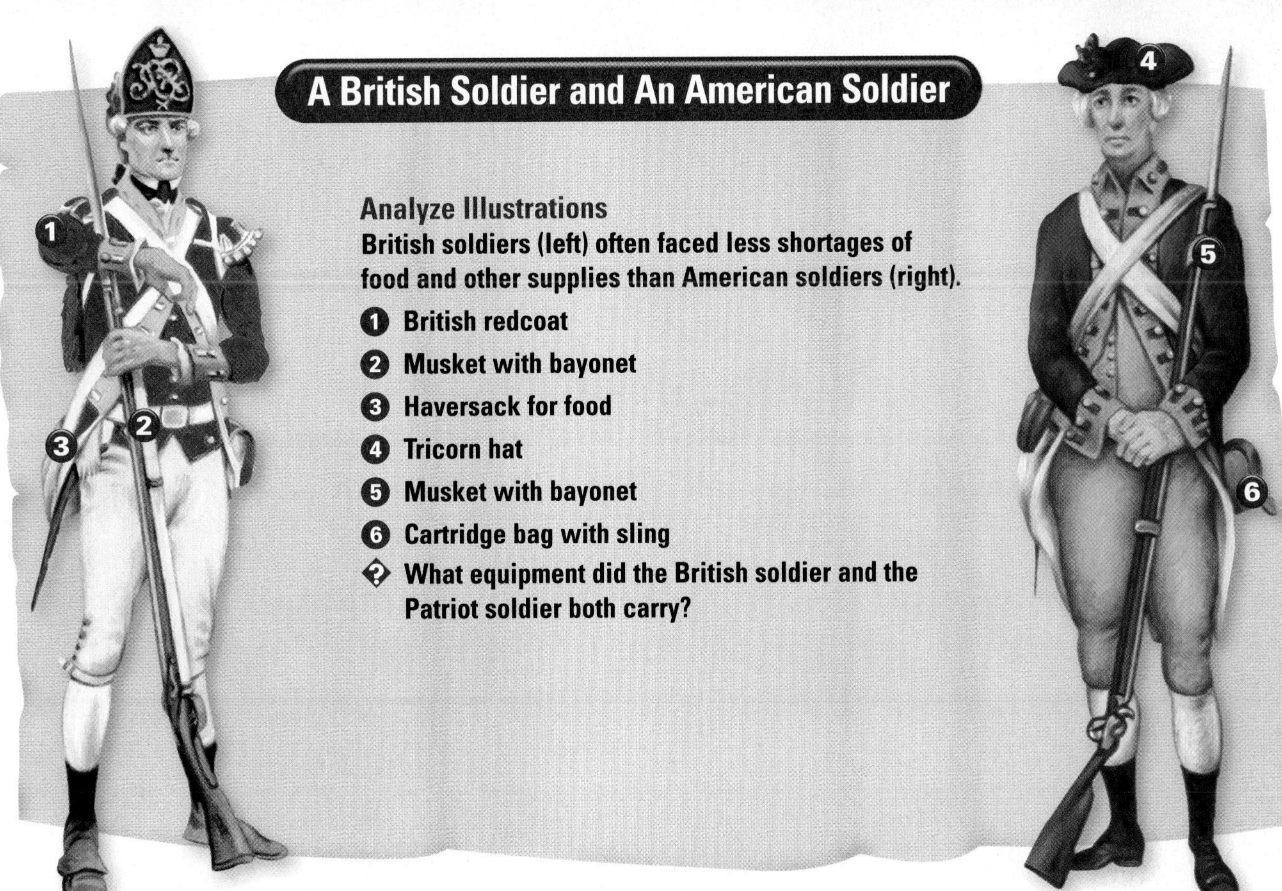

A British Soldier and An American Soldier

Analyze Illustrations
British soldiers (left) often faced less shortages of food and other supplies than American soldiers (right).

1. **British redcoat**
2. **Musket with bayonet**
3. **Haversack for food**
4. **Tricorn hat**
5. **Musket with bayonet**
6. **Cartridge bag with sling**

What equipment did the British soldier and the Patriot soldier both carry?

Comparing Armies

In July 1775 George Washington arrived in Massachusetts to meet the Continental Army. The soldiers wore no uniforms—only their everyday clothes. Many had no guns, so they carried spears and axes. Some had fought in the French and Indian War, but most had no military experience. Many were farmers who had just **enlisted**, or signed up, for duty in the army. Washington was once so frustrated that he threw his hat on the ground and shouted, "Are these the men with which I am to defend America?"*

Keeping the army fed and clothed took huge amounts of supplies. Washington once estimated that his army needed 100,000 barrels of flour and 20 million pounds of meat a year! Congress could not raise enough money to pay for the food needed to feed all the soldiers.

The Continental Army went to war against one of the most powerful armies in the world. The British army was made up of professional soldiers with training and experience. The British had 50,000 soldiers in the colonies. Washington usually had no more than 15,000 soldiers in his army at any one time. The British army also had thousands of **mercenaries**, or hired soldiers. Because many of the mercenaries came from a German region called Hesse-Cassel, Americans called them Hessians.

But the British had problems, too. It was difficult to fight a war more than 3,000 miles from home. Loyalists offered some aid, but the British soldiers still had to wait a long time for supplies and soldiers to replace them.

READING CHECK **CAUSE AND EFFECT**
What geographical problem caused difficulties for the British army?

*George Washington. *Liberty: The American Revolution* by Thomas Fleming. Viking, 1997.

Washington led an attack across the Delaware River and into New Jersey.

Early Battles in the North

By the spring of 1776, Washington and his army had moved south from Massachusetts to New York. They were camped on Long Island when British troops attacked them. Outnumbered four to one, the Americans suffered great losses at the Battle of Long Island.

The British army then decided to chase Washington and what was left of his army. Many soldiers had left after the Battle of Long Island, and Washington had to persuade the others to stay. He and the soldiers who stayed with him did their best to avoid capture by the British. By winter, they had marched through New Jersey to Pennsylvania.

British General William Howe and most of the British army were in New York for the winter. When Washington learned that the Hessian mercenaries stationed at **Trenton**, New Jersey, were not prepared for an attack, he decided to move against them.

On Christmas night, 1776, Washington and his army crossed the icy Delaware River in boats. The troops then marched 9 miles to reach Trenton. There they found the German troops sleeping after spending the day celebrating Christmas. The Americans attacked, and the fighting lasted only an hour before the Hessians surrendered. This victory gave the American soldiers hope for the future.

READING CHECK **DRAW CONCLUSIONS**
Why did Washington decide to attack Trenton on Christmas night?

An Important Victory

In 1777, the British army planned a new campaign. A **campaign** is a series of military operations carried out for a certain goal. The goal of the British was to capture New York so they could separate the 13 colonies and cut off their communications and supplies. They also wanted to use New York City's harbor to land more soldiers and supplies.

The British campaign called for several large groups of soldiers to travel to Albany, New York, to join troops led by British General John Burgoyne. Together they would attack the city from the north, south, and west. This plan might have worked, but the British troops never reached Albany to help Burgoyne. They were delayed by smaller battles along the way.

On September 19, 1777, Continental forces surrounded General Burgoyne's army near the town of **Saratoga**, New York. Burgoyne and his soldiers could not break through the Americans' lines and had to pull back.

The Battle of Saratoga was really two battles that took place over three weeks. During the second main part of the battle, the American commander, **Benedict Arnold**, led a group of soldiers in a daring attack. Although Arnold was wounded badly in the leg, his attack succeeded. As the battle continued, the Americans captured British cannons and supplies. Finally, on October 17, Burgoyne surrendered. The British surrender at Saratoga was a turning point in the war. A **turning point** is an event that causes an important change. Suddenly it looked as if the Americans might have a chance to win the war.

READING CHECK **SUMMARIZE**
Why was the American victory at Saratoga a turning point in the war?

Surrounded in the Battle of Saratoga (below), British General John Burgoyne had to surrender to American General Horatio Gates (inset).

Winter at Valley Forge

In the fall of 1777, the Continental Army once again faced trouble. While trying to keep the British from taking Philadelphia, the Continental Army lost a battle at nearby Brandywine. In late September, British soldiers captured Philadelphia, where they prepared to spend the winter in comfort.

Stunned and exhausted, the weary Continental soldiers retreated to nearby **Valley Forge**, Pennsylvania. Washington chose this location because he wanted to keep watch on the British in Philadelphia.

The Continental Army that set up camp at Valley Forge was a ragged group. Congress did not have the money to send supplies. Most of the soldiers wore clothing they had brought from home, but it had become torn and burned from the soldiers' battles. Some of the men had walked so far that their shoes were falling apart. One young Connecticut soldier wrote that he had "not a scrap of either shoes or stockings to my feet or legs."* He and others wrapped their feet in rags.

Since food was also running low, Washington allowed his soldiers to buy food from farmers around Valley Forge with Continental money from Congress. Also, New York Governor George Clinton sent barrels of salted pork.

Additional help came from the 20-year-old Marquis de Lafayette, who traveled all the way from France to join the Continental Army. Lafayette later described himself as having an American heart. Washington liked the young Frenchman and immediately gave him important duties. Lafayette spent his own

***A Narrative of Some of the Adventures, Dangers, and Sufferings of a Revolutionary Soldier* by Joseph Plumb Martin. Glazier, Masters, and Co., 1830.

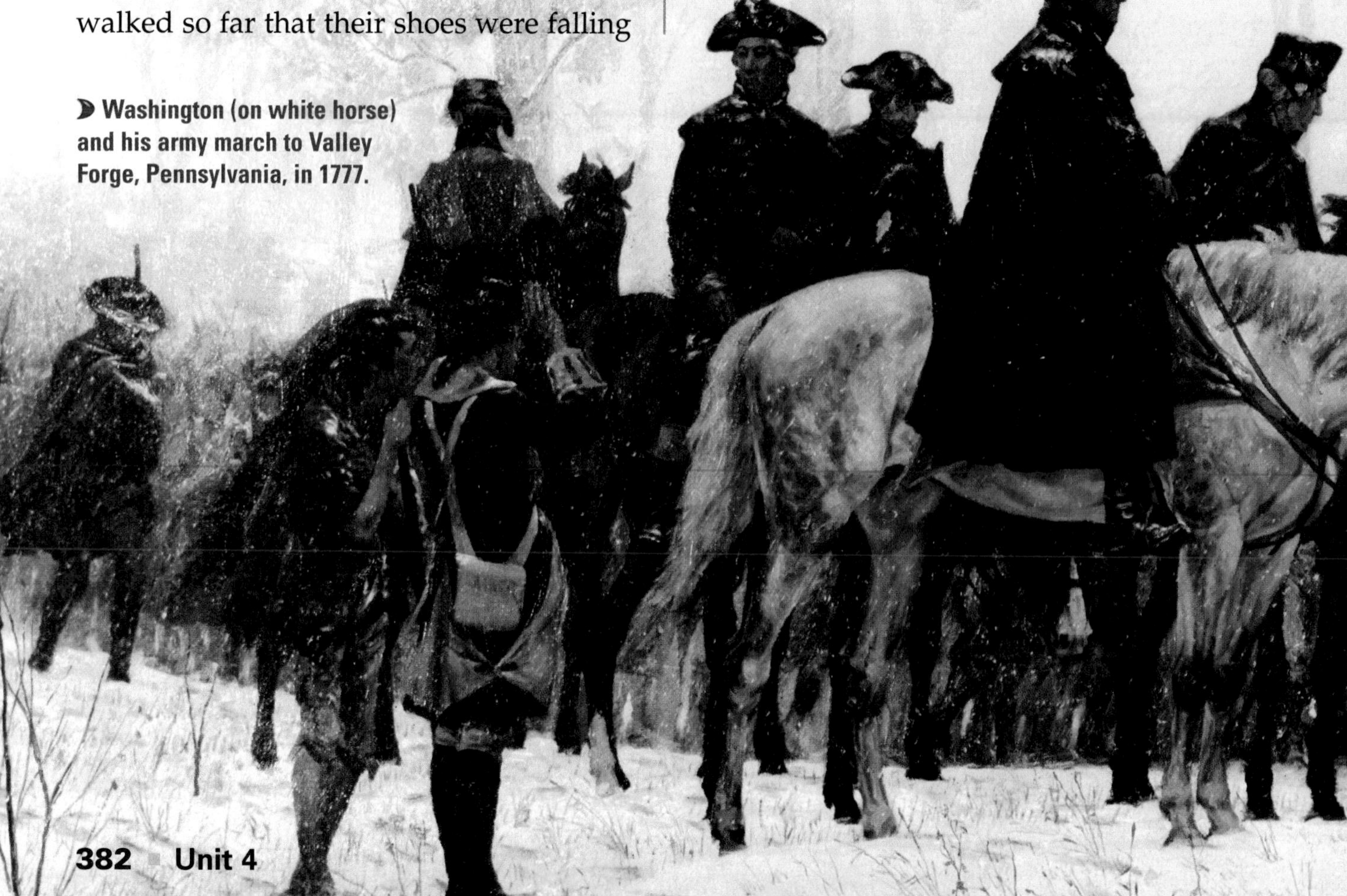

Washington (on white horse) and his army march to Valley Forge, Pennsylvania, in 1777.

money to buy warm clothes for the soldiers he commanded. He was so generous that they began calling him "the soldier's friend."*

Life at Valley Forge improved further when **Friedrich Wilhelm von Steuben** (STOO•buhn) arrived. Von Steuben was a German soldier who had decided to help the Americans by training them to become a skilled fighting force. He taught them how to attack and retreat faster and how to use weapons more effectively. By the spring of 1778, Washington's soldiers had become an organized army.

Friedrich von Steuben

READING CHECK **CAUSE AND EFFECT**
What effect did Friedrich Wilhelm von Steuben have on the Continental Army?

Liberty: The American Revolution by Thomas Fleming. Viking, 1997.

Contributions from Other Nations

While the war raged on in North America, Benjamin Franklin was in France, negotiating with the French government. To **negotiate** is to try to come to an agreement that is acceptable to all the parties involved. Franklin asked the French for supplies and soldiers. He argued that France would benefit from helping defeat its old enemy, Britain.

At first the French offered little help, thinking that Britain would win the war. Then news of the American victory at Saratoga reached France, and the French agreed to support the Americans.

Jorge Farragut was 21 years old when he came from Spain to fight for the Americans in 1776. He later became an officer in the United States Navy.

Other nations also offered to help. In 1781, bankers in the Netherlands gave a large loan to Congress. Russian leaders, through the League of Armed Neutrality, worked to keep the British from blocking trade with the Americans.

Bernardo de Gálvez (GAHL•ves), the governor of Spanish Louisiana, gave guns, food, and money to the Continental Army. Later, he led his own soldiers to capture several British forts. Spanish-born Jorge Farragut (FAIR•uh•guht) fought in the Continental Army and Navy.

READING CHECK **CAUSE AND EFFECT**
What caused the French to join the war in support of the Americans?

Summary

The Continental Army was less experienced than the British army. However, the Americans had some important early victories at Trenton and Saratoga. Other nations helped the Patriot cause.

REVIEW

1. What were some of the important early events of the Revolutionary War?
2. Use the word **campaign** in a sentence about the Revolutionary War.
3. Who led the Americans' negotiations with France?

CRITICAL THINKING

4. ANALYSIS SKILL Why was Valley Forge's relative location important to George Washington?
5. ANALYSIS SKILL What were the costs and benefits of joining the Continental Army?
6. **Write a Speech** Imagine that you are camped with the soldiers at Valley Forge. Write a speech to lift the soldiers' spirits.
7. Focus Skill **CAUSE AND EFFECT** On a separate sheet of paper, copy and complete this graphic organizer.

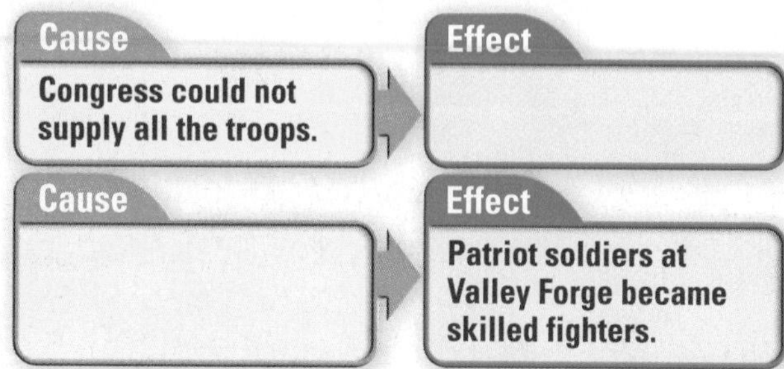

Trustworthiness
Respect
Responsibility
Fairness
Caring
Patriotism

Bernardo de Gálvez

Bernardo de Gálvez was born in Málaga, Spain, in 1746. Gálvez first came to North America in 1762. He traveled with his uncle, who was visiting New Spain. In 1776, he returned to lead a Spanish regiment in Louisiana. One year later, Gálvez became the governor of Spanish Louisiana.

This stamp honors the actions of Gálvez during the Revolutionary War.

During the Revolutionary War, Gálvez chose to help the Americans. He protected New Orleans against British attack, which gave him control of the Mississippi River. Gálvez let American ships use the river to move weapons and food to Patriot forces fighting on the frontier.

In 1779, Spain declared war on Britain. Gálvez captured the British towns of Baton Rouge, Natchez, and Mobile. In 1781, he captured Pensacola. By the time the war ended, Gálvez and his army controlled all of West Florida. After the war, the new United States Congress thanked Bernardo de Gálvez for his help during the American Revolution.

Why Character Counts

How did Gálvez prove his trustworthiness to the Americans?

Bio Brief

1746 — Born 1746

1786 — Died 1786

1777 Gálvez becomes governor of Spanish Louisiana

1781 Gálvez captures the town of Pensacola, Florida

Compare Maps with Different Scales

WHY IT MATTERS

The commanders of the British forces and the American forces used maps to make plans for battle. Most maps have map scales to help you judge distances. Map scales differ depending on how much area is shown. Maps with large scales show less area and more details than maps with small scales. When you want to see all the cities in California, look at a map with a small scale. A map with a large scale might show you the streets and landmarks in San Diego.

WHAT YOU NEED TO KNOW

Look at the map below and the map on page 387. Both show part of Long Island, New York, where the Battle of Long Island took place. On Map A, Long Island looks larger. Map A has a large scale, so more details are shown. On Map B, Long Island looks smaller. Map B has a small scale, so more area is shown.

Each kind of map has value. For example, Map A can be used to see details about the area. Map B can be used to see the surrounding land.

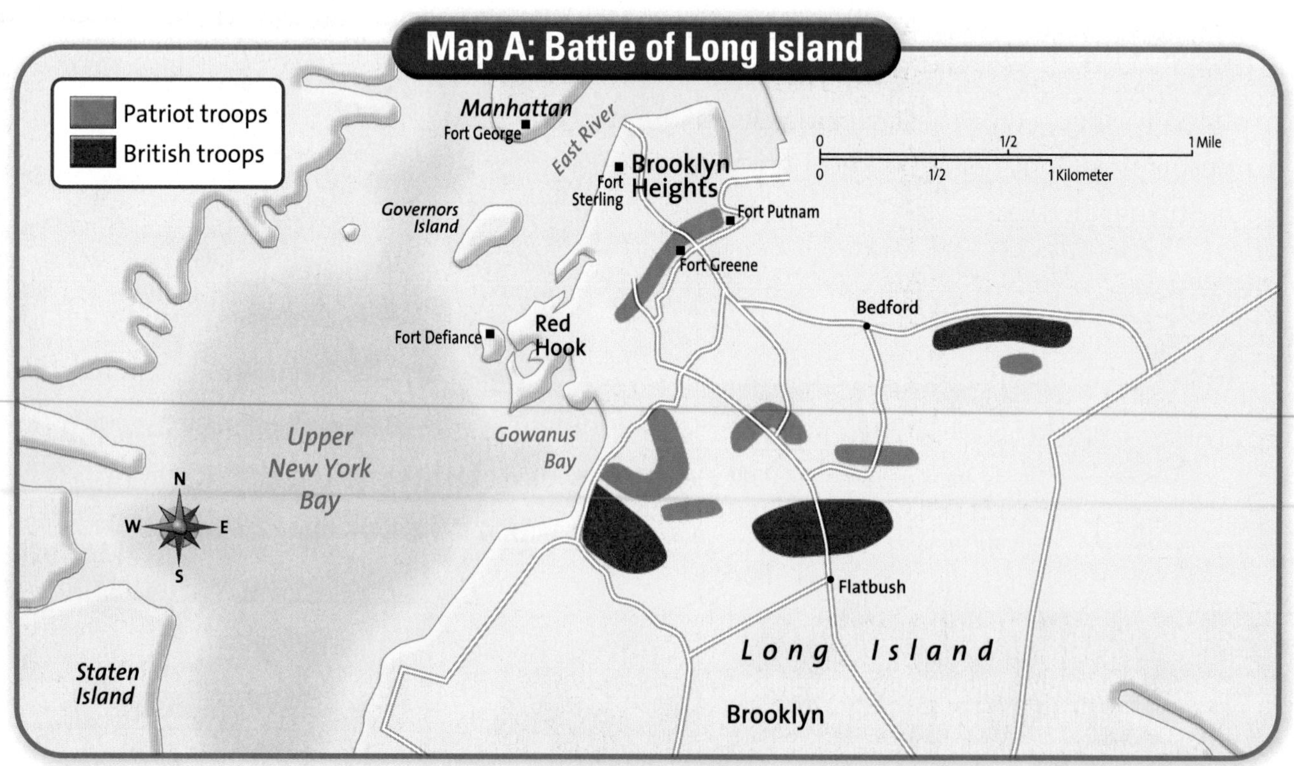

Map B: Battle of Long Island

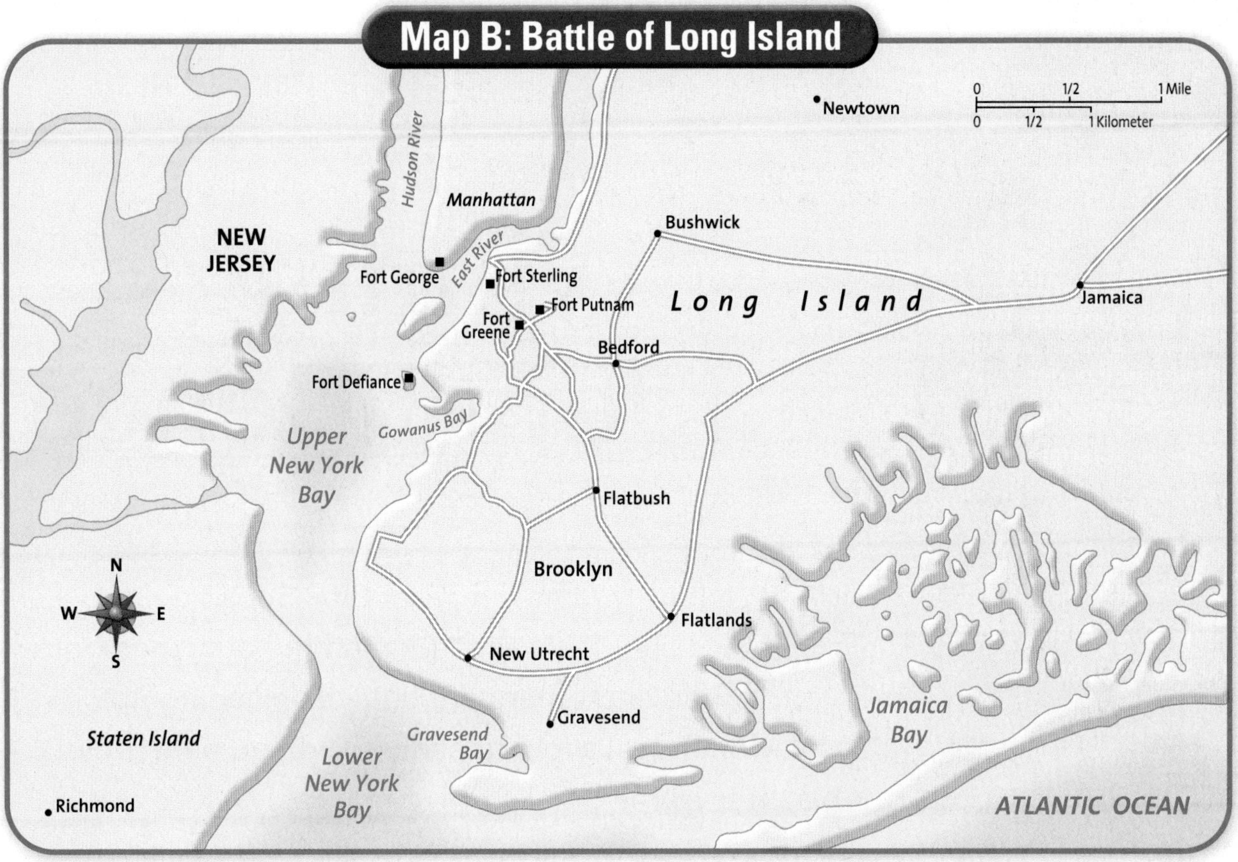

PRACTICE THE SKILL

Use Maps A and B to answer these questions.

1. Which map shows the distance between Patriot troops near Fort Greene and British troops near Flatbush?
2. Which map could you use to find the distance between the Hudson River and Jamaica Bay?
3. What is the distance in miles between Gravesend and Bedford, New York? Which map shows both places?
4. Suppose you are a general in the Continental Army. Which map would you use to plan the retreat into New Jersey? Why?

APPLY WHAT YOU LEARNED

ANALYSIS SKILL When you take trips with your family, you probably use maps to help you find your way. You could use a small-scale map to find interstate and other highways. A large-scale map could help you find the home of a friend who lives in a certain town.

Look at a small-scale map of the state of California. Imagine that you are taking a trip to one of the cities shown on the map. Use the map to find the distance from your hometown to that city.

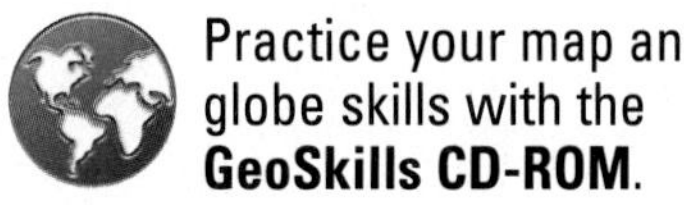

Practice your map and globe skills with the **GeoSkills CD-ROM**.

Lesson 3

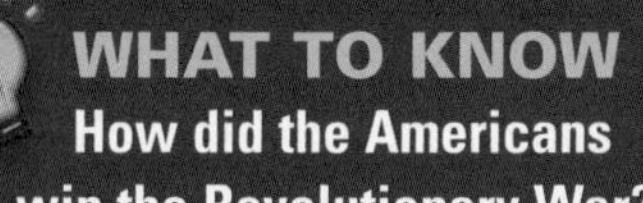

1781 The Battle of Yorktown

1783 Treaty of Paris

WHAT TO KNOW
How did the Americans win the Revolutionary War?

- ✔ Identify the major battles and campaigns of the Revolutionary War.
- ✔ Describe how individuals and other nations contributed to the war's outcome.

VOCABULARY
traitor p. 391

PEOPLE
Nathan Hale
John Paul Jones
Molly Pitcher
Tadeusz Kosciuszko
Benedict Arnold
Nathanael Greene
Charles Cornwallis

PLACES
West Point
Savannah
Charles Town
Cowpens
Guilford Courthouse
Yorktown

CAUSE AND EFFECT

California Standards
HSS 5.6, 5.6.1, 5.6.2, 5.6.3, 5.6.4

Winning Independence

YOU ARE THERE It is 1776 in New York City. Soot from the recent fire has blackened the buildings. You, your father, and others are outside, cleaning up.

A woman says to you sadly, "Did you hear about **Nathan Hale**? Such a brave man."

"He was a spy on our side, right?" you ask her.

"Oh yes," she replies. "When the fire started here, he was captured by the British. Just before he was hanged, he said, 'I only regret that I have but one life to lose for my country.'"*

Brushing soot from his hands, your father says, "That man showed how brave we Patriots can be."

* Nathan Hale. *Liberty: The American Revolution* by Thomas Fleming. Viking, 1997.

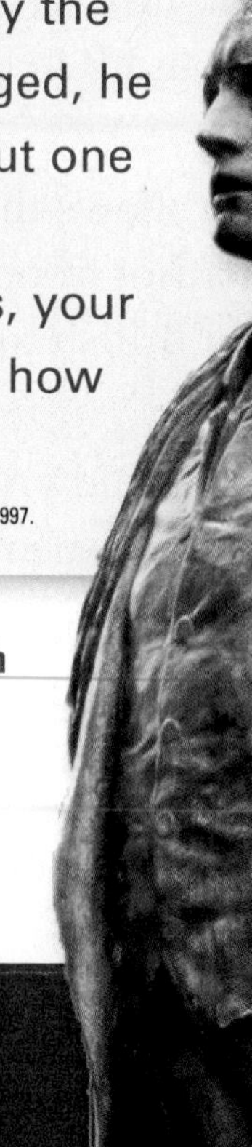

Nathan Hale disguised himself as a Dutch schoolteacher to spy on the British.

Revolutionary Heroes

During the Revolutionary War, Americans were grateful for the efforts of Nathan Hale and other brave Patriots. In 1776, when George Washington asked for volunteers to spy on the British in New York City, Hale volunteered. Hale was following the British when they took control of New York City. A huge fire swept through the city, and as people fled, the British captured Hale. When they discovered he was a spy, they hanged him. The reports of his final words spread quickly, and Hale became a hero.

At sea **John Paul Jones**, an American navy commander, battled larger and better-equipped British ships. In one famous battle in the North Sea near Britain, the British asked Jones to surrender. He replied, "I have not yet begun to fight."* Jones kept fighting until the British ship gave up.

American women also won fame for their bravery during the war. Mary Ludwig Hays McCauley earned the name **Molly Pitcher** by carrying fresh water to American troops during the Battle of Monmouth in New Jersey in 1778. When her husband was wounded, she took his place in battle helping to load the cannons. McCauley stayed beside the cannons for the rest of the battle.

As word of the fight for freedom spread, more volunteers arrived. **Tadeusz Kosciuszko** (kawsh•CHUSH•koh) traveled from Poland to work for the Continental Army. He built walls for defense during the Battle of Saratoga, and he helped design the plans for a fort at **West Point**, New York. Without Kosciuszko's help, the army's defenses would have been much weaker.

READING CHECK **CAUSE AND EFFECT**
What effect did Tadeusz Kosciuszko have on the Battle of Saratoga?

*John Paul Jones. *The Life and Character of the Chevalier John Paul Jones, a Captain in the United States Navy, During the Revolutionary War* by John Henry Sherburne. Wilder and Campbell, 1825.

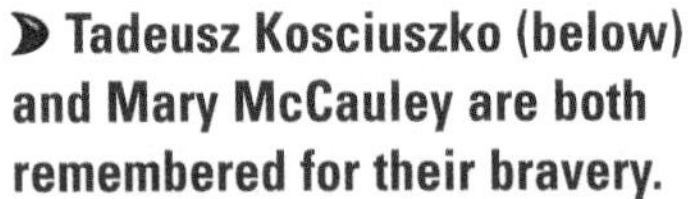
Tadeusz Kosciuszko (below) and Mary McCauley are both remembered for their bravery.

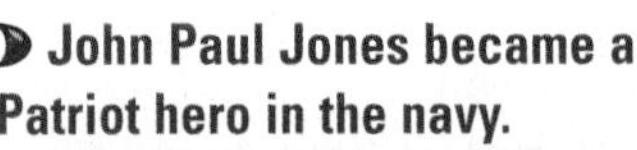
John Paul Jones became a Patriot hero in the navy.

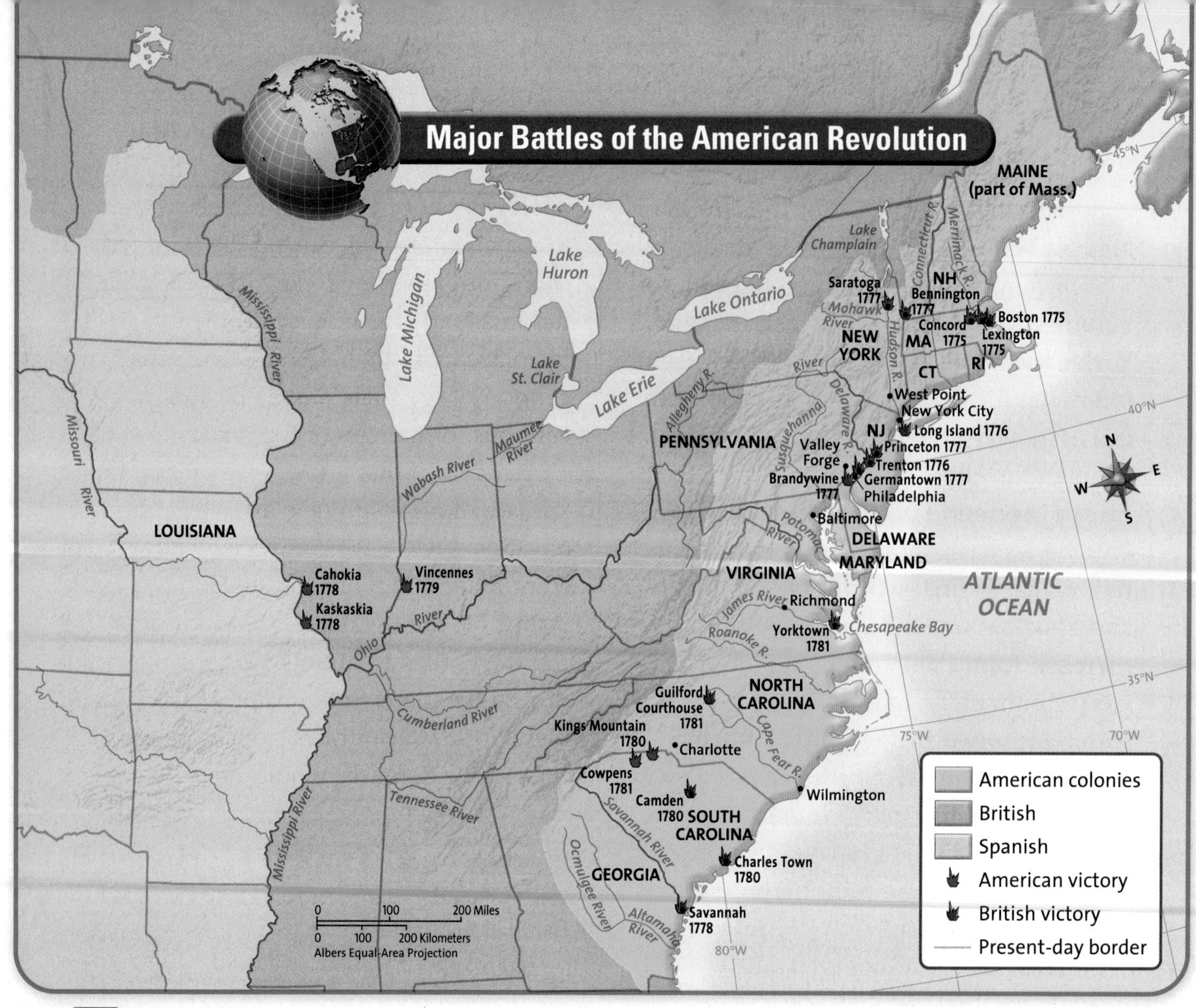

ANALYSIS SKILL Analyze Maps

Regions In which state was the Battle of Cowpens fought?

The War in the South

When the British government learned that the French had begun helping the Americans, British leaders shifted the fighting to the South. They had captured several cities in the North, including Philadelphia and New York City. The British hoped to defeat the Americans in the South before French ships and soldiers could arrive.

The British knew that many Loyalists lived in the South, and they hoped for Loyalist support. British leaders also hoped to capture Southern port cities. The fight would be easier for the British if their navy supplied them from the sea.

Savannah, Georgia, was Britain's first target. On November 25, 1778, about 3,500 British soldiers landed near the town. They quickly overwhelmed the American soldiers who were trying to protect Savannah.

Early in 1780, the British moved north to capture **Charles Town**, later known as Charleston, in South Carolina. There, too, the Continental soldiers were greatly outnumbered and soon lost the battle.

Early in 1781, **Benedict Arnold**, a former Continental Army officer, began leading British attacks on Virginia towns. Arnold had become a **traitor**, or someone who acts against his or her country. Earlier, he had decided to give the British the plans to the American fort at West Point, New York. However, the Americans discovered Arnold's plan before he could carry it out. Arnold began working for the British because he was not satisfied with his rank and salary.

Although the Americans lost several battles to the British, they kept fighting. General **Nathanael Greene**, who led the Continental Army in the South, told his soldiers not to give up. He said,

"We fight, get beat, rise, and fight again."*

Under Greene's leadership, General Daniel Morgan led the Americans to a major victory at **Cowpens**, South Carolina, in January 1781. The Battle of Cowpens was a turning point because it proved that American militia forces could defeat the British.

The British army then pushed into North Carolina. The Americans and British fought a fierce battle at **Guilford Courthouse** in March 1781. However, the British still could not win the war or defeat the American spirit.

READING CHECK **SUMMARIZE**
Why did the British concentrate on the South?

*Nathanael Greene. *Liberty: The American Revolution* by Thomas Fleming. Viking, 1997.

The Battle of Cowpens, South Carolina, was a major victory for the Americans.

Victory at Yorktown

TIME 1781

PLACE Yorktown, Virginia

By the summer of 1781, British General **Charles Cornwallis** had set up his headquarters at **Yorktown**, Virginia. Yorktown was on Chesapeake Bay, a location that made it easy for British ships to deliver supplies. However, Yorktown's location also meant that the town could be surrounded easily. Knowing this, the French and the Americans made a plan to defeat Cornwallis at Yorktown.

Both French and Continental soldiers marched south to surround Yorktown. At the same time, the French navy took control of Chesapeake Bay. The British navy could not get supplies to the British army. General Cornwallis was trapped. In late September, he sent word to his commander in the North:

> **"If you cannot relieve me very soon, you must be prepared to hear the worst."***

"The worst" that Cornwallis warned about did happen. After being surrounded for weeks and under attack from both land and sea, Cornwallis surrendered. One person who was there wrote, "At two o'clock in the evening Oct. 19th, 1781, the British army, led by General Charles O'Hara, marched out of its lines, with colors cased [flags folded] and drums beating a British march."**

READING CHECK **SUMMARIZE**

How did the French contribute to the American victory at Yorktown?

*General Charles Cornwallis, September 1781. South Carolina Historical Society.

***The Revolutionaries* edited by Russell B. Adams, Jr. Time-Life Books, 1996.

French Blockade
The French navy kept British soldiers at Yorktown from getting supplies.

Fighting in the Trenches
Colonel Alexander Hamilton led a large group of American soldiers at Yorktown.

A Closer LOOK

The Battle of Yorktown

The Battle of Yorktown was the last major battle of the Revolutionary War.

1. French soldiers
2. American officers' headquarters
3. American soldiers
4. field where British surrendered
5. British earthworks
6. British soldiers
7. Chesapeake Bay
8. French ships
9. British ships
10. York River

? Why were the British at a disadvantage in the Battle of Yorktown?

The Treaty of Paris

When word of Britain's surrender reached Philadelphia, the Liberty Bell rang out the news. The long fight was over. The Patriots had finally won their independence.

The war had clearly been decided by the victory at Yorktown in 1781. However, the fighting dragged on in some places for more than two years. It was not until April 1782 that the British and Americans sent representatives to Paris, France, to negotiate a peace treaty.

The American representatives, led by Benjamin Franklin, John Adams, and John Jay, stated the terms they wanted in the treaty. Britain had to agree to accept American independence and to remove all British soldiers from American lands.

The British and American representatives talked with one another to work out an agreement. After a year of talks, the Treaty of Paris was signed on September 3, 1783, formally ending the war.

The Treaty of Paris officially named the United States of America as a new country. It also set the new nation's borders. The United States would reach from Georgia in the south to the Great Lakes in the north. The Mississippi River would form its western border.

After the Treaty of Paris was signed, George Washington returned home to Virginia. The war was over, and British troops were leaving the United States. Washington no longer needed to lead the Continental Army. On his way home to Virginia, he stopped in Annapolis, Maryland, where Congress was meeting.

This unfinished painting by Benjamin West shows—from left to right—John Jay, John Adams, and Benjamin Franklin negotiating a peace agreement with British representatives in Paris. The negotiations led to the signing of the Treaty of Paris (right).

At a meeting of Congress, Washington resigns from his position as commander in chief of the Continental Army.

Washington told Congress that since the nation was now at peace, his work was done. He said, "Having now finished the work assigned me, I retire from the great theater of action."* He planned to return to his home and live a quiet life.

READING CHECK **CAUSE AND EFFECT**
What were the effects of the Treaty of Paris?

*George Washington, in an address to the Continental Congress, Annapolis, Maryland, December 23, 1783. *Journals of the Continental Congress* edited by Worthington C. Ford et al. Government Printing Office, 1904–1937.

Summary

American heroes contributed to the war effort. The Americans won at Yorktown in the last important battle of the war. In 1783, the Treaty of Paris brought peace and formally declared the United States a new nation.

REVIEW

1. How did the Americans win the Revolutionary War?
2. Use the term **traitor** in a sentence about Benedict Arnold.
3. How was the Battle of Cowpens a turning point?
4. Who were the American representatives who negotiated the Treaty of Paris?

CRITICAL THINKING

5. **Make It Relevant** Why do you think that American heroes risked their lives in the war? Who do you think are heroes today?
6. **Draw a Medal** Use what you have read to draw a medal of honor for one of the Patriot heroes. Be sure that the medal represents the hero's contribution.
7. Focus Skill **CAUSE AND EFFECT** On a separate sheet of paper, copy and complete this graphic organizer.

Cause	Effect
Many Loyalists lived in the South.	
	The British targeted port cities.

Lesson 4

Time

1750  1790

1787
The Northwest Ordinance is passed

WHAT TO KNOW
How did the American Revolution affect life in the new United States?

- ✓ Explain how state constitutions reflected the ideals of the American Revolution.
- ✓ Evaluate how the Declaration of Independence changed views on slavery.
- ✓ Understand the significance of new land policies and their impact on American Indians.

VOCABULARY
abolitionist p. 397
abolish p. 397
territory p. 399
ordinance p. 399

PEOPLE
Elizabeth Freeman
Michikinikwa
Red Jacket

PLACES
Northwest Territory

CAUSE AND EFFECT

California Standards
HSS 5.6, 5.6.5, 5.6.6, 5.6.7

Consequences of the War

YOU ARE THERE "Slavery is wrong!" a man declares, pounding his fist on the table in front of you. "Just read the Declaration of Independence. It says everybody should have liberty."

Other members of the group nod their heads in agreement. "It's not right that we should win our freedom but deny freedom to slaves," your mother says.

"We should stop slavery altogether," another person says. "But I'm afraid that's going to be hard."

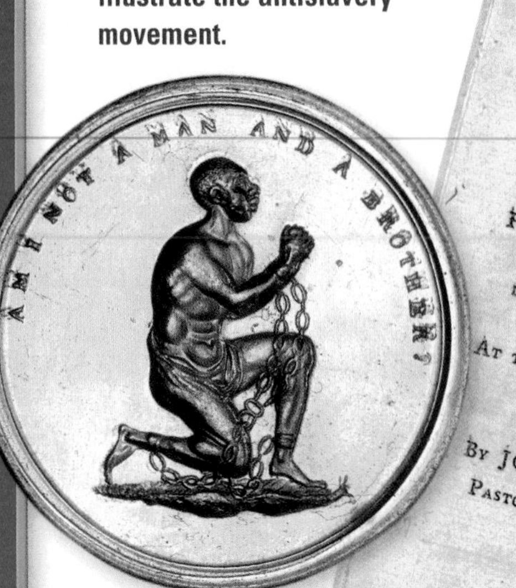

This medal and sermon illustrate the antislavery movement.

THE INJUSTICE AND IMPOLICY OF THE SLAVE TRADE, AND OF THE Slavery of the Africans: ILLUSTRATED IN A SERMON PREACHED BEFORE THE CONNECTICUT SOCIETY FOR THE PROMOTION OF FREEDOM, AND FOR THE RELIEF OF PERSONS UNLAWFULLY HOLDEN IN BONDAGE, AT THEIR ANNUAL MEETING IN NEW-HAVEN, SEPTEMBER 15, 1791. BY JONATHAN EDWARDS, D.D. PASTOR OF A CHURCH IN NEW-HAVEN.

Printed by THOMAS and SAMUEL G

African American ministers were leaders for abolition in the United States.

New Ideas for a New Nation

With freedom from Britain came the opportunity to develop new laws. By 1776, the states had begun to write their own constitutions. Several states used Virginia's state constitution as a model. It began with a list of the basic freedoms of Virginia's citizens, including the right to trial by jury, the freedom to hold elections, and freedom of the press. These were many of the beliefs that people fought for in the American Revolution.

The Declaration of Independence had affected the way many Americans thought about people's rights. The Declaration said that each person had the right to life and liberty. State constitutions, however, did not give this freedom to all people, and most African Americans remained enslaved.

If the Declaration's words were true, many people said, slavery should be stopped. Some groups, including Quakers, spoke out against slavery. In 1775 Quakers formed the country's first **abolitionist** (a•buh•LIH•shuhn•ist), or antislavery, group in Philadelphia.

In Massachusetts, a slave named **Elizabeth Freeman** sued to be free. When asked why she was suing, she answered, "I heard that paper [the Declaration] read yesterday that all [people] are born equal."* The jury agreed, and she won her freedom. Eventually, Massachusetts chose to **abolish**, or end, slavery in 1783.

READING CHECK **CAUSE AND EFFECT**
How did the Declaration of Independence change the way many people viewed slavery?

*Elizabeth Freeman. *Mumbet: The Life and Times of Elizabeth Freeman* by Mary Wilds. Avisson Press, 1999.

Western Settlements

When the Revolutionary War ended, Congress owed huge sums of money to its soldiers. Money was in short supply, though, so Congress developed new land policies. As other nations had done in the past, the United States government used land as a kind of payment for military service. Soldiers received land based on their rank and how long they had served. Some soldiers received hundreds of acres of land.

As a result of this land policy, many former soldiers came to own land in western regions. Not all of the people who moved west, however, were soldiers. Eager to raise money to pay off its debts, Congress sold huge areas of land to settlers, companies, towns, and newly formed states.

As settlers moved west, tensions grew. British troops still occupied forts along the frontier. Spain also claimed lands along the western border. To strengthen its claim on western lands, Congress often just gave land away so people would be encouraged to settle the West.

Aside from the promise of free land, Americans moved to western settlements for other reasons. Many moved to farm land and to start families. Some people were simply eager for adventure. Others hoped to start large farms and become rich. One Georgia man wrote, "I have been trying to get over my desire for a Western plantation, but every time I see a man who has been there, it puts me in a fever."*

READING CHECK SUMMARIZE
What new land policies were developed for former soldiers?

*James Henry Hammond. *Beneath These Waters* by Sharyn Kane and Richard Keeton. National Park Service, 1993.

Settlers moved west of the Appalachians to build new lives.

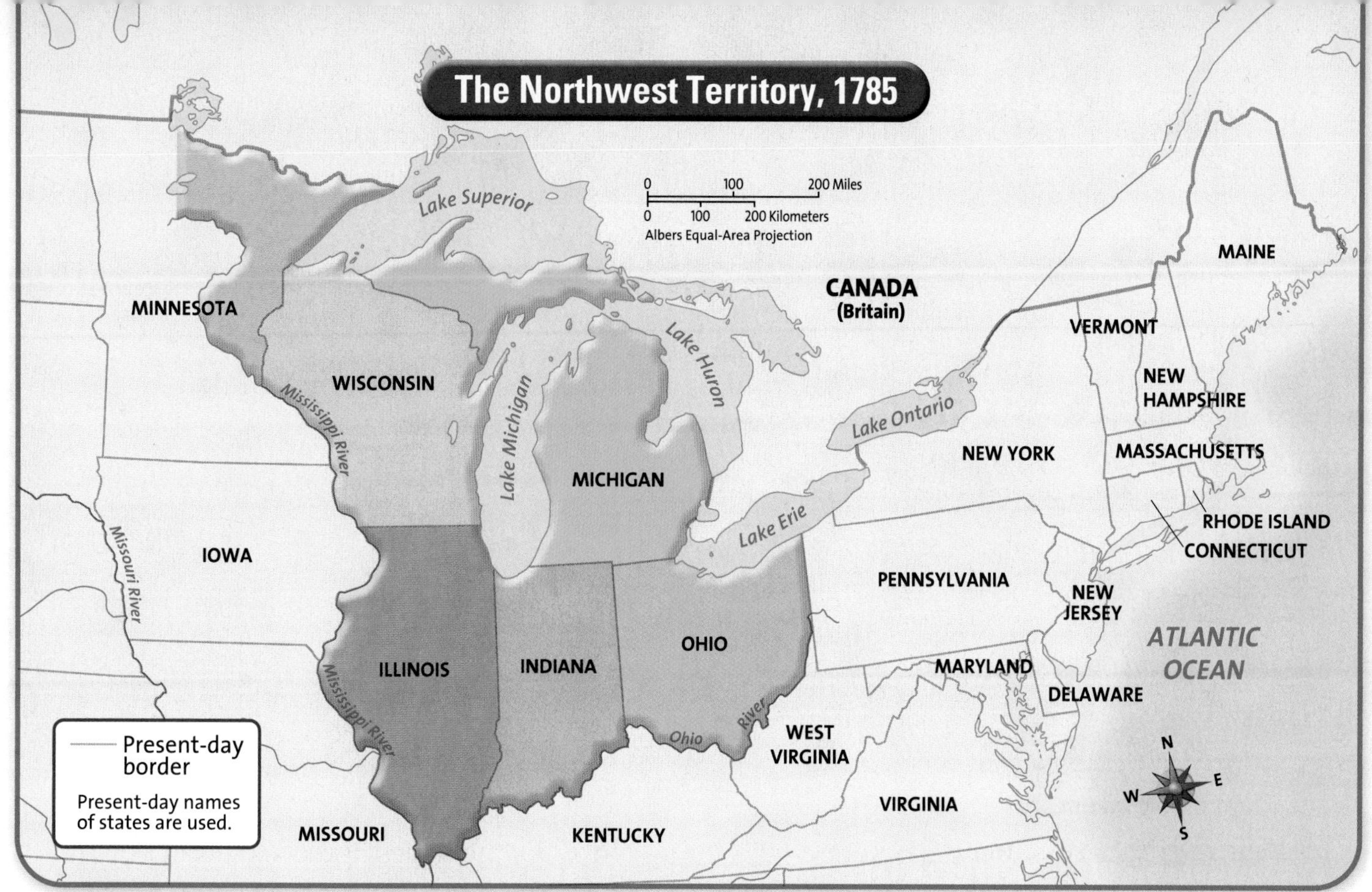

ANALYSIS SKILL Analyze Maps **The Northwest Territory covered more than 260,000 square miles.**

Location **What river formed the western boundary of the Northwest Territory?**

The Northwest Ordinance

Over time, thousands of Americans followed the Ohio River west and settled north of the river in an area that became known as the **Northwest Territory**. A **territory** is land that belongs to a nation but is not a state and is not represented in the national government.

At first there was no plan for how the land should be divided. It was hard to tell where each person's property ended. As a result, many boundary disputes occurred.

Finally in 1787, Congress passed the Northwest Ordinance. This **ordinance**, or set of laws, set up a plan for governing the Northwest Territory and for forming new states from the lands. It said that the Ohio River would form the area's southern boundary. When any region of the Northwest Territory had a population of 60,000 people, it could become a new state.

The new states would be like other states in some ways, but also different. The Northwest Ordinance said, "There shall be neither Slavery nor involuntary Servitude in the said territory. . . ."* Slavery would not be allowed in states formed from the Northwest Territory.

READING CHECK **CAUSE AND EFFECT**
How did the Northwest Ordinance affect slavery?

*"The Northwest Ordinance." *Federal and State Constitutions*, vol. 2, edited by F. N. Thorpe. 1909.

Battles for Land

After the Revolutionary War, the British left most of their forts in the United States. Without British support, it became harder for American Indians to stop settlers from moving to Indian lands. In many areas, tribes fought settlers to keep their lands.

As these tensions grew, **Michikinikwa** (mih•chih•kin•EE•kwah) became a leader for the American Indians of the Northwest Territory. From the Miami tribe of what is now Ohio, Michikinikwa commanded a group of fighters made up of people from many tribes.

In 1794, United States soldiers marched into the Northwest Territory to defeat Michikinikwa. Because he and his warriors took cover among fallen trees, the fight was called the Battle of Fallen Timbers. Michikinikwa's group lost the battle, and the soldiers burned many nearby Indian villages.

In 1795, the tribes agreed to accept the Treaty of Greenville. In this treaty, they gave up most of their land in the Northwest Territory. Many tribes were angered by the American demands for land. After the treaty was signed, they distrusted the United States government.

Some American Indians sold their land to the government or to land companies. The Holland Land Company, for example, wanted to buy much of the land west of the Genesee River from the Seneca Indians in New York. A leader named **Red Jacket** warned his tribe not to sell its land. However, the leaders ignored Red Jacket's advice and signed the Big Tree Treaty, which let the company buy almost all of the Senecas' land.

In the years to come, settlers from the United States moved farther into the western lands. Time and time again, the United States refused to honor its treaties with Indian groups. The lives

Red Jacket warns against the Big Tree Treaty

of the American Indians would never be the same as they had been before the Revolutionary War.

READING CHECK **CAUSE AND EFFECT**
What was the effect of the Treaty of Greenville?

Summary

After the Revolutionary War, the states wrote constitutions and views on slavery changed. Western settlement led to land policies and fights with American Indians.

REVIEW

1. How did the American Revolution affect life in the new United States?
2. Use the terms **territory** and **ordinance** in a sentence about western settlement.
3. How did Congress pay soldiers for their service in the Revolutionary War?

CRITICAL THINKING

4. What ideals of the American Revolution were included in the new state constitutions? Why were they important to the new country's citizens?
5. ANALYSIS SKILL What were the multiple effects of the government selling and giving away western lands?
6. **Write a Persuasive Advertisement** Draw an advertisement that tries to persuade settlers to buy land in the Northwest Territory. List reasons why people should move west.
7. Focus Skill **CAUSE AND EFFECT** On a separate sheet of paper, copy and complete this graphic organizer.

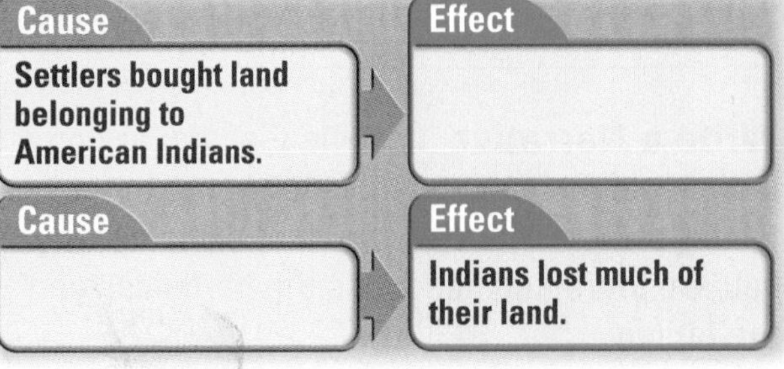

Time

1770

1775

1776
The Americans win the Battle of Trenton

1777
The Americans win the Battle of Saratoga

Reading Social Studies

A **cause** is an event or action that makes something happen.
An **effect** is what happens as a result of that event or action.

Cause and Effect

Complete this graphic organizer to show that you understand the causes and effects of some of the key events of the Revolutionary War. A copy of this graphic organizer appears on page 100 of the Homework and Practice Book.

The Revolutionary War

Cause	Effect
Congress printed more currency.	
	France agreed to help the Americans.
The Treaty of Paris was signed.	

California Writing Prompts

Write a Narrative Imagine that you are one of the soldiers camped at Valley Forge in the winter of 1777. Write a story that explains why you are there and describes the hardships you are facing.

Write a Report Choose one of the people you read about in this chapter and write a report that describes who that person was and what role he or she played in the Revolutionary War.

1780 | 1785 | 1790

1781
The Battle of Yorktown is fought

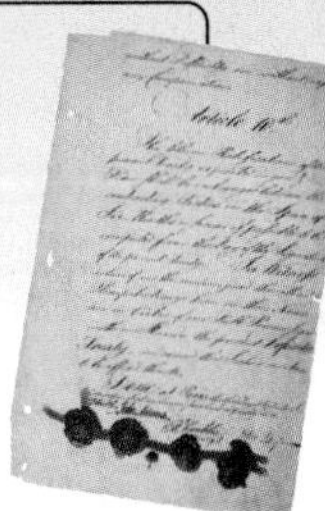

1783
The Treaty of Paris is signed.

Use Vocabulary

Write a sentence or two to explain how each pair of terms is related.

1. **Patriot** (p. 367), **Loyalist** (p. 367)
2. **inflation** (p. 368), **profiteering** (p. 368)
3. **regiment** (p. 370), **enlist** (p. 379)
4. **abolish** (p. 397), **abolitionist** (p. 397)
5. **territory** (p. 399), **ordinance** (p. 399)

Use the Time Line

 **Use the chapter summary time line above to answer these questions.**

6. Did the Battle of Saratoga happen before or after the Battle of Trenton?
7. How many years after the Battle of Yorktown was the Treaty of Paris signed?

Apply Skills

 **Read Parallel Time Lines**

8. Look at the time lines on pages 374 and 375. What happened in America in 1774?

 **Compare Maps with Different Scales**

9. Study the maps on pages 386 and 387. Then write a paragraph describing how the larger and smaller scales affect what information is shown on each map.

Recall Facts

Answer these questions.

10. Why did the Continental Congress have trouble financing the war?
11. Who helped bring water to soldiers at the Battle of Monmouth?
12. Where did the Continental Army spend the winter of 1777?

Write the letter of the best choice.

13. What country helped the Americans win the Battle of Yorktown?
    A France
    B Germany
    C Spain
    D the Netherlands
14. What was the name of the plan for governing the western lands north of the Ohio River?
    A Articles of Confederation
    B Ohio Valley Authority
    C Northwest Ordinance
    D Treaty of Paris

Think Critically

15.  ANALYSIS SKILL Why do you think some American Indians decided to side with the British in the Revolutionary War?
16. ANALYSIS SKILL How did Yorktown's relative location help the Americans?

THE Freedom Trail

GET READY

The Freedom Trail is a $2\frac{1}{2}$-mile walking trail that weaves its way through the city of Boston. The trail connects landmarks that played an important role in America's struggle for independence. Along the Freedom Trail you can stop at places such as Faneuil Hall, where Bostonians protested British taxation policies. You can also walk up to the Bunker Hill Monument which marks the place where American soldiers proved they could fight against the British army. The Freedom Trail is more than just a path between places. Each stop on the trail tells a story about our nation's independence.

LOCATE IT

WHAT TO SEE

The Freedom Trail is marked by red bricks. It gives visitors the opportunity to follow paths once walked by America's first patriots.

A Freedom Trail marker

Faneuil Hall

King's Chapel Burying Ground

Bunker Hill Monument

Statue of Samuel Adams at Faneuil Hall

The Paul Revere House

The State House

A VIRTUAL TOUR

Visit VIRTUAL TOURS at www.harcourtschool.com/hss

Review

THE BIG IDEA

Freedom Freedom was so important to the colonists that they were willing to suffer terrible hardships and years of war to win it.

Summary

The American Revolution

In 1764, Parliament passed a new law to tax the American colonists to help pay the expenses of the French and Indian War. This made many colonists angry. Their anger grew as Parliament tried to enforce even more new tax laws. Many colonists protested. They did not think it was fair to have to pay taxes to a government in which they had no representation.

By 1776, the colonists had decided to declare their independence from Britain. They knew this would mean war against one of the most powerful nations in the world. The colonies had little money and few trained soldiers. Still, they fought.

With the firm leadership of George Washington and the help of citizens and other nations, the Patriots began to win battles. After eight long and hard years of fighting, the Americans won the war.

The Treaty of Paris officially ended the war in 1783 and made the United States a new nation. The nation then faced many difficult challenges. Settlement in the western lands, the problem of slavery, and many other issues had to be dealt with.

Main Ideas and Vocabulary

Read the summary above. Then answer the questions that follow.

1. What does representation mean?
   A freedom to govern on one's own
   B an agreement between two nations
   C the act of speaking for someone else
   D a formal statement
2. Which role did George Washington play in the Revolutionary War?
   A He raised tax money to pay for the war.
   B He negotiated with France for support.
   C He commanded the Continental Army.
   D He wrote the Declaration of Independence.
3. What does the word Patriots mean in the sentence above?
   A hired soldiers
   B colonists who supported independence
   C Britain's American Indian allies
   D colonists who remained loyal to Britain
4. When did the United States officially become a new nation?
   A 1764
   B 1776
   C 1781
   D 1783

Recall Facts

Answer these questions.

5. The French and Indian War began as competition for control of what region?
6. What was the Stamp Act?
7. What was Thomas Jefferson's main job at the Second Continental Congress?
8. How did Mercy Otis Warren contribute to the Patriot cause?
9. How did France help the Americans in the Revolutionary War?
10. Why did some enslaved African Americans fight in the Revolutionary War?

Write the letter of the best choice.

11. Why did colonists boycott British goods?
    - **A** to decrease inflation
    - **B** to practice profiteering
    - **C** to protest British taxes
    - **D** to raise money for the war effort
12. Which key idea is included in the Declaration of Independence?
    - **A** the right to bring grievances to Parliament
    - **B** the right to life and liberty
    - **C** the importance of remaining neutral
    - **D** the abolition of slavery
13. Which battle helped end the Revolutionary War?
    - **A** the Battle of Bunker Hill
    - **B** the Battle of Long Island
    - **C** the Battle of Saratoga
    - **D** the Battle of Yorktown
14. How did the United States government pay many Revolutionary War soldiers?
    - **A** with money the British had to pay after losing the war
    - **B** with positions in the government
    - **C** with grants of western lands
    - **D** with British goods seized in the war

Think Critically

15. ANALYSIS SKILL Do you think the British could have avoided war with the colonists? Explain.

Apply Skills

Compare Historical Maps

ANALYSIS SKILL
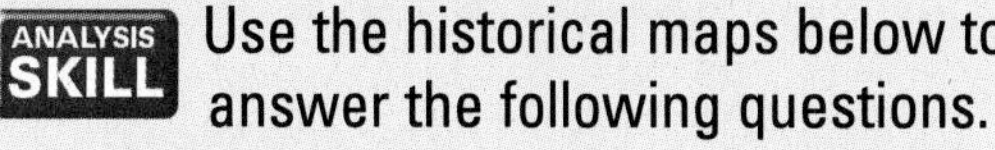
Use the historical maps below to answer the following questions.

16. Why is an area marked in hatch lines on the 1763 map, but not on the 1783 map?
17. What areas shown on the maps changed very little between 1763 and 1783?

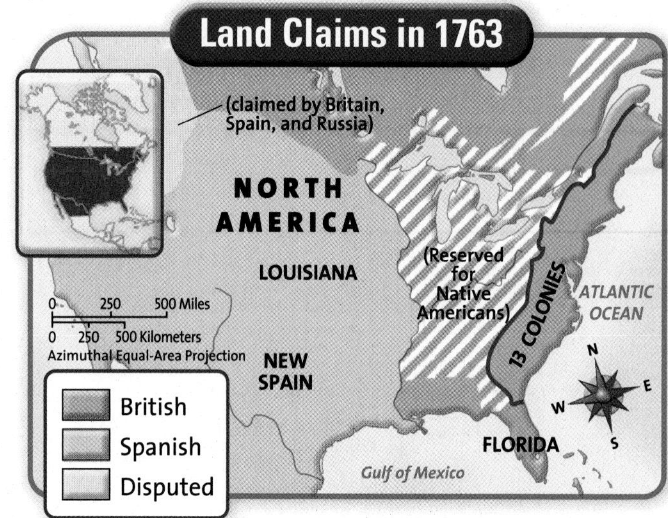

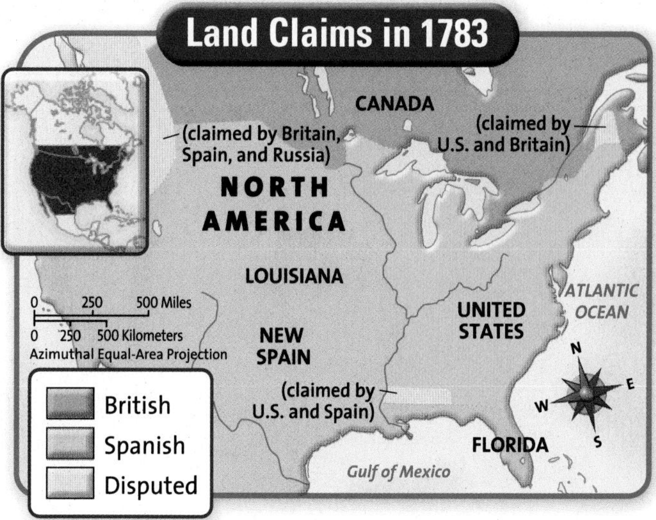

Unit 4 Activities

Read More

- *Travels of the Declaration of Independence* by Evelyn Coleman.

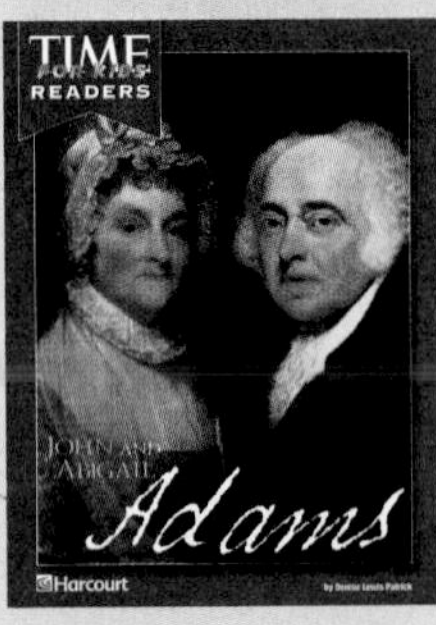

- *John and Abigail Adams* by Denise Lewis Patrick.

- *Victory at Yorktown* by Raymond P. Hill.

Show What You Know

Unit Writing Activity

Write a Summary There were many causes of the Revolutionary War, and its consequences affected everyone in the United States. Write a summary that lists three key causes of the war, tells how the colonists won their freedom, and explains why the war was important. Make sure you have stated the main idea and supporting details.

Unit Project

A Colonial Newspaper Publish a colonial newspaper that tells about the events leading up to the Revolutionary War and how the colonists won their freedom. Decide which people and events you want to include in your newspaper and how you will describe them.

Visit ACTIVITIES at **www.harcourtschool.com/hss**

Governing the Nation

Unit 5

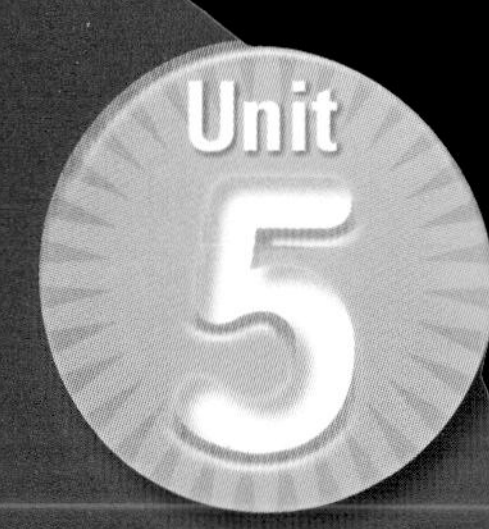

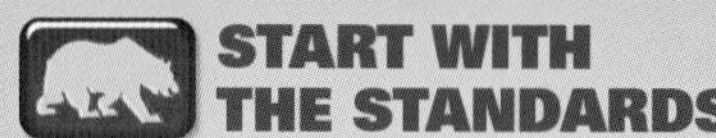

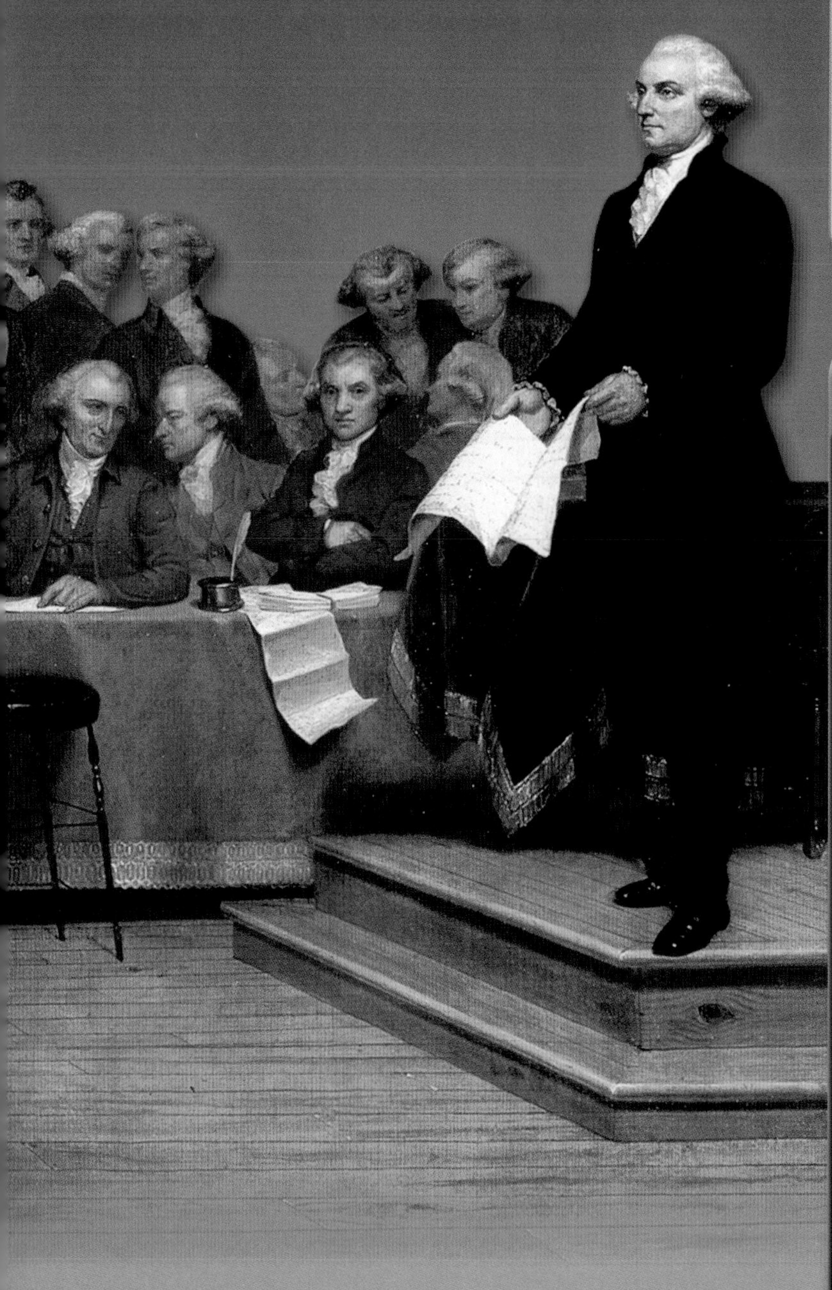

START WITH THE STANDARDS

California History-Social Science Standards

5.7 **Students describe the people and events associated with the development of the U.S. Constitution and analyze the Constitution's significance as the foundation of the American republic.**

The Big Idea

Government and Leadership

The United States Constitution is the foundation of the American republic.

What to Know

- Why did many leaders of the United States feel the need to write a constitution?
- What were some of the major problems faced by the writers of the Constitution?
- How does the Constitution secure our liberty?
- How do people express American ideals?

Show What You Know

- **Unit 5 Test**
- **Writing: A Persuasive Letter**
- **Unit Project: A Constitutional Hall of Fame**

Time

Governing the Nation

1787 The United States Constitution is written, p. 435

1791 The Bill of Rights is added to the Constitution, p. 445

1780 1830 1880

At the Same Time

1781 Los Angeles is founded by the Spanish

1810 The Mexican Revolution begins

Governing the Nation

1920 The Nineteenth Amendment gives women the right to vote, p. 462

1963 Martin Luther King, Jr., leads the March on Washington, D.C., p. 476

1930

1980

PRESENT

James Madison

1751–1836

- Virginia leader who helped organize the Constitutional Convention
- Served as the fourth President of the United States

Gouverneur Morris

1752–1816

- Pennsylvania representative to the Constitutional Convention
- Wrote the Preamble to the United States Constitution

People

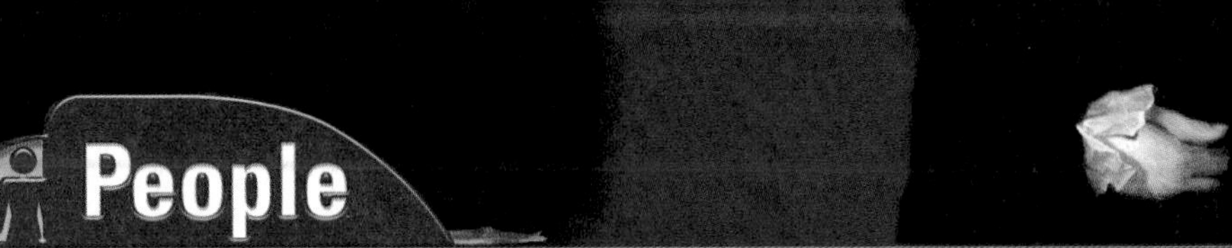

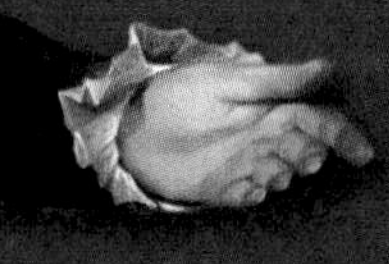

- 1751 • James Madison 1836
- 1752 • Gouverneur Morris 1816
- 1757? • Alexander Hamilton 1804
- 1776 • Mary Pickersgill 1857
- 1779 • Francis Scott Key 1843

Francis Scott Key

1779–1843

- Worked as a lawyer in Washington, D.C.
- Wrote "The Star-Spangled Banner" after the Battle of Fort McHenry

Katharine Lee Bates

1859–1929

- English professor at Wellesley College
- Wrote the poem "America the Beautiful"

Alexander Hamilton

1757?–1804

- New York leader who worked to help ratify the Constitution
- Served as the first Secretary of the Treasury

Mary Pickersgill

1776–1857

- Worked as a flagmaker in Baltimore
- Sewed the flag that inspired "The Star-Spangled Banner"

1900 1950 2000

1859 • Katharine Lee Bates 1929

1927 • Cesar Chavez 1993

1929 • Martin Luther King, Jr. 1968

Cesar Chavez

1927–1993

- Leader of the United Farm Workers
- Led nonviolent protests to get better working conditions for migrant workers

Martin Luther King, Jr.

1929–1968

- African American minister who helped lead the Civil Rights Movement
- Awarded the Nobel Peace Prize for his work

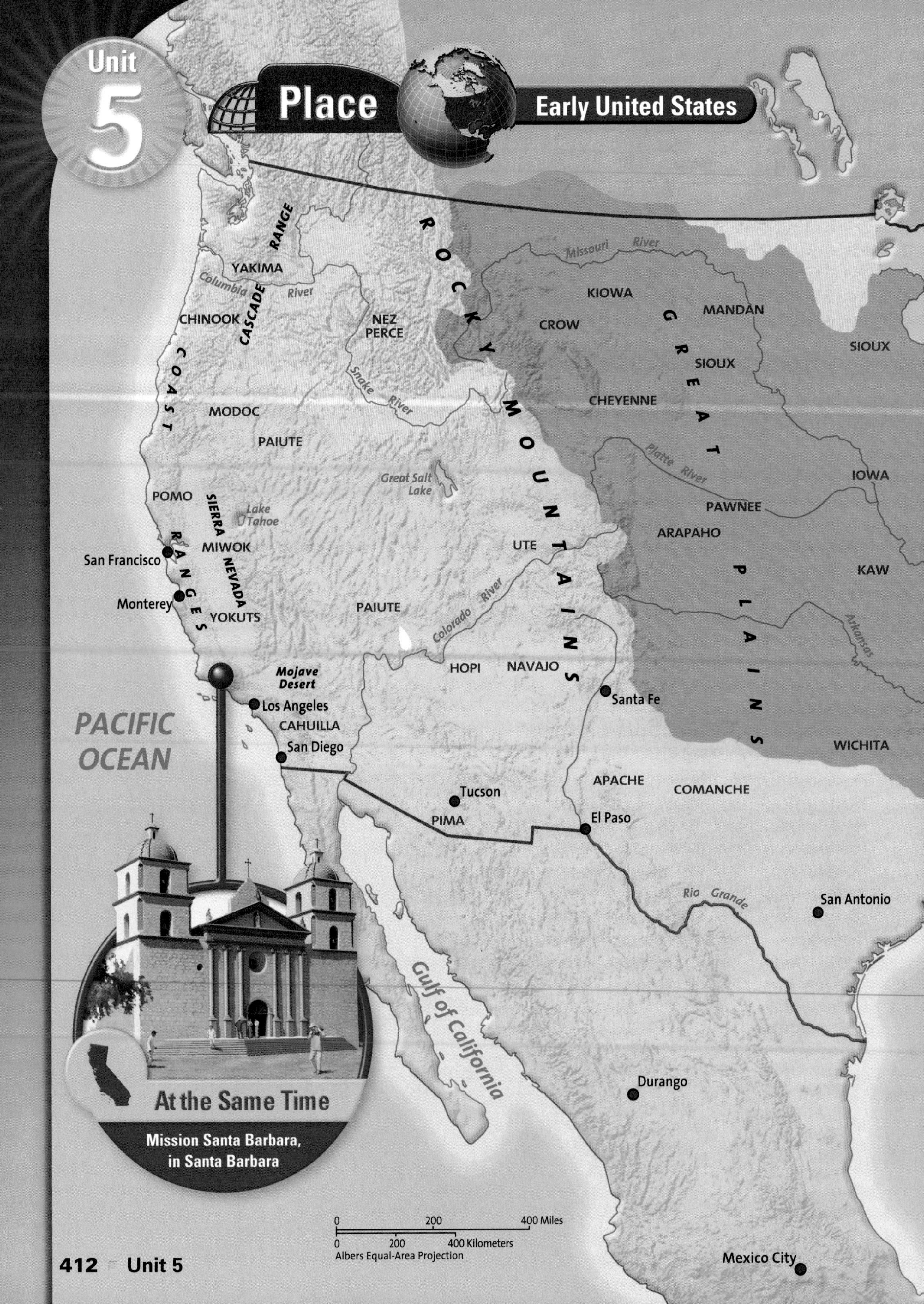

Unit 5
Place
Early United States
ROCKY MOUNTAINS
GREAT PLAINS
CASCADE RANGE
COAST RANGES
SIERRA NEVADA
Missouri River
Columbia River
Snake River
Platte River
Colorado River
Arkansas
Rio Grande
Great Salt Lake
Lake Tahoe
Mojave Desert
PACIFIC OCEAN
Gulf of California
YAKIMA
CHINOOK
NEZ PERCE
KIOWA
MANDAN
CROW
SIOUX
CHEYENNE
MODOC
PAIUTE
IOWA
POMO
PAWNEE
ARAPAHO
MIWOK
UTE
KAW
YOKUTS
HOPI
NAVAJO
CAHUILLA
WICHITA
APACHE
COMANCHE
PIMA
San Francisco
Monterey
Los Angeles
San Diego
Santa Fe
Tucson
El Paso
San Antonio
Durango
Mexico City
0 200 400 Miles
0 200 400 Kilometers
Albers Equal-Area Projection
At the Same Time
Mission Santa Barbara, in Santa Barbara

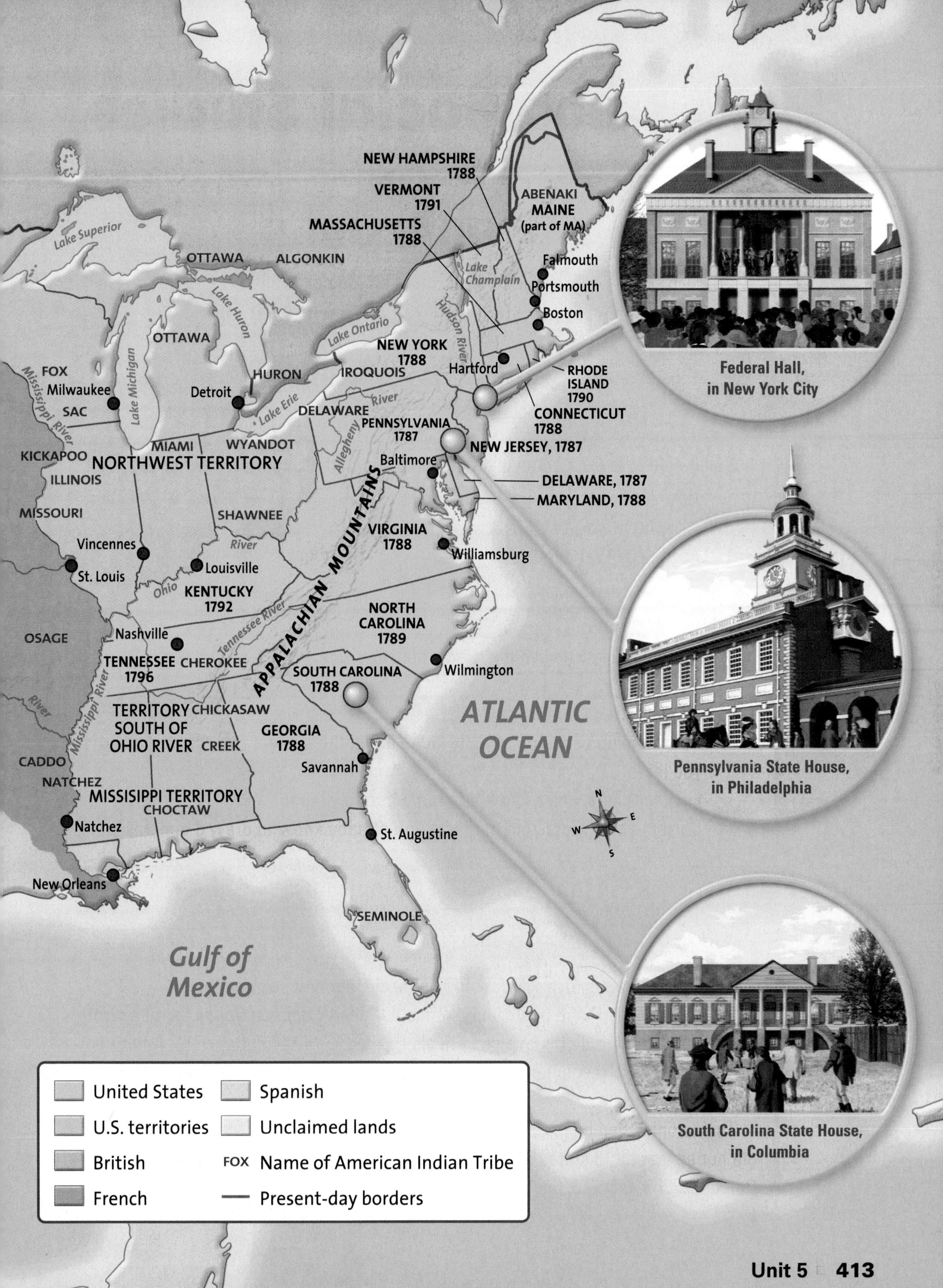

Federal Hall, in New York City

Pennsylvania State House, in Philadelphia

South Carolina State House, in Columbia

Unit 5

Reading Social Studies

Draw Conclusions

A conclusion is a broad statement about an idea or event. It is reached by using what you learn by reading along with what you already know.

Why It Matters

Being able to draw a conclusion can help you better understand what you read.

Evidence
What you learn

Knowledge
What you already know

Conclusion
A broad statement about an idea or event

- ✓ Keep in mind what you already know about the subject and the new facts you learn.
- ✓ Look for clues, and try to figure out what they mean.
- ✓ Combine new facts with the facts you already know to draw a conclusion.

Practice the Skill

Read the paragraphs. Draw a conclusion for the second paragraph.

Evidence
Knowledge
Conclusion

In 1776, Thomas Paine published a pamphlet titled *Common Sense*. In it he wrote that people should rule themselves. He also called for a revolution. (The American colonists fought a revolution against Britain. Thomas Paine helped inspire this revolution.)

The colonies had united to win the Revolutionary War. After the war, many people hoped that all 13 states could act together as one nation under the Articles of Confederation. Instead, the United States government was weak and disorganized.

Apply What You Learned

 **Draw Conclusions** **Read the paragraphs, and answer the questions.**

Freedom Is Just the Beginning

The American colonists had fought hard to win independence from Britain, but the young country still had much work to do. The United States government under the Articles of Confederation was very weak. Because Americans had just fought to rid themselves of one strong and powerful government, they did not want to be ruled by another one.

Most people thought of themselves as citizens of a state first and as Americans second. Each state had its own laws, its own money, and its own soldiers and navy. This created much confusion, and states soon started arguing about taxes, trade, and land ownership. Things were such a mess that some British leaders thought that the Americans might ask the British to come back. Some Americans doubted that they could ever agree to all be part of the same country.

The fighting was over, but the work of making a country had just begun. Someone had to get America organized. Strong leaders, such as Benjamin Franklin, James Madison, and Alexander Hamilton, soon stepped forward to propose a new plan for government in the United States.

Draw Conclusions

1. **What conclusions can you draw about the United States after the Revolutionary War?**
2. **Why did the states begin to argue after the American Revolution?**
3. **What conclusions can you draw about how American leaders would try to organize the United States?**

Study Skills

VOCABULARY

Using a dictionary can help you learn new words that you come across as you read.

- **A dictionary shows all the meanings of a word and tells where the word came from.**
- **You can use a chart to list and organize unfamiliar words that you look up in a dictionary.**

republic (ri-ˊpə-blik) *n.* [from the Latin *respublica*, a public thing] **1. a.** a government whose leader is not a monarch and whose citizens elect leaders and representatives **b.** a political unit, such as a nation, having such a form of government **2.** a group of people freely involved in a specific activity.

Word	Syllables	Origin	Definition
republic	re•pub•lic	Latin	A country that has a central government where the people elect leaders to govern the country.

Apply As You Read

As you read, look up unfamiliar words in the dictionary. Add them to a chart like the one above.

California History-Social Science Standards, Grade 5

5.7 Students describe the people and events associated with the development of the U.S. Constitution and analyze the Constitution's significance as the foundation of the American republic.

CHAPTER 10

The Constitution

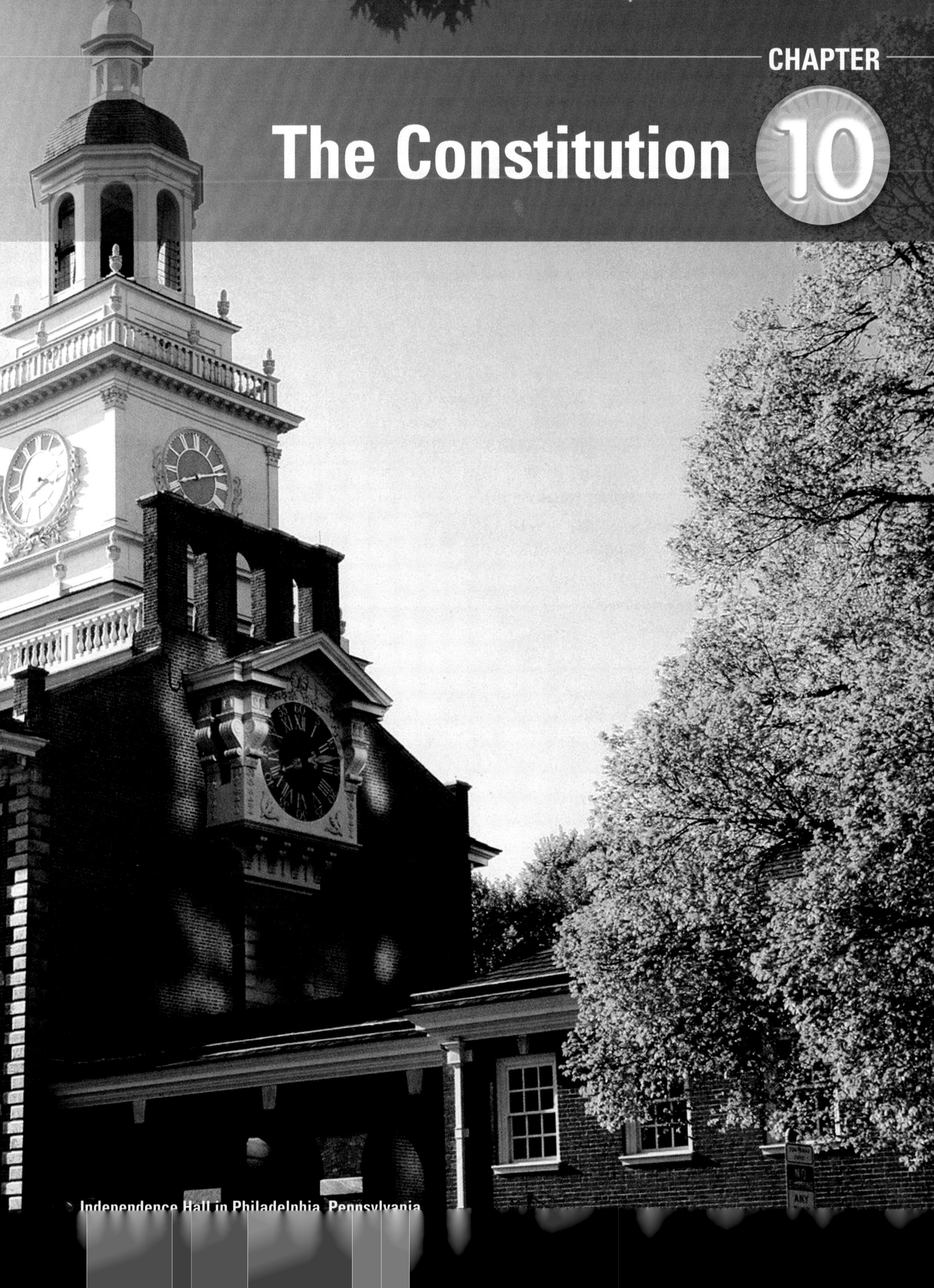

Independence Hall in Philadelphia, Pennsylvania

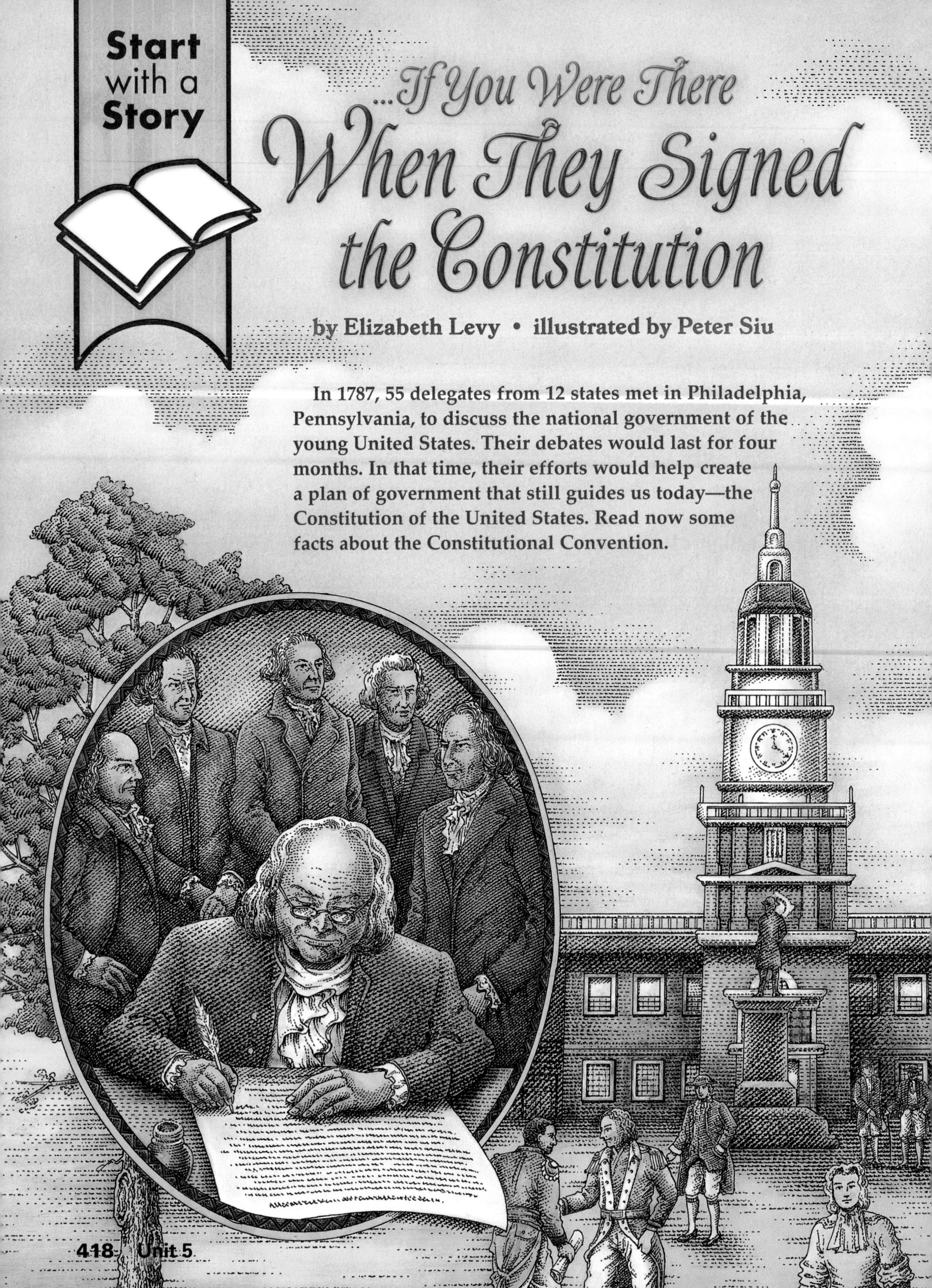

Start with a Story

...If You Were There When They Signed the Constitution

by Elizabeth Levy • illustrated by Peter Siu

In 1787, 55 delegates from 12 states met in Philadelphia, Pennsylvania, to discuss the national government of the young United States. Their debates would last for four months. In that time, their efforts would help create a plan of government that still guides us today—the Constitution of the United States. Read now some facts about the Constitutional Convention.

What is the Constitution?

The Constitution of the United States is the basic law of our nation—like the rules for a game, only these rules are for the government, and all citizens must play.

The Constitution sets up the rules for how laws are made, and who will make the laws. Who will decide if we go to war? Who will have power? You? Me? You can find those answers in the Constitution.

The Constitution of the United States was written in 1787. . . . The men who wrote it wanted their new nation to last. They knew how hard it was to create a government that could change with the times. After all, they had just fought and won a war against a government that had refused to change.

When the Convention finally opened, where did the delegates meet?

They met at the Pennsylvania State House or, as people were already beginning to call it, Independence Hall. It was here that Thomas Jefferson had first read his Declaration of Independence to many of the same men who were now gathering to write the Constitution. . . .

The Convention was mostly held in the East Room, a comfortable room about forty feet by forty feet, probably more than twice the size of your classroom, but smaller than your gym. The delegates sat at round tables covered with green cloths, about three or four to a table.

When you visit Independence Hall, you immediately feel that this is a good room for a debate—not too fancy, yet filled with light from the great tall windows on each side.

Response Corner

1. What does the Constitution do?
2. Imagine that you are helping write a constitution for your school. Write a law you think should be part of your school's constitution. Then write a paragraph defending your law.

Lesson 1

1780 — PRESENT

- 1781 The Articles of Confederation are passed
- 1786 Shays's Rebellion starts
- 1786 The Annapolis Convention meets

The Articles of Confederation

WHAT TO KNOW
What were the weaknesses of the central government under the Articles of Confederation?

- ✓ Describe the shortcomings of the Articles of Confederation.
- ✓ Explain why some leaders wanted to change the Articles of Confederation.

VOCABULARY
commerce p. 422
convention p. 422
arsenal p. 423

PEOPLE
Daniel Shays
James Madison
Patrick Henry

PLACES
Annapolis
Philadelphia

Focus Skill **DRAW CONCLUSIONS**

California Standards
HSS 5.7, 5.7.1

YOU ARE THERE It is 1783, and Congress is meeting at Nassau Hall in New Jersey. Your father is there, serving as a delegate. He has written you many happy letters about meeting General Washington and about the treaty ending the war. However, he worries about the future of the new nation. In his last letter, he wrote that Congress must beg the states for money. You wonder how such a weak Congress can run the government.

Nassau Hall served as the United States capitol for five months in 1783. Congress met there from July to November.

Shortcomings of the Articles

By 1781, the 13 former colonies—now independent states—had approved the Articles of Confederation. Under the Articles, all 13 states formed a confederation known as the United States of America. Each state governed itself, but all were supposed to work together on national issues. However, the shortcomings, or weaknesses, of the Articles made it difficult for the national government to work effectively.

Under the Articles of Confederation, delegates from the states met in a Congress. In order to pass any new law, delegates from at least 9 of the 13 states had to approve it. Often, however, not enough delegates were present to vote. Even when enough delegates were present, they rarely agreed, since no state wanted to be under the control of the other states. If the delegates approved a law, Congress still did not have the power to enforce it.

The Articles limited other powers of the national, or central, government. For example, Congress had the power to declare war, make treaties, and borrow money, but it could not collect taxes. To cover expenses, such as debts from the war, Congress could ask the states for money, but it could not force the states to pay. The Articles also made Congress depend on the states for the nation's defense. Congress could ask for an army, but the states had to provide the soldiers.

READING CHECK **DRAW CONCLUSIONS**
How did the Articles of Confederation limit the power of Congress?

FAST FACT

Nassau Hall was built for the College of New Jersey, now known as Princeton University. George Washington came to Nassau Hall for the student graduation of 1783.

State Currency

Analyze Artifacts

During the 1770s and 1780s, most states printed their own paper money. This led to problems because some states would not accept money from other states.

- **1 Label showing the money was printed in Massachusetts.**
- **2 Label showing how much the money was worth.**
- **3 Picture showing a rising sun.**
- **4 Date the money was printed.**
- **? Why do you think states no longer print their own money?**

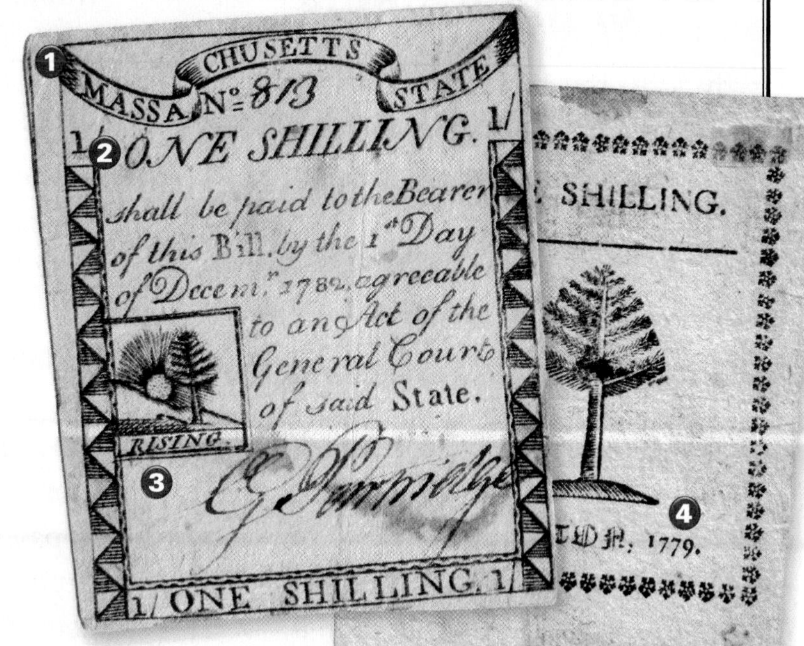

The Annapolis Convention

Under the Articles of Confederation, problems developed with **commerce**, or trade, in the states. Some goods cost much more in one state than in another. Disagreements over trade created problems because the central government could not control trade among the states. In 1786, some leaders called on the states to hold a **convention**, or important meeting, to discuss commerce. The convention was held in **Annapolis,** Maryland, in 1786.

Only five states—Delaware, New Jersey, New York, Pennsylvania, and Virginia—sent delegates to the Annapolis Convention. After much debate, delegates decided that a stronger national government was needed to oversee commerce. This meant changing the Articles of Confederation. To change the Articles, however, all the states had to agree.

The delegates sent a report to the states and to Congress, suggesting that another convention should meet in **Philadelphia**, Pennsylvania, in May 1787. At this convention, representatives from the states would talk not only about commerce but about how to strengthen the Articles of Confederation.

In January 1787, violent events in Massachusetts would demonstrate how little power the central government had under the Articles of Confederation. More leaders began to think that the Articles would have to be changed if the young nation were to survive.

READING CHECK **DRAW CONCLUSIONS**
How could commerce problems be solved?

Shays's Rebellion

TIME 1786–1787
PLACE Massachusetts

Economic problems during the 1780s made life difficult for many people in the United States. Some former soldiers still had not been paid for fighting in the Revolutionary War. Many Americans were poor, yet they had to pay high state taxes. To buy supplies, farmers often had to borrow money and go into debt.

Going into debt caused even more problems for those who could not pay their debts or their taxes. The courts of some states took away their farms or threatened to send those who could not pay to prison. Late in the summer of 1786, poor farmers in Massachusetts protested by refusing to let the courts meet. Armed with pitchforks and guns, the farmers shut down courthouses and destroyed debt records.

These protests, known as Shays's Rebellion, were named for **Daniel Shays**, who had been a captain in the Continental Army. In January 1787, Shays and his followers threatened to take over a Massachusetts **arsenal**, or weapons storehouse, owned by the central government. Under the Articles of Confederation, there was no national army to defend United States property. Because Congress did not have an army to defend the arsenal, the governor of Massachusetts had to send the state militia to stop Shays.

As a result of Shays's Rebellion, many began to fear that the government would be unable to prevent other violent protests. This made many leaders again start thinking about how best to strengthen the central government.

READING CHECK **DRAW CONCLUSIONS**
How did Shays's Rebellion show the weakness of the central government?

During Shays's Rebellion, four of Shays's followers were killed in the attack on the arsenal.

Points of View

Leaders disagreed on how strong the national government should be.

Richard Henry Lee, **a member of Congress**

"... the Confederation ... is a great and fundamental system [of government] ... no change should be admitted until proved to be necessary."

-from *The Letters of Richard Henry Lee*, edited by James Curtis Ballagh. Macmillan, 1911–1914.

John Jay, **Secretary for Foreign Affairs**

"The inefficacy [weakness] of our government becomes daily more and more apparent. Our treasury and our credit are in a sad situation."

-from *The Correspondence and Public Papers of John Jay*, edited by Henry P. Johnston. DaCapo Press, 1971.

It's Your Turn

ANALYSIS SKILL Analyze Points of View
Summarize each person's feelings about the national government.

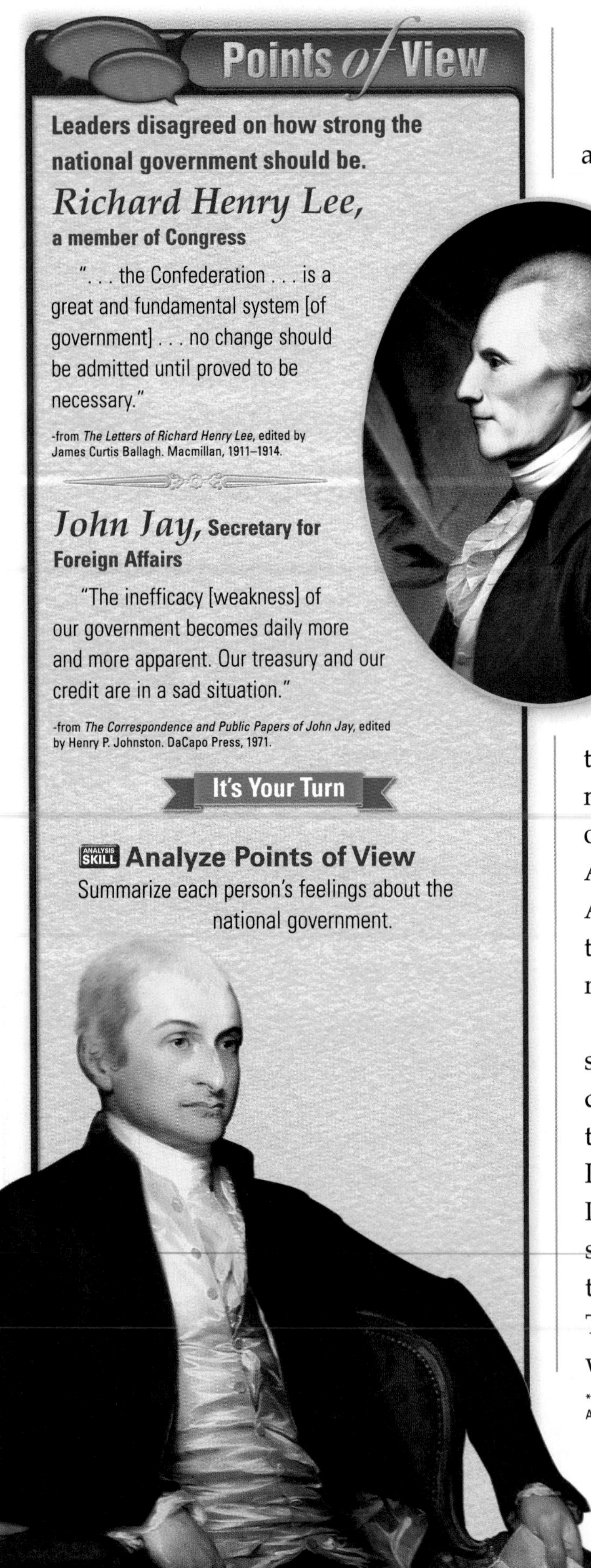

Ideas for Change

After Shays's Rebellion, some people argued that Congress needed more power. **James Madison**, a Virginia leader, believed that the country needed to replace the Articles of Confederation. Other leaders in the United States, such as George Washington and John Adams, agreed with Madison. They wanted a national government that could keep the country from breaking apart. Washington worried that only a "rope of sand" was holding the nation together.*

Others did not agree with this call for a stronger national government. **Patrick Henry**, of Virginia, was one of many leaders who wanted to keep the Articles as they were. Henry argued that Americans had fought the British because they did not want a powerful government ruling their lives.

After Shays's Rebellion, most of the states now agreed to the request of the delegates at the Annapolis Convention to send delegates to a convention in Philadelphia in the spring of 1787. Rhode Island was the only state that refused to send a delegate. Its leaders saw no need to change the Articles of Confederation. They feared a strong national government would threaten the rights of citizens.

*George Washington. *The Papers of George Washington*, edited by W.W. Abbot and Dorothy Twohig. University Press of Virginia, 1991.

John Jay (left) served as the Secretary of Foreign Affairs from 1784 to 1790. Afterward, he served as the first Chief Justice of the United States Supreme Court.

By the end of the Revolutionary War, each of the 13 United States had at least one newspaper.

Soon, leaders on both sides started presenting their views on such political matters by writing letters to newspapers. These letters could then be published for all to read.

READING CHECK **DRAW CONCLUSIONS**
Why did James Madison and others want a stronger central government?

Summary

Under the Articles of Confederation, the United States had a weak central government. Some leaders called for a convention to review the Articles. The call for a strong national government increased after Shays's Rebellion.

REVIEW

1. What were the weaknesses of the central government under the Articles of Confederation?
2. Use the term **commerce** in a sentence about the Annapolis Convention.
3. Why did many farmers face growing debts after the Revolutionary War?

CRITICAL THINKING

4. ANALYSIS SKILL Under the Articles of Confederation, what might happen if a state did not like a law passed by Congress?
5. ANALYSIS SKILL What were some of the causes and effects of Shays's Rebellion?
6. **Write a Letter** The year is 1786. Write a letter to a newspaper in which you argue for changing the Articles of Confederation. Try to persuade your readers that the Articles have shortcomings.
7. Focus Skill **DRAW CONCLUSIONS** On a separate sheet of paper, copy and complete the graphic organizer below.

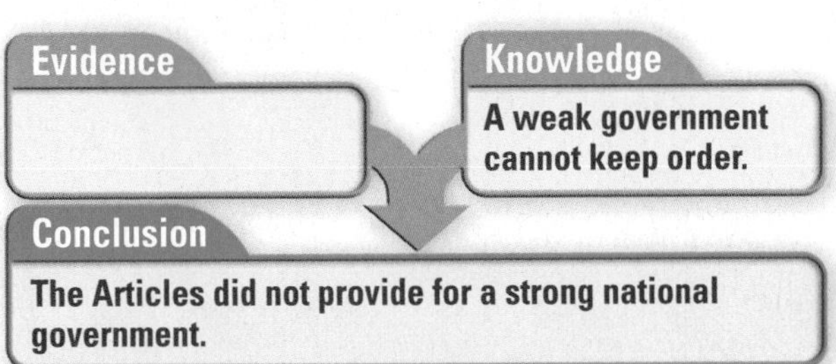

Lesson 2

1780 — PRESENT

1787 The Constitutional Convention begins

1787 The Great Compromise is approved

The Constitutional Convention

WHAT TO KNOW
How was a new plan of government developed at the Constitutional Convention?

- ✓ Describe how the Constitution set up a new plan of government.
- ✓ List the contributions of those who helped write the Constitution.
- ✓ Explain the importance of the Great Compromise.

VOCABULARY
federal system p. 428
republic p. 429
compromise p. 431
bill p. 431

PEOPLE
George Washington
Benjamin Franklin
James Madison
Edmund Randolph
William Paterson
Gouverneur Morris

PLACES
Philadelphia

HSS 5.7, 5.7.2, 5.7.3

YOU ARE THERE The year is 1787. The city of **Philadelphia** has hired you to spread dirt over Chestnut Street in front of the Pennsylvania State House. People keep stopping to ask why you are covering up the cobblestones. You explain that a meeting to fix the Articles of Confederation is going on in the State House. The delegates, who have traveled here from the various states, need quiet so they can work. The dirt will soften the clatter of horses' hooves, helping the delegates concentrate on their work.

Benjamin Franklin arrives at the Pennsylvania State House.

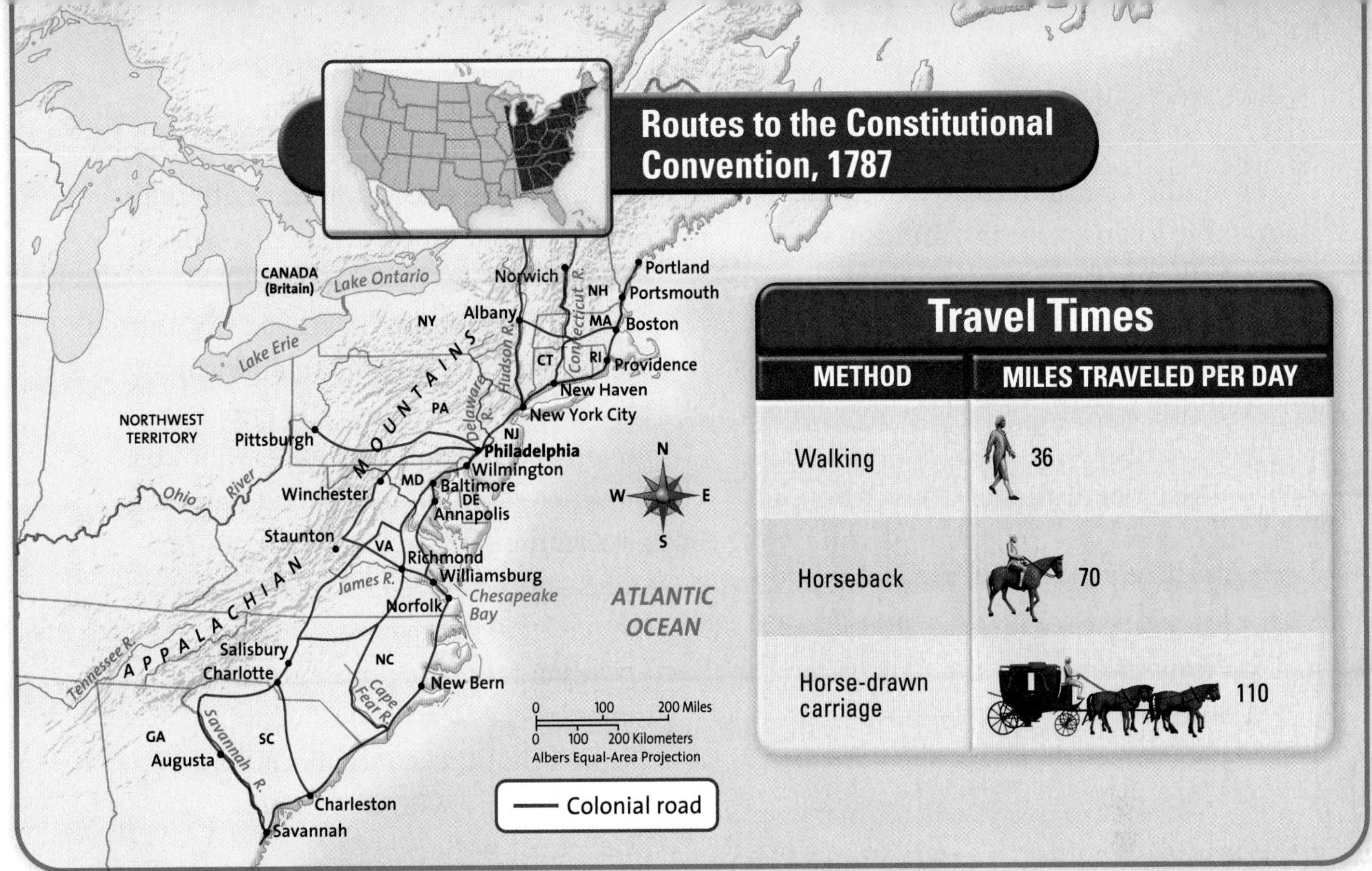

Travel Times

METHOD	MILES TRAVELED PER DAY
Walking	36
Horseback	70
Horse-drawn carriage	110

ANALYSIS SKILL Analyze Maps The map and table above show the routes and travel times to the Constitutional Convention.

Location About how many miles is it from Pittsburgh, Pennsylvania, to Philadelphia?

The Delegates

The delegates to the Philadelphia convention began to gather in May 1787. One of the first to arrive was **George Washington**, from Virginia, who received a hero's welcome for his service in the Revolutionary War. The delegates would elect him president of the convention.

At 5 feet 4 inches tall and 100 pounds, **James Madison**, another Virginia delegate, did not command much attention. Madison was shy and quiet and preferred the company of books to people. Yet Madison's contributions would make him known as the Father of the Constitution.

Benjamin Franklin, of Pennsylvania, made the most colorful entrance. Unable to walk or to ride in a bumpy carriage, the 81-year-old Franklin arrived in a Chinese sedan chair carried by prisoners from the Philadelphia jail.

In all, 55 delegates from 12 states came to the convention at the Pennsylvania State House. Wealthy and educated, the delegates were mainly lawyers, planters, and merchants. All of the delegates were men, and all of them were white. There were no women or enslaved people present at the convention. At that time, not all people had equal rights.

READING CHECK DRAW CONCLUSIONS
Why did the delegates elect George Washington president of the convention?

The Work Begins

From the beginning, the delegates agreed to keep secret the things they talked about. They believed that talking in private would enable them to speak freely and make good decisions. Windows in the State House were covered, and guards stood at the doors.

The Constitutional Convention, as the meeting in Philadelphia came to be known, started on Friday, May 25. At first, the delegates offered ideas on how to improve the Articles of Confederation. Quickly, however, they reached a surprising decision. An entirely new plan of government—a new constitution—needed to be written. In order to write it, the delegates worked hard for the next four months.

One of the issues discussed throughout the convention was the relationship between the states and the national government. Some delegates thought that there should be a strong national government. Others believed that the states should have more power than the national government.

Only a few delegates agreed with George Read of Delaware. He said that the states should be done away with altogether. Even most of those who wanted a strong national government thought that getting rid of the states would be going too far.

Instead, the delegates agreed to strengthen the existing **federal system**,

GEOGRAPHY

Philadelphia

The street map below shows Philadelphia in the late 1700s. Find the State House, where the Constitutional Convention was held. This area of Philadelphia was one of the busiest parts of the city. During the week, people shopped at an open-air public market and children attended the local Quaker school. On the weekends, many people attended services at one of the city's many churches.

in which the power to govern was shared by the national government and the state governments. The states would keep some powers and share other powers with the federal, or national, government.

The federal government would have all power over matters that affected the nation as a whole, such as commerce and defense. To keep power over their own affairs, the states would set up state and local governments, make state laws, and conduct state and local elections.

Both the states and the federal government would have their own court systems. Both would raise money by taxing citizens. However, the states would no longer print money or have armies or navies. In the case of an attack by another country or state, the federal government would have to defend the states.

The delegates set up this federal system so that the new rules of government would be the supreme law of the land. They called their plan the Constitution of the United States of America.

The Constitution helped found the American republic, because it said that voters could participate in both state and national elections. In a **republic**, the people choose representatives to run the government. In this way, the Constitution would guarantee a republican form of government for both the states and the nation.

READING CHECK SUMMARIZE
How is power shared in a federal system?

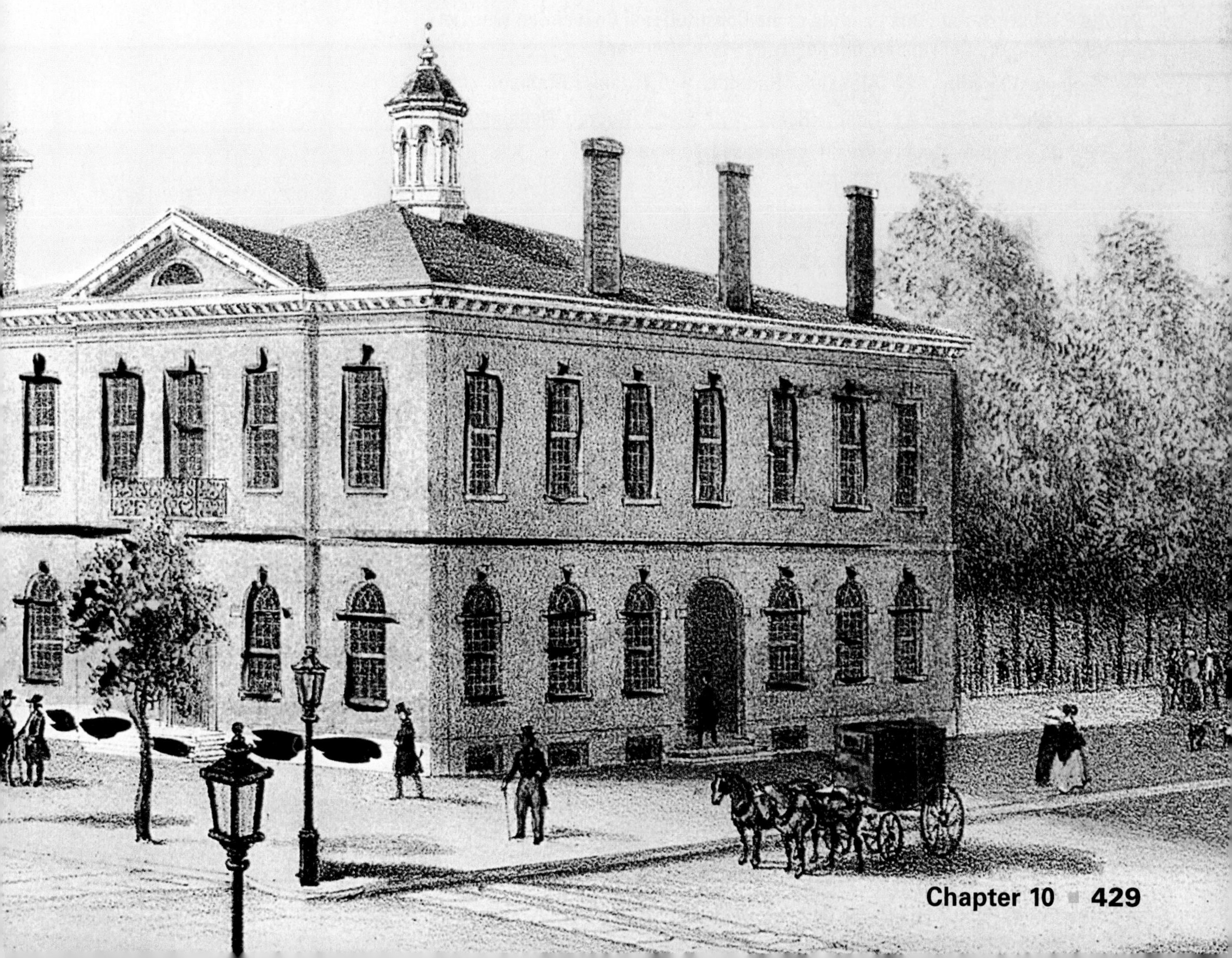

Debate and Compromise

During their work, the delegates to the Constitutional Convention often disagreed with one another. A major disagreement was about how each state would be represented in the new Congress.

Edmund Randolph and the other Virginia delegates introduced a plan for Congress called the Virginia Plan. Under this plan, Congress would have two parts, or houses. The number of representatives that a state would have in both houses would be based on that state's population. States with more people would have more representatives and more votes in Congress. This plan would favor the large states, such as Virginia, Massachusetts, and Pennsylvania, which had many people.

"Not fair!" replied the delegates from the small states. **William Paterson** of New Jersey accused the Virginia Plan of "striking at the existence of the lesser States."* The plan would have given large states control of Congress.

Paterson offered a different plan, called the New Jersey Plan. Under this plan, the new Congress would have one house, in which each state would be equally represented. This plan would give the small states the same number of representatives as the large states.

*William Paterson, June 9, 1787, at the Constitutional Convention, from James Madison's notes. *The Records of the Federal Convention of 1787*, edited by Max Farrand. Yale University Press, 1937.

Analyze Illustrations This painting of the Constitutional Convention was not painted during the Convention, but nearly 80 years afterward.

❶ Benjamin Franklin ❷ Alexander Hamilton ❸ James Madison

❹ Roger Sherman ❺ George Read ❻ George Washington

Why do you think George Washington is seated on a stage?

For weeks, the delegates argued about how states should be represented in Congress. Finally, the delegates realized that in order to reach an agreement, each side would have to give up some of what it wanted. In other words, the delegates would have to make a **compromise**. The delegates decided to set up a committee to work out a compromise.

In one committee meeting, Roger Sherman of Connecticut presented a new plan, called the Connecticut Compromise. It was based on the idea of a two-house Congress. In one house, representation would be based on the population of each state, as in the Virginia Plan. In the other house, each state would be equally represented, as in the New Jersey Plan. Either house could present a **bill**, or an idea for a new law. However, both houses had to approve a bill before it became a law.

Committee members from the large states thought that the compromise gave too much power to the small states. To avoid this, the committee added another idea. Only the house in which representation was based on population would be able to propose tax bills.

The committee presented the Great Compromise, as it became known, to the whole convention. Although the delegates continued to argue, many wanted to make sure that they would have a new plan of government. On July 16, 1787, they approved the Great Compromise.

READING CHECK **DRAW CONCLUSIONS**
Why was the Great Compromise important to the Constitutional Convention?

This detail shows an African American woman at work. Before slavery ended, African Americans were not allowed to vote, hold office, or own property.

Compromises on Slavery

Under Roger Sherman's plan, population would affect each state's representation in Congress. This raised an important issue that troubled many people in the young nation—slavery. Delegates from the northern and the southern states argued about whether enslaved African Americans should be counted when figuring each state's population.

The southern states had many more slaves than the northern states. Delegates from the southern states wanted to count slaves when figuring out how many representatives a state would have in Congress. That way, the southern states could count more people and have more representatives.

Delegates from the northern states did not want slaves to be counted for representation. After all, these delegates argued, slaves were not allowed to vote and did not hold any of the other rights of citizenship. In addition, some delegates wanted slavery to end.

The delegates finally agreed to count three-fifths of the total number of

At the Constitutional Convention, Gouverneur Morris stood out for his attacks on the practice of slavery.

slaves in each state. The Three-fifths Compromise was attached to the Great Compromise. By settling the issue of representation, the delegates moved closer to forming a new government.

After this issue was dealt with, some delegates still spoke out against slavery. **Gouverneur** (guh•ver•NIR) **Morris** of Pennsylvania called slavery "the curse of heaven on the states where it prevailed [existed]."* Other delegates were afraid that if the Constitution stopped states from importing slaves, the southern states would not approve it. The delegates agreed that Congress could not end the slave trade before 1808.

READING CHECK **DRAW CONCLUSIONS**
What issue was settled when delegates agreed to both the Great Compromise and the Three-fifths Compromise?

*Gouverneur Morris. *Original Meanings: Politics and Ideas in the Making of the Constitution* by Jack N. Rakove. Knopf, 1996.

Summary

Instead of just fixing the Articles of Confederation, the delegates at the Constitutional Convention decided to write a new Constitution. The Great Compromise resolved conflicts over representation in the government.

REVIEW

1. How was a new plan of government developed at the Constitutional Convention?
2. Explain how the terms **federal system** and **republic** are related.
3. Who were some of the people associated with the development of the United States Constitution?

CRITICAL THINKING

4. SKILL How did the makers of the Constitution try to fix some of the problems that existed under the Articles of Confederation?
5. **Write a Letter** Imagine you are a delegate. Write a letter to your family explaining the role of compromise at the Constitutional Convention.
6. Focus Skill **DRAW CONCLUSIONS** On a separate sheet of paper, copy and complete the graphic organizer below.

Evidence
The Great Compromise settled the issue of representation.

Knowledge

Conclusion
Compromise played an important role in allowing the Constitutional Convention to move forward.

Lesson 3

Three Branches of Government

WHAT TO KNOW
What are the powers of each of the three branches of government?

- ✓ Explain the purpose of the Constitution as stated in its Preamble.
- ✓ Compare the powers and functions of the three branches of government.

VOCABULARY
principle p. 435
legislative branch p. 436
separation of powers p. 436
executive branch p. 437
electoral college p. 437
veto p. 437
impeach p. 437
judicial branch p. 438
justice p. 438
amendment p. 439

PEOPLE
Gouverneur Morris

PLACES
Philadelphia

DRAW CONCLUSIONS

California Standards
HSS 5.7, 5.7.2, 5.7.3, 5.7.4

YOU ARE THERE

"Fresh berries here!" your father announces to people passing by your fruit cart. It is the summer of 1787 and the weather in **Philadelphia** is hot and muggy. "Be sure those berries look neat, dear," he says.

You sigh as you start to arrange the berry boxes. After a moment, you notice a well-dressed man beside the cart. He pays for some berries and as he walks away you see that he has a wooden leg. "Who was that?" you ask. "That was **Gouverneur Morris**, one of the wisest minds in our country."

➤ Delegates to the Constitutional Convention worked long hours debating and writing the Constitution.

Cultural Heritage

The National Archives

The Declaration of Independence and the United States Constitution are important parts of our nation's heritage. Both documents are held at the National Archives (AR•kyvz) Building in Washington, D.C. Created in 1934, the National Archives preserves the most valuable records of the United States government. For safety, the Constitution and the Declaration of Independence are displayed in airtight cases.

The Preamble

The delegates to the Constitutional Convention wrote the new Constitution with great care. Gouverneur Morris had the job of writing the final version of the Constitution. He spent long hours writing and rewriting each sentence.

In the Preamble, or introduction, to the Constitution, Morris begins with these words:

> **"We the People of the United States . . ."***

Morris had originally written "We the people of the States of New Hampshire, Massachusetts, . . ."** and so on, listing all the states. However, he changed the words to show that the Constitution would make Americans citizens of the nation first and of the states second.

*Constitution of the United States

**Gouverneur Morris. *The Debate on the Constitution* by Bernard Bailyn. Library of America, 1993.

These words also link the Constitution with an idea in the Declaration of Independence. The Declaration said that a government should derive, or get, its power from the people it governs.

The Preamble goes on to explain that the purpose of the Constitution is to create a fairer form of government. This government would be based on some basic **principles**, or rules. One of these principles is the idea of the importance of individual liberty. The Constitution is designed to protect this liberty.

Other principles of the Constitution include justice and peace. Also, the national government would be expected to defend the country and work for the good of the nation.

READING CHECK **DRAW CONCLUSIONS**
Why does the Preamble to the Constitution mention individual liberty?

The Legislative Branch

In Article I, the Constitution describes the **legislative branch**, or lawmaking branch, of the new government. Powers granted, or given, to Congress include making laws, raising an army and a navy, declaring war, and coining and printing money. It would also control commerce.

Under the Articles of Confederation, Congress had been the only branch of the national government. Under the Constitution, three branches share those powers. The delegates created this **separation of powers** to keep any one branch from controlling the government.

Congress became two houses—the House of Representatives and the Senate. Either house could propose most bills. For a bill to become law, a majority in each house would have to vote for it.

Citizens were given the power to vote directly for members of the House of Representatives. Senators would be chosen by their state legislatures. Today, citizens vote directly for members of both houses of Congress.

The number of members each state sent to the House of Representatives would depend on the state's population. Today, the number of representatives in the House is limited to 435. That number is divided among the states, based on their populations. In the Senate, each state has two senators.

Article I outlines other rules for Congress that are still in effect. For example, members of the House of Representatives are elected to two-year terms, while members of the Senate serve six-year terms.

READING CHECK SUMMARIZE
What are the main powers of Congress?

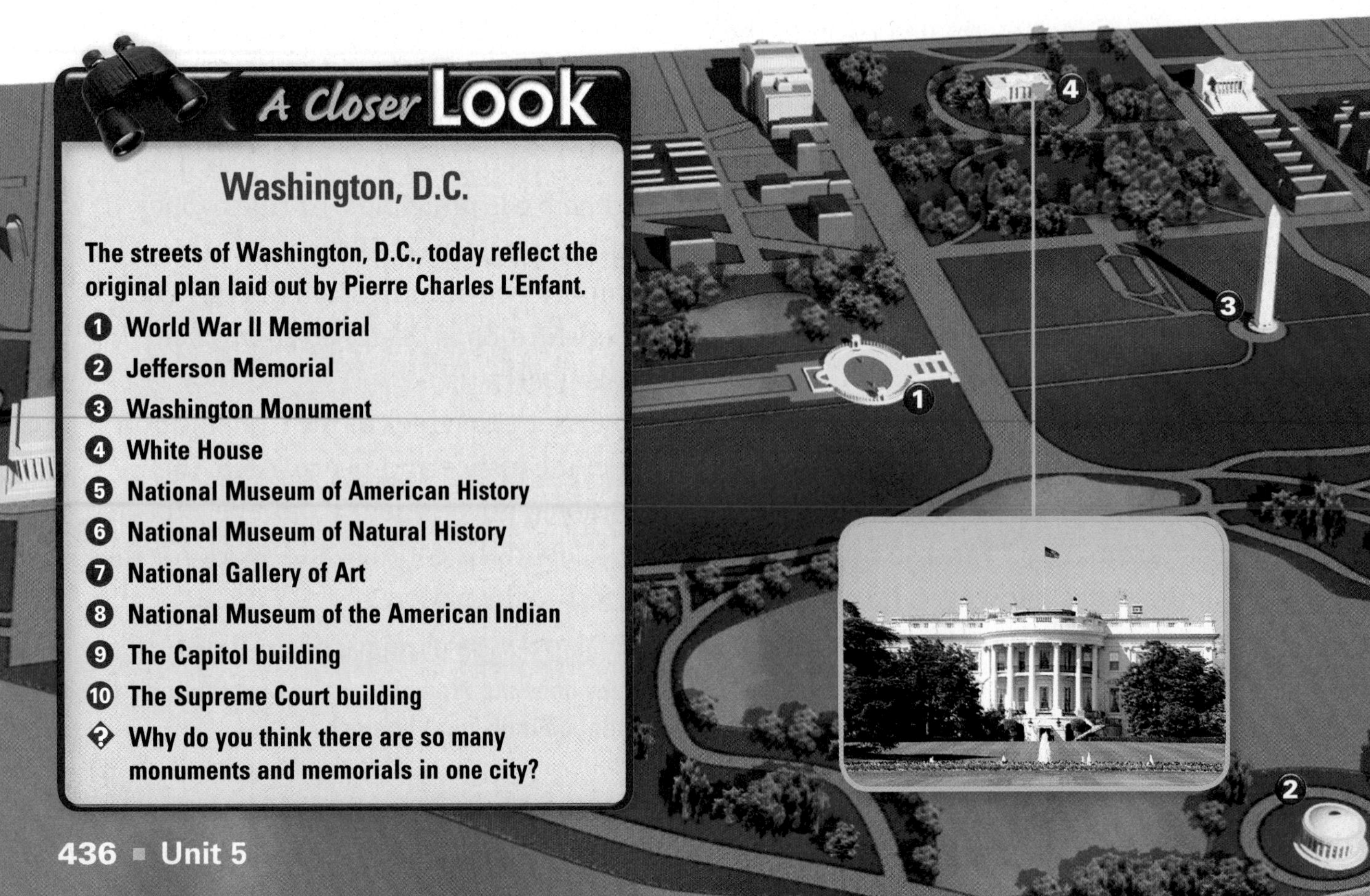

A Closer LOOK

Washington, D.C.

The streets of Washington, D.C., today reflect the original plan laid out by Pierre Charles L'Enfant.

1. World War II Memorial
2. Jefferson Memorial
3. Washington Monument
4. White House
5. National Museum of American History
6. National Museum of Natural History
7. National Gallery of Art
8. National Museum of the American Indian
9. The Capitol building
10. The Supreme Court building

Why do you think there are so many monuments and memorials in one city?

The Executive Branch

In Article II, the Constitution says the power to enforce laws made by Congress is given to the **executive branch**. Some delegates believed that one person should be the chief executive, or leader. Others worried that a single executive would be too much like a monarch.

The delegates finally decided on a single chief executive—the President. Citizens vote for electors, who, in turn, vote for the President. This group of electors is called the **electoral college**.

To be elected President, a person must be at least 35 years old and must have been born in the United States. The President must also have lived in the United States for 14 years. The President is elected to a four-year term.

Once again, the delegates were careful to preserve the separation of powers. They decided that the President would be able to **veto**, or reject, bills passed by Congress. However, Congress could then override the President's veto with a two-thirds majority vote.

The delegates also made the President commander in chief of the United States military. The President's main power, however, would be to "take care that the laws be faithfully executed."* If this duty was not carried out, Congress could **impeach** the President, or accuse the President of crimes. If found guilty, the President could be removed from office.

READING CHECK **DRAW CONCLUSIONS**
Why were the delegates careful to preserve the separation of powers?

*Constitution of the United States

The Judicial Branch

According to Article III of the Constitution, the judicial branch must decide whether laws are working fairly. The **judicial branch** is the court system.

Although the states already had their own courts, the delegates agreed to create a federal court system, too. The courts in this system would decide cases that dealt with the Constitution, treaties, and national laws. They would also decide cases between states and between citizens of different states.

The delegates did not organize the judicial branch in the same way as the other branches. Most of their decisions applied only to the highest court in the United States, which they called the Supreme Court. The Supreme Court would head the judicial branch. Other courts would be created as needed.

The delegates decided that the President would nominate the Supreme Court **justices**, or judges. The Senate would vote whether to approve them. The delegates decided that Supreme Court justices could stay in office for life. This would allow justices to make decisions without worrying about losing their jobs. At first, there were six Supreme Court justices. Today, there are nine.

The Supreme Court has the power to strike down any law that goes against

Housed in this building since 1935, the Supreme Court is the highest court in the United States.

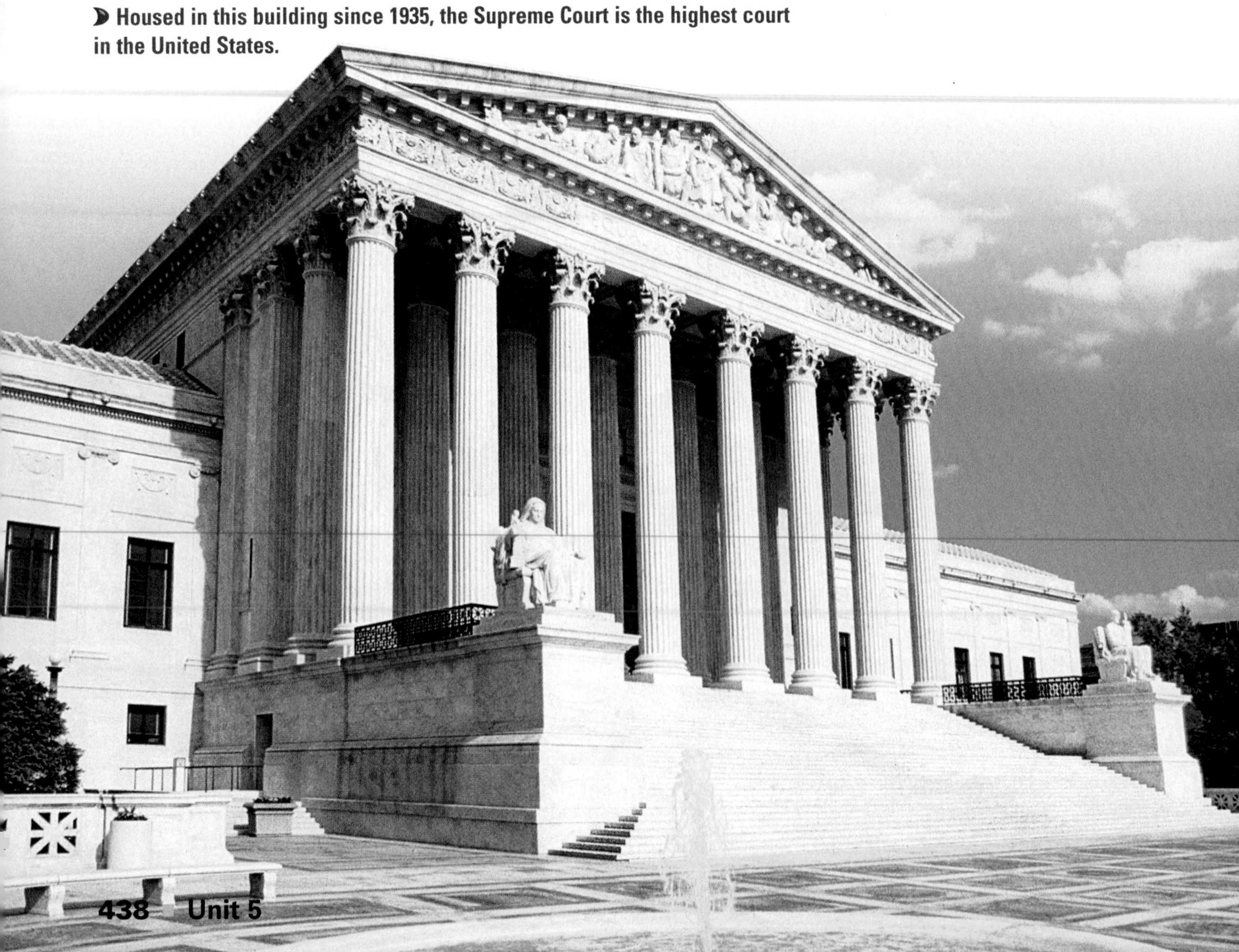

This statue, which represents the authority of law, sits at the entrance to the Supreme Court.

the Constitution. Only by changing the Constitution can Congress restore a law struck down by the Supreme Court.

The delegates understood that as the country grew, it might be necessary to change the Constitution. As part of their work, the delegates agreed on how to make **amendments**, or changes, to the Constitution.

The first step in amending the Constitution requires a two-thirds vote in both houses of Congress or a two-thirds vote of all state legislatures. Then three-fourths of the states have to approve the amendment. This system is set up to give representatives the time they need to study an amendment.

READING CHECK **DRAW CONCLUSIONS**
How does the Supreme Court limit the power of Congress?

Summary

The Constitution divides power among three branches of government—the legislative, the executive, and the judicial.

REVIEW

1. What are the powers of each of the three branches of government?
2. Use the terms **legislative branch**, **executive branch**, and **judicial branch** to explain the **separation of powers**.
3. What powers do citizens have in selecting the President and members of Congress?
4. How can Congress restore a law after the Supreme Court has struck it down?

CRITICAL THINKING

5. ANALYSIS SKILL Do you think the Constitution is important to protecting our liberty today?
6. **Write a Narrative** Imagine you are visiting the nation's capital. Write a story that describes the three branches of government and how they honor the principles of the Constitution.
7. Focus Skill **DRAW CONCLUSIONS**
   On a separate sheet of paper, copy and complete the graphic organizer below.

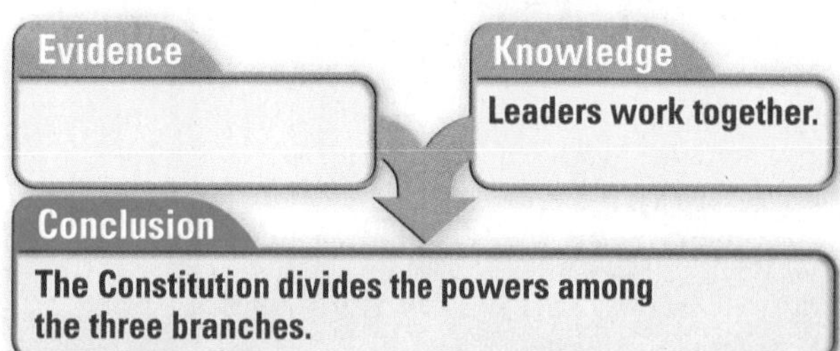

Read a Flowchart

WHY IT MATTERS

Have you ever read something and had a difficult time understanding it? Sometimes information is easier to understand when it is presented in a different way—such as in a flowchart. A **flowchart** is a drawing that shows the order in which things happen. It uses arrows to help you read the steps in the correct order.

WHAT YOU NEED TO KNOW

You can use the following steps to help you read a flowchart.

Step 1 Read the title, and ask yourself what you already know about the subject.

Step 2 Determine the direction in which the information flows.

Step 3 Read the steps in the order shown.

Step 4 Review what you have learned.

PRACTICE THE SKILL

Look at the flowchart on page 441. Use what you know about reading a flowchart to answer the following questions.

1. What happens after both the House and the Senate approve a bill?
2. What happens if the President signs a bill?
3. Where does a bill go if the President vetoes it?
4. How can a bill become a law if the President vetoes it?

APPLY WHAT YOU LEARNED

Make It Relevant With a partner, make a flowchart that explains how something works. Write each step on a strip of paper. Glue the steps—in order—onto a sheet of posterboard, and then connect the steps with arrows. Give your flowchart a title, decorate it with some art, and present it to your classmates.

Congress and the President must often work together to make laws.

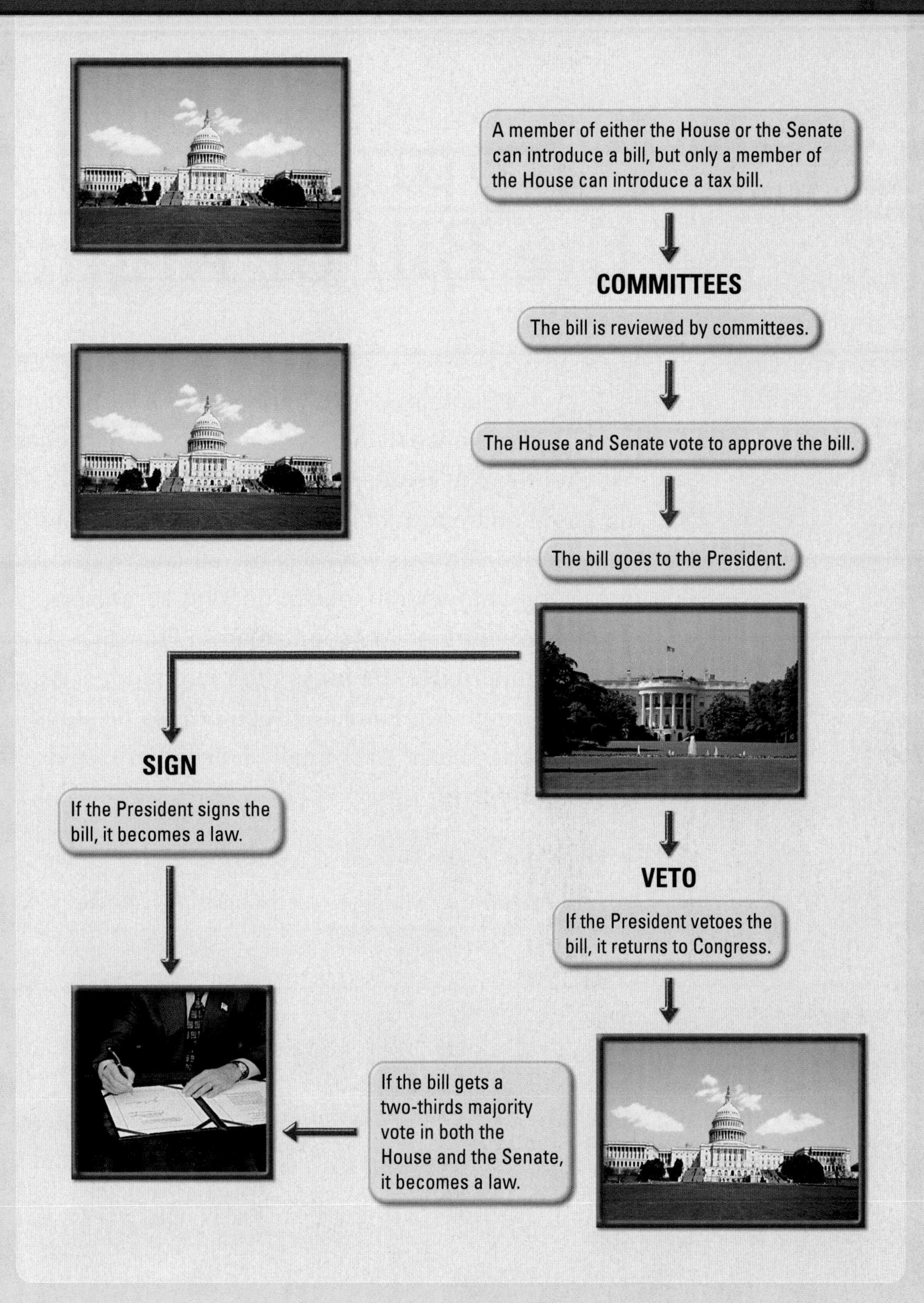

Chart and Graph Skills

Lesson 4

1780 — PRESENT

1787 United States Constitution is completed

1788 The Constitution is ratified

1791 The Bill of Rights is added to the Constitution

Approval and the Bill of Rights

WHAT TO KNOW
What is the Bill of Rights, and why was it added to the Constitution?

- ✓ Describe the struggle to get the Constitution approved.
- ✓ Explain the key rights guaranteed in the Bill of Rights.
- ✓ Describe the development of the United States government.

VOCABULARY
ratify p. 443
Federalists p. 444
Anti-Federalists p. 444
due process of law p. 445
reserved powers p. 445
Cabinet p. 446
political party p. 446

PEOPLE
John Adams
Alexander Hamilton
Thomas Jefferson
Benjamin Banneker

PLACES
Washington, D.C.

DRAW CONCLUSIONS

California Standards
HSS 5.7, 5.7.2, 5.7.3

YOU ARE THERE

It's September 1787, and you're a carpenter's apprentice living in Philadelphia. For the last two months you've heard people around the city talking about an important meeting taking place at the State House. Today is your day off, so you've decided to walk downtown in hopes of hearing some news.

When you arrive, you see Benjamin Franklin leaving the State House. He looks tired but happy. "What's the good news, Mr. Franklin?" you ask, as he steps into his sedan chair. "It is finally finished," he says and waves good-bye.

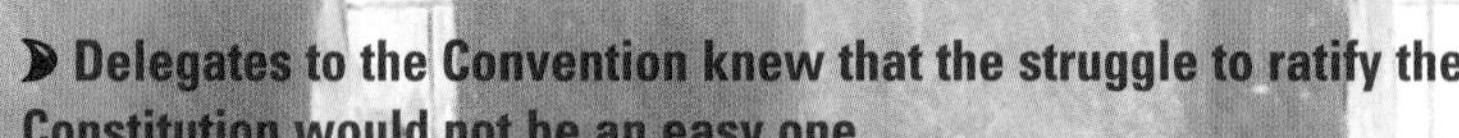

Delegates to the Convention knew that the struggle to ratify the Constitution would not be an easy one.

The Struggle to Ratify

On September 17, 1787, work on the Constitution was completed. Thirty-nine delegates were still present at the Convention and all but three of them—Elbridge Gerry, George Mason, and Edmund Randolph—signed the Constitution. These three delegates did not sign because they disagreed with parts of the final document.

As the delegates were signing the document, Benjamin Franklin stated how confident he felt in the nation's future. During the convention, Franklin had often looked at the chair used by George Washington. Its high back had a carving of the sun on it. Franklin had not been able to decide if the sun was supposed to be rising or setting. Now he said, "I have the happiness to know that it is a rising and not a setting sun."*

*Benjamin Franklin. *Miracle at Philadelphia* by Catherine Drinker Bowen. Little, Brown, 1966.

The Constitution was not yet the law of the land. According to Article VII, 9 of the 13 states had to **ratify**, or approve, the Constitution before it would be official. In each state, voters elected delegates to a state convention. These delegates would vote for or against the Constitution.

At the state conventions, arguments began again. Many state delegates wanted the Constitution to limit the power of the federal government and to protect the basic rights of the people. Some delegates said they would be more willing to approve the Constitution if a bill, or list, of rights were added to it. Supporters of the Constitution promised to propose a bill of rights after the Constitution was ratified.

READING CHECK **DRAW CONCLUSIONS**
What would adding a bill of rights to the Constitution do?

FAST FACT

The Constitution of the United States is the oldest written national constitution. It is also the shortest.

The Vote of Approval

The first state to call for a vote on the Constitution was Delaware. In December 1787, all the Delaware state delegates voted to ratify the Constitution. Later that month, delegates in Pennsylvania and New Jersey also approved the Constitution. In January 1788, delegates in Georgia and Connecticut ratified it.

Those in favor of the Constitution and those against it competed for the support of the remaining eight states. Those citizens who favored the Constitution came to be called **Federalists**. Federalists wanted a strong federal government. Those who disagreed with the Federalists became known as **Anti-Federalists**.

Because the Constitution did not include a bill of rights, the Anti-Federalists feared that the national government would have too much power. The promise of a bill of rights, however, helped change the minds of many people.

In February 1788, Massachusetts ratified the Constitution. In the spring, Maryland and South Carolina did the same. Then, on June 21, 1788, New Hampshire became the ninth state to ratify the Constitution. That was the number of states needed to put the Constitution into effect. Four days later, Virginia also ratified it, and New York followed in July. By the spring of 1789, the new government was at work. Later that year, North Carolina approved the Constitution. Rhode Island gave its approval in 1790.

READING CHECK **DRAW CONCLUSIONS**
Why do you think some Anti-Federalists changed their minds about the Constitution?

Constitution Ratification Vote

STATE	DATE	VOTES FOR	VOTES AGAINST
Delaware	Dec. 7, 1787	30	0
Pennsylvania	Dec. 12, 1787	46	23
New Jersey	Dec. 18, 1787	30	0
Georgia	Jan. 2, 1788	26	0
Connecticut	Jan. 9, 1788	128	40
Massachusetts	Feb. 26, 1788	187	168
Maryland	Apr. 28, 1788	63	11
South Carolina	May 23, 1788	149	73
New Hampshire	June 21, 1788	57	47
Virginia	June 25, 1788	89	79
New York	July 26, 1788	30	27
North Carolina	Nov. 21, 1788	194	77
Rhode Island	May 29, 1790	34	32

Analyze Tables **Alexander Hamilton (below) worked to convince others of the need for a strong federal government. Ratification of the Constitution made such a government possible.**

In which state was the vote closest to being a tie?

Newspapers printed the Bill of Rights so that people could read it.

The Bill of Rights

As promised, not long after the states ratified the Constitution, ten amendments were added to protect the rights of the people. These ten amendments, called the Bill of Rights, became part of the Constitution in 1791.

The First Amendment gives people the freedom to follow any religion, or none at all. It also says the government cannot promote or financially support any religion. The First Amendment also protects freedom of speech, freedom of the press, and the right of people to assemble, or gather together.

The Second Amendment protects people's right to have weapons. The Third Amendment says the government cannot force people to house soldiers in peacetime. The Fourth Amendment protects people against unreasonable searches of their homes.

The Fifth through Eighth Amendments deal with **due process of law**. This term means that people have the right to a fair public trial by a jury. They do not have to testify against themselves in court, and they have the right to have a lawyer defend them. If convicted, they cannot be sentenced to any cruel punishments.

The Ninth Amendment says that the people have many other rights not specifically listed in the Constitution. The Tenth Amendment says that the national government can do only the things that are listed in the Constitution. This means that all other authority, called the **reserved powers**, belongs to the states or to the people.

READING CHECK **DRAW CONCLUSIONS**
Why is the First Amendment important?

The New Government

In 1789, George Washington was elected to be the nation's first President. **John Adams** became the first Vice President. Working with Congress, Washington set up a State Department, a Treasury Department, and a War Department. Together, the heads of these departments and others set up what would come to be known as the **Cabinet**. Cabinet members advise the President.

Two members of Washington's Cabinet began to argue about what was best for the United States. **Alexander Hamilton** wanted a stronger central government. **Thomas Jefferson** wanted less central government. This argument led to the rise of political parties. A **political party** is a group that tries to elect officials who will support its policies. Hamilton's followers formed the Federalist party. Jefferson's supporters became the Democratic-Republican Party, also known as the Jeffersonian Republicans.

In Congress, members of both parties agreed to build a national capital on the Potomac River. George Washington chose the location for the city that came to carry his name. **Benjamin Banneker**, a free African American, helped the architect Pierre Charles L'Enfant plan the nation's capital. In 1800, the federal government was moved from Philadelphia to **Washington, D.C.**

George Washington served as President for two terms, each of which was four years long. Many people wanted him to run for a third term. He refused because he did not think a President should hold power for life. His decision set an example for future Presidents.

Benjamin Banneker helped measure the land, known as the District of Columbia (D.C.), where the national capital was built.

In the election of 1796, the Federalist party, led by Alexander Hamilton, backed John Adams as a candidate for President. The Jeffersonian Republican party backed Thomas Jefferson. When the votes were counted, Adams had won.

On March 4, 1797, John Adams became the second President of the United States. The day he took the oath of office was an important day in history. It was the first time that the United States had changed leaders by means of a peaceful election.

READING CHECK **DRAW CONCLUSIONS**
Why do you think it was necessary for the President to have a Cabinet?

Summary

After a long struggle, the new Constitution was ratified in 1788. In 1789, the new government began with George Washington serving as the first President. The Bill of Rights was added in 1791.

John Adams was the first President to live in what is now the White House.

REVIEW

1. What is the Bill of Rights, and why was it added to the Constitution?
2. Explain the meaning of the term **ratify**.
3. What rights does the Bill of Rights guarantee?
4. What is the role of cabinet members?

CRITICAL THINKING

5. ANALYSIS SKILL Why do you think some delegates felt nervous about signing the Constitution without a bill of rights?
6. ANALYSIS SKILL How does the Bill of Rights support the idea of individual liberty?
7. **Make a Poster** Design a poster that honors the Bill of Rights. List some of the amendments and illustrate your poster with pictures of freedoms that you enjoy.
8. Focus Skill **DRAW CONCLUSIONS**
On a separate sheet of paper, copy and complete the graphic organizer below.

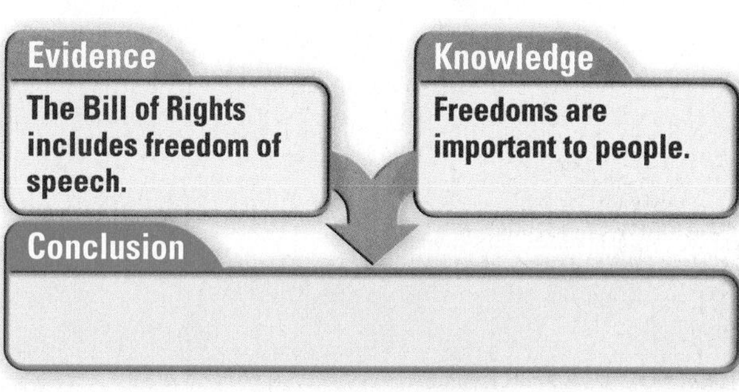

The United States Constitution

Delegates to the Constitutional Convention created a new plan of government. Americans had different ideas about how this plan would affect their state governments and their individual liberties. Here are some points of view that reflect those different ideas about the new Constitution.

In Their Own Words

JOHN ADAMS

John Adams, a Massachusetts leader, writing about the Constitution

“A result of compromise cannot perfectly coincide [agree] with every one’s idea of perfection; but, I hope to hear of its [the Constitution’s] adoption by all states.”

– from *History of the United States of America,* by George Bancroft. Appleton, 1912.

George Mason, a Virginia leader, speaking about the Constitution

"... there never was a government over a very extensive [large] country, without destroying the liberties of the people ... Where is there one exception to this general rule?"

— from "George Mason Fears for the Rights of People" in *The Debate on the Constitution*, by Bernard Bailyn. Library of America, 1993.

George Washington, a Virginia leader, writing about the Constitution

"I sincerely believe it is the best that could be obtained at this time ... the adoption of it [the Constitution] ... is in my opinion desirable."

— from a letter to Patrick Henry in *History of the United States of America*, by George Bancroft. Appleton, 1912.

Mercy Otis Warren, a Massachusetts writer, writing about the Constitution

"There is no security in the [Constitution], either for the rights of conscience or the Liberty of the Press."

— from *An Additional Number of Letters from the Federal Farmer to the Republican*, by Richard Henry Lee. Quadrangle Books, 1962.

It's Your Turn

ANALYSIS SKILL **Analyze Points of View** Work with a classmate to summarize the point of view held by each person. Decide which people supported the Constitution and which people opposed it.

Make It Relevant Explain whether you would have supported the Constitution when it was first written.

Time

1780

1781
The Articles of Confederation are passed

1787
The Constitutional Convention begins

Reading Social Studies

When you **draw conclusions**, you combine facts that you read with facts that you know to understand ideas that are not stated.

Draw Conclusions

Complete this graphic organizer to show that you can draw a conclusion about the Constitutional Convention. A copy of this graphic organizer appears on page 110 of the Homework and Practice Book.

The Constitutional Convention

Evidence

The discussions at the Constitutional Convention were kept secret.

Knowledge

Conclusion

The delegates at the Constitutional Convention did not want others to influence their decisions.

California Writing Prompts

Write a Persuasive Letter Imagine you are living in 1788. You have read the Constitution. Write a letter to the delegates in your state who will decide whether to accept or reject it. Tell them how you want them to vote, and why.

Write a Report Choose one of the delegates who attended the Constitutional Convention. Then write a report, using facts and details about that delegate's role.

1790

1800

1788
The Constitution is ratified

1791
The Bill of Rights is added to the Constitution

Use Vocabulary

Identify the term that correctly matches each definition.

commerce, p. 422
republic, p. 429
impeach, p. 437
amendment, p. 439
ratify, p. 443

1. to accuse of crimes
2. trade
3. a government made up of representatives chosen by the people
4. a change
5. to approve

Use the Time Line

Use the chapter summary time line above to answer these questions.

6. In what year was the Constitution ratified?
7. How many years after the Constitution was ratified was the Bill of Rights added?

Apply Skills

Read a Flowchart

Use the flowchart on page 441 to help you answer these questions.

8. Where is a bill introduced?
9. What happens just before the House and the Senate vote to approve a bill?

Recall Facts

Answer these questions.

10. Under the Articles of Confederation, how were national laws passed?
11. The Great Compromise resolved a conflict about which branch of the federal government?
12. Which branch of the federal government has the power to enforce laws?

Write the letter of the best choice.

13. Who wrote the Preamble to the Constitution?
    A George Washington
    B Benjamin Franklin
    C James Madison
    D Gouverneur Morris
14. Which of the following does the First Amendment protect?
    A the right to bear arms
    B the right to a trial by jury
    C the right to privacy
    D the right to free speech

Think Critically

15. ANALYSIS SKILL Name one primary source and one secondary source that you could use if you wanted to learn more about the Constitution.
16. ANALYSIS SKILL What caused leaders to want to replace the Articles of Confederation?

Study Skills

SKIM AND SCAN

Skimming and scanning are tools that help you quickly learn the main ideas of a lesson.

- **To skim, quickly read the lesson title and the section titles. Look at the visuals, or images, and read the captions. Use this information to identify the main topics.**
- **To scan, look quickly through the text for specific details, such as key words or facts.**

Skim	Scan
Lesson Title: A Constitutional Democracy	**Key Words and Facts:** • The Constitution protects citizens' rights.
Main Idea: The Constitution organizes the government and protects citizens' rights.	• The three branches of government share power.
Section Titles: Powers and Limits, The Branches Work Together ____________	• ____________
Visuals: Election day painting, Checks and Balances diagram. ____________	

Apply As You Read

Before you read each lesson, skim the text to find the main ideas. Then look for key words. If you have questions about a topic, scan the text to find the answers.

California History-Social Science Standards, Grade 5

5.7 Students describe the people and events associated with the development of the U.S. Constitution and analyze the Constitution's significance as the foundation of the American republic.

CHAPTER 11

The American Republic

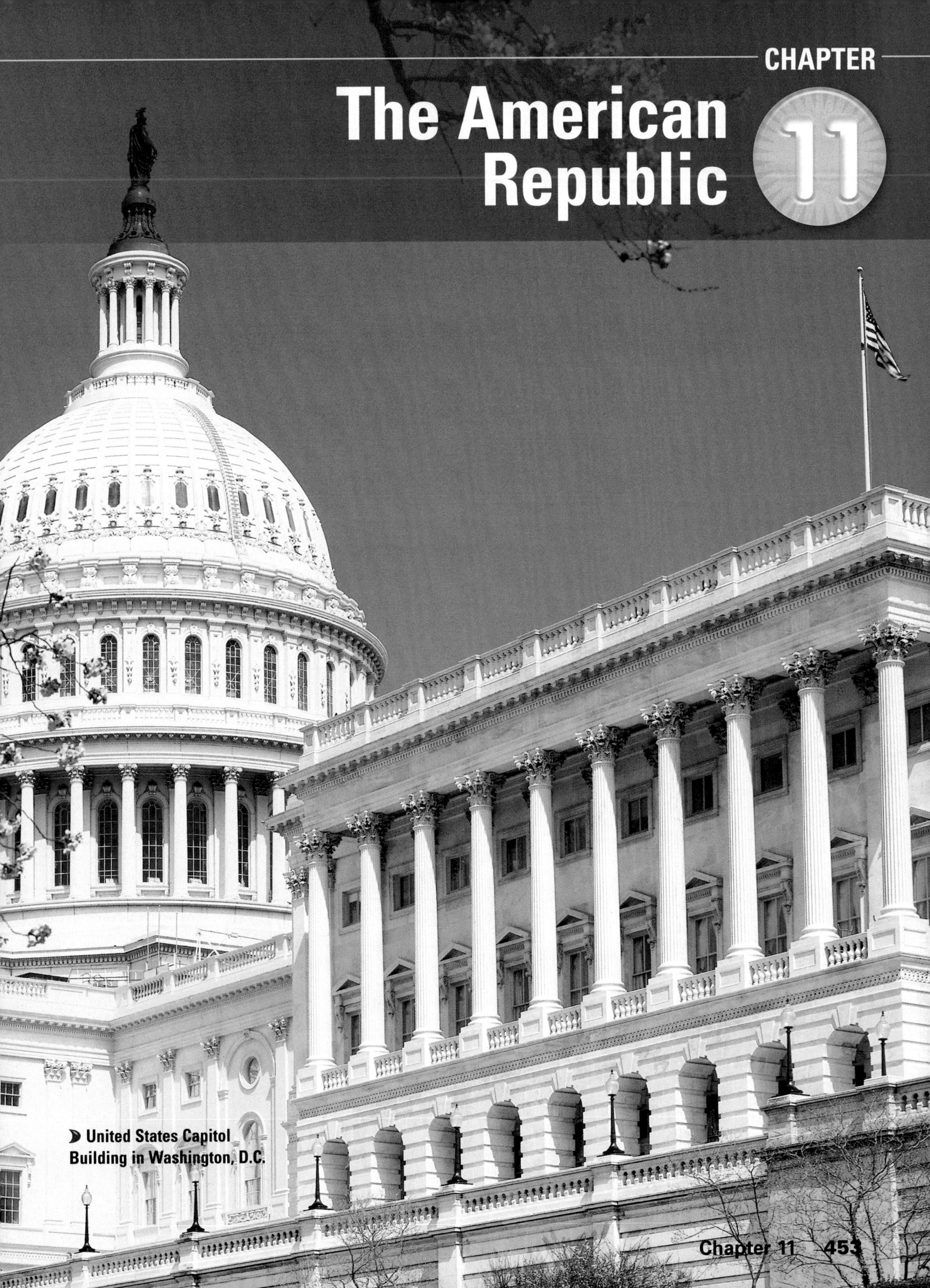

United States Capitol Building in Washington, D.C.

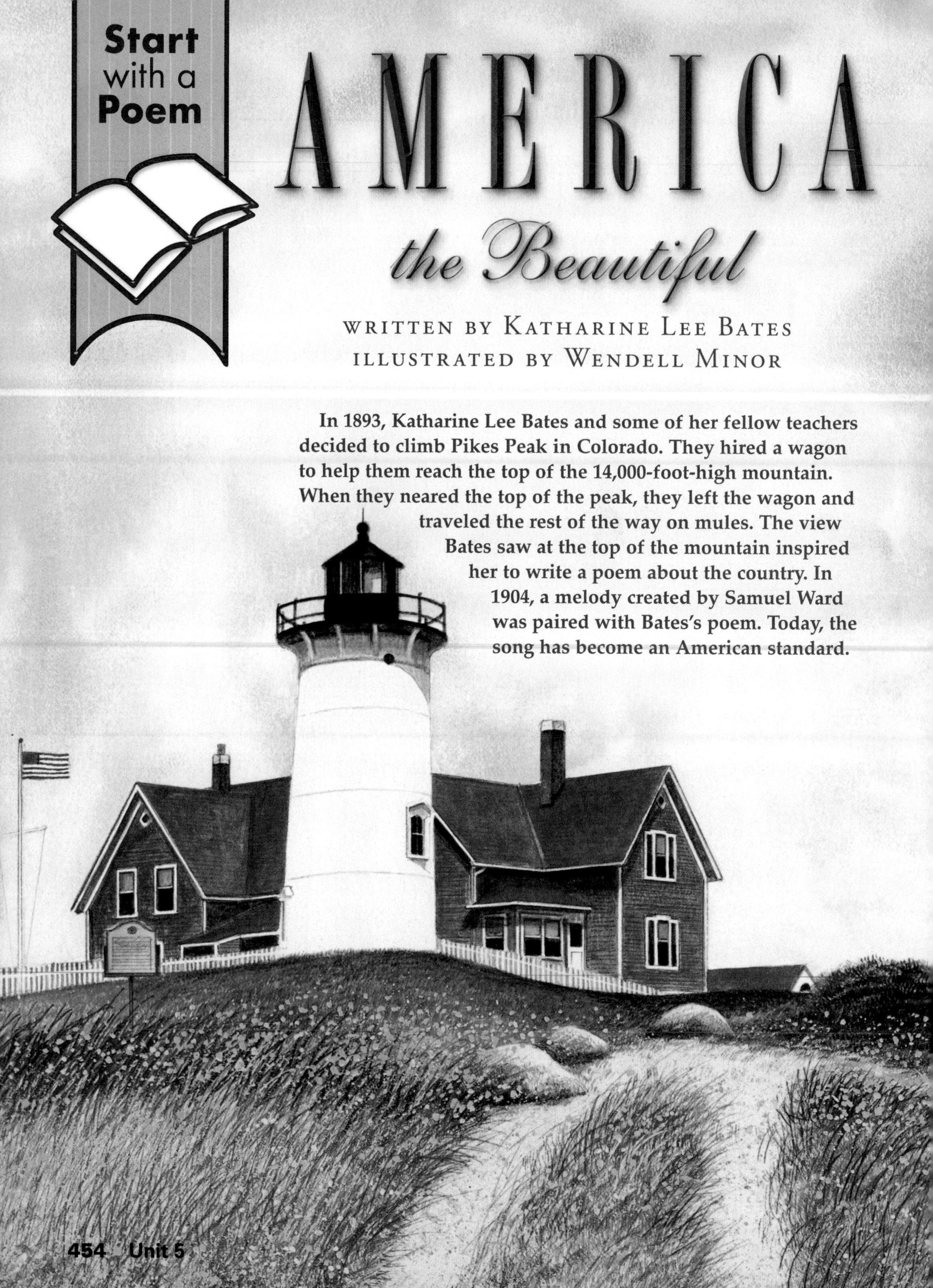

Start with a Poem

AMERICA the Beautiful

WRITTEN BY KATHARINE LEE BATES
ILLUSTRATED BY WENDELL MINOR

In 1893, Katharine Lee Bates and some of her fellow teachers decided to climb Pikes Peak in Colorado. They hired a wagon to help them reach the top of the 14,000-foot-high mountain. When they neared the top of the peak, they left the wagon and traveled the rest of the way on mules. The view Bates saw at the top of the mountain inspired her to write a poem about the country. In 1904, a melody created by Samuel Ward was paired with Bates's poem. Today, the song has become an American standard.

O beautiful for spacious skies,
For amber waves of grain,
For purple mountain majesties
Above the fruited plain!
America! America!
God shed his grace on thee
And crown thy good with brotherhood
From sea to shining sea!

O beautiful for pilgrim feet
Whose stern, impassioned stress
A thoroughfare for freedom beat
Across the wilderness!
America! America!
God mend thine every flaw,
Confirm thy soul in self-control,
Thy liberty in law!

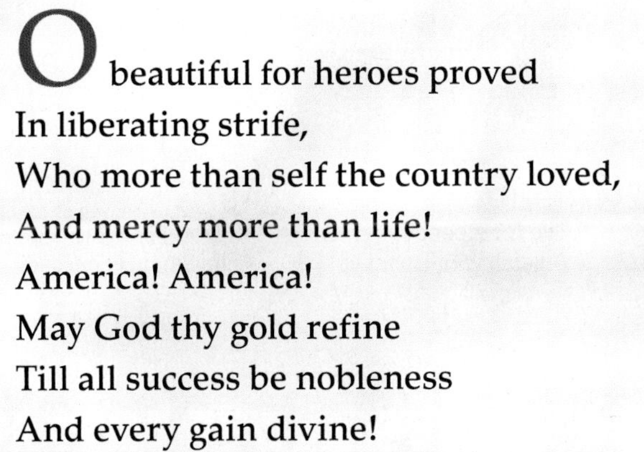

O beautiful for heroes proved
In liberating strife,
Who more than self the country loved,
And mercy more than life!
America! America!
May God thy gold refine
Till all success be nobleness
And every gain divine!

O beautiful for patriot dream
That sees beyond the years
Thine alabaster cities gleam
Undimmed by human tears!
America! America!
God shed His grace on thee
And crown thy good with brotherhood
From sea to shining sea!

Response Corner

1. How does the poem reflect how the author feels about America?
2. Using Bates's poem as a model, write a poem about your thoughts about America. Share your poem with the class.

Lesson 1

Time

1780 — PRESENT

1920 The Nineteenth Amendment is passed

1971 The Twenty-sixth Amendment is passed

WHAT TO KNOW
How does the Constitution help protect citizens' rights by both empowering and limiting the federal government?

- Identify the principles of a constitutional democracy.
- Learn how the authority of a democratic government comes from its people.
- Compare the powers granted to citizens, to the three branches of the federal government, and to the states.

VOCABULARY
democracy p. 458
checks and balances p. 459

DRAW CONCLUSIONS

HSS 5.7, 5.7.3, 5.7.4

A Constitutional Democracy

YOU ARE THERE

The year is 1789. You're excited because you're going to town tomorrow with your father. He will be voting in the first elections under the Constitution. He tells you that he feels proud to be part of a constitutional democracy. In a **democracy**, the people rule, and they are free to make choices about their lives and their government.

Election Day in Philadelphia, Pennsylvania

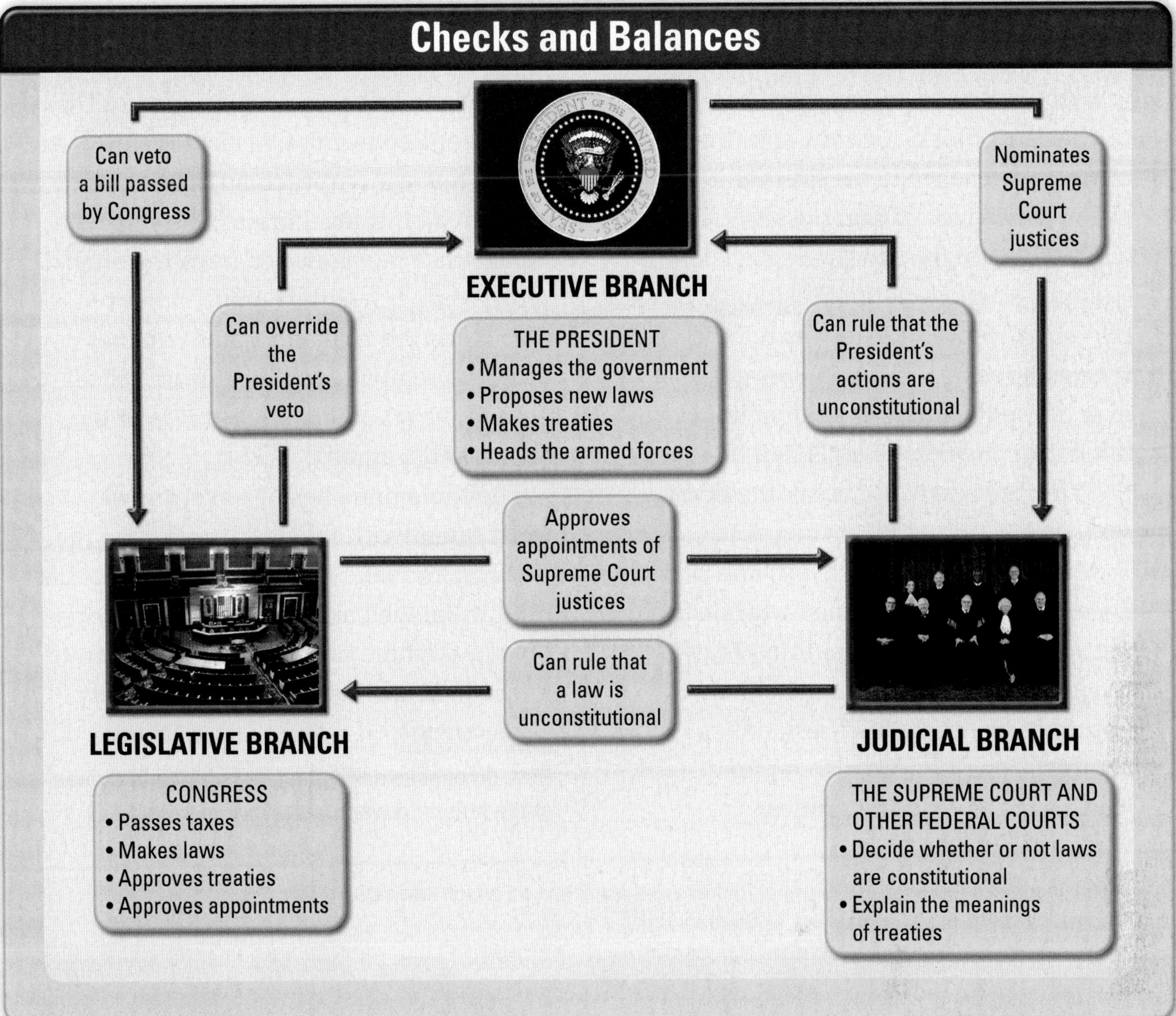

Analyze Diagrams

How can the President check the authority of Congress?

Sharing Powers

The Constitution had to empower the federal government, or give it enough power to govern the nation. At the same time, states and citizens had to be protected from that power.

The checks, or limits, on federal power are outlined in the Constitution. It describes in detail how the federal government's power is shared among its three main branches.

Each branch is given different powers by the Constitution in a way that allows each branch to watch over the others. This system of **checks and balances** keeps any one branch from becoming too powerful or misusing its authority. This system was developed in the hope that it would allow the nation to form "a more perfect union."*

READING CHECK **DRAW CONCLUSIONS**
How does the Constitution both empower and limit the federal government?

*The Constitution of the United States.

Checks and Balances

Each branch of government has ways to check, or block, the power of the others. For example, the President can check the power of Congress by vetoing a bill that Congress has passed. Then Congress can check the President's power by voting to override, or cancel, the veto. If this happens, a bill becomes a law even if the President is against it. If a bill before the Senate ends in a tie vote, the Vice President can break the tie by voting.

Another example of checks and balances is the way Supreme Court justices are selected. The President nominates the justices. Then the Senate either approves or rejects the President's choices. Congress can also remove justices if they commit crimes.

The Constitution describes how a government official can be brought to trial for treason, bribery, or other crimes. The House of Representatives is the only group that can impeach an official in the executive or judicial branch. To impeach means that the House charges the official with a crime. It is the Senate, however, that holds the trial and votes whether or not to remove an official from office. To remove an official, two-thirds of the Senate must agree.

The three branches of government must often work together to exercise their powers. To make laws and treaties, to use military power, and to protect individual liberty, all three branches must cooperate in order to use their powers effectively.

READING CHECK **DRAW CONCLUSIONS**
How do checks and balances help the branches of the federal government work together?

This painting shows the old House of Representatives chamber, which was used from 1807 to 1857. Today, it is known as Statuary Hall.

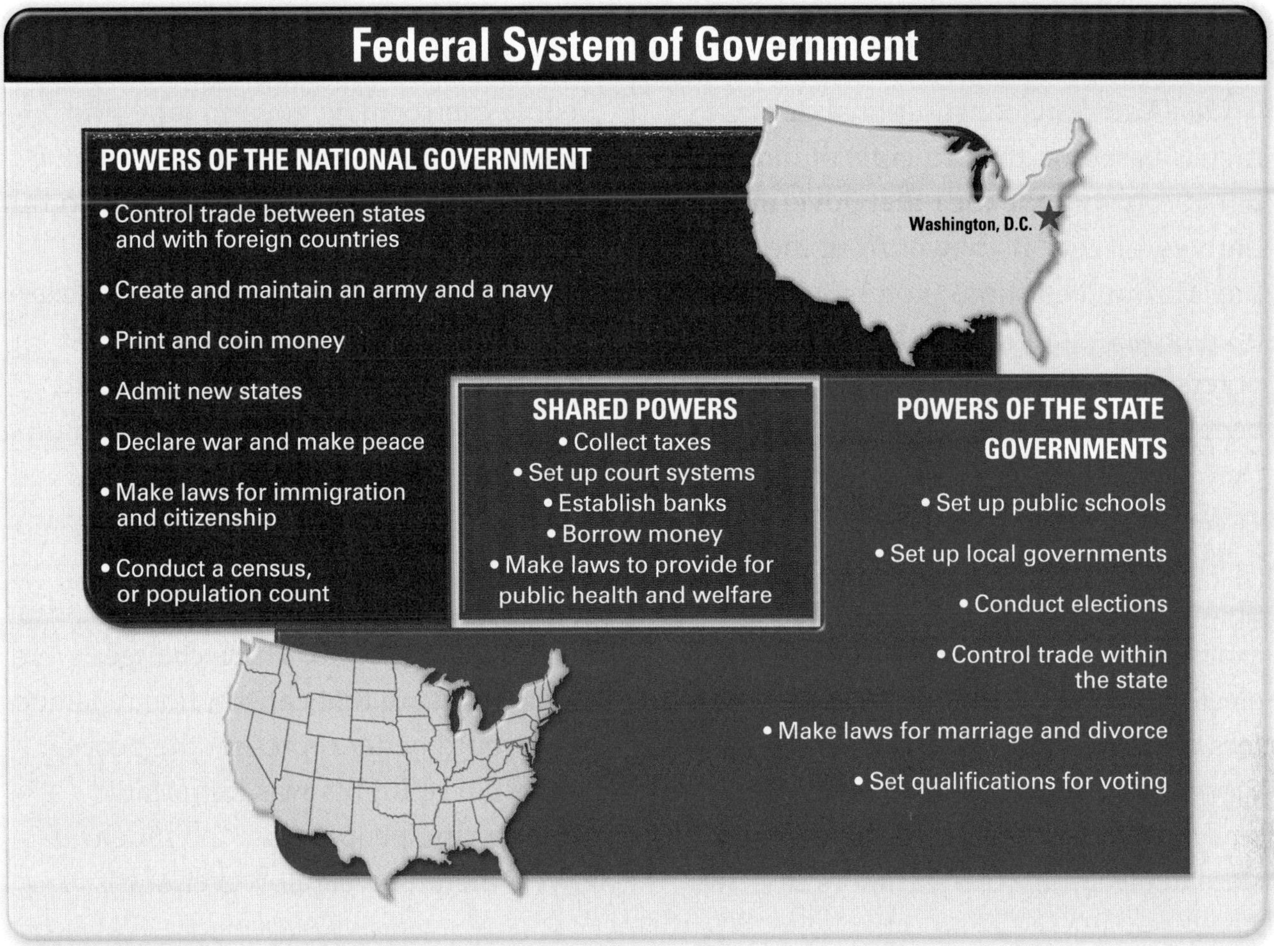

Federal System of Government

POWERS OF THE NATIONAL GOVERNMENT

- Control trade between states and with foreign countries
- Create and maintain an army and a navy
- Print and coin money
- Admit new states
- Declare war and make peace
- Make laws for immigration and citizenship
- Conduct a census, or population count

SHARED POWERS

- Collect taxes
- Set up court systems
- Establish banks
- Borrow money
- Make laws to provide for public health and welfare

POWERS OF THE STATE GOVERNMENTS

- Set up public schools
- Set up local governments
- Conduct elections
- Control trade within the state
- Make laws for marriage and divorce
- Set qualifications for voting

Washington, D.C.

Analyze Charts

Why do you think state governments need the power to set up local governments?

State Powers

The writers of the Constitution were careful to preserve the powers of the states. The Tenth Amendment deals with this issue. It says that any powers not clearly given to the federal government or denied to the states by the Constitution belong to the states or the people. For example, state governments can build and manage state highways and state parks. They oversee public schools and state colleges and universities. Just as the federal government does, state governments provide many services and help people solve problems.

The Constitution limits the way the powers of the federal government can be applied to the states. For example, Congress cannot favor one state over another in making trade agreements or in collecting taxes. Congress also cannot tax goods moving from one state to another.

Powers that the states do not have are listed in the Constitution. For example, states cannot print money, raise armies, or make treaties with other countries. They cannot set up agreements with other states without the approval of Congress.

READING CHECK **DRAW CONCLUSIONS**
Why does the Constitution include a general protection of states' rights?

Rights of Citizens

Our American constitutional democracy is based on the principle of individual liberty and the idea that government derives, or gets, its power from the people. Through elections, voters select their own representatives and leaders. If the voters do not like certain laws that have been passed, they can elect officials who they think will change the laws.

Several amendments have been added to the Constitution to give the people greater control over their leaders. For example, state legislatures originally elected senators. In 1913, to make senators more responsible to the people they represent, the Seventeenth Amendment was adopted. It allows the voters of each state to elect their own senators directly.

Limiting the amount of time that public officials can hold office is another way people can regulate government. The Twenty-second Amendment says that a President cannot serve more than two full terms in office.

Voting is one way that people can exercise control over their government. At first, this right was not extended to all people. Women were not given the right to vote in national elections until the Nineteenth Amendment was adopted in 1920. In 1971, the Twenty-sixth Amendment lowered the voting age from 21 years of age to 18. These changes were made to ensure that constitutional democracy would better represent the people.

The Bill of Rights was important in protecting people from too much government power. However, the

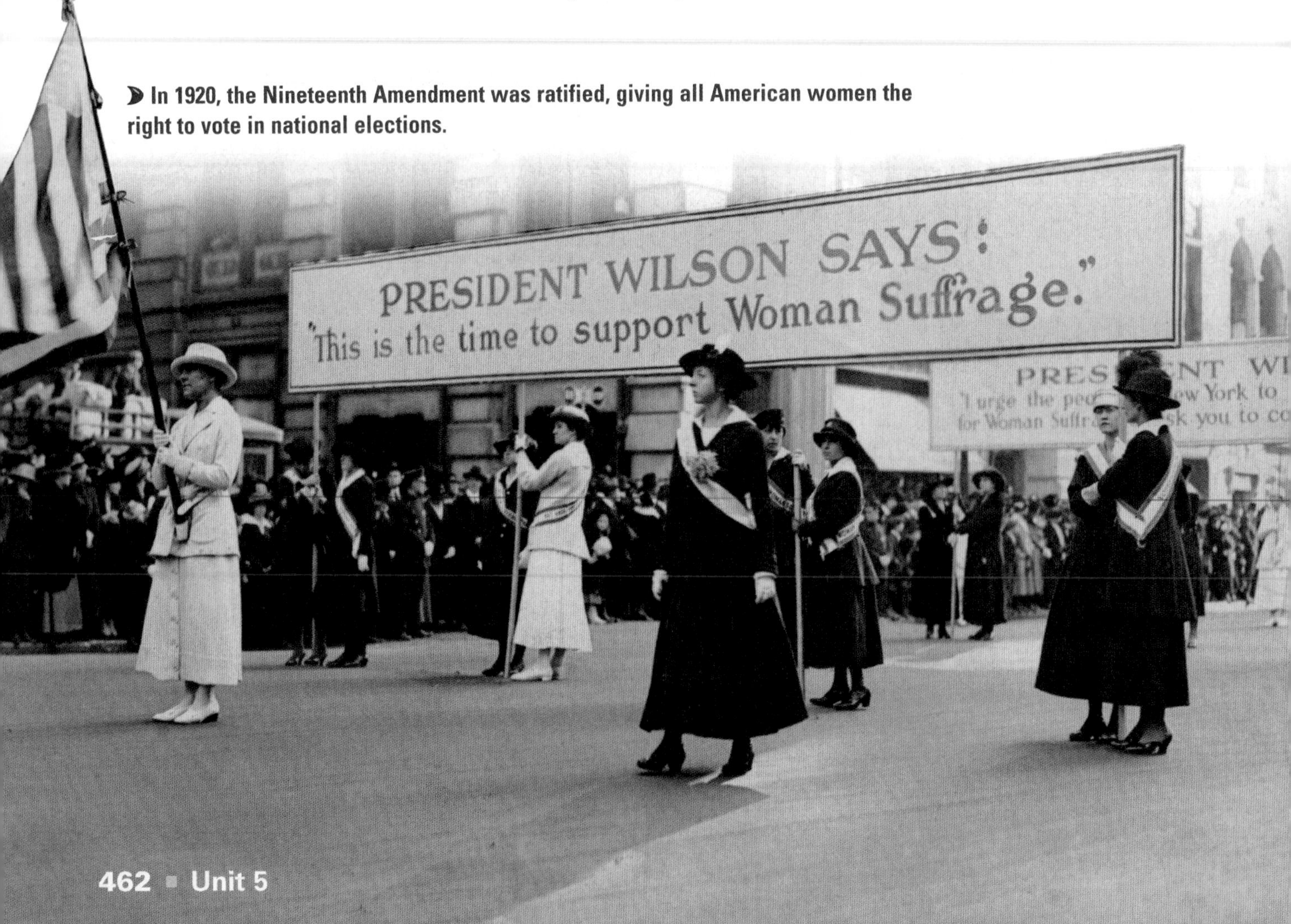

In 1920, the Nineteenth Amendment was ratified, giving all American women the right to vote in national elections.

Constitution also made the federal government responsible for protecting the people. Congress has the power to raise money to defend the United States and to provide services for its people by collecting tariffs, or taxes, on goods. In this way, the Constitution makes sure that the government has the resources needed to serve its citizens.

READING CHECK **DRAW CONCLUSIONS**
How can people take part in our American constitutional democracy?

Summary

In our constitutional democracy, the power to govern comes from the people. The Constitution separates the powers of the federal government and state governments. The federal government's powers operate by a system of checks and balances among the legislative, executive, and judicial branches.

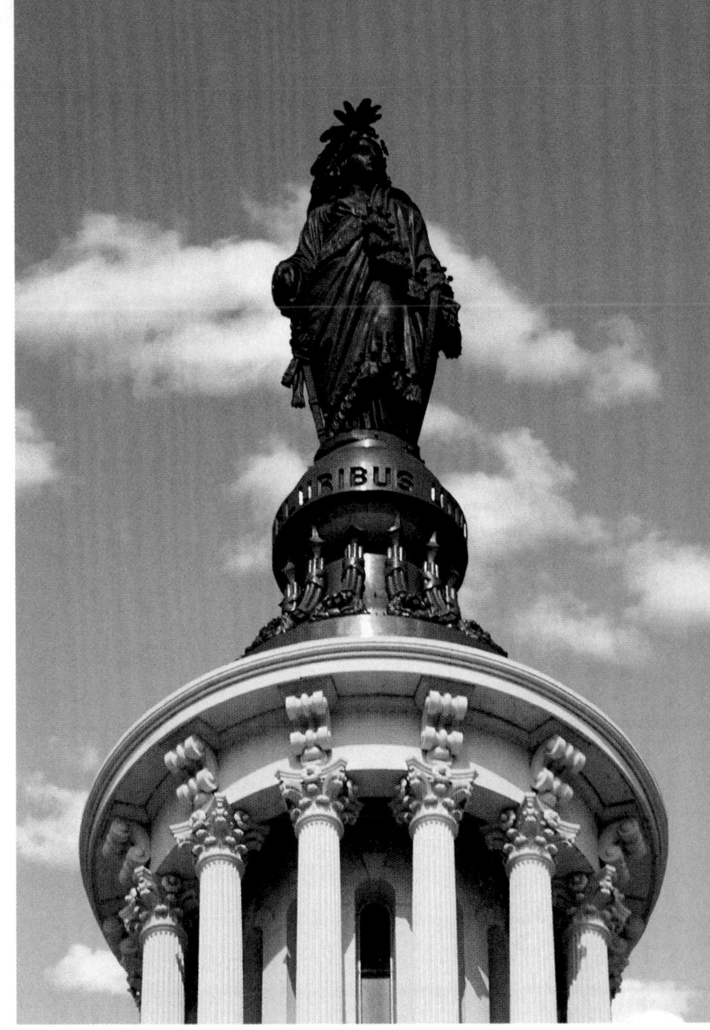

This statue representing freedom stands atop the Capitol building in Washington, D.C.

REVIEW

1. How does the Constitution help protect citizens' rights by both empowering and limiting the federal government?
2. Use the term **checks and balances** to explain how it keeps any one branch of the federal government from becoming too powerful.
3. How does the Constitution prevent Congress from favoring one state over another?

CRITICAL THINKING

4. ANALYSIS SKILL How did the Nineteenth Amendment expand democracy?
5. **Make a Chart** List at least three powers given to the federal government, to the states, and to citizens. Explain how the Constitution empowers and limits each group.
6. Focus Skill **DRAW CONCLUSIONS** On a separate sheet of paper, copy and complete the graphic organizer below.

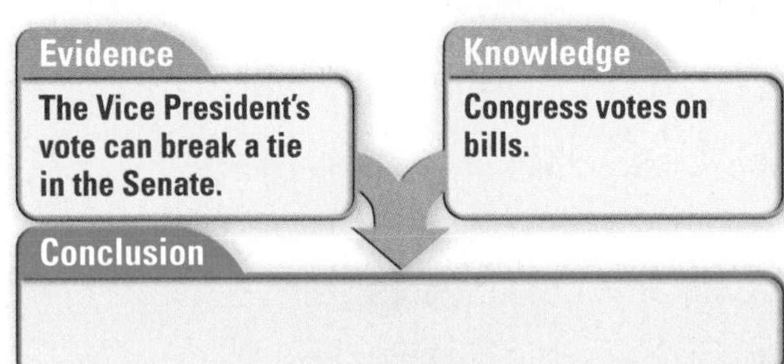

Read a Population Map

WHY IT MATTERS

In 1790, the first census was taken. It counted the people living in the United States and showed where they lived. The population density map on page 465 shows the results of the first census. **Population density** is the average number of people living in an area of a certain size, usually one square mile or one square kilometer. Knowing how to read population density maps will help you understand population information.

WHAT YOU NEED TO KNOW

You can use these steps to learn how to read a population density map.

Step 1 **Read the title of the map. Think about what you know about the people in this place, at this time.**

Pitcher showing state populations from the first census

Step 2 **Study the key. Compare its colors with those on the map.**

Step 3 **Put the visual information shown on the map into your own words.**

PRACTICE THE SKILL

The map on page 465 shows population density. Use the map to answer the following questions.

1. Which state is more densely populated, Massachusetts or Georgia?
2. What is the population density of the area in which New York City is located?
3. Find Nashville, Philadelphia, and Richmond. Which place has the highest population density?
4. Which part of the country had the highest population density in 1790, the northern or the southern states?

APPLY WHAT YOU LEARNED

ANALYSIS SKILL Choose five of the cities shown on the population density map. List the population density of each city. Then make a bar graph comparing the population densities of the cities you chose.

Practice your map and globe skills with the **GeoSkills CD-ROM.**

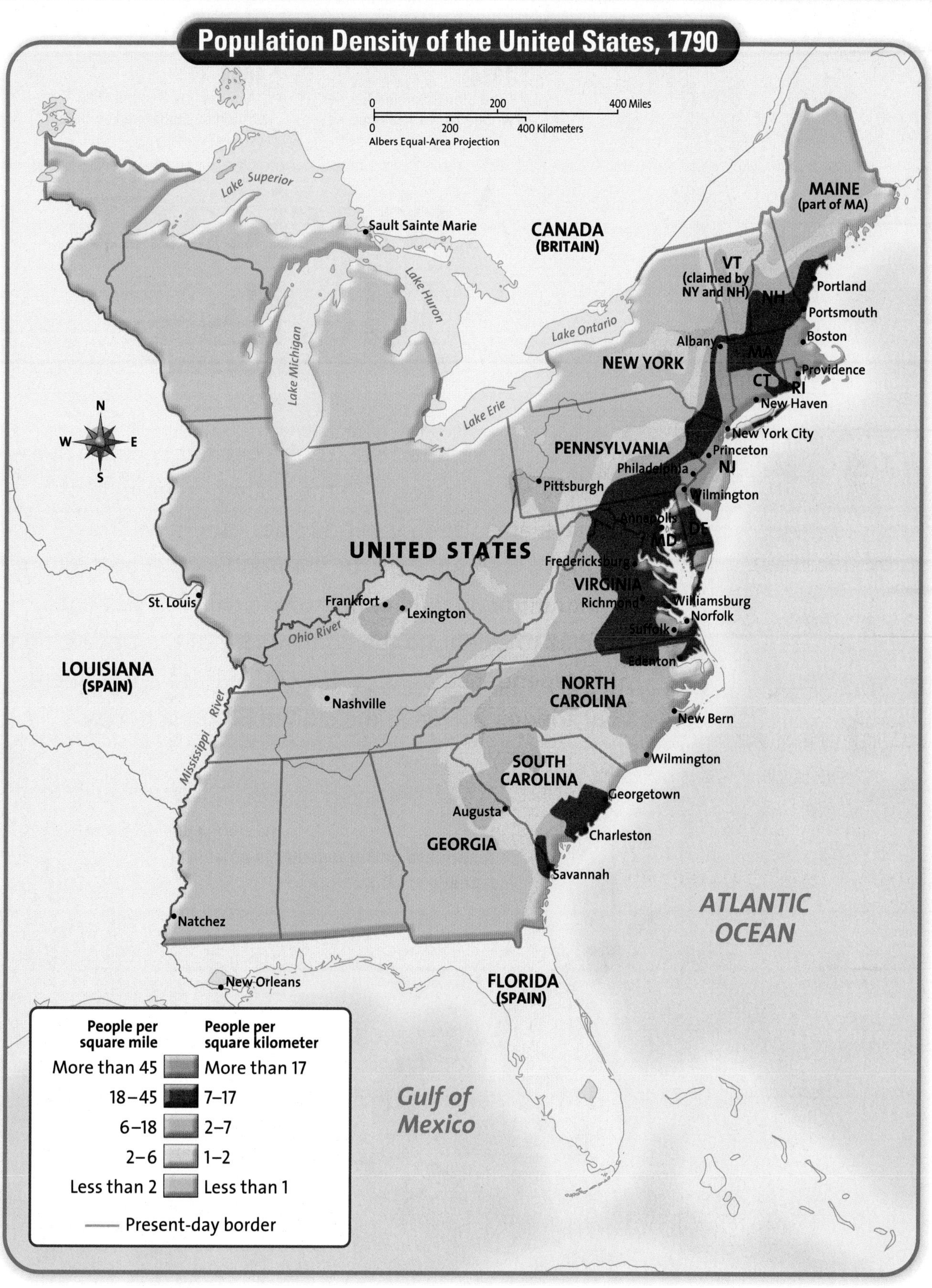

Map and Globe Skills

Lesson 2

Time

1780 — PRESENT

1814 "The Star-Spangled Banner" is written by Francis Scott Key

1893 "America the Beautiful" is written by Katharine Lee Bates

WHAT TO KNOW
What are the ideals that make up the American creed?

- ✓ Explain how the citizens of the United States are responsible for safeguarding, or protecting, the liberty of individuals.
- ✓ Explain why respect for the rule of law and the preservation of the Constitution are important to the American creed.
- ✓ Identify songs that express American ideals.

VOCABULARY
creed p. 467
ideal p. 467
patriotism p. 468

PEOPLE
Mary Pickersgill
Francis Scott Key
Katharine Lee Bates

DRAW CONCLUSIONS

California Standards
HSS 5.7, 5.7.5, 5.7.6

American Ideals

YOU ARE THERE The year is 1818. You're excited because summer has come to the rolling green hills of Pennsylvania. Soon you and your family will travel by wagon to Springs Park for the first Festival of Candles. At nighttime on July 4, the town's children will light candles to celebrate the anniversary of the Declaration of Independence on July 4, 1776. In this way, you and your friends will wish the United States a happy birthday.

➤ Americans gather together to celebrate Independence Day.

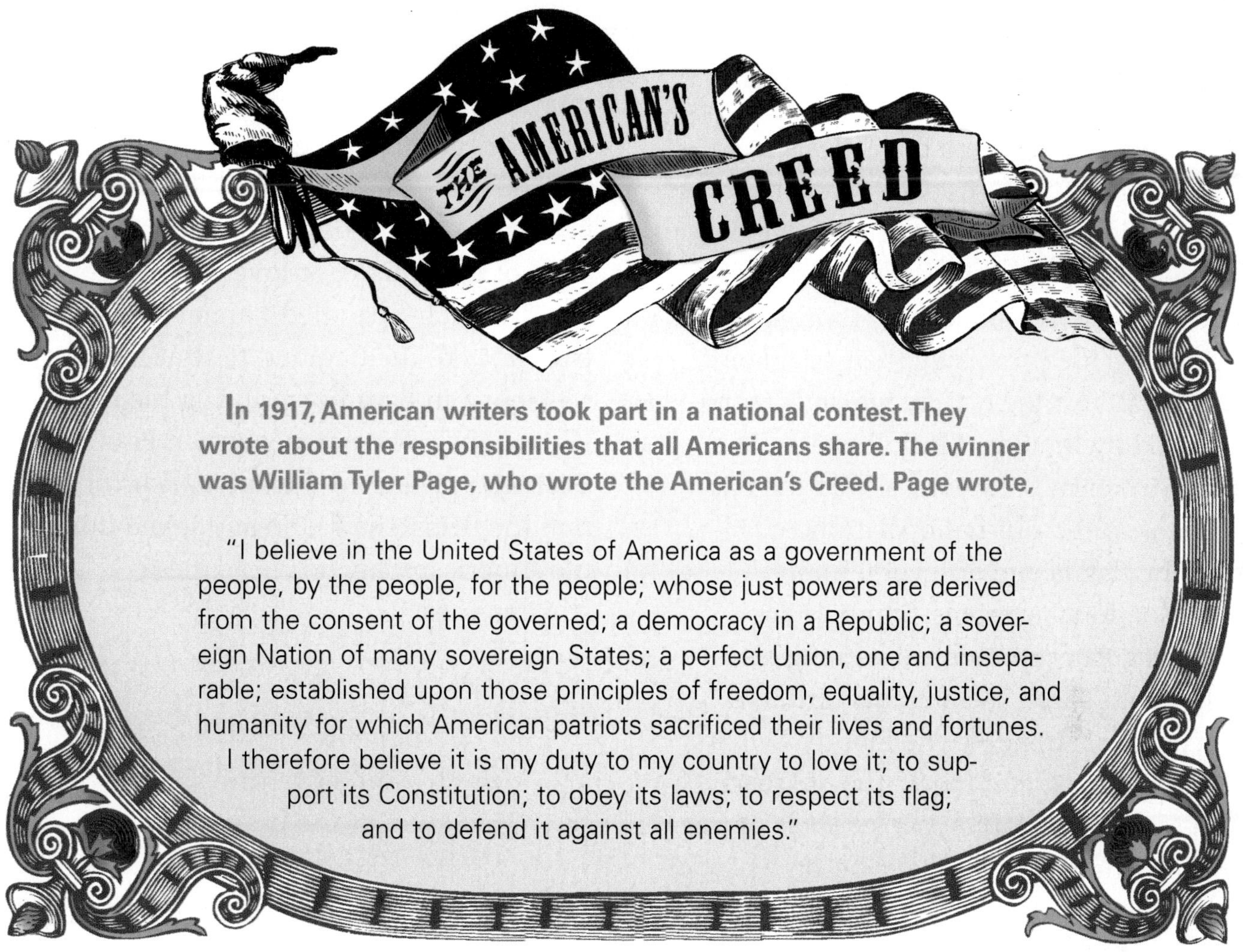

In 1917, American writers took part in a national contest. They wrote about the responsibilities that all Americans share. The winner was William Tyler Page, who wrote the American's Creed. Page wrote,

"I believe in the United States of America as a government of the people, by the people, for the people; whose just powers are derived from the consent of the governed; a democracy in a Republic; a sovereign Nation of many sovereign States; a perfect Union, one and inseparable; established upon those principles of freedom, equality, justice, and humanity for which American patriots sacrificed their lives and fortunes. I therefore believe it is my duty to my country to love it; to support its Constitution; to obey its laws; to respect its flag; and to defend it against all enemies."

American Ideals

Our constitutional democracy is based on the principle of majority rule. In the United States, all citizens over the age of eighteen have the right to vote. By voting in elections, citizens make choices for all the people in their communities, states, and nation. However, all people in the United States, even those who do not agree with the majority, have certain rights. The Constitution protects the rights of those in the minority, and the majority cannot take away their rights. This principle helps to safeguard the liberty of individual Americans.

Because government's powers come from the people, laws must be applied equally to all people, and government cannot limit the right of people to share their ideas or opinions. However, citizens also have responsibilities to government. They must respect the rule of law, and if they choose to work for change, they must do so in lawful ways. They must also help preserve the Constitution.

These principles are at the heart of the American **creed**. This system of beliefs calls on citizens to protect the rights of individuals, to respect the rule of law, and to uphold the Constitution. United States history can be seen as an attempt to put these **ideals**, or goals, into practice.

READING CHECK **DRAW CONCLUSIONS**
What could happen if the Constitution did not protect minority rights?

Expressing Ideals

Americans express their ideals in a number of ways. In many schools across the nation, students say the Pledge of Allegiance, which was originally written in 1892. A pledge is a promise, and students are promising their allegiance, or loyalty, to the nation, which is represented by the flag. **Mary Pickersgill**, a flagmaker in Baltimore, sewed the flag that inspired our national anthem.

The flag is one of several important national symbols. Symbols are images that represent something else. The bald eagle, the national bird, is a symbol of strength. The Liberty Bell, in Philadelphia, and the Statue of Liberty, in New York Harbor, are symbols of freedom. These symbols have become part of the nation's identity, and they represent important American ideals.

Americans also sing songs that express their ideals. "The Star-Spangled Banner" is the national anthem. An anthem is a song of **patriotism**, or love of one's country. "The Star-Spangled Banner" tells the true story of the flag that flew at Fort McHenry, in Baltimore, during the War of 1812. The poem's writer, **Francis Scott Key**, watched the battle. Fearful that the British had won and taken down the American flag, he wrote these stirring lines:

> **"Oh, say, does that star-spangled banner yet wave**
> **O'er the land of the free and the home of the brave?"**

Children IN HISTORY

Caroline Pickersgill

In 1813, the Pickersgill family of Baltimore took on an unusual sewing project. The commander of Fort McHenry wanted the family to make the largest American flag ever flown.

Thirteen-year-old Caroline Pickersgill helped her mother Mary make the flag. They worked steadily for six weeks. The finished flag was 42 feet wide and 30 feet tall. Each star measured 2 feet across.

A year later, the British attacked Fort McHenry. After 25 hours of cannon fire, the Pickersgills' star-spangled banner still flew over the fort. Francis Scott Key told the story of that flag in what became our national anthem.

Make It Relevant **What are some examples of patriotic symbols in your school?**

Another patriotic song, "America the Beautiful" by **Katharine Lee Bates**, is a hymn. A hymn is a song of praise. "America the Beautiful" praises the country's physical beauty and its history. Like the national symbols, these songs encourage love of country and national unity.

READING CHECK **DRAW CONCLUSIONS**
What feelings does the national anthem express?

In the United States, fireworks are often used to celebrate the Fourth of July.

Summary

Several basic political ideals have shaped American democracy. The American creed is based on ideals that are found in the Constitution. Americans express the nation's ideals through the Pledge of Allegiance and songs such as the national anthem.

REVIEW

1. What are the ideals that make up the American creed?
2. Use the term **ideal** in a sentence about individual freedom.
3. What song became the national anthem?

CRITICAL THINKING

4. SKILL What caused Francis Scott Key to write "The Star-Spangled Banner?"
5. SKILL Why do you think national symbols continue to be important to people today?
6. **Write a Poem or Song** Write a poem or song that expresses an American ideal by telling about an event you have studied in American history.
7. **DRAW CONCLUSIONS**
On a separate sheet of paper, copy and complete the graphic organizer below.

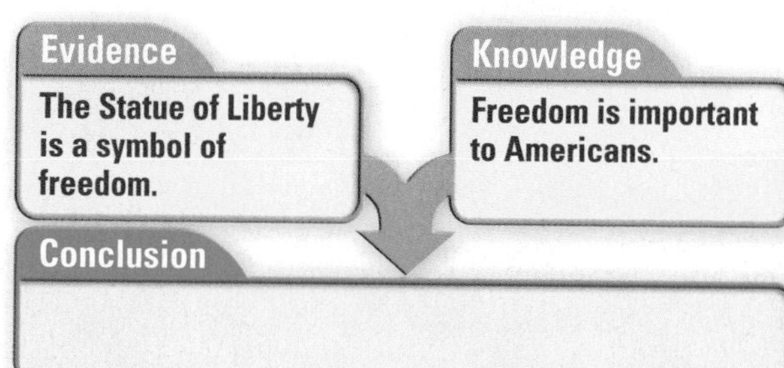

Read an Editorial Cartoon

WHY IT MATTERS

Cartoons that express opinions about politics or about the government are called editorial cartoons. Editorial cartoons have appeared in magazines and newspapers since the late 1700s. These cartoons are examples of the free expression of ideas and opinions that is protected by the First Amendment to the Constitution.

Editorial cartoons sometimes contain symbols. Some symbols used again and again by cartoonists have come to represent the same thing. For example, the Statue of Liberty stands for freedom, and a dove means peace. Uncle Sam—an older, bearded man wearing stars and stripes—represents the United States. The donkey is the symbol for the Democratic party, while the elephant is the symbol for the Republican party.

Most editorial cartoonists have strong opinions, and their cartoons can be critical. Often they are also amusing. Studying editorial cartoons can help you understand different points of view about current events and historical events.

The donkey (left) is the symbol of the Democratic party, and the elephant (right) is the symbol of the Republican party.

In this cartoon, President George W. Bush walks a tightrope while trying to balance the Democratic donkey and the Republican elephant.

WHAT YOU NEED TO KNOW

You can use the following steps to help you interpret, or explain, editorial cartoons.

Step 1 **Identify the symbols and characters in the cartoon.**

Step 2 **Read any captions or labels.**

Step 3 **Determine the issue or event described in the cartoon.**

Step 4 **Decide what the cartoonist is trying to say in the cartoon.**

Uncle Sam is a symbol of the United States.

PRACTICE THE SKILL

Look at the cartoon on this page, and then answer the following questions.

1. What does the cartoon suggest about the office of the President?
2. Why would the President have to balance these two forces?

APPLY WHAT YOU LEARNED

Make It Relevant Draw an editorial cartoon that shows your opinion about a freedom that you enjoy. For example, this could be an activity that you enjoy with friends or family, a holiday, or an important event.

PRIMARY SOURCES

Patriotic Artifacts

Patriotic artifacts come in many different shapes and forms. One way that Americans have long shown their patriotism is by honoring the United States flag. The first United States flag was designed in 1777. It had 13 stars and 13 strips symbolizing the original 13 states. The colors on the flag are also symbolic. Red stands for bravery, white stands for purity, and blue stands for justice. Over the years, the flag has appeared on posters, clothes, and even toys.

No one is sure who made the first United States flag, but many early flagmakers were women.

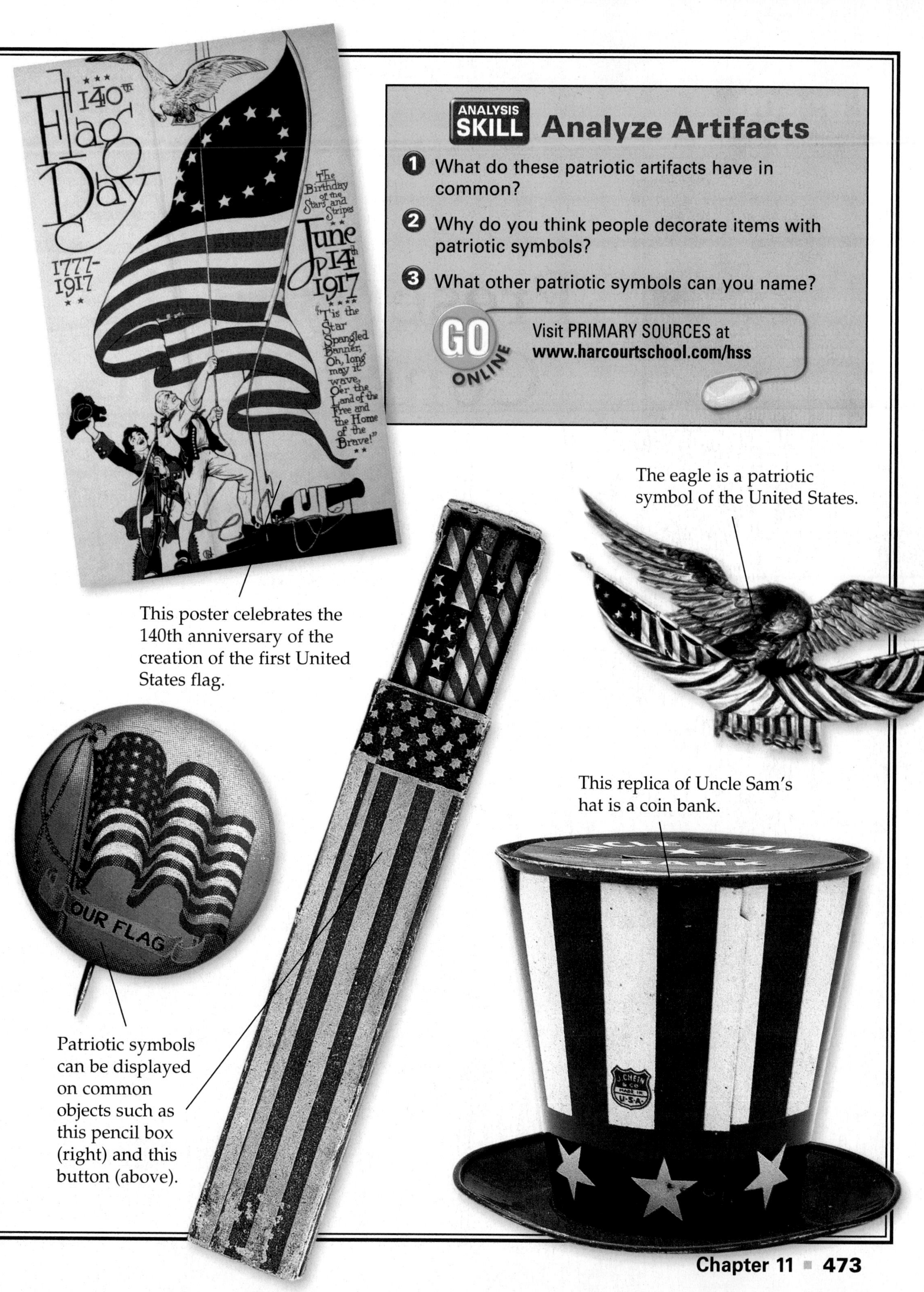

ANALYSIS SKILL Analyze Artifacts

1. What do these patriotic artifacts have in common?
2. Why do you think people decorate items with patriotic symbols?
3. What other patriotic symbols can you name?

GO ONLINE Visit PRIMARY SOURCES at **www.harcourtschool.com/hss**

This poster celebrates the 140th anniversary of the creation of the first United States flag.

The eagle is a patriotic symbol of the United States.

This replica of Uncle Sam's hat is a coin bank.

Patriotic symbols can be displayed on common objects such as this pencil box (right) and this button (above).

Lesson 3

Time

1780		PRESENT
1964 The Civil Rights Act is passed	**1965** The Voting Rights Act is passed	**1990** The Americans with Disabilities Act is passed

WHAT TO KNOW
Why is it important for citizens to preserve the Constitution?

- ✓ Explain how citizens and government leaders work to preserve the Constitution.
- ✓ Tell how individuals have used the Constitution to safeguard the liberty of individual Americans.

VOCABULARY
naturalization p. 475
civil rights p. 476

PEOPLE
Martin Luther King, Jr.
Cesar Chavez
Justin Dart
Earl Warren

DRAW CONCLUSIONS

California Standards
HSS 5.7, 5.7.4, 5.7.5

Preserving the Constitution

YOU ARE THERE You're standing on the balcony of Federal Hall in New York City on April 30, 1789. George Washington is taking the oath of office as the first President of the United States. You hear Washington say, "I will . . . to the best of my ability, preserve, protect, and defend the Constitution of the United States." You wonder if future Americans will meet the challenge of preserving, protecting, and defending the Constitution.

George Washington takes the oath of office.

Each year, thousands of immigrants are sworn in as United States citizens.

FAST FACT

In 2003, almost 706,000 immigrants became citizens of the United States. Nearly one of every five immigrants planned to settle in New York City or Los Angeles.

Supporting the Constitution

Americans elected to office, such as members of the House of Representatives and the Senate, take an oath to preserve the Constitution. Like the President, they are expected to uphold its ideals.

Others who take an oath to defend the Constitution are immigrants who are becoming citizens. These immigrants must go through **naturalization**, which is the process of becoming a legal citizen of the United States. To apply for citizenship, an immigrant must be at least 18 years old. He or she must also have lived in the United States for at least five years, or three years if married to a United States citizen.

Persons applying for citizenship must also pass a test on United States government and history. They must be able to write and speak English. Those who pass these tests must take an oath promising their allegiance to the United States. Part of the oath says, "I will support and defend the Constitution of the United States of America against all enemies, foreign and domestic."*

Meeting the challenge of upholding the Constitution has sometimes meant adding amendments. Since the Constitution was written, 27 amendments have been added to it. Many of these amendments have helped bring equal rights to different groups.

READING CHECK **DRAW CONCLUSIONS**
Why do you think elected officials must take an oath to preserve the Constitution?

*Oath of Allegiance to the United States of America.

EXPANDING CIVIL RIGHTS IN AMERICA
1865-1954

The Thirteenth Amendment outlaws slavery

The Fourteenth Amendment grants voting rights to African American men

Rights for Everyone

Voting is just one of the rights guaranteed to citizens of the United States. However, some groups of people in the United States did not always share in those rights. For many years, African Americans, American Indians, Asian Americans, Hispanic Americans, and others were denied those rights.

Members of these groups often did not get the same freedoms or opportunities as other Americans. They could not get certain jobs or live in certain areas. Their children often had to go to schools that were not as good as the schools that most other American children attended.

In the 1950s, many people worked to end these unfair ways. Their work became known as the Civil Rights movement. **Civil rights** are the rights of citizens to equal treatment under the law.

One of the movement's leaders was **Martin Luther King, Jr.,** an African American minister from Georgia. He encouraged African Americans to use nonviolent ways to gain their civil rights. Over many years, he and millions of other people took part in marches and protests to show their support for civil rights.

In 1963, King and other civil rights leaders organized a march in Washington, D.C. More than 250,000 people took part. In a speech there, King told of his hopes for equality. He said,

> **"I have a dream that my four little children will one day live in a nation where they will not be judged by the color of their skin, but by the content of their character."***

*Martin Luther King, Jr. *A Testament of Hope: The Essential Writings and Speeches of Martin Luther King, Jr.*, edited by James M. Washington. Harper Collins, 1991.

EXPANDING CIVIL RIGHTS IN AMERICA
1955–PRESENT

The Civil Rights Act of 1964 is passed

The Voting Rights Act of 1965 is passed

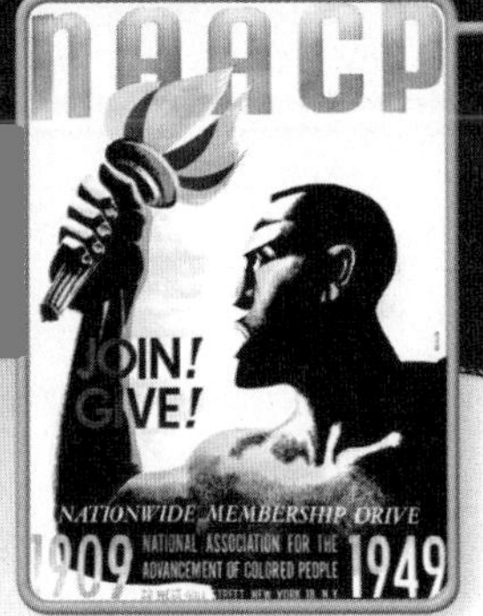

The National Association for the Advancement of Colored People (NAACP) is founded

Amendment grants women the right to vote

Education outlaws school segregation

About a year after the march in Washington, Congress passed the Civil Rights Act of 1964. This law states that all Americans have the right to use public places and services. It also says that employers cannot refuse to hire people because of their race, religion, national origin, or gender. The next year, Congress passed the Voting Rights Act. This law helps make sure that all Americans can vote in elections.

Following the lead of the African American Civil Rights movement, other groups also worked for equal rights. Native Americans formed the American Indian Movement (AIM) to work for their rights.

To improve the lives of migrant farmworkers, **Cesar Chavez** helped form a group that later became the United Farm Workers (UFW). This group helps get better wages and working conditions for farmworkers, many of whom are Mexican Americans.

By the 1960s, many women had jobs outside the home, but they often earned less than men who had the same kinds of jobs. As other groups had, women began to work together for equal rights. New laws were passed that said employers must treat men and women equally.

Other people, such as **Justin Dart**, worked hard to get the Americans with Disabilities Act (ADA) passed in 1990. This law says that Americans with disabilities must be given the same rights and opportunities as other citizens.

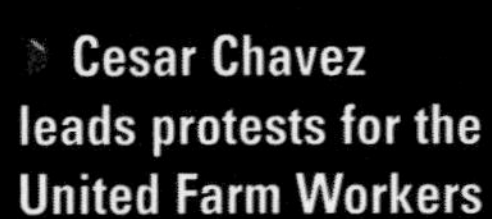

Cesar Chavez leads protests for the United Farm Workers

The American Indian Movement is founded

The Americans with Disabilities Act is passed

1966

1968

1990

The Constitution is kept at the National Archives Building in Washington, D.C.

As society grows and changes, the work of preserving the Constitution continues. **Earl Warren**, former chief justice of the United States, said that the Supreme Court has the duty "to apply to ever changing conditions the never changing principles of freedom."*

READING CHECK **DRAW CONCLUSIONS**
How can individuals preserve the ideals of the Constitution?

*Earl Warren. *The Bill of Rights: How We Got It And What It Means* by Milton Meltzer. Thomas Crowell, 1990.

Summary

Throughout the history of the United States, citizens have had to work to preserve the Constitution. Through amendments and other laws, the ideals of freedom and equality have been extended to more Americans. These changes were made by citizens working together for equal treatment under the law.

REVIEW

1. Why is it important for citizens to preserve the Constitution?
2. Use the term **civil rights** to describe the work of Cesar Chavez.
3. What did Martin Luther King, Jr., do to help preserve the ideals set forth in the Constitution?

CRITICAL THINKING

4. ANALYSIS SKILL What were some of the effects of the Civil Rights movement?
5. ANALYSIS SKILL Put these events in order from first to last: the Americans with Disabilities Act is passed, the NAACP is founded, the United Farm Workers is founded.
6. **Write a Letter** Write a letter to your representative in Congress, identifying a problem and possible solutions to it. Be sure your solutions are based on principles that uphold the Constitution.
7. Focus Skill **DRAW CONCLUSIONS**
On a separate sheet of paper, copy and complete the graphic organizer below.

Evidence	Knowledge
Amendments were added to protect individual rights.	**Not every American had equal rights in the past.**

Conclusion

Martin Luther King, Jr.

*"I have a dream that one day this nation will rise up and live out the true meaning of its creed: 'We hold these truths to be self-evident, that all men are created equal.'"**

Biography

Trustworthiness
Respect
Responsibility
Fairness
Caring
Patriotism

Why Character Counts

How did King's actions show how much he cared for his fellow human beings?

Growing up, Martin Luther King, Jr., saw that African Americans did not have the same rights as other Americans. King wanted to make the United States a nation where all people were treated equally. He spent much of his life trying to achieve his dream of equality.

250,000 people attended the March on Washington.

King was born in Atlanta, Georgia, in 1929. His father was a minister, and he also became a minister. While at college, King developed strong public-speaking skills.

He put those skills to work as a minister in Montgomery, Alabama. In 1955, King led a bus boycott that helped African Americans win equal treatment on the city's buses. His success brought him national fame. Afterward, he organized peaceful protests throughout the South in support of equal rights. In 1964, King won the Nobel Peace Prize for his work.

*Martin Luther King, Jr., August 1963. *In Our Own Words*, edited by R. Torricelli and A. Caroll. Kodansha International, 1999.

Bio Brief

1929 — Born 1929

1968 — Died 1968

1955 Leads the successful Montgomery bus boycott

1963 Leads the March on Washington, where he gives his "I Have a Dream" speech

GO ONLINE

Interactive Multimedia Biographies
Visit MULTIMEDIA BIOGRAPHIES at www.harcourtschool.com/hss

Act as a Responsible Citizen

WHY IT MATTERS

Citizens have many rights, and with those rights come many responsibilities to their country, state, and community. With the right to vote, for example, comes the responsibility to vote. Responsible citizens are aware of what is happening in their community. When they see a problem, they take action to help solve it.

WHAT YOU NEED TO KNOW

You read how Cesar Chavez acted as a responsible citizen when he helped organize the United Farm Workers to improve wages and working conditions for farmworkers. Acting responsibly is an important part of being an active citizen, but acting as a responsible citizen requires some special thought. Here are some steps that you can follow to help you act responsibly.

Step 1 Identify a problem around you.

Step 2 Learn about the problem, and think of ways to solve it.

The word *huelga* means "strike" in Spanish.

In 1965, Cesar Chavez and the United Farm Workers led a boycott against grapes, forcing grape growers to give the workers more pay.

Step 3 **Decide what you can do to help, either on your own or with other people.**

Step 4 **Take action, but always look for safe solutions. If you cannot solve the problem yourself, get help from others, such as your family, a police officer, or a community official.**

Step 5 **Review your actions to see if the results are what you expected.**

PRACTICE THE SKILL

Answer these questions.

1. What problem did Cesar Chavez see?
2. What actions did he take to solve the problem?
3. How did Cesar Chavez get help from other people?

APPLY WHAT YOU LEARNED

Make It Relevant Use the steps on this page to decide on ways you might act as a responsible citizen of your school or community.

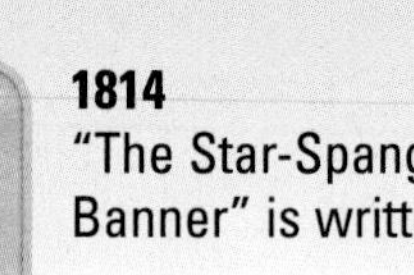

1814
"The Star-Spangled Banner" is written

Reading Social Studies

When you **draw conclusions,** you combine facts that you read with facts that you know to understand ideas that are not stated.

Draw Conclusions

Complete this graphic organizer to show that you can draw a conclusion about how people have worked to preserve American ideals. A copy of this graphic organizer appears on page 120 of the Homework and Practice Book.

Working for Equality

Evidence
In 1963, more than 250,000 people marched for civil rights.

Knowledge
Calling attention to injustice often helps bring change.

Conclusion

California Writing Prompts

Write a Research Report Choose one of the patriotic symbols described in this chapter. Research facts and details about it. Then write a report that explains why the symbol is important to Americans today.

Write a Persuasive Speech Choose one person whom you admire for his or her work to protect the Constitution. Write a speech to persuade your listeners of the importance of this person's work.

1900 | 1950 | PRESENT

1913
The Seventeenth Amendment is passed

1920
The Nineteenth Amendment is passed

1964
The Civil Rights Act is passed

Use Vocabulary

Identify the term that correctly matches each definition.

democracy, p. 458
creed, p. 467
patriotism, p. 468
naturalization, p. 475
civil rights, p. 476

1. the process of becoming a citizen
2. love of country
3. a government system in which the people rule
4. the rights of citizens to equal treatment under the law
5. a system of beliefs

Use the Time Line

Use the chapter summary time line above to answer these questions.

6. In what century were the Seventeenth and Nineteenth Amendments passed?
7. When was "The Star-Spangled Banner" written?

Apply Skills

Read a Population Map

8. Study the map on page 465. Which city had the higher population density, Pittsburgh or Albany?
9. What was the population density of Nashville?

Recall Facts

Answer these questions.

10. How can the President limit the power of Congress?
11. What are two important ideals of the American creed?
12. What story do the words of "The Star-Spangled Banner" tell?

Write the letter of the best choice.

13. Which of the following is a power shared by state governments and the federal government?
    A collecting taxes
    B making immigration laws
    C printing money
    D declaring war
14. Which of the following is NOT a symbol of the United States?
    A the Statue of Liberty
    B the bald eagle
    C the maple leaf
    D the Liberty Bell

Think Critically

15. ANALYSIS SKILL Explain the effects of the Twenty-second Amendment on the Executive Branch.
16. ANALYSIS SKILL In time order from earliest to most recent, list three groups that have worked for equal rights.

The National Constitution Center

GET READY

Where can you be sworn in as President of the United States, enter a voting booth and vote for your favorite President, or take the seat of a Supreme Court justice? You can do all these things at the National Constitution Center in Philadelphia. Opened in July 2003, the Center is dedicated to preserving the history of the United States Constitution. Visitors to the Center's museum can see a film about the Constitution and enjoy more than 100 interactive exhibits that show the importance of the Constitution in American life. The Center also encourages visitors to take an active role as citizens. It offers computers that visitors can use to e-mail elected officials and a viewing area where large screens and a news ticker display today's constitutional news.

LOCATE IT

WHAT TO SEE

At the American National Tree, visitors can learn about 100 Americans whose lives illustrate the principles in the Constitution.

In the 350-seat, star-shaped theater, an actor and a film explain the major themes of the Constitution from 1787 to the present day.

In Signers Hall, visitors can walk around 42 life-size bronze statues. They represent the 39 delegates who signed the Constitution and the 3 who refused.

A VIRTUAL TOUR

GO ONLINE

Visit VIRTUAL TOURS at **www.harcourtschool.com/hss**

Review

THE BIG IDEA

Government and Leadership The United States Constitution is the foundation of the American republic.

Summary

Governing the Nation

The Articles of Confederation set up the United States' first national government. After a few years, though, many of the nation's leaders agreed that this government was not strong enough. Leaders gathered at a convention to improve the Articles. Then they decided to replace them instead.

The delegates faced conflicts, which they resolved through compromise. Finally, they agreed on a plan of government, described in the Constitution. It established the three branches of the federal government—the executive, the legislative, and the judicial branches. Checks and balances kept any one branch from having too much power. All 13 states ratified the Constitution.

In 1791, the Bill of Rights was added. These first ten amendments guaranteed certain rights and freedoms for American citizens. Over the years, more amendments have been added to the Constitution. They help ensure that all Americans enjoy the rights provided in the Constitution.

Americans today express the ideals found in the Constitution in many ways, such as by saying the Pledge of Allegiance and by singing the national anthem.

Main Ideas and Vocabulary

Read the summary above. Then answer the questions that follow.

1. What is a convention?
- **A** a plan of government
- **B** a disagreement
- **C** an important meeting
- **D** a change

2. What is the purpose of checks and balances?
- **A** to keep one branch of the government from having too much power
- **B** to keep states from printing money
- **C** to make sure leaders never compromise
- **D** to stop the states from going to war

3. What does ratified mean?
- **A** attended
- **B** approved
- **C** wrote
- **D** vetoed

4. What is the Bill of Rights?
- **A** the introduction to the Constitution
- **B** a list of judges' responsibilities
- **C** part of the Articles of Confederation
- **D** the first ten amendments to the Constitution

Recall Facts

Answer these questions.

5. Under the Articles of Confederation, how were national laws passed?
6. What were two important conflicts at the Constitutional Convention?
7. What idea was called the Great Compromise?
8. What are two responsibilities that American citizens have to the government?
9. In the federal system of government, what two authorities share power?

Write the letter of the best choice.

10. Which leader wanted to keep the Articles of Confederation?
    A George Washington
    B James Madison
    C Patrick Henry
    D Benjamin Franklin
11. Where does a constitutional democracy get its power?
    A from the President
    B from Congress
    C from laws
    D from the people
12. Which power is shared by the national and state governments?
    A print and coin money
    B collect taxes
    C declare war and make peace
    D make treaties with other countries
13. Which of the following is an important American political principle?
    A majority rule
    B limited freedom
    C judicial veto
    D unlimited government

Think Critically

14. ANALYSIS SKILL Summarize Shays's Rebellion and explain the problems that led to it.
15. ANALYSIS SKILL If a meeting such as the Constitutional Convention was held today, do you think it should be kept secret?

Apply Skills

Read a Population Density Map

ANALYSIS SKILL Use the population density map below to answer the following questions.

16. What color is used to show a population density of 2–6 people per square mile?
17. Which part of Virginia had the lowest population density in 1790?
18. Which part of Virginia had the highest population density in 1790?

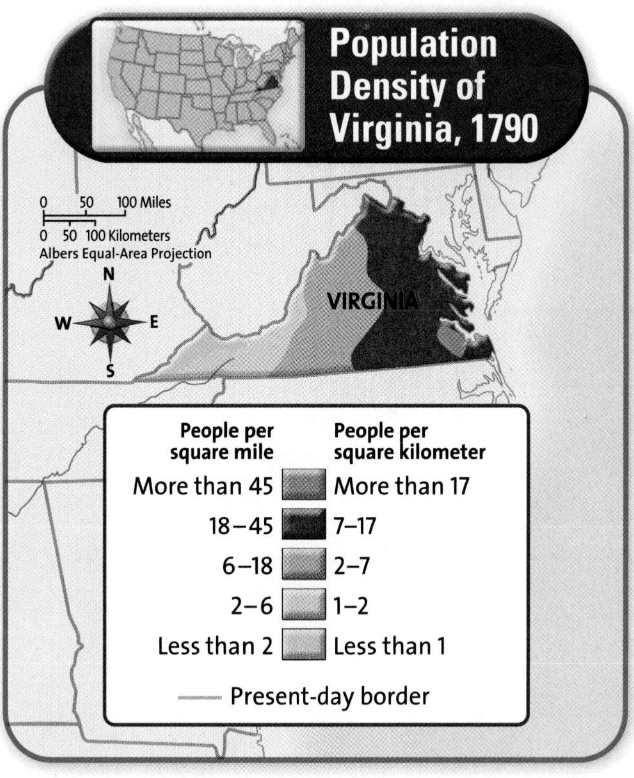

Unit 5

Activities

Read More

■ *The Star-Spangled Banner* by Lisa deMauro.

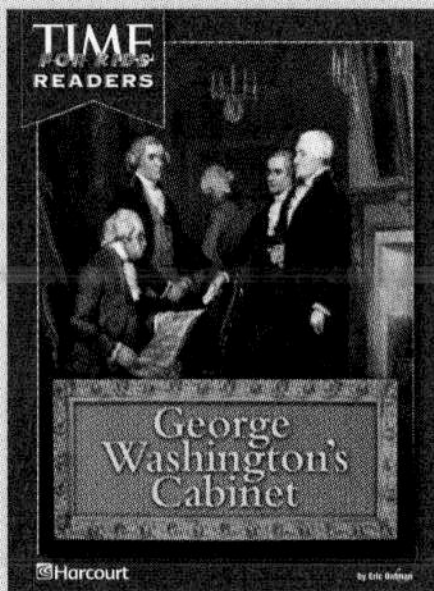

■ *George Washington's Cabinet* by Eric Oatman.

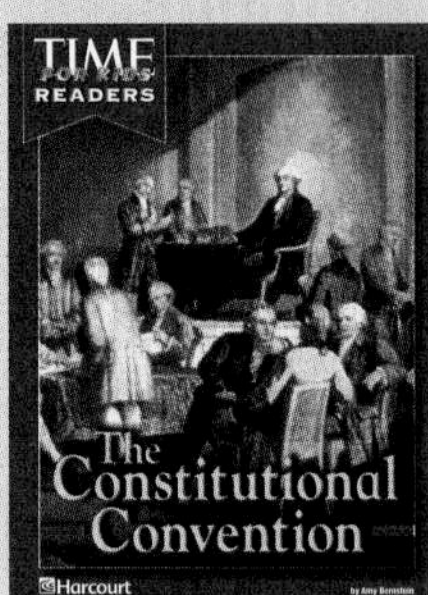

■ *The Constitutional Convention* by Amy Bernstein.

Show What You Know

Unit Writing Activity

Write a Persuasive Letter Imagine that you are writing to a student in another country. The student has asked you why the Constitution is an important document to the people of the United States. Write a persuasive letter to convince him or her of the Constitution's significance and how it is the foundation of the American republic. Clearly state your position, and provide evidence to support it.

Unit Project

A Constitutional Hall of Fame Plan a Hall of Fame to honor the United States Constitution. Choose important people, events, and ideas that you want to highlight in your Hall of Fame. Then show these different topics through posters, displays, poems, and narratives.

GO ONLINE Visit ACTIVITIES at **www.harcourtschool.com/hss**

Western Expansion

START WITH THE STANDARDS

California History-Social Science Standards

5.3 Students describe the cooperation and conflict that existed among the American Indians and between the Indian nations and the new settlers.

5.8 Students trace the colonization, immigration, and settlement patterns of the American people from 1789 to the mid-1800s, with emphasis on the role of economic incentives, effects of the physical and political geography, and transportation systems.

The Big Idea

Growth and Change

The United States expanded as its population and economy grew and as new lands were acquired.

WHAT TO KNOW

- ✓ How did immigration impact the early United States?
- ✓ How did geography and transportation affect western settlement?
- ✓ How did western settlement affect American Indian groups?
- ✓ What kind of changes did the United States face in the early 1800s?

Show What You Know

★ Unit 6 Test

Writing: A Narrative

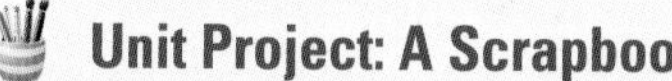

Unit Project: A Scrapbook

Unit 6

Time

Western Expansion

1803 The United States makes the Louisiana Purchase, p. 515

1811 Work begins on the National Road, p. 503

1825 The Erie Canal opens, p. 504

1800

1810

1820

Western Expansion

1846 The Mexican-American War begins, p. 560

1848 Gold is discovered in California, p. 562

1850 California becomes a state, p. 564

1830

1840

1850

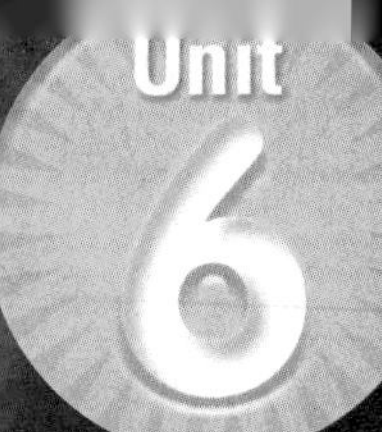

Miguel Hidalgo y Costilla

1753–1811

- Catholic priest who helped begin the Mexican Revolution
- Worked to end slavery in Mexico

Andrew Jackson

1767–1845

- General in the United States Army
- Served as the seventh President of the United States

People

1750 | 1810 | 1840

- 1753 • Miguel Hidalgo y Costilla 1811
- 1767 • Andrew Jackson 1845
- 1774 • Meriwether Lewis 1809
- 1786? • Sacagawea 1812?
- 1790 • Chief John Ross
- 1813 • John C. Frémont
- 1820? • Harriet Tubman
- 1828 • Yung Wing

John Ross

1790–1866

- Chief of the Cherokee Nation
- Led the Cherokees on the journey known as the "Trail of Tears"

John C. Frémont

1813–1890

- Western explorer known as the Great Pathfinder
- Elected as one of California's first United States senators

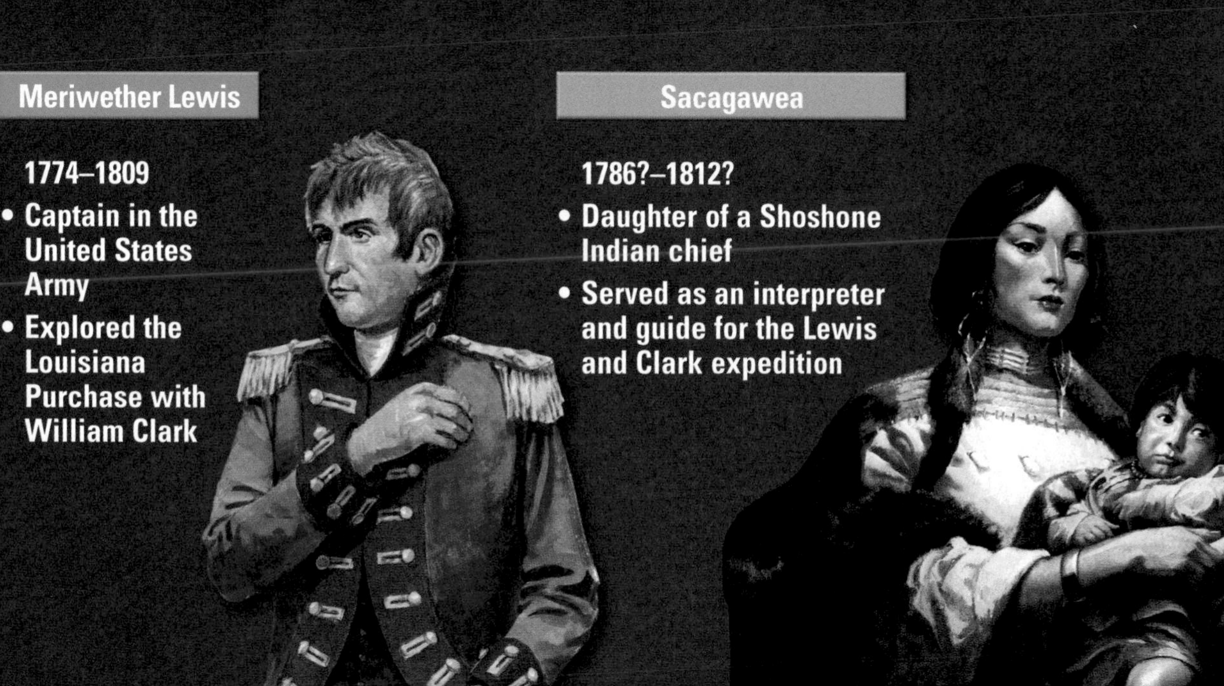

Meriwether Lewis

1774–1809
- Captain in the United States Army
- Explored the Louisiana Purchase with William Clark

Sacagawea

1786?–1812?
- Daughter of a Shoshone Indian chief
- Served as an interpreter and guide for the Lewis and Clark expedition

1870 1900 1930

1866

1890

1913

1912

Harriet Tubman

1820?–1913
- Led hundreds of enslaved people to freedom along the Underground Railroad
- Leader in the abolitionist movement

Yung Wing

1828–1912
- First Asian immigrant to graduate from an American university
- Helped other Chinese students receive American educations

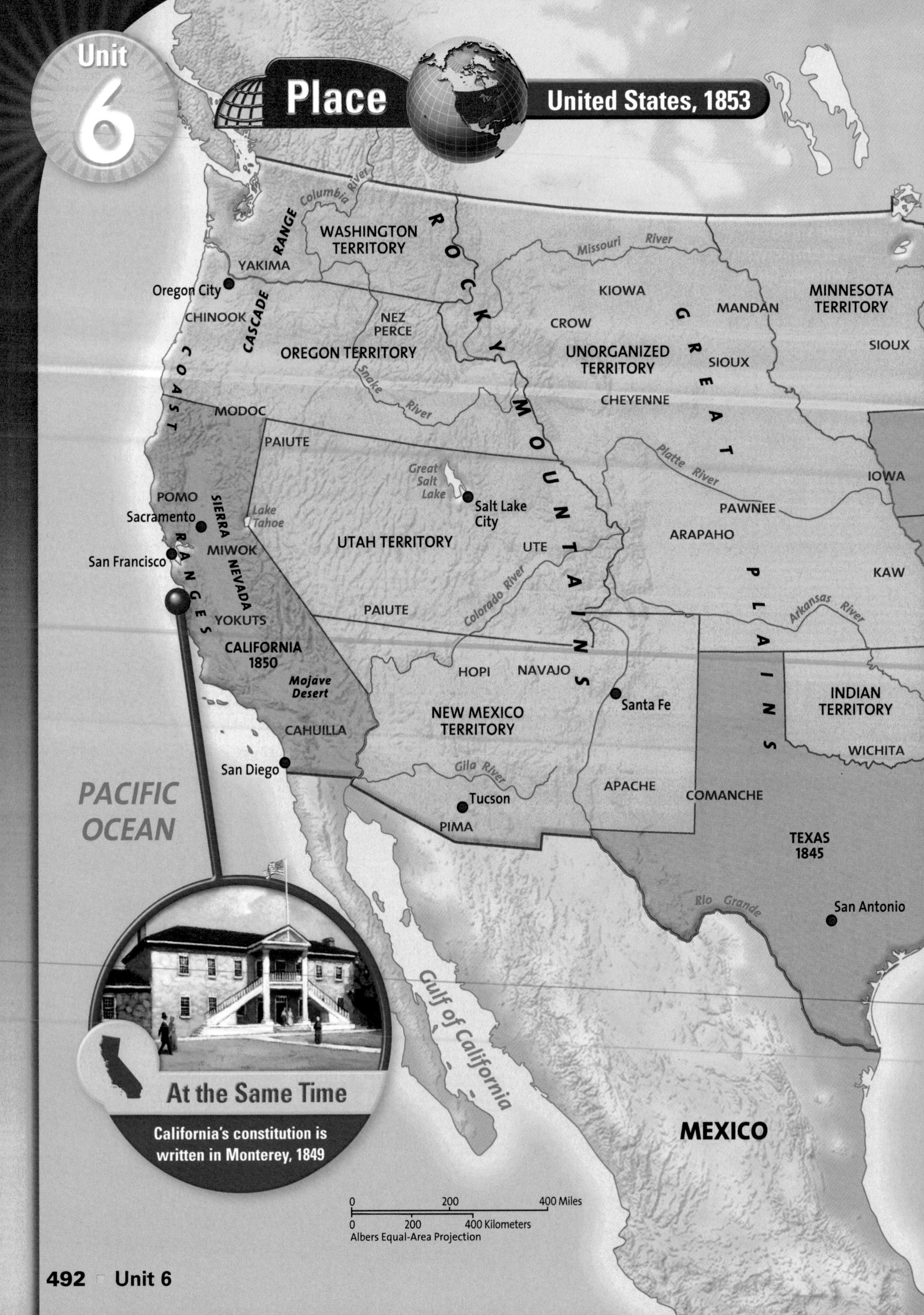
Unit 6
Place
United States, 1853
WASHINGTON TERRITORY
OREGON TERRITORY
UNORGANIZED TERRITORY
MINNESOTA TERRITORY
UTAH TERRITORY
NEW MEXICO TERRITORY
INDIAN TERRITORY
CALIFORNIA 1850
TEXAS 1845
IOWA
MEXICO
PACIFIC OCEAN
Gulf of California
ROCKY MOUNTAINS
GREAT PLAINS
CASCADE RANGE
COAST RANGES
SIERRA NEVADA
Mojave Desert
Columbia River
Snake River
Missouri River
Platte River
Colorado River
Arkansas River
Gila River
Rio Grande
Great Salt Lake
Lake Tahoe
Oregon City
Sacramento
San Francisco
Salt Lake City
Santa Fe
San Diego
Tucson
San Antonio
YAKIMA
CHINOOK
NEZ PERCE
MODOC
PAIUTE
POMO
MIWOK
YOKUTS
CAHUILLA
KIOWA
CROW
MANDAN
SIOUX
CHEYENNE
PAWNEE
ARAPAHO
UTE
KAW
HOPI
NAVAJO
APACHE
COMANCHE
WICHITA
PIMA
0 200 400 Miles
0 200 400 Kilometers
Albers Equal-Area Projection
At the Same Time
California's constitution is written in Monterey, 1849

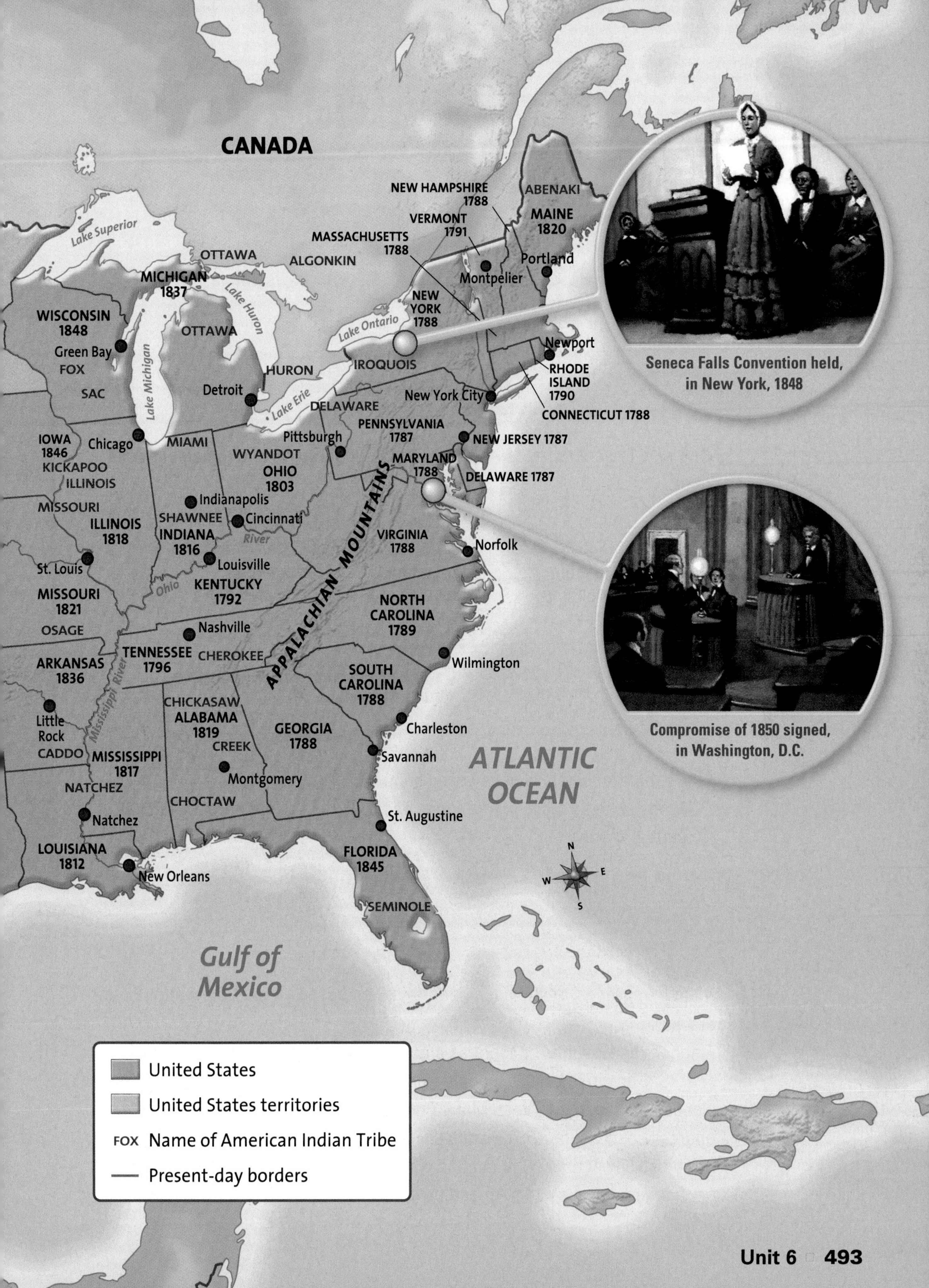

Seneca Falls Convention held, in New York, 1848

Compromise of 1850 signed, in Washington, D.C.

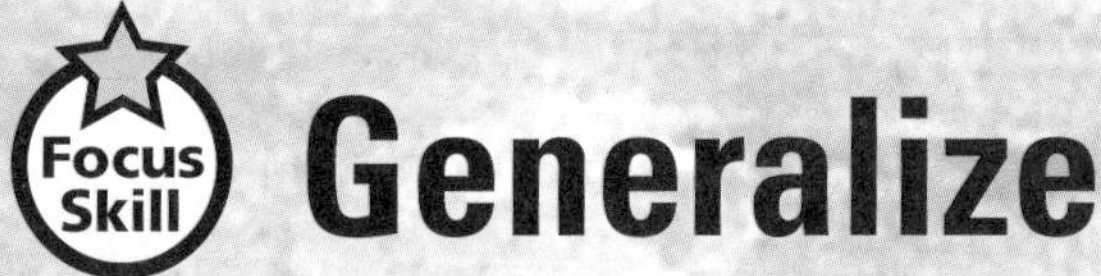

Unit 6 Reading Social Studies

Focus Skill Generalize

When you generalize, you make a statement that shows how a group of facts are related.

Why It Matters

Being able to generalize can help you better understand and remember what you read.

Facts

Information presented in a passage	Information presented in a passage	Information presented in a passage

Generalization

General statement about that information

- ✓ A generalization is always based on facts.
- ✓ Words such as *most, many, some, generally,* and *usually* are clues to generalizations.

Practice the Skill

Read the paragraphs, and make a generalization based on the information in the second paragraph.

"America the Beautiful" describes a country that stretches "from sea to shining sea." Starting in the 1800s, people from many different states began looking for new lands to settle in the West. Many Americans were moving west.

Facts: Congress passed a land ordinance dividing western lands into townships. Each township had 36 sections. One section was for public schools. The rest were sold.

Generalization: (The ordinance was a system for settlement.)

Apply What You Learned

 **Generalize Read the paragraphs, and answer the questions.**

Growing in Many Ways

The new American government counted its citizens for the first time in 1790. From that year on, the United States has taken a census every ten years. The results show how the nation has grown.

In 1790, only about 3 percent of all Americans lived in the biggest cities—Salem, Boston, New York, Philadelphia, Baltimore, and Charleston. Two percent lived in other cities, and 95 percent of Americans lived on farms. The 4 million people in the United States in 1790 included nearly 700,000 African Americans. Most African Americans were enslaved and lived in the South.

The second census was taken in 1800. By that time nearly 1 million settlers lived on the frontier. That was a big change. Tennessee had become a state in 1796, and four years later, it had a population of more than 100,000 people. Kentucky had almost 221,000 people, and it was a state, too.

In 1800, Ohio had more than 45,000 people. It had a larger population than 11 of the original 13 states. Only New York and Pennsylvania had more people than Ohio. Ohio became a state three years after the 1800 census. As the nation grew, people continued to move farther west.

Generalize

1. **What generalization can you make about where most Americans lived in 1790?**
2. **Where did most African Americans live in 1790?**
3. **What generalization can you make about the changes in frontier areas between 1790 and 1800?**

Study Skills

MAKE AN OUTLINE

Making an outline can help you organize the main ideas and details you read about.

- **Topics in an outline are shown by Roman numerals.**
- **Main ideas about each topic are shown by capital letters.**
- **Details about each main idea are shown by numbers.**

The Changing Frontier

I. A Growing Population
  A. A New Wave of Immigrants
    1. New immigrants arrived from England, Scotland, Ireland, and Germany
    2. Immigrants came to escape hardships, for new opportunities, and for freedom
  B. Through the Cumberland Gap
    1.
    2.
  C. Using Waterways
    1.
    2.
II. Pioneer Life

Apply As You Read

As you read this chapter, remember to pay attention to the topics, main ideas, and details. Use that information to complete an outline of the chapter.

California History-Social Science Standards, Grade 5

5.3 Students describe the cooperation and conflict that existed among the American Indians and between the Indian nations and the new settlers.
5.8 Students trace the colonization, immigration, and settlement patterns of the American people from 1789 to the mid-1800s, with emphasis on the role of economic incentives, effects of the physical and political geography, and transportation systems.

CHAPTER 12 The Changing Frontier

Reenactors of the Lewis and Clark expedition, near St. Charles, Missouri

Start with a Story

MY NAME IS YORK

by Elizabeth Van Steenwyk illustrated by Bill Farnsworth

In 1803, York, an enslaved African American, and his owner, William Clark, joined an expedition to explore lands west of the Mississippi River. In time, more than 300 people joined the group, including an American Indian woman named Sacajawea (sa•kuh•juh•WEE•uh) and her husband, Charbonneau (CHAR•buh•noh).

High plains and deep forests challenge us, and our bodies strain against the work we endure to pass through them. Mountains grow higher, gorges deeper, as we search for the westward waterway. We pause to admire a great fall of water that tumbles into white foam below.

Captain Clark explores a deep ravine with Sacajawea and Charbonneau while I wait above to enjoy the warmth of sky and sun.

Suddenly the sky darkens. Angry clouds release a torrent. I find shelter beneath a chalky overhang and then I remember: Captain Clark and the others have not returned.

ravine a small, narrow steep-sided valley

torrent a rushing, violent stream of liquid

I run to the cliff's edge and see their desperate struggle as water rises in the ravine. Sacajawea hands her small son to me. Then I reach out to her and Charbonneau. But where is Captain Clark?

Now he struggles upward too, before I reach out to pull him to safety. When he can speak, he tells me that his compass is lost. Later, he finds it and I wonder: Will that compass one day point my way to freedom?

We cross the Bitterroot Mountains where snow still drifts. Food grows scarce, but we share what we have with the Nez Perce and they with us. Sacajawea digs for wild artichokes, but there are few. We miss the abundance of plump chokecherries and greens that grew near the great falls.

Men, women, and children gather near me to touch my color and I, in turn, touch theirs. We marvel at our sameness. They begin to call me Great Medicine.

We pass through many canyons before arriving at a sagebrush plain. A river begins and we follow its growth along a tumbling course. Through high country it winds as rocks project into its current. Rapids create mighty hazards as we move ever west in tired boats.

Then we overcome a final thrust of mountains and there is the scent of ocean in the air. Soon we stand where water and land unite and rejoice in our success. We have found a waterway to the western sea.

Response Corner

1. How did York prove to be a valuable member of the expedition?
2. Imagine that you are a member of this expedition. Write a journal entry describing an experience that you might have had on the trip.

Lesson 1

1811 The Cumberland Road is started

1825 The Erie Canal opens

WHAT TO KNOW
How did the United States grow during the early 1800s?

- ✓ Explain where many of the people came from who immigrated to the United States from Europe.
- ✓ Describe how and why immigrants traveled into the Ohio and Mississippi Valleys through the Cumberland Gap.

VOCABULARY
pathfinder p. 502
flatboat p. 504
canal p. 504
lock p. 505

PEOPLE
Daniel Boone
Robert Fulton

PLACES
Cumberland Gap
Erie Canal

GENERALIZE

California Standards
HSS 5.8, 5.8.1

A Growing Population

YOU ARE THERE

The winter of 1800 has been hard in Scotland, and all that your family has left to eat are a few potatoes. Outside, the air is cold and damp, and it's not much warmer inside. You miss your older brother, Sean. He left for the United States a year ago, and you haven't heard from him since.

Then your father bursts into the cottage. Waving a letter in the air, he says, "It's from Sean! He says we can join him on his farm in the Ohio Valley!" You can barely feel the cold anymore. Your family is moving to the United States!

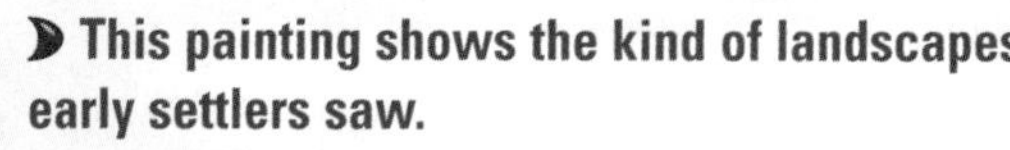

➤ This painting shows the kind of landscapes early settlers saw.

Small rowboats were used to take immigrants to the larger ships that traveled to the United States.

New Waves of Immigrants

In the late 1700s and early 1800s, many new immigrants arrived in the United States. They came mostly from England, Scotland, Ireland, and Germany. Many Scots-Irish immigrants arrived between 1789 and 1850. The Scots-Irish were people from Scotland who had settled in Ireland.

Many immigrants came to the United States to escape hardships. Others came because of economic incentives—the chance to make money. Because land was plentiful, people could buy it fairly cheaply and start their own farms and businesses.

Few other countries in the world offered the freedom and opportunities that were available in the United States. Americans did not have to obey the wishes of a king. They could also choose from many different places to live. Benjamin Franklin once wrote that the United States offered,

> **"... good climate, fertile soil, wholesome air, free governments, wise laws, liberty, a good people to live among, and a hearty welcome."***

To reach the United States, immigrants from Europe boarded ships sailing west. They arrived in Atlantic port cities such as Boston, New York City, and Philadelphia. Many immigrants then moved farther inland to start farms in the Ohio and Mississippi Valleys. Traveling to these areas was not easy. The Appalachian Mountains stood as a barrier to traveling west.

READING CHECK GENERALIZE
What economic incentives brought immigrants to the United States?

*Benjamin Franklin. *Benjamin Franklin: Writings.* Library of America, 1987.

The Wilderness Road

As early as 1775, people wanted to settle in what is now Kentucky. However, the unmarked American Indian trails that led over the Appalachian Mountains were too narrow for wagons. Daniel Boone was hired to build a road. He and about 30 workers cut trees to widen and connect several of the American Indian trails. The Wilderness Road that Boone built made it much easier for settlers to reach Kentucky. By 1792, more than 100,000 people had traveled along the Wilderness Road.

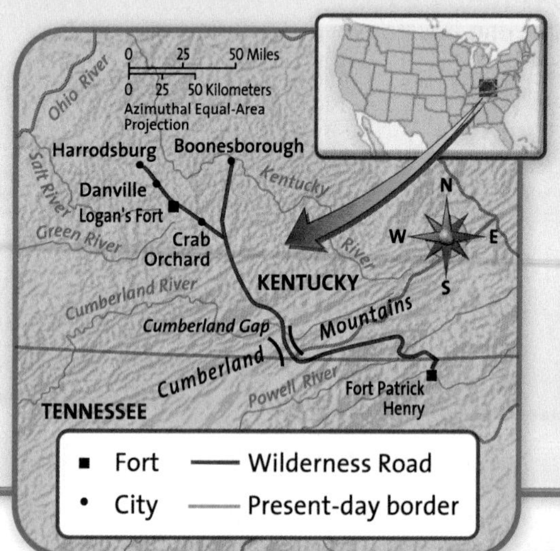

Through the Cumberland Gap

One path to the west led through the **Cumberland Gap**. Located near where present-day Kentucky, Virginia, and Tennessee meet, the path through the Cumberland Gap had long been used by American Indians.

Among the first settlers to use the trail through the Cumberland Gap was a pathfinder named **Daniel Boone**. A **pathfinder** is someone who finds a way through an unfamiliar region. In 1769, Boone explored the land west of the Cumberland Gap, later called Kentucky. Boone was then hired to clear a road into Kentucky. This trail later became known as the Wilderness Road.

As land became more expensive in Virginia and the Carolinas, more people moved west toward the frontier. Traveling along the Wilderness Road was

➤ **Daniel Boone helped many settlers travel through the Cumberland Gap.**

The National Road helped to make mail delivery faster and easier.

not easy, however. There were no places to buy supplies on the early frontier. Settlers had to bring their clothing, furniture, and tools with them. To transport these goods over the Cumberland Gap, people used overland wagons. These large wagons could hold thousands of pounds of belongings. Overland wagons were also strong enough to make the trip on the rough Wilderness Road.

With their wagons loaded, settlers set out over the mountains. Until the late 1700s, Kentucky had few American settlers. One traveler there during the early 1800s wrote, "I often went 10 miles by narrow paths without meeting a house, and nearly lost myself."* Settlers were arriving in increasing numbers, however.

In 1790, about 110,000 settlers were already living on the western side of the Appalachian Mountains. By 1800—just ten years later—that number had grown to more than 385,000. Many of the new settlers built homes along the Ohio River. Some of these new settlements were near American Indian lands.

The need for better transportation grew as the number of settlers grew. In response, the federal government began building roads. Work on the Cumberland Road, also known as the National Road, started in 1811. By 1818, the Cumberland Road connected Maryland to the western side of Virginia. This road was wide enough for wagons. Travelers going farther west often continued their journeys by boat along the Ohio River.

READING CHECK GENERALIZE

How were overland wagons important to settlers?

*C. S. Rafinesque. *A Life of Travels and Researches in North America and South Europe.* F. Turner, 1836.

Using Waterways

Moving goods by horse and wagon was hard, slow work. In the early 1800s, waterways provided an easier way to move people and goods. Large boats and rafts could carry more people and goods than wagons could.

Rivers crossed much of the land. Farmers used these waterways to ship crops to markets on the Atlantic coast. They used **flatboats**, or large floating rafts made of boards that were tied together. Each flatboat was about 40 feet long and could be used in shallow rivers.

Faster methods of traveling along waterways soon took over. In the late 1700s, inventors built boats powered by steam engines. **Robert Fulton** built a steamboat in which a steam engine turned a huge paddle wheel. It could travel upriver at about 5 miles per hour. Steamboats became a common form of transportation for settlers traveling west.

Where no waterways existed, people built canals. A **canal** is a waterway dug across the land to connect bodies of water. The best-known of these, the **Erie Canal**, connected Lake Erie and the Hudson River in New York. When it was finished in 1825, the Erie Canal was 363 miles long.

A Closer Look

The Erie Canal

Many families lived and worked on the boats that moved people and goods up and down the Erie Canal. Each person on the boat had a job. A father might captain a ship, while a mother might cook for the crew. Even the children worked by guiding the mules that towed boats through the canal.

1. **Gates controlled by balance beams**
2. **Watertight gates**
3. **Towing rope**
4. **Canal towpath**

◈ How were boats moved through a lock?

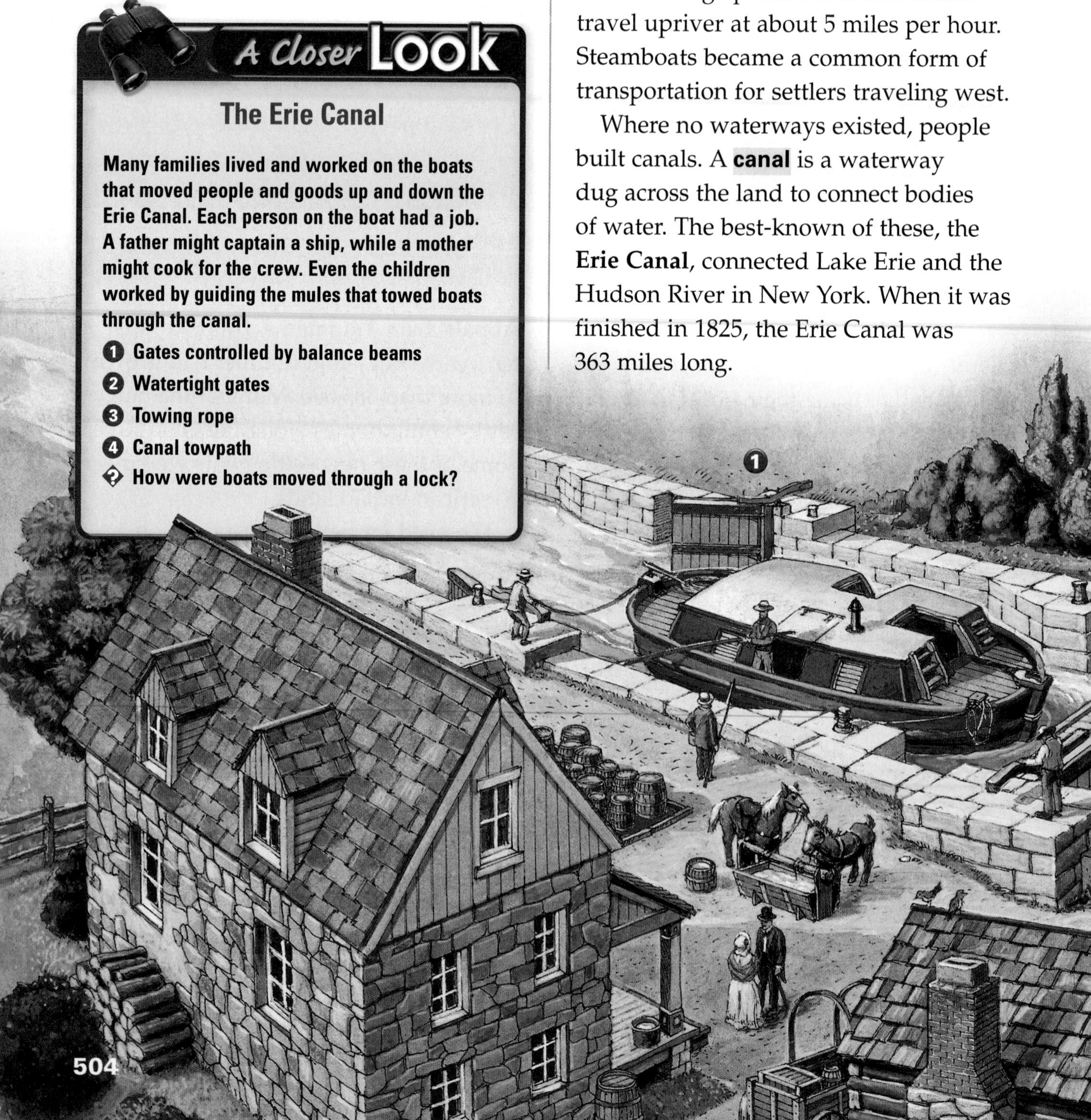

At the point where water levels differed, the canal had **locks**, or sections of water held between gates. A lock is like an elevator for boats. When one gate is opened, water flows in and raises a boat to the level of the water in the next lock. Then the other gate opens, and the boat moves onward. The process is reversed when a boat needs to be lowered.

Before the Erie Canal was built, it took 20 days to ship a ton of goods from Buffalo to New York City. After the canal opened, it took just 8 days. Soon, canals were being built in many different states.

READING CHECK **GENERALIZE**
How did canals change the way settlers could travel to the west?

Summary

In the early 1800s new waves of immigrants came to the United States. Settlers used overland wagons to travel through the Cumberland Gap. Others used flatboats or steamboats to travel on the Ohio and Mississippi Rivers.

REVIEW

1. How did the United States grow during the early 1800s?
2. Write a sentence that includes the terms **lock** and **canal**.
3. How did steamboats change river travel?

CRITICAL THINKING

4. ANALYSIS SKILL Why were economic incentives important to new immigrants?
5. ANALYSIS SKILL Why do you think many new settlers chose to live near the Ohio River?
6. **Write an Advertisement** Imagine that you are a writer during the early 1800s. Write an advertisement encouraging people to settle on the frontier.
7. Focus Skill **GENERALIZE**
On a separate sheet of paper, copy and complete the graphic organizer.

Facts

The Cumberland Gap was cleared to provide a road to Kentucky.	People were soon able to travel west quickly by canal.

Generalization

Compare Graphs

WHY IT MATTERS

Suppose you want to give a presentation on immigration to the United States during the early 1800s. You might want to show a lot of information in a brief, clear way. One way to do this is by using graphs. Knowing how to read and put together graphs will allow you to compare a lot of information at once.

WHAT YOU NEED TO KNOW

Different kinds of graphs illustrate information in different ways. A bar graph uses bars and is useful for quick comparisons. The bar graph on page 507 shows immigration to the United States between 1820 and 1830. A circle graph can also make comparisons. The circle graph on page 507 shows immigration from Britain, Ireland, and Germany in 1820. A line graph shows change over time. The line graph on page 507 shows the population of the United States from 1820 to 1850.

In the early 1800s, most immigrants came to the United States from Britain, Germany, and Ireland.

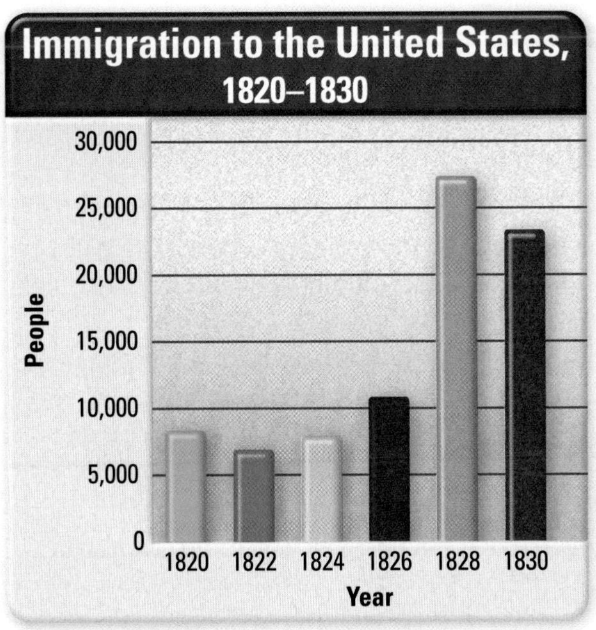

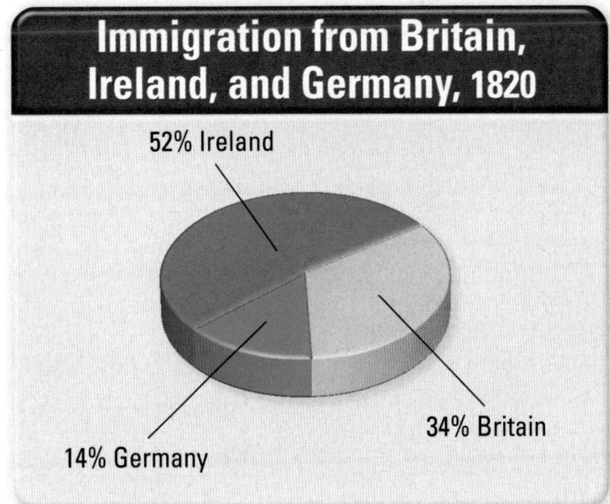

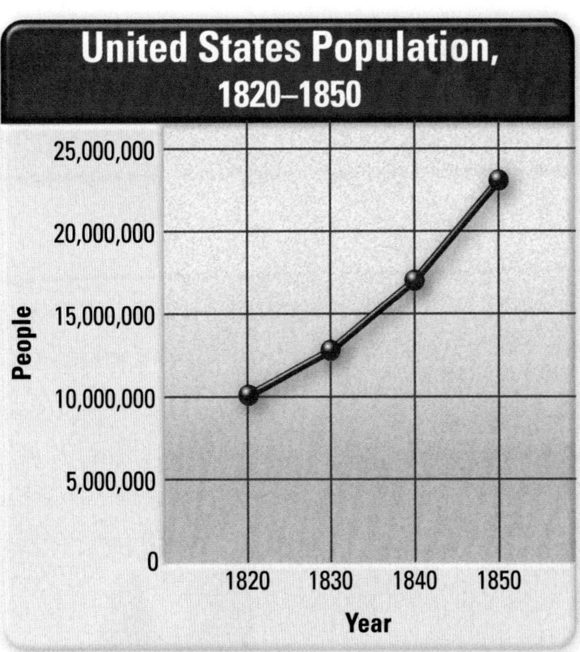

PRACTICE THE SKILL

Compare the information in the bar, circle, and line graphs by answering the following questions. Think about the advantages and disadvantages of each kind of graph.

1. In 1820, did Ireland or Britain have more immigrants arriving in the United States? In which graph did you find the answer?
2. About how many people immigrated to the United States in 1826?
3. Look at the line graph. What happened to the population of the United States over time?
4. Was the number of immigrants in 1828 greater than or less than the number of immigrants in 1830?

APPLY WHAT YOU LEARNED

Use the information in the circle graph to write a paragraph summarizing information about immigration. Share your paragraph with a partner, and compare your summaries.

Lesson 2

1800 | 1825 | 1850

1803 Ohio becomes the seventeenth state

1820 About 145,000 settlers live in Indiana

WHAT TO KNOW
How did pioneers use natural resources to meet their needs?

- Describe how early pioneers met the many challenges of life on the frontier.
- Identify the new states formed as the United States grew.

VOCABULARY
pioneer p. 509
tall tale p. 511

PEOPLE
Abraham Lincoln
Daniel Drake
Mike Fink
John Chapman
Paul Bunyan

PLACES
Vermont
Kentucky
Tennessee
Ohio

GENERALIZE

California Standards
HSS 5.8, 5.8.1, 5.8.3

Pioneer Life

YOU ARE THERE

It's a cold morning on your family's farm near the Ohio River. As your father comes into the cabin with an armful of firewood, you hop up to help him.

"This land is amazing," he says, grinning at you. "And I have some great news for you. There's another family that is building a cabin to the east. I hear they have a son your age." You're about to get neighbors! It's been more than a month since you've seen any children except your older sister.

The first settlers in Orange, Ohio, had very few neighbors.

At the New Salem State Historic Site in Petersburg, Illinois, historical reenactors show what life was like for pioneer families in Illinois.

A Frontier Home

Areas to the west of the Appalachian Mountains were growing fast. In 1800, about 5,000 people lived in the area that is now Indiana. By 1820, about 140,000 more settlers had moved there. Life in the western settlements was often hard, but natural resources were plentiful.

One of the most important natural resources for the **pioneers**, or people who were first to settle a place, was trees. Most early pioneers lived in cabins built of logs from large trees. The logs were fitted into place on top of one another, and any gaps between them were filled with moss or mud. Many early log cabins were no more than 20 feet wide and had only one or two rooms. If a cabin had windows at all, they were small and often covered with greased paper instead of glass. Pioneers burned wood in their fireplaces to heat their homes and to cook their food. The fireplaces also provided light in the evening.

Some pioneers did not even have a cabin. In 1816, Thomas and Nancy Lincoln and their young son, **Abraham Lincoln**, traveled to the Northwest Territory. Instead of living in a cabin, they spent much of the winter in a three-sided shelter of branches and logs. Young Abraham Lincoln, who would one day become President of the United States, lived a hard life on the frontier.

READING CHECK **GENERALIZE**
Why were trees a valuable resource for pioneers?

To iron clothes, women heated irons on wood-burning stoves.

Children IN HISTORY

Daniel Drake

For Daniel Drake, life on the Kentucky farm where he lived was filled with chores. Up before sunrise, Daniel fed horses, cows, and pigs. On washing day, he brought water from the spring and helped scrub the clothes. He was also responsible for tending the fire, watching the younger children, and plowing the fields. However, Daniel did not spend his entire life on the family farm. As an adult, he became a well known doctor on the frontier.

Make It Relevant How were Daniel's chores similar to and different from the kinds of chores children do today?

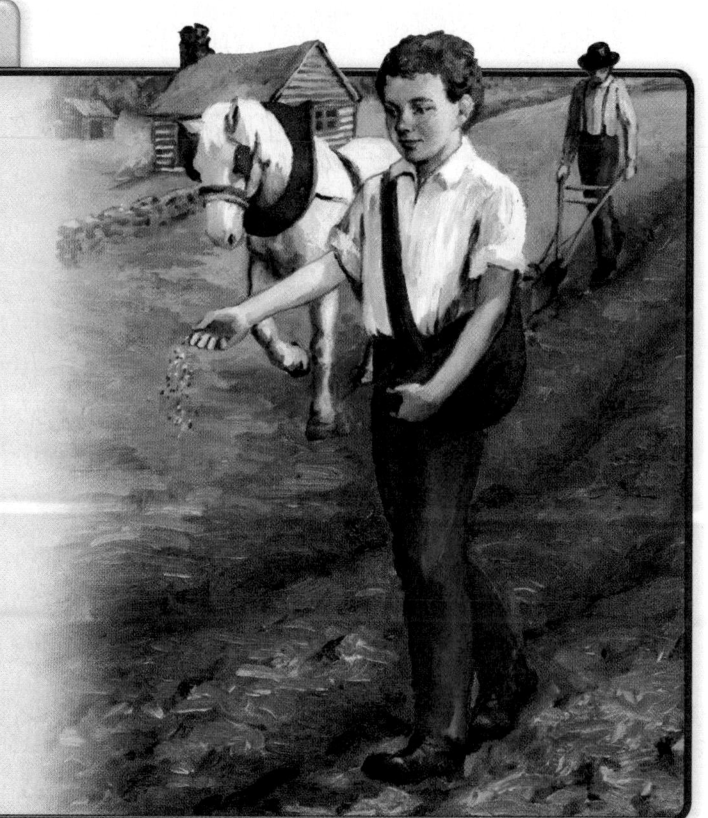

Working Together

On frontier farms, everyone worked hard. Most pioneers woke up before dawn to begin their work. Men and boys took care of the animals and the crops. They used tools such as shovels and rakes that they had made out of wood.

Women and girls also cared for farm animals and did many other chores. One pioneer woman wrote,

> **"... each woman is, at times at least, her own cook, nurse, seamstress and school-ma'am."***

People on the frontier often taught their own children, since schools were not built in an area until enough pioneers lived nearby. Even then, most children attended school for only part of the year.

Most pioneer children had little time for school. They began working at a very young age. **Daniel Drake** lived on a frontier farm in Kentucky. By the time he was 8 years old, Daniel was already helping his father plant crops in the fields.

Pioneer families had to work hard to do everyday chores. For example, washing clothes could take all day. Pioneers made their own laundry soap from ashes and animal fat. Families carried buckets of water from a nearby river or stream, and each piece of clothing had to be scrubbed until it was clean.

READING CHECK SUMMARIZE
Why did many pioneer children attend school only part of the year?

*Mary Clavers. *A New Home—Who'll Follow?* C. S. Francis & Co., 1855.

Legendary Pioneers

People who settled the frontier faced great challenges. Some pioneers became so famous that people made up stories about them. One example was **Mike Fink**, who worked as a sailor on the Mississippi River. Some of the stories about him are **tall tales**, or exaggerated adventure stories. One tall tale says that Fink ran away from home when he was just two days old. Another says that he could wrestle alligators and snapping turtles.

Many tall tales were about people who lived on the frontier. **John Chapman** was one such person. Chapman spent much of his life traveling through Pennsylvania, Ohio, Indiana, and Illinois, planting trees. Stories said he gave apple seeds to all the settlers he met, so he became known as Johnny Appleseed.

Not all tall tales were about real people. People in the Northwest Territory often told stories about a logger named **Paul Bunyan**. One popular song about Paul Bunyan said

> **"He was born up in Wisconsin**
> **And was thirty-five feet tall."***

This story is obviously made up. Nobody is 35 feet tall! But the brave deeds told in Paul Bunyan stories had some truth. Loggers had to be strong because they cut down huge trees.

READING CHECK **GENERALIZE**

In what area of the country did most tall tale figures live?

*Earl Clifton Beck. *Songs of the Michigan Lumberjacks*. University of Michigan Press, 1941.

A tall tale says that the large footsteps of Paul Bunyan and Babe the Blue Ox created Minnesota's 10,000 lakes.

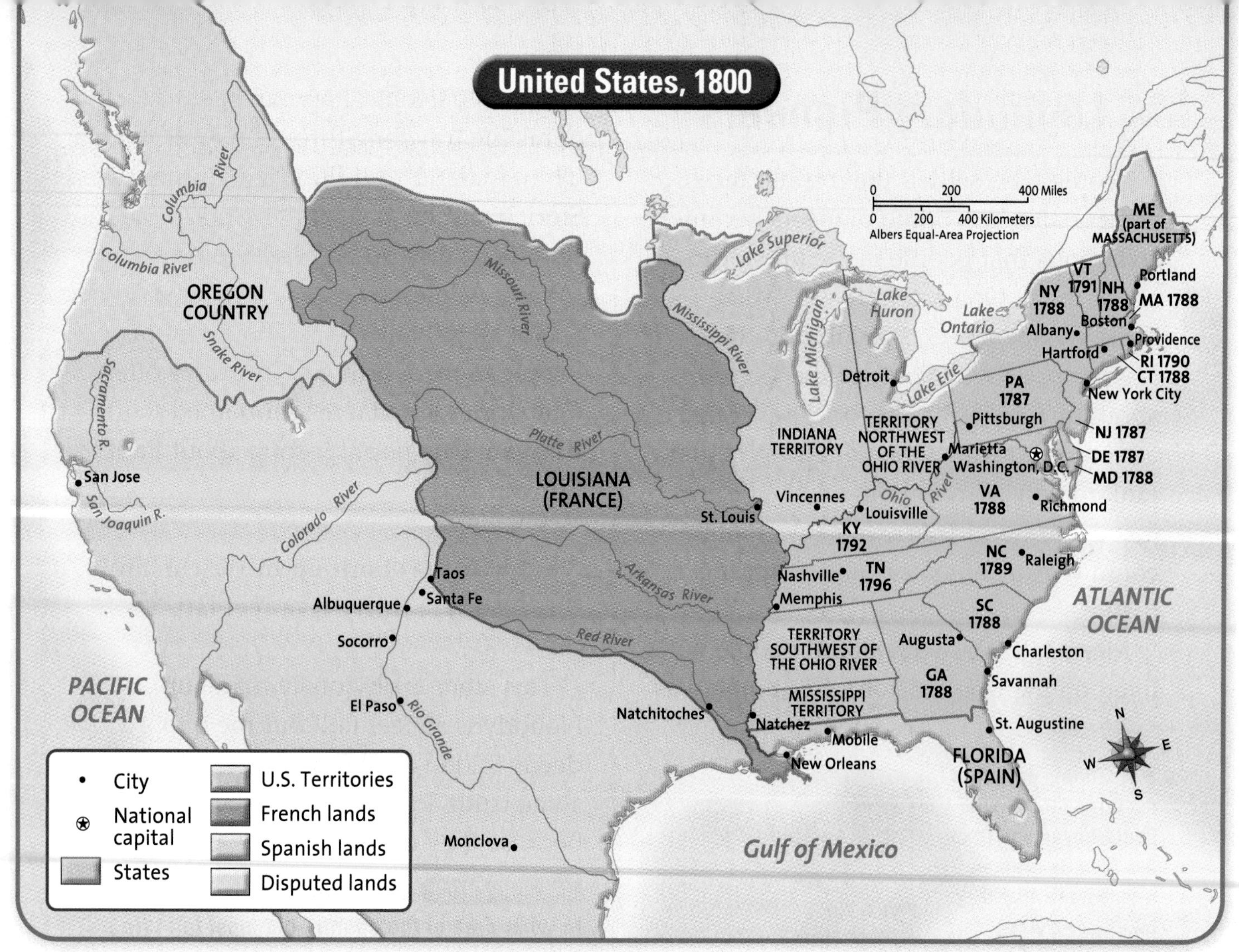

ANALYSIS SKILL Analyze Maps

Location What were the two westernmost states in 1800?

New States

In 1791, **Vermont** was added to the original 13 states. As pioneers settled western areas, other new states began to form. The first state west of the Appalachian Mountains was admitted in 1792. Its name, **Kentucky**, was taken from an Iroquois Indian word meaning "land of tomorrow."

Sometimes people disagreed about the forming of new states. During the 1780s, one group in North Carolina tried to form the "State of Franklin." John Sevier, a former soldier, was elected as governor there in 1785. However, North Carolina soon sent soldiers to take the land back.

In 1796, John Sevier became the first governor of another place—**Tennessee**. This time, the area he governed was admitted into the United States. Tennessee was named after Tanasi, a Cherokee village.

The addition of new states did not stop with Kentucky and Tennessee. The Northwest Territory was growing fast, too. People used the Ohio River and the many other rivers in the region for travel, and before long, people began to build towns along many of those rivers.

Those people came from many different backgrounds. Some were free African Americans who had moved there because slavery was not allowed in the Northwest Territory.

In 1788, pioneers founded Marietta, the oldest permanent settlement in what is now **Ohio**. The Ohio River helped make Marietta an important trading center for the Northwest Territory. Soon, other towns were built in Ohio. By 1800, more than 45,000 people lived in Ohio, and in 1803, it became the seventeenth state. Over time, as people moved farther west, this pattern of settlement, growth, and statehood repeated itself across the Northwest Territory.

READING CHECK **GENERALIZE**
Why did some African Americans choose to settle in the Northwest Territory?

Summary

Starting in the early 1800s, more people began to settle in the Northwest Territory area. As more settlers moved west, new states formed.

REVIEW

1. How did pioneers use natural resources to meet their needs?
2. Use the term **pioneer** in a sentence that gives its meaning.
3. How did rivers affect where people settled?

CRITICAL THINKING

4. ANALYSIS SKILL Why did pioneers choose to go to places where they would face challenges and hardships?
5. **Write a Tall Tale** Choose a real life pioneer. Then write an exciting adventure story about that person.
6. Focus Skill **GENERALIZE**
On a separate sheet of paper, copy and complete the graphic organizer.

Facts

Generalization

Settlers worked hard on frontier farms.

This painting shows Marietta, Ohio, in 1835.

Lesson 3

Time

1800 | 1825 | 1850

1803 The United States purchases Louisiana from France

1805 Lewis and Clark reach the Pacific Ocean

1806 Zebulon Pike explores the Southwest

Exploring the West

WHAT TO KNOW
What lands did the United States gain from the Louisiana Purchase?

- ✓ Explain why President Jefferson agreed to buy Louisiana from France.
- ✓ Describe the expedition to explore the lands of the Louisiana Purchase.

VOCABULARY
trespass p. 518

PEOPLE
Thomas Jefferson
Napoleon Bonaparte
Meriwether Lewis
William Clark
York
Sacagawea
Zebulon Pike

PLACES
Fort Mandan
Pikes Peak

Focus Skill **GENERALIZE**

California Standards
HSS 5.3, 5.8, 5.8.3

YOU ARE THERE

Sunlight warms the crowd in the New Orleans city square. Like everybody else, you are watching the men in the center of the square. They are raising a red-and-white striped flag.

"Look, that's the American flag," people whisper to each other as the flag unfurls in the wind. As of today, December 20, 1803, New Orleans no longer belongs to France. Your home is now on land owned by the United States!

➤ The United States flag is raised over New Orleans.

ANALYSIS SKILL Analyze Maps

Place What river marked the western border of the United States before the Louisiana Purchase?

The Louisiana Purchase

On March 4, 1801, **Thomas Jefferson** became the third President of the United States. At his inauguration, Jefferson spoke of his hopes, calling the United States "a rising nation, spread over a wide and fruitful land."* He knew, however, that the nation faced some serious problems.

One problem was that the United States had no ports of its own on the Gulf of Mexico. Farmers who lived in western areas had to ship their goods down the Mississippi River to New Orleans, which at the time was under Spain's control. There, they could sell the goods to ships sailing for Europe and other areas.

Soon after Jefferson became President, Spain gave New Orleans and the rest of Louisiana back to France. Jefferson feared that if the French controlled Louisiana, they could stop settlers from moving farther west.

Jefferson sent representatives to France to ask **Napoleon Bonaparte** (nuh•POH•lee•yuhn BOH•nuh•part), the leader of France, to sell New Orleans and nearby lands. At the time, France was preparing for war with Britain. Napoleon needed money to fight the British, so he offered to sell all of Louisiana—more than 800,000 square miles—for just $15 million. On April 30, 1803, the agreement became official, doubling the size of the United States. The sale of this huge territory became known as the Louisiana Purchase.

READING CHECK GENERALIZE
Why did France agree to sell Louisiana?

*Thomas Jefferson. *Jefferson's Call for Nationhood: The First Inaugural Address.* Texas A&M University Press, 2003.

Exploring Louisiana

Few people in the United States knew much about the nation's new lands that stretched from the Mississippi River to the Rocky Mountains and from New Orleans north to Canada. To identify what resources the area had, President Jefferson asked Congress for money for an expedition to explore the land.

Jefferson chose **Meriwether Lewis** to lead the expedition. A former Army officer, Lewis had served in the Northwest Territory. He chose a friend named **William Clark** to help lead the expedition. Clark was responsible for keeping records and making maps.

Lewis and Clark put together a group of about 30 people, most of whom were soldiers, and called the group the Corps of Discovery. One member of the group was **York**, an enslaved African American owned by William Clark. York was highly skilled in hunting and fishing.

In May 1804, the group left its camp near present-day St. Louis and traveled up the Missouri River by boat. By October, the expedition reached present-day North Dakota, where it had to stop for the winter. The group built a small camp near a Mandan Indian village and named it **Fort Mandan**.

At Fort Mandan, Lewis and Clark hired a French fur trader to translate Indian languages for them. The fur trader was married to a Shoshone (shuh•SHOH•nee) woman named **Sacagawea** (sa•kuh•juh•WEE•uh). Lewis and Clark asked her to help guide the expedition through the Shoshone lands.

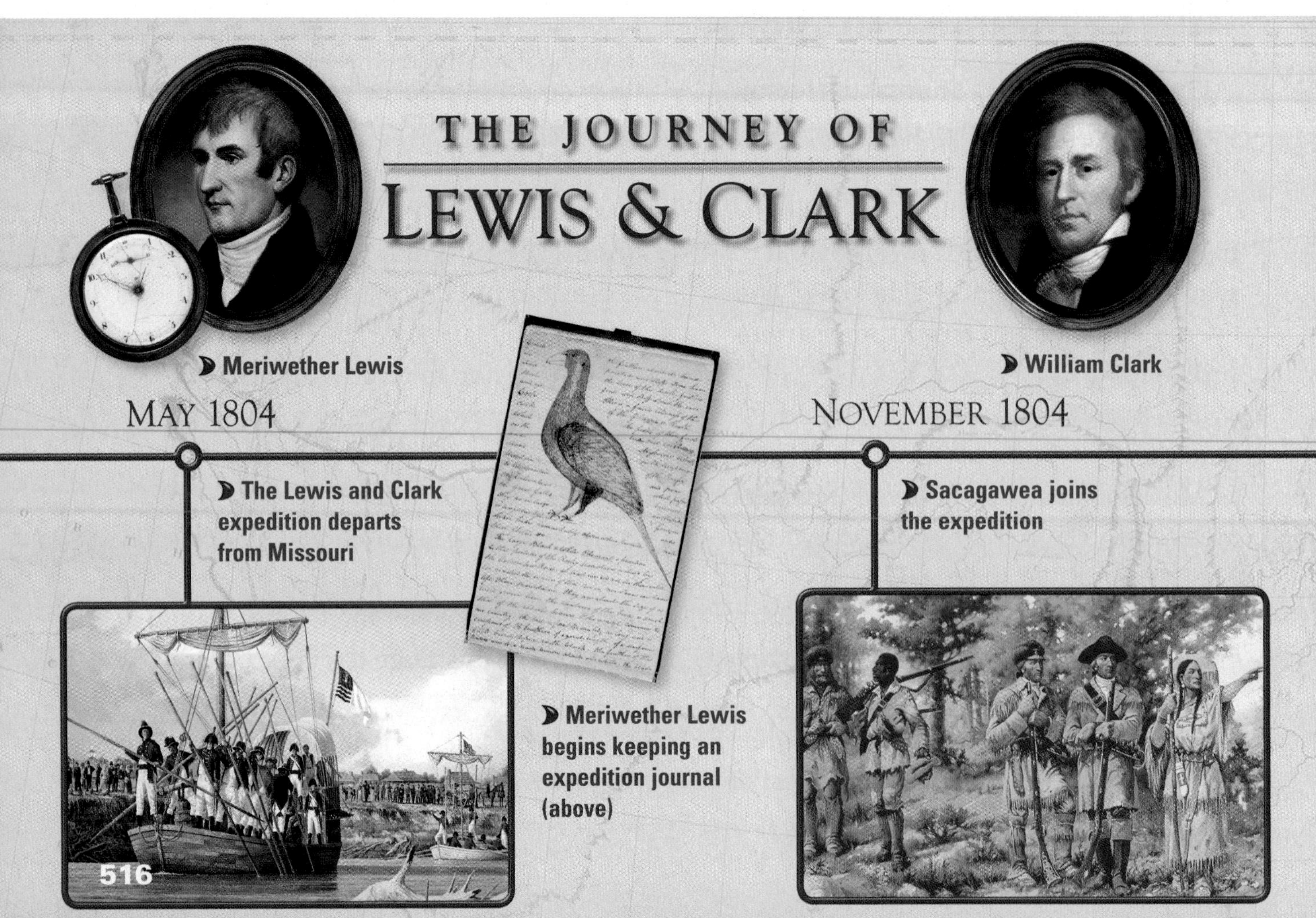

Meriwether Lewis

William Clark

The Lewis and Clark expedition departs from Missouri

Sacagawea joins the expedition

Meriwether Lewis begins keeping an expedition journal (above)

In the spring of 1805, the Lewis and Clark expedition set out again, moving farther up the Missouri River toward the Rocky Mountains. With Sacagawea's help, the expedition bought horses from the Shoshone to continue the journey through the mountain passes of the Rockies. After crossing the mountains, the explorers built boats and rowed down the Clearwater, Snake, and Columbia Rivers toward the Pacific coast.

In November 1805, after traveling for more than a year and covering more than 3,000 miles, the Lewis and Clark expedition reached the Pacific Ocean. On that day, Clark wrote in his journal:

> "Ocian [Ocean] in view! O! the joy!"*

In March 1806, the Corps of Discovery began the long journey back to St. Louis. It reached St. Louis in September. Despite the dangers the group had faced, all but one member returned safely. The Corps of Discovery had done everything that President Jefferson had asked of it.

Lewis and Clark had drawn maps to show the relative locations of mountain passes and major rivers. They had spoken to many different American Indian groups along the way. They also brought back seeds, plants, and even live animals. In later years, the work of Lewis and Clark helped American settlers find their way to the Pacific coast.

READING CHECK **GENERALIZE**
How did American Indian groups help Lewis and Clark during their expedition?

*William Clark. *The Journals of Lewis and Clark.* Mariner Books, 1997.

The expedition reaches the Pacific Ocean

The expedition returns to St. Louis

The expedition reaches Montana

Many American Indian leaders travel to Washington, D.C., to meet with President Jefferson (shown on the peace medal below)

Pike's Journey

In 1806, another expedition set off, to explore the southwestern section of the Louisiana Purchase. Captain **Zebulon Pike** led a small group that made discoveries about the geography of the region. In present-day Colorado, Pike saw a "blue mountain" in the distance. Today, that mountain is known as **Pikes Peak**, after Zebulon Pike.

The expedition followed the Rocky Mountains south. Along the way, the explorers crossed into Spanish land without realizing it. The Spanish quickly arrested Pike and the others for **trespassing**, or entering their land without permission. Pike spent several months with the Spanish before being released. When he returned to the United States, he described the route he had taken to the Spanish lands and explained that the people living there needed manufactured goods. Traders from the United States soon headed into the Southwest to begin trading with Spanish settlers.

Zebulon Pike

READING CHECK **GENERALIZE**
How did Zebulon Pike's expedition affect trade with Spain?

Summary

In 1803, the United States bought Louisiana from France. The Louisiana Purchase added a huge area of land to the United States. Meriwether Lewis, William Clark, and Zebulon Pike explored this new area.

REVIEW

1. What lands did the United States gain from the Louisiana Purchase?
2. Use the term **trespassing** in a sentence about Zebulon Pike.
3. What was Sacagawea's part in the Lewis and Clark expedition?

CRITICAL THINKING

4. ANALYSIS SKILL Why was New Orleans' relative location important to the United States?
5. ANALYSIS SKILL What were some of the costs and benefits of the Lewis and Clark expedition?
6. **Write an Editorial** Imagine that the Louisiana Purchase has just taken place. Write an editorial agreeing or disagreeing with Jefferson's decision to send explorers into the new lands.
7. Focus Skill **GENERALIZE**
On a separate sheet of paper, copy and complete the graphic organizer.

Facts

Lewis and Clark explored the northwestern part of the Louisiana Purchase.	Zebulon Pike explored the southwestern part of the Louisiana Purchase.

Generalization

Sacagawea

Biography

Trustworthiness
Respect
Responsibility
Fairness
Caring
Patriotism

Sacagawea, a Shoshone Indian, was born in what is now the state of Idaho. In 1800, she was kidnapped by another Indian group and taken away from her people. As a young woman, she married a French trader named Toussaint Charbonneau. When Lewis and Clark hired Charbonneau for their expedition, they asked Sacagawea to come along to work as a translator.

Sacagawea helped find routes for the explorers to follow. She also carried her baby, Jean Baptiste, along with her for the entire journey. Lewis and Clark both praised Sacagawea's bravery. One day, the boat she was riding in tipped over. Charbonneau panicked, but Sacagawea calmly saved the journals and supplies.

In 1994 Sacagawea was honored with this stamp.

In time, the Corps of Discovery reached the lands of the Shoshone Indians. To Sacagawea's surprise, she discovered that her brother, Cameahwait (KAM•ah•wait), had become a Shoshone leader. However, Sacagawea chose to remain with the Corps of Discovery.

After the Lewis and Clark expedition ended, Sacagawea and Charbonneau moved to Fort Manuel, in what is now South Dakota. They remained there until her death in about 1812.

Why Character Counts

How did Sacagawea's actions with the Corps of Discovery show her trustworthiness?

Bio Brief

1786 Born 1786?

1800 Sacagawea is kidnapped and taken to North Dakota

1804 Sacagawea joins the Lewis and Clark expedition

1812 Died 1812?

Interactive Multimedia Biographies
Visit **MULTIMEDIA BIOGRAPHIES** at
www.harcourtschool.com/hss

Make a Thoughtful Decision

WHY IT MATTERS

While leading their famous expedition through the Louisiana Purchase, Lewis and Clark had to make many thoughtful decisions. These decisions had important consequences for the expedition. A **consequence** is what happens because of an action. The decisions you make can have good or bad consequences. To make a thoughtful decision, you must think about the possible consequences before you act.

WHAT YOU NEED TO KNOW

Here are some steps you can use to help you make a thoughtful decision.

Step 1 **Make a list of choices to help you reach your goal.**

Step 2 **Gather information you will need to make a good decision.**

Step 3 **Predict consequences, and compare them.**

Step 4 **Make a choice, and take action.**

PRACTICE THE SKILL

Imagine that you are looking for a route to the Pacific coast. As the leader of your expedition, you will have to make many important choices. Your ability to make thoughtful decisions may determine the survival of your group. Page 521 lists two of the important decisions that you will face. Think about the possible consequences of each choice, and make thoughtful decisions. Explain the steps you followed in making each decision.

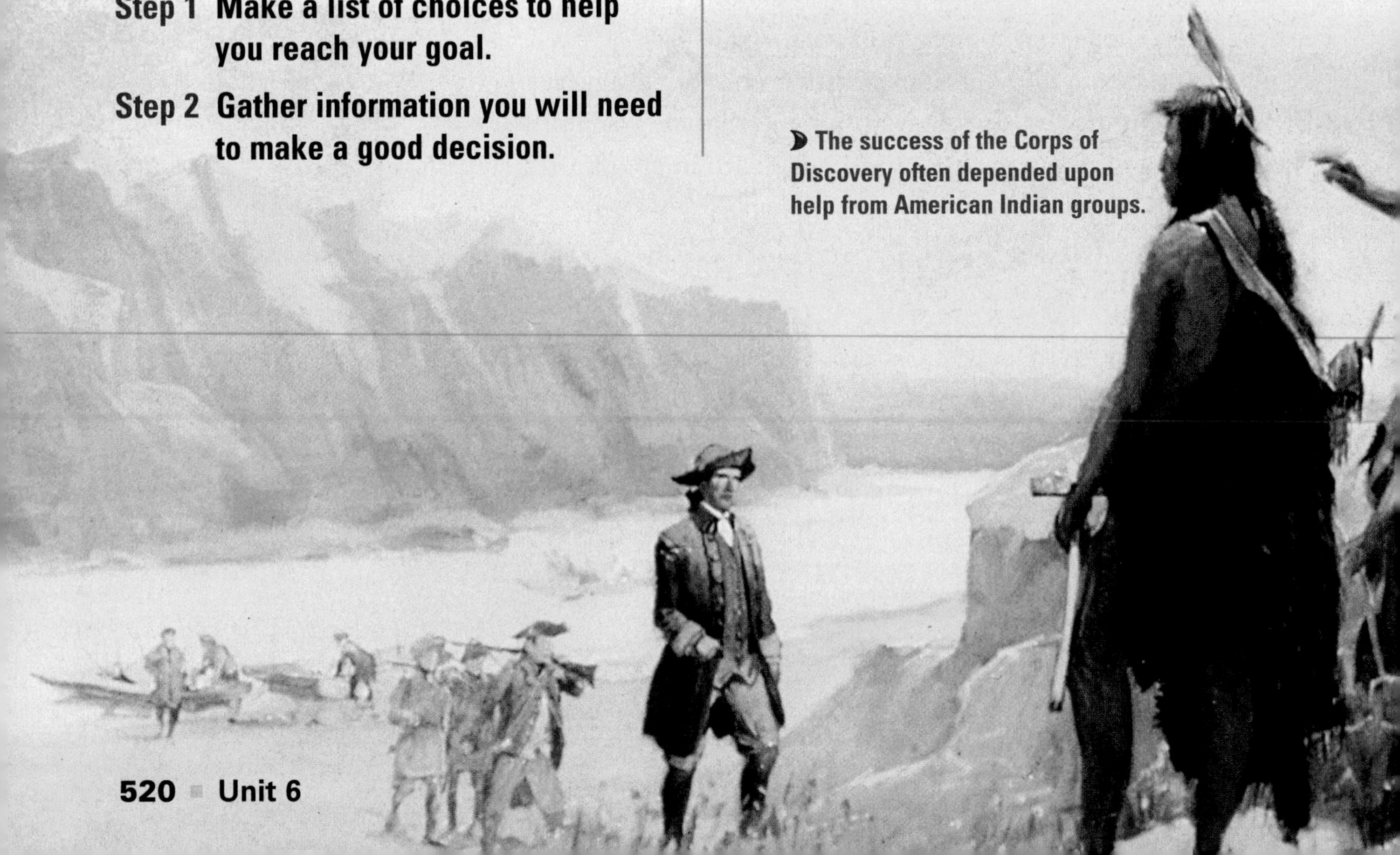

The success of the Corps of Discovery often depended upon help from American Indian groups.

1. You are gathering supplies for your upcoming expedition. Should you buy enough food to last the entire trip, or should you bring less than you will need and add to your supplies by hunting and gathering food along the way? Remember that during the journey you must carry all the supplies you bring.
2. After you begin your journey, you stop at a trading post. There, you meet two French traders and a Plains Indian who can each speak more than one language. Should you hire them to help you communicate with the different groups living in the area, or should you save your money and limit the number of people in your group?

APPLY WHAT YOU LEARNED

Make It Relevant Think about a decision you made at school this week. What steps did you follow? What choices did you have? What were the consequences of the choices that you made? Do you think your decision was a thoughtful one? Explain your answer to a family member.

Lesson 4

1800 — 1825 — 1850

- **1808** Tecumseh and his brother establish Prophetstown
- **1812** The United States declares war on Britain
- **1814** British soldiers capture Washington, D.C.

WHAT TO KNOW
What events led Britain and the United States to go to war again?

- Explain how Tecumseh tried to unite American Indian groups.
- Describe the events of the War of 1812.

VOCABULARY
encroach p. 523

PEOPLE
Tecumseh
James Madison
Dolley Madison
Francis Scott Key
Andrew Jackson

PLACES
Prophetstown
Fort McHenry

GENERALIZE

California Standards
HSS 5.3, 5.3.6

The War of 1812

YOU ARE THERE

Hundreds of Shawnee people have gathered to hear Chief **Tecumseh** (tuh•KUHM•suh) speak today. The cold wind slaps against your back as you listen to his words.

Lifting up his hands, Tecumseh raises his voice: "Will we let ourselves be destroyed in our turn without making an effort worthy of our race?"*

Cheers as loud as thunder burst from the crowd. "He's right!" your friend shouts. "A hundred years from now, people will still talk of our bravery!"

*Tecumseh. *Encyclopedia of Native American Tribes* by Carl Waldman. Checkmark Books, 1999.

The Shawnee considered Tecumseh a great warrior. This compass was given to him by British General Sir Isaac Brock.

Tecumseh visited most of the tribes west of the Appalachian Mountains and east of the Mississippi River, seeking members for his confederation.

Tecumseh's Plan

As settlers moved west, they settled on lands that belonged to American Indians. Many times, the United States Army tried to drive the Indians away. In Canada, the British chose to help the Indians and to encourage them to fight the Americans.

Some Indian leaders began calling on their people to join together to fight the settlers. Chief Tecumseh of the Shawnee tribe was one such leader. Tecumseh tried to persuade the Indian nations to join together against the United States. He said they should work together to stop settlers, who had encroached on their lands. To **encroach** is to move beyond established borders.

In 1808, Tecumseh and his brother, Tenskwatawa (ten•SKWAHT•uh•wah), known by settlers as the Prophet, established in what is now Indiana a village called **Prophetstown**. Tecumseh hoped that Indians from different groups would come together at Prophetstown to defend their lands. Some tribes agreed to unite. Others, though, did not want an alliance with former enemies.

Still, Tecumseh continued his efforts. He used strong words in his speeches. Tecumseh believed that Indian groups needed to set aside their differences. He said, "Brothers, we must be united . . . we must fight each other's battles."*

Tecumseh urged Indians to join with the British. The British offered help because they hoped to stop the United States from growing larger. Tensions grew between the United States and Britain. Soon the two nations would be at war again.

READING CHECK **GENERALIZE**

Why did Chief Tecumseh ask other Indian nations to join together against the settlers?

*Tecumseh. *Tecumseh: A Life* by John Sugden. Owl Books, 1999.

A Second War with Britain

Americans grew angry with the British for many reasons. In the early 1800s Britain was often at war with France. To stop Americans from trading with France and other nations, the British navy captured American trading ships at sea. In June 1812, President **James Madison** asked Congress to declare war on Britain, and its members quickly agreed.

At that time, Britain had the strongest navy in the world, and Britain's navy soon set up a blockade along the Atlantic coast. Although the tiny United States Navy had only 16 ships, it won several important battles, including the Battle of Lake Erie in 1813.

American soldiers then crossed into British Canada. On October 5, 1813, they fought in the Battle of the Thames (TEMZ), defeating the British and their Indian allies. Chief Tecumseh was among those killed in the fighting. After his death, the partnerships he had built among Indian groups ended.

British forces also won battles. In August 1814, British soldiers closed in on Washington, D.C. As fighting came closer, First Lady **Dolley Madison** began packing at the White House. As she escaped, she was able to save important government papers and a portrait of George Washington. That evening, the British set fire to the White House, the Capitol, and the Library of Congress.

With the city of Washington in flames, the British sailed to Baltimore, which

During the War of 1812, many naval battles were fought.

was protected by **Fort McHenry**. Although British ships bombed the fort for many hours, the Americans did not give up. The sight of the American flag waving over the fort after the battle made **Francis Scott Key** so proud that he wrote a poem that later became a song—"The Star-Spangled Banner."

When they could not beat the Americans at Baltimore, the British sailed south to New Orleans. American troops were waiting for them there. After fierce fighting, General **Andrew Jackson** forced the British out. At that time, however, the United States had already won the war. On December 24, 1814—two weeks before the battle—the British and the Americans had signed a peace treaty in Europe. Because news traveled slowly at that time, word of the peace treaty did not reach New Orleans in time to prevent the battle.

Dolley Madison

READING CHECK **CAUSE AND EFFECT**
What event caused Francis Scott Key to write "The Star-Spangled Banner"?

Summary

Chief Tecumseh tried to persuade Indians to unite against American settlers. Britain offered to help the Indians. Tensions between Britain and the United States led to the War of 1812.

REVIEW

1. What events led Britain and the United States to go to war again?
2. Use the term **encroach** in a sentence about Tecumseh.
3. Who led American troops to victory in the Battle of New Orleans?

CRITICAL THINKING

4. ANALYSIS SKILL Why do you think the partnerships Tecumseh built among Indian groups ended after his death?
5. ANALYSIS SKILL Why was the relative location of Washington, D.C. important to the British during the War of 1812?
6. **Write an Interview** Imagine that you are a newspaper reporter during the War of 1812. Write a list of questions to ask Francis Scott Key about his poem "The Star-Spangled Banner."
7. Focus Skill **GENERALIZE**
On a separate sheet of paper, copy and complete the graphic organizer.

Facts

The British encouraged American Indian groups to fight settlers from the United States.	Tecumseh argued that American Indians should ally with the British.

Generalization

Lesson 5

1827 The Cherokee constitution is written

1835 The Second Seminole War begins

1838 The Cherokee are forced to leave their homelands

WHAT TO KNOW
How did life change for American Indians in the early 1800s?

- ✓ Describe the actions taken by Seminole Indians to avoid being forced off their lands.
- ✓ Explain how Chief John Ross worked to protect the Cherokee.
- ✓ Describe the hardships the Cherokee suffered on the Trail of Tears.

VOCABULARY
reservation p. 527
assimilate p. 528

PEOPLE
Chief Osceola
Andrew Jackson
Sequoyah
Chief John Ross
John Marshall

PLACES
Florida
Georgia
North Carolina

GENERALIZE

HSS 5.3, 5.3.4, 5.3.6, 5.8

American Indian Life Changes

YOU ARE THERE Chief **Osceola** (ah•see•OH•luh) holds his head high as he looks out over you and your fellow Seminole Indians. "The United States Army is attacking our people to the north," he says. "They want to drive us away."

The thought of leaving your village makes you sad. Just then, you hear a splash in the nearby marsh. Is it just an alligator, or are soldiers already coming? You grab your sister's hand and hold it tightly.

"We won't give up," Osceola says. He looks right at you. "We will fight to keep our lands."

The Dade Massacre, an ambush of United States soldiers by the Seminole, marked the beginning of the Second Seminole War.

The Seminole Wars

For many years, American settlers and Seminole Indians had battled each other. Settlers grew angry when the Seminole, who lived in Spanish **Florida**, gave shelter to escaped slaves. In 1818, General **Andrew Jackson** led soldiers into Florida. The fighting that resulted became known as the First Seminole War.

Chief Osceola

The next year, in 1819, Spain agreed to give Florida to the United States. The United States government soon forced all the Seminole onto a reservation in Florida. A **reservation** is an area of land set aside by the government for use only by American Indians. In 1829, when Andrew Jackson became President, he ordered the Seminole to move to lands to the west. Many Seminole did not want to abandon their homes. They decided to stay and fight.

In 1835, the Second Seminole War began. This time, **Chief Osceola** was the Seminole leader. Under Osceola's command, Seminole families hid in southern Florida. They began attacking American soldiers and then hiding out in the swamps. The soldiers were not used to Florida's heat and it was hard for them to fight in swamps and marshes. For a short time, it seemed as if the Seminole might win.

Then an American general promised Osceola peace talks. When Osceola appeared at the meeting, he was captured and put into prison instead. Osceola died in prison. After his death, many Seminole decided to move west. Others followed in 1858, after the Seminole lost a third war.

READING CHECK **GENERALIZE**
Why did the Second Seminole War begin?

FAST FACT

The term *Seminole* comes from the Spanish word *cimarron,* which means "wild runaway." The Seminole Indians were given this name because there were many escaped slaves who became Seminole.

Indian Removal

The Seminoles were not the only Indian group to be forced west. During the early 1800s, Cherokee lands stretched through **Georgia**, Alabama, Tennessee, and **North Carolina**. As more settlers moved in, problems began.

At first, the Cherokee hoped to live peacefully with settlers. They had **assimilated** to, or adopted, American ways of life. Some sent their children to American schools to learn to read and write English.

Although they had assimilated to American ways of life, the Cherokee wanted to preserve their own language and culture. A Cherokee named **Sequoyah** (sih•KWOY•uh) created a written alphabet for his people's language. Soon thousands of Cherokee people learned to read and write in their own language.

In 1827, the Cherokee used Sequoyah's alphabet to write their own constitution. It stated that the new Cherokee Nation would elect chiefs and representatives. In this way, the Cherokee government was similar to the government of the United States.

Many Americans still did not respect the Cherokee government. They wanted all the Cherokee to leave. When gold was discovered on Cherokee lands, matters grew worse. President Andrew Jackson took the side of the settlers.

In 1830, Jackson signed the Indian Removal Act, which broke many treaties between American Indians and the United States. It said that the Indians east of the Mississippi River had to give up their lands. In exchange, they would be

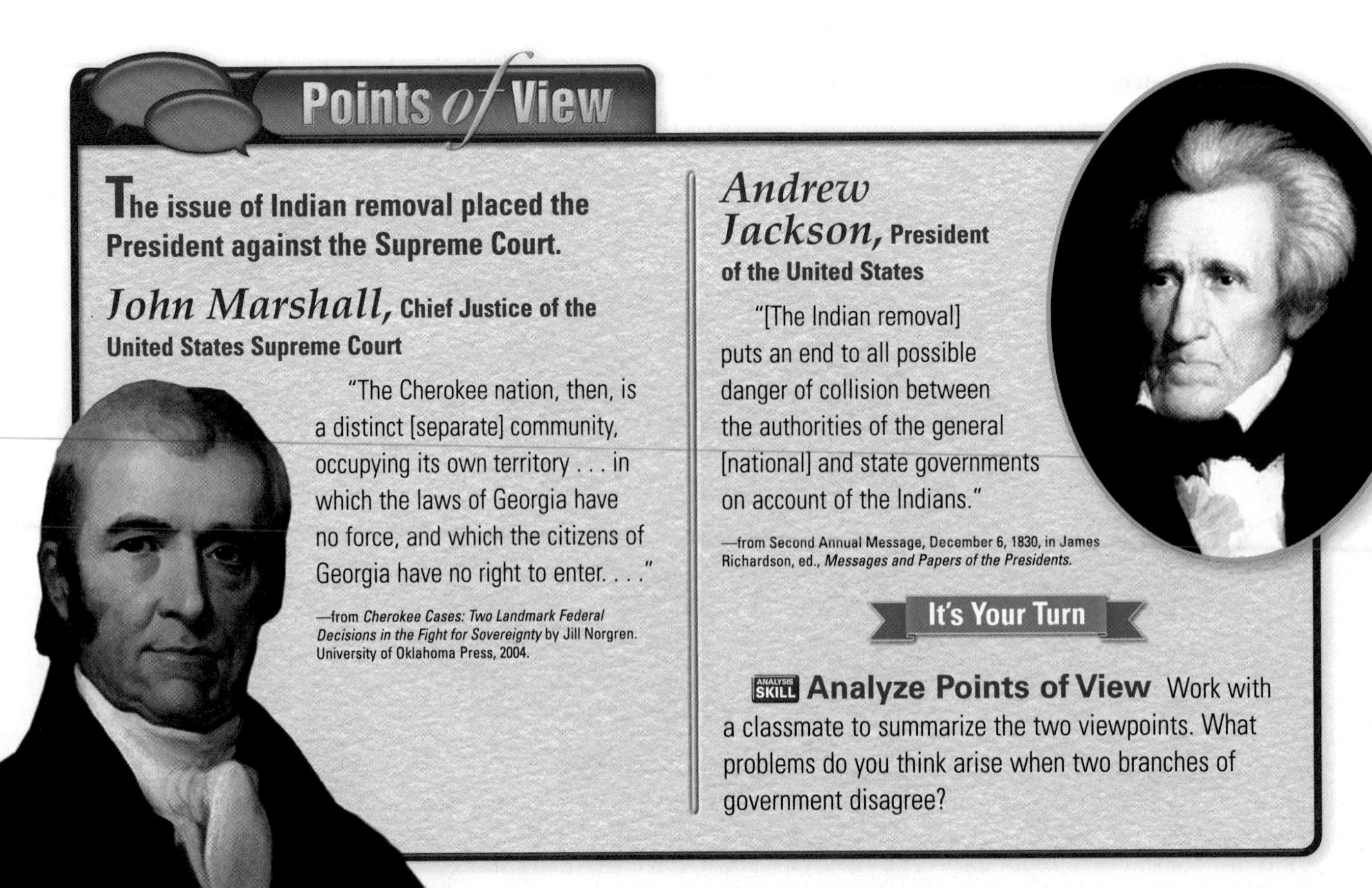

Points of View

The issue of Indian removal placed the President against the Supreme Court.

***John Marshall,* Chief Justice of the United States Supreme Court**

"The Cherokee nation, then, is a distinct [separate] community, occupying its own territory . . . in which the laws of Georgia have no force, and which the citizens of Georgia have no right to enter. . . ."

—from *Cherokee Cases: Two Landmark Federal Decisions in the Fight for Sovereignty* by Jill Norgren. University of Oklahoma Press, 2004.

***Andrew Jackson,* President of the United States**

"[The Indian removal] puts an end to all possible danger of collision between the authorities of the general [national] and state governments on account of the Indians."

—from Second Annual Message, December 6, 1830, in James Richardson, ed., *Messages and Papers of the Presidents.*

It's Your Turn

ANALYSIS SKILL **Analyze Points of View** Work with a classmate to summarize the two viewpoints. What problems do you think arise when two branches of government disagree?

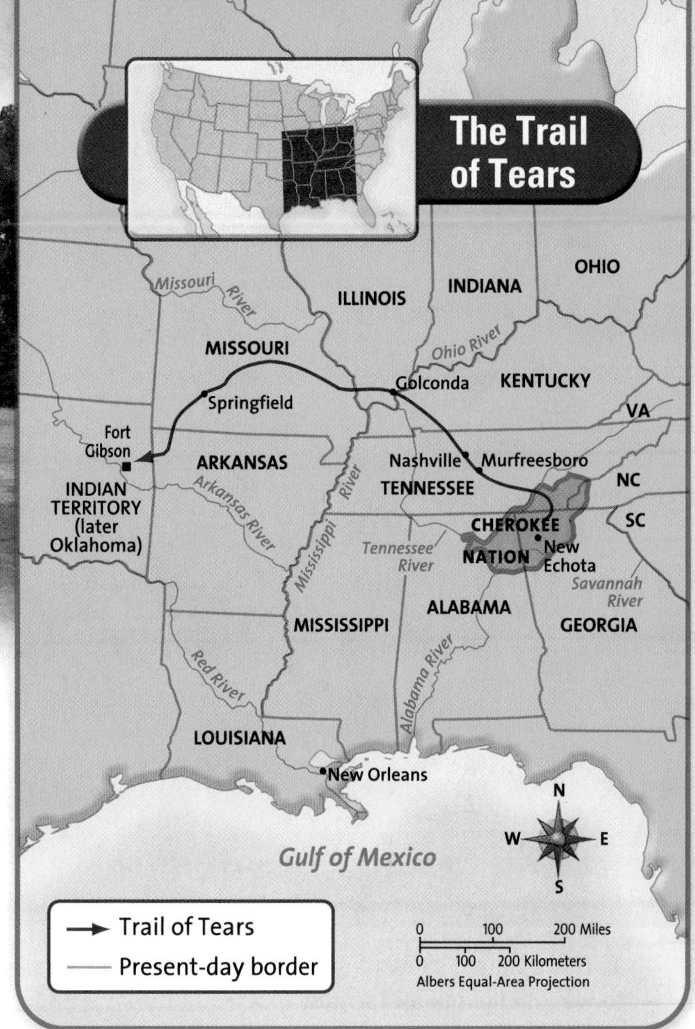

ANALYSIS SKILL Analyze Maps This cabin remains in the Cherokee capital of New Echota in Georgia.

Movement What direction did the Trail of Tears follow?

given lands west of the Mississippi River, in the Indian Territory. This area spread across most of what is now Oklahoma.

The Cherokee would not agree to give up their lands. To push them out, the Georgia government gave away their land to American settlers. To protest these wrongs, Cherokee Chief **John Ross** took the case to court. Ross argued for his people's rights before the Supreme Court in Washington, D.C.

In 1832, the Supreme Court ruled in favor of the Cherokee Nation. Chief Justice **John Marshall** said that the state of Georgia could not take their lands. When the Cherokee heard about the Supreme Court ruling, they held celebration feasts.

However, their celebrations soon ended. According to the Constitution, it is the job of the President to enforce Supreme Court rulings, but President Jackson chose not to obey the Court. Instead, Jackson said, "John Marshall has made his decision, now let him enforce it."*

In 1835, the United States government persuaded several Cherokee to sign a treaty giving their people's lands in the Southeast to the United States. More than 16,000 Cherokee protested the treaty, but their protests did no good.

Martin Van Buren was elected as the next United States President. At first, the Cherokee hoped Van Buren would act justly, but he agreed with Andrew Jackson. On March 27, 1838, Van Buren sent the United States Army to force the remaining Cherokee to move west.

READING CHECK GENERALIZE

How did Andrew Jackson view the rights of American Indians?

*Andrew Jackson. "Expansion and Exodus." *The Native Americans: An Illustrated History*, edited by David Hurst Thomas. Turner Publishing, 1993.

This painting shows a group of Cherokee on the Trail of Tears. Many were forced to walk to the Indian Territory.

The Trail of Tears

In 1838, about 7,000 United States soldiers, led by General Winfield Scott, arrived on Cherokee lands. The soldiers built small forts in which to gather Indians for the journey west. They then began forcing all Cherokee families out of their homes and into the forts.

General Scott asked the Cherokee to leave their homes willingly. Scott wrote that in the forts "you will find food for all, and clothing for the destitute [poor] . . . and in comfort, be transported to your new homes."* Scott's words proved to be untrue.

*Winfield Scott. *The Trail of Tears: The Cherokee Journey from Home*, by Marlene Targ Brill. The Millbrook Press, 1995.

A Cherokee child carried this doll on the journey.

The Cherokee families who stayed in the forts were given moldy food to eat. Hundreds died from disease.

Only a small number of Cherokee were lucky enough to escape from the soldiers. They hid in the forests and survived by gathering wild foods. They eventually managed to buy land in North Carolina. There, they began a new settlement.

By the time Chief John Ross returned from Washington, D.C., the Cherokee were being forced west. They had to walk about 800 miles to the Indian Territory. Along the way, they were given little food and water. Bad weather made the journey even more difficult. In places, the Cherokee had to struggle through knee-deep mud. On the plains, they walked through freezing blizzards.

Ross and his family left with the last group of Cherokee. One night, his wife, Quatie Ross, gave her only blanket to a child. She then became sick and died.

One of every four Cherokee did not survive the journey to the new lands. So many people died along the way that the survivors called the path "the place where they cried." Later, the journey became known as the Trail of Tears. Other Indian groups—including the Chickasaw, the Choctaw, and the Creek—were also forced to leave their lands. They, too, died by the thousands on the Trail of Tears.

READING CHECK **SUMMARIZE**
Why did the journey west by the Cherokee and other Indian groups become known as the Trail of Tears?

Summary

In the early 1800s, American Indians struggled to keep their lands. President Jackson signed the Indian Removal Act, which broke many treaties. The Cherokee were forced to move west on the Trail of Tears.

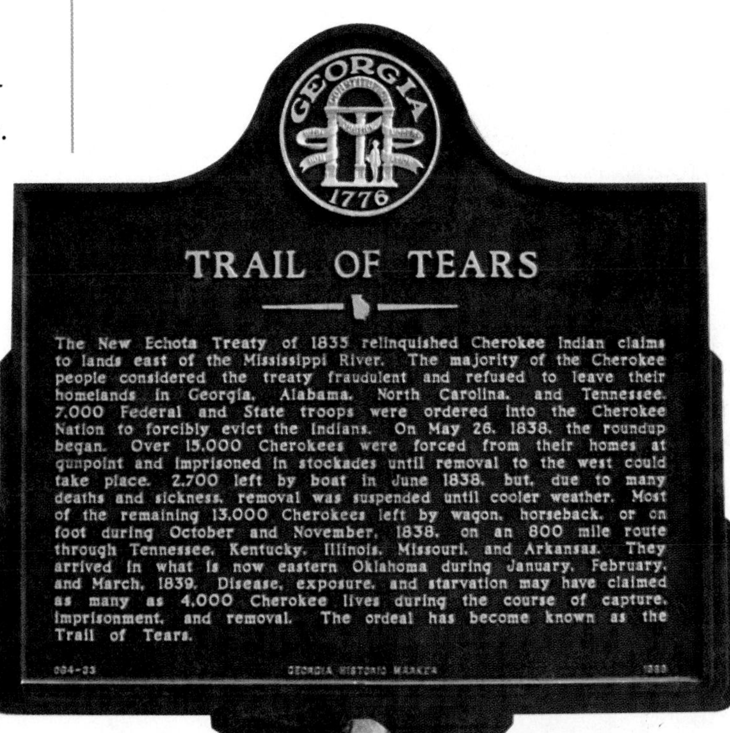

➤ **This plaque in Georgia marks the beginning of the Trail of Tears.**

REVIEW

1. How did life change for American Indians during the early 1800s?
2. Use the word **reservation** in a sentence about the Seminole.
3. In what way was the government of the Cherokee Nation similar to that of the United States?

CRITICAL THINKING

4. ANALYSIS SKILL Why might the Cherokee have wanted to learn Sequoyah's writing system?
5. ANALYSIS SKILL In what way did Chief John Ross try to achieve a peaceful solution for the Cherokee?
6. **Draw a Scene** Draw a scene showing the hardships the Cherokee faced on the Trail of Tears.
7. Focus Skill **GENERALIZE**
On a separate sheet of paper, copy and complete the graphic organizer.

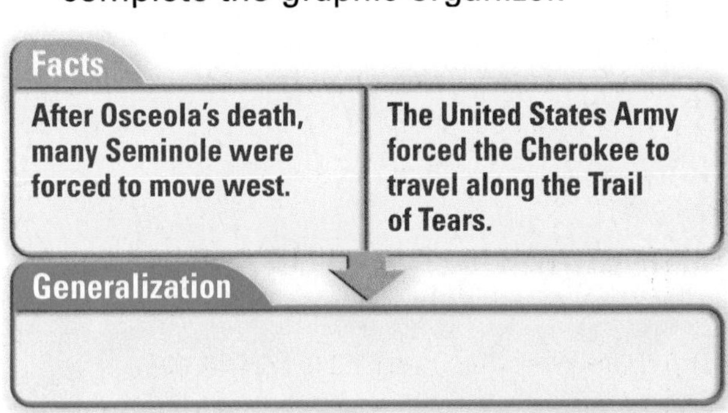

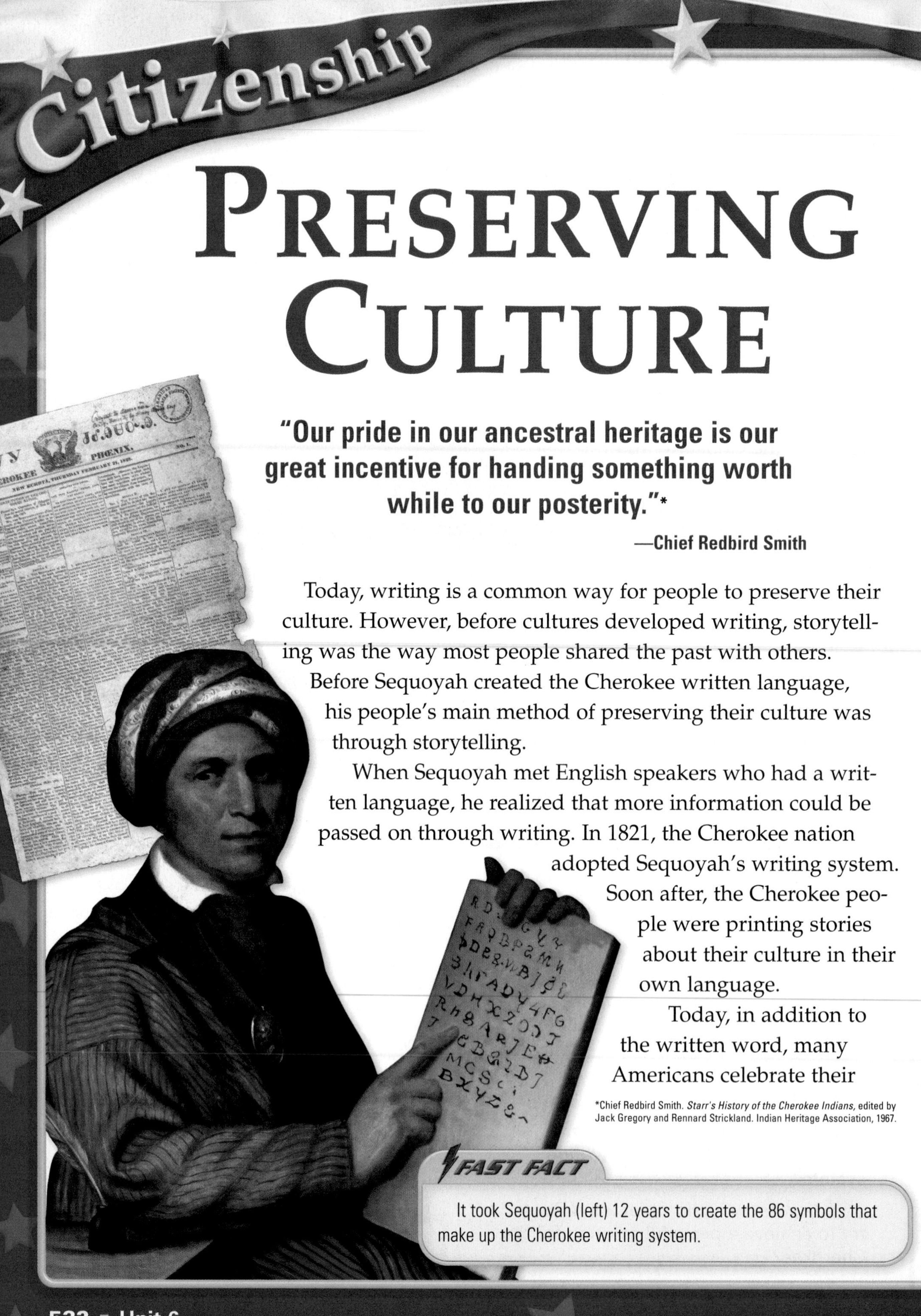

Citizenship

Preserving Culture

"Our pride in our ancestral heritage is our great incentive for handing something worth while to our posterity."*

—Chief Redbird Smith

Today, writing is a common way for people to preserve their culture. However, before cultures developed writing, storytelling was the way most people shared the past with others. Before Sequoyah created the Cherokee written language, his people's main method of preserving their culture was through storytelling.

When Sequoyah met English speakers who had a written language, he realized that more information could be passed on through writing. In 1821, the Cherokee nation adopted Sequoyah's writing system. Soon after, the Cherokee people were printing stories about their culture in their own language.

Today, in addition to the written word, many Americans celebrate their

*Chief Redbird Smith. *Starr's History of the Cherokee Indians*, edited by Jack Gregory and Rennard Strickland. Indian Heritage Association, 1967.

FAST FACT

It took Sequoyah (left) 12 years to create the 86 symbols that make up the Cherokee writing system.

customs as a way of preserving their heritage. Customs such as storytelling, songwriting, art, and cooking allow people to participate in culture. These activities often form a special part of cultural celebrations or rituals of worship. Museums and organizations are also important in preserving cultural history, helping people bridge the gap between the past and the present.

People from all over the world still share their culture through stories. Writing is an important skill that helps preserve culture.

Think About It!

Make It Relevant **Americans preserve their cultures in many ways. How do different groups in your community preserve their cultures?**

Families prepare special dishes and participate in special ceremonies to celebrate and preserve their heritages.

Chapter 12 Review

Time

1800 — 1810

1803
The Louisiana Purchase is made

1805
Lewis and Clark reach the Pacific

Reading Social Studies

When you make a **generalization,** you summarize a group of facts and show how they are related.

Generalize

Complete this graphic organizer to make generalizations about life on the frontier during the early 1800s. A copy of this graphic organizer appears on page 132 of the Homework and Practice Book.

Living on the Frontier

Facts		

Generalization

Most frontier families lived on farms.

California Writing Prompts

Write a Narrative Imagine that you live on the frontier with your family in the early 1800s. Write a story describing what a typical day for you is like. Include descriptions of your family's home and your chores.

Write a Persuasive Speech Think about why people decided to journey west. Imagine that you are living in the 1840s and want your family to move west. Write a speech to try to persuade your family to move.

1820

1830

1825
The Erie Canal opens

1830
The Indian Removal Act is signed

Use Vocabulary

Write a sentence or two to explain how each pair of terms is related.

1. **canal** (p. 504), **lock** (p. 505)
2. **pathfinder** (p. 502), **pioneer** (p. 509)
3. **encroach** (p. 523), **trespassing** (p. 518)
4. **assimilate** (p. 528), **reservation** (p. 527)

Use the Time Line

Use the chapter summary time line above to answer these questions.

5. When was the Indian Removal Act signed?
6. When did Lewis and Clark reach the Pacific Ocean?

Apply Skills

Compare Graphs

7. Choose two of the graphs on page 507. Then write a paragraph describing how the two graphs are alike and how they are different.

Make a Thoughtful Decision

8. Imagine that the year is 1790 and a friend has asked you to immigrate with her to the United States. What steps would you follow to come to a decision?

Recall Facts

Answer these questions.

9. From where did most immigrants to the United States come in the late 1700s and early 1800s?
10. What was the Indian Removal Act?

Write the letter of the best choice.

11. What was the purpose of the Erie Canal?
    - **A** to provide a way for wagons to cross the Appalachian Mountains
    - **B** to provide a waterway connecting the Great Lakes and the Atlantic Ocean
    - **C** to provide jobs for immigrants
    - **D** to provide a port along the Gulf of Mexico
12. What was the first state west of the Appalachian Mountains to join the United States?
    - **A** Illinois
    - **B** Indiana
    - **C** Kentucky
    - **D** Ohio

Think Critically

13. ANALYSIS SKILL What were some of the costs and benefits of the Louisiana Purchase?
14. ANALYSIS SKILL How do you think Sequoyah's writing system affected the Cherokee people?

Study Skills

WRITE TO LEARN

Writing about what you read can help you better understand and remember information.

- **Write down the information that you learn from each lesson.**
- **Write your own response to the new information you learned.**

Moving West	
What I Learned	Personal Response
John C. Frémont explored and mapped the Oregon Country.	It must have been difficult to travel in a new area without a map to use as a guide.
Settlers to the Oregon Country had to carry all the supplies they would need.	

Apply As You Read

As you read the chapter, stop after each lesson to write what you learned and your reaction to it.

California History-Social Science Standards, Grade 5

5.3 Students describe the cooperation and conflict that existed among the American Indians and between the Indian nations and the new settlers.
5.8 Students trace the colonization, immigration, and settlement patterns of the American people from 1789 to the mid-1800s, with emphasis on the role of economic incentives, effects of the physical and political geography, and transportation systems.

CHAPTER

Moving West 13

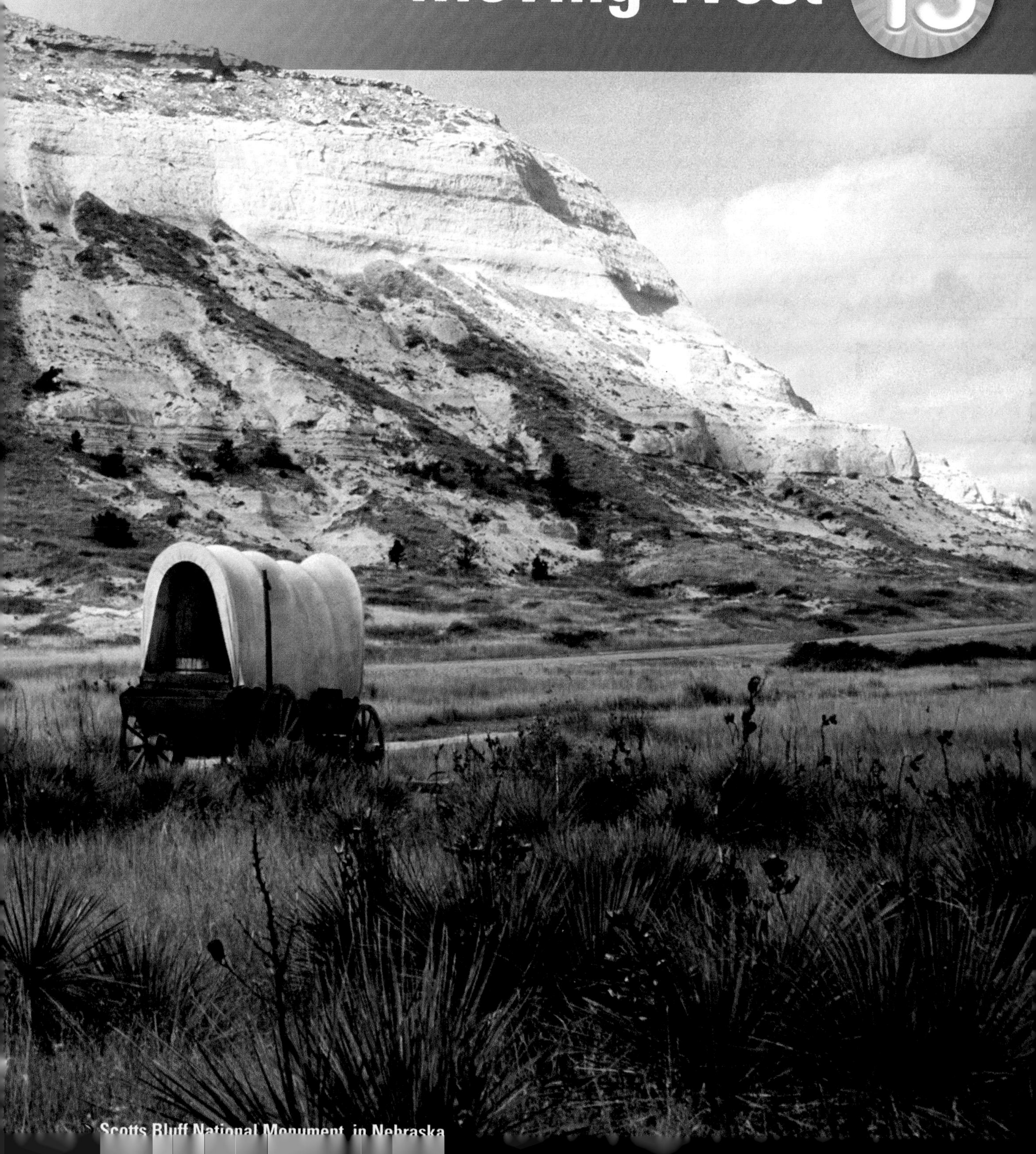

Scotts Bluff National Monument, in Nebraska

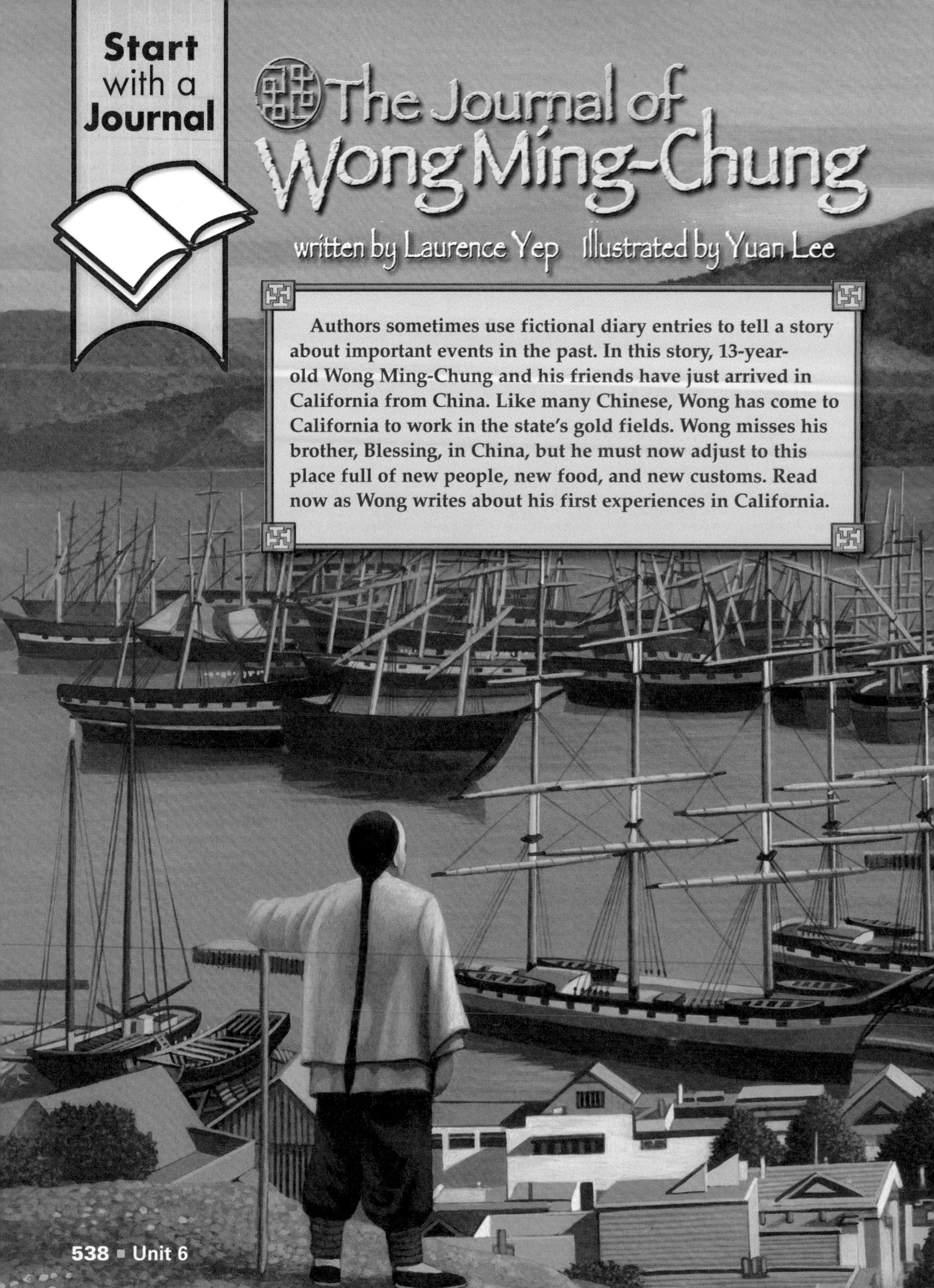

Start with a Journal

The Journal of Wong Ming-Chung

written by Laurence Yep illustrated by Yuan Lee

Authors sometimes use fictional diary entries to tell a story about important events in the past. In this story, 13-year-old Wong Ming-Chung and his friends have just arrived in California from China. Like many Chinese, Wong has come to California to work in the state's gold fields. Wong misses his brother, Blessing, in China, but he must now adjust to this place full of new people, new food, and new customs. Read now as Wong writes about his first experiences in California.

June 18
San Francisco, or First City

The Golden Mountain is stranger, scarier, funnier, sadder and more wonderful than I ever imagined. Now that I am here I will use only the American calendar.

When we got off the ship, I thought I was in the middle of a forest. Except I could hear the ocean. Then I realized the tall poles were the masts of ships. I was surrounded by hundreds of empty boats. They jam the harbor like fish in my village pond. I bet I could have walked from one deck to another across the bay.

I didn't see any sailors. Instead, I saw laundry hanging from lines as if people were using the boats as houses. Then I saw one ship that literally had a house built on top of it. Maybe all the sailors had left their ships to find gold too.

Big, loud machines were pounding logs vertically into the mud a half-kilometer from shore. Real houses perched on top of logs that had already been driven in. Men and machines were filling in the shoreline to make more space. In some places, they weren't even bothering to move the ship, but were just filling the dirt around it. Blessing would have loved the machines.

First City nestles at the foot of steep hills between the shore and the hill-sides. A few houses lie scattered on the slopes. Instead of building on the hills, they're expanding into the water.

Though it's summer, the air is as chilly here as the winter back home.

I have to stop now. They're calling for us to register.

First City the Chinese name given to San Francisco

register to officially record entry into a country

Golden Mountain The Chinese name for California.

Response Corner

1. What are some sights and sounds that Wong describes?
2. Imagine moving to a new place where you can't even speak the language. Write a journal entry describing what your first day might be like.

Lesson 1

1800 — 1850

1836 Marcus and Narcissa Whitman settle in Oregon

1843 John C. Frémont begins his explorations of the West

1847 Mormon settlers arrive in Utah

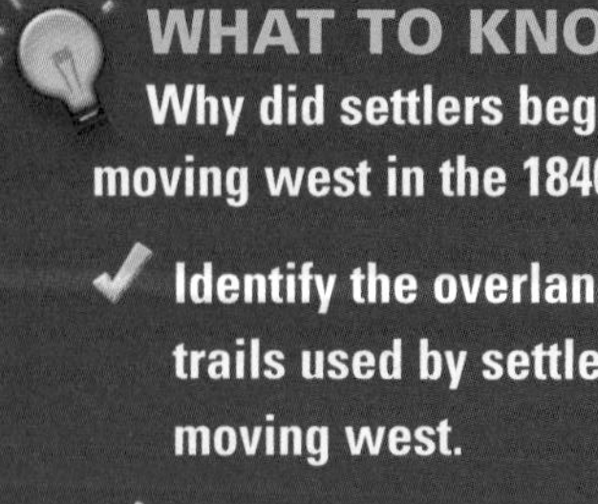

WHAT TO KNOW
Why did settlers begin moving west in the 1840s?

- Identify the overland trails used by settlers moving west.
- Understand how geography influenced westward migration.

VOCABULARY
wagon train p. 542
ford p. 542

PEOPLE
Jedediah Smith
John C. Frémont
Marcus Whitman
Narcissa Whitman
William Becknell
Brigham Young

PLACES
Oregon Trail
Oregon Country
Santa Fe Trail
Old Spanish Trail
California Trail
Mormon Trail

GENERALIZE

HSS 5.3, 5.3.5, 5.8, 5.8.3, 5.8.4

Western Trails

YOU ARE THERE Independence, Missouri, seems like the most exciting place in the world to live. It is 1845, and your father's supply store can barely keep goods on the shelves. Every day, more people are arriving.

"Look at all the people," your younger sister says, tugging at your sleeve. "Where are they going?" Outside, dozens of overland wagons are rolling by. The sun is rising, and people are eager to leave.

"The **Oregon Trail** begins here," you tell her. "It goes almost all the way to the Pacific Ocean." Someday, you decide, you too will follow the trail!

➤ Jedediah Smith found a pass through the Rocky Mountains.

Fur traders and trappers were among the first to settle in the West.

Western Pathfinders

Many early western settlers were those who made a living in the fur trade. As more trappers and fur traders moved west, though, the number of wild animals declined. Trappers and traders had to look for other kinds of work. Some became pathfinders for settlers who wanted to move to lands with fertile soil and good rainfall.

Travelers moving west needed the pathfinders to show them safe trails and mountain passes. With help from American Indians, a trapper named **Jedediah Smith** found the South Pass across the Rocky Mountains. Eventually, the South Pass became part of the trail to the **Oregon Country**, in the Pacific Northwest. It was not really a country, but a region made up of parts of present-day Canada, Washington, Idaho, Montana, and Oregon.

In 1843, the United States government hired **John C. Frémont** to explore, map, and report on the West. Frémont wrote that his expeditions were meant "to show the face and character of the country."*

John C. Frémont

Frémont made several journeys during which he charted trails in Utah and California. He also mapped the Oregon Trail—the path to the Oregon Country. As newspapers across the country published Frémont's reports of the West, "Oregon fever" swept across the nation.

READING CHECK GENERALIZE
Which areas of the United States did John Frémont map?

*John C. Frémont. *Report of the Exploring Expedition to the Rocky Mountains and to Oregon and North California.* Gates and Seaton, 1845.

The Oregon Trail

Oregon began to attract settlers even before it was owned by the United States. In 1836, **Marcus** and **Narcissa Whitman** set up a Christian mission near the Walla Walla Valley. In letters to her family, Narcissa Whitman described the beautiful valleys and rich soil of the Oregon Country. Her letters, later published, helped attract settlers to Oregon.

For most settlers, the journey began in Independence, Missouri. Sometimes wagons arrived together, and other times separately. The pioneers waited in Independence until enough wagons had gathered to make a **wagon train**. Then they hired a guide and headed west.

After leaving Independence, the wagon trains headed northwest to the Platte River in Nebraska. Then they followed the Platte west across the Great Plains, toward the Rocky Mountains.

Each person helped during the journey. Even children had chores to do, such as gathering wood for campfires. Older children walked beside the oxen during the day, while the wagon train was moving.

Pioneers ran into problems because of the rough land around them. Wagon trains often had to **ford**, or cross, deep rivers. Fording a river was dangerous. If a wagon tipped over, all its goods could be lost. There was no way for settlers to replace the supplies they had packed.

Another hardship on the trail was the changing climate. Some parts of the trail passed through hot, dry deserts, while other parts led through freezing mountain passes. Along the way, travelers

faced severe storms. One settler wrote that she spent "two hours and a half with the ice water running onto me, and the hailstones beating upon my head. . . ."*

Despite all the difficulties, however, few settlers turned back. Some even left messages of encouragement along the way. One landmark they looked for was Independence Rock, in present-day Wyoming. The rock was given this name because most settlers reached it around the Fourth of July. Many pioneers carved their names into this huge, granite rock.

Wagon trains then used the South Pass to cross the Rocky Mountains. After crossing present-day Idaho, they came to a place called the Columbia River. This area of the river was filled with rapids and whirlpools. It was one of the most dangerous parts of the journey. To get their wagons downriver, some pioneers built huge wooden rafts.

In 1846, Sam Barlow built a land route that allowed settlers to avoid fording the river. Travelers had to pay five dollars per wagon to use the road. Many did so gladly, because it was much safer than rafting down the river.

Finally, the settlers reached Oregon's fertile Willamette Valley. There, the tired travelers usually received food, clothing, and shelter from other settlers in the valley. Soon after recovering from their journey, the newcomers rushed to claim free pieces of land. A family could claim 640 acres and pay nothing! As soon as the settlers had their property, they built houses and farms.

READING CHECK SUMMARIZE
How did climate affect western pioneers?

*Mary Rockwood Powers. *A Woman's Overland Journey to California.* Glen Adams, 1987.

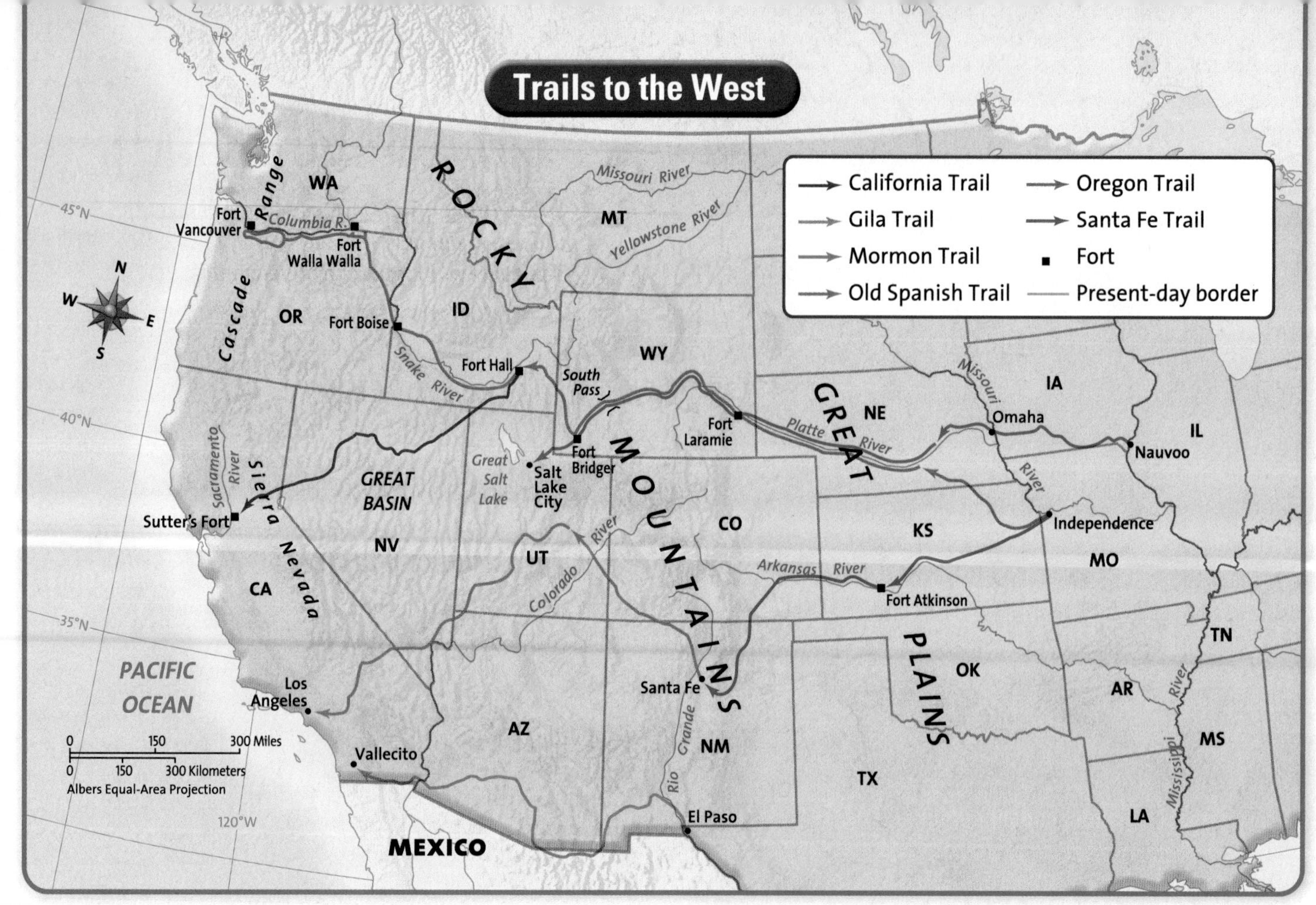

ANALYSIS SKILL Analyze Maps

Movement Which trail led to Sutter's Fort?

Other Trails West

Independence, Missouri, was also the starting point for other trails west. In 1821, a Missouri trader named **William Becknell** opened the **Santa Fe Trail**. It ran from Independence to Santa Fe in New Mexico. It covered about 780 miles.

Merchants used the Santa Fe Trail for trade. Wagons on the trail carried silver and furs from the West to cities in the East. In 1846, the Santa Fe Trail became a military route, with forts to protect travelers. Three years later, mail carriers started using the trail for mail service.

New Mexico was just one destination for people traveling the Santa Fe Trail. A newer part of the trail, called the **Old Spanish Trail**, crossed the Rio Grande and the Colorado River. It linked Santa Fe to Los Angeles in California.

When settlers on the Oregon Trail reached the southeastern part of what is now Idaho, some turned southwest toward California. Known as the **California Trail**, this trail became the main overland route to California.

Many settlers came to California to start farms and ranches. Travelers on the California Trail had to bring enough water to cross the deserts of what is now Nevada. They also had to try to pass the Sierra Nevada before winter. Heavy snowfall could make this mountain range difficult to pass. If they reached the end of the trail, they often found good land.

Other trails led from many of the southern states to Texas. Newcomers followed these routes to start farms and ranches in Texas. Many of the settlers came to Texas by land. Some settlers from the North and the upper South took a ferry, or a flat-bottomed boat, across the Red River. Then they traveled to the area that is now part of the city of Dallas. Many families from the South came to Texas by boat and settled along the Gulf coast, or around Austin and San Antonio.

Another important pathway west was the **Mormon Trail**. It led to the Great Salt Lake, in present-day Utah. Mormons are members of the Church of Jesus Christ of Latter-day Saints. In the 1840s, their religion was still new, and many places in the eastern United States did not welcome Mormons. They decided to go west to form their own communities.

In 1846, **Brigham Young** led a group of Mormons on a 1,000-mile journey from Illinois to Utah. He and his followers reached the Great Salt Lake valley in July 1847. Young told the Mormons that they should build a city in the valley.

By 1847, about 2,000 Mormons had moved to the new settlement of Salt Lake City. The Great Salt Lake region grew fast, and it soon became known as the Utah Territory. Brigham Young became the territory's first governor.

READING CHECK **GENERALIZE**
Why did the Mormons travel to the Great Salt Lake valley?

A typical wagon had about 2,000 pounds of tools and supplies.

When settlers first started moving west, some American Indians helped guide them.

American Indians React

Most of the overland trails to the West had been American Indian footpaths. For centuries, Indians had traveled these paths to trade with each other. When settlers began using the trails during the late 1830s, they were crossing over the Indians' western lands. At first, the newcomers and Indians traded goods with one another. Some Indians even worked as scouts for the settlers, guiding the wagon trains across the rough trails.

However, over time, Indians began to worry about the thousands of new settlers. The Indians saw that this westward migration was a threat to their hunting grounds. At times, they attacked the wagon trains. At other times, the settlers attacked the Indians. To protect and support the settlers, the United States army built forts along the trails.

The migration of settlers pushed American Indians farther west, forcing them to compete for land. As a result, internecine conflicts started among tribes. In the present-day states of South Dakota, Nebraska, and Wyoming, the Lakota Sioux fought with other Indians over hunting grounds. In 1851, the Lakota and other tribes signed the Horse Creek Treaty with the United States. In the treaty, the Indians agreed to stop attacking settlers as well as each other. The peace was soon broken, however, as more settlers arrived.

READING CHECK **GENERALIZE**
Why did some western Indian tribes begin to fight among themselves in the 1840s?

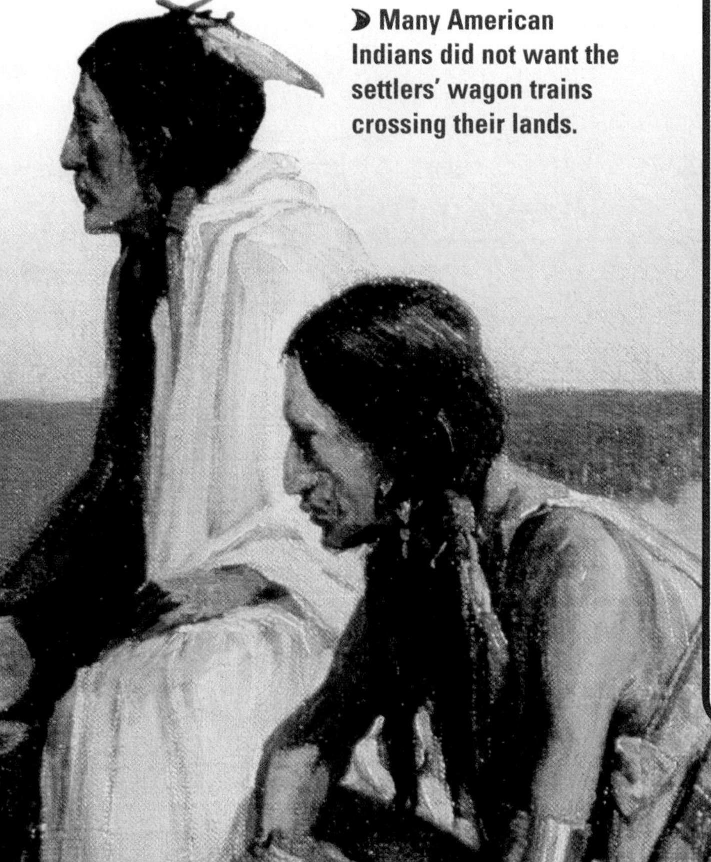

Many American Indians did not want the settlers' wagon trains crossing their lands.

Summary

Starting in the 1840s, thousands of American settlers moved to the areas west of the Rocky Mountains. They followed trails once used by Indians and trappers. Most moved to the West for better opportunities. The arrival of the new settlers led to conflicts with American Indians.

REVIEW

1.  Why did settlers begin moving west in the 1840s?
2. Use the term **ford** to write a sentence about traveling on a western trail.
3. What challenges did pioneers face along the overland trails to the West?

CRITICAL THINKING

4. ANALYSIS SKILL How might the number of settlers heading west have affected people living in Independence, Missouri?
5. ANALYSIS SKILL What were some of the costs and benefits of traveling the Oregon Trail?
6. **Write a Diary Entry** Imagine that you are a pioneer traveling along the Oregon Trail. Write a diary entry about one of the challenges you and your family face along the way.
7. Focus Skill **GENERALIZE**
   On a separate sheet of paper, copy and complete the graphic organizer below.

Facts

Generalization

Settlers traveling the Oregon Trail faced a difficult journey.

PRIMARY SOURCES

Western Trail Goods

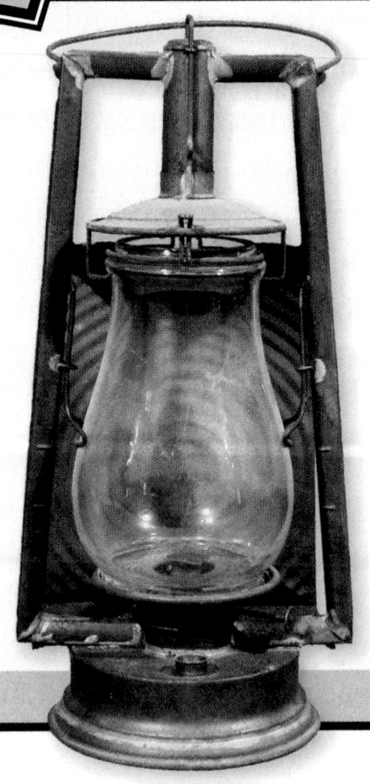

Pioneers heading west had to think carefully about the goods they would need on their journey. They might encounter harsh weather, hunger, or illness, so they had to plan for all these problems. There were few places along the way where they could get more supplies so they had to pack everything they needed in their wagons.

For pioneers heading west, the wagon was like a mobile home. All of their most valuable possessions were packed inside.

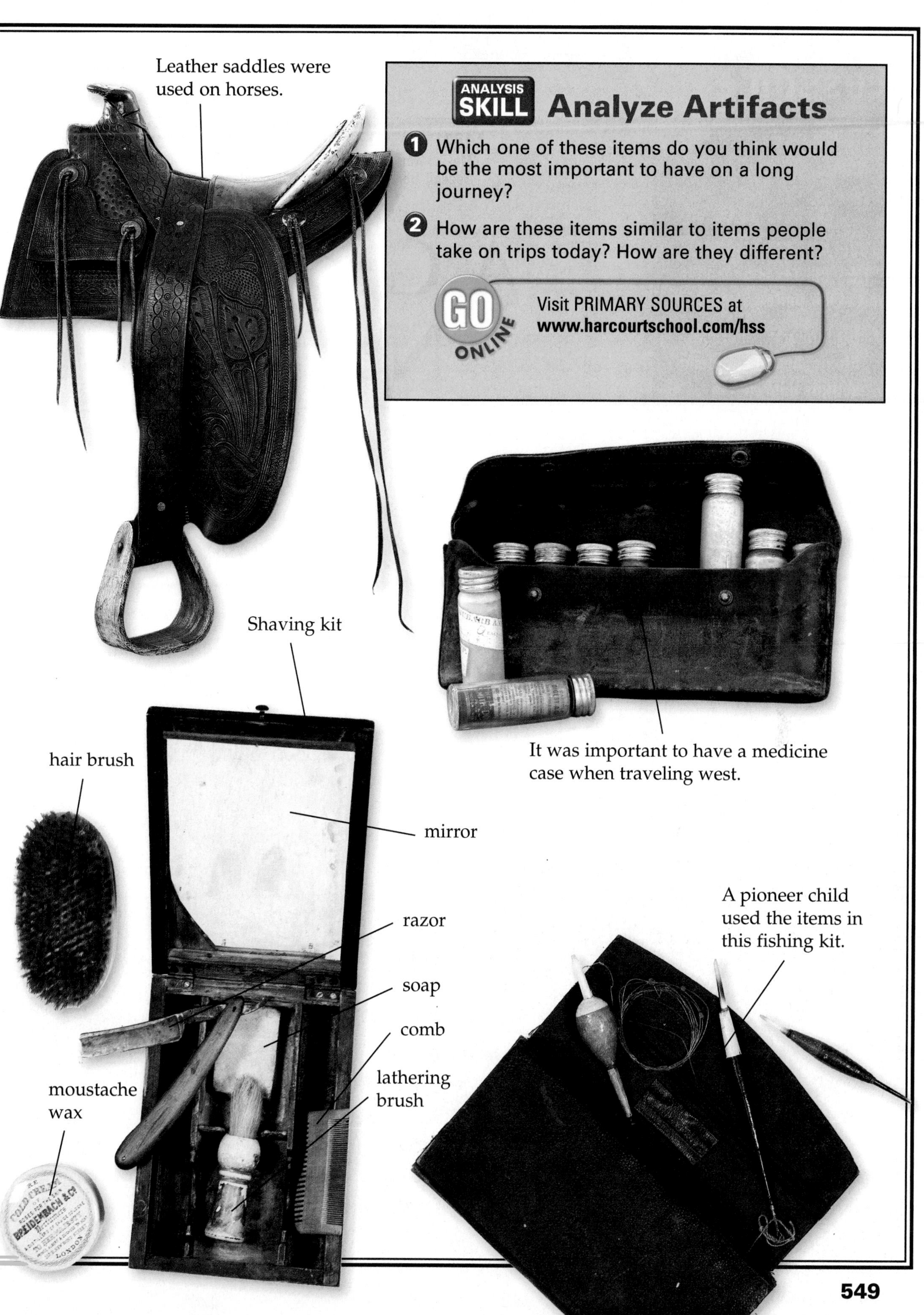

ANALYSIS SKILL Analyze Artifacts

1. Which one of these items do you think would be the most important to have on a long journey?
2. How are these items similar to items people take on trips today? How are they different?

GO ONLINE Visit PRIMARY SOURCES at **www.harcourtschool.com/hss**

Lesson 2

Time

1800 1850

1821 Mexico wins its freedom from Spain

1836 Texas declares its independence

1845 Texas becomes a state

WHAT TO KNOW
How did Texas become a part of the United States?

- Explain why American, Mexican, and European settlers migrated to Texas.
- Relate the significance of the Texas Revolution.
- Describe how Texas became a state.

VOCABULARY
annex p. 553
slave state p. 553
free state p. 553

PEOPLE
Miguel Hidalgo y Costilla
Stephen Austin
Antonio López de Santa Anna
Sam Houston
Juan Seguín
José Antonio Navarro

PLACES
Austin
Alamo

GENERALIZE

California Standards
HSS 5.8, 5.8.5, 5.8.6

A Growing Nation

YOU ARE THERE It is 1825, and your family's wagon train has finally reached **Austin**, Texas. Just ahead, a group of people is coming to greet your wagon train. You try to remember how to say "hello" in Spanish.

"Hello," one of the boys says as he walks up to your wagon. He grins at you. "Welcome to Texas."

"You speak English!" you say with surprise.

"Of course," he says. "We're from Kentucky. Hundreds of families from many states live here."

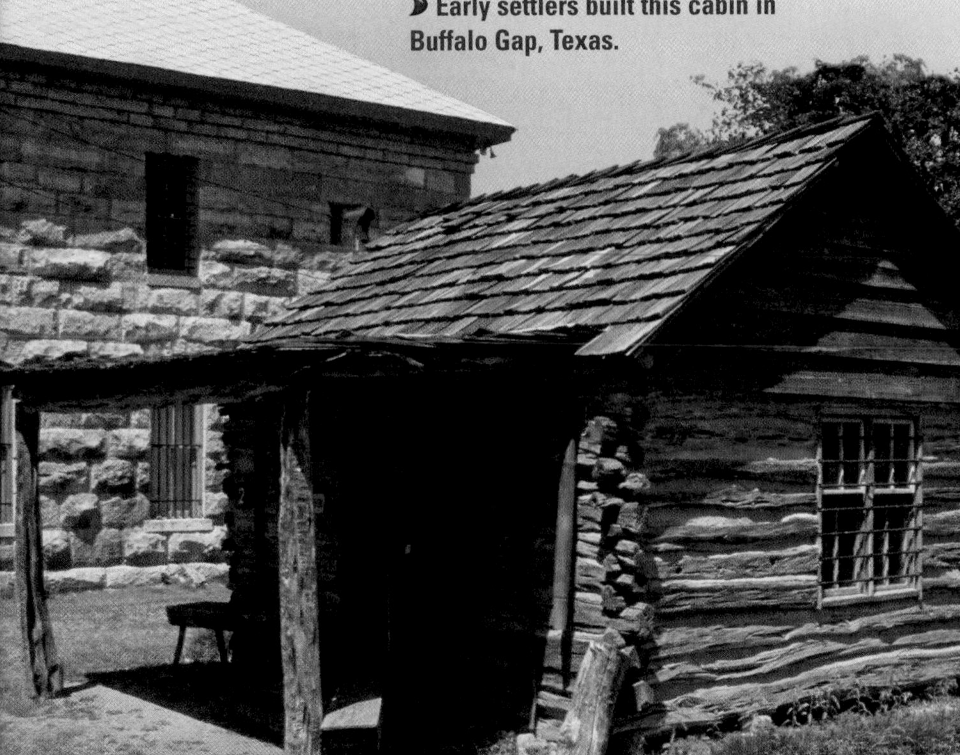

Early settlers built this cabin in Buffalo Gap, Texas.

Cultural Heritage

Vaqueros

Spanish and Mexican *vaqueros*, or cowhands, strongly influenced American culture in the West. Vaqueros used a *lazo*, or rope lasso, to catch their cattle. They wore leather leggings called *chaparejos* to protect their legs from thorny bushes. Americans soon began calling these leggings "chaps." The vaquero's *sombrero*, or large hat, developed into the American cowboy hat. American cowhands who wore cowboy hats and chaps copied the vaquero style.

New Settlements in Texas

Among the newcomers to the West were settlers who had moved farther north in Mexico. During the early 1800s, Spain still controlled Mexico, which included Texas and other places in the southwestern part of what is now the United States. However, many Mexicans felt ignored by the Spanish government and wanted to govern themselves. In 1810, a Mexican priest named **Miguel Hidalgo y Costilla** (mee•GEL ee•DAHL•goh ee kohs•TEE•yah) began the Mexican independence movement.

When Mexico won its independence from Spain in 1821, the new Mexican government took control of much of the Southwest. Since few people lived in Texas, Mexico wanted more settlers to move there. Mexico's leaders gave land grants in Texas in order to encourage Mexican settlers, or Tejanos (tay•HAH•nohs), to migrate into central and southern Texas.

Not all newcomers to Texas came from Mexico. In 1824, **Stephen Austin**, a Missouri businessperson, convinced 300 families from the United States to move to Texas. By 1830, thousands of immigrants from the United States and Europe had set up communities in Texas.

As more Americans arrived in Texas, the Mexican government's worries grew. In 1830, it tried to stop more Americans from settling in Texas. It also wanted the settlers already there to pay more taxes. The laws angered the settlers. In 1834, fighting broke out when Mexico's new leader, General **Antonio López de Santa Anna**, sent troops to Texas to enforce his laws.

READING CHECK **GENERALIZE**
How did Mexico encourage settlers to move to Texas?

The Texas War for Independence

Many Texans decided they no longer wanted to be governed by Mexico. In 1836, a group of them approved the Texas Declaration of Independence. It said that Texas was an independent nation and was no longer part of Mexico. **Sam Houston** was chosen as the commander of the new Texas army.

General Santa Anna was determined to keep Texas for Mexico. He led about 5,000 soldiers toward San Antonio, Texas. About 180 American soldiers made a stand at the San Antonio de Valero Mission, or the **Alamo**. Among them were James Bowie and Davy Crockett, two well-known American pioneers.

For 13 days, the Texans were besieged. Then, on March 6, 1836, Mexican troops made a final attack on the Alamo. Mexican soldiers poured into the fort and captured the defenders. All the defenders were put to death—except for a few women, children, and slaves.

Santa Anna then fought Sam Houston and his army at San Jacinto. As the Texas soldiers ran into battle, they shouted, "Remember the Alamo!"* The Texas army surprised the Mexican forces and after a brief battle they captured Santa Anna.

After his defeat at the Battle of San Jacinto, Santa Anna agreed to move his troops south of the Rio Grande. With Santa Anna's surrender, the Texas War for Independence ended.

READING CHECK **GENERALIZE**
What happened at the Alamo?

*_Heroes of the Alamo_, edited by A.G. Adair and M.G. Crockett. Second Edition, 1957.

During the Battle of San Jacinto (below), the Texas forces captured this flag (right) carried by Santa Anna's army.

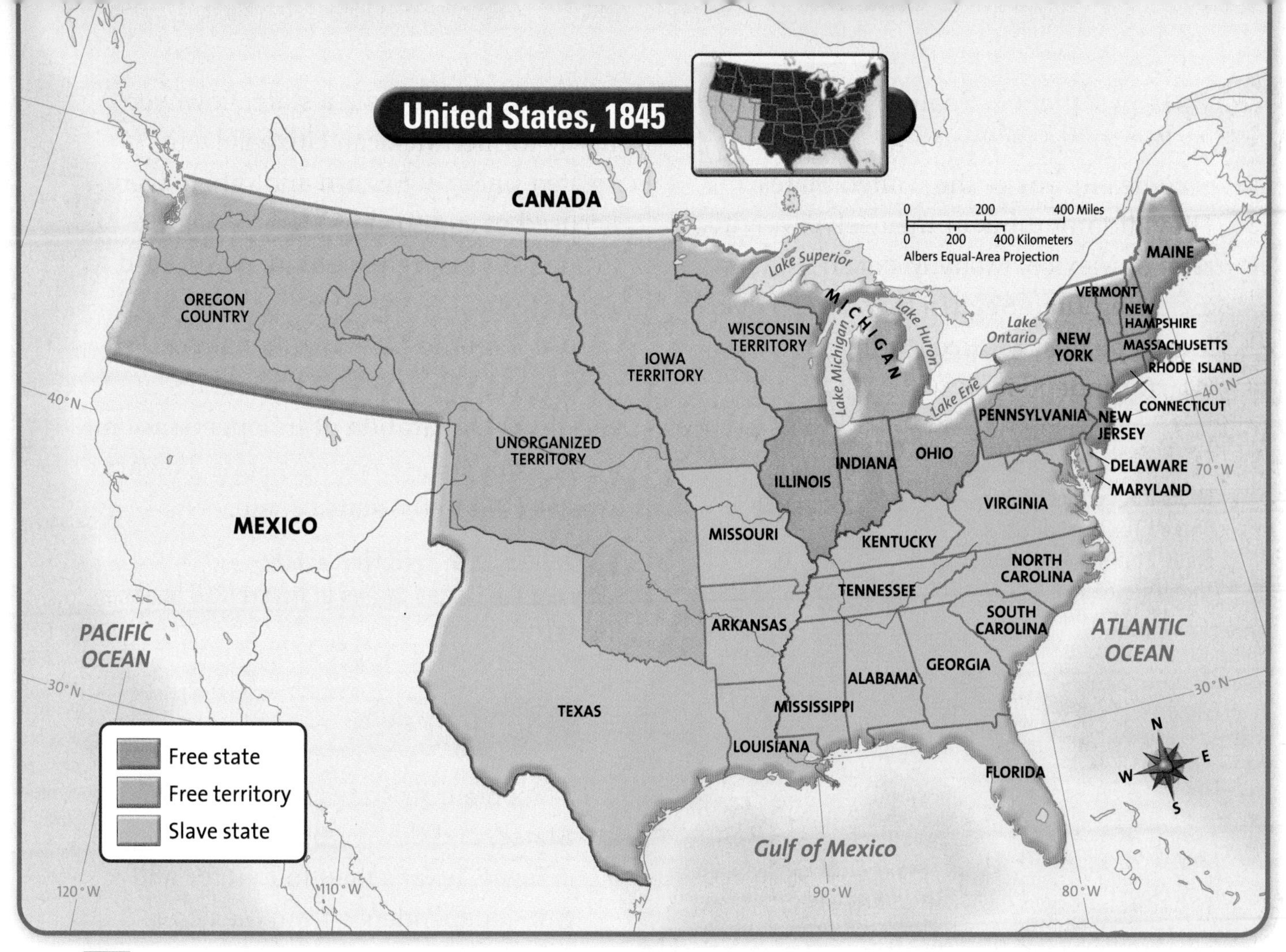

Analyze Maps

Regions How many states allowed slavery in 1845?

Texas Becomes a State

Shortly after Texas became independent, Texans voted to join the United States. However, the government of the United States refused to **annex**, or add on, Texas as a state. Some people worried that making Texas a state might start a war with Mexico. They also argued about the issue of slavery in Texas.

In the 1840s, the United States was divided between slave states and free states. Slavery was allowed in the **slave states**, which were mostly in the South. Slavery was not allowed in the **free states**, located in the North. By 1845, Texas had at least 30,000 slaves. Proponents, or supporters, of slavery wanted Texas to become a state, while abolitionists opposed adding another slave state.

While people in the United States argued, Texas remained an independent republic. Then, James K. Polk ran for President of the United States in 1844, pledging to make Texas part of the United States. Polk won the election, but before he took office, President John Tyler asked the United States Congress to pass an agreement to make Texas a state. On December 29, 1845, Texas officially became the twenty-eighth state.

Many settlers of Spanish and Mexican descent chose to remain in Texas and become citizens of the United States. They did not think of themselves as citizens of Mexico. Many Mexican settlers, including **Juan Seguín** (say•GEEN), had fought against Mexico during the Texas War for Independence.

After Texas became a state, however, many former Mexican citizens were treated unfairly. Seguín and others were accused of supporting Mexico. Seguín argued for his rights, but he was forced to leave Texas.

José Antonio Navarro—a native Texan—had been one of the signers of the Texas Declaration of Independence in 1836. After Texas became a state, Navarro was elected to the state senate.

READING CHECK **GENERALIZE**
Why did the United States at first refuse to annex Texas?

José Antonio Navarro helped Texas become a state. This stamp celebrates Texas statehood.

Summary

People from Mexico, the United States, and Europe built communities in Texas. Texans then fought for and won independence from Mexico. Despite disagreements over slavery, Texas became a state.

REVIEW

1. How did Texas become a part of the United States?
2. Use the terms **slave state** and **free state** in a sentence about Texas statehood.
3. Who was José Antonio Navarro?

CRITICAL THINKING

4. ANALYSIS SKILL How did the relative location of Texas affect who settled there?
5. ANALYSIS SKILL What were the multiple causes and effects of the Texas War for Independence?
6. **Write a Diary Entry** Imagine that you live in Texas in 1845. Write a diary entry telling what you think about the decision to become part of the United States.
7. Focus Skill **GENERALIZE**
On a separate sheet of paper, copy and complete the graphic organizer below.

Facts

Texans approved the Texas Declaration of Independence.	Sam Houston and his army won the Battle of San Jacinto.

Generalization

Miguel Hidalgo

Biography

Trustworthiness
Respect
Responsibility
Fairness
Caring
Patriotism

Every year on September 16, Mexico pays tribute to Miguel Hidalgo y Costilla, who helped begin the movement for Mexico's independence. Hidalgo wanted freedom for the people of Mexico.

In 1810, Hidalgo, a Mexican priest, planned a revolution against the Spanish government. Hidalgo and many others felt that Mexico should be free from Spanish rule. However, his plan was discovered, and several of his friends were arrested. On September 15, 1810, he rang the bells of his church in the city of Dolores as a protest against Spain. He called on all Mexicans to join him in a fight for independence.

The church in Dolores still stands today.

Thousands joined Hidalgo, and his army took over several Mexican cities. Yet when they reached the capital, Mexico City, Hidalgo realized his army was no match for the heavily armed Spanish soldiers. On Hidalgo's orders, the Mexicans turned back. In 1811, Hidalgo was captured by the Spanish and sentenced to death, making him one of the first people to give his life for Mexico's independence.

Why Character Counts

How did Miguel Hidalgo show he cared about the people of Mexico?

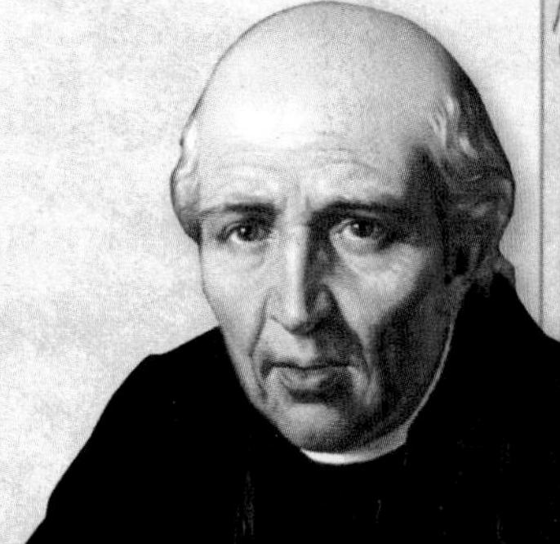

Bio Brief

1753 — Born 1753

1811 — Died 1811

1778 Hidalgo becomes a priest

1810 Hidalgo calls on Mexicans to unite against Spain

GO ONLINE Interactive Multimedia Biographies Visit MULTIMEDIA BIOGRAPHIES at www.harcourtschool.com/hss

Solve a Problem

WHY IT MATTERS

Like Texans in the 1830s, people everywhere face problems at one time or another. Many people face more than one problem at the same time. Think about a problem you have faced recently. Were you able to solve it? Did you wish you could have found a better way to solve the problem? Knowing how to solve problems is a skill that you will use all your life.

WHAT YOU NEED TO KNOW

Here are some steps you can use to help you solve a problem.

Step 1 Identify the problem.

Step 2 Gather information.

Step 3 List possible solutions.

Step 4 Consider the advantages and disadvantages of each solution.

Step 5 Choose the best solution.

Step 6 Try your solution.

Step 7 Think about how well your solution helped solve the problem.

PRACTICE THE SKILL

Imagine that it is the mid-1800s. You have been preparing for a long time to move away from your homeland. At last, you are ready to start a new life in the the new state of Texas. One problem that you now face, however, is that there is not enough money for your family members to go with you. They must remain in your homeland while you search for new opportunities. Think about how to solve the problem of having to move to a new country without your family.

1. How might some immigrants have solved the problem of moving to the United States without their families?

Immigrants often came to the United States on their own.

This painting shows a family of Scottish immigrants outside their new farm home. Often several generations of a family would live together.

2. How might they have carried out this solution?
3. How well might the immigrants' solution have helped them?
4. Do you think this was the best way for immigrants to solve this problem?
5. What other solution might have helped immigrants be with their families?

APPLY WHAT YOU LEARNED

Make It Relevant Identify a problem in your community or school. Use the steps shown to write a plan for solving the problem. What solution did you choose? Why do you think that your solution will help solve the problem?

Lesson 3

Time

1800 — 1850

1846 The Mexican-American War begins

1848 The California gold rush begins

WHAT TO KNOW
How did Oregon, California, and other western lands become part of the United States?

- Understand the Mexican-American War's significance.
- Describe the physical characteristics of states and territories in 1850.
- Discuss life in California during the gold rush.

VOCABULARY
manifest destiny p. 559
cession p. 561
gold rush p. 562
forty-niner p. 562

PEOPLE
James K. Polk
James Gadsden
John Sutter
Mariano Vallejo

PLACES
Oregon Territory
Mexico City
Monterey
Los Angeles
San Francisco

GENERALIZE

California Standards
HSS 5.8, 5.8.2, 5.8.4, 5.8.6

From Ocean to Ocean

YOU ARE THERE

"This valley looks like paradise," your mother says, wiping the trail dust from her hands. "I didn't know Oregon would be this beautiful."

Green and yellow fields stretch as far as you can see. It has been months since your wagon train set out on the Oregon Trail, but the long journey is finally at an end. Oregon will be your new home.

"Can we go see the Pacific Ocean now?" you ask.

Your mother laughs. "It's not as close as you think, but one day we will."

The Oregon Conflict

During the 1840s, much of the Pacific Northwest was claimed by both the United States and Britain. However, settlers moving to Oregon from the United States felt that they had a right to the land. At the time, many people in the United States believed in the idea of **manifest destiny**. They thought that the United States was meant to stretch from the Atlantic Ocean to the Pacific Ocean.

As the number of settlers in the Northwest increased, Britain and the United States argued about the border of the Oregon Country. President **James K. Polk** was a strong supporter of manifest destiny. Polk wanted to set the border between the United States and Canada far to the north. The British thought the border should be farther south. For a time, it looked as if arguments over the Oregon Country might cause another war between the United States and Britain. In 1846, the two countries agreed to sign the Oregon Treaty. The treaty established the northern border of the Oregon Country.

In 1848, Congress created the **Oregon Territory**, which included present-day Oregon, Idaho, Washington, and parts of Wyoming and Montana. Afterward, a movement to make Oregon a state began. The people of the territory agreed that Oregon would not be a slave state. This led to a national debate on whether to admit another free state. Finally, on February 14, 1859, President James Buchanan signed a bill making Oregon the thirty-third state.

READING CHECK **GENERALIZE**
How was the Oregon boundary conflict settled?

After a long journey on the Oregon Trail, wagon trains arrived in the Pacific Northwest.

War with Mexico

American army drum

During the time that the United States was settling its conflict with Britain, a dispute arose with Mexico. The United States claimed that the Rio Grande formed the southern border of Texas. Mexico said that the boundary was actually the Nueces (nu•AY•sahs) River, about 100 miles north of the Rio Grande.

In 1845, President Polk sent John Slidell to Mexico. Slidell offered Mexico $30 million for California, New Mexico, and Texas lands north of Mexico. The Mexican leaders refused to meet with Slidell. They said they did not want to sell their lands to the United States.

In response, President Polk sent about 3,500 United States soldiers to the area between the Nueces River and the Rio Grande. General Zachary Taylor, who commanded the soldiers, ordered them to build a fort on the land Mexico claimed. Taylor also blockaded the mouth of the Rio Grande.

Mexico sent soldiers to protect its claim to the Rio Grande. On May 6, 1846, American and Mexican soldiers fought at Palo Alto. The next day, the two sides battled each other again. In both battles, the United States Army drove Mexican soldiers back.

By that time, President Polk had already begun writing a message of war to Congress. On May 13, 1846, Congress declared war on Mexico, and the Mexican-American War officially began.

Not all Americans agreed with the war. For example, Northerners felt that the war could cause the expansion of slavery into the west. Some said that the United States government wanted to go to war to take Mexico's lands. However, those who disagreed with the war could not stop it.

General Zachary Taylor directs troops at Buena Vista, in northern Mexico, during the Mexican-American War.

The Mexican-American War divided people in the United States.

President James K. Polk, 1846

"As war exists, and, notwithstanding all our efforts to avoid it, exists by the act of Mexico herself, we are called upon . . . [to protect] the interests of our country."

—from *Changing Interpretations of America's Past,* Volume 1, edited by Jim R. McClellan. Dushkin, 2000.

Horace Greeley, 1846

"People of the United States! Your rulers are precipitating [throwing] you into a fathomless abyss [bottomless pit] of crime and calamity [distress]!"

—from *Changing Interpretations of America's Past,* Volume 1, edited by Jim R. McClellan. Dushkin, 2000.

It's Your Turn

ANALYSIS SKILL **Analyze Points of View** Summarize each person's feelings about the Mexican-American War. Then explain the reasons for each point of view.

United States soldiers marched south to try to capture Mexico's capital, **Mexico City**. They soon won a battle at Buena Vista. One month later, the United States Navy captured Veracruz.

Santa Anna led the Mexican army as it prepared to defend Mexico City. After a hard fight, the Mexican army was defeated. The United States captured Mexico City on September 14, 1847. The Mexican-American War was over.

In 1848, the United States and Mexico signed the Treaty of Guadalupe Hidalgo (gwah•dah•LOO•pay ee•DAHL•goh). Under this treaty, Mexico gave the United States a huge region known as the Mexican Cession. A **cession**, or concession, is something given up. The Mexican Cession included all of present-day California, Nevada, Utah, and parts of New Mexico, Arizona, Colorado, and Wyoming. In return, the United States paid Mexico $15 million.

When the Mexican-American War ended, about 80,000 Mexicans remained in areas that now belonged to the United States. Most of them stayed and became citizens of the United States. They felt connected to the land because their ancestors had lived there since the 1700s. One Mexican American said, "We were the pioneers of the Pacific Coast, building towns and missions while General Washington was carrying on the War of the Revolution."*

In 1853, the United States gained even more land when **James Gadsden**, the United States minister to Mexico, bought the rest of New Mexico and Arizona from Mexico. The Gadsden Purchase brought the southern continental United States to its present size. It also set the border between the United States and Mexico.

READING CHECK **GENERALIZE**
Why did the United States and Mexico go to war in 1846?

*Guadalupe Vallejo. "Ranch Mission Days in California." *The Century Magazine.* Vol. XLI, December 1890.

California Grows

In the 1840s, California was a land of large ranches with a few small towns, such as **Monterey** and **Los Angeles**. At that time, most people in California were either Californios, as the Spanish-speaking people there called themselves, or American Indians. Their lives changed greatly after the United States gained California in the Mexican Cession. They would soon change even more.

In 1848, workers building a sawmill for **John Sutter** along the bank of the South Fork of the American River found some gold nuggets in the river. Soon most of the workers left to search for more gold.

Communication across the country was still slow in 1848. As a result, it took a while for people to hear about the gold in California. However, once word got out, a **gold rush** began. In a short time, about 80,000 gold seekers arrived in California from other parts of the United States as well as from Europe and Asia. They were called **forty-niners** because many of them arrived in 1849.

Many forty-niners had made their way west along the overland trails. Others had reached the Pacific coast by sailing around Cape Horn at the southern tip of South America or by crossing the Isthmus of Panama. For the forty-niners, gold was their economic incentive—they hoped to become rich. Although most did not find enough gold to become wealthy, a few

GEOGRAPHY

Marshall Gold Discovery State Historic Park

No one is sure who first found gold in California, but James Marshall claimed that he was the one. While leading workers at Sutter's Mill, Marshall said that he found the first gold nuggets in a nearby riverbed. Today, the site of the discovery is part of the Marshall Gold Discovery State Historic Park, in Coloma, California.

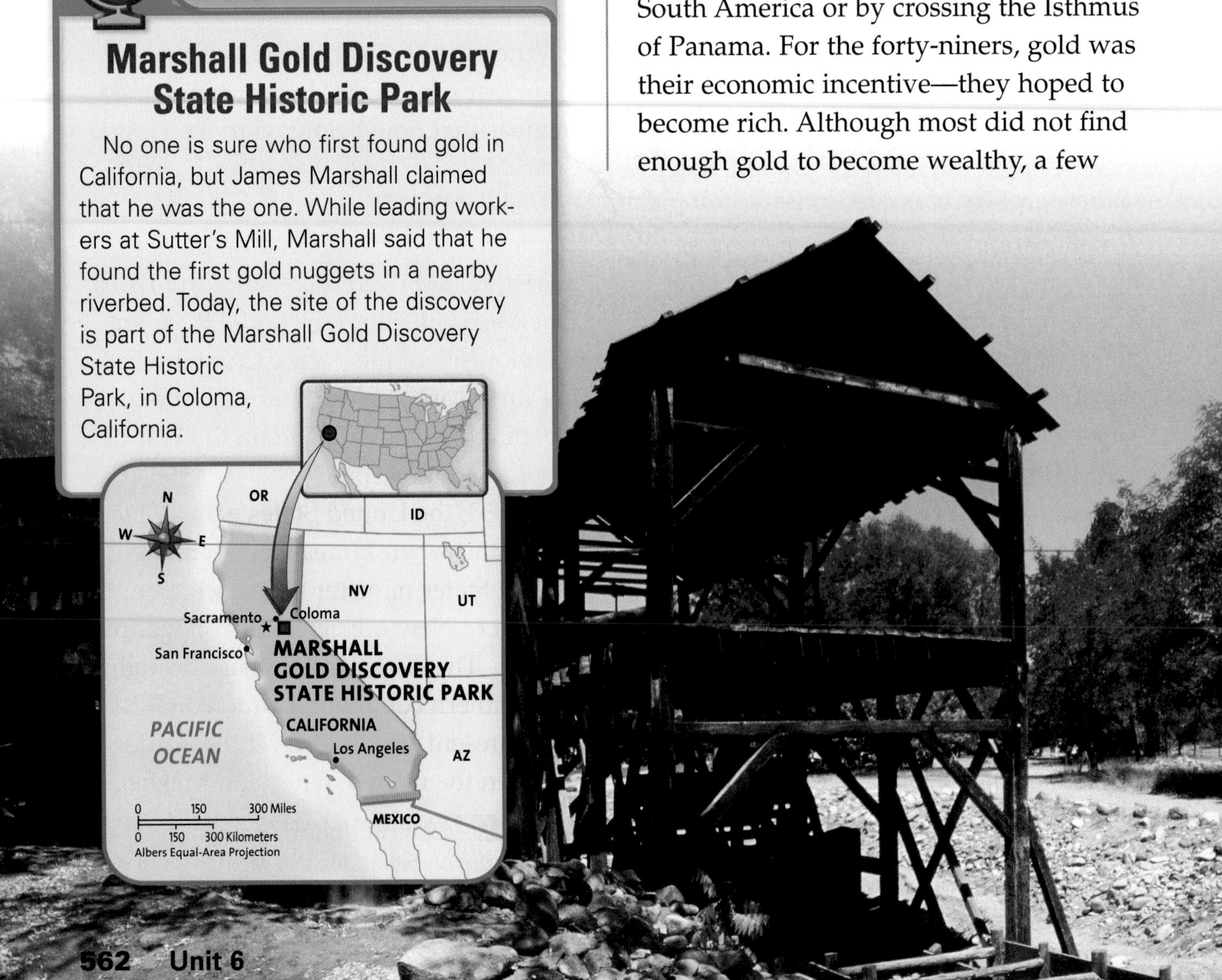

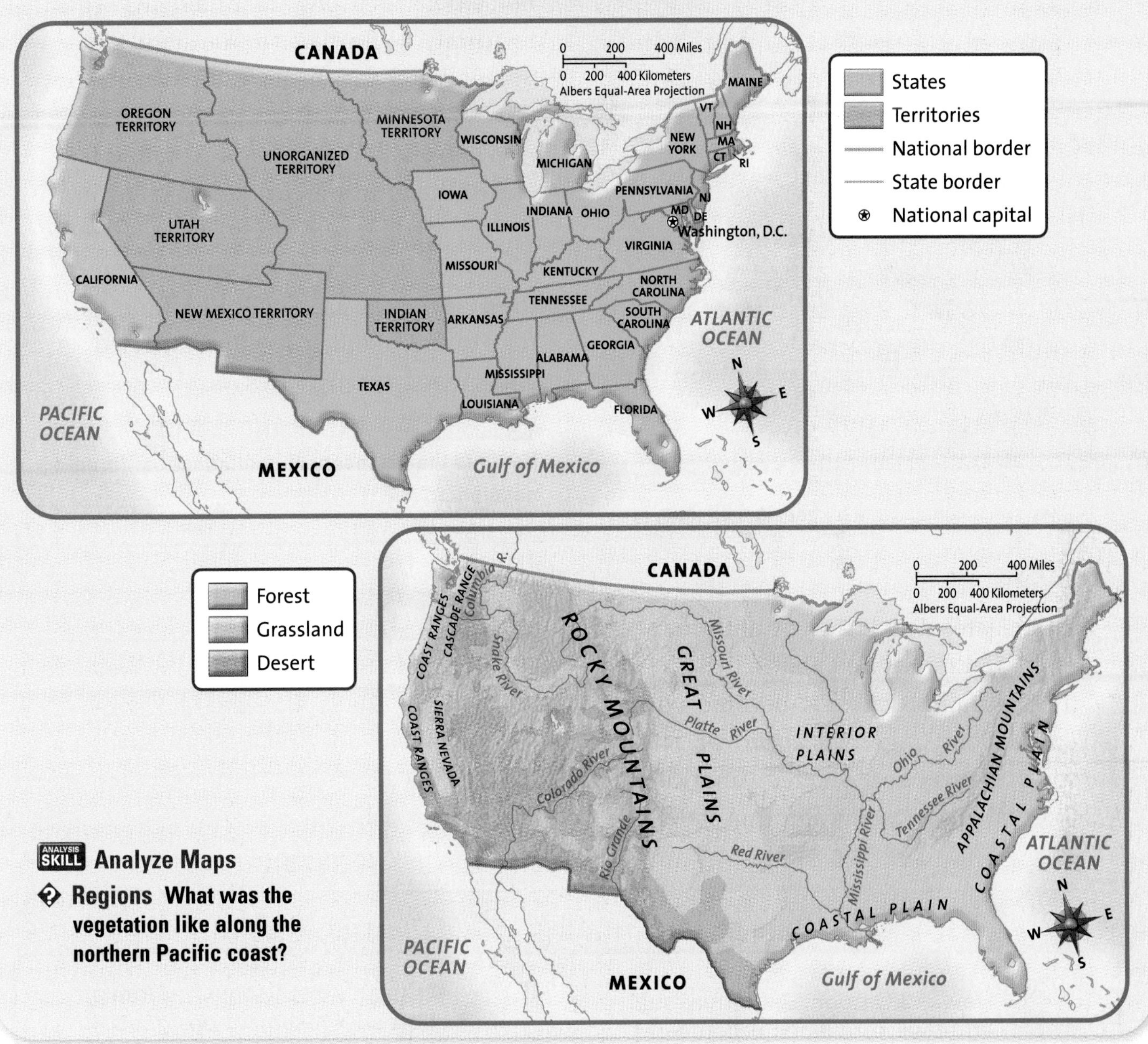

ANALYSIS SKILL Analyze Maps

Regions What was the vegetation like along the northern Pacific coast?

struck it rich. One man described how he broke open a rock to find ". . . bright, yellow gold, in little pieces . . ."*

Gold was not the only valuable resource in California. For many years, New England sailors had traveled there to trade for cattle hides and tallow, or animal fat, which was used in oil lamps. Whalers hunted in the oceans, and sea traders took sea otter and seal furs to markets in the East.

At that time, ships from Atlantic ports had to sail around Cape Horn to reach the Pacific Ocean. California's resources were so rich, however, that traders willingly made the dangerous voyage.

By 1849, California's population had grown to about 100,000 people. That same year, a group of delegates met at Monterey to discuss statehood for California. Among them was **Mariano Vallejo**, a former Mexican army general. Together,

*Gould Buffum. "Six Months in the Gold Mines." *The United States Democratic Review.* J. & H.G. Langley, July 1850.

Chinese immigrants pan for gold in California, in the 1850s.

the delegates decided that California should join the United States.

Before California could become a state, Congress had to give its approval. The issue of slavery still divided Americans. Slave states opposed California statehood because slavery was not legal there. After fierce debates, Congress finally agreed to admit California as a free state. On September 9, 1850, California became the thirty-first state.

When California became a state it had one of the most diverse populations in the country. During the gold rush, people had come to California from all over the world. Many Chinese immigrants, for example, settled in **San Francisco** and other growing cities.

READING CHECK CAUSE AND EFFECT
How did the discovery of gold affect California's population?

Summary

The United States added many western lands in the 1800s. After the Mexican-American War, the United States claimed most of the Southwest. In 1850, California became the thirty-first state.

REVIEW

1. How did Oregon, California, and other western lands become part of the United States?
2. Write a sentence about California's history, using the terms **gold rush** and **forty-niner**.
3. What lands did the Mexican Cession give to the United States?

CRITICAL THINKING

4. **Make It Relevant** Would you have been willing to move to California to find gold? Why or why not?
5. ANALYSIS SKILL What would be the possible benefits and costs of joining the gold rush?
6. **Write an Advertisement** Write a short advertisement designed to attract people to California's goldfields. List reasons why people should come.
7. Focus Skill **GENERALIZE**
On a separate sheet of paper, copy and complete the graphic organizer.

Facts

Generalization

California's population represented a diversity of cultures.

Yung Wing

*"Knowledge is power, and power is greater than riches."**

Not all early Asian immigrants to the United States settled on the west coast. Yung Wing arrived in the United States in 1847 to attend school in Connecticut. He later became the first Asian to graduate from an American university. From 1850 to 1854, Wing attended Yale University in Connecticut.

Yung Wing enrolled in Yale University in 1850.

Wing was born in 1828 near Macao, China. He first attended a school set up by American missionaries. When one of the missionaries returned home, Wing accompanied him.

Wing succeeded at Yale in spite of the trouble he sometimes faced from those who did not want him there. After he graduated, he wanted to help other Chinese students study in the United States. In 1872, he helped establish the Chinese Educational Mission, which brought Chinese students to the United States. The program lasted for only nine years, but the students who were involved had a strong impact on their homeland and in the United States.

Wing himself became a diplomat, representing China in the United States. In 1875, he married Mary Kellogg, and the couple had two children. Wing died in Hartford, Connecticut in 1912.

Yung Wing. *My Life in China and America.* Arno Press, 1978.

Why Character Counts

How did Yung Wing show he cared about educating others?

Bio Brief

1828 — Born 1828

1854 Wing graduates from Yale University

1872 Wing helps start a program for Chinese students to study in the United States

1912 — Died 1912

Identify Changing Borders

WHY IT MATTERS

Historical maps give important information about places as they were in the past. By studying a historical map, you can see how a place and its borders have changed over time. Seeing those changes on a historical map can help you understand the changes and how they came about.

WHAT YOU NEED TO KNOW

This chapter describes how the United States grew over time. The map on page 567 uses colors to show how the country's borders changed from the late 1700s to the mid-1800s. It uses labels to identify the different regions and to give the year in which each one became part of the United States.

PRACTICE THE SKILL

Use the map on page 567 to answer these questions.

1. What color is used to show the United States as it was in 1783?
2. In what year did the Gadsden Purchase take place?

A surveyor sets a property line at Castroville, Texas, in the 1840s.

The Growth of the United States

Present-day border

RUSSIA
ALASKA PURCHASE 1867
CANADA
0 200 400 Miles
0 400 Kilometers
PACIFIC OCEAN
CANADA
TREATY WITH BRITAIN 1842
0 200 400 Miles
0 200 400 Kilometers
Albers Equal-Area Projection
TREATY WITH BRITAIN 1818
Lake Superior
Lake Michigan
Lake Huron
Lake Ontario
Lake Erie
OREGON TERRITORY 1846
LOUISIANA PURCHASE 1803
40°N
70°W
MEXICAN CESSION 1848
UNITED STATES 1783
ATLANTIC OCEAN
PACIFIC OCEAN
GADSDEN PURCHASE 1853
TEXAS ANNEXATION 1845
30°N
1810
1812
1813
FLORIDA 1819
120°W
HAWAII ANNEXATION 1898
PACIFIC OCEAN
0 100 Miles
0 100 Kilometers
MEXICO
Gulf of Mexico
110°W
90°W
80°W
N E S W

3. In what year was Texas annexed by the United States?
4. What country shared a border with the Oregon Territory?
5. What area was added to the United States in 1803?

APPLY WHAT YOU LEARNED

ANALYSIS SKILL Study the map on this page. Then use what you see to write a paragraph describing how the borders of the United States have changed since 1783.

Practice your map and globe skills with the **GeoSkills CD-ROM**.

Lesson 4

Time

1800 — 1850

1790 The first textile mill in the United States opens

1845 The Great Irish Famine begins

1848 The Seneca Falls Convention is held

New People and New Ideas

WHAT TO KNOW
How did new people and new inventions change life in the United States?

- ✔ Trace the effects of new transportation systems.
- ✔ Identify how economic incentives attracted new immigrants.
- ✔ Describe the struggle between slavery's proponents and opponents.

VOCABULARY
Industrial Revolution p. 569
cotton gin p. 569
interchangeable parts p. 569
telegraph p. 571
Underground Railroad p. 573

PEOPLE
Harriet Tubman
Frederick Douglass
Lucretia Mott
Elizabeth Cady Stanton
Susan B. Anthony

PLACES
Seneca Falls

GENERALIZE

California Standards
HSS 5.4.6, 5.8, 5.8.1

YOU ARE THERE Today, you are visiting your father at the textile mill where he works. The building is huge—gears and belts are everywhere. They make so much noise you have to cover your ears with your hands.

"Look," your father says, pointing upward. "It used to take your grandmother weeks to make this much cloth at her loom." Above you, huge machines are weaving sheets of wool cloth. Lengths of yellow, blue, and red cloth take shape as you watch.

"Can you show me how the machines work?" you ask. You've never seen anything so exciting!

The Industrial Revolution

In the early 1800s, new inventions changed the way people lived and worked in the United States. People began using machines to make large quantities of goods. This period became known as the **Industrial Revolution**.

The Industrial Revolution began during the late 1700s, when Britain developed huge machines to spin thread and weave textiles, or cloth. In 1790, the first American textile mill opened in Rhode Island. It marked the beginning of large-scale manufacturing in the United States.

In 1793, Eli Whitney developed the **cotton gin**. It was used on southern plantations to remove seeds from cotton quickly, which meant that more cotton could be shipped to textile mills. Whitney also invented a system of **interchangeable parts** to make guns. These parts were exactly alike. If one part was damaged, another part could instantly be put in its place.

As more factories were built—mostly in the North—more workers were needed to run them. Men, women, and even children went to work in factories, usually for little money. Women who worked at textile mills in Lowell, Massachusetts, were paid only about $12 a month.

Despite the low pay, factory workers were paid better than poor farmworkers. Factory jobs provided an economic incentive for many European immigrants. Most of these new immigrants settled in cities in the North, where industries had grown very quickly. For the most part, the South remained an agricultural region.

READING CHECK **GENERALIZE**
Why did many new immigrants choose to settle in cities in the North?

A Closer LOOK

A Textile Mill

With the invention of the the steam engine, textile mills no longer depended on running water as a power source.

1. **The steam engine turned the gears that drove the different machines inside the mill.**
2. **First, machines spun cotton or wool into yarn.**
3. **Next, machines prepared the yarn for weaving.**
4. **Finally, machines wove the yarn into cloth.**

What powered all of the machines in the mill?

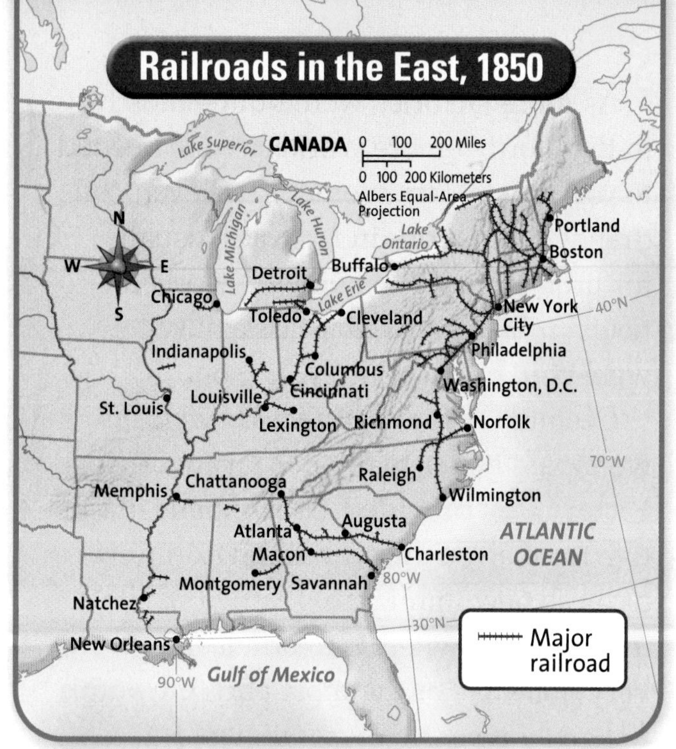

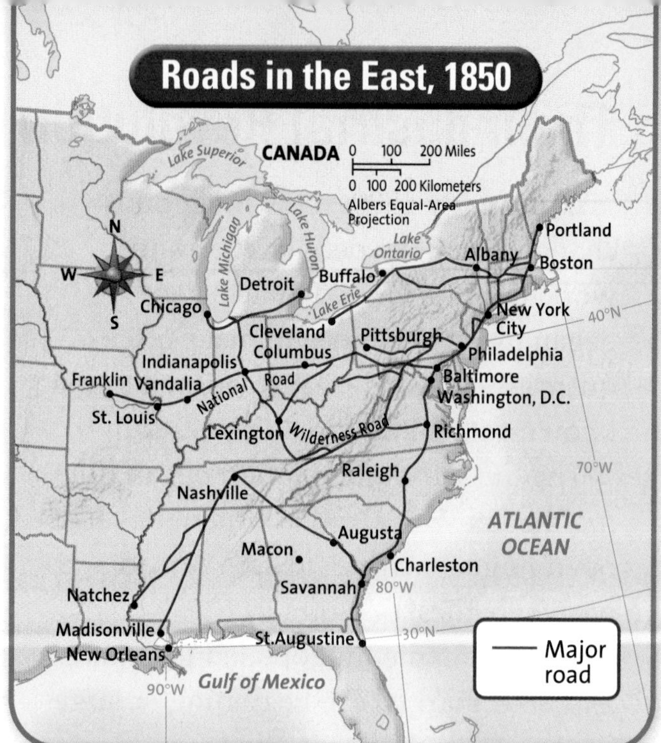

ANALYSIS SKILL Analyze Maps

Location What was the westernmost city with a railroad link in 1850?

Travel and Communication

During the mid-1800s, the Industrial Revolution changed settlement patterns in the United States. By 1860, about one of every five Americans lived in a city. As cities grew, people developed faster systems of transportation to travel between the cities.

By 1860, there were more than 1,000 steamboats running on rivers in the United States. Many people chose to travel on steamboats because they were cheaper and faster than sailboats.

Before long, steamboats began to affect the growth of cities in the West. New immigrants and traders settled in the areas where steamboats docked. Most major western cities rose up around river ports. Cincinnati, on the Ohio River, and

The railroad attracted new people and businesses to towns located along the train routes.

St. Louis, on the Mississippi River, both developed in this way.

Steamboats were so successful that inventors began using steam engines in railroad engines, or locomotives. The first locomotive made in the United States was the Tom Thumb, built in 1830 for the Baltimore & Ohio Railroad.

Before the Tom Thumb, railroad companies had used horses to pull railroad cars. The new steam engines made railway travel much faster. Railroads grew quickly after 1830. By 1850, about 9,000 miles of track crossed the nation.

Many of these railroad routes joined cities in the East. Railroads carried raw materials from farms in the South and the West. Factories and mills in the North used the raw materials to make manufactured goods, which were then taken to market on railroad cars.

Railroads transported people as well as goods. Many cities and towns grew near railroad stops. As people came to depend on railroad travel, even more tracks were built. By the late 1800s, railroads would stretch from coast to coast.

New inventions also changed the way people communicated. In the early 1800s, messages had been sent by messenger or by mail. A message traveling from one part of the country to another could take weeks to arrive.

In 1837, Samuel F. B. Morse invented a faster way to communicate. His invention, called the **telegraph**, sent messages from one machine to another along a wire. To do this, Morse invented a code system in which electronic "dots" and "dashes"—short and long taps on a key—stood for letters of the alphabet. Today, this code is known as Morse code.

One telegraph operator sent Morse code across a wire. At the other end, a different operator translated the code back into letters and words. Suddenly messages that once took days or weeks to send took only seconds!

By 1866, a working telegraph cable had been laid all the way across the floor of the Atlantic Ocean. The queen of England and the President of the United States exchanged the first telegraph messages sent across the ocean.

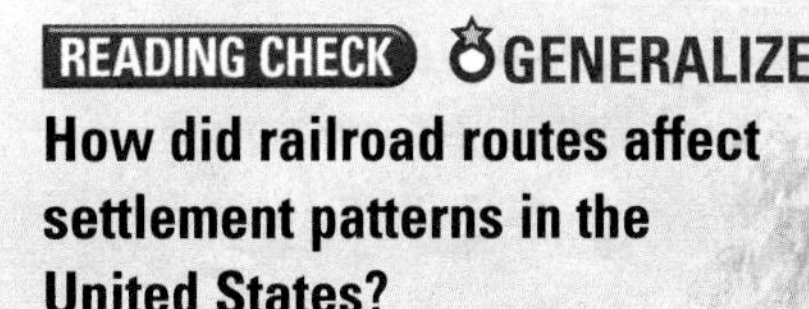

READING CHECK **GENERALIZE**
How did railroad routes affect settlement patterns in the United States?

Many immigrants sailed to New York City in search of new opportunities and a better life in the United States.

Changes in Population

During the 1800s, a growing number of immigrants from Europe arrived in the United States. Their journey was made faster by changes in transportation. On a sailing ship, it had taken an average of two months for European immigrants to cross the Atlantic Ocean. Steamships crossing the ocean made the voyage much faster.

New transportation systems also affected immigration patterns within the United States. For example, many immigrants moved to areas to be near railroads. Thousands of Irish workers settled where they could take jobs building the railroads. Scandinavian immigrants often moved to the Great Lakes and Great Plains regions because railroad companies were offering free land to settlers.

During the 1840s, there was a huge increase in the number of Irish immigrants who came to the United States. Between 1845 and 1850, a disease killed most of Ireland's potato crops, the main diet of many Irish farm families. People began calling this time the Great Irish Famine. A famine (FA•min) is a time when food is limited and people starve.

During the Great Irish Famine, more than 1 million people starved to death. Many of those who survived chose to move to the United States. They immigrated to places such as Boston and New York City and began new lives.

READING CHECK **GENERALIZE**
Why did many Irish people immigrate to the United States during the 1840s?

Working for Change

As life in the United States changed, more slaves sought their freedom. Abolitionists, or people who wanted to abolish slavery, began the **Underground Railroad**—not an actual railroad, but secret routes along which runaway slaves traveled. These routes led to free states in the North and to Canada. Former slaves such as **Harriet Tubman** worked as guides for the runaways.

Many of the escaped slaves settled in the North. One former slave named **Frederick Douglass** settled in New York. Douglass felt strongly about the wrongs of slavery. He began an abolitionist newspaper named the *North Star*.

▸ **Frederick Douglass**

Like some other abolitionists, Douglass also spoke out in support of women's rights. In 1848, he attended a women's rights convention held in **Seneca Falls**, New York. **Lucretia Mott** and **Elizabeth Cady Stanton** organized the convention to protest the fact that women were not allowed to vote or to hold public office.

Mott and Stanton argued that women should be given the same rights as men. Stanton wrote a Declaration of Sentiments, which she modeled after the Declaration of Independence. Her Declaration began by

The Underground Railroad

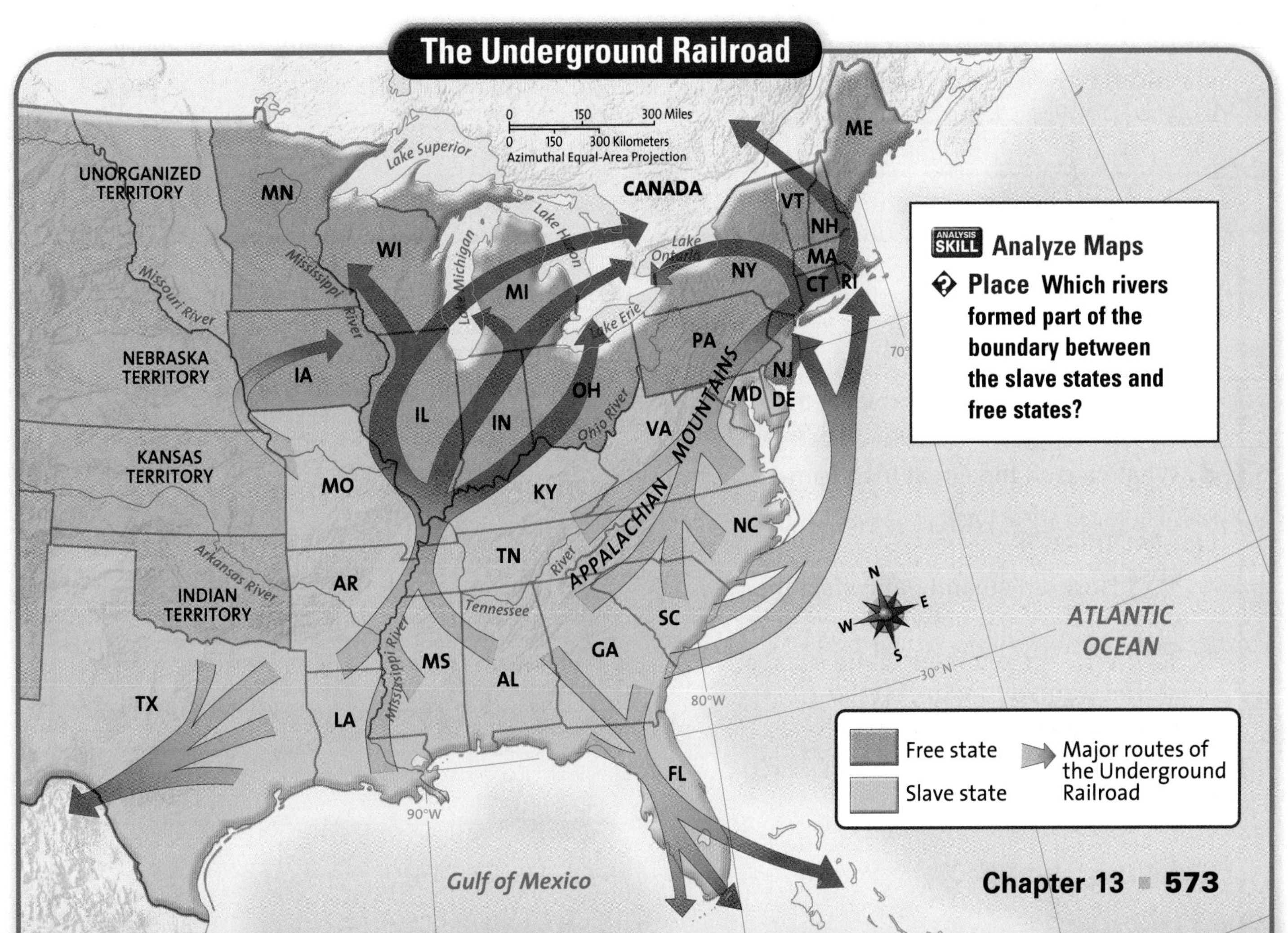

ANALYSIS SKILL Analyze Maps

Place Which rivers formed part of the boundary between the slave states and free states?

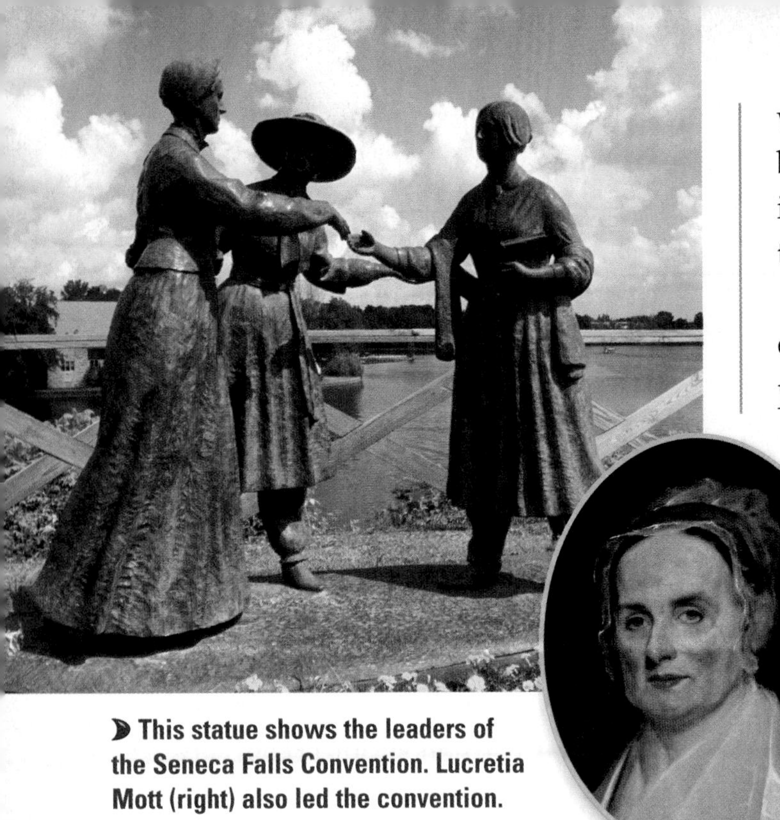

This statue shows the leaders of the Seneca Falls Convention. Lucretia Mott (right) also led the convention.

saying, "We hold these truths to be self-evident; that all men and women are created equal."*

Susan B. Anthony also worked for women's rights. She argued that women should have the right to vote. Many years would pass before Anthony's arguments became widely accepted. In 1869, women in the Wyoming Territory won the right to vote in elections there.

African Americans had not yet gained equal rights, either. When Congress passed the Compromise of 1850, one of the laws made it easier for slave owners to recover escaped slaves. Disagreements about slavery grew violent. They would eventually tear the United States apart.

READING CHECK **GENERALIZE**
How did the Underground Railroad help escaped slaves gain their freedom?

*Elizabeth Cady Stanton. *A History of Woman Suffrage.* Fowler and Wells, 1889.

Summary

New inventions led to the Industrial Revolution. Steamboats and railroads made travel easier. However, the nation faced rising disagreements over slavery and women's rights.

REVIEW

1. How did new people and new inventions change life in the United States?
2. Write a sentence that explains the meaning of the term **Industrial Revolution**.
3. What caused the Great Irish Famine?

CRITICAL THINKING

4. ANALYSIS SKILL How did steamboats affect the way cities in the West grew?
5. ANALYSIS SKILL Why do you think some escaped slaves wanted to work on the Underground Railroad?
6. **Write an Advertisement** Imagine that you are a writer during the early 1850s. Write an advertisement encouraging people to use the telegraph to send messages.
7. Focus Skill **GENERALIZE**
On a separate sheet of paper, copy and complete the graphic organizer.

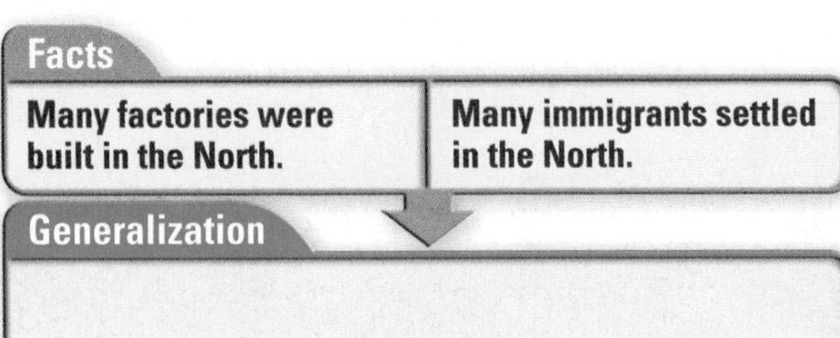

Harriet Tubman

Biography

Trustworthiness
Respect
Responsibility
Fairness
Caring
Patriotism

*"I was the conductor of the Underground Railroad for eight years, and I can say what most conductors can't say—I never ran my train off the track and I never lost a passenger."**

Harriet Tubman was born an enslaved person in Bucktown, Maryland. In 1849, when Tubman was about 29 years old, she heard rumors that she was about to be sold. To avoid being sold, she set out for the North, making her secret way to Philadelphia and freedom.

This postage stamp honors Harriet Tubman.

Tubman could have started a new life and forgotten about her past. However, she could not forget about the enslaved people she had left behind. She decided to try to bring as many enslaved people to freedom as she could. In 1850, she made her first trip back to the South to guide runaways on the Underground Railroad. She would make 18 more trips. In all, she rescued more than 300 people.

Later in life, Tubman continued to find ways to care for other people. For example, she opened a home where older African Americans could live and get care. The house stayed open even after her death.

*Harriet Tubman. *Bound for the Promised Land: Harriet Tubman, Portrait of an American Hero* by Kate Larson. Ballantine, 2004.

Why Character Counts

How did Harriet Tubman show that she cared about others?

Bio Brief

1820 Born 1820

1911 Died 1911

1849 Tubman escapes from Maryland

1860 Tubman makes her nineteenth and last trip to the South

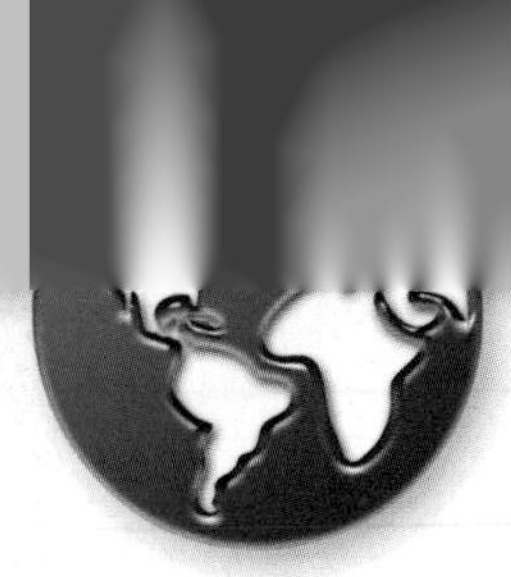

Read a Time Zone Map

WHY IT MATTERS

For centuries, people used the sun to determine their local time. When the sun was at its highest point in the sky, it was noon. Since the sun is at its highest point at different times in different places, the United States had more than 100 time zones! This made scheduling train travel difficult.

Sandford Fleming of Canada and Charles Dowd of the United States developed the idea of dividing Earth into standard time zones. A **time zone** is a region in which a single time is observed.

WHAT YOU NEED TO KNOW

Fleming recommended that the world be organized into 24 different time zones. In each new time zone to the west, the time is one hour earlier than in the time zone just before that.

The map on page 577 shows the time zones in the Western Hemisphere. Find Los Angeles, in the Pacific time zone. Now find Salt Lake City in the mountain time zone. The time in the Pacific time zone is one hour earlier than in the mountain time zone. If it is 5:00 P.M. in the Pacific time zone, it is 6:00 P.M. in the mountain time zone.

PRACTICE THE SKILL

Use the time zone map of the Western Hemisphere on page 577 to answer these questions.

1. How are colors used on the time zone map?
2. In what time zone are New York City, Philadelphia, and Washington, D.C.?
3. If it is 10:00 A.M. in Chicago, Illinois, what time is it in San Diego, California?
4. If you traveled from Houston, Texas, to Los Angeles, California, through how many time zones would you pass?

Before standard time zones, scheduling train stops was difficult because every town kept its own time.

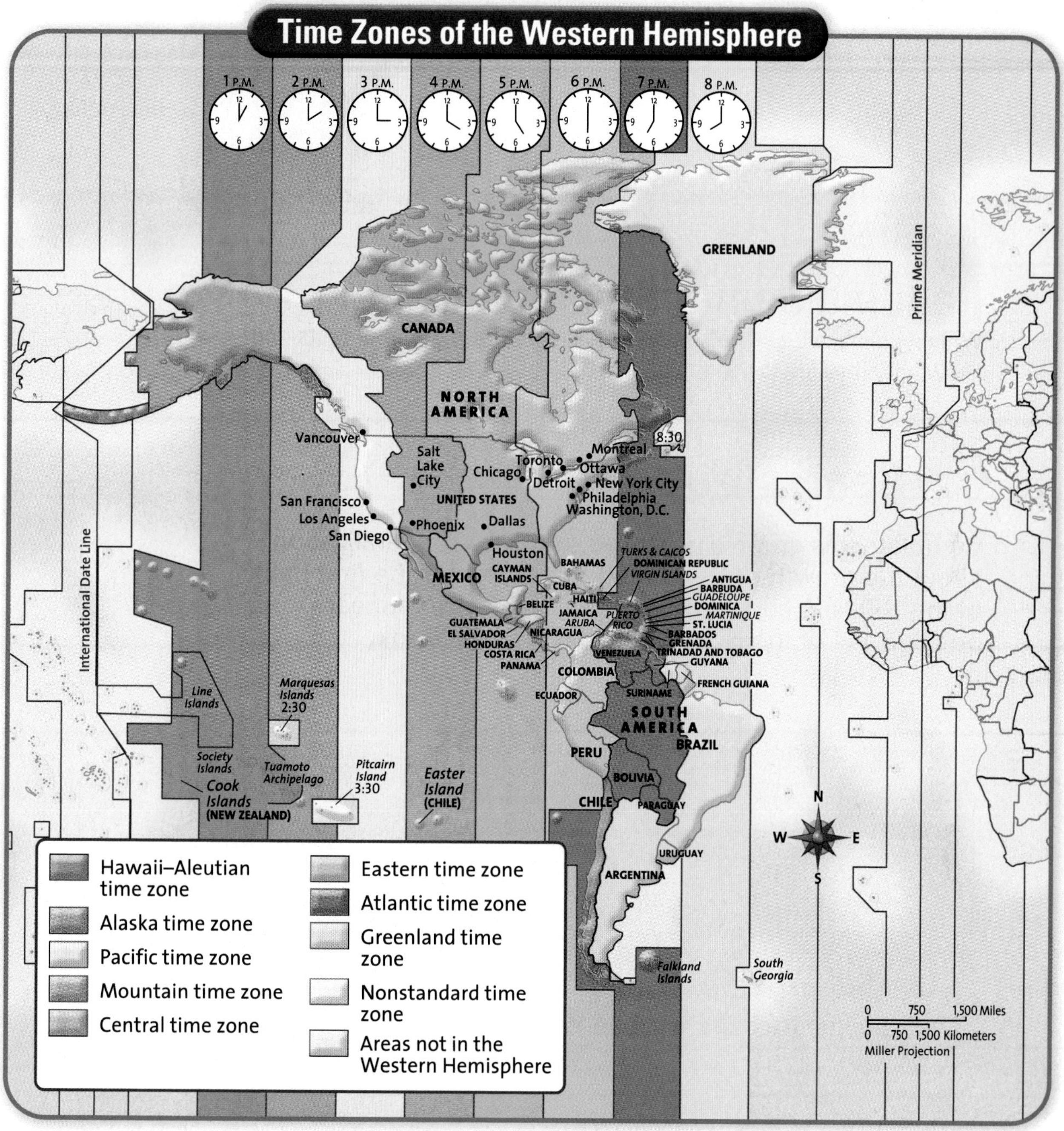

Time Zones of the Western Hemisphere

1 P.M. | 2 P.M. | 3 P.M. | 4 P.M. | 5 P.M. | 6 P.M. | 7 P.M. | 8 P.M.

- Hawaii–Aleutian time zone
- Alaska time zone
- Pacific time zone
- Mountain time zone
- Central time zone
- Eastern time zone
- Atlantic time zone
- Greenland time zone
- Nonstandard time zone
- Areas not in the Western Hemisphere

0 750 1,500 Miles
0 750 1,500 Kilometers
Miller Projection

APPLY WHAT YOU LEARNED

ANALYSIS SKILL Make up two questions about the map on this page. Write your questions on the front of a sheet of paper and the answers on the back. Exchange papers with a classmate, and check each other's answers.

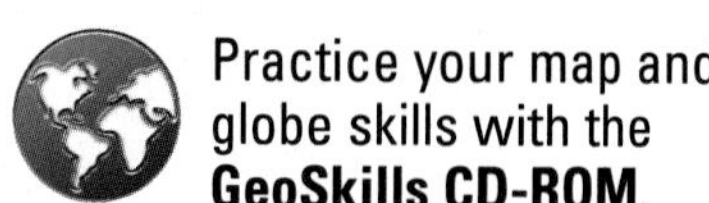

Practice your map and globe skills with the **GeoSkills CD-ROM**.

Chapter 13 Review

Time

1820

1830

1843
John C. Frémont maps the Oregon Trail

Reading Social Studies

When you make a **generalization,** you summarize a group of facts and show how they are related.

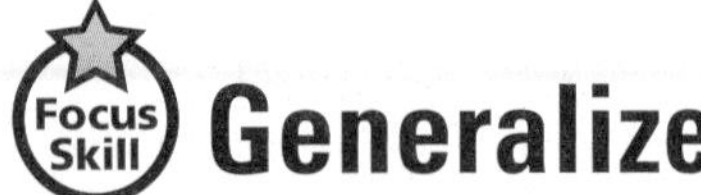

Generalize

Complete this graphic organizer to make a generalization about the growth of the United States during the first half of the 1800s. A copy of this graphic organizer appears on page 144 of the Homework and Practice Book.

Moving West

Facts

Generalization

Most people traveled west on wagon trails.

California Writing Prompts

Write a Narrative Imagine that you have just completed a journey on the Oregon Trail. Write a story, describing where your journey started and ended and the different physical features you saw along the way.

Write a Persuasive Letter Imagine that you are the mayor of San Francisco, California, in 1849. Write a letter to a newspaper to persuade people to settle in San Francisco. Be sure to offer reasons to support your proposal.

1845
Texas becomes a state

1846
The Mexican-American War begins

1848
The California gold rush begins

Use Vocabulary

Identify the term at the right that best relates to each term below.

ford, p. 542
slave state, p. 553
manifest destiny, p. 559
gold rush, p. 562
interchangeable parts, p. 569

1. forty-niner
2. wagon train
3. Oregon Territory
4. Industrial Revolution
5. Underground Railroad

Use the Time Line

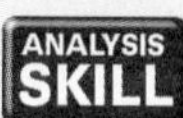

Use the chapter summary time line above to answer these questions.

6. Did Texas become a state before or after the Mexican-American War began?
7. How many years after Frémont mapped the Oregon Trail was gold discovered in California?

Apply Skills

Solve a Problem

8. How did the United States and Britain solve the problem of their land claim disputes in the Oregon Country?

ANALYSIS SKILL **Identify Changing Borders**

9. Study the map on page 567. What was the western border of the U.S. in 1783?

Recall Facts

Answer these questions.

10. Why did settlers from Mexico move to California and Texas?
11. Where in the West did Mormons first settle?
12. Why did the Lakota Sioux fight with other Indian tribes in the 1840s?
13. Who was Antonio López de Santa Anna?

Write the letter of the best choice.

14. Which of these states was once part of Mexico?
    A Florida
    B Oregon
    C Texas
    D Ohio
15. Which of these western trails did settlers use to reach the Willamette Valley?
    A California Trail
    B Mormon Trail
    C Oregon Trail
    D Santa Fe Trail

Think Critically

16. ANALYSIS SKILL Why do you think members of Congress argued over admitting new states as slave states or as free states?
17. ANALYSIS SKILL How did the steamship and the locomotive affect where people settled in the United States?

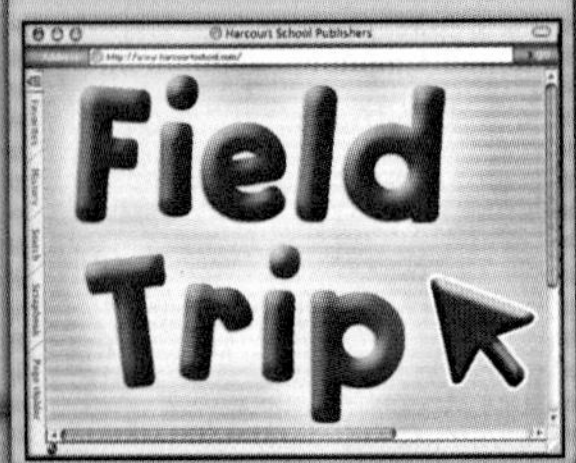

END OF *the* OREGON TRAIL

INTERPRETIVE CENTER

GET READY

For many settlers traveling to Oregon Country, the last stop on their journey was a grassy meadow known as Abernathy Green. Here, they could graze their animals and set up camp. Today, Abernathy Green—in Oregon City, Oregon—is the location of the End of the Oregon Trail Interpretive Center.

This museum is dedicated to preserving the history, heritage, and spirit of the brave pioneers who traveled the Oregon Trail. Visitors to the center can watch a video and try making traditional crafts. They can also walk through exhibits that show the Pacific Northwest from the time when fur traders and American Indians roamed the area to the coming of the railroad.

LOCATE IT

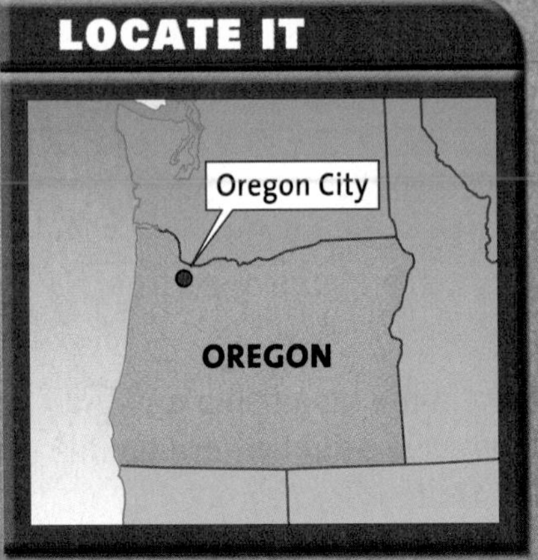

WHAT TO SEE

Buildings shaped like covered wagons contain the museum's exhibits.

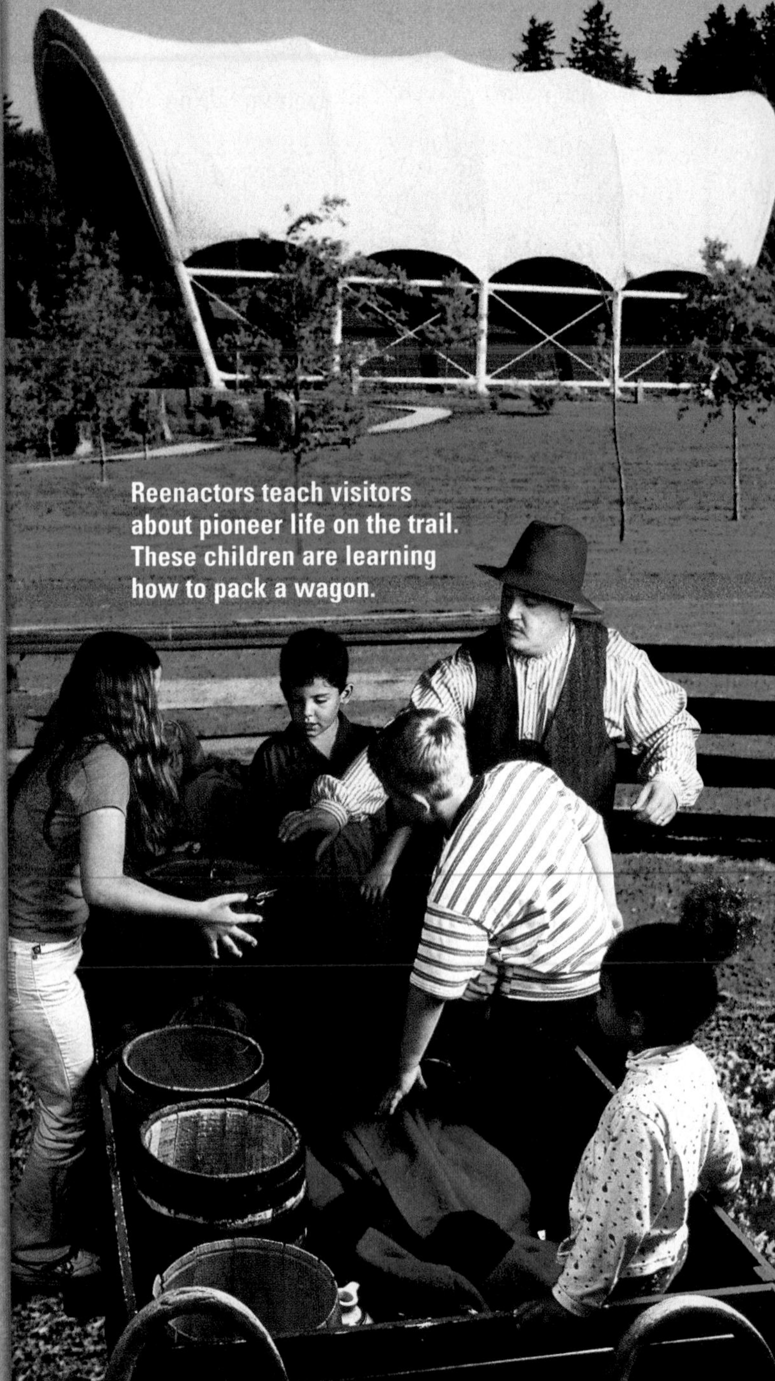

Reenactors teach visitors about pioneer life on the trail. These children are learning how to pack a wagon.

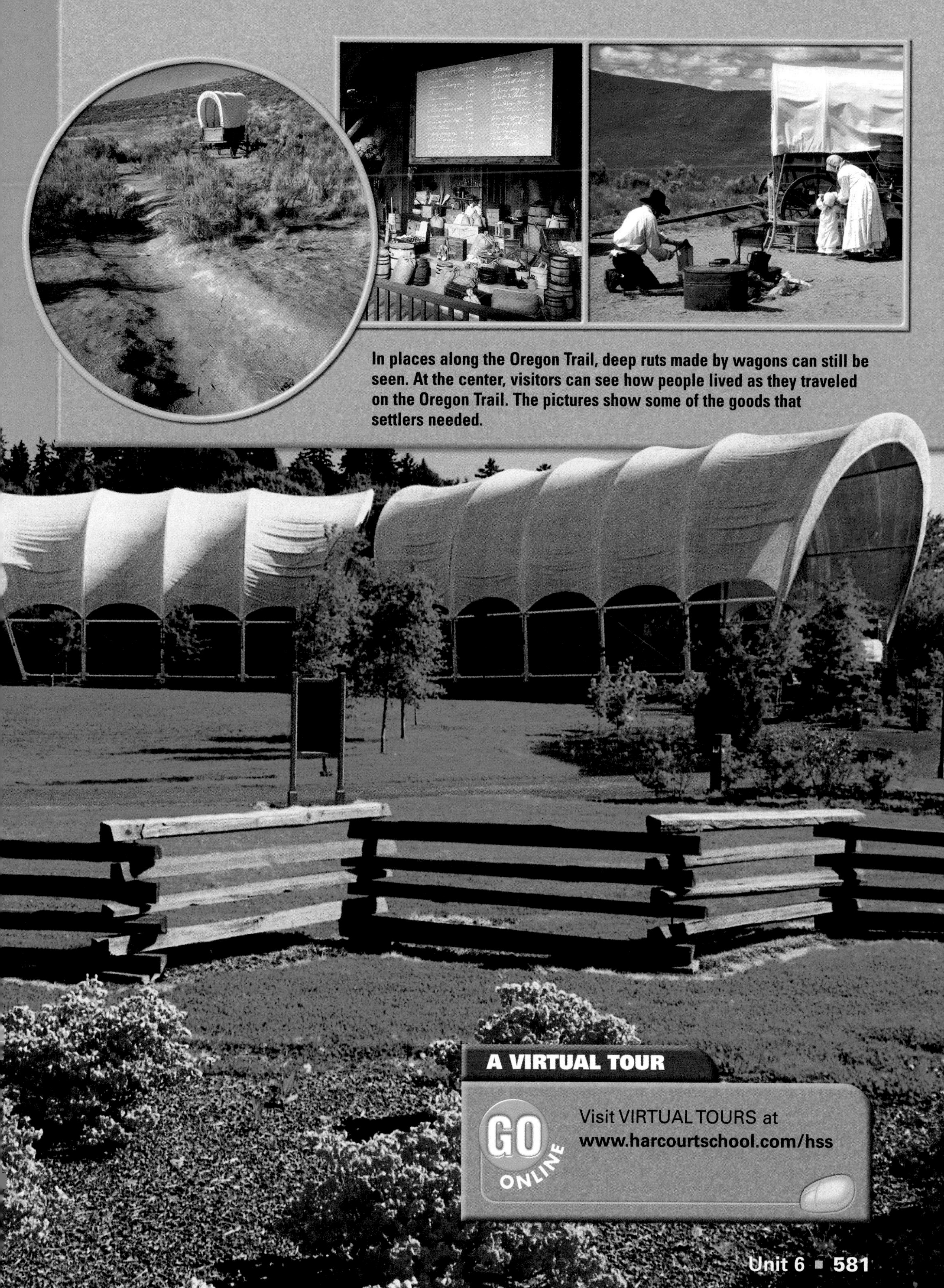

In places along the Oregon Trail, deep ruts made by wagons can still be seen. At the center, visitors can see how people lived as they traveled on the Oregon Trail. The pictures show some of the goods that settlers needed.

A VIRTUAL TOUR

GO ONLINE

Visit VIRTUAL TOURS at **www.harcourtschool.com/hss**

Review

THE BIG IDEA

Growth and Change The United States expanded as its population and economy grew and as new lands were acquired.

Summary

Western Expansion

Waves of immigrants poured into the United States during the late 1700s and early 1800s. From eastern port cities, many of them moved west in search of open lands. Some of those pioneers used the Wilderness Road to cross the Appalachian Mountains, and then used boats and wagons to travel farther west.

After the Louisiana Purchase in 1803, the United States extended west to the Rocky Mountains. Still, many Americans wanted more land. They believed in manifest destiny. Families and traders began using wagon trails to cross the Rockies and settle in the Oregon Country.

Other settlers moved to southwestern lands. After winning independence from Mexico, Texas joined the United States. After the Mexican-American War, California and many other southwestern lands were sold to the United States.

By 1850, the United States stretched from sea to sea. Railroads, canals, telegraphs, and other technology helped different regions of the nation connect. But the issue of slavery still divided the nation.

Main Ideas and Vocabulary

Read the summary above. Then answer the questions that follow.

1. What does the term pioneers mean?
   - **A** people who are first to settle a new place
   - **B** people who start new businesses
   - **C** people who leave one country to live in another
   - **D** people who mine gold
2. What formed the western border of the United States after 1803?
   - **A** the Appalachian Mountains
   - **B** the Mississippi River
   - **C** the Pacific Ocean
   - **D** the Rocky Mountains
3. What was the main goal expressed by the idea of manifest destiny?
   - **A** religious freedom
   - **B** abolishing slavery
   - **C** extending land claims
   - **D** increasing immigration
4. When was California sold to the United States?
   - **A** after the Mexican-American War
   - **B** after the American Revolution
   - **C** after the Battle of the Alamo
   - **D** after the War of 1812

Recall Facts

Answer these questions.

5. Why did many immigrants move to the United States?
6. Why was the Erie Canal built?
7. How did pioneer families work together to complete all of their chores?
8. Why did people choose to move west?
9. What issue caused conflict when western territories tried to become states?

Write the letter of the best choice.

10. Which of these explorers was arrested for trespassing on Spanish lands?
    A John C. Frémont
    B Meriwether Lewis
    C Zebulon Pike
    D Jedediah Smith
11. How did most pioneers cross the Rocky Mountains?
    A by using the South Pass
    B by using the Cumberland Gap
    C by using the Wilderness Road
    D by using the Erie Canal
12. During which war did the Mexican army attack the Alamo?
    A the War of 1812
    B the American Revolution
    C the Mexican-American War
    D the Texas War for Independence
13. Which treaty ended the Mexican-American War?
    A Treaty of Paris
    B Oregon Treaty
    C Treaty of Ghent
    D Treaty of Guadalupe Hidalgo

Think Critically

14. ANALYSIS SKILL What were some of the costs and benefits of building canals?
15. ANALYSIS SKILL How do you think the idea of manifest destiny affected American Indians?

Apply Skills

Identify Border Changes

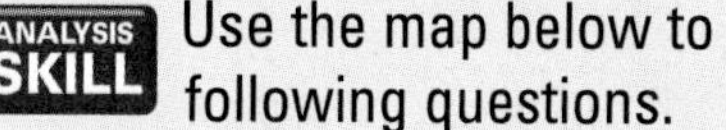
ANALYSIS SKILL Use the map below to answer the following questions.

16. What territory did the Columbia River pass through?
17. What body of water formed the eastern border of the Louisiana Purchase?
18. What year was the last land addition made?
19. What body of water bordered the Oregon Territory and the Mexican Cession?

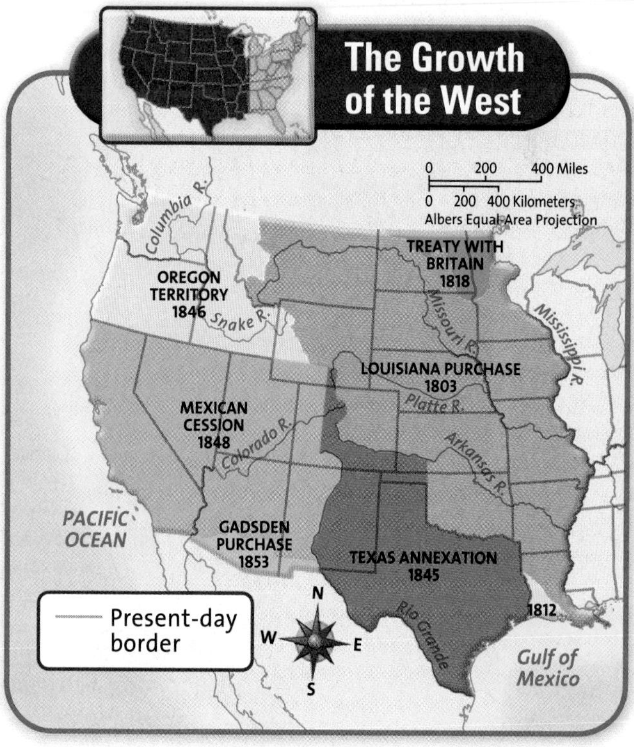

Unit 6 Activities

Read More

- *Tecumseh* by Stefan Petrucha.

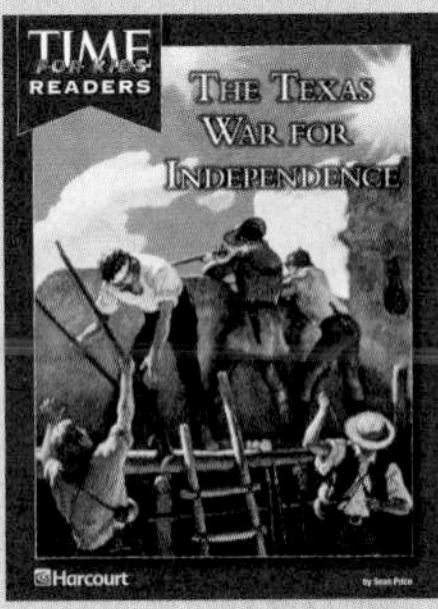

- *The Texas War for Independence* by Sean Price.

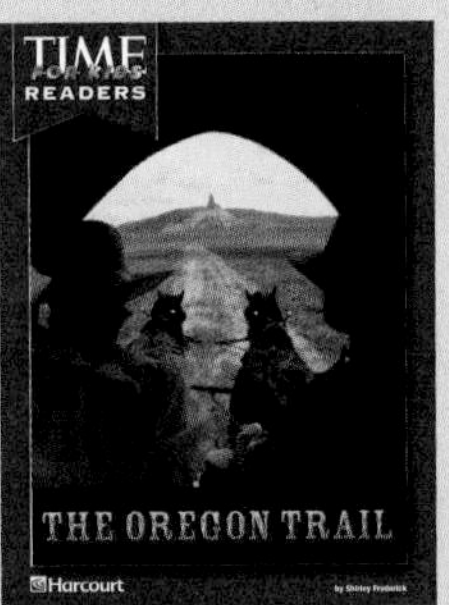

- *The Oregon Trail* by Shirley Frederick.

Show What You Know

Unit Writing Activity

Write a Narrative Write a narrative that describes the first meeting between a settler and an American Indian. In the narrative, the settler should tell where his or her group is from, why they want to settle a new area, and how they traveled there. The American Indian should also give his or her point of view. Make sure your narrative has a setting, a plot, and clearly shows the conflicts that may result.

Unit Project

A Scrapbook Design a scrapbook about the western expansion of the United States. Decide which people, places, and events to include and how you will show information about each. You should make drawings and paintings, write poems and tall tales, and draw maps to put into your scrapbook.

Visit ACTIVITIES at **www.harcourtschool.com/hss**

For Your Reference

From Past to Present

Since 1850, the United States has continued to grow and change. It has overcome great challenges from abroad and has expanded freedom and opportunity for its citizens at home.

E pluribus unum

("Out of many, one")

—motto on the Seal of the United States

1 A Changing Nation

The United States changed greatly in the 1800s. As manufacturing grew, new cities sprang up. Many people moved from farms to cities to work in the factories. Millions of immigrants also came to the United States to find jobs and start new lives in a new country. The greatest change to the United States in the 1800s, however, resulted from the Civil War.

The End of Slavery

In 1860, people in the United States remained deeply divided over whether slavery should be allowed. Many in the North wanted to see it abolished, while many in the South claimed that their economy depended on it. They felt that the federal government should not be able to make laws either to abolish or to limit slavery.

Many Southerners also believed that states had the right to secede from, or leave, the Union—the United States— if they chose to do so. Many feared that **Abraham Lincoln**, who was running for President at the time, might outlaw slavery if he were elected. Lincoln won the election, and in the months that followed, eleven Southern states seceded from the Union. They formed a new country they called the Confederate States of America, or the Confederacy.

President Lincoln said that states could not secede, and he promised to hold on to United States forts and other property located in those

The nation grew in the 1800s.

Abraham Lincoln met with his cabinet to discuss the Emancipation Proclamation.

states. In April 1861, Confederate soldiers defeated the Union troops stationed at Fort Sumter in South Carolina. This battle marked the beginning of the American Civil War.

During the war, President Lincoln made an important decision. On January 1, 1863, he issued the **Emancipation Proclamation**. This was an order stating that all enslaved people living in parts of the South that were still fighting against the Union would be "then, thenceforward, and forever free."*

After four years of hardships, the Civil War finally came to an end in April 1865, when the Confederate army surrendered. The United States was one nation again.

* Abraham Lincoln. *The Emancipation Proclamation* by John Hope Franklin. Doubleday, 1963.

Citizenship for African Americans

After the Civil War, three amendments were added to the Constitution. The Thirteenth Amendment ended slavery. The Fourteenth Amendment said that all citizens had equal rights under the law. The Fifteenth Amendment gave African American men the right to vote.

As free citizens, African Americans made many contributions to the nation. They became teachers and scientists, started businesses, and were elected to office. **Hiram Revels** of Mississippi became the first African American to be elected to the United States Senate.

Hiram Revels

Booker T. Washington

George Washington Carver

Over time, however, state governments in the South passed laws that made it very difficult, if not impossible, for African Americans to vote. Other new laws led to segregation, or the practice of separating people into different groups based on their race or culture. For example, African Americans had to go to separate schools and ride in separate train cars.

Even with these new hardships, African Americans continued to contribute to the economic, political, and cultural development of the United States. Among them was **Booker T. Washington**, who helped found the Tuskegee Institute—a trade school for African Americans—in Alabama. **George Washington Carver**, a scientist and teacher at the Tuskegee Institute, helped the South build a stronger economy. He encouraged farmers there to grow peanuts and sweet potatoes, and he invented new ways to use these crops. He and his students showed that more than 300 products could be made from peanuts, including ink, shampoo, and dyes.

Thurgood Marshall, who later became a Supreme Court justice, argued against school segregation so that students, like Linda Brown (right), could get an education.

Expanding Freedoms

African Americans continued to work to gain civil rights. Both **Ida B. Wells** and **W. E. B. Du Bois** (doo•BOYS) were leaders in that effort. Wells wrote newspaper articles about violence against African Americans. DuBois's writings called for equality for African Americans, women, and other groups.

Progress toward equal rights was slow, but in 1954, the United States Supreme Court issued an important ruling. In a case called *Brown v. Board of Education*, the Court ruled that an African American girl named **Linda Brown** had the right to attend a public school in Topeka, Kansas. It also ordered the integration of all public schools in the United States. Integration is the inclusion of different people in a group as equals. Courts later ruled that segregation in all public places was also unconstitutional.

African Americans were not the only group that struggled to win the rights promised in the Constitution. Women gained the vote in 1920, when the Nineteenth Amendment was ratified. In 1924, Congress passed a law making all American Indians in the United States citizens with the right to vote. In 1971, the voting age for all Americans was lowered from 21 to 18.

By the 1970s, new laws were passed saying that employers must treat men and women equally, and that all jobs had to be open to both men and women. In 1975, laws were passed that said Indian tribes could run their own businesses and education programs.

REVIEW

1. **What was the Emancipation Proclamation?**
2. **Which amendment officially ended slavery in the United States?**
3. **What did the Court rule in *Brown v. Board of Education*?**

➤ **Martin Luther King, Jr., (shown at center) marched in support of new civil rights laws.**

2 A Nation of Immigrants

➤ **Most immigrants who came to the United States were searching for a better life.**

In the 1850s, writer **Herman Melville** said, "We are not a nation so much as a world."* He was saying that the United States is made up of people from many other places. So many people in the United States—or their parents, grandparents, or earlier ancestors—have come from other places that our country is often called a nation of immigrants. These people have contributed to building the United States and making it what it is today.

*Herman Melville. *Redburn: His First Voyage.* Viking Press, 1983.

New States, New People

By the late 1800s, the United States was one of the most powerful nations in the world. The country continued to grow as new states were added to the Union. In 1959, the number of states reached 50 when Alaska and Hawaii were admitted.

During this time, the United States added to its land in other ways. As a result of winning the Spanish-American War in 1898, the United States gained control of Cuba, Puerto Rico, Guam, and the Philippine Islands. Both Cuba and the Philippines later became independent countries, but Puerto Rico and Guam remain part of the United States today.

As the United States grew in area, its population also grew. People continued to immigrate to the United States from all parts of the world, and the country became a diverse nation of many races, religions, and national origins.

Immigrants added to the nation's economic, cultural, and social life. They brought new skills, new languages, and new ways of life to the United States. They farmed and started businesses, helped build railroads and cities, and worked in factories and mines. They became teachers and scientists, writers of literature and music, and artists in the entertainment industry.

Immigrants have also shared their cultures with people born in the United States. Their foods, holidays, musical styles, dances, and games have given Americans a richer life.

New Waves of Immigrants

Between 1820 and 1920, more than 30 million people immigrated to the United States. Faster ships made crossing the oceans easier, and cheaper fares allowed more people to make the trip.

The newcomers came from all over the world. Among them were thousands of people, including many from China, who came to California during the gold rush. In about 1900, a smaller wave of immigrants came from Asia. Most of these Asian newcomers were from Japan. They arrived at the immigration station at Angel Island, in San Francisco Bay, and settled along the Pacific coast.

People from Mexico and other parts of Latin America also continued to move to the United States in the 1900s. Many of them settled in Texas, New Mexico, Arizona, and southern California. Many immigrants from Cuba also settled in Florida.

Most immigrants who arrived before 1870 came from northern and western Europe. After 1870, most came from Italy, Greece, Poland, Hungary, Russia, and other countries in southern and eastern Europe. Most of these people arrived at the immigration station on Ellis Island, in New York Harbor.

Beginning in 1886, a new sight greeted immigrants who arrived in New York. It was the Statue of Liberty, a gift to the people of the United States of America from the people of France.

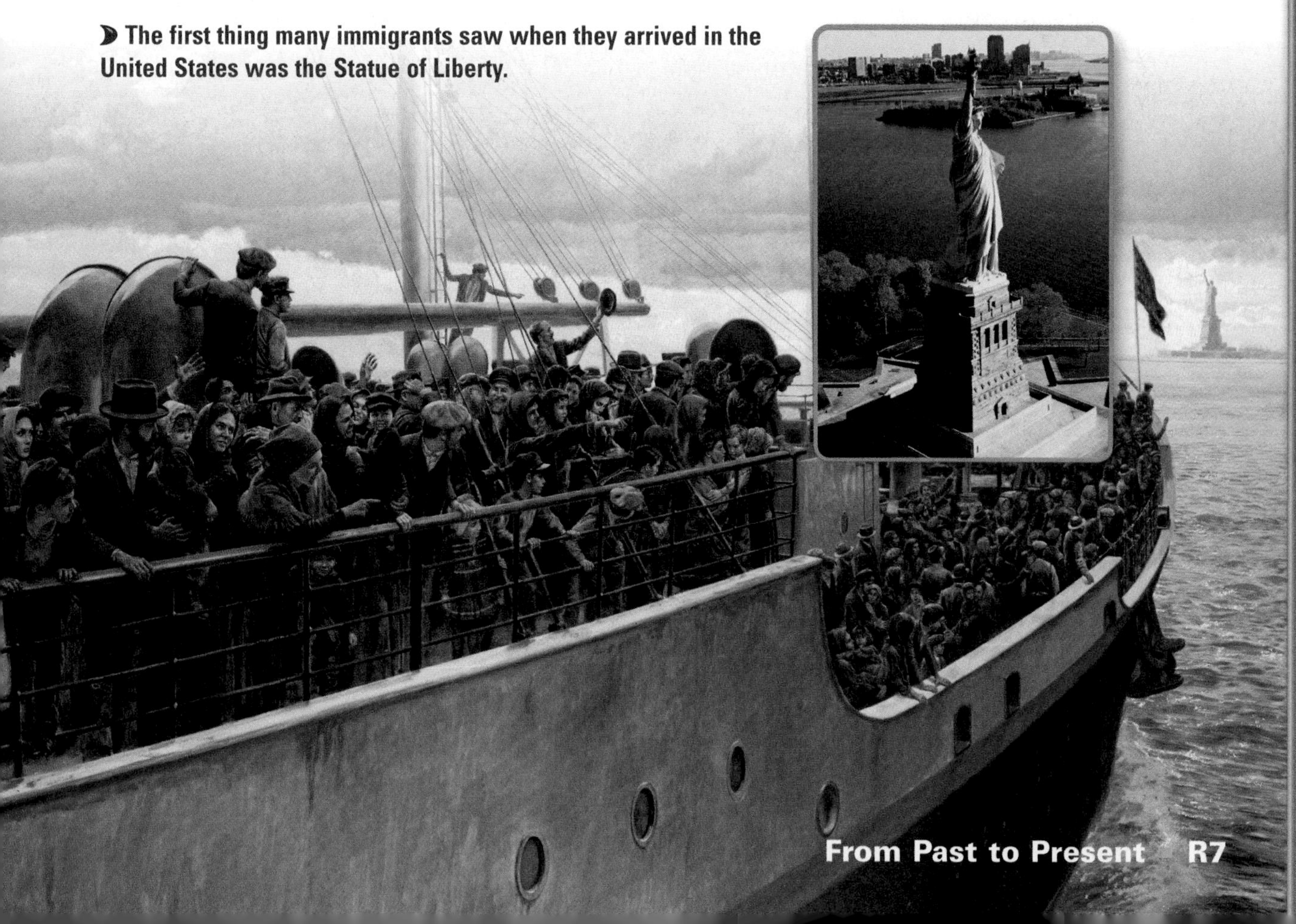

The first thing many immigrants saw when they arrived in the United States was the Statue of Liberty.

Carved into the base of the Statue of Liberty is the poem "The New Colossus," written by **Emma Lazarus**. It describes how the Statue of Liberty welcomes immigrants to the United States. The poem ends,

> **". . . Give me your tired, your poor,**
> **Your huddled masses yearning to breathe free,**
> **The wretched refuse of your teeming shore.**
> **Send these, the homeless, tempest-tost to me,**
> **I lift my lamp beside the golden door!"***

Today, the Statue of Liberty is a symbol of the United States. It reminds all Americans of the ideals and many freedoms they share.

Overcoming Hardships

For many immigrants, coming to the United States meant an opportunity for a better life. Many came to escape hardships in their homelands. In the United States, with hard work and ability, they could hope for a brighter future. For many, it also meant being free for the first time in their lives.

However, coming to the United States involved new hardships. The immigrants had to leave their homes and their friends and relatives behind and move to an unfamiliar land. Often they did not know anyone in their new community. They had to learn a new language as well as ways of doing things, and this took time and effort.

*Emma Lazarus. *Emma Lazarus: Selected Poems and Other Writings*, edited by Gregory Eiselein. Broadview Press, 2002.

This photograph from 1900 shows a busy day on Mulberry Street, on the Lower East Side of New York City.

When they reached the United States many immigrants worked under poor conditions in factories.

Many immigrants faced another kind of hardship in their new country—discrimination. Discrimination is the unfair treatment of people because of their religion, their race, their national origin, or other characteristics that make them different.

During the late 1800s, the United States faced economic hard times. Many businesses closed, and many workers lost their jobs. Some people began to blame their problems on immigrants. They thought that immigrants were taking their jobs, and some immigrants' homes and businesses were attacked.

There was a growing demand for Congress to limit the number of immigrants. Over the next 50 years, Congress passed a series of laws that limited the number of immigrants allowed to enter the United States each year. These laws severely limited or even banned immigration from certain regions of the world, especially Asia.

Immigration Continues

Immigrants continue to make important contributions to American life. Today, of the more than 290 million people living in the United States, more than 32 million were born in another country. That is more than 1 of every 10 people in the United States.

Most immigrants who came to the United States in the late 1800s and early 1900s were from countries in Europe. Today, immigrants come from all over the world, especially from Asia and Latin America. In fact, more than half of all foreign-born people in the United States today are from Latin American countries. About one-fourth are from countries in Asia, such as China, Japan, India, and the Philippines. The rest are from Europe, Africa, Australia, and other areas.

Most people who live in the United States today are either immigrants or the descendants of immigrants.

Many different cultural celebrations take place across the United States.

Some people's families have been living in the United States for many years. Other immigrants have come only recently. Instead of arriving on ships, as immigrants did in the past, most immigrants today arrive by plane at one of the nation's international airports.

Many Americans continue to take part in the customs and traditions unique to their cultures. Some immigrants still speak the languages of their native countries. Cultural differences among Americans can also be seen in the foods we eat, the music we listen to, and the religious groups we belong to. This adds to the diversity of American culture.

Although Americans are different from one another, we are united because we also have much in common. We all live under a constitutional democracy, and we are united by basic American ideals—freedom, opportunity, belief in individual rights, and respect for all people and their differences.

REVIEW

1. **How did immigration help make the United States a more diverse nation?**
2. **How was immigration before 1870 different from immigration after 1870?**
3. **What hardships did many immigrants face?**
4. **What unites Americans today?**

New Challenges to Freedom

The United States entered the twentieth century as a strong nation. During the 1900s, it used its power to defend freedom around the world. World War I was the first of many challenges the United States and its allies faced.

World War I

In the early 1900s, nations across Europe formed alliances in which the members of each alliance promised to help one another if they were attacked. In southern Europe, Serbia and Austria-Hungary shared a border. On June 28, 1914, a Serb shot and killed Austria-Hungary's Archduke Francis Ferdinand and his wife. In response, Austria-Hungary declared war on Serbia.

The allies of each of the two nations came to its aid. On one side were the Central Powers, which included Austria-Hungary, Germany, and the Ottoman Empire. On the other side were the Allied Powers, or Allies. They included Serbia, Britain, France, Russia, and Italy.

Most people in the United States wanted to stay out of the war. In 1917, however, the United States joined the war on the side of the Allied Powers. One reason was that Britain and France, who were allies of the United States, needed help. Another reason was that German submarines had begun attacking American ships.

Soldiers preparing for World War I stand for inspection at the University of California.

In asking Congress to declare war on Germany, President **Woodrow Wilson** said, "The world must be made safe for democracy."*

With more men leaving their jobs to go and fight in the war, there were fewer workers at home. The need for workers helped African Americans and women. Between 1914 and 1919, as part of what became known as the **Great Migration**, half a million African Americans left the South and moved to northern cities to find jobs in factories making war materials. Thousands of women also found jobs in factories.

The United States helped the Allies win the war, which ended in 1918, seventeen months after the first American soldiers arrived in Europe. Before the fighting stopped, however, about 53,000 Americans had been killed.

*Woodrow Wilson. *The Politics of Woodrow Wilson*, edited by August Heckscher. Harper, 1956.

The Great Depression

A decade after World War I ended, European nations were still struggling to rebuild their economies. The United States, however, was enjoying prosperity.

Many Americans invested in the stock market as a way to make more money. In the stock market, people buy and sell stocks, or shares in businesses. Some people used all of their savings and even borrowed large sums of money to invest.

Beginning in the fall of 1929, some investors decided to take their money out of the stock market. This caused stock prices to fall. As prices fell, more investors decided to sell. Soon panicked stockholders were trying to sell all of their stocks. On October 29, 1929,

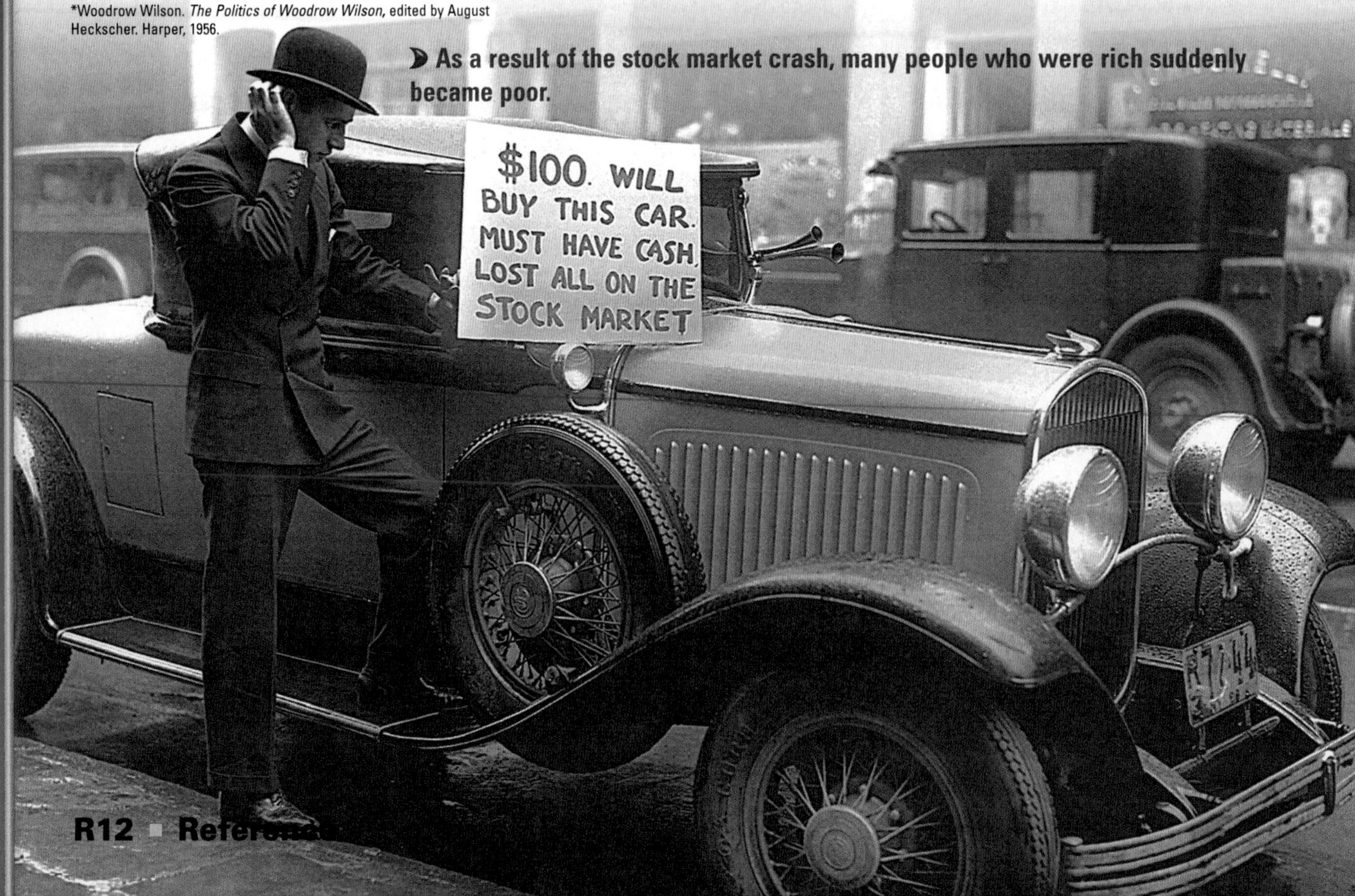

As a result of the stock market crash, many people who were rich suddenly became poor.

American newspapers (above) announce the invasion of Poland by the Germans. The United States did not enter the war until the Japanese bombed Pearl Harbor in Hawaii.

the stock market crashed, or failed. Nearly everyone who owned stocks lost money.

The stock market crash contributed to a worldwide economic depression. It was a time of widespread unemployment and hunger. One of every four American workers was without a job. This depression, which continued through the 1930s, was so bad that it became known as the **Great Depression**.

In 1932, **Franklin D. Roosevelt** was elected President. He promised the American people a "New Deal," and he worked with Congress to start many new programs to put people back to work and end the depression. The New Deal gave Americans hope that the country was on the road to better times. In Europe, however, there was no New Deal and little hope for the future.

World War II

The Great Depression was especially hard for people in Germany. Germany had agreed to pay large sums of money to the countries it had attacked in World War I, but its economy was in ruins.

In 1933, **Adolf Hitler** became the leader of Germany and ruled as a dictator. Hitler was the leader of a political party in Germany called the National Socialists, or Nazis. He promised to make Germany a powerful country once again and began to rebuild its army.

The Berlin Wall separated East Germany and West Germany for 28 years.

Hitler and his followers used force against people who disagreed with them. They put many of these people into prisons called concentration camps. Millions of Jews, whom Hitler blamed for Germany's problems, were sent to these camps and killed. This mass murder became known as the **Holocaust**.

German troops began invading neighboring countries, and in 1939, war broke out. Dictators had also ruled Italy and Japan. They, too, invaded nearby countries, and war spread.

On December 7, 1941, Japanese war planes attacked the United States Navy base at Pearl Harbor, Hawaii. The next day, the United States declared war on Japan. Three days later, Germany and Italy declared war on the United States.

Germany, Italy, and Japan were known as the Axis powers. The United States joined with the Allies, which included Britain, France, and the Soviet Union. The Allies defeated Germany in May 1945. Japan surrendered in August after the United States dropped atomic bombs on two Japanese cities. World War II was over.

After the war, the Soviet Union began to pressure eastern European nations to adopt a form of government known as communism. Under communism, the government owns all land and businesses, and people often have little freedom. By 1950, China also had a communist government.

Democratic nations were in constant conflict with the Soviet Union and other communist countries. This hostility between democratic nations and communist nations became known as the **Cold War**. It was mostly a conflict of words, but fighting occurred in places such as Korea and Vietnam.

During the 1980s, the people of eastern Europe rebelled against communism. Eventually, the Soviet Union abandoned communism and broke up into several nations. The Cold War was over. The United States stood alone as the world's most powerful nation and the only superpower.

New Challenges

At the end of the twentieth century, the United States continued to promote democratic values around the world. However, the nation faced a new kind of danger—terrorism. Terrorism is the deliberate use of violence to further a cause. Terrorists do not fight on behalf of a country. They make surprise attacks on civilians, or non-military people. Bombings and other acts of terrorism have occurred in the United States and around the world.

On the morning of September 11, 2001, terrorists hijacked, or illegally took control of, four commercial jet airplanes. They flew a plane into each of the two towers of the World Trade Center in New York City. The towers caught fire and later collapsed. They flew another plane into the Pentagon, the nation's military headquarters, near Washington, D.C. The fourth plane, believed to be headed for the nation's capital, crashed in an empty field in Pennsylvania. All together nearly 3,000 Americans died in the attacks.

Leaders of the United States soon learned that many of the terrorists had been trained in parts of Afghanistan. To end Afghanistan's support of terrorists, the United States and its allies overthrew its rulers.

In 2003, President **George W. Bush** declared that Saddam Hussein, the leader of Iraq, was a danger to the world. Along with some of its allies, the United States defeated the Iraqi army and arrested Hussein.

REVIEW

1. **How did the Great Depression affect Americans?**
2. **In what ways has terrorism affected the United States?**

More than 40,000 people worked in the World Trade Center buildings. Before their destruction, the towers were the tallest buildings in New York City.

New Ideas and New Inventions

From 1850 to the present, the economy of the United States has changed. New ideas and new inventions have transformed the lives of people in the United States and the rest of the world.

New Technologies

The late 1800s was a time of invention and progress. The telephone and the electric lightbulb were introduced. Improvements in steelmaking allowed for the building of more railroads and the construction of very large buildings and bridges.

Changes were taking place in transportation, too. When the first cars were built in the early 1900s, they were too expensive for most people to afford. **Henry Ford** changed that. He developed a system of mass production using an assembly line. Instead of being built one at a time, Ford's cars were assembled, or put together, as they moved past a line of workers. This new technology saved Ford money, allowing him to produce less-expensive cars.

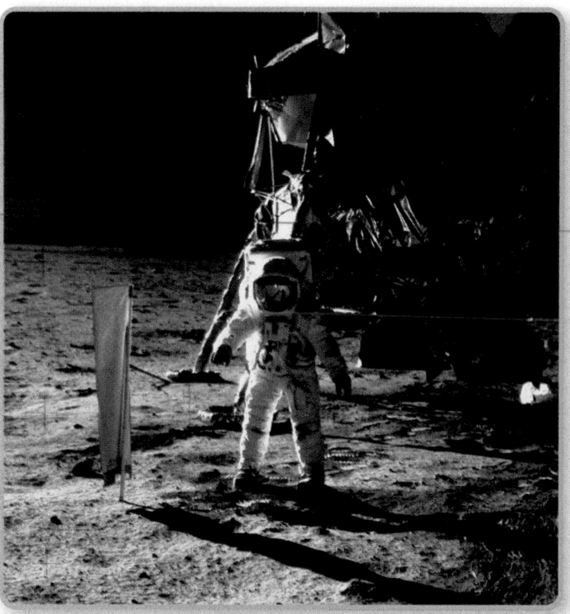

Following Ford's lead, other companies produced goods faster and more cheaply than ever before. The economy now depended more on making goods and less on growing things. Consumers rushed to buy washing machines, vacuum cleaners, radios, and other electrical goods for the home. The first movies were made at this time, too.

In 1946, scientists built the first computer. Computers changed the American economy as much as the assembly line did. They also made

Scientists developed special equipment to be used on the moon.

space travel possible. In 1969, astronaut **Neil Armstrong** became the first person to step foot on the moon. Today, computers allow satellites to orbit Earth, sending and receiving everything from television programs to weather information.

New technologies have made it possible to take music almost anywhere.

Changing Lives

New technologies continue to change the daily lives of many Americans. Cell phones allow people to communicate wherever they go. Satellites let viewers choose from hundreds of television programs.

The Internet, which links computers around the world, is changing the way people do almost everything. Instead of sending letters through the mail, people can send e-mails that travel around the world in seconds. Instead of driving to a store, consumers can buy nearly anything they need online. Instead of reading a newspaper or watching the news on TV, people can read the news online or watch video clips. Instead of buying compact discs, music lovers can pay to download songs from online stores to their computers. Instead of going to a library, students can do research online. Wireless technology allows people to do all of these things almost anywhere.

These changes have created new kinds of jobs and new ways of working. More people work at home, using their computers to do their jobs. A small business in the United States can set up a Web site and sell its products to people everywhere.

REVIEW

1. **How did the assembly line affect the economy of the United States?**
2. **How does technology continue to affect the lives of many Americans?**

Computers allow people to gather and exchange information faster than ever before.

The World: Political

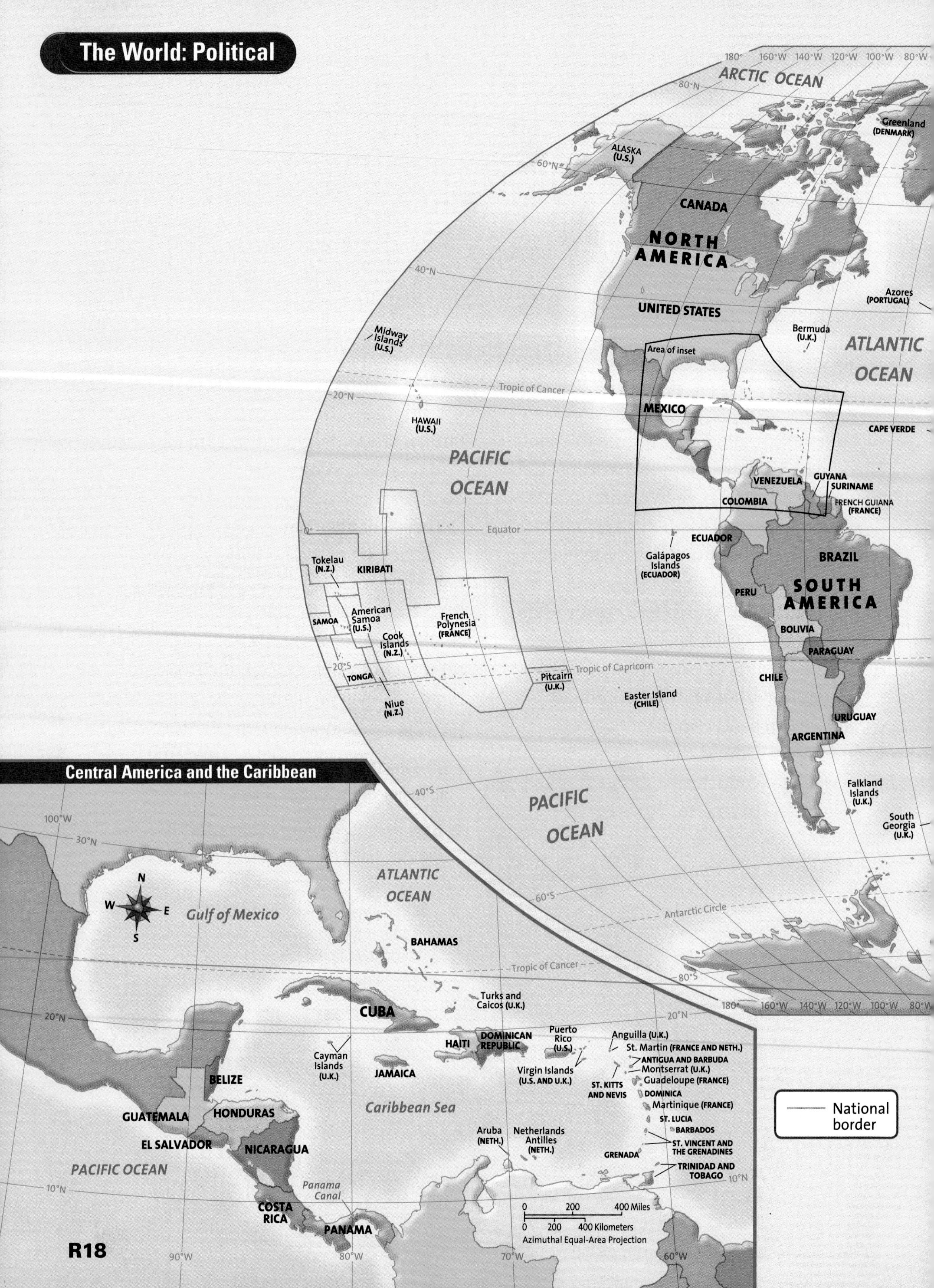

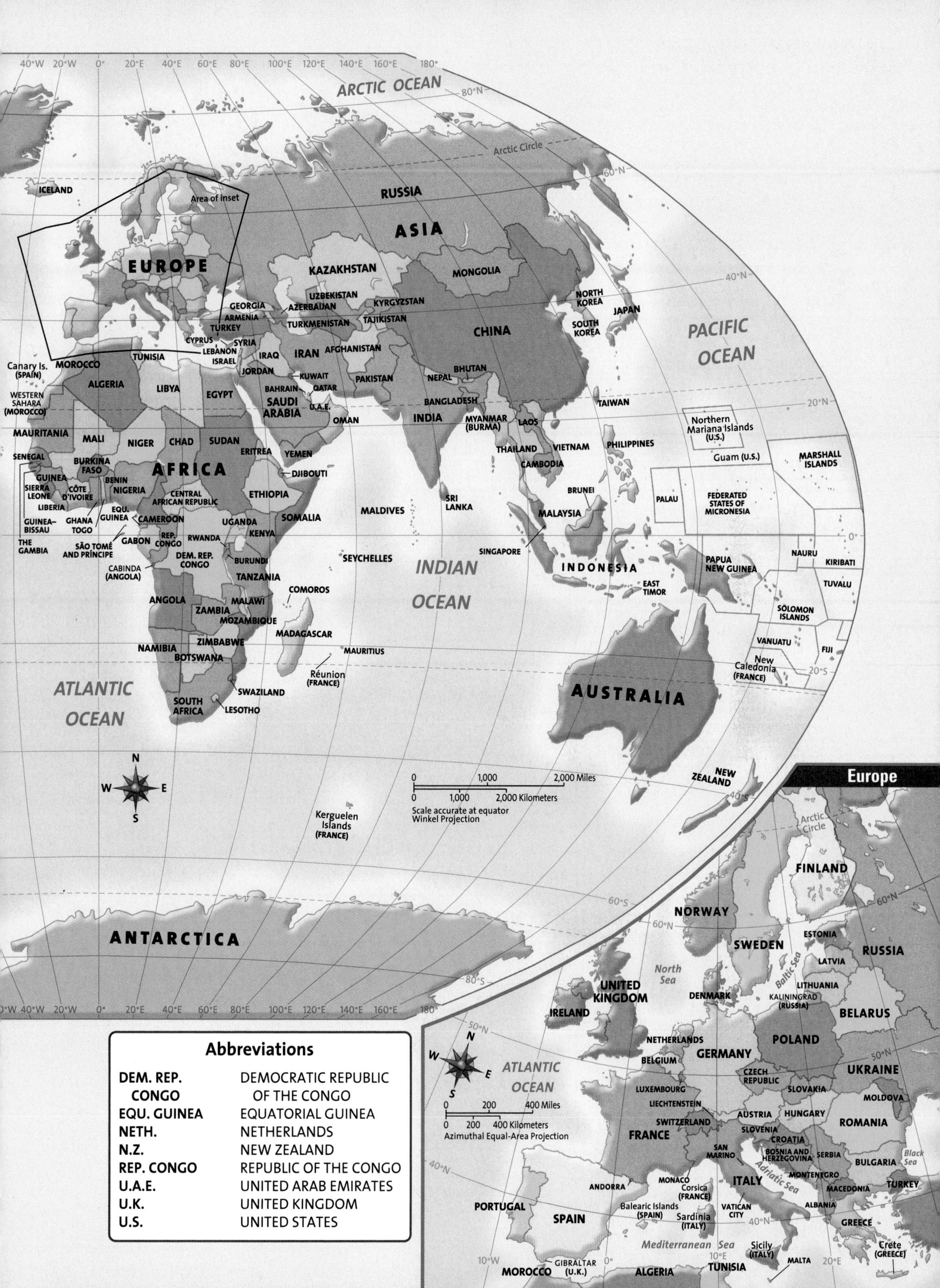
ARCTIC OCEAN
Arctic Circle
Area of inset
ICELAND
RUSSIA
ASIA
EUROPE
KAZAKHSTAN
MONGOLIA
UZBEKISTAN
KYRGYZSTAN
GEORGIA
AZERBAIJAN
ARMENIA
TURKEY
TURKMENISTAN
TAJIKISTAN
NORTH KOREA
SOUTH KOREA
JAPAN
CHINA
PACIFIC OCEAN
CYPRUS
SYRIA
LEBANON
ISRAEL
IRAQ
IRAN
AFGHANISTAN
JORDAN
KUWAIT
BAHRAIN
QATAR
SAUDI ARABIA
U.A.E.
OMAN
PAKISTAN
NEPAL
BHUTAN
BANGLADESH
INDIA
MYANMAR (BURMA)
LAOS
TAIWAN
Canary Is. (SPAIN)
MOROCCO
TUNISIA
WESTERN SAHARA (MOROCCO)
ALGERIA
LIBYA
EGYPT
MAURITANIA
MALI
NIGER
CHAD
SUDAN
ERITREA
YEMEN
SENEGAL
BURKINA FASO
AFRICA
DJIBOUTI
GUINEA
SIERRA LEONE
LIBERIA
CÔTE D'IVOIRE
BENIN
NIGERIA
CENTRAL AFRICAN REPUBLIC
ETHIOPIA
GUINEA-BISSAU
THE GAMBIA
GHANA
TOGO
EQU. GUINEA
CAMEROON
UGANDA
SOMALIA
KENYA
GABON
REP. CONGO
RWANDA
SÃO TOMÉ AND PRÍNCIPE
DEM. REP. CONGO
BURUNDI
CABINDA (ANGOLA)
TANZANIA
SEYCHELLES
MALDIVES
SRI LANKA
THAILAND
VIETNAM
CAMBODIA
PHILIPPINES
BRUNEI
MALAYSIA
SINGAPORE
INDONESIA
EAST TIMOR
INDIAN OCEAN
Northern Mariana Islands (U.S.)
Guam (U.S.)
MARSHALL ISLANDS
PALAU
FEDERATED STATES OF MICRONESIA
PAPUA NEW GUINEA
NAURU
KIRIBATI
TUVALU
SOLOMON ISLANDS
VANUATU
FIJI
New Caledonia (FRANCE)
COMOROS
ANGOLA
MALAWI
ZAMBIA
MOZAMBIQUE
MADAGASCAR
MAURITIUS
Réunion (FRANCE)
NAMIBIA
ZIMBABWE
BOTSWANA
SWAZILAND
SOUTH AFRICA
LESOTHO
ATLANTIC OCEAN
AUSTRALIA
NEW ZEALAND
0 1,000 2,000 Miles
0 1,000 2,000 Kilometers
Scale accurate at equator
Winkel Projection
Kerguelen Islands (FRANCE)
ANTARCTICA
N
S
E
W
40°W 20°W 0° 20°E 40°E 60°E 80°E 100°E 120°E 140°E 160°E 180°
80°N
60°N
40°N
20°N
0°
20°S
40°S
60°S
80°S
Abbreviations
DEM. REP. CONGO DEMOCRATIC REPUBLIC OF THE CONGO
EQU. GUINEA EQUATORIAL GUINEA
NETH. NETHERLANDS
N.Z. NEW ZEALAND
REP. CONGO REPUBLIC OF THE CONGO
U.A.E. UNITED ARAB EMIRATES
U.K. UNITED KINGDOM
U.S. UNITED STATES
Europe
Arctic Circle
FINLAND
NORWAY
ESTONIA
SWEDEN
RUSSIA
LATVIA
North Sea
Baltic Sea
LITHUANIA
UNITED KINGDOM
DENMARK
KALININGRAD (RUSSIA)
IRELAND
BELARUS
NETHERLANDS
POLAND
GERMANY
BELGIUM
ATLANTIC OCEAN
CZECH REPUBLIC
UKRAINE
LUXEMBOURG
SLOVAKIA
MOLDOVA
LIECHTENSTEIN
0 200 400 Miles
0 200 400 Kilometers
Azimuthal Equal-Area Projection
AUSTRIA
HUNGARY
SWITZERLAND
ROMANIA
FRANCE
SLOVENIA
CROATIA
SAN MARINO
BOSNIA AND HERZEGOVINA
SERBIA
Black Sea
BULGARIA
Adriatic Sea
MONTENEGRO
MONACO
ANDORRA
Corsica (FRANCE)
ITALY
MACEDONIA
TURKEY
PORTUGAL
Balearic Islands (SPAIN)
Sardinia (ITALY)
VATICAN CITY
ALBANIA
SPAIN
GREECE
Mediterranean Sea
Sicily (ITALY)
Crete (GREECE)
GIBRALTAR (U.K.)
MALTA
MOROCCO
ALGERIA
TUNISIA
10°W 0° 10°E 20°E
40°N
50°N
60°N

The World: Physical

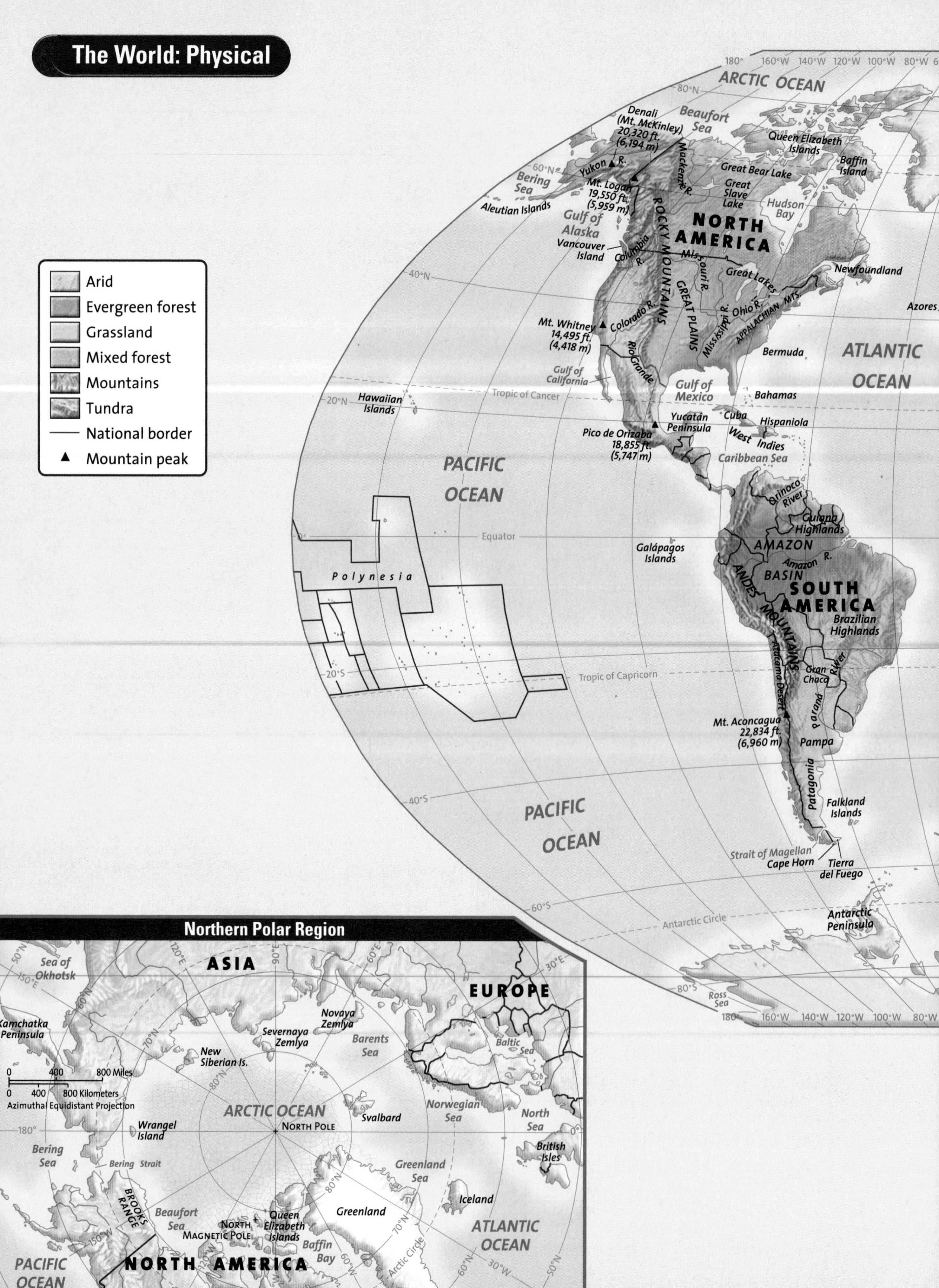

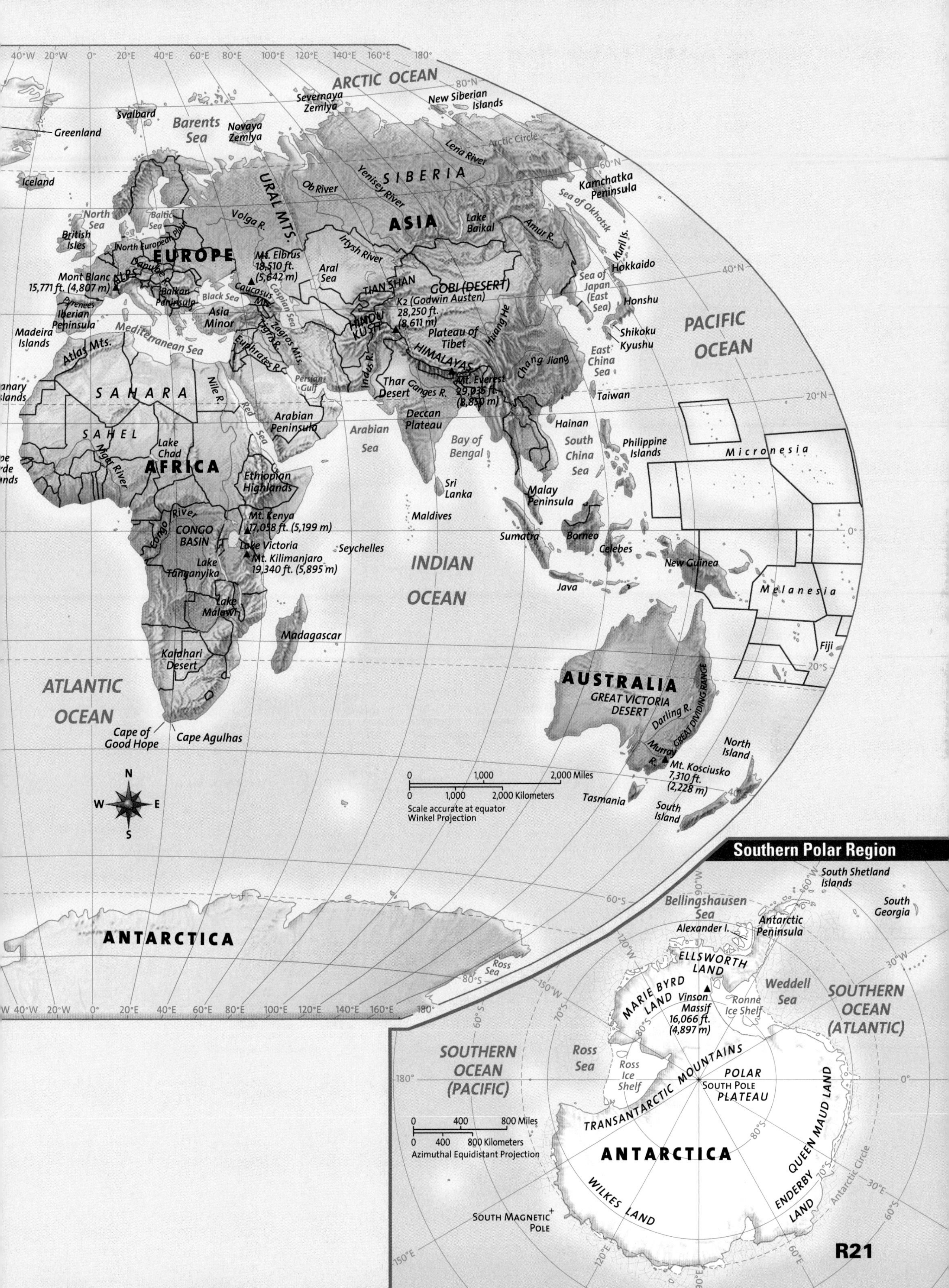

ARCTIC OCEAN
Severnaya Zemlya
New Siberian Islands
Svalbard
Greenland
Barents Sea
Novaya Zemlya
Arctic Circle
Lena River
Iceland
SIBERIA
URAL MTS.
Ob River
Yenisey River
Kamchatka Peninsula
Sea of Okhotsk
North Sea
Baltic Sea
British Isles
North European Plain
Volga R.
ASIA
Lake Baikal
Amur R.
Kuril Is.
EUROPE
Mt. Elbrus 18,510 ft. (5,642 m)
Irtysh River
Hokkaido
Mont Blanc 15,771 ft. (4,807 m)
ALPS
Danube R.
Balkan Peninsula
Aral Sea
Caucasus Mts.
Caspian Sea
TIAN SHAN
GOBI (DESERT)
Sea of Japan (East Sea)
Honshu
Pyrenees
Iberian Peninsula
Black Sea
Asia Minor
Zagros Mts.
HINDU KUSH
K2 (Godwin Austen) 28,250 ft. (8,611 m)
Plateau of Tibet
Huang He
PACIFIC OCEAN
Shikoku
Kyushu
Madeira Islands
Atlas Mts.
Mediterranean Sea
Tigris R.
Euphrates R.
Indus R.
HIMALAYAS
Chang Jiang
East China Sea
Canary Islands
SAHARA
Nile R.
Persian Gulf
Thar Desert
Ganges R.
Mt. Everest 29,035 ft. (8,850 m)
Taiwan
Red Sea
Arabian Peninsula
Deccan Plateau
Hainan
SAHEL
Arabian Sea
Bay of Bengal
South China Sea
Philippine Islands
Lake Chad
Micronesia
Niger River
AFRICA
Ethiopian Highlands
Sri Lanka
Malay Peninsula
Congo River
Mt. Kenya 17,058 ft. (5,199 m)
Maldives
CONGO BASIN
Lake Victoria
Sumatra
Borneo
Celebes
Seychelles
Mt. Kilimanjaro 19,340 ft. (5,895 m)
INDIAN OCEAN
New Guinea
Lake Tanganyika
Java
Melanesia
Lake Malawi
Madagascar
Fiji
Kalahari Desert
AUSTRALIA
GREAT VICTORIA DESERT
GREAT DIVIDING RANGE
Darling R.
ATLANTIC OCEAN
Cape of Good Hope
Cape Agulhas
Murray R.
North Island
Mt. Kosciusko 7,310 ft. (2,228 m)
0 1,000 2,000 Miles
0 1,000 2,000 Kilometers
Scale accurate at equator
Winkel Projection
Tasmania
South Island
N
W
E
S
ANTARCTICA
Ross Sea
Southern Polar Region
South Shetland Islands
Bellingshausen Sea
South Georgia
Antarctic Peninsula
Alexander I.
ELLSWORTH LAND
MARIE BYRD LAND
Vinson Massif 16,066 ft. (4,897 m)
Ronne Ice Shelf
Weddell Sea
SOUTHERN OCEAN (ATLANTIC)
SOUTHERN OCEAN (PACIFIC)
Ross Sea
Ross Ice Shelf
TRANSANTARCTIC MOUNTAINS
POLAR PLATEAU
SOUTH POLE
QUEEN MAUD LAND
0 400 800 Miles
0 400 800 Kilometers
Azimuthal Equidistant Projection
ANTARCTICA
WILKES LAND
ENDERBY LAND
Antarctic Circle
SOUTH MAGNETIC POLE

Western Hemisphere: Political

Western Hemisphere: Physical

United States: Overview

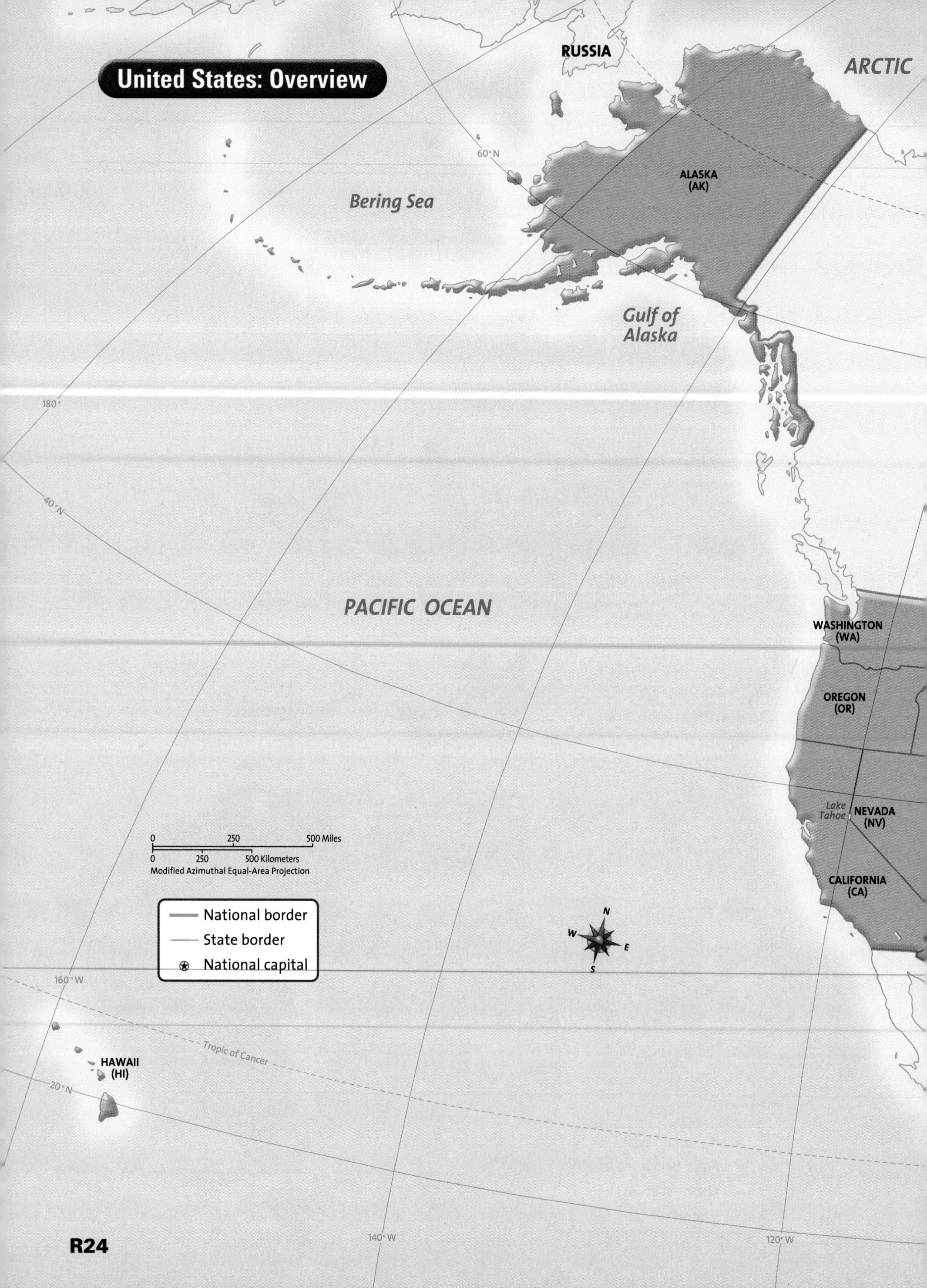

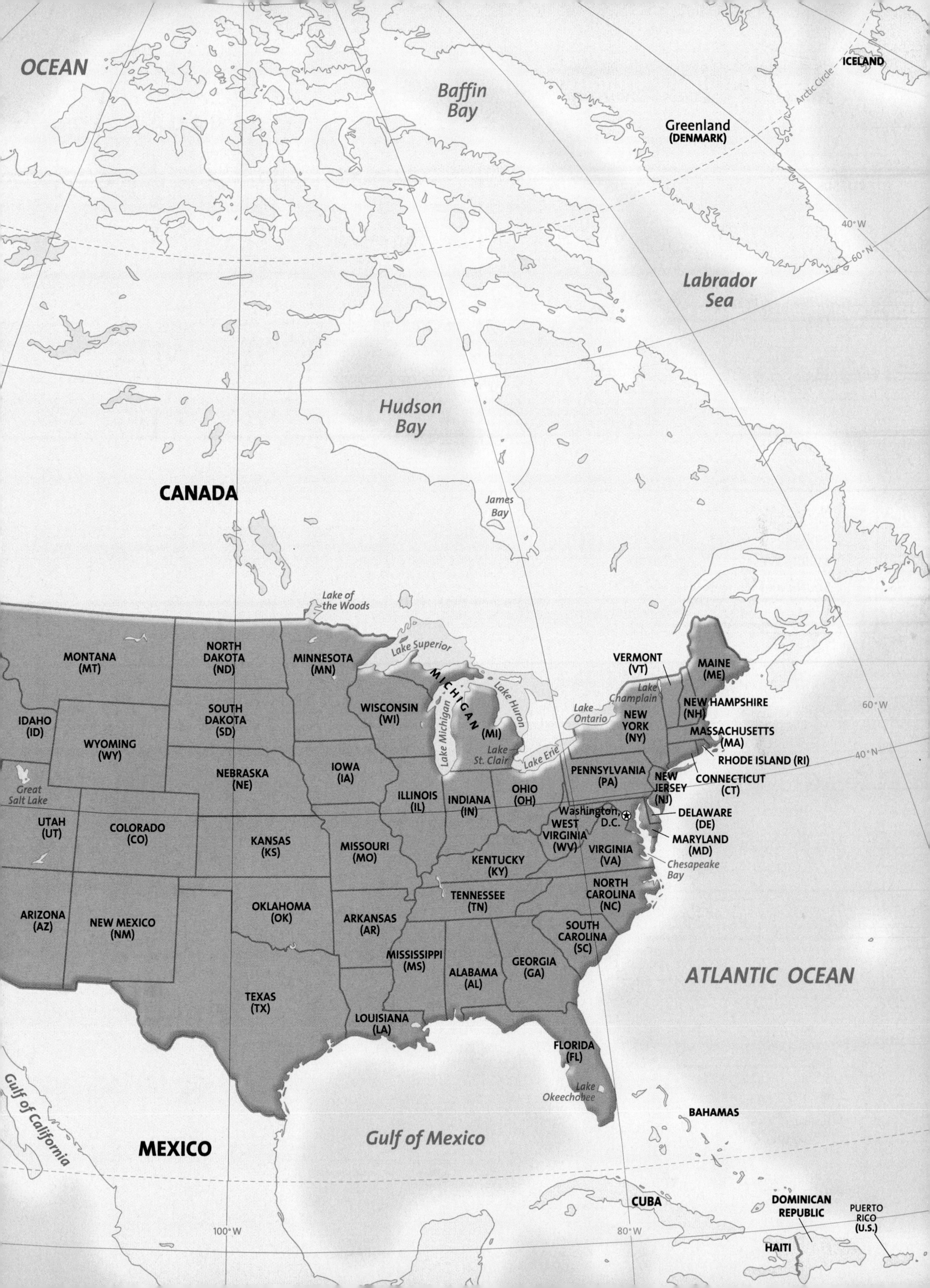

OCEAN
ICELAND
Baffin Bay
Arctic Circle
Greenland
(DENMARK)
40° W
60° N
Labrador Sea
Hudson Bay
CANADA
James Bay
Lake of the Woods
Lake Superior
MONTANA
(MT)
NORTH DAKOTA
(ND)
MINNESOTA
(MN)
MICHIGAN
(MI)
Lake Huron
VERMONT
(VT)
MAINE
(ME)
Lake Champlain
NEW HAMPSHIRE
(NH)
IDAHO
(ID)
SOUTH DAKOTA
(SD)
WISCONSIN
(WI)
Lake Michigan
Lake Ontario
NEW YORK
(NY)
MASSACHUSETTS
(MA)
60° W
WYOMING
(WY)
Lake St. Clair
Lake Erie
RHODE ISLAND (RI)
40° N
NEBRASKA
(NE)
IOWA
(IA)
PENNSYLVANIA
(PA)
NEW JERSEY
(NJ)
CONNECTICUT
(CT)
Great Salt Lake
ILLINOIS
(IL)
INDIANA
(IN)
OHIO
(OH)
Washington, D.C.
DELAWARE
(DE)
UTAH
(UT)
COLORADO
(CO)
KANSAS
(KS)
MISSOURI
(MO)
WEST VIRGINIA
(WV)
MARYLAND
(MD)
KENTUCKY
(KY)
VIRGINIA
(VA)
Chesapeake Bay
NORTH CAROLINA
(NC)
TENNESSEE
(TN)
ARIZONA
(AZ)
NEW MEXICO
(NM)
OKLAHOMA
(OK)
ARKANSAS
(AR)
SOUTH CAROLINA
(SC)
MISSISSIPPI
(MS)
ALABAMA
(AL)
GEORGIA
(GA)
ATLANTIC OCEAN
TEXAS
(TX)
LOUISIANA
(LA)
FLORIDA
(FL)
Lake Okeechobee
Gulf of California
BAHAMAS
MEXICO
Gulf of Mexico
CUBA
DOMINICAN REPUBLIC
PUERTO RICO
(U.S.)
100° W
80° W
HAITI

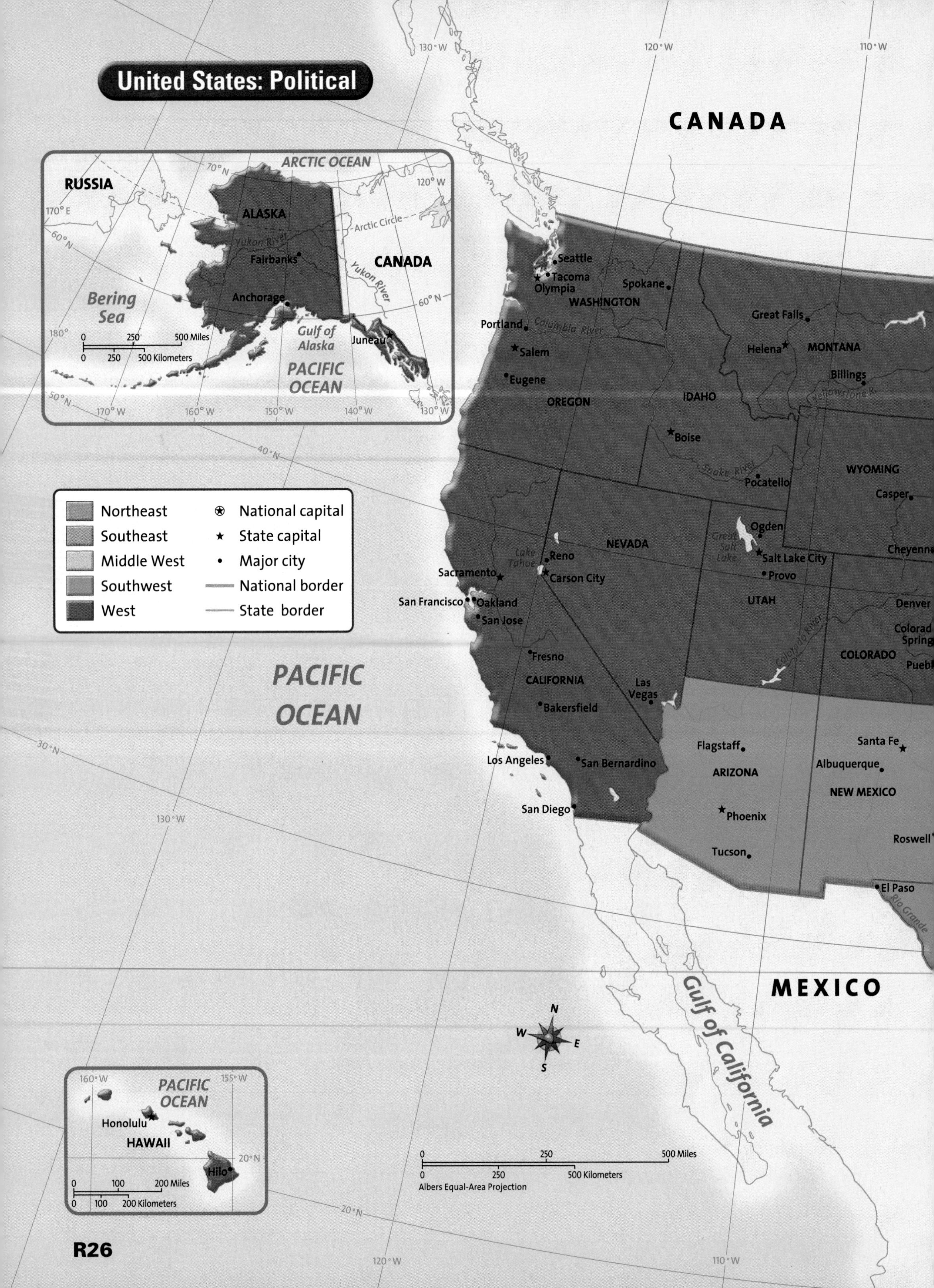

United States: Political
CANADA
RUSSIA
ARCTIC OCEAN
ALASKA
Arctic Circle
Yukon River
Fairbanks
CANADA
Bering Sea
Anchorage
Gulf of Alaska
Juneau
PACIFIC OCEAN
0 250 500 Miles
0 250 500 Kilometers
Northeast
Southeast
Middle West
Southwest
West
National capital
State capital
Major city
National border
State border
Seattle
Tacoma
Olympia
WASHINGTON
Spokane
Portland
Columbia River
Salem
Eugene
OREGON
Great Falls
Helena
MONTANA
Billings
Yellowstone R.
IDAHO
Boise
Snake River
Pocatello
WYOMING
Casper
Cheyenne
Ogden
Great Salt Lake
Salt Lake City
Provo
UTAH
NEVADA
Reno
Lake Tahoe
Carson City
Sacramento
San Francisco
Oakland
San Jose
Fresno
CALIFORNIA
Las Vegas
Bakersfield
Denver
Colorado River
COLORADO
PACIFIC OCEAN
Los Angeles
San Bernardino
San Diego
Flagstaff
ARIZONA
Phoenix
Tucson
Santa Fe
Albuquerque
NEW MEXICO
Roswell
El Paso
Rio Grande
MEXICO
Gulf of California
N
W
E
S
0 250 500 Miles
0 250 500 Kilometers
Albers Equal-Area Projection
PACIFIC OCEAN
Honolulu
HAWAII
Hilo
0 100 200 Miles
0 100 200 Kilometers

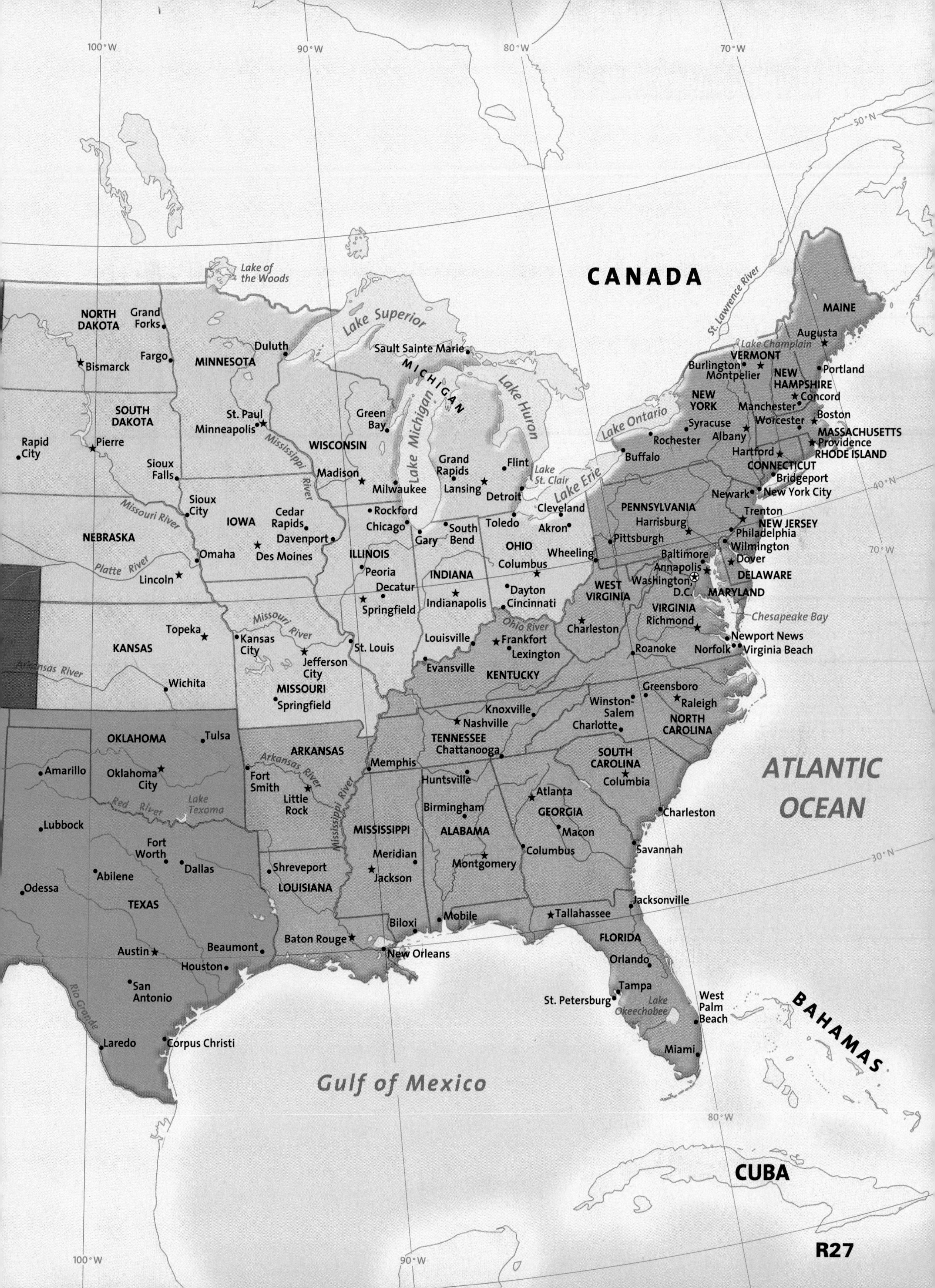

100°W
90°W
80°W
70°W
50°N
40°N
30°N
70°W
80°W
100°W
90°W
CANADA
Lake of the Woods
Lake Superior
Lake Michigan
Lake Huron
Lake Ontario
Lake Erie
Lake St. Clair
St. Lawrence River
Lake Champlain
NORTH DAKOTA
Grand Forks
Fargo
Bismarck
MINNESOTA
Duluth
St. Paul
Minneapolis
SOUTH DAKOTA
Pierre
Rapid City
Sioux Falls
Mississippi River
WISCONSIN
Green Bay
Madison
Milwaukee
MICHIGAN
Sault Sainte Marie
Grand Rapids
Lansing
Flint
Detroit
IOWA
Sioux City
Cedar Rapids
Davenport
Des Moines
Missouri River
NEBRASKA
Omaha
Lincoln
Platte River
ILLINOIS
Rockford
Chicago
Gary
South Bend
Peoria
Decatur
Springfield
INDIANA
Indianapolis
OHIO
Toledo
Cleveland
Akron
Columbus
Dayton
Cincinnati
Wheeling
PENNSYLVANIA
Pittsburgh
Harrisburg
Philadelphia
NEW YORK
Buffalo
Rochester
Syracuse
Albany
New York City
MAINE
Augusta
Portland
VERMONT
Burlington
Montpelier
NEW HAMPSHIRE
Concord
Manchester
MASSACHUSETTS
Boston
Worcester
Providence
RHODE ISLAND
Hartford
CONNECTICUT
Bridgeport
Newark
Trenton
NEW JERSEY
Wilmington
Dover
DELAWARE
Baltimore
Annapolis
Washington, D.C.
MARYLAND
WEST VIRGINIA
Charleston
VIRGINIA
Richmond
Chesapeake Bay
Newport News
Norfolk
Virginia Beach
Roanoke
KANSAS
Topeka
Kansas City
Wichita
Arkansas River
MISSOURI
Jefferson City
St. Louis
Springfield
Ohio River
Louisville
Frankfort
Lexington
Evansville
KENTUCKY
Greensboro
Winston-Salem
Raleigh
NORTH CAROLINA
Charlotte
Knoxville
Nashville
TENNESSEE
Chattanooga
Memphis
OKLAHOMA
Tulsa
Oklahoma City
Amarillo
Red River
Lake Texoma
ARKANSAS
Fort Smith
Little Rock
Mississippi River
SOUTH CAROLINA
Columbia
Charleston
ATLANTIC OCEAN
Huntsville
Birmingham
Atlanta
GEORGIA
Macon
MISSISSIPPI
ALABAMA
Meridian
Jackson
Montgomery
Columbus
Savannah
Lubbock
Fort Worth
Dallas
Abilene
Odessa
TEXAS
Shreveport
LOUISIANA
Jacksonville
Tallahassee
Biloxi
Mobile
Baton Rouge
New Orleans
FLORIDA
Orlando
Tampa
St. Petersburg
Lake Okeechobee
West Palm Beach
Miami
Austin
Beaumont
Houston
San Antonio
Rio Grande
Laredo
Corpus Christi
BAHAMAS
Gulf of Mexico
CUBA

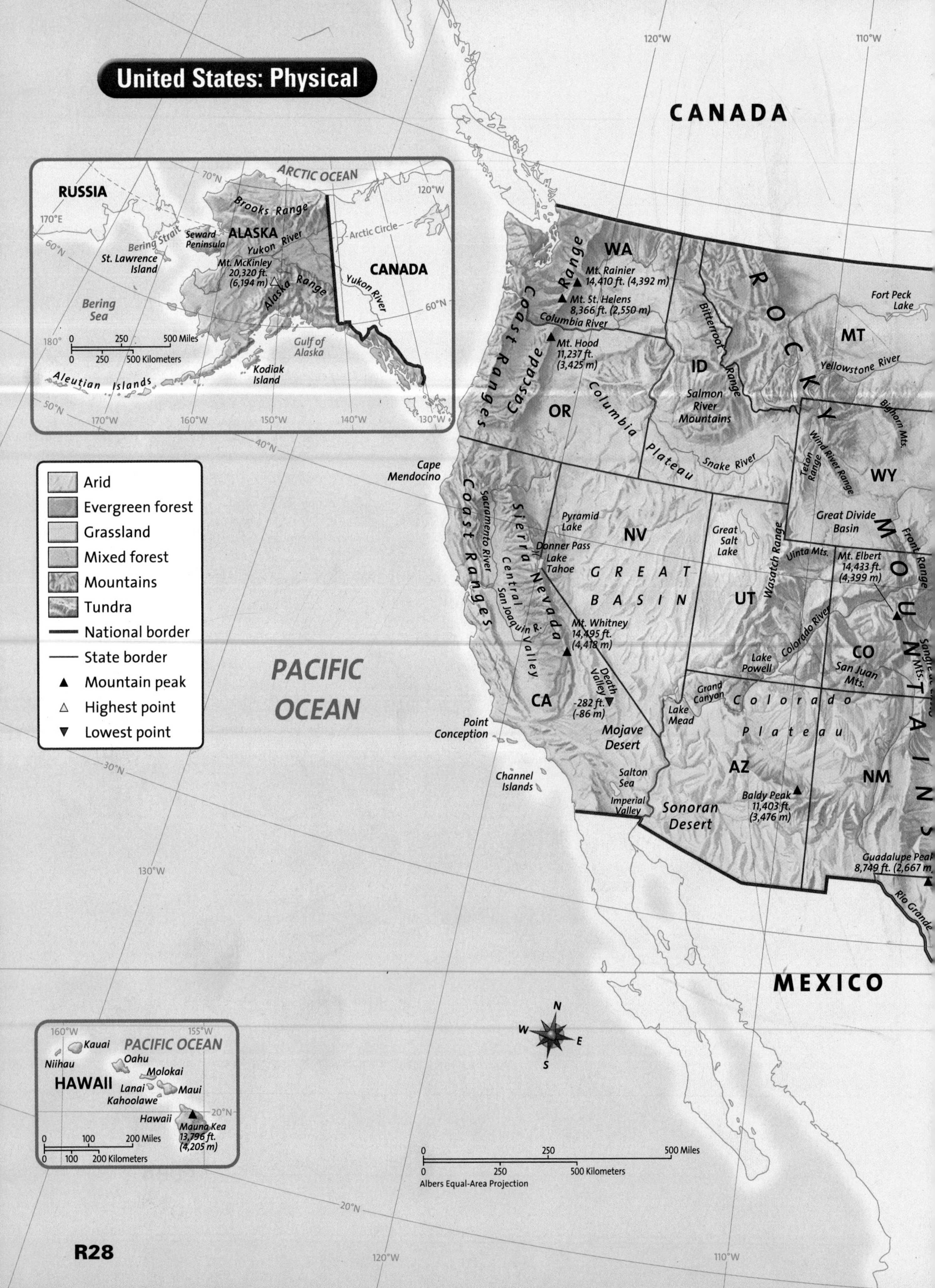
United States: Physical
CANADA
ARCTIC OCEAN
RUSSIA
ALASKA
Brooks Range
Seward Peninsula
Bering Strait
St. Lawrence Island
Yukon River
Mt. McKinley 20,320 ft. (6,194 m)
Alaska Range
Arctic Circle
Bering Sea
Gulf of Alaska
Kodiak Island
Aleutian Islands
0 250 500 Miles
0 250 500 Kilometers
Arid
Evergreen forest
Grassland
Mixed forest
Mountains
Tundra
National border
State border
Mountain peak
Highest point
Lowest point
WA
Mt. Rainier 14,410 ft. (4,392 m)
Mt. St. Helens 8,366 ft. (2,550 m)
Columbia River
Mt. Hood 11,237 ft. (3,425 m)
Cascade Range
Coast Ranges
OR
Columbia Plateau
ID
Bitterroot Range
Salmon River Mountains
Snake River
MT
Fort Peck Lake
Yellowstone River
Bighorn Mts.
WY
Teton Range
Wind River Range
Great Divide Basin
ROCKY MOUNTAINS
Cape Mendocino
Sacramento River
Sierra Nevada
Central Valley
San Joaquin R.
Pyramid Lake
Donner Pass
Lake Tahoe
NV
GREAT BASIN
Great Salt Lake
Wasatch Range
Uinta Mts.
UT
Mt. Elbert 14,433 ft. (4,399 m)
Front Range
CO
San Juan Mts.
Colorado River
Lake Powell
Mt. Whitney 14,495 ft. (4,418 m)
Death Valley
-282 ft. (-86 m)
CA
PACIFIC OCEAN
Point Conception
Mojave Desert
Grand Canyon
Lake Mead
Colorado Plateau
Channel Islands
Salton Sea
Imperial Valley
AZ
Sonoran Desert
Baldy Peak 11,403 ft. (3,476 m)
NM
Guadalupe Peak 8,749 ft. (2,667 m)
Rio Grande
MEXICO
N
S
E
W
Kauai
Niihau
Oahu
Molokai
HAWAII
Lanai
Maui
Kahoolawe
Hawaii
Mauna Kea 13,796 ft. (4,205 m)
0 100 200 Miles
0 100 200 Kilometers
0 250 500 Miles
0 250 500 Kilometers
Albers Equal-Area Projection

CANADA
ATLANTIC OCEAN
Gulf of Mexico
BAHAMAS
CUBA
ME
NH
VT
MA
RI
CT
NY
NJ
PA
DE
MD
VA
WV
OH
KY
TN
NC
SC
GA
FL
AL
MS
LA
AR
MO
IL
IN
MI
WI
MN
IA
ND
SD
NE
KS
OK
TX
GREAT PLAINS
INTERIOR PLAINS
CENTRAL PLAINS
APPALACHIAN MOUNTAINS
PIEDMONT
COASTAL PLAIN
Lake of the Woods
Upper Red Lake
Lower Red Lake
Leech Lake
Mille Lacs Lake
Mesabi Range
Isle Royale
Lake Superior
Keweenaw Peninsula
Upper Peninsula
Lake Michigan
Lower Peninsula
Lake Huron
Lake St. Clair
Lake Erie
Lake Ontario
Niagara Falls
Lake Sakakawea
Lake Oahe
Black Hills
Missouri River
Mississippi River
Wisconsin River
Lake Winnebago
Sand Hills
North Platte R.
Platte River
South Platte R.
Smoky Hills
Red Hills
Illinois River
Wabash River
Ohio River
Missouri River
Lake of the Ozarks
Harry S. Truman Reservoir
Ozark Plateau
Lake Barkley
Cumberland Gap
Cumberland R.
Tennessee R.
Mt. Mitchell 6,684 ft. (2,037 m)
Arkansas River
Canadian River
Ouachita Mountains
Lake Texoma
Red River
Mississippi River
Llano Estacado
Sabine River
Brazos River
Edwards Plateau
Pecos River
Colorado River
Sam Rayburn Reservoir
Toledo Bend Reservoir
Lake Maurepas
Lake Pontchartrain
Galveston Bay
Rio Grande
Mississippi Delta
Mobile Bay
Tombigbee R.
Alabama R.
Chattahoochee R.
Stone Mountain
Clark Hill Lake
Savannah River
Oconee R.
Ocmulgee R.
Altamaha R.
Okefenokee Swamp
St. Johns River
Cape Canaveral
Tampa Bay
Lake Okeechobee
Everglades
Cape Sable
Florida Keys
Straits of Florida
St. Lawrence River
Moosehead Lake
Mt. Katahdin 5,269 ft. (1,606 m)
Lake Champlain
Mt. Washington 6,288 ft. (1,917 m)
White Mts.
Green Mts.
Adirondack Mountains
Finger Lakes
Connecticut R.
Hudson R.
Cape Ann
Cape Cod
Long Island
Allegheny Mts.
Potomac R.
Delaware Bay
Cape Charles
Chesapeake Bay
James R.
Roanoke R.
Albemarle Sound
Cape Hatteras
Cape Fear River
Cape Fear
100°W
90°W
80°W
70°W
50°N
40°N
30°N

California: Political

★ State capital
● County seat
• Other city
National border
State border
County border

0 — 75 — 150 Miles
0 — 75 — 150 Kilometers
Albers Equal-Area Projection

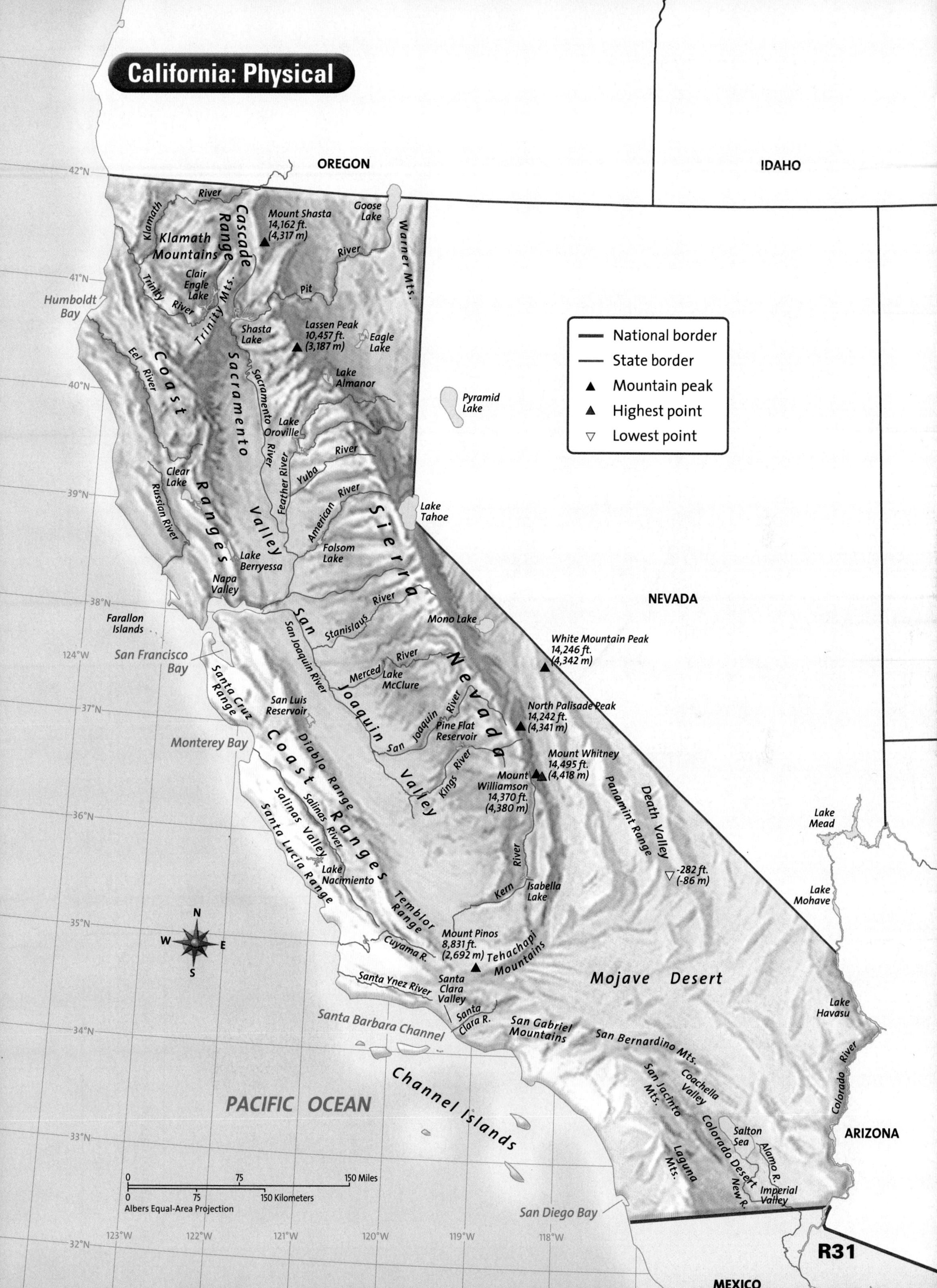

California: Physical
OREGON
IDAHO
NEVADA
ARIZONA
MEXICO
PACIFIC OCEAN
National border
State border
Mountain peak
Highest point
Lowest point
Klamath River
Klamath Mountains
Cascade Range
Mount Shasta 14,162 ft. (4,317 m)
Goose Lake
Warner Mts.
Pit River
Trinity River
Clair Engle Lake
Trinity Mts.
Humboldt Bay
Shasta Lake
Lassen Peak 10,457 ft. (3,187 m)
Eagle Lake
Lake Almanor
Eel River
Coast Ranges
Sacramento Valley
Sacramento River
Pyramid Lake
Lake Oroville
Feather River
Yuba River
Clear Lake
Russian River
American River
Lake Tahoe
Sierra Nevada
Lake Berryessa
Folsom Lake
Napa Valley
Farallon Islands
San Francisco Bay
Stanislaus River
Mono Lake
San Joaquin Valley
San Joaquin River
White Mountain Peak 14,246 ft. (4,342 m)
Merced River
Lake McClure
Santa Cruz Range
San Luis Reservoir
North Palisade Peak 14,242 ft. (4,341 m)
Pine Flat Reservoir
Monterey Bay
Diablo Range
Kings River
Mount Whitney 14,495 ft. (4,418 m)
Mount Williamson 14,370 ft. (4,380 m)
Panamint Range
Death Valley
Salinas Valley
Salinas River
Santa Lucia Range
Lake Nacimiento
Lake Mead
Kern River
Isabella Lake
-282 ft. (-86 m)
Lake Mohave
Temblor Range
Mount Pinos 8,831 ft. (2,692 m)
Cuyama R.
Tehachapi Mountains
Mojave Desert
Santa Ynez River
Santa Clara Valley
Lake Havasu
Santa Barbara Channel
Santa Clara R.
San Gabriel Mountains
San Bernardino Mts.
Channel Islands
San Jacinto Mts.
Coachella Valley
Colorado River
Salton Sea
Colorado Desert
Laguna Mts.
Alamo R.
New R.
Imperial Valley
San Diego Bay
N
W
E
S
0
75
150 Miles
150 Kilometers
Albers Equal-Area Projection
42°N
41°N
40°N
39°N
38°N
37°N
36°N
35°N
34°N
33°N
32°N
124°W
123°W
122°W
121°W
120°W
119°W
118°W

Canada

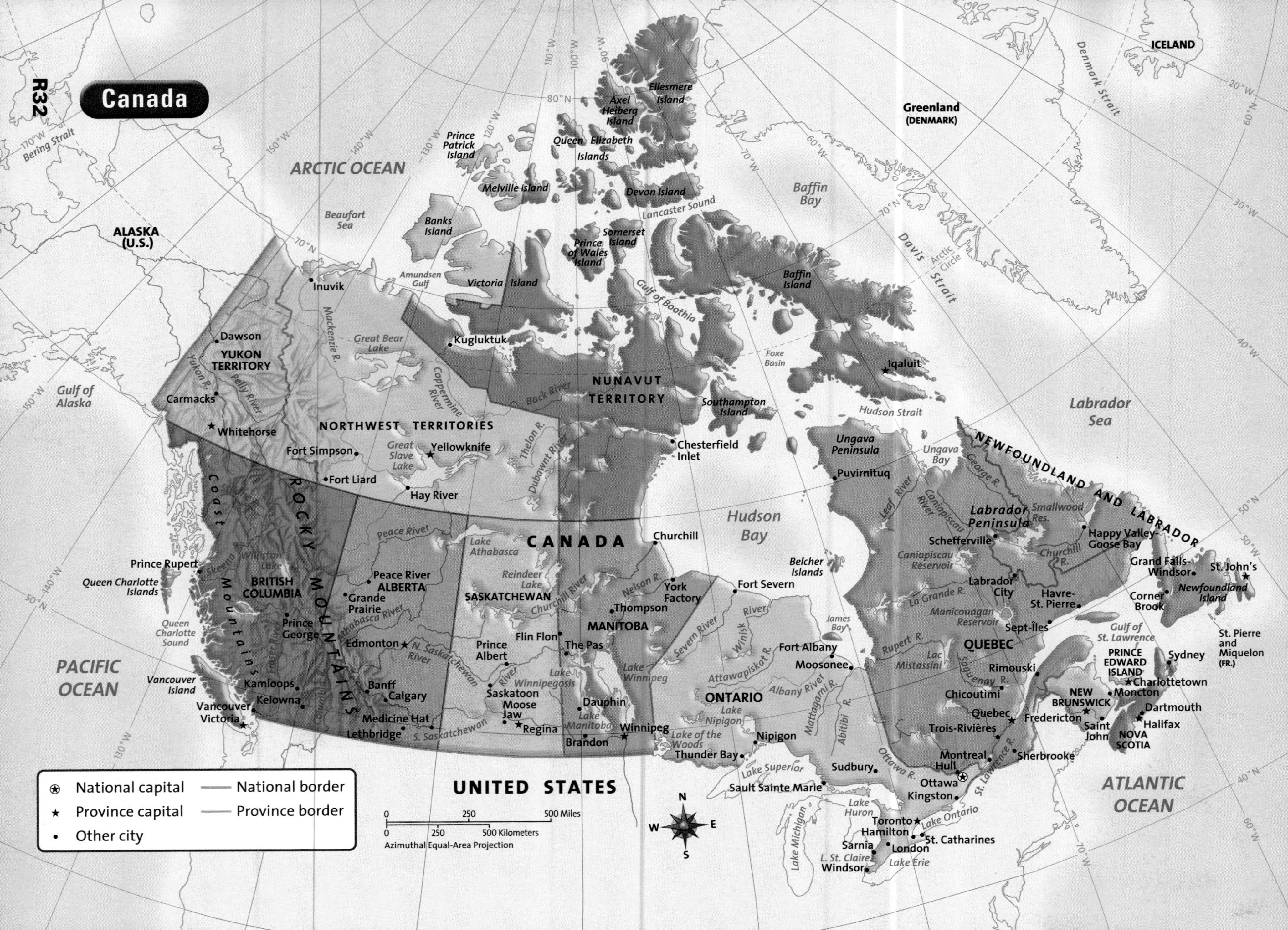
ARCTIC OCEAN
Beaufort Sea
ALASKA (U.S.)
Bering Strait
Gulf of Alaska
PACIFIC OCEAN
Greenland (DENMARK)
ICELAND
Denmark Strait
Baffin Bay
Davis Strait
Arctic Circle
Labrador Sea
ATLANTIC OCEAN
UNITED STATES
CANADA
YUKON TERRITORY
NORTHWEST TERRITORIES
NUNAVUT TERRITORY
BRITISH COLUMBIA
ALBERTA
SASKATCHEWAN
MANITOBA
ONTARIO
QUEBEC
NEWFOUNDLAND AND LABRADOR
NEW BRUNSWICK
PRINCE EDWARD ISLAND
NOVA SCOTIA
ROCKY MOUNTAINS
Coast Mountains
Prince Patrick Island
Queen Elizabeth Islands
Ellesmere Island
Axel Heiberg Island
Melville Island
Devon Island
Lancaster Sound
Banks Island
Somerset Island
Prince of Wales Island
Victoria Island
Amundsen Gulf
Gulf of Boothia
Baffin Island
Foxe Basin
Southampton Island
Hudson Strait
Hudson Bay
James Bay
Belcher Islands
Ungava Peninsula
Ungava Bay
Labrador Peninsula
Smallwood Res.
Caniapiscau Reservoir
Manicouagan Reservoir
Gulf of St. Lawrence
Newfoundland Island
St. Pierre and Miquelon (FR.)
Queen Charlotte Islands
Queen Charlotte Sound
Vancouver Island
Great Bear Lake
Great Slave Lake
Lake Athabasca
Reindeer Lake
Lake Winnipegosis
Lake Manitoba
Lake Winnipeg
Lake of the Woods
Lake Nipigon
Lake Superior
Lake Michigan
Lake Huron
L. St. Claire
Lake Erie
Lake Ontario
Lac Mistassini
Williston Lake
Yukon R.
Pelly River
Mackenzie R.
Coppermine River
Back River
Thelon R.
Dubawnt River
Peace River
Athabasca River
N. Saskatchewan River
S. Saskatchewan
Churchill River
Nelson R.
Severn River
Winisk River
Attawapiskat R.
Albany River
Mattagami R.
Abitibi R.
Ottawa R.
St. Lawrence R.
Saguenay R.
Rupert R.
La Grande R.
Caniapiscau River
Leaf River
George R.
Churchill R.
Stikine R.
Skeena R.
Fraser River
Columbia R.
Inuvik
Dawson
Carmacks
Whitehorse
Fort Simpson
Fort Liard
Yellowknife
Hay River
Kugluktuk
Iqaluit
Chesterfield Inlet
Puvirnituq
Prince Rupert
Prince George
Peace River
Grande Prairie
Edmonton
Kamloops
Kelowna
Vancouver
Victoria
Banff
Calgary
Medicine Hat
Lethbridge
Prince Albert
Saskatoon
Moose Jaw
Regina
Flin Flon
The Pas
Dauphin
Brandon
Winnipeg
Thompson
Churchill
York Factory
Fort Severn
Fort Albany
Moosonee
Nipigon
Thunder Bay
Sault Sainte Marie
Sudbury
Toronto
Hamilton
St. Catharines
London
Sarnia
Windsor
Kingston
Ottawa
Hull
Montreal
Trois-Rivières
Quebec
Sherbrooke
Chicoutimi
Rimouski
Sept-Îles
Havre-St. Pierre
Labrador City
Schefferville
Happy Valley-Goose Bay
Grand Falls-Windsor
Corner Brook
St. John's
Fredericton
Saint John
Moncton
Charlottetown
Sydney
Dartmouth
Halifax
80°N
70°N
60°N
50°N
40°N
170°W
150°W
140°W
130°W
120°W
110°W
100°W
90°W
70°W
60°W
40°W
30°W
20°W
N
E
S
W
National capital
Province capital
Other city
National border
Province border
0 250 500 Miles
0 250 500 Kilometers
Azimuthal Equal-Area Projection

Mexico

UNITED STATES
MEXICO
Gulf of Mexico
PACIFIC OCEAN
Bay of Campeche
Caribbean Sea
Gulf of California
Gulf of Tehuantepec
Baja California
Yucatán Peninsula
Isthmus of Tehuantepec
Sonoran Desert
SIERRA MADRE OCCIDENTAL
SIERRA MADRE ORIENTAL
SIERRA MADRE DEL SUR
Rio Grande
Rio Bravo
Conchos R.
Yaqui R.
Santiago R.
Lerma R.
Balsas River
Usumacinta R.
Lake Chapala
Yucatán Channel
Tropic of Cancer
30°N
20°N
110°W
100°W
90°W
N
S
E
W
BAJA CALIFORNIA
BAJA CALIFORNIA SUR
SONORA
CHIHUAHUA
COAHUILA
NUEVO LEÓN
TAMAULIPAS
SINALOA
DURANGO
ZACATECAS
SAN LUIS POTOSÍ
NAYARIT
AGUASCALIENTES
GUANAJUATO
QUERÉTARO
HIDALGO
JALISCO
COLIMA
MICHOACÁN
MÉXICO
DISTRITO FEDERAL
TLAXCALA
MORELOS
PUEBLA
VERACRUZ
GUERRERO
OAXACA
TABASCO
CHIAPAS
CAMPECHE
YUCATÁN
QUINTANA ROO
BELIZE
GUATEMALA
HONDURAS
EL SALVADOR
Tijuana
Mexicali
Ensenada
Puerto Peñasco
Guadalupe
Cedros Island
Eugenia Point
Nogales
Hermosillo
Guaymas
Ciudad Obregón
Navojoa
Nueva Casas Grandes
Ciudad Juárez
Villa Ahumada
Chihuahua
Delicias
Hidalgo del Parral
Loreto
La Paz
San Lucas
Cape San Lucas
Los Mochis
Culiacán
Mazatlán
Durango
Torreón
Nuevo Laredo
Monclova
Saltillo
Monterrey
Reynosa
Matamoros
Ciudad Victoria
Concepción del Oro
Fresnillo
Zacatecas
Ciudad Mante
Tampico
Ciudad de Valles
San Luis Potosí
Aguascalientes
León
Irapuato
Guanajuato
Querétaro
Marías Islands
San Blas
Tepic
Puerto Vallarta
Cape Corrientes
Guadalajara
Revillagigedo Islands
Socorro Island
Colima
Tecomán
Morelia
Uruapán
Mexico City
Toluca
Pachuca
Tlaxcala
Puebla
Cuernavaca
Poza Rica
Jalapa Enríquez
Veracruz
Lázaro Cárdenas
Chilpancingo
Acapulco
Oaxaca
Puerto Escondido
Salina Cruz
Coatzacoalcos
Villahermosa
Tuxtla Gutiérrez
Comitán
Tapachula
Ciudad del Carmen
Campeche
Mérida
Cancún
Cozumel Island
Chetumal
National border
State border
National capital
State capital
Other city
0
150
300 Miles
0
150
300 Kilometers
Azimuthal Equal-Area Projection

Almanac

Facts About the States

State Flag	State	Year of Statehood	Population*	Area (sq. mi.)	Capital	Origin of State Name
	Alabama	1819	4,500,752	50,750	Montgomery	Choctaw, *alba ayamule*, "one who clears land and gathers food from it"
	Alaska	1959	648,818	570,374	Juneau	Aleut, *alayeska*, "great land"
	Arizona	1912	5,580,811	113,642	Phoenix	Papago, *arizonac*, "place of the small spring"
ARKANSAS	**Arkansas**	1836	2,725,714	52,075	Little Rock	Quapaw, "the downstream people"
CALIFORNIA REPUBLIC	**California**	1850	35,484,453	155,973	Sacramento	Spanish, a fictional island
	Colorado	1876	4,550,688	103,730	Denver	Spanish, "red land" or "red earth"
	Connecticut	1788	3,483,372	4,845	Hartford	Mohican, *quinnitukqut*, "at the long tidal river"
	Delaware	1787	817,491	1,955	Dover	Named for Lord de la Warr
	Florida	1845	17,019,068	54,153	Tallahassee	Spanish, "filled with flowers"
	Georgia	1788	8,684,715	57,919	Atlanta	Named for King George II of England
	Hawaii	1959	1,257,608	6,450	Honolulu	Polynesian, *hawaiki* or *owykee*, "homeland"
	Idaho	1890	1,366,332	82,751	Boise	Invented name with unknown meaning

State Flag	State	Year of Statehood	Population*	Area (sq. mi.)	Capital	Origin of State Name
	Illinois	1818	12,653,544	55,593	Springfield	Algonquin, *iliniwek,* "men" or "warriors"
	Indiana	1816	6,195,643	35,870	Indianapolis	*Indian* + *a*, "land of the Indians"
	Iowa	1846	2,944,062	55,875	Des Moines	Dakota, *ayuba*, "beautiful land"
	Kansas	1861	2,723,507	81,823	Topeka	Sioux, "land of the south wind people"
	Kentucky	1792	4,117,827	39,732	Frankfort	Iroquoian, *ken-tah-ten*, "land of tomorrow"
	Louisiana	1812	4,496,334	43,566	Baton Rouge	Named for King Louis XIV of France
	Maine	1820	1,305,728	30,865	Augusta	Named after a French province
	Maryland	1788	5,508,909	9,775	Annapolis	Named for Henrietta Maria, Queen Consort of Charles I of England
	Massachusetts	1788	6,433,422	7,838	Boston	Massachusetts American Indian tribe, "at the big hill" or "place of the big hill"
	Michigan	1837	10,079,985	56,809	Lansing	Ojibwa, "large lake"
	Minnesota	1858	5,059,375	79,617	St. Paul	Dakota Sioux, "sky-blue water"
	Mississippi	1817	2,881,281	46,914	Jackson	Indian word meaning "great waters" or "father of waters"
	Missouri	1821	5,704,484	68,898	Jefferson City	Named after the Missouri Indian tribe. *Missouri* means "town of the large canoes."

* latest available population figures

State Flag	State	Year of Statehood	Population*	Area (sq. mi.)	Capital	Origin of State Name
MONTANA	**Montana**	1889	917,621	145,566	Helena	Spanish, "mountainous"
	Nebraska	1867	1,739,291	76,878	Lincoln	From an Oto Indian word meaning "flat water"
	Nevada	1864	2,241,154	109,806	Carson City	Spanish, "snowy" or "snowed upon"
	New Hampshire	1788	1,287,687	8,969	Concord	Named for Hampshire County, England
	New Jersey	1787	8,638,396	7,419	Trenton	Named for the Isle of Jersey
	New Mexico	1912	1,874,614	121,365	Santa Fe	Named by Spanish explorers from Mexico
	New York	1788	19,190,115	47,224	Albany	Named after the Duke of York
N★C	**North Carolina**	1789	8,407,248	48,718	Raleigh	Named after King Charles II of England
	North Dakota	1889	633,837	70,704	Bismarck	Sioux, *dakota*, "friend" or "ally"
	Ohio	1803	11,435,798	40,953	Columbus	Iroquois, *oheo*, "great water"
OKLAHOMA	**Oklahoma**	1907	3,511,532	68,679	Oklahoma City	Choctaw, "red people"
STATE OF OREGON 1859	**Oregon**	1859	3,559,596	96,003	Salem	Unknown; generally accepted that it was taken from the writings of Maj. Robert Rogers, an English army officer
	Pennsylvania	1787	12,365,455	44,820	Harrisburg	*Penn + sylvania*, meaning "Penn's *woods*"

State Flag	State	Year of Statehood	Population*	Area (sq. mi.)	Capital	Origin of State Name
	Rhode Island	1790	1,076,164	1,045	Providence	From the Greek island of Rhodes
	South Carolina	1788	4,147,152	30,111	Columbia	Named after King Charles II of England
	South Dakota	1889	764,309	75,898	Pierre	Sioux, *dakota*, "friend"or "ally"
	Tennessee	1796	5,841,748	41,220	Nashville	Name of a Cherokee village
	Texas	1845	22,118,509	261,914	Austin	Native American, *tejas*, "friend" or "ally"
	Utah	1896	2,351,467	82,168	Salt Lake City	From the Ute tribe, meaning "people of the mountains"
	Vermont	1791	619,107	9,249	Montpelier	French, *vert*, "green," and *mont*, "mountain"
	Virginia	1788	7,386,330	39,598	Richmond	Named after Queen Elizabeth I of England
	Washington	1889	6,131,445	66,582	Olympia	Named for George Washington
	West Virginia	1863	1,810,354	24,087	Charleston	From the English-named state of Virginia
WISCONSIN 1848	**Wisconsin**	1848	5,472,299	54,314	Madison	Possibly Algonquian, "the place where we live"
	Wyoming	1890	501,242	97,105	Cheyenne	From Delaware Indian word meaning "land of vast plains"
	District of Columbia		563,384	67		Named after Christopher Columbus

* latest available population figures

Almanac
Facts About the Presidents

ATLAS/ALMANAC

1 George Washington

1732–1799
Birthplace: *Westmoreland County, VA*
Home State: *VA*
Political Party: *None*
Age at Inauguration: *57*
Served: *1789–1797*
Vice President: *John Adams*

2 John Adams

1735–1826
Birthplace: *Braintree, MA*
Home State: *MA*
Political Party: *Federalist*
Age at Inauguration: *61*
Served: *1797–1801*
Vice President: *Thomas Jefferson*

3 Thomas Jefferson

1743–1826
Birthplace: *Albemarle County, VA*
Home State: *VA*
Political Party: *Democratic-Republican*
Age at Inauguration: *57*
Served: *1801–1809*
Vice Presidents: *Aaron Burr, George Clinton*

4 James Madison

1751–1836
Birthplace: *Port Conway, VA*
Home State: *VA*
Political Party: *Democratic-Republican*
Age at Inauguration: *57*
Served: *1809–1817*
Vice Presidents: *George Clinton, Elbridge Gerry*

5 James Monroe

1758–1831
Birthplace: *Westmoreland County, VA*
Home State: *VA*
Political Party: *Democratic-Republican*
Age at Inauguration: *58*
Served: *1817–1825*
Vice President: *Daniel D. Tompkins*

6 John Quincy Adams

1767–1848
Birthplace: *Braintree, MA*
Home State: *MA*
Political Party: *Democratic-Republican*
Age at Inauguration: *57*
Served: *1825–1829*
Vice President: *John C. Calhoun*

7 Andrew Jackson

1767–1845
Birthplace: *Waxhaw settlement, SC*
Home State: *TN*
Political Party: *Democratic*
Age at Inauguration: *61*
Served: *1829–1837*
Vice Presidents: *John C. Calhoun, Martin Van Buren*

8 Martin Van Buren

1782–1862
Birthplace: *Kinderhook, NY*
Home State: *NY*
Political Party: *Democratic*
Age at Inauguration: *54*
Served: *1837–1841*
Vice President: *Richard M. Johnson*

9 William H. Harrison

1773–1841
Birthplace: *Berkeley, VA*
Home State: *OH*
Political Party: *Whig*
Age at Inauguration: *68*
Served: *1841*
Vice President: *John Tyler*

10 John Tyler

1790–1862
Birthplace: *Greenway, VA*
Home State: *VA*
Political Party: *Whig*
Age at Inauguration: *51*
Served: *1841–1845*
Vice President: *none*

11 James K. Polk

1795–1849
Birthplace: *near Pineville, NC*
Home State: *TN*
Political Party: *Democratic*
Age at Inauguration: *49*
Served: *1845–1849*
Vice President: *George M. Dallas*

12 Zachary Taylor

1784–1850
Birthplace: *Orange County, VA*
Home State: *LA*
Political Party: *Whig*
Age at Inauguration: *64*
Served: *1849–1850*
Vice President: *Millard Fillmore*

13 Millard Fillmore

1800–1874
Birthplace: *Locke, NY*
Home State: *NY*
Political Party: *Whig*
Age at Inauguration: *50*
Served: *1850–1853*
Vice President: *none*

14 Franklin Pierce

1804–1869
Birthplace: *Hillsboro, NH*
Home State: *NH*
Political Party: *Democratic*
Age at Inauguration: *48*
Served: *1853–1857*
Vice President: *William R. King*

Home State refers to the state of residence when elected.

15 James Buchanan

1791–1868
Birthplace: *near Mercersburg, PA*
Home State: *PA*
Political Party: *Democratic*
Age at Inauguration: *65*
Served: *1857–1861*
Vice President: *John C. Breckinridge*

16 Abraham Lincoln

1809–1865
Birthplace: *near Hodgenville, KY*
Home State: *IL*
Political Party: *Republican*
Age at Inauguration: *52*
Served: *1861–1865*
Vice Presidents: *Hannibal Hamlin, Andrew Johnson*

17 Andrew Johnson

1808–1875
Birthplace: *Raleigh, NC*
Home State: *TN*
Political Party: *National Union*
Age at Inauguration: *56*
Served: *1865–1869*
Vice President: *none*

18 Ulysses S. Grant

1822–1885
Birthplace: *Point Pleasant, OH*
Home State: *IL*
Political Party: *Republican*
Age at Inauguration: *46*
Served: *1869–1877*
Vice Presidents: *Schuyler Colfax, Henry Wilson*

19 Rutherford B. Hayes

1822–1893
Birthplace: *near Delaware, OH*
Home State: *OH*
Political Party: *Republican*
Age at Inauguration: *54*
Served: *1877–1881*
Vice President: *William A. Wheeler*

20 James A. Garfield

1831–1881
Birthplace: *Orange, OH*
Home State: *OH*
Political Party: *Republican*
Age at Inauguration: *49*
Served: *1881*
Vice President: *Chester A. Arthur*

21 Chester A. Arthur

1829–1886
Birthplace: *Fairfield, VT*
Home State: *NY*
Political Party: *Republican*
Age at Inauguration: *51*
Served: *1881–1885*
Vice President: *none*

22 Grover Cleveland

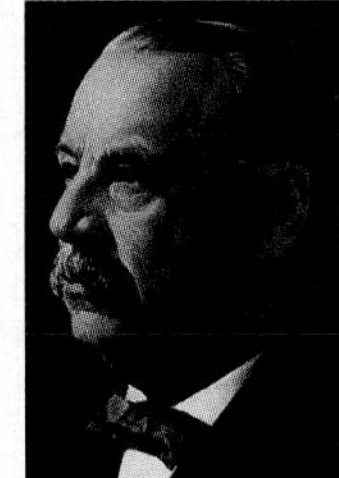

1837–1908
Birthplace: *Caldwell, NJ*
Home State: *NY*
Political Party: *Democratic*
Age at Inauguration: *47*
Served: *1885–1889*
Vice President: *Thomas A. Hendricks*

23 Benjamin Harrison

1833–1901
Birthplace: *North Bend, OH*
Home State: *IN*
Political Party: *Republican*
Age at Inauguration: *55*
Served: *1889–1893*
Vice President: *Levi P. Morton*

24 Grover Cleveland

1837–1908
Birthplace: *Caldwell, NJ*
Home State: *NY*
Political Party: *Democratic*
Age at Inauguration: *55*
Served: *1893–1897*
Vice President: *Adlai E. Stevenson*

25 William McKinley

1843–1901
Birthplace: *Niles, OH*
Home State: *OH*
Political Party: *Republican*
Age at Inauguration: *54*
Served: *1897–1901*
Vice Presidents: *Garret A. Hobart, Theodore Roosevelt*

26 Theodore Roosevelt

1858–1919
Birthplace: *New York, NY*
Home State: *NY*
Political Party: *Republican*
Age at Inauguration: *42*
Served: *1901–1909*
Vice President: *Charles W. Fairbanks*

27 William H. Taft

1857–1930
Birthplace: *Cincinnati, OH*
Home State: *OH*
Political Party: *Republican*
Age at Inauguration: *51*
Served: *1909–1913*
Vice President: *James S. Sherman*

28 Woodrow Wilson

1856–1924
Birthplace: *Staunton, VA*
Home State: *NJ*
Political Party: *Democratic*
Age at Inauguration: *56*
Served: *1913–1921*
Vice President: *Thomas R. Marshall*

29 Warren G. Harding

1865–1923
Birthplace: *Blooming Grove, OH*
Home State: *OH*
Political Party: *Republican*
Age at Inauguration: *55*
Served: *1921–1923*
Vice President: *Calvin Coolidge*

ATLAS/ALMANAC

30 Calvin Coolidge

1872–1933
Birthplace: *Plymouth Notch, VT*
Home State: *MA*
Political Party: *Republican*
Age at Inauguration: *51*
Served: *1923–1929*
Vice President: *Charles G. Dawes*

31 Herbert Hoover

1874–1964
Birthplace: *West Branch, IA*
Home State: *CA*
Political Party: *Republican*
Age at Inauguration: *54*
Served: *1929–1933*
Vice President: *Charles Curtis*

32 Franklin D. Roosevelt

1882–1945
Birthplace: *Hyde Park, NY*
Home State: *NY*
Political Party: *Democratic*
Age at Inauguration: *51*
Served: *1933–1945*
Vice Presidents: *John N. Garner, Henry A. Wallace, Harry S. Truman*

33 Harry S. Truman

1884–1972
Birthplace: *Lamar, MO*
Home State: *MO*
Political Party: *Democratic*
Age at Inauguration: *60*
Served: *1945–1953*
Vice President: *Alben W. Barkley*

34 Dwight D. Eisenhower

1890–1969
Birthplace: *Denison, TX*
Home State: *NY*
Political Party: *Republican*
Age at Inauguration: *62*
Served: *1953–1961*
Vice President: *Richard M. Nixon*

35 John F. Kennedy

1917–1963
Birthplace: *Brookline, MA*
Home State: *MA*
Political Party: *Democratic*
Age at Inauguration: *43*
Served: *1961–1963*
Vice President: *Lyndon B. Johnson*

36 Lyndon B. Johnson

1908–1973
Birthplace: *near Stonewall, TX*
Home State: *TX*
Political Party: *Democratic*
Age at Inauguration: *55*
Served: *1963–1969*
Vice President: *Hubert H. Humphrey*

37 Richard M. Nixon

1913–1994
Birthplace: *Yorba Linda, CA*
Home State: *NY*
Political Party: *Republican*
Age at Inauguration: *56*
Served: *1969–1974*
Vice Presidents: *Spiro T. Agnew, Gerald R. Ford*

38 Gerald R. Ford

1913–
Birthplace: *Omaha, NE*
Home State: *MI*
Political Party: *Republican*
Age at Inauguration: *61*
Served: *1974–1977*
Vice President: *Nelson A. Rockefeller*

39 Jimmy Carter

1924–
Birthplace: *Plains, GA*
Home State: *GA*
Political Party: *Democratic*
Age at Inauguration: *52*
Served: *1977–1981*
Vice President: *Walter F. Mondale*

40 Ronald W. Reagan

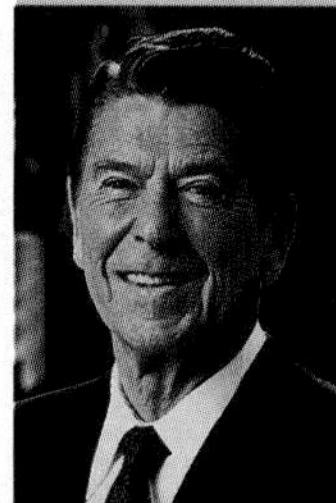

1911–2004
Birthplace: *Tampico, IL*
Home State: *CA*
Political Party: *Republican*
Age at Inauguration: *69*
Served: *1981–1989*
Vice President: *George Bush*

41 George Bush

1924–
Birthplace: *Milton, MA*
Home State: *TX*
Political Party: *Republican*
Age at Inauguration: *64*
Served: *1989–1993*
Vice President: *Dan Quayle*

42 William Clinton

1946–
Birthplace: *Hope, AR*
Home State: *AR*
Political Party: *Democratic*
Age at Inauguration: *46*
Served: *1993–2001*
Vice President: *Albert Gore*

43 George W. Bush

1946–
Birthplace: *New Haven, CT*
Home State: *TX*
Political Party: *Republican*
Age at Inauguration: *54*
Served: *2001–*
Vice President: *Richard Cheney*

Home State refers to the state of residence when elected.

American Documents

THE DECLARATION OF INDEPENDENCE

In Congress, July 4, 1776.
The unanimous Declaration of the thirteen United States of America,

When in the Course of human events it becomes necessary for one people to dissolve the political bands which have connected them with another, and to assume among the powers of the earth, the separate and equal station to which the Laws of Nature and of Nature's God entitle them, a decent respect to the opinions of mankind requires that they should declare the causes which impel them to the separation.

Preamble
The Preamble tells why the Declaration was written. It states that the members of the Continental Congress believed the colonies had the right to break away from Britain and become a free nation.

We hold these truths to be self-evident, that all men are created equal, that they are endowed by their Creator with certain unalienable Rights, that among these are Life, Liberty and the pursuit of Happiness.

That to secure these rights, Governments are instituted among Men, deriving their just powers from the consent of the governed,

That whenever any Form of Government becomes destructive of these ends, it is the Right of the People to alter or to abolish it, and to institute new Government, laying its foundation on such principles and organizing its powers in such form, as to them shall seem most likely to effect their Safety and Happiness. Prudence, indeed, will dictate that Governments long established should not be changed for light and transient causes; and accordingly all experience hath shown, that mankind are more disposed to suffer, while evils are sufferable, than to right themselves by abolishing the forms to which they are accustomed. But when a long train of abuses and usurpations, pursuing invariably the same Object evinces a design to reduce them under absolute Despotism, it is their right, it is their duty, to throw off such Government, and to provide new Guards for their future security.

A Statement of Rights
The opening part of the Declaration tells what rights-the members of the Continental Congress believed that all people have. All people are equal in having the rights to life, liberty, and the pursuit of happiness. The main purpose of a government is to protect the rights of the people who consent to be governed by it. These rights cannot be taken away. When a government tries to take these rights away from the people, the people have the right to change the government or do away with it. The people can then form a new government that respects these rights.

Such has been the patient sufferance of these Colonies; and such is now the necessity which constrains them to alter their former Systems of Government. The history of the present King of Great Britain is a history of repeated injuries and usurpations, all having in direct object the establishment of an absolute Tyranny over these States. To prove this, let Facts be submitted to a candid world.

Charges Against the King
The Declaration lists more than 25 charges against the king. He was mistreating the colonists, the Declaration says, in order to gain total control over the colonies.

He has refused his Assent to Laws, the most wholesome and necessary for the public good.

He has forbidden his Governors to pass Laws of immediate and pressing importance, unless suspended in their operation till his Assent should be obtained; and when so suspended, he has utterly neglected to attend to them.

The king rejected many laws passed by colonial legislatures.

AMERICAN DOCUMENTS

He has refused to pass other Laws for the accommodation of large districts of people, unless those people would relinquish the right of Representation in the Legislature, a right inestimable to them and formidable to tyrants only.

The king made the colonial legislatures meet at inconvenient times and places.

He has called together legislative bodies at places unusual, uncomfortable, and distant from the depository of their public Records, for the sole purpose of fatiguing them into compliance with his measures.

The king and the king's governors often dissolved colonial legislatures for disobeying their orders.

He has dissolved Representative Houses repeatedly, for opposing with manly firmness his invasions on the rights of the people.

He has refused for a long time, after such dissolutions, to cause others to be elected; whereby the Legislative powers, incapable of Annihilation, have returned to the People at large for their exercise; the State remaining in the mean time exposed to all the dangers of invasion from without, and convulsions within.

AMERICAN DOCUMENTS

The king stopped people from moving to the colonies and into the western lands.

He has endeavored to prevent the population of these States; for that purpose obstructing the Laws for Naturalization of Foreigners; refusing to pass others to encourage their migrations hither, and raising the conditions of new Appropriations of Lands.

The king prevented the colonists from choosing their own judges. The king chose the judges, and they served only as long as the king was satisfied with them.

He has obstructed the Administration of Justice, by refusing his Assent to Laws for establishing Judiciary powers.

He has made Judges dependent on his Will alone, for the tenure of their offices, and the amount and payment of their salaries.

The king hired people to help collect taxes in the colonies.

He has erected a multitude of New Offices, and sent hither swarms of Officers to harass our people, and eat out their substance.

The king appointed General Thomas Gage, commander of Britain's military forces in the Americas, as governor of Massachusetts.

He has kept among us, in times of peace, Standing Armies without the Consent of our legislatures.

He has affected to render the Military independent of and superior to the Civil power.

He has combined with others to subject us to a jurisdiction foreign to our constitution, and unacknowledged by our laws; giving his Assent to their Acts of pretended Legislation:

The king expected the colonists to provide housing and supplies for the British soldiers in the colonies.

For quartering large bodies of armed troops among us:

For protecting them, by a mock Trial, from punishment for any Murders which they should commit on the Inhabitants of these States:

For cutting off our Trade with all parts of the world:

The king and Parliament demanded that colonists pay many taxes, even though the colonists did not agree to pay them.

For imposing Taxes on us without our Consent:

Colonists were tried by British naval courts, which had no juries.

For depriving us in many cases, of the benefits of Trial by Jury:

Colonists accused of treason were sent to Britain to be tried.

For transporting us beyond Seas to be tried for pretended offenses:

For abolishing the free System of English Laws in a neighboring Province, establishing therein an Arbitrary government, and enlarging its Boundaries so as to render it at once an example and fit instrument for introducing the same absolute rule into these Colonies:

For taking away our Charters, abolishing our most valuable Laws, and altering fundamentally the Forms of our Governments:

For suspending our own Legislatures, and declaring themselves invested with power to legislate for us in all cases whatsoever.

He has abdicated Government here, by declaring us out of his Protection and waging War against us.

The king allowed General Gage to take military action to enforce British laws in the colonies.

He has plundered our seas, ravaged our Coasts, burnt our towns, and destroyed the lives of our people.

He is at this time transporting large Armies of foreign Mercenaries to complete the works of death, desolation and tyranny, already begun with circumstances of Cruelty & perfidy scarcely paralleled in the most barbarous ages, and totally unworthy the Head of a civilized nation.

The king hired Hessian mercenaries and sent them to fight the colonists.

He has constrained our fellow Citizens taken Captive on the high Seas to bear Arms against their Country, to become the executioners of their friends and Brethren, or to fall themselves by their Hands.

He has excited domestic insurrections amongst us, and has endeavored to bring on the inhabitants of our frontiers, the merciless Indian Savages, whose known rule of warfare, is an undistinguished destruction of all ages, sexes and conditions.

The king's governor in Virginia promised freedom to all enslaved people who joined the British forces. The British also planned to use Indians to fight the colonists.

In every stage of these Oppressions We have Petitioned for Redress in the most humble terms: Our repeated Petitions have been answered only by repeated injury. A Prince, whose character is thus marked by every act which may define a Tyrant, is unfit to be the ruler of a free people.

The Declaration explained the efforts of the colonists to avoid separation from Britain. But the colonists said that the king had ignored their protests. Because of the many charges against the king, the writers of the Declaration concluded that he was not fit to rule free people.

Nor have We been wanting in attentions to our British brethren. We have warned them from time to time of attempts by their legislature to extend an unwarrantable jurisdiction over us. We have reminded them of the circumstances of our emigration and settlement here. We have appealed to their native justice and magnanimity, and we have conjured them by the ties of our common kindred to disavow these usurpations, which, would inevitably interrupt our connections and correspondence. They too have been deaf to the voice of justice and of consanguinity. We must, therefore, acquiesce in the necessity, which denounces our Separation, and hold them, as we hold the rest of mankind, Enemies in War, in Peace Friends.

We, therefore, the Representatives of the united States of America, in General Congress, Assembled, appealing to the Supreme Judge of the world for the rectitude of our intentions, do, in the Name, and by Authority of the good People of these Colonies, solemnly publish and declare, That these United Colonies are, and of Right ought to be Free and Independent States; that they are Absolved from all Allegiance to the British Crown, and that all political connection between them and the State of Great Britain, is and ought to be totally dissolved; and that as Free and Independent States, they have full Power to levy War, conclude Peace, contract Alliances, establish Commerce, and to do all other Acts and Things which Independent States may of right do.

A Statement of Independence
The writers declared that the colonies were now free and independent states. All ties with Britain were broken. As free and independent states, they had the right to make war and peace, to trade, and to do all the things free countries could do.

To support the Declaration, the signers promised one another their lives, their fortunes, and their honor.

And for the support of this Declaration, with a firm reliance on the protection of divine Providence, we mutually pledge to each other our Lives, our Fortunes and our sacred Honor.

John Hancock

NEW HAMPSHIRE
Josiah Bartlett
William Whipple
Matthew Thornton

MASSACHUSETTS
John Adams
Samuel Adams
Robert Treat Paine
Elbridge Gerry

NEW YORK
William Floyd
Philip Livingston
Francis Lewis
Lewis Morris

RHODE ISLAND
Stephen Hopkins
William Ellery

NEW JERSEY
Richard Stockton
John Witherspoon
Francis Hopkinson
John Hart
Abraham Clark

PENNSYLVANIA
Robert Morris
Benjamin Rush
Benjamin Franklin
John Morton
George Clymer
James Smith
George Taylor
James Wilson
George Ross

DELAWARE
Caesar Rodney
George Read
Thomas McKean

MARYLAND
Samuel Chase
William Paca
Thomas Stone
Charles Carroll of Carrollton

NORTH CAROLINA
William Hopper
Joseph Hewes
John Penn

VIRGINIA
George Wythe
Richard Henry Lee
Thomas Jefferson
Benjamin Harrison
Thomas Nelson, Jr.
Francis Lightfoot Lee
Carter Braxton

SOUTH CAROLINA
Edward Rutledge
Thomas Heyward, Jr.
Thomas Lynch, Jr.
Arthur Middleton

CONNECTICUT
Roger Sherman
Samuel Huntington
William Williams
Oliver Wolcott

GEORGIA
Button Gwinnett
Lyman Hall
George Walton

Members of the Continental Congress stated that copies of the Declaration should be sent to all Committees of Correspondence and to commanders of the troops and that it should be read in every state.

Resolved, That copies of the Declaration be sent to the several assemblies, conventions, and committees, or councils of safety, and to the several commanding officers of the continental troops; that it be proclaimed in each of the United States, at the head of the army.

The Constitution of The United States of America

Preamble*

We the people of the United States, in order to form a more perfect Union, establish justice, insure domestic tranquillity, provide for the common defense, promote the general welfare, and secure the blessings of liberty to ourselves and our posterity, do ordain and establish this Constitution for the United States of America.

Preamble
The introduction to the Constitution states the purposes for writing it. The writers wanted to set up a fairer form of government and to secure peace and freedom for themselves and for future generations.

ARTICLE I
THE LEGISLATIVE BRANCH
SECTION 1. CONGRESS

All legislative powers herein granted shall be vested in a Congress of the United States, which shall consist of a Senate and House of Representatives.

Congress
Congress has the authority to make laws. Congress is made up of two groups of lawmakers: the Senate and the House of Representatives.

SECTION 2. THE HOUSE OF REPRESENTATIVES

(1) The House of Representatives shall be composed of members chosen every second year by the people of the several states, and the electors in each state shall have the qualifications requisite for electors of the most numerous branch of the state legislature.

(1) Election and Term of Members
Qualified voters are to elect members of the House of Representatives every two years. Anyone whom state law allows to vote for a state's legislators may also vote for its representatives to Congress.

(2) No person shall be a Representative who shall not have attained to the age of-twenty-five years, and been seven years a citizen of the United States, and who shall not, when elected, be an inhabitant of that state in which he shall be chosen.

(2) Qualifications
Members of the House of Representatives must be at least 25 years old. They must have been citizens of the United States for at least seven years. They must live in the state that they will represent.

(3) Representatives [*and direct taxes*]** shall be apportioned among the several states which may be included within this Union, according to their respective numbers [*which shall be determined by adding to the whole number of free persons, including those bound to service for a term of years, and excluding Indians not taxed, three-fifths of all other persons*]. The actual enumeration shall be made within three years after the first meeting of the Congress of the United States, and within every subsequent term of ten years, in such manner as they shall by law direct. The number of Representatives shall not exceed one for every 30,000, but each state shall have at least one Representative [*; and until such enumeration shall be made, the State of New Hampshire shall be entitled to choose three; Massachusetts eight; Rhode Island and Providence Plantations one; Connecticut five; New York six; New Jersey four; Pennsylvania eight; Delaware one; Maryland six; Virginia ten; North Carolina five; South Carolina five; and Georgia three*].

(3) Determining Apportionment
The number of representatives a state may have depends on the number of people living in each state. Every ten years the federal government must take a census, or count, of the population in every state. Every state will have at least one representative.

*Titles have been added to make the Constitution easier to read. They did not appear in the original document.

**The parts of the Constitution that no longer apply are printed in italics within brackets [ ]. These portions have been changed or set aside by later amendments.

AMERICAN DOCUMENTS

(4) Filling Vacancies
If there is a vacancy in the House of Representatives, the governor of the state involved must call a special election to fill it.

(4) When vacancies happen in the representation from any state, the executive authority thereof shall issue writs of election to fill such vacancies.

(5) Special Authority
The House of Representatives chooses a Speaker as its presiding officer. It also chooses other officers as appropriate. The House is the only government branch that may impeach, or charge, an official in the executive branch or a judge of the federal courts for failing to carry out his or her duties. These cases are then tried in the Senate.

(5) The House of Representatives shall choose their Speaker and other officers; and shall have the sole power of impeachment.

SECTION 3. THE SENATE

(1) Number, Term, and Selection of Members
Each state is represented by two senators. Until Amendment 17 was passed, state legislatures chose the senators for their states. Each senator serves a six-year term and has one vote in Congress.

(1) The Senate of the United States shall be composed of two Senators from each state [*chosen by the legislature thereof*], for six years, and each Senator shall have one vote.

(2) Overlapping Terms and Filling Vacancies
One-third of the senators are elected every two years for a six-year term. This grouping allows at least two-thirds of the experienced senators to remain in the Senate after each election. Amendment 17 permits state governors to appoint a replacement to fill a vacancy until the next election is held.

(2) [*Immediately after they shall be assembled in consequence of the first election, they shall be divided as equally as may be into three classes. The seats of the Senators of the first class shall be vacated at the expiration of the second year, of the second class at the expiration of the fourth year, and of the third class at the expiration of the sixth year, so that one-third may be chosen every second year; and if vacancies happen by resignation, or otherwise, during the recess of the legislature of any state, the executive thereof may make temporary appointments until the next meeting of the legislature, which shall then fill such vacancies.*]

(3) Qualifications
Senators must be at least 30 years old. They must have been citizens of the United States for at least nine years. They must live in the state that they will represent.

(3) No person shall be a Senator who shall not have attained to the age of thirty years, and been nine years a citizen of the United States, and who shall not, when elected, be an inhabitant of that state for which he shall be chosen.

(4) President of the Senate
The Vice President acts as chief officer of the Senate but does not vote unless there is a tie.

(4) The Vice President of the United States shall be President of the Senate, but shall have no vote, unless they be equally divided.

(5) Other Officers
The Senate chooses its other officers and a president pro tempore, who serves if the Vice President is not present or if the Vice President becomes President. *Pro tempore* is a Latin term meaning "for the time being."

(5) The Senate shall choose their other officers, and also a President *pro tempore*, in the absence of the Vice President, or when he shall exercise the office of the President of the United States.

(6) The Senate shall have the sole power to try all impeachments. When sitting for that purpose, they shall be on oath or affirmation. When the President of the United States is tried, the Chief Justice shall preside; and no person shall be convicted without the concurrence of two-thirds of the members present.

(6) Impeachment Trials
If the House of Representatives votes in favor of impeachment, the Senate holds a trial. A two-thirds vote is required to convict a person who has been impeached.

(7) Judgment in cases of impeachment shall not extend further than to removal from office, and disqualification to hold and enjoy any office of honor, trust, or profit under the United States; but the party convicted shall nevertheless be liable and subject to indictment, trial, judgment, and punishment, according to law.

(7) Penalty for Conviction
If convicted in an impeachment case, an official is removed from office and may also be banned from ever holding office in the United States government again. The convicted person may also be tried in a regular court of law for any crimes.

SECTION 4. ELECTIONS AND MEETINGS

(1) The times, places, and manner of holding elections for Senators and Representatives shall be prescribed in each state by the legislature thereof; but the Congress may at any time by law make or alter such regulations, [*except as to the places of choosing Senators*].

(1) Holding Elections
Each state makes its own rules about electing senators and representatives. However, Congress may change these rules. Today congressional elections are held on the Tuesday after the first Monday in November, in even-numbered years.

(2) The Congress shall assemble at least once in every year, [*and such meeting shall be on the first Monday in December, unless they shall by law appoint a different day*].

(2) Meetings
The Constitution requires Congress to meet at least once a year. That day is the first Monday in December, unless Congress sets a different day. Amendment 20 changed this date to January 3.

SECTION 5. RULES OF PROCEDURE

(1) Each house shall be the judge of the elections, returns and qualifications of its own members, and a majority of each shall constitute a quorum to do business; but a smaller number may adjourn from day to day, and may be authorized to compel the attendance of absent members, in such manner and under such penalties as each house may provide.

(1) Organization
Each house of Congress may decide if its members have been elected fairly and are entitled to hold office. Each house may do business only when a quorum—a majority of its members—is present. By less than a majority vote, each house may compel absent members to attend.

(2) Each house may determine the rules of its proceedings, punish its members for disorderly behavior, and, with the concurrence of two-thirds, expel a member.

(2) Rules
Each house may decide its own rules for doing business, punish its members, and expel a member from office if two-thirds of the members agree.

(3) Each house shall keep a journal of its proceedings, and from time to time publish the same, excepting such parts as may in their judgment require secrecy; and the yeas and nays of the members of either house on any question shall, at the desire of one-fifth of those present, be entered on the journal.

(3) Journal
The Constitution requires each house to keep records of its activities and to publish these records from time to time. The House Journal and the Senate Journal are published at the end of each session. How each member voted must be recorded if one-fifth of the members ask for this to be done.

(4) Adjournment
When Congress is in session, neither house may take a recess for more than three days without the consent of the other.

(4) Neither house, during the session of Congress, shall, without the consent of the other, adjourn for more than three days, nor to any other place than that in which the two houses shall be sitting.

SECTION 6. PRIVILEGES AND RESTRICTIONS

(1) Pay and Privileges
Members of Congress set their own salaries, which are to be paid by the federal government. Members cannot be arrested or sued for anything they say while Congress is in session. This privilege is called congressional immunity. Members of Congress may be arrested while Congress is in session only if they commit a crime.

(1) The Senators and Representatives shall receive a compensation for their services, to be ascertained by law and paid out of the Treasury of the United States. They shall in all cases, except treason, felony, and breach of the peace, be privileged from arrest during their attendance at the session of their respective houses, and in going to and returning from the same; and for any speech or debate in either house, they shall not be questioned in any other place.

(2) Restrictions
Members of Congress may not hold any other federal office while serving in Congress. A member may not resign from office and then take a government position created during that member's term of office or for which the pay has been increased during that member's term of office.

(2) No Senator or Representative shall, during the time for which he was elected, be appointed to any civil office under the authority of the United States, which shall have been created, or the emoluments whereof shall have been increased, during such time; and no person holding any office under the United States shall be a member of either house during his continuance in office.

SECTION 7. MAKING LAWS

(1) Money-Raising Bills
All money-raising bills must be introduced first in the House of Representatives, but the Senate may suggest changes.

(1) All bills for raising revenue shall originate in the House of Representatives; but the Senate may propose or concur with amendments as on other bills.

(2) How a Bill Becomes a Law
After a bill has been passed by both the House of Representatives and the Senate, it must be sent to the President. If the President approves and signs the bill, it becomes law. The President can also veto, or refuse to sign, the bill. Congress can override a veto by passing the bill again by a two-thirds majority. If the President does not act within ten days, one of two things will happen. If Congress is still in session, the bill becomes a law. If Congress ends its session within that same ten-day period, the bill does not become a law.

(2) Every bill which shall have passed the House of Representatives and the Senate shall, before it become a law, be presented to the President of the United States; if he approve, he shall sign it, but if not, he shall return it, with his objections, to that house in which it shall have originated, who shall enter the objections at large on their journal, and proceed to reconsider it. If after such reconsideration two-thirds of that house shall agree to pass the bill, it shall be sent, together with the objections, to the other house, by which it shall likewise be reconsidered, and, if approved by two-thirds of that house, it shall become a law. But in all such cases the votes of both houses shall be determined by yeas and nays, and the names of the persons voting for and against the bill shall be entered on the journal of each house respectively. If any bill shall not be returned by the President within ten days (Sundays excepted) after it shall have been presented to him, the same bill shall be a law, in like manner as if he had signed it, unless the Congress by their adjournment prevent its return, in which case it shall not be a law.

(3) Orders and Resolutions
All attempts by Congress to make law must be submitted to the President for the President's agreement or veto. Congress may decide on its own when to end the session. Other such acts must be signed or vetoed by the President.

(3) Every order, resolution, or vote to which the concurrence of the Senate and House of Representatives may be necessary (except on a question of adjournment) shall be presented to the President of the United States; and before the same shall take effect, shall be approved by him, or being disapproved by him, shall be repassed by two-thirds of the Senate and House of Representatives, according to the rules and limitations prescribed in the case of a bill.

SECTION 8. POWERS DELEGATED TO CONGRESS

The Congress shall have power

(1) To lay and collect taxes, duties, imposts and excises, to pay the debts and provide for the common defense and general welfare of the United States; but all duties, imposts and excises shall be uniform throughout the United States;

(1) Taxation
Congress has the authority to raise money to pay debts, defend the United States, and provide services for its people by collecting taxes or tariffs on foreign goods. All taxes must be applied equally in all states.

(2) To borrow money on the credit of the United States;

(2) Borrowing Money
Congress may borrow money for the federal government's use. This is usually done by selling government bonds.

(3) To regulate commerce with foreign nations, and among the several states and with the Indian tribes;

(3) Commerce
Congress can control trade with other countries, with Indian nations, and between states.

(4) To establish an uniform rule of naturalization, and uniform laws on the subject of bankruptcies throughout the United States;

(4) Naturalization and Bankruptcy
Congress decides what requirements people from other countries must meet to become United States citizens. Congress can also pass laws to protect people who are bankrupt, or cannot pay their debts.

(5) To coin money, regulate the value thereof, and of foreign coin, and fix the standard of weights and measures;

(5) Coins, Weights, and Measures
Congress can coin money and decide its value. Congress may also decide on the system of weights and measures to be used throughout the nation.

(6) To provide for the punishment of counterfeiting the securities and current coin of the United States;

(6) Counterfeiting
Congress may pass laws to punish people who make fake money or bonds.

(7) To establish post offices and post roads;

(7) Postal Service
Congress can build post offices and make rules about the postal system and the roads used for mail delivery.

(8) To promote the progress of science and useful arts by securing for limited times to authors and inventors the exclusive right to their respective writings and discoveries;

(8) Copyrights and Patents
Congress can issue patents and copyrights to inventors and authors to protect the ownership of their works.

(9) To constitute tribunals inferior to the Supreme Court;

(9) Federal Courts
Congress can establish a system of federal courts under the Supreme Court.

(10) To define and punish piracies and felonies committed on the high seas and offenses against the law of nations;

(10) Crimes at Sea
Congress can pass laws to punish people for crimes committed at sea. Congress may also punish United States citizens for breaking international law.

(11) Declaring War
Only Congress can declare war.

(11) To declare war, grant letters of marque and reprisal, and make rules concerning captures on land and water;

(12) The Army
Congress can establish an army, but it cannot vote money to support it for more than two years. This part of the Constitution was written to keep the army under Congressional control.

(12) To raise and support armies, but no appropriation of money to that use shall be for a longer term than two years;

(13) The Navy
Congress can establish a navy and vote money to support it for as long as necessary. No time limit was set because people thought the navy was less of a threat to people's liberty than the army was.

(13) To provide and maintain a navy;

(14) Military Regulations
Congress makes the rules that guide and govern all the armed forces.

(14) To make rules for the government and regulation of the land and naval forces;

(15) The Militia
Each state may organize some or all of its citizens into a militia, or military force, capable of fighting to protect the state. The militia can be called into federal service by the President, as authorized by Congress, to enforce laws, to stop uprisings against the government, or to protect the people in case of floods, earthquakes, and other disasters.

(15) To provide for calling forth the militia to execute the laws of the Union, suppress insurrections and repel invasions;

(16) Control of the Militia
Congress may help each state arm, train, and organize its citizens into an armed military force. Each state may appoint its own officers and train this force according to rules set by Congress.

(16) To provide for organizing, arming, and disciplining the militia, and for governing such part of them as may be employed in the service of the United States, reserving to the states, respectively, the appointment of the officers, and the authority of training the militia according to the discipline prescribed by Congress;

(17) National Capital and Other Property
Congress may pass laws to govern the nation's capital (Washington, D.C.) and any land owned by the government.

(17) To exercise exclusive legislation in all cases whatsoever, over such district (not exceeding ten miles square) as may, by cession of particular states, and the acceptance of Congress, become the seat of government of the United States, and to exercise like authority over all places purchased by the consent of the legislature of the state in which the same shall be, for the erection of forts, magazines, arsenals, dock-yards, and other needful buildings; —and

(18) Other Necessary Laws
The Constitution allows Congress to make laws that are necessary to enforce the powers listed in Article I. This clause has two conflicting interpretations. One is that Congress can only do what is absolutely necessary to carry out the powers listed in Article I and in other parts of the Constitution. The other view is that Congress can do whatever is reasonably helpful to carrying out those powers, so its authority becomes very broad though not unlimited.

(18) To make all laws which shall be necessary and proper for carrying into execution the foregoing powers, and all other powers vested by this Constitution in the government of the United States, or in any department or officer thereof.

SECTION 9. POWERS DENIED TO CONGRESS

(1) [*The migration or importation of such persons as any of the states now existing shall think proper to admit shall not be prohibited by the Congress prior to the year 1808; but a tax or duty may be imposed on such importation, not exceeding 10 dollars for each person.*]

(1) Slave Trade
Some authority is not given to Congress. Congress could not prevent the slave trade until 1808, but it could put a tax of ten dollars on each slave brought into the United States. After 1808, this section no longer applied, and Congress banned the slave trade.

(2) The privilege of the writ of habeas corpus shall not be suspended, unless when in cases of rebellion or invasion the public safety may require it.

(2) Habeas Corpus
A writ of habeas corpus entitles a person to a hearing before a judge. The judge must then decide if there is good reason for that person to have been arrested. If not, that person must be released. The government is not allowed to take this privilege away except during a national emergency, such as an invasion or a rebellion.

(3) No bill of attainder or ex post facto law shall be passed.

(3) Special Laws
Congress cannot pass laws that impose punishment on a named individual or group. Congress also cannot pass laws that punish a person for an action that was legal when it was done.

(4) [*No capitation or other direct tax shall be laid, unless in proportion to the census or enumeration herein before directed to be taken.*]

(4) Direct Taxes
Congress cannot set a direct tax on people—as opposed to taxes on transactions, such as on imports into the country, or on sales of certain goods—unless it is in proportion to the total population. Amendment 16, which provides for the income tax, is an exception.

(5) No tax or duty shall be laid on articles exported from any state.

(5) Export Taxes
Congress cannot tax goods sent from one state to another or from a state to another country.

(6) No preference shall be given by any regulation of commerce or revenue to the ports of one state over those of another; nor shall vessels bound to, or from, one state, be obliged to enter, clear, or pay duties in another.

(6) Ports
When making trade laws, Congress cannot favor one state over another. Congress cannot require ships from one state to pay a duty to enter another state.

(7) No money shall be drawn from the Treasury, but in consequence of appropriations made by law; and a regular statement and account of the receipts and expenditures of all public money shall be published from time to time.

(7) Public Money
The government cannot spend money from the treasury unless Congress passes a law allowing it to do so. A written record must be kept of all money spent by the government.

(8) No title of nobility shall be granted by the United States; and no person holding any office of profit or trust under them, shall, without the consent of the Congress, accept of any present, emolument, office, or title, of any kind whatever, from any king, prince, or foreign state.

(8) Titles of Nobility and Gifts
The United States government cannot grant titles of nobility. Government officials cannot accept gifts from other countries without the permission of Congress. This clause was intended to prevent government officials from being bribed by other nations.

(1) Complete Restrictions
The Constitution does not allow states to act as if they were individual countries. No state government may make a treaty with other countries. No state can print or coin its own money.

(2) Partial Restrictions
No state government can tax imported goods or exported goods without the consent of Congress. States may charge a limited fee to inspect these goods, but profits must be given to the United States Treasury.

(3) Other Restrictions
No state government may tax ships entering its ports unless Congress approves. No state may keep an army or navy during times of peace other than its citizen-soldier militia. No state can enter into agreements, or "compacts," with other states without the consent of Congress.

SECTION 10. POWERS DENIED TO THE STATES

(1) No state shall enter into any treaty, alliance, or confederation; grant letters of marque and reprisal; coin money; emit bills of credit; make anything but gold and silver coin a tender in payment of debts; pass any bill of attainder, ex post facto law, or law impairing the obligation of contracts, or grant any title of nobility.

(2) No state shall, without the consent of the Congress, lay any imposts or duties on imports or exports, except what may be absolutely necessary for executing its inspection laws; and the net produce of all duties and imposts, laid by any state on imports or exports, shall be for the use of the Treasury of the United States; and all such laws shall be subject to the revision and control of the Congress.

(3) No state shall, without the consent of Congress, lay any duty of tonnage, keep troops, or ships of war in time of peace, enter into any agreement or compact with another state, or with a foreign power, or engage in war, unless actually invaded, or in such imminent danger as will not admit of delay.

(1) Term of Office
The President has the authority to carry out our nation's laws. The term of office for both the President and the Vice President is four years.

(2) The Electoral College
This group of people is to be chosen by the voters of each state to elect the President and Vice President. The number of electors in each state is equal to the combined number of senators and representatives that state has in Congress.

(3) Election Process
This clause describes in detail how the electors were to choose the President and Vice President. In 1804 Amendment 12 changed the process for electing the President and the Vice President.

ARTICLE II
THE EXECUTIVE BRANCH

SECTION 1. PRESIDENT AND VICE PRESIDENT

(1) The executive power shall be vested in a President of the United States of America. He shall hold his office during the term of four years, and together with the Vice President, chosen for the same term, be elected as follows:

(2) Each state shall appoint, in such manner as the legislature thereof may direct, a number of electors, equal to the whole number of Senators and Representatives to which the state may be entitled in the Congress; but no Senator or Representative, or person holding an office of trust or profit under the United States, shall be appointed an elector.

(3) [*The electors shall meet in their respective states, and vote by ballot for two persons, of whom one at least shall not be an inhabitant of the same state with themselves. And they-shall make a list of all the persons voted for, and of the number of votes for each; which list they shall sign and certify, and transmit sealed to the seat of the government of the United States, directed to the president of the Senate. The president of the Senate shall, in the presence of the Senate and House of Representatives, open all the certificates, and the votes shall then be counted. The person having the greatest number of votes shall be the President, if such number be a majority of the whole number of electors appointed; and if there be more than one who have such majority, and have an equal number of votes, then the House of Representatives shall immediately choose by ballot one of them for President; and if no person have a majority, then from the five highest on the list the said House shall in like manner choose the President. But in choosing the President the votes shall be taken by states, the representation from each state having one vote: A quorum-for this purpose shall consist*

of a member or members from two-thirds of the states, and a majority of all the states shall be necessary to a choice. In every case, after the choice of the President, the person having the greatest number of votes of the electors shall be the Vice President. But if there should remain two or more who have equal votes, the Senate shall choose from them by ballot the Vice President.]

(4) The Congress may determine the time of choosing the electors, and the day on which they shall give their votes; which day shall be the same throughout the United States.

(4) Time of Elections
Congress decides the day the electors are to be elected and the day they are to vote.

(5) No person except a natural-born citizen [*or a citizen of the United States, at the time of the adoption of this Constitution,*] shall be eligible to the office of the President; neither shall any person be eligible to that office who shall not have attained to the age of thirty-five years, and been fourteen years a resident within the United States.

(5) Qualifications
The President must be at least 35 years old, be a citizen of the United States by birth, and have been living in the United States for 14 years or more.

(6) [*In case of the removal of the President from office, or of his death, resignation, or inability to discharge the powers and duties of the said office, the same shall devolve on the Vice President, and the Congress may by law provide for the case of removal, death, resignation or inability, both of the President and Vice President, declaring what officer shall then act as President, and such officer shall act accordingly, until the disability be removed, or a President shall be elected.*]

(6) Vacancies
If the President dies, resigns, or is removed from office, the Vice President becomes President.

(7) The President shall, at stated times, receive for his services, a compensation, which shall neither be increased nor diminished during the period for which he shall have been elected, and he shall not receive within that period any other emolument from the United States, or any of them.

(7) Salary
The President receives a salary that cannot be raised or lowered during a term of office. The President may not be paid any additional salary by the federal government or any state or local government. Today the President's salary is $400,000 a year, plus expenses for things such as housing, travel, and entertainment.

(8) Before he enter on the execution of his office, he shall take the following oath or affirmation:—"I do solemnly swear (or affirm) that I will faithfully execute the office of President of the United States, and will to the best of my ability, preserve, protect, and defend the Constitution of the United States."

(8) Oath of Office
Before taking office, the President must promise to perform the duties faithfully and to protect the country's form of government. Usually the Chief Justice of the Supreme Court administers the oath of office.

SECTION 2. POWERS OF THE PRESIDENT

(1) The President shall be Commander in Chief of the Army and Navy of the United States, and of the militia of the several states, when called into the actual service of the United States; he may require the opinion, in writing, of the principal officer in each of the executive departments, upon any subject relating to the duties of their respective offices, and he shall have power to grant reprieves and pardons for offenses against the United States, except in cases of impeachment.

(1) The President's Leadership
The President is the commander of the nation's armed forces and of the militia when it is in service of the nation. All heads of government departments must respond to the President's requests for their opinions. The President can pardon people, or excuse them from punishment for crimes they committed.

(2) Treaties and Appointments The President has the authority to make treaties, but they must be approved by a two-thirds vote of the Senate. The President nominates justices to the Supreme Court, ambassadors to other countries, and other federal officials with the Senate's approval. Congress may allow the President to appoint some officials without Senate confirmation. It may also let courts or heads of federal departments appoint some officials.

(2) He shall have power, by and with the advice and consent of the Senate, to make treaties, provided two-thirds of the senators present concur; and he shall nominate, and by and with the advice and consent of the Senate, shall appoint ambassadors, other public ministers and consuls, judges of the Supreme Court, and all other officers of the United States, whose appointments are not herein otherwise provided for, and which shall be established by law; but the Congress may by law vest the appointment of such inferior officers, as they think proper, in the President alone, in the courts of law, or in the heads of departments.

(3) Filling Vacancies If a government official's position becomes vacant when the Senate is not in session, the President can make a temporary appointment.

(3) The President shall have power to fill up all vacancies that may happen during the recess of the Senate, by granting commissions which shall expire at the end of their next session.

Duties The President must report to Congress on the condition of the country. This report is now presented in the annual State of the Union message. The President is also responsible for enforcing federal laws.

SECTION 3. DUTIES OF THE PRESIDENT

He shall from time to time give to the Congress information of the state of the Union, and recommend to their consideration such measures as he shall judge necessary and expedient; he may, on extraordinary occasions, convene both houses, or either of them, and in case of disagreement between them, with respect to the time of adjournment, he may adjourn them to such time as he shall think proper; he shall receive ambassadors and other public ministers; he shall take care that the laws be faithfully executed, and shall commission all the officers of the United States.

Impeachment The President, the Vice President, or any government official will be removed from office if impeached, or accused, and then found guilty of treason, bribery, or other serious crimes.

SECTION 4. IMPEACHMENT

The President, Vice President and all civil officers of the United States, shall be removed from office on impeachment for, and conviction of, treason, bribery, or other high crimes and misdemeanors.

ARTICLE III
THE JUDICIAL BRANCH

Federal Courts The authority to decide legal cases is granted to a Supreme Court and to a system of lower courts established by Congress. The Supreme Court is the highest court in the land. Justices and judges are in their offices for life, subject to good behavior.

SECTION 1. FEDERAL COURTS

The judicial power of the United States shall be vested in one Supreme Court, and in such inferior courts as the Congress may from time to time ordain and establish. The judges, both of the supreme and inferior courts, shall hold their offices during good behavior, and shall, at stated times, receive for their services a compensation, which shall not be diminished during their continuance in office.

SECTION 2. AUTHORITY OF THE FEDERAL COURTS

(1) General Authority Federal courts have the authority to decide cases that arise under the Constitution, laws, and treaties of the United States. They also have the authority to settle disagreements among states and among citizens of different states.

(1) The judicial power shall extend to all cases, in law and equity, arising under this Constitution, the laws of the United States, and treaties made or which shall be made, under their authority; to all cases affecting ambassadors, other public ministers and consuls; to all cases of admiralty and maritime jurisdiction; to controversies to which the United States shall be a party; to controversies between two or more states; [*between a state and citizens of another state;*]

between citizens of different states; —between citizens of the same state claiming lands under grants of different states, [*and between a state or the citizens thereof, and foreign states, citizens, or subjects.*]

(2) In all cases affecting ambassadors, other public ministers and consuls, and those in which a state shall be party, the Supreme Court shall have original jurisdiction. In all the other cases before mentioned, the Supreme Court shall have appellate jurisdiction, both as to law and fact, with such exceptions, and under such regulations as the Congress shall make.

(2) Supreme Court
The Supreme Court can decide certain cases being tried for the first time. It can review cases that have already been tried in a lower court if the decision has been appealed, or questioned, by one side.

(3) The trial of all crimes, except in cases of impeachment, shall be by jury; and such trial shall be held in the state where the said crimes shall have been committed; but when not committed within any state, the trial shall be at such place or places as the Congress may by law have directed.

(3) Trial by Jury
The Constitution guarantees a trial by jury for every person charged with a federal crime. Amendments 5, 6, and 7 extend and clarify a person's right to a trial by jury.

SECTION 3. TREASON

(1) Treason against the United States shall consist only in levying war against them, or in adhering to their enemies, giving them aid and comfort. No person shall be convicted of treason unless on the testimony of two witnesses to the same overt act, or on confession in open court.

(1) Definition of Treason
Acts that may be considered treason are making war against the United States or helping its enemies. A person cannot be convicted of attempting to overthrow the government unless there are two witnesses to the act or the person confesses in court to treason.

(2) The Congress shall have power to declare the punishment of treason, but no attainder of treason shall work corruption of blood, or forfeiture except during the life of the person attainted.

(2) Punishment for Treason
Congress can decide the punishment for treason, within certain limits.

ARTICLE IV
RELATIONS AMONG STATES

SECTION 1. OFFICIAL RECORDS

Full faith and credit shall be given in each state to the public acts, records, and judicial proceedings of every other state. And the Congress may by general laws prescribe the manner in which such acts, records, and proceedings shall be proved, and the effect thereof.

Official Records
Each state must honor the official records and judicial decisions of other states.

SECTION 2. PRIVILEGES OF THE CITIZENS

(1) The citizens of each state shall be entitled to all privileges and immunities of citizens in the several states.

(1) Privileges
A citizen moving from one state to another has the same rights as other citizens living in that person's new state of residence. In some cases, such as voting, people may be required to live in their new state for a certain length of time before obtaining the same privileges as citizens there.

(2) A person charged in any state with treason, felony, or other crime, who shall flee from justice, and be found in another state, shall on demand of the executive authority of the state from which he fled, be delivered up, to be removed to the state having jurisdiction of the crime.

(2) Extradition
At a state governor's request, a person who is charged with a crime in a state and who tries to escape justice by crossing into another state may be returned to the state in which the crime was committed.

(3) Fugitive Slaves
The original Constitution required that runaway slaves be returned to their owners. Amendment 13 abolished slavery, eliminating the need for this clause.

(3) [*No person held to service or labor in one state, under the laws thereof, escaping into another, shall in consequence of any law or regulation therein, be discharged from such service or labor, but shall be delivered up on claim of the party to whom such service or labor may be due.*]

SECTION 3. NEW STATES AND TERRITORIES

(1) Admission of New States
Congress has the authority to admit new states to the Union. The Supreme Court has held that all new states have the same rights as existing states.

(1) New states may be admitted by the Congress into this Union; but no new state shall be formed or erected within the jurisdiction of any other state; nor any state be formed by the junction of two or more states, or parts of states, without the consent of the legislatures of the states concerned as well as of the Congress.

(2) Federal Property
The Constitution allows Congress to make or change laws governing federal property. This applies to territories and federally owned land within states, such as national parks.

(2) The Congress shall have power to dispose of and make all needful rules and regulations respecting the territory or other property belonging to the United States; and nothing in this Constitution shall be so construed as to prejudice any claims of the United States, or of any particular state.

Guarantees to the States
The federal government guarantees that every state shall have a republican form of government. The United States must also protect the states against invasion and help the states deal with rebellion or local violence.

SECTION 4. GUARANTEES TO THE STATES

The United States shall guarantee to every state in this Union a republican form of government, and shall protect each of them against invasion; and on application of the legislature, or of the executive (when the legislature cannot be convened) against domestic violence.

Amending the Constitution
Changes to the Constitution may be proposed by a two-thirds vote of both the House of Representatives and the Senate or by a national convention called by Congress when asked by two-thirds of the states. For a proposed amendment to become law, the legislatures or conventions in three-fourths of the states must approve it.

ARTICLE V
AMENDING THE CONSTITUTION

The Congress, whenever two-thirds of both houses shall deem it necessary, shall propose amendments to this Constitution, or, on the application of the legislatures of two-thirds of the several states, shall call a convention for proposing amendments, which, in either case, shall be valid to all intents and purposes, as part of this Constitution, when ratified by the legislatures of three-fourths of the several states, or by conventions in three-fourths thereof, as the one or the other mode of ratification may be proposed by the Congress; provided that [*no amendment which may be made prior to the year 1808 shall in any manner affect the first and fourth clauses in the Ninth Section of the First Article; and that*] no state, without its consent, shall be deprived of its equal suffrage in the Senate.

ARTICLE VI
GENERAL PROVISIONS

(1) Public Debt
Any debt owed by the United States before the Constitution went into effect was to be honored.

(1) All debts contracted and engagements entered into, before the adoption of this Constitution, shall be as valid against the United States under this Constitution, as under the Confederation.

(2) Federal Supremacy
This clause declares that the Constitution, federal laws, and treaties are the highest law in the nation. Whenever a state law and a federal law are found to disagree, the federal law must be obeyed so long as it is constitutional.

(2) This Constitution, and the laws of the United States which shall be made in pursuance thereof, and all treaties made, or which shall be made, under the authority of the United States, shall be the supreme law of the land; and the judges in every state shall be bound thereby, anything in the Constitution or laws of any state to the contrary notwithstanding.

(3) The Senators and Representatives before mentioned, and the members of the several state legislatures, and all executive and judicial officers, both of the United States and of the several states, shall be bound by oath or affirmation, to support this Constitution; but no religious test shall ever be required as a qualification to any office or public trust under the United States.

(3) Oaths of Office
All federal and state officials must promise to follow and enforce the Constitution. These officials cannot be required to follow a particular religion or satisfy any religious test.

ARTICLE VII
RATIFICATION

Ratification
In order for the Constitution to become law, 9 of the 13 states had to approve it. Special conventions were held for this purpose. The process took 9 months to complete.

The ratification of the conventions of nine states, shall be sufficient for the establishment of this Constitution between the states so ratifying the same.

Done in convention by the unanimous consent of the states present the seventeenth day of September in the year of our Lord one thousand seven hundred and eighty seven and of the independence of the United States of America the Twelfth. In witness whereof we have hereunto subscribed our names.

George Washington—President and deputy from Virginia

DELAWARE
George Read
Gunning Bedford, Jr.
John Dickinson
Richard Bassett
Jacob Broom

MARYLAND
James McHenry
Daniel of St. Thomas Jenifer
Daniel Carroll

VIRGINIA
John Blair
James Madison, Jr.

NORTH CAROLINA
William Blount
Richard Dobbs Spaight
Hugh Williamson

SOUTH CAROLINA
John Rutledge
Charles Cotesworth Pinckney
Charles Pinckney
Pierce Butler

GEORGIA
William Few
Abraham Baldwin

NEW HAMPSHIRE
John Langdon
Nicholas Gilman

MASSACHUSETTS
Nathaniel Gorham
Rufus King

CONNECTICUT
William Samuel Johnson
Roger Sherman

NEW YORK
Alexander Hamilton

NEW JERSEY
William Livingston
David Brearley
William Paterson
Jonathan Dayton

PENNSYLVANIA
Benjamin Franklin
Thomas Mifflin
Robert Morris
George Clymer
Thomas FitzSimons
Jared Ingersoll
James Wilson
Gouverneur Morris

ATTEST: William Jackson, secretary

AMERICAN DOCUMENTS

Freedom of Religion, Speech, Press, Assembly, and Petition
The Constitution provides for the freedoms of religion, speech, the press, peaceable assembly, and petition for redress of grievances. It also prohibits Congress from establishing religion.

AMENDMENT 1 (1791)***
FREEDOM OF RELIGION, SPEECH, PRESS, ASSEMBLY, AND PETITION

Congress shall make no law respecting an establishment of religion, or prohibiting the free exercise thereof; or abridging the freedom of speech, or of the press; or the right of the people peaceably to assemble, and to petition the government for a redress of grievances.

Weapons
People disagree about the meaning of this amendment. Some think it protects the right of state governments to arm their own state militias. Others think it protects the right of individual people to own guns, as a means of maintaining an armed citizenry that can act as a check and balance on government power.

AMENDMENT 2 (1791)
WEAPONS

A well-regulated militia, being necessary to the security of a free state, the right of the people to keep and bear arms shall not be infringed.

Housing Soldiers
The federal government cannot force people to house soldiers in their homes during peacetime. However, Congress may pass laws allowing this during wartime.

AMENDMENT 3 (1791)
HOUSING SOLDIERS

No soldier shall, in time of peace, be quartered in any house, without the consent of the owner; nor in time of war, but in a manner to be prescribed by law.

Searches and Seizures
This amendment protects people's privacy and safety. Subject to certain exceptions, a law officer cannot search a person or a person's home and belongings unless a judge has issued a valid search warrant. There must be good reason for the search. The warrant must describe the place to be searched and the people or things to be seized, or taken.

AMENDMENT 4 (1791)
SEARCHES AND SEIZURES

The right of the people to be secure in their persons, houses, papers, and effects, against unreasonable searches and seizures, shall not be violated; and no warrants shall issue but upon probable cause, supported by oath or affirmation, and particularly describing the place to be searched, and the persons or things to be seized.

Rights of Accused Persons
If a person is accused of a crime that is punishable by death or of any other serious crime, a grand jury must decide if there is enough evidence to hold a trial. People cannot be tried twice for the same crime, nor can they be forced to testify against themselves. No person shall be fined, jailed, or executed by the government unless the person has been given a fair trial. The government cannot take a person's property for public use unless fair payment is made.

AMENDMENT 5 (1791)
RIGHTS OF ACCUSED PERSONS

No person shall be held to answer for a capital, or otherwise infamous crime, unless on a presentment or indictment of a grand jury, except in cases arising in the land or naval forces, or in the militia, when in actual service in time of war or public danger; nor shall any person be subject for the same offense to be twice put in jeopardy of life or limb; nor shall be compelled in any criminal case to be a witness against himself; nor be deprived of life, liberty, or property, without due process of law; nor shall private property be taken for public use without just compensation.

*** The date beside each amendment is the year that the amendment was ratified and became part of the Constitution.

AMENDMENT 6 (1791)
RIGHTS RELATED TO CRIMINAL TRIALS

In all criminal prosecutions, the accused shall enjoy the right to a speedy and public trial, by an impartial jury of the state and district wherein the crime shall have been committed, which district shall have been previously ascertained by law, and to be informed of the nature and cause of the accusation; to be confronted with the witnesses against him; to have compulsory process for obtaining witnesses in his favor, and to have the assistance of counsel for his defense.

Rights Related to Criminal Trials
A person accused of a crime has the right to a public trial by an impartial jury, locally chosen. The trial must be held within a reasonable amount of time. The accused person must be told of all charges and has the right to see, hear, and question any witnesses and to call his or her own witnesses. The government must allow the accused to have a lawyer. This has also been interpreted as requiring the government to provide a lawyer free of charge to a person who is accused of a serious crime and who is unable to pay for legal services.

AMENDMENT 7 (1791)
JURY TRIAL IN CIVIL CASES

In suits at common law, where the value in controversy shall exceed 20 dollars, the right of trial by jury shall be preserved, and no fact tried by a jury shall be otherwise re-examined in any court of the United States, than according to the rules of the common law.

Jury Trial in Civil Cases
In most federal civil cases involving more than 20 dollars, a jury trial is guaranteed. Civil cases are those disputes between two or more people over money, property, personal injury, or legal rights. Usually civil cases are not tried in federal courts unless they involve a federal law, rather than just state law, or much larger sums of money are involved.

AMENDMENT 8 (1791)
BAIL AND PUNISHMENT

Excessive bail shall not be required, nor excessive fines imposed, nor cruel and unusual punishments inflicted.

Bail and Punishment
Courts cannot punish convicted criminals in cruel and unusual ways and cannot impose fines that are too high. Bail is money put up as a guarantee that an accused person will appear for trial. In certain cases bail can be denied altogether.

AMENDMENT 9 (1791)
RIGHTS OF THE PEOPLE

The enumeration in the Constitution, of certain rights, shall not be construed to deny or disparage others retained by the people.

Rights of the People
People disagree about the meaning of this amendment. Some think it authorizes courts to protect certain individual rights even though those rights are not expressly stated in the Bill of Rights. Others think the amendment recognizes that state laws may protect a wide range of individual rights that are not mentioned in the Bill of Rights but that those unenumerated rights may be defined or repealed by the democratic process in each state.

AMENDMENT 10 (1791)
POWERS OF THE STATES AND THE PEOPLE

The powers not delegated to the United States by the Constitution, nor prohibited by it to the states, are reserved to the states respectively, or to the people.

Powers of the States and the People
Any powers not given to the federal government or denied to the states belong to the states or to the people.

AMENDMENT 11 (1798)
SUITS AGAINST STATES

The judicial power of the United States shall not be construed to extend to any suit in law or equity, commenced or prosecuted against one of the United States or citizens of another state, or by citizens or subjects of any foreign state.

Suits Against States
A citizen of one state or of a foreign country cannot sue another state in federal court.

Election of President and Vice President
This amendment replaces the part of Article II, Section 1, that originally explained the process of electing the President and Vice President. Amendment 12 was an important step in the development of the two-party system. It allows a party to nominate its own candidates for both President and Vice President.

AMENDMENT 12 (1804)
ELECTION OF PRESIDENT AND VICE PRESIDENT

The electors shall meet in their respective states, and vote by ballot for President and Vice President, one of whom, at least, shall not be an inhabitant of the same state with themselves; they shall name in their ballots the person voted for as President, and in distinct ballots the person voted for as Vice President, and they shall make distinct lists of all persons voted for as President, and of all persons voted for as Vice President, and of the number of votes for each, which lists they shall sign and certify, and transmit, sealed, to the seat of government of the United States, directed to the President of the Senate; the President of the Senate shall, in the presence of the Senate and House of Representatives, open all the certificates, and the votes shall then be counted; the person having the greatest number of votes for President shall be the President, if such a number be a majority of the whole number of electors appointed; and if no person have such majority; then from the persons having the highest numbers not exceeding three on the list of those voted for as President, the House of Representatives shall choose immediately, by ballot, the President. But in choosing the President, the votes shall be taken by states, the representation from each state having one vote; a quorum for this purpose shall consist of a member or members from two thirds of the states, and a majority of all the states shall be necessary to a choice. [*And if the House of Representatives shall not choose a President whenever the right of choice shall devolve upon them, before the fourth day of March next following, then the Vice President shall act as President, as in the case of the death or other constitutional disability of the President.*] The person having the greatest number of votes as Vice President, shall be the Vice President, if such number be a majority of the whole number of electors appointed, and if no person have a majority, then, from the two highest numbers on the list the Senate shall choose the Vice President; a quorum for the purpose shall consist of two thirds of the whole number of Senators, and a majority of the whole number shall be necessary to a choice. But no person constitutionally ineligible to the office of President shall be eligible to that of Vice President of the United States.

End of Slavery
People cannot be forced to work against their will unless they have been tried for and convicted of a crime for which this means of punishment is ordered. However, there are historical exceptions where compulsory work is permitted, such as the military draft and jury duty. Congress may enforce this by law.

AMENDMENT 13 (1865)
END OF SLAVERY

SECTION 1. ABOLITION

Neither slavery nor involuntary servitude, except as a punishment for crime whereof the party shall have been duly convicted, shall exist within the United States, or any place subject to their jurisdiction.

SECTION 2. ENFORCEMENT

Congress shall have power to enforce this article by appropriate legislation.

Citizenship
All persons born or naturalized in the United States are citizens of the United States and of the state in which they live. State governments may not deny any citizen the full rights of citizenship. This amendment also guarantees that no state may take away a person's life, liberty, or property without following the procedure prescribed by law. All citizens must be protected equally under law.

AMENDMENT 14 (1868)
RIGHTS OF CITIZENS

SECTION 1. CITIZENSHIP

All persons born or naturalized in the United States and subject to the jurisdiction thereof, are citizens of the United States and of the state wherein they reside. No state shall make or enforce any law which shall abridge the privileges or immunities of citizens of the United States, nor shall any state deprive any person of life, liberty, or property, without due process of law; nor deny to any person within its jurisdiction the equal protection of the laws.

SECTION 2. NUMBER OF REPRESENTATIVES

Representatives shall be apportioned among the several states according to their respective numbers, counting the whole number of persons in each state, [*excluding Indians not taxed*]. But when the right to vote at any election for the choice of electors for President and Vice President of the United States, representatives in Congress, the executive and judicial officers of a state, or the members of the legislature thereof, is denied to any of the [*male*] inhabitants of such state, being [*twenty-one years of age and*] citizens of the United States, or in any way abridged, except for participation in rebellion or other crime, the basis of representation therein shall be reduced in the proportion which the number of such [*male*] citizens shall bear to the whole number of [*male*] citizens [*twenty-one years of age*] in such state.

Number of Representatives
Each state's representation in Congress is based on its total population. Any state denying eligible citizens the right to vote will have its representation in Congress decreased. This clause abolished the Three-fifths Compromise in Article I, Section 2. Later amendments granted women the right to vote and lowered the voting age to 18.

SECTION 3. PENALTY FOR REBELLION

No person shall be a Senator or Representative in Congress, or elector of President and Vice President, or hold any office, civil or military, under the United States, or under any state, who, having previously taken an oath, as a member of Congress, or as an officer of the United States, or as a member of any state legislature, or as an executive or judicial officer of any state, to support the Constitution of the United States, shall have engaged in insurrection or rebellion against the same, or given aid or comfort to the enemies thereof. But Congress may, by a vote of two thirds of each house, remove such disability.

Penalty for Rebellion
No person who has rebelled against the United States may hold federal office. This clause was originally added to punish the leaders of the Confederacy for failing to support the Constitution of the United States.

SECTION 4. GOVERNMENT DEBT

The validity of the public debt of the United States, authorized by law, including debts incurred for payment of pensions and bounties for services in suppressing insurrection or rebellion, shall not be questioned. But neither the United States nor any state shall assume or pay any debt or obligation incurred in aid of insurrection or rebellion against the United States, [*or any claim for the loss or emancipation of any slave*;] but all such debts, obligations, and claims shall be held illegal and void.

Government Debt
The federal government is responsible for all federal public debts. It is not responsible, however, for Confederate debts or for debts that result from any rebellion against the United States.

SECTION 5. ENFORCEMENT

The Congress shall have power to enforce, by appropriate legislation, the provisions of this article.

Enforcement
Congress may enforce these provisions by law.

AMENDMENT 15 (1870)
VOTING RIGHTS

SECTION 1. RIGHT TO VOTE

The right of citizens of the United States to vote shall not be denied or abridged by the United States or by any state on account of race, color, or previous condition of servitude.

Right to Vote
No state may prevent a citizen from voting because of race or color or condition of previous servitude.

SECTION 2. ENFORCEMENT

The Congress shall have power to enforce this article by appropriate legislation.

AMENDMENT 16 (1913)
INCOME TAX

The Congress shall have power to lay and collect taxes on incomes, from whatever source derived, without apportionment among the several states, and without regard to any census or enumeration.

Income Tax
Congress has the power to collect taxes on its citizens, based on their personal incomes, rather than requiring the states to impose and collect such taxes.

AMERICAN DOCUMENTS

Direct Election of Senators
Originally, state legislatures elected senators. This amendment allows the people of each state to elect their own senators directly. The idea is to make senators more responsible to the people they represent.

AMENDMENT 17 (1913)
DIRECT ELECTION OF SENATORS
SECTION 1. METHOD OF ELECTION

The Senate of the United States shall be composed of two Senators from each state, elected by the people thereof, for six years; and each Senator shall have one vote. The electors in each state shall have the qualifications requisite for electors of the most numerous branch of the state legislatures.

SECTION 2. VACANCIES

When vacancies happen in the representation of any state in the Senate, the executive authority of such state shall issue writs of election to fill such vacancies: *Provided*, that the legislature of any state may empower the executive thereof to make temporary appointments until the people fill the vacancies by election as the legislature may direct.

SECTION 3. EXCEPTION

[*This amendment shall not be so construed as to affect the election or term of any Senator chosen before it becomes valid as part of the Constitution.*]

Prohibition
This amendment made it illegal to make, sell, or transport liquor within the United States or to transport it out of the United States or its territories. Amendment 18 was the first to include a time limit for approval. If not ratified within seven years, it would be repealed, or canceled. Many later amendments have included similar time limits.

AMENDMENT 18 (1919)
BAN ON ALCOHOLIC DRINKS
SECTION 1. PROHIBITION

[*After one year from the ratification of this article the manufacture, sale, or transportation of intoxicating liquors within, the importation thereof into, or the exportation thereof from the United States and all territory subject to the jurisdiction thereof for beverage purposes is hereby prohibited.*]

SECTION 2. ENFORCEMENT

[*The Congress and the several states shall have concurrent power to enforce this article by appropriate legislation.*]

SECTION 3. RATIFICATION

[*This article shall be inoperative unless it shall have been ratified as an amendment to the Constitution by the legislatures of the several states as provided in the Constitution, within seven years from the date of the submission hereof to the states by the Congress.*]

Women's Voting Rights
This amendment protected the right of women throughout the United States to vote.

AMENDMENT 19 (1920)
WOMEN'S VOTING RIGHTS
SECTION 1. RIGHT TO VOTE

The right of citizens of the United States to vote shall not be denied or abridged by the United States or by any state on account of sex.

SECTION 2. ENFORCEMENT

Congress shall have power to enforce this article by appropriate legislation.

Terms of Office
The terms of the President and the Vice President begin on January 20, in the year following their election. Members of Congress take office on January 3. Before this amendment newly elected members of Congress did not begin their terms until March 4. This meant that those who had run for reelection and been defeated remained in office for four months.

AMENDMENT 20 (1933)
TERMS OF OFFICE
SECTION 1. BEGINNING OF TERMS

The terms of the President and Vice President shall end at noon on the 20th day of January, and the terms of Senators and Representatives at noon on the 3rd day of January, of the years in which such terms would have ended if this article had not been ratified; and the terms of their successors shall then begin.

SECTION 2. SESSIONS OF CONGRESS

The Congress shall assemble at least once in every year, and such meeting shall begin at noon on the 3rd day of January, unless they shall by law appoint a different day.

Sessions of Congress
Congress meets at least once a year, beginning at noon on January 3. Congress had previously met at least once a year beginning on the first Monday of December.

SECTION 3. PRESIDENTIAL SUCCESSION

If, at the time fixed for the beginning of the term of the President, the President-elect shall have died, the Vice President-elect shall become President. If a President shall not have been chosen before the time fixed for the beginning of his term, or if the President-elect shall have failed to qualify, then the Vice President-elect shall act as President until a President shall have qualified; and the Congress may by law provide for the case wherein neither a President-elect nor a Vice President-elect shall have qualified, declaring who shall then act as President, or the manner in which one who is to act shall be selected and such person shall act accordingly until a President or Vice President shall be qualified.

Presidential Succession
If the newly elected President dies before January 20, the newly elected Vice President becomes President on that date. If a President has not been chosen by January 20 or does not meet the requirements for being President, the newly elected Vice President becomes President. Congress may enact a law that indicates who will temporarily serve as President if neither the newly elected President nor the newly elected Vice President meets the requirements for office.

SECTION 4. ELECTIONS DECIDED BY CONGRESS

The Congress may by law provide for the case of the death of any of the persons from whom the House of Representatives may choose a President whenever the right of choice shall have devolved upon them, and for the case of the death of any of the persons from whom the Senate may choose a Vice President whenever the right of choice shall have devolved upon them.

SECTION 5. EFFECTIVE DATE

[*Sections 1 and 2 shall take effect on the 15th day of October following the ratification of this article.*]

SECTION 6. RATIFICATION

[*This article shall be inoperative unless it shall have been ratified as an amendment to the Constitution by the legislatures of three fourths of the several states within seven years from the date of its submission.*]

AMENDMENT 21 (1933)
END OF PROHIBITION

SECTION 1. REPEAL OF AMENDMENT 18

The eighteenth article of amendment to the Constitution of the United States is hereby repealed.

SECTION 2. STATE LAWS

The transportation or importation into any state, territory, or possession of the United States for delivery or use therein of intoxicating liquors, in violation of the laws thereof, is hereby prohibited.

SECTION 3. RATIFICATION

[*This article shall be inoperative unless it shall have been ratified as an amendment to the Constitution by conventions in the several states, as provided in the Constitution within seven years from the date of the submission hereof to the states by Congress.*]

End of Prohibition
This amendment repealed Amendment 18. This is the only amendment to be ratified by state conventions instead of by state legislatures. Congress felt that this would give people's opinions about prohibition a better chance to be heard.

Two-Term limit for Presidents
A President may not serve more than two full terms in office. Any President who serves less than two years of a previous President's term may be elected for two more terms.

AMENDMENT 22 (1951)
TWO-TERM LIMIT FOR PRESIDENTS
SECTION 1. TWO-TERM LIMIT

No person shall be elected to the office of the President more than twice, and no person who has held the office of President, or acted as President, for more than two years of a term to which some other person was elected President shall be elected to the office of the President more than once. [*But this article shall not apply to any person holding the office of President when this article was proposed by the Congress, and shall not prevent any person who may be holding the office of President, or acting as President, during the term within which this article becomes operative from holding the office of President, or acting as President, during the remainder of such term.*]

SECTION 2. RATIFICATION

[*This article shall be inoperative unless it shall have been ratified as an amendment to the Constitution by the legislatures of three-fourths of the several states within seven years from the date of its submission to the states by the Congress.*]

AMERICAN DOCUMENTS

Presidential Electors for District of Columbia
This amendment grants three electoral votes to the national capital.

AMENDMENT 23 (1961)
PRESIDENTIAL ELECTORS FOR DISTRICT OF COLUMBIA
SECTION 1. NUMBER OF ELECTORS

The District constituting the seat of Government of the United States shall appoint in such manner as Congress may direct:

A number of electors of President and Vice President equal to the whole number of Senators and Representatives in Congress to which the District would be entitled if it were a state, but in no event more than the least populous state; they shall be in addition to those appointed by the states, but they shall be considered, for the purposes of the election of President and Vice President, to be electors appointed by a state, and they shall meet in the District and perform such duties as provided by the twelfth article of amendment.

SECTION 2. ENFORCEMENT

The Congress shall have power to enforce this article by appropriate legislation.

Ban on Poll Taxes
No United States citizen may be prevented from voting in a federal election because of failing to pay a tax to vote. Poll taxes had been used in some states to prevent African Americans from voting.

AMENDMENT 24 (1964)
BAN ON POLL TAXES
SECTION 1. POLL TAX ILLEGAL

The right of citizens of the United States to vote in any primary or other election for President or Vice President, for electors for President or Vice President, or for Senator or Representative in Congress, shall not be denied or abridged by the United States or any state by reason of failure to pay any poll tax or other tax.

SECTION 2. ENFORCEMENT

The Congress shall have power to enforce this article by appropriate legislation.

Presidential Vacancy
If the President is removed from office or resigns from or dies while in office, the Vice President becomes President.

AMENDMENT 25 (1967)
PRESIDENTIAL SUCCESSION
SECTION 1. PRESIDENTIAL VACANCY

In case of the removal of the President from office or of his death or resignation, the Vice President shall become President.

SECTION 2. VICE PRESIDENTIAL VACANCY

Whenever there is a vacancy in the office of the Vice President, the President shall nominate a Vice President who shall take the office upon confirmation by a majority vote of both houses of Congress.

Vice Presidential Vacancy
If the office of the Vice President becomes open, the President names someone to assume that office and that person becomes Vice President if both houses of Congress approve by a majority vote.

SECTION 3. PRESIDENTIAL DISABILITY

Whenever the President transmits to the President pro tempore of the Senate and the Speaker of the House of Representatives his written declaration that he is unable to discharge the powers and duties of his office, and until he transmits to them a written declaration to the contrary, such powers and duties shall be discharged by the Vice President as Acting President.

Presidential Disability
This section explains in detail what happens if the President cannot continue in office because of sickness or any other reason. The Vice President takes over as acting President until the President is able to resume office.

SECTION 4. DETERMINING PRESIDENTIAL DISABILITY

Whenever the Vice President and a majority of either the principal officers of the executive departments or of such other body as Congress may by law provide, transmit to the President pro tempore of the Senate and the Speaker of the House of Representatives their written declaration that the President is unable to discharge the powers and duties of his office, the Vice President shall immediately assume the powers and duties of the office as Acting President.

Thereafter, when the President transmits to the President pro tempore of the Senate and the Speaker of the House of Representatives his written declaration that no inability exists, he shall resume the powers and duties of his office unless the Vice President and a majority of either the principal officers of the executive department or of such other body as Congress may by law provide, transmit within four days to the President pro tempore of the Senate and the Speaker of the House of Representatives their written declaration that the President is unable to discharge the powers and duties of his office. Thereupon Congress shall decide the issue, assembling within 48 hours for that purpose if not in session. If the Congress, within 21 days after receipt of the latter written declaration, or, if Congress is not in session, within 21 days after Congress is required to assemble, determines by two-thirds vote of both houses that the President is unable to discharge the powers and duties of his office, the Vice President shall continue to discharge the same as Acting President; otherwise the President shall resume the powers and duties of his office.

Determining Presidential Disability
If the Vice President and a majority of the Cabinet inform the Speaker of the House and the president pro tempore of the Senate that the President cannot carry out his or her duties, the Vice President then serves as acting President. To regain the office, the President has to inform the Speaker and the president pro tempore in writing that he or she is again able to serve. But, if the Vice President and a majority of the Cabinet disagree with the President and inform the Speaker and the president pro tempore that the President is still unable to serve, then Congress decides who will hold the office of President.

AMENDMENT 26 (1971)
VOTING AGE

SECTION 1. RIGHT TO VOTE

The right of citizens of the United States, who are 18 years of age or older, to vote shall not be denied or abridged by the United States or any state on account of age.

SECTION 2. ENFORCEMENT

The Congress shall have the power to enforce this article by appropriate legislation.

Voting Age
All citizens 18 years or older have the right to vote. Formerly, the voting age was 21 in most states.

AMENDMENT 27 (1992)
CONGRESSIONAL PAY

No law, varying the compensation for the services of the Senators and Representatives, shall take effect, until an election of Representatives shall have intervened.

Congressional Pay
A law raising or lowering the salaries for members of Congress cannot be passed for that session of Congress.

"The Star-Spangled Banner" was written by Francis Scott Key in September 1814 and adopted as the national anthem in March 1931. The army and navy had recognized it as such long before Congress approved it.

During the War of 1812, Francis Scott Key spent a night aboard a British warship in the Chesapeake Bay while trying to arrange for the release of an American prisoner. The battle raged throughout the night, while the Americans were held on the ship. The next morning, when the smoke from the cannons finally cleared, Francis Scott Key was thrilled to see the American flag still waving proudly above Fort McHenry. It symbolized the victory of the Americans.

There are four verses to the national anthem. In these four verses, Key wrote about how he felt when he saw the flag still waving over Fort McHenry. He wrote that the flag was a symbol of the freedom for which the people had fought so hard. Key also told about the pride he had in his country and the great hopes he had for the future of the United States.

The National Anthem

The Star-Spangled Banner

(1)

Oh, say can you see by the dawn's early light
What so proudly we hail'd at the twilight's last gleaming,
Whose broad stripes and bright stars through the perilous fight
O'er the ramparts we watch'd were so gallantly streaming?
And the rockets' red glare, the bombs bursting in air,
Gave proof through the night that our flag was still there.
Oh, say does that star-spangled banner yet wave
O'er the land of the free and the home of the brave?

(2)

On the shore dimly seen through the mists of the deep,
Where the foe's haughty host in dread silence reposes,
What is that which the breeze, o'er the towering steep,
As it fitfully blows, half conceals, half discloses?
Now it catches the gleam of the morning's first beam,
In full glory reflected now shines in the stream.
'Tis the star-spangled banner, oh, long may it wave
O'er the land of the free and the home of the brave!

(3)

And where is that band who so vauntingly swore
That the havoc of war and the battle's confusion
A home and a country should leave us no more?
Their blood has wash'd out their foul footstep's pollution.
No refuge could save the hireling and slave
From the terror of flight or the gloom of the grave,
And the star-spangled banner in triumph doth wave
O'er the land of the free and the home of the brave.

(4)

Oh, thus be it ever when freemen shall stand
Between their lov'd home and the war's desolation!
Blest with vict'ry and peace may the heav'n-rescued land
Praise the power that hath made and preserv'd us a nation!
Then conquer we must, when our cause it is just,
And this be our motto, "In God is our Trust,"
And the star-spangled banner in triumph shall wave
O'er the land of the free and the home of the brave.

The Pledge of Allegiance

I pledge allegiance to the Flag
of the United States of America,
and to the Republic
for which it stands,
one Nation under God, indivisible,
with liberty and justice for all.

The flag is a symbol of the United States of America. The Pledge of Allegiance says that the people of the United States promise to stand up for the flag, their country, and the basic beliefs of freedom and fairness upon which the country was established.

Research Handbook

Before you can write a report or complete a project, you must gather information about your topic. You can find some information in your textbook. Other sources of information are technology resources, print resources, and community resources.

Technology Resources
- Internet
- Computer disk
- Television and radio

Print Resources
- Almanac
- Atlas
- Dictionary
- Encyclopedia
- Nonfiction book
- Periodical
- Thesaurus

Community Resources
- Teacher
- Museum curator
- Community leader
- Older citizen

Technology Resources

The main technology resources you can use for researching information are the Internet and computer disks. Your school or local library may have CD-ROMs or DVDs that contain information about your topic. Other media, such as television and radio, can also be good sources of current information.

Using the Internet

The Internet contains vast amounts of information. By using a computer to go online, you can read documents, see pictures and artworks, listen to music, take a virtual tour of a museum or other location, and read about current events.

Information that you find online is always changing. Keep in mind that some websites that you find might contain mistakes or incorrect information. To get accurate information, be sure to visit only trusted websites, such as museum and government sites. Also, try to find two or more websites that give the same facts.

Plan Your Search

- Identify the topic to be researched.
- Make a list of questions that you want to answer about your topic.

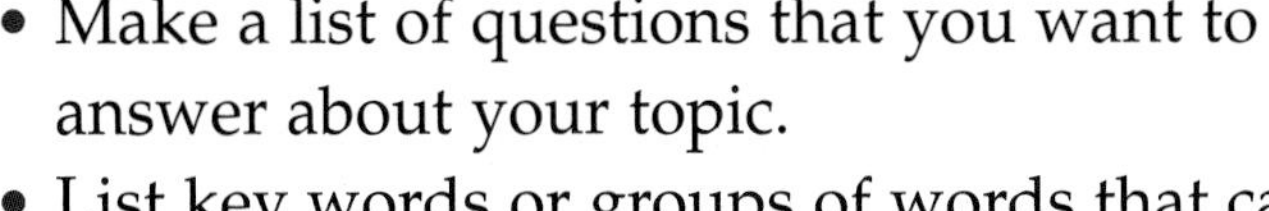

- List key words or groups of words that can be used to write or talk about your topic.
- Look for good online resources to find answers to your questions.
- Choose the steps you will take to find the information you need.

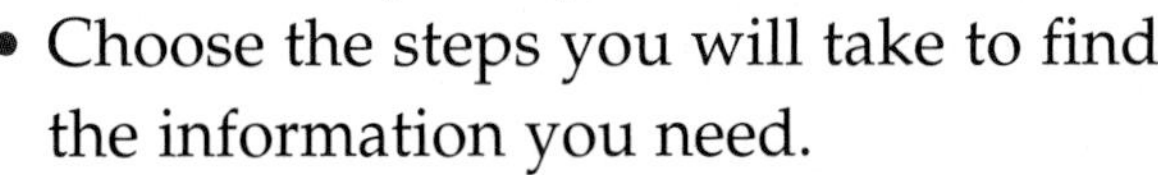

Use a Search Engine

A search engine is an online collection of websites that can be sorted by entering a key word or group of words. There are many different search engines available. You may want to ask a librarian, a teacher, or a parent for suggestions on which search engine to use.

Search by Subject To search by subject, or topic, use a search engine. Choose from the list of key words that you made while planning your search, and enter a key word or group of words in the search engine field on your screen. Then click SEARCH or GO. You will see a list of available websites that have to do with your topic. Click on the site or sites you think will be most helpful. If you do not find enough websites listed, think of other key words or related words, and search again.

RIVERDALE HIGH SCHOOL SEARCH

Web Images People News

Enter your subject here▶ Sacramento

Search Advanced Search

Visit Sacramento
Visit Sacramento! Learn about Sacramento's various tourist destinations and....
www.visitsacramento.com/

Historic Sacramento
This site is a collection of photographs of historic Sacramento since 1848....
www.historicsacramento.com/

Sacramento Information
A history of Sacramento, California....
www.sacramentoinfo.com/

Search by Address Each website has its own address, called a Uniform Resource Locator, or URL for short. To get to a website using a URL, simply type the URL in the LOCATION/GO TO box on your screen and hit ENTER or click GO.

Use Bookmarks The bookmark feature is an Internet tool for keeping and organizing URLs. If you find a website that seems especially helpful, you can save the URL so that you can quickly and easily return to it later. Click BOOKMARKS or FAVORITES at the top of your screen, and choose ADD. Your computer makes a copy of the URL and keeps a record of it.

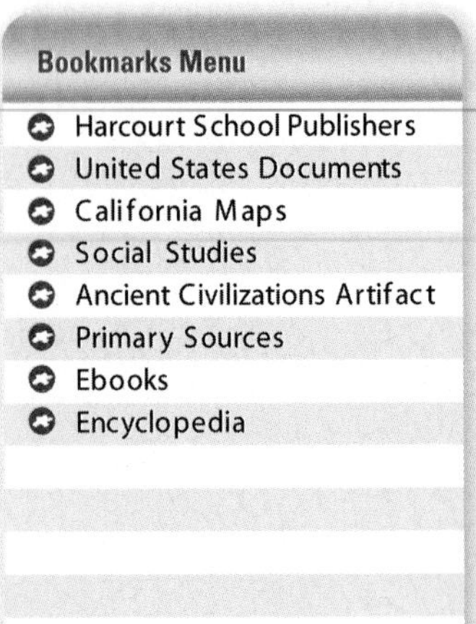

Print Resources

Books in libraries are organized through a system of numbers. Every book has its own number called a call number. The call number tells where in the library the book can be found. Some reference books, such as encyclopedias, are usually kept in a separate section of a library. Each book there has R or RE—for *reference*—on its spine. Most reference books can only be used in the library. Most libraries also have a special section for periodicals, which include magazines and newspapers.

Almanac

An almanac is a book or electronic resource that contains facts about different subjects. The subjects are listed in alphabetical order in an index, and many number-based facts are shown in tables or charts. New almanacs are published each year, so they have the most current information.

Atlas

An atlas is a book of maps that gives information about places. Different kinds of atlases show different places at different times. Your teacher or librarian can help you find the kind of atlas you need for your research.

Dictionary

A dictionary gives the correct spelling of words and their definitions, or meanings. It also gives the words' pronunciations, or how to say the words aloud. In addition, many dictionaries have lists of foreign words, abbreviations, well-known people, and place names.

de•mand\di-ˊmand*n* **1:** to ask with authority **2:** the desire or need for a product or service
de•pend\di-ˊpend*vi* **1:** to be undecided **2:** to rely on for help
de•pos•it\di-ˊpä-zit*vb* **1:** to put money into a bank account **2:** to place for safekeeping or as a pledge

Dictionary entry

RESEARCH HANDBOOK

Encyclopedia

An encyclopedia is a book or set of books that gives information about many different topics. The topics are arranged alphabetically. An encyclopedia is a good source to use when beginning your research. In addition to words, electronic encyclopedias often have sound and video clips as well.

Capitol, United States, houses the United States legislative branch, or Congress. The Capitol building is in Washington, D.C., on Capitol Hill. The Capitol is a government building and a symbol of the United States. Visitors from different countries visit the Capitol each year. The public can go inside and see where the House of Representatives and the Senate meet.

In 1792 the government held a special contest. Architects from around the country competed to see whose design for the Capitol would be chosen. Amateur architect and doctor William Thornton submitted the winning entry. In 1793, construction of the Capitol began. Congress held its first meeting in the new Capitol in 1800. During the War of 1812, British troops set fire to the building in the year 1814. Congress could not return to the Capitol until 1819.

The Capitol is modeled on the architecture used by Romans. The Capitol's 540 rooms include offices and reception rooms. In these rooms are keepsakes from United States history and works of art from memorable artists. The center of the Capitol, also known as the Rotunda, is beneath the dome. It is more than 95 feet in diameter and 185 feet high. The large center dome is painted white to match the rest of the marble building. On top of the dome is the Statue of Freedom. The statue is a woman with a headdress of eagle feathers, holding a shield and sword.

Many state funerals for famous United States citizens, such as Abraham Lincoln and Ronald Reagan, have been held in the Rotunda under the dome ceiling. Painted in 1865, *The Apotheosis of George Washington* by an Italian painter Constantino Brumidi, decorates the dome ceiling.

To the north of the Rotunda is the Senate wing of the Capitol. This wing has rooms open to the public where visitors can watch the Senate in session. The old Supreme court chamber is also housed in this wing. The chamber looks much like it did in 1859. This is where the court met during 1810 to 1859. The President's room is also located on the Senate side. It is one of the most decorated rooms. Portraits of George Washington and a large bronze chandelier decorate this room.

South of the Rotunda is the House of Representatives wing. Located in this wing are the House Chamber and the Statuary Hall. The House Chamber has rooms open to the public for viewing. The Statuary Hall contains statues of notable Americans. In 1857, an extension to the House wing was completed. Thomas Ustick Walter, co-founder of the American Institute of Architects, built it. Walter is responsible for the fireproof cast-iron dome on top of the building's center completed in 1866. It replaced the small wood-constructed dome built in 1824.

In 1962, architect J. George Stewart completed the eastward expansion of the Capitol's center. Today, the Capitol covers 4 acres and has five levels. It is part of the Capitol Complex.

The Capitol Complex consists of the United States Botanical Garden Conservatory, United States Supreme Court, office buildings for the House of Representatives and Senate, and the Library of Congress.

Chapter 1 • 217

Encyclopedia article

Nonfiction Books

A nonfiction book gives facts about real people, places, and things. All nonfiction books in a library are arranged in order and by category according to their call numbers. To find a book's call number, you use a library's card file or computer catalog. You can search for a book in the catalog by subject, author, or title.

Periodicals

A periodical is published each day, each week, or each month. Periodicals are good resources for current information on topics not yet found in books. Many libraries have a guide that lists magazine articles by subject. Two such guides are the *Children's Magazine Guide* and the *Readers' Guide to Periodical Literature.* The entries in guides are usually in alphabetical order by subject, author, or title.

Thesaurus

A thesaurus (thih•SAWR•uhs) gives synonyms, or words that mean the same or nearly the same as another word. A thesaurus also gives antonyms, or words that have the opposite meanings. Using a thesaurus can help you find words that better describe your topic and make your writing more interesting.

Community Resources

Many times, people in your community can tell you information about your research topic. You can learn facts, opinions, or points of view by asking these people thoughtful questions. Before you talk to any of them, always ask a teacher or a parent for permission.

Listening to Find Information

It is important to plan ahead whenever you talk with people as part of your research. Planning ahead will help you gather the information you need. Follow these tips as you gather information from people in your community.

Before

- Find out more about the topic you want to discuss.
- Think about the kind of information you still need.
- Consider the best way to gather the information you need.
- List the people you want to talk to.
- Make a list of useful questions you want to ask. Make sure your questions are clear and effective.

During

- Speak clearly and loudly enough when asking questions.
- Listen carefully. Make sure you are getting the information you need, and revise your questions based on what you hear. You may also think of new questions to ask.
- Think about the speaker's perspective, tone of voice, and word choice. Use these clues to evaluate whether the speaker is a good source of information about your topic.
- Be polite. Do not interrupt or argue with the person who is speaking.
- Take notes to help you remember important ideas and details.
- Write down the person's exact words if you think you will want to quote them in your report. If possible, use a tape recorder. Be sure to ask the speaker for permission in advance.

After

- Thank the person you spoke with.
- Follow up by writing a thank-you note.

Writing to Get Information

You can also write to people in your community to gather information. You can write an e-mail or a letter. Keep these ideas in mind as you write:

- Write neatly or use a computer.
- Say who you are and why you are writing. Be clear and specific about what you want to know.
- Carefully check your spelling and punctuation.
- If you are writing a letter, provide a self-addressed, stamped envelope for the person to send you a response.
- Thank the person.

222 Central Avenue
Bakersfield, CA 93301
October 25, 20- -

Northern Regional Tourism Division
Attn: Ms. Stephanie Nguyen
123 Main Street
Sacramento, CA 94211

Dear Ms. Nguyen:

My name is David Thomas, and I am writing this letter to see if you can send me some information about scenic attractions in the state of California. My family is planning a vacation next month, and we would like to visit some of the attractions in the northern part of the state. Please send a brochure listing the scenic attractions and a highway map. I understand this is a service you provide for those planning vacations in the area. I am excited about visiting your part of the state.

Thank you for your help.

Sincerely,

David Thomas

David Thomas
222 Central Avenue
Bakersfield, CA 93301

Bureau of Tourism
Attn: Stephanie Nguyen
123 Main Street
Sacramento, CA 94211

RESEARCH HANDBOOK

Reporting

Written Reports

Your teacher may ask you to write a report about the information you find. Knowing how to write a report will help you make good use of the information. The following tips will help you write your report.

Before Writing

- Choose a main idea or topic.
- Think of questions about your topic. Questions should be clear and focus on specific ideas about your topic.
- Gather information from two or more sources. You may use print resources, technology resources, or community resources. Be sure to look for answers to your questions.
- Take notes on the information you find.
- Review your notes to be sure you have the information you need. Write down ideas and details about your topic to put in your report.
- Use your notes to make an outline of the information you found. Organize your ideas in a way that is easy to understand.

Outline

The California Capitol Building

I. Where, when, and why the capitol building was constructed

A. The capitol building was built in Sacramento.

1. In 1849, the capital was in San Jose.
2. In 1852, the capital moved from San Jose to Vallejo.
3. Since Vallejo was not a good place for a capitol building, the capital moved to Sacramento.

B. The population of California increased, creating a need for a capitol building.

1. People wanted a symbol to represent the state of California.
2. In 1854, Sacramento's statehouse became the new capitol building.

C. Many important decisions are made in the capitol building.

1. Government representatives make new laws.
2. Government officials meet to talk about California issues.

D. Knowing about the state capitol is important for good citizenship.

1. The building includes information everyone should know.
2. Citizens vote for people who represent them.

Bibliography

Hernandez, Elizabeth. *Sacramento Through the Years.* San Antonio, Texas: Old Alamo Press, 2004

Wyatt, Adam. *The History of California.* Philadelphia, Pennsylvania: Scenic River Publishing, 2003

Bibliography Card

Wyatt, Adam. *The History of California.* Philadelphia, Pennsylvania: Scenic River Publishing, 2003, page 25.

San Jose was the first state capital of California. Eventually the state government moved to Sacramento in 1854.

THE CALIFORNIA CAPITOL BUILDING	
Reading Notes	**Class Notes**
• The California Legislature first met at the Capitol building in 1869 • Government representatives make laws in the Capitol building • Government representatives vote on issues there • The capital of California was San Jose in 1849 • In 1852, the capital moved to Vallejo • The Sacramento statehouse became the new Capitol building	• Visitors can tour the offices of the California attorney general, secretary of state, treasurer, and governor • Outside the building is a statue of Junipero Serra • Around the building are 40 acres of garden • The capital moved from San Jose to Vallejo to Sacramento, when the statehouse became the Capitol building • The Capitol building is a symbol for the people of California • The Capitol building was built out of the statehouse and took four more years to complete

Citing Sources

An important part of research and writing is citing sources. When you cite a source, you keep a written record of where you got your information. The list of sources will be presented as a bibliography. A bibliography is a list of the books, periodicals, and other sources that you used to find the information in your report.

RESEARCH HANDBOOK

Write a First Draft

- Use your notes and your outline to write a draft of your report. Keep in mind that your purpose is to share information.
- Write in paragraph form. Develop your topic with facts, details, examples, and explanations. Each paragraph should focus on one new idea.
- Get all your ideas down on paper. You can revise your draft and correct errors in the next step.

Revise

- Read over your draft. Does it make sense? Does your report have a beginning, a middle, and an end? Have you answered all your questions?
- Rewrite sentences that are unclear or poorly worded. Move sentences that seem out of place.
- Add details when needed to support your ideas.
- If too many sentences are alike, make some sentences shorter or longer to keep your report interesting.
- Check any quotations to be sure you have shown someone's exact words and that you have noted the source correctly.

Proofread and Edit

- Proofread your report, checking for errors.
- Correct any errors in spelling, capitalization, or punctuation. If you are writing your report on a computer, use the spell-check feature.
- Use a thesaurus to find words that better describe your topic or that make your report more interesting.

Publish

- Make a neat, clean copy of your report.
- Include illustrations, maps, or other drawings to help explain your topic.

Rough draft

Allison Cesareo
Social Studies

A History of the Capitol Building in Sacramento, California

The capitol Building in Sacramento California is a very important place. The capitol building is the place where our state government works on making new laws. It is also where our government officials meet to talk about important issues happening in California. Many people do not know about the history of the capitol building because it was build before many of today's California citizens were born. There are many interesting historical facts about the Capital building in Sacramento, California. It is important to know ~~who made the decision to build it~~, where it was built, when it was built, and what happens in the capitol building today.

The capitol Building in Sacramento was not always the location of our state's government offices. ~~A long time ago~~, the capitol of California was located in San Jose ~~in the year 1849~~. In 1852 the capital of California moved from San jose to Vallejo, California. At that time, Vallejo was not a good place for the capitol building. The work on the building took a long time and it was very expensive. ~~Then~~, in 1853, the capital moved to Benicia where it remained until the city of Sacramento offered its courthouse as the new capitol building. In 1854, Sacramento's courthouse became the new statehouse. The building that the first session held its meeting in, is not the same building that serves as today's capitol building. When the capital first moved to Sacramento, members of the legislature were happy to have a place to meet that would stand as a symbol of the great State of California. But, soon after, the city began to grow. As the population increased, so did the need for a new Capitol building.

Final draft

Allison Cesareo
Social Studies

A History of the Capitol Building in Sacramento, California

The capitol building in Sacramento, California, is a very important place. The capitol building is the place where our government representatives make new laws. It is also where our government officials meet to talk about important issues happening in California. Many people do not know about the history of the capitol building because it was built before many of today's California citizens were born. There are many interesting historical facts about the capitol building, which is located in Sacramento, California. It is important to know where it was built, when it was built, and what happens in the capitol building today.

The capitol building in Sacramento was not always the location of our state's government offices. In 1849, the capitol of California was located in San Jose. In 1852, California's capital moved from San Jose to Vallejo, California. At that time, Vallejo was not a good place for the capitol building because work on the building took a long time and it was very expensive. In 1853, the capital of California moved to Benicia where it remained until the city of Sacramento offered its courthouse as the new capitol building. In 1854, Sacramento's courthouse became the new statehouse. The building in Sacramento that held the first state sesssion in 1854 is not the same building that served as today's California capitol building.

When the state capital was first moved to Sacramento, members of the legislature were happy to have a nice place to meet that would serve as a symbol of the great state of California. But, soon after, the city began to grow. As the population increased, so did the need for a new Capitol building.

Proofreading marks and their meanings	
Mark	**Meaning**
∧	Insert word.
∧,	Insert comma.
¶	Start a new paragraph.
≡ (cap)	Use capital letter.
~	Delete.
(lc)	Use lowercase letter.

Listening to Find Information

Sometimes in class you may be asked to give an oral presentation. Like a written report, the purpose of an oral presentation is to share information. These tips will help you prepare an oral presentation:

- Follow the steps described in Before Writing to gather and organize information.
- Use your notes to plan and organize your presentation. Include an introduction and a conclusion in your report.
- Prepare note cards that you can refer to as you speak.
- Prepare visuals such as illustrations, diagrams, maps, or other graphics to help listeners better understand your topic.
- Give your audience a controlling idea about your topic. A controlling idea is the main idea that you support with facts and details.
- Practice your presentation.
- Be sure to speak clearly and loudly enough. Keep your listeners interested in your report by using facial expressions and hand movements.

Biographical Dictionary

The Biographical Dictionary provides information about many of the people introduced in this book. Names are listed alphabetically by last name. Pronunciation guides are provided for hard-to-pronounce names. Following each name are the birth and death dates of that person. If the person is still alive, only the year of birth appears. A brief description of the person's main achievement is then given. The page number that follows tells where the main discussion of that person appears in this book. (You can check the Index for other page references.) Guide names at the top of each page help you quickly locate the name you need to find.

BIOGRAPHICAL DICTIONARY

A

Adams, Abigail *1744–1818* Massachusetts woman and wife of John Adams who supported the Patriot cause. p. 369

Adams, John *1735–1826* Massachusetts leader who served as a member of Congress and later as the second President of the United States. p. 349

Adams, Samuel *1722–1803* American Revolutionary leader who set up a Committee of Correspondence in Boston and helped form the Sons of Liberty. p. 328

Anthony, Susan B. *1820–1906* Womans-suffrage leader who worked for the equal rights of women. p. 574

Armistead, James *1760?–1830* African American who served as a spy for the Patriots during the Revolutionary War. p. 370

Arnold, Benedict *1741–1801* Continental Army officer who later became a traitor and worked for the British during the Revolutionary War. p. 381

Attucks, Crispus (A•tuhks) *1725?–1770* African American patriot who was killed during the Boston Massacre. p. 332

Austin, Stephen F. *1793–1836* American pioneer who started an American settlement in Texas. p. 551

B

Balboa, Vasco Núñez de (bahl•BOH•uh, NOON•yay day) *1475–1519* Spanish explorer who reached the Pacific Ocean in 1513. p. 123

Banneker, Benjamin *1731–1806* Free African American who helped survey the land for the new capital of the United States. p. 446

Barlow, Sam *1795–1867* American pathfinder who built the Barlow Road, which helped settlers traveling on the Oregon Trail. p. 543

Bates, Katharine Lee *1859–1929* American educator and poet who wrote "America the Beautiful." p. 469

Becknell, William *1796?–1865* American pioneer from Missouri who mapped the Santa Fe Trail. p. 544

Berkeley, Lord John *1607–1678* Proprietor, with Sir George Carteret, of the New Jersey Colony. p. 244

Bonaparte, Napoleon (BOH•nuh•part, nuh•POH•lee•yuhn) *1769–1821* French leader who sold Louisiana to the United States in 1803. p. 515

Boone, Daniel *1734–1820* American pathfinder who was one of the first settlers to cross the Appalachian Mountains. p. 502

Bowie, James *1796–1836* American soldier killed at the Battle of the Alamo during the Texas War for Independence. p. 552

Braddock, Edward *1695–1755* Commander of British forces during the early years of the French and Indian War. p. 321

Bradford, William *1590–1657* English Pilgrim settler and governor of the Plymouth Colony. p. 172

Brown, Linda *1943–* African American student whose family was among a group that challenged public school segregation in Kansas. R5

Burgoyne, John (ber•GOYN) *1722–1792* British general who lost the Battle of Saratoga during the Revolutionary War. p. 381

Burke, Edmund *1729–1797* British leader during the American Revolution who advised the British government to compromise with the colonists. p. 338

Caboto, Giovanni (kah•BOH•toh) *1450?–1499?* Italian explorer, also known as John Cabot, who explored Newfoundland for the English. p. 121

Cabrillo, Juan Rodriguez *1500?–1543* Spanish explorer who was the first European to explore the west coast of North America. p. 131

Calvert, Cecilius *1605–1675* Son of George Calvert; established the Maryland Colony. p. 273

Calvert, George *1580?–1632* Member of the Virginia Company and the first Lord Baltimore; received the original charter for Maryland. p. 273

Carteret, Sir George *c. 1610–1680* Proprietor, with Lord John Berkeley, of the New Jersey Colony. p. 244

Cartier, Jacques (kar•TYAY, ZHAHK) *1491–1557* French explorer who explored the eastern coast of what is now Canada. p. 177

Carver, George Washington *1864–1943* African American scientist who developed new products using peanuts, sweet potatoes, and soybeans. R4

Champlain, Samuel de (sham•PLAYN) *1567?–1635* French explorer who founded the Quebec settlement in what is now Canada. p. 177

Chapman, John *1774–1845* American pioneer, known as Johnny Appleseed, who planted trees in the Northwest Territory. p. 511

Charles II *1630–1685* English king who granted charters for the New Hampshire Colony and the Carolina Colony. p. 240

Chavez, Cesar *1927–1993* Mexican American labor leader and organizer of the United Farm Workers. p. 477

Clark, William *1770–1838* American explorer who aided Meriwether Lewis during an expedition through the Louisiana Purchase. p. 516

Columbus, Christopher *1451–1506* Italian explorer who sailed for Spain. He was searching for a western route to Asia but instead reached islands near the Americas. p. 114

Cornwallis, Charles *1738–1805* British general who surrendered at the Battle of Yorktown, resulting in victory for the Americans in the Revolutionary War. p. 392

Coronado, Francisco Vásquez de (kawr•oh•NAH•doh) *1510?–1554* Spanish explorer who led an expedition through southwestern North America searching for the Seven Cities of Gold. p. 131

Cortes, Hernando (kawr•TEZ) *1485–1547* Spanish conquistador who led a group that defeated the Aztecs in what is now Mexico. p. 130

Crockett, Davy *1786–1836* American pioneer who was killed while defending the Alamo. p. 552

D

Dart, Justin *1930–* Civil rights leader who helped promote the Americans with Disabilities Act (ADA). p. 477

Deganawida (deh•gahn•uh•WEE•duh) *1500s* Legendary Iroquois holy man who called for an end to the fighting among the Iroquois, which led to the formation of the Iroquois League. p. 77

de Soto, Hernando (day SOH•toh) *1496?–1542* Spanish explorer who led an expedition through southeastern North America. p. 132

Dickinson, John *1732–1808* Member of the Continental Congress who helped write the Articles of Confederation, which were adopted in 1781. p. 343

Douglass, Frederick *1817–1895* African American abolitionist who escaped from slavery and became a famous speaker and writer. p. 573

Drake, Daniel *1785–1852* Pioneer doctor and educator. p. 510

Du Bois, W. E. B. (doo•BOYS) *1868–1963* African American teacher and writer who helped found the National Association for the Advancement of Colored People (NAACP). R5

Edwards, Jonathan *1703–1758* Massachusetts minister who helped lead the Great Awakening. p. 252

Elizabeth I *1533–1603* Queen of England from 1558 to 1603. p. 161

Equiano, Olaudah (ek•wee•AH•noh, OH•luh•dah) *1750?–1797* African who was kidnapped and sold into slavery. He late wrote a book about his life and gave speeches against slavery. p. 289

Estevanico (es•tay•vahn•EE•koh) *1474?–1539* African enslaved person who went on an expedition in search of the Seven Cities of Gold. p. 130

Farragut, Jorge (FAIR•uh•guht, HAWR•hay) *1755–1817* Spanish-born soldier who fought in the Continental Army and Navy. p. 384

Ferdinand II *1452–1516* King of Spain who, with Queen Isabella, funded Christopher Columbus's voyages. He also helped lead the Spanish Reconquista. p. 115

Fink, Mike *1770?–1823?* Pioneer and sailor on the Mississippi. His adventures have been exaggerated in tall tales. p. 511

Forten, James *1766–1842* Free African American who, as a 14 year-old, volunteered to join the Continental Navy during the Revolutionary War. p. 370

Franklin, Benjamin *1706–1790* American leader and delegate to the Constitutional Convention. He was also a respected scientist and business leader. p. 254

Freeman, Elizabeth *1742?–1829* African American woman from Massachusetts who sued for, and won, her freedom in 1780. p. 397

Frémont, John C. *1813–1890* American pathfinder who made maps of the West. p. 541

Fulton, Robert *1765–1815* American engineer and inventor who created the first commercial steamboat. p. 504

G

Gadsden, James *1788–1858* United States minister to Mexico who arranged to buy parts of present-day New Mexico and Arizona from Mexico—known as the Gadsden Purchase. p. 561

Gage, Thomas *1721–1787* Governor of Massachusetts and a leader in the British army during the Revolutionary War. p. 344

Gálvez, Bernardo de (GAHL•ves) *1746–1786* Spanish governor of Louisiana who helped the Americans in the Revolutionary War. p. 384

George II *1683–1760* British king who chartered the Georgia Colony. p. 276

George III *1738–1820* King of Britain during the Revolutionary War. p. 326

Gerry, Elbridge *1744–1814* Massachusetts delegate to the Constitutional Convention. p. 443

Greeley, Horace *1811–1872* American journalist and political leader; publisher of a newspaper called the *New York Tribune*. p. 561

Greene, Nathanael *1742–1786* Continental Army officer who forced the British out of Georgia and the Carolinas. p. 391

Grenville, George *1712–1770* British prime minister who passed the Stamp Act in 1765. p. 327

Gutenberg, Johannes *1390–1468* German inventor of an improved printing press. p. 111

Hale, Nathan *1755–1776* American Revolutionary hero who was hanged by the British for spying for the Patriots. p. 388

Hamilton, Alexander *1755–1804* American leader in calling for the Constitutional Convention and winning support for it. He favored a strong national government. p. 446

Hancock, John *1737–1793* Leader of the Sons of Liberty in Massachusetts. p. 340

Henry *1394–1460* Henry the Navigator, prince of Portugal, who set up the first European school for training sailors in navigation. p. 112

Henry VIII *1491–1547* English King who started the Church of England. p. 171

Henry, Patrick *1736–1799* Virginia leader who spoke out against British policies and later opposed the Constitution. p. 333

Hiawatha (hy•uh•WAH•thuh) *1500s* Onondaga chief who persuaded other Iroquois tribes to form the Iroquois League. p. 77

Hidalgo, Miguel *1753–1811* Mexican priest who called for a revolution against Spain in 1810. p. 555

Hooker, Thomas *1586?–1647* Minister who helped form the Connecticut Colony. p. 218

Houston, Sam *1793–1863* President of the Republic of Texas and, later, governor of the state of Texas. p. 552

Hudson, Henry *1570?–1611* English explorer who claimed a large area of what is now New York for the Dutch. p. 142

Hutchinson, Anne Marbury *1591–1643* English colonist who was banished from the Massachusetts Colony because of her religious beliefs. p. 213

I

Isabella I *1451–1504* Queen of Spain who, with King Ferdinand, funded Christopher Columbus's voyages. She also helped lead the Spanish Reconquista. p. 115

J

Jackson, Andrew *1767–1845* Seventh President of the United States. He ordered the removal of many American Indian groups from their lands. p. 527

James I *1566–1625* King of England in the early 1600s. The James River and Jamestown were named for him. p. 162

James, the Duke of York *1633–1701?* English leader who took over New Netherland from the Dutch and set up New York and New Jersey. p. 243

Jay, John *1745–1829* American leader who became the first Chief Justice of the United States Supreme Court. p. 424

Jefferson, Thomas *1743–1826* Third President of the United States and the main writer of the Declaration of Independence. He also purchased Louisiana from France in 1803. p. 349

Joliet, Louis (zhohl•YAY, loo•EE) *1645–1700* French fur trader who with Jacques Marquette and five others explored North America for France. p. 180

Jones, John Paul *1747–1792* American naval officer during the Revolutionary War. p. 389

K

Key, Francis Scott *1779–1843* American lawyer and poet who wrote "The Star-Spangled Banner." p. 468

King, Martin Luther, Jr. *1929–1968* African American civil rights leader who worked to end unfair treatment of African Americans. He won the Nobel Peace Prize in 1964. p. 479

Kosciuszko, Tadeusz (kawsh•CHUSH•koh) *1746–1817* Polish soldier who helped the Americans in the Revolutionary War. p. 389

L

La Salle, Sieur de (luh•SAL) *1643–1687* French explorer who found the mouth of the Mississippi River and claimed the Mississippi Valley for France. p. 180

Lafayette, Marquis de (lah•fee•ET) *1757–1834* French soldier who fought alongside the Americans in the Revolutionary War. p. 378

Las Casas, Bartolomé de (lahs KAH•sahs, bar•toh•loh•MAY day) *1474–1566* Spanish missionary who spent much of his life trying to help American Indians. p. 156

Law, John *1671–1729* Scottish banker who was appointed proprietor of the Lousiana region. p. 182

Lee, Richard Henry *1732–1794* American Revolutionary leader who believed the colonies should become independent from Britain. p. 349

L'Enfant, Pierre Charles *1754–1825* French-born American engineer who designed the original layout of Washington, D.C. p. 446

Lewis, Meriwether *1774–1809* American explorer chosen by Thomas Jefferson to explore the lands of the Louisiana Purchase. p. 516

Lincoln, Abraham *1809–1865* Sixteenth President of the United States, leader of the Union in the Civil War, and signer of the Emancipation Proclamation. p. 509

Logan *1725?–1780?* Prominent American Indian leader and member of the Mingo tribe who fought against the Americans in the Revolutionary War. p. 371

Louis XIV *1638–1715* King of France from 1643 to 1715. p. 180

Ludington, Sybil *1761–1839* New York woman who, when she was 16, rode to warn American soldiers of a British attack in 1777. p. 369

Luther, Martin *1483–1546* German religious leader who began the Protestant Reformation by protesting the policies of the Catholic Church. p. 133

M

Madison, Dolley *1768–1849* Wife of James Madison and First Lady during the War of 1812. p. 524

Madison, James *1751–1836* Fourth President of the United States. He helped write the United States Constitution. p. 424

Magellan, Ferdinand (muh•JEH•luhn) *1480?–1521* Portuguese explorer who led an expedition to sail west to Asia in 1519. He died on the voyage, but one of his ships returned to Spain and became the first ship to sail around the world. p. 124

Marquette, Jacques (mahr•KET, ZHAHK) *1637–1675* Catholic missionary who knew several American Indian languages. With Louis Joliet, he explored North America for France. p. 180

Marshall, John *1755–1835* Chief Justice of the Supreme Court who ruled that the United States should protect the Cherokee Indians and their lands in Georgia. p. 528

Mason, George *1725–1792* Virginia delegate to the Constitutional Convention who later opposed the Constitution. p. 449

McCauley, Mary Ludwig Hays *1754?–1832* Pennsylvania woman who earned the nickname Molly Pitcher because she carried water to American soldiers during the Battle of Monmouth in the Revolutionary War. p. 389

Menéndez de Avilés, Pedro (may•NAYN•days day ah•vee•LAYS) *1519–1574* Spanish leader who helped build the settlement at St. Augustine, Florida, the first permanent European settlement in what is now the United States. p. 157

Metacomet *1639?–1676* Leader of the Wampanoag Indians. Called King Philip by the English. Led King Philip's War in New England. p. 211

Minuit, Peter *1580–1638* Dutch leader of New Netherland who purchased Manhattan Island. p. 178

Morris, Gouverneur (guh•ver•NIR) *1752–1816* American leader who helped write the United States Constitution. p. 433

Morse, Samuel F. B. *1791–1872* American inventor who developed the telegraph and the Morse code. p. 571

Motecuhzoma (moh•tay•kwah•SOH•mah) *1466–1520* Emperor of the Aztecs at the time of the arrival of the Spanish. p. 130

Mott, Lucretia *1793–1880* American reformer who helped organize the Seneca Falls Convention. p. 573

N

Navarro, José Antonio (nah•VAR•roh hoh•SAY ahn•TOH•nee•oh) *1795–1871* A signer of the Texas Declaration of Independence. p. 554

Niza, Marcos de (day NEE•sah) *1495–1558* Spanish priest who was sent on an expedition to find the Seven Cities of Gold. p. 130

BIOGRAPHICAL DICTIONARY

Oglethorpe, James *1696–1785* English leader who founded the Georgia Colony. p. 276

Osceola *1804–1838* Leader of the Seminole Indians in Florida. p. 527

Otis, James *1725–1783* Massachusetts colonist who spoke out against British taxes and called for "no taxation without representation." p. 327

P

Paine, Thomas *1737–1809* Author of *Common Sense,* in which he attacked King George III and called for a revolution to make the colonies independent. p. 348

Parker, John *1729–1775* Leader of the Minutemen in Massachusetts. p. 340

Paterson, William *1745–1806* New Jersey delegate to the Constitutional Convention who submitted the New Jersey Plan, under which each state would have one vote, regardless of population. p. 430

Penn, William *1644–1718* Founder of the Pennsylvania Colony. Penn was a Quaker who made Pennsylvania a refuge for settlers who wanted religious freedom. p. 245

Philip II *1527–1598* King of Spain and son of Emperor Charles V and Isabella of Portugal. p. 154

Pickersgill, Caroline *c. 1800–?* Helped her mother make the flag that inspired the writing of "The Star-Spangled Banner." p. 468

Pickersgill, Mary *1776–1857* Baltimore woman who, along with her daughter Caroline, sewed a flag for Ft. McHenry that later inspired "The Star-Spangled Banner." p. 468

Pike, Zebulon *1779–1813* American explorer who led an expedition to explore the southwestern part of the Louisiana Purchase. p. 518

Pinckney, Eliza Lucas *1722?–1793* South Carolina colonist who experimented with growing indigo plants. p. 291

Pitt, William *1708–1778* British leader of Parliament during the French and Indian War. p. 321

Pocahontas (poh•kuh•HAHN•tuhs) *1595–1617* Daughter of Chief Powhatan. She married English settler John Rolfe. p. 163

Polk, James K. *1795–1849* Eleventh President of the United States. Led the United States during the Mexican American War. p. 559

Polo, Marco *1254–1324* Italian explorer who spent many years in Asia in the late 1200s. He wrote a famous book about his travels. p. 110

Ponce de Leon, Juan (POHN•say day lay•OHN) *1460–1521* Spanish explorer who claimed what is now Florida for Spain in 1513. p. 129

Pontiac *1720?–1769?* Ottawa Indian chief who led a rebellion against the British to stop the loss of Indian hunting lands. p. 322

Powhatan (pow•uh•TAN) *1550–1521* Algonquian Indian chief who governed the area that later became the Virginia Colony. He was the fater of Pocahontas. p. 163

Putnam, Israel *1718–1790* American commander in the Revolutionary War who fought at the Battle of Bunker Hill. p. 344

Raleigh, Sir Walter (RAH•lee) *1554–1618* English explorer who helped set up England's first colony in North America, on Roanoke Island near North Carolina p. 161

Randolph, Edmund *1753–1813* Virginia delegate to the Constitutional Convention who wrote the Virginia Plan, which stated that the number of representatives a state would have in Congress should be based on the population of the state. p. 430

Revels, Hiram *1827?–1901* Minister from Mississippi who became the first African American elected to the United States Senate. p. R3

Revere, Paul *1735–1818* Massachusetts colonist who warned the Patriots that the British were marching toward Concord. p. 341

Rolfe, John *1585–1622* Jamestown settler who discovered a method of drying tobacco that led to great profits. p. 164

Ross, John *1790–1866* Chief of the Cherokee Nation. He fought to prevent the loss of the Cherokee lands. Led his people on the Trail of Tears. p. 529

S

Sacagawea (sa•kuh•juh•WEE•uh) *1786?–1812?* Shoshone woman who was an interpreter for the Lewis and Clark expedition. p. 516

Salem, Peter *1750?–1816* African American who fought alongside the Minutemen at Concord and at the Battle of Bunker Hill. p. 370

Samoset *1590?–1653?* American Indian who spoke English and who helped English settlers at Plymouth. p. 173

Sampson, Deborah *1760–1827* Massachusetts woman who disguised herself as a soldier to fight for the Americans in the Revolutionary War. p. 369

Santa Anna, Antonio López de *1794–1876* Mexican general who led his country during the Mexican American War. p. 551

Scott, Winfield *1786–1866* American general who took part in the Cherokee Removal. p. 530

Seguín, Juan (say•GEEN) *1806–1889* Tejano settler who helped defend the Alamo. p. 554

Sequoyah (sih•KWOY•uh) *1765?–1843* Cherokee leader who created a writing system for the Cherokee language. p. 528

Sevier, John *1745–1815* First governor of Tennessee. p. 512

Shays, Daniel *1747?–1825* Leader of a farmers' rebellion in Massachusetts in 1787. p. 423

Sherman, Roger *1721–1793* Connecticut delegate to the Constitutional Convention who worked out the compromise in which Congress would have two houses—one based on state population and one with two members from each state. p. 431

Slidell, John *1793–1871* American leader who tried to purchase New Mexico and California from Mexico. p. 560

Smith, Jedediah Strong *1799–1831* American pathfinder and trader; he traveled overland to California in the late 1820s. p. 541

Smith, John *1580–1631* English explorer and leader of the Jamestown settlement. p. 163

Stanton, Elizabeth Cady *1815–1902* American reformer who helped organize the Seneca Falls Convention and wrote the Declaration of Sentiments. p. 573

Steuben, Friedrich, Baron von (vahn STOO•buhn) *1730–1794* German soldier who helped train American troops during the Revolutionary War. p. 383

Stevenson, Robert Louis *1850–1894* Scottish author, poet, and essayist. His writings include *Kidnapped* and *Treasure Island.* p. 16

Stuyvesant, Peter (STY•vuh•suhnt) *1610?–1672* Dutch governor of New Netherland. p. 242

Sutter, John *1803–1880* American pioneer who owned the sawmill where gold was discovered in 1848, leading to the California gold rush. p. 562

T

Tamanend *1776–1857* Lenni Lenape Indian chief who established peaceful relations with William Penn and the Pennsylvania settlers. p. 247

Tapahonso, Luci *1953–* Navajo poet and author. p. 59

Taylor, Zachary *1784–1850* United States Army General during the Mexican American War; later became the twelfth President of the United States. p. 560

Tecumseh (tuh•KUHM•suh) *1768–1813* Shawnee leader of Indians in the Northwest Territory. He wanted to stop Americans from settling on Indian lands. p. 522

Tenskwatawa (ten•SKWAHT•uh•wah) *1768–1834* Shawnee leader and brother of Tecumseh. p. 523

Thayendanegea (thay•en•da•NEG•ah) *1742–1807* Known as Joseph Brant; Mohawk leader who helped the British during the Revolutionary War. p. 371

Tisquantum *1585?–1622* American Indian who spoke English and who helped English settlers at Plymouth. p. 173

Tubman, Harriet *1820–1913* African American abolitionist and former slave who helped lead others to freedom along the Underground Railroad. p. 573

Tyler, John *1790–1862* Tenth President of the United States. He asked for Texas to be admitted as a state. p. 553

BIOGRAPHICAL DICTIONARY

V

Verrazano, Giovanni (ver•uh•ZAH•noh) *1458?–1528?* Italian explorer who explored what is now New York Bay while searching for the Northwest Passage. p. 140

Vespucci, Amerigo (veh•SPOO•chee, uh•MAIR•ih•goh) *1454–1512* Italian explorer who made several voyages from Europe to South America. He determined that the land he reached was part of a new continent, which was later named America in his honor. p. 122

W

Warren, Earl *1891–1974* Chief Justice of the Supreme Court who wrote the 1954 decision against school segregation. p. 478

Warren, Mercy Otis *1728–1814* Massachusetts colonist who wrote poems and plays supporting the Patriot cause. p. 369

Washington, Booker T. *1856?–1915* African American educator who helped found the Tuskegee Institute in Alabama. R4

Washington, George *1732–1799* First President of the United States and leader of the Continental Army during the Revolutionary War. p. 320

Washington, Martha *1731–1802* Wife of George Washington. p. 369

Wheatley, Phillis *1753?–1784* African woman who was brought to Massachusetts and sold as an enslaved person. She later became a famous poet and supported the Patriots during the Revolutionary War. p. 347

Whitefield, George *1714–1770* English minister who helped lead the Great Awakening. p. 252

Whitman, Narcissa *1808–1847* American missionary and pioneer who, along with her husband Marcus, founded a mission in the Oregon Country. p. 542

Whitney, Eli *1765–1825* American inventor who developed the cotton gin and interchangeable parts. p. 569

Williams, Roger *1603?–1683* Founder of Providence in what is now Rhode Island. He was forced to leave the Massachusetts Colony because he disagreed with its leaders. p. 208

Wing, Yung *1828–1912* Chinese student who became the first Asian to graduate from an American university. He later served as a representative to the United States. p. 565

Winthrop, John *1588–1649* Puritan leader who served as governor of the Massachusetts Colony. p. 207

Y

York *1800s* Enslaved African American whose hunting and fishing skills contributed to the Lewis and Clark expedition. p. 516

Young, Brigham *1801–1877* Mormon leader who helped the Mormons settle in the Great Salt Lake valley. p. 545

Gazetteer

The Gazetteer is a geographical dictionary that can help you locate places discussed in this book. Place names are listed alphabetically. Hard-to-pronounce names are followed by pronunciation guides. A description of the place is then given. The absolute location, or latitude and longitude, of each city is provided. The page number that follows tells where each place is shown on a map. Guide words at the top of each page help you locate the place name you need to find.

A

Adena (uh•DEE•nuh) An ancient settlement of the Mound Builders; located in southern Ohio. (40°N, 81°W) p. 38

Africa Second-largest continent on Earth. p. I16

Alaska Range A mountain range in central Alaska. p. 16

Albany (AWL•buh•nee) The capital of New York; located in the eastern part of the state, on the Hudson River. (42°N, 74°W) p. 15

Aleutian Islands (uh•LOO•shuhn) A chain of volcanic islands, extending west from the Alaska Peninsula; located between the northern Pacific Ocean and the Bering Sea. p. 16

Allegheny River (a•luh•GAY•nee) A river in the northeastern United States; flows southwest to join the Monongahela River in Pennsylvania, forming the Ohio River. p. 413

Annapolis (uh•NA•puh•luhs) The capital of Maryland; located on Chesapeake Bay. (39°N, 76°W) p. 15

Antarctica One of Earth's seven continents. p. I16

Appalachian Mountains (a•puh•LAY•chuhn) A mountain system of eastern North America; extends from southeastern Quebec, Canada, to central Alabama. p. R29

Arctic Ocean One of Earth's four oceans; located north of the Arctic Circle. p. 25

Arkansas River A tributary of the Mississippi River, beginning in central Colorado and ending in southeastern Arkansas. p. 515

Asia Largest continent on Earth. p. I16

Atlanta The capital of Georgia; located in the northwest-central part of the state. (34°N, 84°W) p. 15

Atlantic Ocean Second-largest ocean; separates North and South America from Europe and Africa. p. 15

Augusta The capital of Maine; located in the eastern part of the state. (44°N, 70°W) p. 15

Austin The capital of Texas; located in the southern part of the state near the lower Colorado River. (30°N, 97°W) p. 15

Australia A country; smallest continent on Earth. p. I16

B

Baffin Bay A bay that connects the Arctic Ocean to the Atlantic Ocean; located between Canada and Greenland. p. 16

Baja California A peninsula in northwestern Mexico. p. 16

Baltimore A major seaport in Maryland; located on the upper end of Chesapeake Bay. (39°N, 77°W) p. 197

Baton Rouge (BA•tuhn• ROOZH) The capital of Louisiana; located in the southeastern part of the state. (30°N, 91°W) p. 15

Beaufort Sea (BOH•fert) That part of the Arctic Ocean between northeastern Alaska and the Canadian Arctic Islands. p. 16

Bering Strait A narrow strip of water; separates Asia from North America. p. 25

Bismarck The capital of North Dakota; located in the southern part of the state, near the Missouri River. (47°N, 101°W) p. 15

Black Sea A large inland sea between Europe and Asia. p. R21

Boise The capital of Idaho; located in the southern part of the state. (43°N, 116°W) p. 15

Bonampak An ancient settlement of the Mayan civilization; located in present-day southeastern Mexico. (16°N, 91°W) p. 38

Boston The capital of Massachusetts; located in the eastern part of the state. (42°N, 71°W) p. 15

Boston Harbor The western section of Massachusetts Bay; located in eastern Massachusetts; the city of Boston is located at its western end. p. 331

Brandywine A battlefield on Brandywine Creek in southeastern Pennsylvania; site of a major Revolutionary War battle in 1777. (40°N, 76°W) p. 390

Brooklyn Heights The site of a Revolutionary War battle. It is now part of the borough of Brooklyn. (41°N, 74°W) p. 386

Brooks Range A mountain range crossing northern Alaska. p. 16

Cahokia (kuh•HOH•kee•uh) A village in southwestern Illinois; site of an ancient settlement of the Mound Builders. (39°N, 90°W) p. 38

Cambridge A city in northeastern Massachusetts; located near Boston. (42°N, 71°W) p. 340

Camden A city in north-central South Carolina; site of a major Revolutionary War battle in 1780. (34°N, 81°W) p. 390

Canyon de Chelly (SHAY) A settlement of the Ancient Puebloans; located in present-day northeastern Arizona. p. 38

Cape Cod A peninsula of southeastern Massachusetts, extending into the Atlantic Ocean and enclosing Cape Cod Bay. (42°N, 70°W) p. 177

Cape Fear River A river in central and southeastern North Carolina; formed by the Deep and Haw Rivers; flows southeast into the Atlantic Ocean. p. 275

Carson City The capital of Nevada; located in the western part of the state near Lake Tahoe. (39°N, 120°W) p. 15

Cascade Range A mountain range in the western United States; a continuation of the Sierra Nevada; extends north from California to Washington. p. 16

Central Plains The eastern part of the Interior Plains. p. 16

Chaco Canyon (CHAH•koh) A settlement of the Ancient Puebloans; located in present-day northwestern New Mexico. (37°N, 108°W) p. 38

Charles River A river in eastern Massachusetts; separates Boston from Cambridge; flows into Boston Bay. p. 331

Charleston A city in southeastern South Carolina; a major port on the Atlantic Ocean; once known as Charles Town. (33°N, 80°W) p. 226

Charleston The capital of West Virginia; located in the southern part of the state. (38°N, 81°W) p. 15

Charlestown A city in Massachusetts; located on Boston Harbor between the mouths of the Charles and Mystic Rivers. p. 340

Charlotte The largest city in North Carolina; located in the south-central part of the state. (35°N, 81°W) p. 427

Cherokee Nation (CHAIR•uh•kee) A Native American nation located in present-day northern Georgia, eastern Alabama, southern Tennessee, and western North Carolina. p. 529

Chesapeake Bay An inlet of the Atlantic Ocean; surrounded by Virginia and Maryland. p. 275

Cheyenne (shy•AN) The capital of Wyoming; located in the southeastern part of the state. (41°N, 105°W) p. 15

Chicago A city in Illinois; located on Lake Michigan; the third-largest city in the United States. (42°N, 88°W) p. 493

Chickamauga (chik•uh•MAW•guh) A city in northwestern Georgia; site of a Civil War battle in 1863. (35°N, 85°W) p. 470

Cincinnati (sin•suh•NA•tee) A large city in southwestern Ohio; located on the Ohio River. (39°N, 84°W) p. 493

Coast Mountains A mountain range in western British Columbia and southern Alaska; a continuation of the Cascade Range. p. 16

Coast Ranges Mountains along the Pacific coast of North America, extending from Alaska to Baja California. p. 16

Coastal Plain Low, mostly flat land that stretches inland from the Atlantic Ocean and the Gulf of Mexico. p. 16

Colorado River A river in the southwestern United States; its basin extends from the Rocky Mountains to the Sierra Nevada; flows into the Gulf of California. p. 38

Columbia The capital of South Carolina; located in the center of the state. (34°N, 81°W) p. 15

Columbia River A river that begins in the Rocky Mountains in southwestern Canada, forms the Washington-Oregon border, and empties into the Pacific Ocean; supplies much of that area's hydroelectricity. p. 544

Columbus The capital of Ohio; located in the center of the state. (40°N, 83°W) p. 15

Compostela (kahm•poh•STEH•lah) A city in west-central Mexico. (21°N, 105°W) p. 131

Concord The capital of New Hampshire; located in the southern part of the state. (43°N, 71°W) p. 15

Concord A town in northeastern Massachusetts, near Boston; site of a major Revolutionary War battle in 1775. (42°N, 71°W) p. 340

Concord River A river in northeastern Massachusetts; formed by the junction of the Sudbury and Assabet Rivers; flows north into the Merrimack River at Lowell. p. 340

Connecticut River The longest river in New England; begins in New Hampshire and empties into Long Island Sound, New York. p. 390

Copán (koh•PAHN) An ancient settlement of the Mayan civilization; located in present-day Honduras, in northern Central America. (15°N, 89°W) p. 38

Cowpens A town in northwestern South Carolina; located near the site of a major Revolutionary War battle in 1781. (35°N, 82°W) p. 390

Crab Orchard An ancient settlement of the Mound Builders; located in present-day southern Illinois. (38°N, 89°W) p. 38

Cuba An island country in the Caribbean; the largest island of the West Indies. (22°N, 79°W) p. 16

D

Delaware Bay An inlet of the Atlantic Ocean; located between southern New Jersey and Delaware. p. 245

Denver The capital of Colorado; located in the northern part of the state. (40°N, 105°W) p. 15

Des Moines (dih•MOYN) The capital of Iowa; located in the southern part of the state. (41°N, 94°W) p. 15

Dickson An ancient settlement of the Mound Builders; located in present-day central Illinois. p. 38

Dover The capital of Delaware located in the central part of the state. (39°N, 76°W) p. 15

E

Edenton (EE•duhn•tuhn) A town in northeastern North Carolina; located on Albemarle Sound, near the mouth of the Chowan River. (36°N, 77°W) p. 275

Emerald Mound An ancient settlement of the Mound Builders; located in present-day southwestern Mississippi. (32°N, 91°W) p. 38

Eureka A city in northern California that developed as an arrival point for gold miners in the 1850s. p. 20

Europe One of Earth's seven continents. p. I16

F

Fall River A city and port in southeastern Massachusetts; in the nineteenth century it was one of the largest centers in the United States for cotton mills and textile machinery work. (41°N, 71°W) p. 225

Falmouth (FAL•muhth) A town in southwestern Maine. (44°N, 70°W) p. 413

Fort Atkinson A fort in southern Kansas; located on the Santa Fe Trail. (43°N, 89°W) p. 544

Fort Boise (BOY•zee) A fort in eastern Oregon; located on the Snake River and on the Oregon Trail. p. 544

Fort Bridger A present-day village in southwestern Wyoming; once an important station on the Oregon Trail. (41°N, 110°W) p. 544

Fort Crown Point A French fort; located in northeastern New York, on the shore of Lake Champlain. p. 321

Fort Cumberland A British fort located in northeastern West Virginia, on its border with Maryland. p. 321

Fort Duquesne (doo•KAYN) A French fort in present-day Pittsburgh, Pennsylvania; captured by the British and a new fort built and named Fort Pitt. (40°N, 80°W) p. 321

Fort Edward A British fort in New York, on the Hudson River; a present-day village. (43°N, 74°W) p. 321

Fort Frontenac (FRAHN•tuh•nak) A French fort once located on the site of present-day Kingston, Ontario, in southeastern Canada; destroyed by the British in 1758. (44°N, 76°W) p. 321

Fort Gibson A fort in eastern Oklahoma; end of the Trail of Tears. (36°N, 95°W) p. 529

Fort Hall A fort in southeastern Idaho; located on the Snake River, at a junction on the Oregon Trail. p. 544

Fort Laramie A fort in southeastern Wyoming; located on the Oregon Trail. (42°N, 105°W) p. 544

Fort Ligonier (lig•uh•NIR) A British fort; located in southern Pennsylvania near the Ohio River. p. 321

Fort Mandan A fort in present-day central North Dakota, on the Missouri River; site of a winter camp for the Lewis and Clark expedition. (48°N, 104°W) p. 515

Fort Necessity A British fort located in southwestern Pennsylvania; located in present-day Great Meadows. (38°N, 80°W) p. 321

Fort Niagara A fort located in western New York, at the mouth of the Niagara River. (43°N, 79°W) p. 321

GAZETTEER

Fort Oswego A British fort; located in western New York, on the shore of Lake Ontario. (43°N, 77°W) p. 321

Fort Ticonderoga (ty•kahn•der•OH•gah) A fort on Lake Champlain, in northeastern New York. (44°N, 73°W) p. 321

Fort Vancouver A fort in southwestern Washington, on the Columbia River; the western end of the Oregon Trail; present-day Vancouver. (45°N, 123°W) p. 544

Fort Walla Walla A fort in southeastern Washington; located on the Oregon Trail. (46°N, 118°W) p. 544

Fort William Henry A British fort located in eastern New York. (43°N, 74°W) p. 321

Frankfort The capital of Kentucky; located in the northern part of the state. (38°N, 85°W) p. 15

Gulf of Alaska A northern inlet of the Pacific Ocean; located between the Alaska Peninsula and the southwestern coast of Canada. p. 16

Gulf of California An inlet of the Pacific Ocean; located between Baja California and the northwestern coast of Mexico. p. 16

Gulf of Mexico An inlet of the Atlantic Ocean; located on the southeastern coast of North America; surrounded by the United States, Cuba, and Mexico. p. 16

Gulf of St. Lawrence A deep gulf on the Atlantic Ocean; located on the eastern coast of Canada, between Newfoundland island and the Canadian mainland. p. 145

Gulf Stream One of the strongest ocean currents in the world; the stream starts in the Gulf of Mexico, travels through the Straits of Florida, and flows north into the Atlantic Ocean. p. 129

G

Germantown A residential section of present-day Philadelphia, on Wissahickon Creek, in southeastern Pennsylvania; site of a major Revolutionary War battle in 1777. (40°N, 75°W) p. 390

Golconda (gahl•KAHN•duh) A city in the southeastern comer of Illinois; a point on the Trail of Tears. (37°N, 88°W) p. 529

Great Basin One of the driest parts of the United States; located in Nevada, Utah, California, Idaho, Wyoming, and Oregon; includes the Great Salt Lake Desert, the Mojave Desert, and Death Valley. p. 16

Great Lakes A chain of five lakes; located in central North America; the largest group of freshwater lakes in the world. p. 16

Great Plains A continental slope in western North America; borders the eastern base of the Rocky Mountains from Canada to New Mexico and Texas. p. 16

Great Salt Lake The largest lake in the Great Basin; located in northwestern Utah. p. 16

Great Wagon Road A former route used in the mid-1700s by colonists moving to settle in the backcountry. p. 277

Greenland The largest island on Earth; located in the northern Atlantic Ocean, east of Canada. p. 16

Guilford Courthouse (GIL•ferd) A location in north-central North Carolina, near Greensboro; site of a major Revolutionary War battle in 1781. (36°N, 80°W) p. 90

H

Harrisburg The capital of Pennsylvania; located in the southern part of the state, near the Susquehanna River. (40°N, 77°W) p. 15

Hartford The capital of Connecticut; located in the center of the state, near the Connecticut River. (42°N, 73°W) p. 15

Havana The capital of Cuba; located on the northwestern coast of the country. (23°N, 82°W) p. 131

Hawaiian Islands A state; a chain of volcanic and coral islands; located in the north-central Pacific Ocean. p. 15

Hawikuh (hah•wee•KOO) A former village in southwestern North America; located on the route of the Spanish explorer Coronado in present-day northwestern New Mexico. p. 131

Helena (HEH•luh•nuh) The capital of Montana; located in the western part of the state. (46°N, 112°W) p. 15

Hispaniola (ees•pah•NYOH•lah) An island in the West Indies made up of Haiti and the Dominican Republic; located in the Caribbean Sea between Cuba and Puerto Rico. p. 131

Honolulu The capital of Hawaii; located on the island of Oahu. (21°N, 158°W) p. 15

Hopewell An ancient settlement of the Mound Builders; located in present-day southern Ohio. (39°N, 83°W) p. 38

Hudson Bay An inland sea in east central Canada surrounded by the Northwest Territories, Manitoba, Ontario, and Quebec. p. 139

Hudson River A river in the northeastern United States beginning in upper New York and flowing into the Atlantic Ocean; named for the explorer Henry Hudson. p. 139

Independence A city in western Missouri; the starting point of the Oregon and Santa Fe Trails. (39°N, 94°W) p. 544

Indian Ocean One of Earth's four oceans; located east of Africa, south of Asia, west of Australia, and north of Antarctica. p. R19

Indianapolis (in•dee•uh•NE•puh•luhs) The capital of Indiana; located in the center of the state. (40°N, 86°W) p. 15

Interior Plains One of the major plains regions of the United States, located between the Appalachian Mountains and the Rocky Mountains; includes the Central Plains and the Great Plains. p. 16

Jackson The capital of Mississippi; located in the southern part of the state. (32°N, 90°W) p. 15

Jamaica (juh•MAY•kuh) An island country in the West Indies; south of Cuba. p. 131

Jamestown The first permanent English settlement in the Americas; located in eastern Virginia, on the shore of the James River. (37°N, 76°W) p. 275

Jefferson City The capital of Missouri; located in the center of the state, near the Missouri River. (38°N, 92°W) p. 15

Juneau (JOO•noh) The capital of Alaska; located in the southeastern part of the state. (55°N, 120°W) p. 15

Kaskaskia (kas•KAS•kee•uh) A village in southwestern Illinois; site of a major Revolutionary War battle in 1778. (38°N, 90°W) p. 390

Kennebec River (KEN•uh•bek) A river in west central and southern Maine; flows south from Moosehead Lake to the Atlantic Ocean. p. 210

Kings Mountain A ridge in northern South Carolina and southern North Carolina; site of a Revolutionary War battle in 1780. p. 390

La Venta An ancient settlement of the Olmec; located in present-day southern Mexico, on an island near the Tonalá River. (18°N, 94°W) p. 38

Labrador A peninsula in northeastern North America; once known as Markland. p. 16

Labrador Sea Located south of Greenland and northeast of North America. p. 16

Lake Champlain (sham•PLAYN) A lake between New York and Vermont. p. 139

Lake Erie The fourth-largest of the Great Lakes; borders Canada and the United States. p. 139

Lake Huron The second-largest of the Great Lakes; borders Canada and the United States. p. 139

Lake Michigan The third-largest of the Great Lakes; borders Michigan, Illinois, Indiana, and Wisconsin. p. 139

Lake Okeechobee (oh•kuh•CHOH•bee) A large lake in south Florida. p. R26

Lake Ontario The smallest of the Great Lakes; borders Canada and the United States. p. 139

Lake Superior The largest of the Great Lakes; borders Canada and the United States. p. 139

Lake Tahoe A lake on the California-Nevada border. p. R26

Lancaster A city in southeastern Pennsylvania. (40°N, 76°W) p. 245

Lansing The capital of Michigan; located in the southern part of the state. (43°N, 85°W) p. 15

Lexington A town in northeastern Massachusetts; site of the first battle of the Revolutionary War in 1775. (42°N, 71°W) p. 340

Lincoln The capital of Nebraska; located in the southeastern part of the state. (41°N, 97°W) p. 15

Little Rock The capital of Arkansas; located in the center of the state, near the Arkansas River. (35°N, 92°W) p. 15

Long Island An island located east of New York City and south of Connecticut; lies between Long Island Sound and the Atlantic Ocean. p. 386

Los Adaes Site of a mission of New Spain; located in present-day eastern Texas. p. 157

Los Angeles The largest city in California, located next to the Pacific Ocean, founded by Spanish settlers in 1781. (34°N, 119°W) p. 26

Louisiana Purchase A territory in the west-central United States; it doubled the size of the nation when it was purchased from France in 1803; extended from the Mississippi River to the Rocky Mountains and from the Gulf of Mexico to Canada. p. 515

Macon (MAY•kuhn) A city in central Georgia; located on the Ocmulgee River. (33°N, 84°W) p. 570

Madison The capital of Wisconsin; located in the southern part of the state. (43°N, 89°W) p. 15

Marshall Gold Discovery State Historic Park A park in eastern California located at the site where James Marshall discovered gold in 1848; setting of the California gold rush of 1849. p. 562

Massachusetts Bay An inlet of the Atlantic Ocean; on the eastern coast of Massachusetts; extends from Cape Ann to Cape Cod. p. 210

Medford A city in northeastern Massachusetts, north of Boston. (42°N, 71°W) p. 340

Mediterranean Sea (meh•duh•tuh•RAY•nee•uhn) An inland sea, enclosed by Europe on the west and north, Asia on the east, and Africa on the south. p. R20

Menotomy Town in northeastern Massachusetts where Minutemen attacked British forces after the Battles of Lexington and Concord. p. 340

Merced A city in central California located near the Merced River. p. 20

Merrimack River A river in southern New Hampshire and northeastern Massachusetts; empties into the Atlantic Ocean. p. 210

Mesa Verde (MAY•suh VAIR•day) A settlement of the Ancient Puebloans; located in present-day southwestern Colorado. (37°N, 108°W) p. 38

Mexico City A city on the southern edge of the Central Plateau of Mexico; the present-day capital of Mexico. (19°N, 99°W) p. 157

Mississippi River A river in the United States; located centrally, its source is Lake Itasca in Minnesota; flows south into the Gulf of Mexico. p. 16

Missouri River A tributary of the Mississippi River; located centrally, it begins in Montana and ends at St. Louis, Missouri. p. 515

Montgomery The capital of Alabama; located in the southern part of the state. (32°N, 86°W) p. 15

Montpelier (mahnt•PEEL•yer) The capital of Vermont; located in the northern part of the state (44°N, 72°W) p. 15

Montreal The second-largest city in present-day Canada; located in southern Quebec, on Mimtreat Island on the north bank of the St. Lawrence River. (46°N, 73°W). p. R32

Morristown A town in northern New Jersey; a campsite for the Continental Army during the Revolutionary War. (41°N, 74°W) p. 245

Moundville An ancient settlement of the Mound Builders; located in present-day central Alabama. (33°N, 88°W) p. 38

Murfreesboro A city in central Tennessee; located on the west fork of the Stones River; a site on the Trail of Tears. (36°N, 86°W) p. 529

N

Narragansett Bay An inlet of the Atlantic Ocean in southeastern Rhode Island. p. 210

Nashville The capital of Tennessee; located in the center of the state near the Cumberland River. (36°N, 87°W) p. 15

Natchitoches (NAK•uh•tahsh) The first settlement in present-day Louisiana; located in the northwest-central part of the state. (32°N, 93°W) p. 515

Nauvoo (naw•VOO) A city in western Illinois; located on the Mississippi River; beginning of the Mormon Trail. (41°N, 91°W) p. 548

New Amsterdam A Dutch city on Manhattan Island; later became New York City. (41°N, 74°W) p. 211

New Bedford A city in southeastern Massachusetts founded by English settlers in 1634; an early shipping and whaling center. (41°N, 70°W) p. 225

New Bern A city and port in southeastern North Carolina. (35°N, 77°W) p. 197

New Echota (ih•KOHT•uh) An American Indian town in northwestern Georgia; chosen as the capital of the Cherokee Nation in 1819. (34°N, 85°W) p. 529

New France The possessions of France in North America from 1534 to 1763; included Canada, the Great Lakes region, and Louisiana. p. 319

New Guinea (GIH•nee) An island of the eastern Malay Archipelago; located in the western Pacific Ocean, north of Australia. p R21

New Haven A city in southern Connecticut; located on New Haven Harbor. (41°N, 73°W) p. 210

New London A city in southeastern Connecticut; located on Long Island Sound at the mouth of the Thames River. (41°N, 72°W) p. 297

New Orleans The largest city in Louisiana; a major port located between the Mississippi River and Lake Pontchartrain. (30°N, 90°W) p. 182

New Spain The former Spanish possessions from 1535 to 1821; included the southwestern United States, Mexico, Central America north of Panama, the West Indies, and the Philippines. p. 157

Newfoundland An island off the eastern coast of Canada; located north of Nova Scotia and a part of Newfoundland and Laborador province. p. 145

Newport A city on the southern end of Rhode Island; located at the mouth of Narragansett Bay. (41°N, 71°W) p. 225

Newton A city in south-central Kansas. (38°N, 97°W) p. 488

Norfolk (NAWR•fawk) A city in southeastern Virginia; located on the Elizabeth River. (37°N, 76°W) p. 226

North America One of Earth's seven continents. p. I16

North Pole The northernmost point on Earth. p. R20

Nova Scotia (NOH•vuh SKOH•shuh) A province of Canada; located in eastern Canada on a peninsula. p. R32

Ocmulgee (ohk•MUHL•gee) An ancient settlement of the Mound Builders; located in present-day central Georgia. p. 38

Ocmulgee River A river in central Georgia; formed by the junction of the Yellow and South Rivers; flows south to join the Altamaha River. p. 390

Oconee River (oh•KOH•nee) A river in central Georgia; flows south and southeast to join the Ocmulgee and form the Altamaha River. p. 275

Ogallala (oh•guh•LAH•luh) A city in western Nebraska on the South Platte River. (41°N, 102°W) p. 546

Ohio River A tributary of the Mississippi River, beginning in Pittsburgh, Pennsylvania, and ending at Cairo, Illinois. p. 399

Oklahoma City The capital of Oklahoma; located in the center of the state, near the Canadian River. (35°N, 98°W) p. 15

Old Spanish Trail Part of the Santa Fe Trail that linked Santa Fe to Los Angeles. p. 544

Olympia (oh•LIM•pee•uh) The capital of Washington; located in the western part of the state near Puget Sound. (47°N, 123°W) p. 15

Omaha (OH•muh•hah) The largest city in Nebraska; located in the eastern part of the state, on the Missouri River. (41°N, 96°W) p. 544

Oregon Country A former region in western North America; located between the Pacific coast and the Rocky Mountains, from the northern border of California to Alaska. p. 515

Oregon Trail A former route to the Oregon Country; extended from the Missouri River northwest to the Columbia River in Oregon. p. 544

Pacific Ocean Largest body of water on Earth; extending from Arctic Circle to Antarctic regions, separating North and South America from Australia and Asia. p. 25

Palenque (pah•LENG•kay) An ancient settlement of Mayan civilization; located in present-day southern Mexico. (18°N, 92°W) p. 38

Pee Dee River A river in North Carolina and South Carolina; forms where the Yadkin and Uharie Rivers meet; empties into Winyah Bay. p. 275

Philadelphia A city in southeastern Pennsylvania, on the Delaware River; a major United States port. (40°N, 75°W) p. 245

Philippine Islands A group of more than 7,000 islands off the coast of southeastern Asia, making up the country of the Philippines. p. R21

Phoenix The capital of Arizona; located in the southern part of the state. (33°N, 112°W) p. 15

Piedmont Area of high land on the eastern side of the Appalachian Mountains. p. 16

Pierre (PIR) The capital of South Dakota; located in the center of the state, near the Missouri River. (44°N, 100°W) p. 15

Pikes Peak A mountain in east-central Colorado; part of the Rocky Mountains. p. 515

Platte River (PLAT) A river in central Nebraska; flows east into the Missouri River below Omaha. p. 515

Plymouth A town in southeastern Massachusetts, on Plymouth Bay; site of the first settlement built by the Pilgrims, who sailed on the *Mayflower*. (42°N, 71°W) p. 210

Portland A port city in southwestern Maine; located on Casco Bay. (44°N, 70°W) p. 427

Portsmouth (PAWRT•smuhth) A port city in southeastern New Hampshire; located at the mouth of the Piscataqua River. (43°N, 71°W) p. 197

Potomac River (puh•TOH•muhk) A river on the Coastal Plain of the United States; begins in West Virginia and flows into Chesapeake Bay; Washington, D.C., is located on this river. p. 275

Princeton A township in west-central New Jersey; site of a major Revolutionary War battle. (40°N, 75°W) p. 390

Providence (PRAH•vuh•duhns) The capital of Rhode Island; located in the northern part of the state, near the Providence River. (42°N, 71°W) p. 15

Pueblo Bonito (PWEH•bloh boh•NEE•toh) Largest of the prehistoric pueblo ruins; located in Chaco Canyon. p. 38

Puerto Rico An island of the West Indies; located southeast of Florida; a commonwealth of the United States. p. R18

Q

Quebec (kwih•BEK) The capital of the province of Quebec, Canada; located on the northern side of the St. Lawrence River; the first successful French settlement in the Americas; established in 1608. (47°N, 71°W) p. R32

R

Raleigh (RAH•lee) The capital of North Carolina; located in the eastern part of the state. (36°N, 79°W) p. 15

Red River A tributary of the Mississippi River; rises in eastern New Mexico, flows across Louisiana and into the Mississippi River; forms much of the Texas-Oklahoma border. p. 515

Richmond The capital of Virginia; a port city located in the east-central part of the state. (38°N, 77°W) p. 15

Rio Grande A river in southwestern North America; it begins in Colorado and flows into the Gulf of Mexico; forms the border between Texas and Mexico. p. 515

Roanoke River A river in southern Virginia and northeastern North Carolina; flows east and southeast across the North Carolina border and into Albemarle Sound. p. 277

Rocky Mountains A range of mountains in the western United States and Canada, extending from Alaska to New Mexico; these mountains divide rivers that flow east from those that flow west. p. 16

S

Sacramento (sa•kruh•MEN•toh) The capital of California; located in the northern part of the state, near the Sacramento River. (39°N, 122°W) p. 15

Sacramento River A river in northwestern California; rises near Mt. Shasta and flows south into Suisun Bay. p. 544

Salem (SAY•luhm) The capital of Oregon; located in the western part of the state. (45°N, 123°W) p. 15

Salt Lake City The capital of Utah; located in the northern part of the state near the Great Salt Lake. (41°N, 112°W) p. 15

San Antonio A city in south-central Texas; located on the San Antonio River; site of the Alamo. (29°N, 98°W) p. 492

San Diego A large port city in southern California; located on San Diego Bay. (33°N, 117°W) p. 57

San Francisco The second-largest city in California; located in the northern part of San Francisco Bay. (38°N, 123°W) p. 157

San Gabriel A city in southwestern California, eight miles east of Los Angeles; it began as a mission in 1771. (34°N, 118°W) p. 512

San Lorenzo An ancient settlement of the Olmec; located in present-day southern Mexico. (29°N, 113°W) p. 38

San Miguel Island One of the five islands off the coast of southern California that make up Channel Islands National Park. p. 26

San Salvador One of the islands in the southern Bahamas; Christopher Columbus landed there in 1492. p. 124

Santa Barbara A coastal city about 80 miles north of Los Angeles; former site of a Spanish mission. (34°N, 120°W) p. 26

Santa Fe (SAN•tah FAY) The capital of New Mexico located in the north-central part of the state. (35°N, 106°W) p. 15

Santa Fe Trail A former commercial route to the western United States; extended from western Missouri to Santa Fe, in central New Mexico. p. 544

Santee River A river in southeast-central South Carolina; formed by the junction of the Congaree and Wateree Rivers; flows southeast into the Atlantic Ocean. p. 275

Saratoga A village on the western bank of the Hudson River in eastern New York; site of a major Revolutionary War battle in 1777; present-day Schuylerville. (43°N, 74°W) p. 390

Savannah The oldest city in Georgia; located in the southeastern part of the state, near the Savannah River. (32°N, 81°W) p. 275

Savannah River A river that forms the border between Georgia and South Carolina; flows into the Atlantic Ocean at Savannah, Georgia. p. 275

Serpent Mound An ancient settlement of the Mound Builders; located in present-day southern Ohio. (39°N, 83°W) p. 38

Sierra Madre Occidental (ahk•sih•den•TAHL) A mountain range in western Mexico, running parallel to the Pacific coast. p. 16

Sierra Madre Oriental (awr•ee•en•TAHL) A mountain range in eastern Mexico, running parallel to the coast along the Gulf of Mexico. p. 16

Sierra Nevada A mountain range in eastern California that runs parallel to the Coast Ranges. p. 16

Snake River A river that begins in the Rocky Mountains and flows west into the Pacific Ocean; part of the Oregon Trail ran along this river. p. 515

South America One of Earth's seven continents. p. I16

South Pass A pass in southwestern Wyoming; crosses the Continental Divide; part of the Oregon Trail. p. 544

South Pole The southernmost point on Earth. p. R20

Spiro An ancient settlement of the Mound Builders; located in eastern Oklahoma. (35°N, 95°W) p. 38

Springfield The capital of Illinois; located in the center of the state. (40°N, 90°W) p. 15

Springfield A city in southwestern Missouri; a point on the Trail of Tears. (37°N, 93°W) p. 529

St. Augustine (AW•guh•steen) A city on the coast of northeastern Florida; the oldest city founded by Europeans in the United States. (30°N, 81°W) p. 131

St. Lawrence River A river in northeastern North America; begins at Lake Ontario and flows into the Atlantic Ocean; forms part of the border between the United States and Canada. p. 139

St. Louis A major port city in east-central Missouri; known as the Gateway to the West. (38°N, 90°W) p. 512

St. Paul The capital of Minnesota; located in the southeastern part of the state near the Mississippi River. (45°N, 93°W) p. 15

Susquehanna River (suhs•kwuh•HA•nuh) A river in Maryland, Pennsylvania, and central New York; rises in Otsego Lake, New York, and empties into northern Chesapeake Bay. p. 390

Tallahassee (ta•luh•HA•see) The capital of Florida; located in the northwestern part of the state. (30°N, 84°W) p. 15

Tenochtitlán (tay•nohch•tee•LAHN) The ancient capital of the Aztec Empire, now the site of Mexico City. (19°N, 99°W) p. 131

Tikal (tih•KAHL) An ancient settlement of the Mayan civilization; located in present-day Guatemala, in Central America. (17°N, 89°W) p. 38

Topeka The capital of Kansas; located in the northeastern part of the state. (39°N, 96°W) p. 15

Trail of Tears A trail that was the result of the Indian Removal Act of 1830; extended from the Cherokee Nation to Fort Gibson, in the Indian Territory. p. 529

Trenton The capital of New Jersey located in the west central part of the state. (40°N, 74°W) p. 15

Tres Zapotes (TRAYS sah•POH•tays) An ancient settlement of the Olmec; located in southern Mexico. (18°N, 95°W) p. 38

Tucson (TOO•sahn) A city in southern Arizona; located on the Santa Cruz River. (32°N, 111°W) p. 157

Turtle Mound An ancient settlement of the Mound Builders; located on the present-day east-central coast of Florida. (29°N, 81°W) p. 38

Valley Forge A site in southeastern Pennsylvania, where the Continental Army camped during the winter of 1777. (40°N, 77°W) p. 390

Vincennes (vihn•SENZ) A town in southwestern Indiana; site of a Revolutionary War battle in 1779. (39°N, 88°W) p. 390

Wabash River (WAW•bash) A river in western Ohio and Indiana; flows west and south to the Ohio River, to form part of the Indiana-Illinois border. p. 390

Washington, D.C. The capital of the United States; located between Maryland and Virginia, on the Potomac River in a special district that is not part of any state. (39°N, 77°W) p. 15

West Indies The islands enclosing the Caribbean Sea, stretching from Florida in North America to Venezuela in South America. p. R20

West Point A United States military post since the Revolutionary War; located in southeastern New York on the western side of the Hudson River. p. 390

Williamsburg A city in southeastern Virginia; located on a peninsula between the James and York Rivers; capital of the Virginia Colony. p. 275

Wilmington A coastal city in southeastern North Carolina; located along the Cape Fear River. p. 275

Yellowstone River A river in northwestern Wyoming, southeastern Montana, and northwestern North Dakota; flows northeast to the Missouri River. p. 515

Yorktown A small town in southeastern Virginia; located on Chesapeake Bay; site of the last major Revolutionary War battle in 1781. (37°N, 76°W) p. 390

Yucatan Peninsula A peninsula in southeastern Mexico and northeastern Central America. p. 16

GAZETTEER

Glossary

The Glossary contains important history and social science words and their definitions, listed in alphabetical order. Each word is respelled as it would be in a dictionary. When you see the mark ´ after a syllable, pronounce that syllable with more force. The page number at the end of the definition tells where the word is first used in this book. Guide words at the top of each page help you quickly locate the word you need to find.

add, āce, câre, pälm; end, ēqual; it, īce; odd, ōpen, ôrder; to͝ok, po͞ol; up, bûrn; yo͞o as *u* in *fuse*; oil; pout; ə as *a* in *above*, *e* in *sicken*, *i* in *possible*, *o* in *melon*, *u* in *circus*; check; ring; thin; this; zh as in *vision*

A

abolish (ə•bä´lish) To end. p. 397

abolitionist (a•bə•li´shən•ist) A person who wanted to end slavery. p. 397

absolute location (ab´sə•lo͞ot lō•kā´shən) The exact location of a place on Earth, or its lines of latitude and longitude. p. 22

adapt (ə•dapt´) To adjust ways of living to land and resources. p. I15, 53

adobe (ə•dō´bē) A brick made of sun-dried clay and straw. p. 53

agriculture (a´grə•kul•chər) Farming. p. 30

alliance (ə•lī´ənts) A formal agreement between countries or groups of people. p. 320

ally (a´lī) A partner. p. 180

amendment (ə•mend´mənt) An addition or change to the Constitution. p. 439

ancestor (an´ses•tər) An early family member. p. 25

annex (ə•neks´) To add on. p. 553

Anti-Federalist (an´tī•fe´də•rə•list) A citizen who was against ratification of the Constitution. p. 444

apprentice (ə•pren´təs) A person who learns a trade by living with the family of a skilled worker and training for several years. p. 260

arsenal (är´sə•nəl) A place used for storing weapons. p. 423

Articles of Confederation (är´ti•kəls uv kən•fe•də•rā´shən) The United States' first plan of government. p. 352

artifact (är´tə•fakt) An object made by early people. p. 26

artisan (är´tə•zən) A craft worker. p. 260

assimilate (ə•si´mə•lāt) To adopt the culture traits of a population or group. p. 528

B

backcountry (bak´kən•trē) The land between the Coastal Plain and the Appalachian Mountains. p. 277

barter (bär´tər) To exchange goods, usually without using money. p. 64

benefit (be´nə•fit) Something that is gained. p. 114

bill (bil) An idea for a new law. p. 431

blockade (blä•kād´) To use warships to prevent other ships from entering or leaving a harbor. p. 338

borderlands (bôr´dər•landz) Areas of land on or near the borders between countries, colonies, or regions that serve as barriers. p. 157

boycott (boi´kät) To refuse to buy or use goods or services. p. 329

broker (brō´kər) A person who is paid to buy and sell for someone else. p. 292

budget (bu´jət) A plan for spending money. p. 327

C

Cabinet (ka´bə•nit) A group of the President's most important advisers. p. 446

campaign (kam•pān´) A campaign is a series of military operations carried out for a certain goal. p. 381

canal (kə•nal´) A waterway dug across land. p. 504

cardinal direction (kärd´nəl də•rek´shən) One of the main directions: north, south, east, or west. p. I21

cash crop (kash krop) A crop that people raise to sell rather than to use themselves. p. 164

GLOSSARY

century (sen´chə•rē) A period of 100 years. p. 32

ceremony (ser´ə•mō•nē) A series of actions performed during a special event. p. 55

cession (se´shən) Something that is given up, such as land. p. 561

character traits (kâr´ik•tər trāts) A person's qualities and ways of acting. p. I5

charter (chär´tər) An official paper in which certain rights are given by a government to a person, group, or business. p. 207

checks and balances (cheks and ba´lən•səz) A system that gives each branch of government different powers so that each branch can watch over the authority of the others. p. 459

chronology (krə•nä´lə•jē) Time order. p. I3

circle graph (sûr´kəl graf) A round chart that can be divided into pieces, or parts, often referred to as a pie graph. p. 280

civil rights (si´vəl rīts) The rights of citizens to equal treatment under the law. p. 476

civilization (si•və•lə•zā´shən) A culture that usually has cities with well-developed forms of government, religion, and learning. p. 37

clan (klan) A group of families that are related to one another. p. 62

class (klas) A group of people who are alike in some way. Classes are treated with different amounts of respect in a society. p. 38

classify (kla´sə•fī) To group together. p. 88

climate (klī´mət) The kind of weather a place has most often, year after year. p. 16

coerce (kō•ərs´) To bring about by force or threat. p. 338

colony (kä´lə•nē) A land ruled by a distant country. p. 155

commander in chief (kə•man´dər in chēf´) A person who is in control of all the armed forces of a nation. p. 343

commerce (kä´mərs) Trade. p. 422

Committees of Correspondence (kə•mi´tēs uv kôr•ə•spän´dənts) Members of a committee who would write letters that would be sent to the other colonies, keeping the colonies informed and united in a common cause. p. 328

common (kä´mən) An open area where sheep and cattle graze, village green. p. 216

compact (käm´pakt) An agreement. p. 172

compass rose (kum´pəs rōz) A circular direction marker on a map. p. I21

compromise (käm′prə•mīz) To give up some of what you want in order to reach an agreement. p. 80

confederation (kən•fe•də•rā´shən) A loosely united group of governments working together. p. 77

congress (kän´grəs) A formal meeting of government representatives who have the authority to make laws. p. 339

conquistador (kän•kēs´tə•dôr) Any of the Spanish conquerors in the Americas during the early 1500s. p. 129

consent (kən•sent´) Agreement. p. 209

consequence (kän´sə•kwens) Something that happens because of an action. p. 520

constitution (kän•stə•tōō´shən) A written plan of government. p. 275

continent (kän´tə•nənt) A large land mass. p. I16

contour line (kän´tōōr līn) A line on a drawing or map that connects all points of equal elevation. p. 144

convention (kən•ven´shən) An important meeting. p. 422

cost (kost) The effort made to achieve or gain something p. 114

cotton gin (kä´tən jin) A machine that removed seeds from cotton fibers much more quickly than workers could by hand. p. 569

council (koun´sel) A group that makes laws. p. 72

Counter-Reformation (koun´tər re•fər•mā´shən) A time when the Catholic church banned books that were against its teachings and used its courts to punish people who protested Catholic rules and beliefs. p. 133

creed (krēd) A system of beliefs. p. 467

cultural region (kul´chə•rəl rē´jən) An area in which people share some ways of life. p. 42

culture (kul´chər) A way of life. p. 31

custom (kus´təm) A practice or usage common to a particular group, place, or individual. p. 37

D

debtor (de´tər) A person who was put in prison for owing money. p. 276

decade (de´kād) A period of ten years. p. 32

declaration (de•klə•rā´shən) An official statement. p. 349

delegate (de′li•gət) A representative. p. 320

democracy (di•mä´krə•sē) A form of government in which the people have power to make choices about their lives and government, either directly or through representation. p. 458

dissent (di•sent´) A difference of opinion. p. 208

diversity (də•vûr'sə•tē) Differences, such as those among different peoples. p. 251

division of labor (də•vi´zhən uv lā´bər) Work that is divided so that each worker does a small part of a larger job. p. 54

documentary source (dä•kyə•men´tə•rē sōrs´) An item produced at the time an event takes place, often by a person who experienced the event. p. 334

due process of law (do͞o prä´ses uv lô) The principle that guarantees the right to a fair public trial. p. 445

dugout (dug´out) A boat made from a large, hollowed-out log. p. 61

E

earthwork (ûrth´wərk) A wall made of dirt or stone. p. 344

economy (i•kä´nə•mē) The way people of a state, region, or country use resources to meet their needs. p. 63

electoral college (i•lek´tə•rəl kä´lij) A group of officials chosen by citizens to vote for the President and Vice President. p. 437

elevation (e•lə•vā´shən) The height of land in relation to sea level. p. 144

empire (em'pīr) A collection of lands ruled by the nation that conquered them. p. 113

encroach (in•krōch') To move onto without asking permission. p. 523

enlist (in•list´) To join or to sign up. p. 379

entrepreneur (än•trə•prə•nûr´) A person who sets up and runs a business. p. 114

environment (en•vī´rən•mənt) Surroundings. p. 18

equator (i•kwā´tər) The imaginary line that divides Earth into the Northern and Southern Hemispheres. p. I16

established church (is•ta´blisht chûrch) A church supported by the government. p. 165

ethnic group (eth´nik gro͞op) A group made up of people from the same country, people of the same race, or people with a common way of life. p. 280

evidence (e´və•dəns) Proof. p. I2

executive branch (ig•ze´kyə•tiv branch) A branch of government whose main job is to see that laws passed by the legislative branch are carried out. p. 437

expedition (ek•spə•di´shən) A journey. p. 112

expel (ik•spel´) To force to leave. p. 208

export (ek´spôrt) A product that leaves a country. p. 226

F

fact (fakt) A statement that can be checked and proved to be true. p. 136

federal system (fe´də•rəl sis´təm) A system of government in which the authority to govern is shared by the central and state governments. p. 428

Federalist (fe´də•rə•list) After the American Revolution, a citizen who wanted a strong national government and was in favor of ratifying the Constitution. p. 444

flatboat (flat´bōt) A large boat with a flat bottom and square ends. p. 504

flow chart (flō chärt) A diagram that shows the order in which things happen. p. 440

ford (fōrd) To cross a body of water. p. 542

forty-niner (fôr•tē•nī´nər) A gold seeker who arrived in California in 1849. p. 562

free market (frē mär´kət) An economic system where people are free to choose the goods and services they buy and produce. p. 223

free state (frē´ stāt) A state that did not allow slavery before the Civil War. p. 553

frontier (frən•tir´) The land that lies beyond settled areas. p. 212

G

generation (je•nə•rā´shən) The average time between the birth of parents and the birth of their children. p. 27

gold rush (gōld rush) A sudden rush of new people to an area where gold has been found. p. 562

government (gu´vərn•mənt) A system by which people of a community, state, or nation use leaders and laws to help people live together. p. 37

governor (guv´ər•nər) The head of the executive branch of state government. p. 166

grant (grant) A sum of money or other payment given for a particular purpose. p. 129

Great Awakening (grāt ə•wā´kən•ing) A religious movement started in the Middle Colonies that called for greater freedom of choice in religion. p. 252

grid system (grid sis´təm) An arrangement of lines that divide a map into squares. p. I22

grievance (grē´vəns) A complaint. p. 351

H

hacienda (ä•sē•en´dä) A large estate where cattle and sheep are raised. p. 158

harpoon (här•po͞on´) A long spear with a sharp shell point. p. 60

hemisphere (he´mə•sfir) One half of Earth. p. I17

hieroglyph (hī•´rə•glif) A picture or symbol that stands for sounds, words, or ideas. p. 38

hogan (hō´gän) A cone-shaped Navajo shelter built by covering a log frame with bark and mud. p. 56

human feature (hyo͞o´mən fē´chər) Something created by humans, such as a building or road, that alters the land. p. I14

I

ideal (ī•dēl´) A goal. p. 467

igloo (i´glo͞o) A house made of snow or ice. p. 86

immigrant (i´mi•grənt) A person who comes into a country to make a new home. p. 251

impeach (im•pēch´) To accuse a government official, such as the President, of "treason, bribery, or other high crimes and misdemeanors." p. 437

imperial policy (im•pir´ē•əl pä´lə•sē) Laws and orders issued by the British government. p. 328

import (im´pôrt) A product brought into a country. p. 226

indentured servant (in•den´chərd sûr´vənt) A person who agreed to work for another person without pay for a certain length of time in exchange for passage to North America. p. 164

independence (in•də•pen´dəns) The freedom to govern on one's own. p. 349

indigo (in´di•gō) A plant from which a blue dye can be made. p. 291

Industrial Revolution (in•dus´trē•əl re•və•lo͞o´shən) The period of time during the 1700s and 1800s in which machines took the place of hand tools to manufacture goods. p. 569

industry (in´dəs•trē) All the businesses that make one kind of product or provide one kind of service. p. 224

inflation (in•flā´shən) An economic condition in which more money is needed to buy goods and services than was needed earlier. p. 368

inset map (in´set map) A smaller map within a larger one. p. I20

institutionalize (in•stə•to͞o´shə•nə•līz) To make a part of life. p. 283

interchangeable parts (in•tər•chān´jə•bəl pärts) Identical copies of parts made by machines so that if one part breaks, an identical one can be installed. p. 569

interdependence (in•tər•di•pen´dəns) Dependence on others for goods and services. p. 292

interest (in´trəst) The money a bank or a borrower pays for the use of money. p. 262

intermediate direction (in•tər•mē´dē•it də•rek´shən) One of the in-between directions: northeast, northwest, southeast, southwest. p. I21

internecine (in•tər•ne´•sēn) Marked by fighting between groups. p. 180

interpret (in•tər´prət) To explain. p. I2

isthmus (is´məs) A narrow strip of land that connects two larger land areas. p. 123

J

judicial branch (jo͞o•di´shəl branch) The branch of government that settles differences about the meaning of the laws. p. 438

justice (jus´təs) Fairness. p. 245

justice (jus´təs) A judge. p. 438

GLOSSARY

kayak (kī´ak) A one-person canoe made of waterproof skins stretched over wood or bone. p. 86

land use (land yo͞os) The way in which most of the land in a place is used. p. 296

landform region (land´fôrm rē´jən) One of the areas that make up Earth's surface, such as mountains, hills, or plains. p. 15

legend (le'jənd) A story handed down over time, often to explain the past. p. 27

legislative branch (le'jəs•lā•tiv branch) The branch of government that makes the laws. p. 436

legislature (le'jəs•lā•chər) The lawmaking branch of a colony, a state government, or the national government. p. 165

line graph (līn graf) A chart that uses one or more lines to show changes over time. p. 230

lines of latitude (līnz uv la´tə•to͞od) Lines on a map or globe that run east and west; also called parallels. p. 22

lines of longitude (līnz uv lon´jə•to͞od) Lines on a map or globe that run north and south; also called meridians. p. 22

location (lō•kā´shən) The place where something can be found. p. I14

locator (lō´kā•tər) A small map or picture of a globe that shows where an area on the main map is found in a state, on a continent, or in the world. p. I21

lock (läk) A part of a canal in which the water level can be raised or lowered to bring ships to the level of the next part of the canal. p. 505

lodge (läj) A circular house of the Plains Indians. p. 70

longhouse (lông´hous) A long wooden building in which several related families lived together. p. 62

Loyalist (loi´ə•list) A person who remained loyal to the British king. p. 367

majority rule (mə•jôr´ə•tē ro͞ol) The political idea that the majority of an organized group should have the power to make decisions for the whole group. p. 172

manifest destiny (ma´nə•fest des´tə•nē) The belief, shared by many Americans, that the United States should one day stretch from the Atlantic Ocean to the Pacific Ocean. p. 559

map legend (map le´jənd) A part of a map that explains what the symbols on the map stand for. p. I20

map scale (map skāl) A part of a map that compares a distance on the map to a distance in the real world. p. I21

map title (map tī´təl) Words on a map that tell the subject of the map. p. I20

mercenary (mûr´sən•er•ē) A soldier who serves for pay in the military of a foreign nation. p. 379

meridian (mə•ri´dē•ən) A line of longitude that runs from the North Pole to the South Pole. p. 22

Middle Passage (mi´dəl pa´sij) The travel of enslaved Africans from Africa to the West Indies. p. 226

migration (mī•grā´shən) The movement of people. p. 25

militia (mə•li´shə) A volunteer army. p. 254

millennium (mə•le´nē•əm) A period of 1,000 years. p. 32

Minutemen (mi'nət•man) A member of the Massachusetts colony militia who could quickly be ready to fight the British. p. 340

mission (mi'shən) A small religious community. p. 157

missionary (mi´shə•ner•ē) A person sent out by a church to spread its religion. p. 133

modify (mä´də•fī) To change. p. I15

monopoly (mə•no´pə•lē) The complete control of a product or service. p. 337

mutiny (myo͞o´tə•nē) To rebel against the leader of one's group. p. 143

naturalization (na•chə•rə•lə•zā'shən) The process of becoming an American citizen by living in the country for five years and then passing a test. p. 475

naval store (nā´vəl stōr) A product that is used to build and repair a ship. p. 224

navigation (na•və•gā´shən) The method of planning and controlling the course of a ship. p. 112

negotiate (ni•gō´shē•āt) To talk with another to work out an agreement. p. 383

GLOSSARY

network (net´wərk) A system. p. 64

neutral (no̅o̅´trəl) Not taking a side in a disagreement. p. 367

nomad (nō´mad) A wanderer who has no settled home. p. 28

Northwest Passage (nôrth´west pa´sij) A waterway in North America thought to connect the Atlantic Ocean and the Pacific Ocean. p. 139

O

olive branch (ä´liv branch) An ancient symbol of peace. p. 345

opinion (ə•pin´yən) A statement that tells what a person thinks or believes. p. 136

opportunity cost (ä•pər•to̅o̅´nə•tē kôst) The value of the thing a person gives up in order to get something else. p. 262

ordinance (ôr´də•nəns) A law or set of laws. p. 399

overseer (ō´vər•sē•ər) A hired person who watched field slaves as they worked. p. 284

P

palisade (pa•lə•sād´) A wall made of sharpened tree trunks to protect a village from enemies or wild animals. p. 76

parallel (par´ə•lel) A line of latitude. It is called this because parallels are always the same distance from one another. p. 22

parallel time lines (par´ə•lel tīm līnz) Two or more time lines that show the same period of time. p. 374

Parliament (pär´lə•mənt) The lawmaking body of the British government. p. 321

pathfinder (path´fīn•dər) Someone who finds a way through an unknown region. p. 502

Patriot (pā´trē•ət) A colonist who was against British rule and supported the rebel cause in the American colonies. p. 367

patriotism (pā´trē•ə•ti•zəm) Love of one's country. p. 468

percent (pər•sent´) One-hundredth of the total whole. p. 281

petition (pə•ti´shən) A signed request made to an official person or organization. p. 339

physical feature (fi´zi•kəl fē´chər) A land feature that has been made by nature. p. I14

pilgrim (pil´grəm) A person who makes a journey for religious reasons. p. 171

pioneer (pī•ə•nir´) A person who is first to settle a new place. p. 509

plantation (plan•tā´shən) A huge farm. p. 156

planter (plan´tər) A plantation owner. p. 284

point of view (point uv vyo̅o̅) A person's perspective. p. I4

political party (pə•li´ti•kəl pär´tē) A group whose members seek to elect government officials who share the group's points of view about many issues. p. 446

population density (po•pyə•lā´shən den´sə•tē) The number of people who live within 1 square mile or 1 square kilometer of land. p. 464

potlatch (pät´lach) A special American Indian gathering or celebration with feasting and dancing. p. 64

preamble (prē´am•bəl) An introduction; first part. p. 350

presidio (prā•sē´dē•ō) A Spanish fort. p. 157

primary source (prī´mer•ē sôrs) A record of an event made by a person who saw or took part in it. p. 168

prime meridian (prīm mə•ri´dē•ən) The imaginary line that divides Earth into the Western Hemisphere and the Eastern Hemisphere. p. I17

principle (prin´sə•pəl) A rule that is used in deciding how to behave. p. 435

proclamation (prä•klə•mā´shən) A public announcement. p. 322

profiteering (prä•fə•tir´ing) Charging an extra-high price for a good or service. p. 368

proprietary colony (prə•prī´ə•ter•ē kä´lə•nē) A colony owned and ruled by one person who was chosen by a king or queen. p. 182

proprietor (prə•prī´ə•tər) An owner. p. 245

prosperity (präs•per´ə•tē) Economic success. p. 258

public office (pub´lik ô´fəs) A job a person is elected to do. p. 217

pueblo (pwe´blō) A Spanish word for *village*. p. 40

Q

quarter (kwôr´tər) To provide or pay for housing. p. 338

R

ratify (ra′tə•fī) To approve. p. 443

raw material (rô mə•tir′ē•əl) A resource that can be used to make a product. p. 161

Reconquista (rā•kōn•kēs′tä) The plan to make Spain all Catholic; also called the Reconquest. p. 115

reform (ri•fôrm′) A change. p. 133

Reformation (re•fər•mā′shən) A Christian movement that began in sixteenth-century Europe as an attempt to reform the Roman Catholic Church; resulted in the founding of Protestantism. p. 133

refuge (re′fyōōj) A safe place. p. 244

regiment (re′jə•mənt) A large, organized group of soldiers. p. 370

region (rē′jən) An area of Earth in which many features are similar. p. I15

relative location (re′lə•tiv lō•kā′shən) The position of one place in relation to another. p. 22

religious toleration (ri•li′jəs tä•lə•rā′shən) Acceptance of religious differences. p. 252

repeal (ri•pēl′) To cancel, or undo, a law. p. 329

represent (re•pri•zent′) To speak for. p. 165

representation (re•pri•zen•tā′shən) The act of speaking on behalf of someone else. p. 327

republic (ri•pub′lik) A form of government in which people elect representatives to govern the country. p. 429

research (ri•sûrch′) To investigate. p. I2

reservation (re•zər•vā′shən) Land set aside by the government for use by American Indians. On reservations, Indians govern themselves. p. 527

reserved powers (ri•zûrvd′ pou′ərz) Authority that belongs to the states or to the people, not to the national government. p. 445

resolution (re•zə•lōō′shən) A formal statement of the feelings of a group of people about an important topic. p. 349

revolution (re•və•lōō′shən) A sudden, great change, such as the overthrow of an established government. p. 341

royal colony (roi′əl kä′lə•nē) A colony ruled directly by a monarch. p. 166

secondary source (se′kən•der•ē sôrs) A record of an event written by someone who was not present at the time. p. 168

sedition (sə•di′shən) Speech or behavior that causes other people to work against a government. p. 209

self-government (self•gu′vərn•mənt) A system of government in which people make their own laws. p. 172

separation of powers (se•pə•rā′shən uv pou′erz) The division of the national government into three branches instead of into one all-powerful branch. p. 436

slave state (slāv stāt) A state that allowed slavery before the Civil War. p. 553

slavery (slā′və•rē) The practice of holding people against their will and making them carry out orders. p. 156

sod (sod) Earth cut into blocks or mats, held together by grass and its roots. p. 70

staple (stā′pəl) Something that is always needed and used, such as milk or bread. p. 53

stock (stäk) A share of ownership in a business. p. 162

surplus (sûr′pləs) An amount that is more than what is needed. p. 54

tall tale (täl tāl) An exaggerated adventure story. p. 511

technology (tek•nä′lə•jē) The use of scientific knowledge and tools to make or do something. p. 111

telegraph (te′lə•graf) A machine that used electricity to send messages over wires. p. 571

tepee (tē′pē) A cone-shaped tent made from wooden poles and buffalo skins. p. 71

territory (ter′ə•tôr•ē) Land that belongs to a national government but is not a state. p. 399

theory (thē′ə•rē) An idea based on study and research. p. 25

time line (tīm līn) A diagram that shows events that took place during a certain period of time. p. 32

time zone (tīm zōn) A region in which a single time is used. p. 576

totem pole (tō′təm pōl) A tall wooden post carved with shapes of animals and people and representing a family's history and importance. p. 63

town meeting (toun mē′ting) An assembly in the New England Colonies in which male landowners could take part in government. p. 217

trade-off (trād´ôf) The giving up of one thing to get another. p. 262

tradition (trə•dish´ən) A custom, a way of life, or an idea that has been handed down from the past. p. 38

traitor (trā´tər) One who works against one's own government. p. 391

travois (trə•voi´) A device made of two poles fastened to a dog's harness, used to carry possessions. p. 71

treason (trē´zən) The act of working against one's own government. p. 327

treaty (trē´tē) An agreement between nations about peace, trade, or other matters. p. 125

trespass (tres´pas) To go onto someone else's property without asking permission. p. 518

trial by jury (trī´əl bī jûr´ē) The right of a person accused of a crime to be tried by a jury, or group, of fellow citizens. p. 245

triangular trade route (trī•ang´gyə•lər trād ro͞ot) A shipping route that linked England, the English colonies in North America, and the west coast of Africa, forming an imaginary triangle in the Atlantic Ocean. p. 226

turning point (tûr´ning point) A single event that causes important and dramatic change. p. 381

Underground Railroad (un'dər•ground rāl'rōd) A system of escape routes for enslaved people, leading to free land. p. 573

veto (vē´tō) To reject. p. 437

wagon train (wa´gən trān) A group of wagons, each pulled by horses or oxen. p. 542

wampum (wäm´pəm) Beads made from cut and polished seashells, used to keep records, send messages to other tribes, barter for goods, or give as gifts. p. 77

wigwam (wig´wäm) A round, bark-covered American Indian shelter. p. 78

Index

The Index lets you know where information about important people, places, and events appears in the book. All entries are listed in alphabetical order. For each entry, the page reference indicates where information about that entry can be found in the text. Page references for illustrations are set in italic type. An italic *m* indicates a map. Page references set in boldface type indicate the pages on which vocabulary terms are defined. Guide words at the top of each page help you identify which words appear on which page.

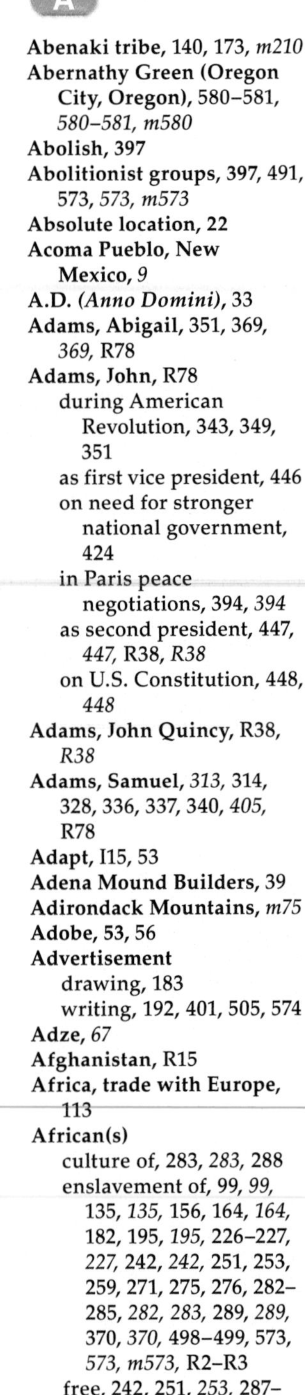

INDEX

INDEX

F

G

H

I

N

Q

R

Y

Z

For permission to reprint copyrighted material, grateful acknowledgment is made to the following sources:

Atheneum Books for Young Readers, an imprint of Simon & Schuster Children's Publishing Division: From *The Courage of Sarah Noble* by Alice Dalgliesh. Text copyright © 1952 by Alice Dalgliesh and Leonard Weisgard; text copyright renewed © 1982 by Margaret B. Evans and Leonard Weisgard.

BookStop Literary Agency, on behalf of Steve Lowe: From *The Log of Christopher Columbus*, selections by Steve Lowe, translated by Robert H. Fuson. Compilation copyright © 1992 by Steve Lowe; translation copyright 1987 by Robert H. Fuson.

Coward-McCann, A Division of Penguin Young Readers Group, A Member of Penguin Group (USA) Inc., 345 Hudson St., New York, NY 10014: From *Phoebe the Spy* by Judith Berry Griffin, illustrated by Margot Tomes. Text copyright © 1977 by Judith Berry Griffin; illustrations copyright © 1977 by Margot Tomes. Originally titled *Phoebe and the General.*

Sally Crum, 2498 S. Broadway, Grand Junction, CO 81503: From *Race to the Moonrise: An Ancient Journey* by Sally Crum. Text copyright © by Sally Crum.

Harcourt, Inc.: "If We Should Travel," and "Far From Here" from *Between Earth and Sky: Legends of Native American Sacred Places* by Joseph Bruchac. Text copyright © 1996 by Joseph Bruchac.

HarperCollins Publishers: From *Stranded at Plimouth Plantation 1626* by Gary Bowen. Copyright © 1994 by Gary Bowen. Illustrations by Charles Santore from *Paul Revere's Ride: The Landlord's Tale* by Henry Wadsworth Longfellow. Illustrations copyright © 2003 by Charles Santore.

Houghton Mifflin Company: From *Molly Bannaky* by Alice McGill, illustrated by Chris K. Soentpiet. Text copyright © 1999 by Alice McGill; illustrations copyright © 1999 by Chris Soentpiet.

Mary Laychak, on behalf of Northland Publishing Company, Flagstaff, AZ: From *My Name Is York* by Elizabeth Van Steenwyk, illustrated by Bill Farnsworth. Text copyright © 1997 by The Donald and Elizabeth Van Steenwyk Family Trust; illustrations copyright © 1997 by Bill Farnsworth.

Philomel Books, A Division of Penguin Young Readers Group, A Member of Penguin Group (USA) Inc., 345 Hudson St., New York, NY 10014: Illustrations by Robert Sabuda from *The Log of Christopher Columbus*, selections by Steve Lowe, translated by Robert H. Fuson. Illustrations copyright © 1992 by Robert Sabuda.

G. P. Putnam's Sons, A Division of Penguin Young Readers Group, A Member of Penguin Group (USA) Inc., 345 Hudson St., New York, NY 10014: Illustrations by Wendell Minor from *America the Beautiful* by Katharine Lee Bates. Illustrations copyright © 2003 by Wendell Minor.

Random House Children's Books, a division of Random House, Inc.: From *Ben Franklin of Old Philadelphia* by Margaret Cousins. Text copyright 1952 by Margaret Cousins; text copyright renewed 1980 by Margaret Cousins.

Scholastic Inc.: From *If You Were There When They Signed the Constitution* by Elizabeth Levy. Text copyright © 1987 by Elizabeth Levy.

From *My Name Is America: The Journal of Wong Ming-Chung, A Chinese Miner*, a Dear America Book by Laurence Yep. Text copyright © 2000 by Laurence Yep.

The University of Arizona Press: From "It Has Always Been This Way" in *Sa'anii Dahataal/ The Women Are Singing: Poems and Stories* by Luci Tapahonso. Text copyright © 1993 by Luci Tapahonso.

PHOTO CREDITS

PLACEMENT KEY: (t) top; (b) bottom; (l) left; (r) right; (c) center; (bg) background; (fg) foreground; (i) inset.

COVER

Hisham F. Ibrahim/PictureQuest (Statue of George Washington); Joseph Sohm; Visions of America/Corbis (United States Constitution); Muench Photography (Cumash Painted Cave); Photographer: Dennis Degnan/Corbis (Independence Hall); Harcourt (Colonial flag).

INTRODUCTION

I2 Marilyn ""Angel"" Wynn/Nativestock.com; I2 The Granger Collection, New York; I2 The Granger Collection, New York; I2 Courtesy of APVA Preservation Virginia; I3 Missouri Historical Society, St. Louis; I3 Victoria and Albert Museum London/Eileen Tweedy/Art Archive; I3 Bettmann/Corbis; I3 Social History Division/Smithsonian Institution, National Museum of American History; I3 Atwater Kent Museum of Philadelphia, Courtesy of Historical Society of Pennsylvania Collection/Bridgeman Art Library; I4 Bettmann/Corbis; I4 Freelance Photography Guild/Corbis; I4 David R. Frazier Photolibrary, Inc./Alamy Images; I4 akg-images; I5 Smithsonian Institution, NNC, Jeff Tinsley; I5 Library of Congress Rare Book and Special Collections Division. Washington, D.C.; I5 Bettmann/Corbis; I5 Hulton Archive/Getty Images;I5 Bettmann/Corbis; I6 Archivo Iconografico, S.A./Corbis; I6 Royalty-Free/Corbis; I7 Museum of the City of New York/Corbis; I7 John Slemp/Look South; I7 Marilyn "Angel" Wynn/Nativestock.com; I7 Science Museum, London / Topham-HIP/The Image Works, Inc.; I7 US Postal Service Licensing Group; I14 Gala/SuperStock; I14 Mitchell Funk/Image Bank/Getty Images; I15 Vince Streano/Corbis

UNIT 1

Opener 1-2 The Granger Collection, New York; 7 Yoshio Tomii/SuperStock; 14-15 James Randklev; Visions of America/Corbis; 17 Charles Cook/Lonely Planet Images; 18-19 MacDuff Everton/Corbis; 21 PhotoDisc; 26 Tom & Susan Bean; 27 (b) Lawrence Migdale/Photo Researchers, Inc.; 27 (t) Marilyn "Angel" Wynn /Nativestock.com; 29 Werner Forman/Art Resource, NY; 31 (l) John Maier, Jr./The Image Works, Inc.; 31 (r) Werner Forman/Art Resource, NY; 35 (c) Corbis; 35 (t) Fulcrum Publishing; 37 (inset) Yoshio Tomii/SuperStock; 37 (t) Kenneth Garrett; 39 (b) Martin Pate, Newnan, GA. Courtesy Southeast Archeological Center, National Park Service; 39 (t) Werner Forman/Art Resource, NY; 40-41 Liz Hymans/Corbis; 41 (t) Richard Sisk/Panoramic Images; 42 Peter Harholdt/ Corbis; 45 Yoshio Tomii/SuperStock; 54 PlaceStockPhoto.com; 55 Courtesy of the Phoebe Apperson Hearst Museum of Anthropology and the Regents of the University of California, 17-194; 56 Robert Harding Picture Library/Alamy Images; 57 Paul Chesley/Stone/Getty Images; 58 Branson Reynolds/Index Stock Imagery; 59 (l) Jim Cowlin/Adstock Photos; 59 (r) Monty Roessel Photography; 60 (b) Peter Harholdt/Corbis; 60 (t) Werner Forman/Art Resource, NY; 64-65 Dave G. Houser/Corbis; 65 (t) www.canadianheritage.ca ID #23257, National Archives of Canada C-74714; 66 (b) Rolf Hicker/Panoramic Images; 66 (t) Alaska State Library, William A. Kelly Photograph Collection, Photographer: Elbridge W Merrill; 67 (bc) Alaska State Library, Early Prints Photograph Collection; 67 (bl) Edenshaw, Charles (attributed to), Canadian: Haida 1839-1920, Model Totem Pole c 1890/1905, Argillite, 19.6 x 4.0 x 4.0 cm, Art Gallery of Ontario, Gift of Roy G. Cole, Rosseau, Ontario, 1997; 67 (br) Patrick J. Endres/Alaska Photographics; 67 (c) Alaska State Museum; 67 (t) Alaska State Museum; 68-69 Natural Exposures, Inc.; 69 (inset) Lowell Georgia/Corbis; 72 (b) South Dakota State Historical Society; 72 (t) Nativestock.com; 73 Greenwich Workshop Inc.; 75 Ian Dagnall/Alamy Images; 78 The Mariners' Museum/Corbis; 79 Canadian Museum of Civilization; 80 Newberry Library, Chicago/ SuperStock; 81 Larry Downing/Reuters /Corbis; 83 (b) Myrleen Cate/PhotoEdit; 83 (c) Bob Daemmrich/Stock Boston; 83 (t) Myrleen Ferguson Cate/PhotoEdit; 85 Werner Forman/Art Resource, NY; 86-87 Bryan & Cherry Alexander Photography; 87 (l) Werner Forman/Art Resource, NY; 87 (r) Bryan & Cherry Alexander Photography; 88 The Granger Collection, New York; 89 Westwind Enterprises; 92 Jerry Jacka Photography; 92 Russ Finley Photography; 92 (c) Jerry Jacka Photography; 93 (br) Bob Rowan; Progressive Image/Corbis; 93 (tl) Russ Finley Photography; 93 (tr) Tom Bean/ Corbis; 94 PlaceStockPhoto.com

UNIT 2

Opener 96-97 The Granger Collection, New York; 98 (tl) Giraudon/Art Resource, NY; 98 (tr) MITHRA-INDEX/Bridgeman Art Library; 102 Japack Company/Corbis; 103 Larry Benvenuti/GTPhoto; 110 (l) The Granger Collection, New York; 110 (r) The Art Archive; 111 Stock Montage/SuperStock; 112 National Maritime Museum; 114 akg-images; 115 The Granger Collection, New

York; 118 (bl) Science Museum, London/Topham-HIP/The Image Works, Inc.; 118 (br) Science Museum, London /Topham-HIP/The Image Works, Inc.; 118 (t) Bettmann/Corbis; 119 (b) Archivo Iconografico, S.A./Corbis; 119 (l) Science Museum, London/Topham-HIP/The Image Works, Inc.; 119 (r) Science Museum, London/Topham-HIP/The Image Works, Inc.; 121 Mark Lewis Photography/Mira.com; 122 (l) SuperStock; 122 (r) Stefano Bianchetti/Corbis; 123 Stephen St. John/National Geographic Image Collection; 124 (c) North Wind Picture Archives; 124 (cl) Image Select/Art Resource, NY; 124 (r) Marine Museum Lisbon/Dagli Orti/Art Archive; 125 Copyright The British Museum; 126NASA; 127 (b) Florida Museum of Natural History; 127 (c) Courtesy of Robert S. McElvaine; 127 (t) Frank Trapper/Corbis/Sygma; 128 The Cummer Museum of Art and Gardens, Jacksonville/SuperStock; 129 M.T. O'Keefe/Robertstock.com; 131 (c) San Diego Historical Society; 131 (cl) Stock Montage; 131 (cr) Ms. Nevin Kempthorne, Courtesy of The National Park Service; 131 (l) The Granger Collection, New York; 131 (r) Hernando De Soto Historical Society; 134 Giraudon/Art Resource, NY; 136-137 "Coronado's Expedition Crossing the Llano Estacado", Courtesy of Abell-Hanger Foundation and of the Permian Basin Petroleum Museum, Library and Hall of Fame of Midland, Texas where this painting is on permanent display; 138 New-York Historical Society, New York, USA/Bridgeman Art Library; 139 (b) The Granger Collection, New York; 139 (c) The Granger Collection, New York; 139 (t) The Granger Collection, New York; 140-141 Giraudon/Art Resource, NY; 142 (c) Bettmann/Corbis; 142 (l) Scala/Art Resource, NY; 142 (r) Bettmann/Corbis; 143 David David Gallery /SuperStock; 147 David David Gallery/SuperStock; 147 Stephen St. John/National Geographic Image Collection; 156 Robert Frerck/Odyssey Productions, Chicago; 157 Jeffrey L. Rotman/Corbis; 159 (l) Bridgeman Art Library; 159 (r) akg-images; 160 akg-images; 161 Fort Raleigh National Historic Site/National Park Service; 162 (inset) Private Collection/Bridgeman Art Library; 164 Colonial Williamsburg Foundation; 165 Library of Virginia; 166 The Granger Collection, New York; 167 New-York Historical Society, New York, USA/Bridgeman Art Library; 168 The Granger Collection, New York; 168 (c) Private Collection/Bridgeman Art Library; 168 (cr) Courtesy of APVA Preservation Virginia; 168 (l) Bettmann/Corbis; 168 (r) Courtesy of APVA Preservation Virginia; 169 (c) Richard T. Nowitz/Corbis; 169 (r) Courtesy of APVA Preservation Virginia; 170 Copyright © Reproduced with permission from the Thomas Ross Collection, www.rosscollection.co.uk; 172 The Granger Collection, New York; 173 Dave G. Houser/Corbis; 174 The Granger Collection, New York; 175 Gibson Stock Photography; 176 Confederation Life Collection by permission of the Syndics of Cambridge University Library; 178 Dave Bartruff/Corbis; 180 Nik Wheeler/Corbis; 181 Patrick and Beatrice Haggerty Museum of Art, Marquette University, Milwaukee, WI; 181 (bl) The Granger Collection, New York; 181 (r) The Granger Collection, New York; 182 The Granger Collection, New York; 187 The Granger Collection, New York; 187 Copyright © Reproduced with permission from the Thomas Ross Collection, www.rosscollection.co.uk; 188 David Olsen/Stone/Getty Images; 188 (inset) Richard Cummins/Corbis; 189 (c) Lowell Georgia/Corbis; 189 (t) James L. Amos/Corbis; 190 Sisse Brimberg/National Geographic Image Collection

UNIT 3

Opener 192-193 SuperStock; 194 Stock Montage; 194 The Corcoran Gallery of Art/Corbis; 194 Royal Albert Memorial Museum, Exeter, Devon, UK/Bridgeman Art Library; 199 Richard T. Nowitz/Corbis; 199 Dorothy Littell Greco/The Image Works, Inc.; 200 James L. Amos/Corbis; 206 G.E. Kidder Smith, Courtesy Kidder Smith Collection, Rotch Visual Collections, M.I.T.; 207 Bettmann/Corbis; 207 National Gallery of Victoria, Melbourne, Australia/Bridgeman Art Library; 207 (b) Stock Montage; 208 Geoffrey Clements/Corbis; 209 The Granger Collection, New York; 210 James Blair/PhotoDisc; 211 Shelburne Museum; 212 Museum of Art, Rhode Island School of Design, Gift of Mr. Robert Winthrop, Photography by Del Bogart; 214 (l) Bettmann/Corbis; 214 (r) BrianSmith.com Photography; 215 New-York Historical Society, New York, USA/Bridgeman Art Library; 218 Todd Gipstein/National Geographic Image Collection; 220 (b) The Granger Collection, New York; 220 (t) Blackwell History of Education Museum; 222 Lee Snider/Corbis; 223 Prints & Photographs Division, [LC-USZC2-3223]; 224 Joseph H. Bailey/National Geographic Image Collection; 225 The Mariners' Museum; 227 (inset) Bridgeman Art Library; 227 (l) Maritime Museum Kronborg Castle Denmark/Dagli Orti/Art Archive; 228 The Granger Collection, New York; 228 Annie Griffiths Belt/Corbis; 229 The Granger Collection, New York; 229 Embroidered by: Sally Jackson, Massachusetts (probably Boston) born about 1760, Sampler, American 1771, Plain weave lined embroidered with silk in cross, split, French knot and stem stiches. 76.2 x 50.8 cm (30 x 20 in), Museum of Fine Arts, Boston, Museum purchase with funds donated anonymously and Frank B. Bernis Fund, 2001.739; 229 Courtesy of APVA Preservation Virginia; 229 Colonial Williamsburg Foundation; 229 Colonial Williamsburg Foundation; 230 Farrell Grehan/Corbis; 231 Paul Johnson/Index Stock Imagery; 232 National Gallery of Victoria, Melbourne, Australia/Bridgeman Art Library; 233 Geoffrey Clements/Corbis; 233 Shelburne Museum; 240 National Portrait Gallery, London/SuperStock; 241 L.F. Tantillo; 242 (b) The Granger Collection, New York; 242 (t) Museum of International Folk Art. Santa Fe, New Mexico. Photo by: Blair Clark; 243 The Granger Collection, New York; 244 SuperStock; 244 Haverford College Quaker and Special Collections; 244 Museum of the City of New York/Corbis; 244 Peter Gridley/Taxi/Getty Images; 245 Hulton Archive/Getty Images; 246 (l) The Newark Museum/Art Resource, NY; 246 (r) Haverford College Library, Haverford, PA., Quaker Collection, Burlington (NJ) Meetinghouse, coll. no. 912; 247 Courtesy of the Historical Society of Pennsylvania, Atwater Kent Museum of Philadelphia; 248 The Maryland Historical Society, Baltimore, Maryland; 248 Lee Snider/Corbis; 248 Bettmann/Corbis; 249 Comstock Images/Alamy Images; 250 Albany Institute of History & Art; 251 Darlene Bordwell/Ambient Light Photography; 252 (l) American Tract Society; 252 (r) Francis G. Mayer/Corbis; 253 Abby Aldrich Folk Art Museum, Colonial Williamsburg Foundation, Williamsburg, VA; 254 Michael Sheldon/Art Resource, NY; 255 (l) CIGNA Museum & Art Collection; 255 (r) Winterthur Museum, Garden & Library; 258 The New-York Historical Society; 259 (tc) Christie's Images; 259 (tl) Victoria and Albert Museum London / Eileen Tweedy/Art Archive; 259 (tr) Christie's Images; 260 Colonial Williamsburg Foundation; 261 Colonial Williamsburg Foundation; 262 Colonial Williamsburg Foundation; 263 Colonial Williamsburg Foundation; 264 Stapleton Collection/Corbis; 265 Francis G. Mayer/Corbis; 265 The Granger Collection, New York; 272 The Maryland Historical Society, Baltimore, Maryland; 273 Courtesy of The Maryland Commission on Artistic Property of the Maryland State Archives; 274 Courtesy of The Maryland Commission on Artistic Property of the Maryland State Archives; 275 Hulton Archive/Getty Images; 276 Corpus Christi College, Oxford, UK/Bridgeman Art Library; 278 Bettmann/Corbis; 279 (l) Kelly Culpepper/Transparencies, Inc.; 279 (r) Peabody Essex Museum, Salem, Massachusetts, USA/Bridgeman Art Library; 280 Colonial Williamsburg Foundation; 281 Colonial Williamsburg Foundation; 282 Virginia Historical Society, Richmond, Virginia; 283 Virginia Museum of Fine Arts, Richmond. Gift of Edgar William and Bernice Chrysler Garbisch. Photo: Wen Hwa Ts'ao; 283 (r) Morris Museum of Art, Augusta, Georgia; 286 Colonial Williamsburg Foundation; 287 Courtesy of the Historical Archaeology Collections of the Florida Museum of Natural History, photo by James Quine; 288 SuperStock; 289 Royal Albert Memorial Museum, Exeter, Devon, UK/Bridgeman Art Library; 290 Ferens Art Gallery, Hull City Museums and Art Galleries, UK/Bridgeman Art Library; 291 Painet Stock Photos; 293 American Numismatic Society; 294 Courtesy of Enoch Pratt Free Library, State Library Resource Center, Baltimore, MD; 294 (inset) National Park Service, Harpers Ferry Center Commissioned Art Collection, artist Greg Harlin of Wood Ronasville Harlin, Inc.; 295 David David Gallery/SuperStock; 296 John Mead/Science Photo Library/Photo Researchers, Inc.; 297 David Shopper/Index Stock Imagery; 298 Courtesy of The Maryland Commission on Artistic Property of the Maryland State Archives; 299 Courtesy of Enoch Pratt Free Library, State Library Resource Center, Baltimore, MD; 299 Corpus Christi College, Oxford, UK/Bridgeman Art Library; 300 Colonial Williamsburg Foundation; 300 (b) Mary Ann and Bryan Hemphill; 300 (c) Houserstock, Inc.; 301 Mary Ann and Bryan Hemphill; 301 Colonial Williamsburg Foundation; 301 (c) PictureQuest

UNIT 4

Opener 304-305 Francis G. Mayer/Corbis; 307 The Granger Collection, New York; 311 The Granger Collection, New York; 312 James P Blair/PhotoDisc; 318 Larry Olsen Photography; 320 Historical Art Prints; 321 Gift of Dr. J. C. Webster, McCord Museum of Canadian History, Montreal; 322 (b) Reynolds Museum, Winston Salem, North Carolina,

USA/Bridgeman Art Library; 322 (t) Detroit Historical Museums & Society; 326 By Courtesy of The National Portrait Gallery, London; 327 Metropolitan Museum of Art; 328 The Granger Collection, New York; 329 (b) Boston Public Library; 329 (t) Colonial Williamsburg Foundation; 331 Massachusetts Historical Society, Boston, MA, USA/ Bridgeman Art Library; 332 (c) Stock Montage; 332 (l) Massachusetts Historical Society, Boston, MA, USA/Bridgeman Art Library; 337 American Antiquarian Society; 339 Bettmann/Corbis; 341 Janelco; 342 The Granger Collection, New York; 343 J. McGrail /Robertstock.com; 344 Atwater Kent Museum of Philadelphia, Courtesy of Historical Society of Pennsylvania Collection/Bridgeman Art Library; 346 Hulton Archive/Getty Images; 347 The Pierpont Morgan Library/Art Resource, NY; 347 Stock Montage; 348 (l) Stock Montage; 348 (r) National Portrait Gallery, London/ SuperStock; 349 Thomas Jefferson Writing the Declaration of Independence, Howard Pyle, 1853-1911, Delaware Art Museum; 351 (l) Stock Barrow; 351 (r) Lee Snider Photo Images; 352 Bettmann/Corbis; 353 (l) Historical Society of Pennsylvania; 353 (r) Milne Special Collections and Archives/ University of New Hampshire Library; 354 Delaware Art Museum, Wilmington, USA, Howard Pyle Collection/Bridgeman Art Library; 358 Gift of Dr. J. C. Webster, McCord Museum of Canadian History, Montreal; 366 Ted Spiegel/Corbis; 367 The Connecticut Historical Society Museum, Hartford, Connecticut; 368 (c) The Granger Collection, New York; 368 (t) The Granger Collection, New York; 369 (l) Christie's Images/SuperStock; 369 (r) The Granger Collection, New York; 370 David Wagner; 370 The Granger Collection, New York; 371 American Numismatic Society; 371 (c) Independence National Historical Park; 371 (r) Historical Art Prints; 372 Johnson Hall (Sir William Johnson Presenting Medals to the Indian Chiefs of the Six Nations at Johnstown, N.Y., 1772), Edward Lamson Henry (1841-1919), 1903, Oil on canvas, Albany Institute of History & Art Purchase, 1993.44; 375 J. McGrail /Robertstock.com; 376 Smithsonian Institution, National Museum of American History; 377 Smithsonian Institution, National Museum of American History; 378 Courtesy of The Maryland Commission on Artistic Property of the Maryland State Archives; 380 Metropolitan Museum of Art, New York, USA/Bridgeman Art Library; 381 Fort Ticonderoga; 381 (inset) The Granger Collection, New York; 382 SuperStock; 383 akg-images; 385 The Granger Collection, New York; 388 Lee Snider/Corbis; 389 (c) Bettmann/Corbis; 389 (l) Chopin birthplace Poland / Dagli Orti/Art Archive; 389 (r) The Granger Collection, New York; 391 Don Troiani/Historical Art Prints; 394 Winterthur Museum, Garden & Library; 395 Hulton Archive/Getty Images; 396 (l) The British Museum/Topham-HIP/ The Image Works, Inc.; 396 (r) Rare Book and Special Collections Division, Library of Congress; 397 The Granger Collection, New York; 398 Indianapolis Museum of Art, USA/Bridgeman Art Library; 400 Lowe Art Museum/SuperStock; 400 (l) North Wind Picture Archives; 400 (r) The Granger Collection, New York; 401 (c) Atwater Kent Museum of Philadelphia, Courtesy of Historical Society of Pennsylvania Collection/Bridgeman Art Library; 401 (l) SuperStock; 401 (r) New-York Historical Society, New York, USA/Bridgeman Art Library; 402 Metropolitan Museum of Art, New York, USA/Bridgeman Art Library; 404 (inset) Stock Boston; 404 (r) Gibson Stock Photography; 405 (bl) Ed Young/Corbis; 405 (br) Danilo Donadoni/Bruce Coleman Inc.; 405 (cl) Dave G. Houser/Corbis; 405 (cr) Dave G. Houser/Corbis; 405 (tc) Susan Cole Kelly Photographer; 405 (tl) Tibor Bognar/Corbis; 405 (tr) Richard Cummins/Corbis; 406 Colonial Williamsburg Foundation

UNIT 5

Opener 408-409 Gift of Edgar William and Bernice Chrysler Garbish, 50.2.1, Virginia Museum of Fine Arts; 410 SuperStock; 410 Atwater Kent Museum of Philadelphia, Courtesy of Historical Society of Pennsylvania Collection/Bridgeman Art Library; 411 Archivo Iconografico, S.A./Corbis; 420 Walter Choroszewski; 422 American Numismatic Society; 422 The Granger Collection, New York; 424 (b) National Portrait Gallery, Smithsonian Institution/Art Resource, NY; 424 (t) National Portrait Gallery, Smithsonian Institution/Art Resource, NY; 425 Künstler Enterprises; 426 SuperStock; 428 Bettmann/Corbis; 430 Independence National Historical Park; 432 The Metropolitan Museum of Art, Morris K. Jessup Fund, 1940. (40.40) Photograph © 1985 The Metropolitan Museum of Art; 433 Atwater Kent Museum of Philadelphia, Courtesy of Historical Society of Pennsylvania Collection/Bridgeman Art Library; 434 Gift of Edgar William and Bernice Chrysler Garbish, Virginia Museum of Fine Arts; 435 Dennis Brack/Stock Photo; 436 (b) Jeff Greenberg/Danita Delimont Stock Photography; 436 (c) George Gibbons/Taxi/ Getty Images; 437 Jon Feingersh/Masterfile; 438 Jurgen Vogt/Image Bank/Getty Images; 439 Royalty-Free/Corbis; 440 Brooks Kraft/ Corbis; 441 (bl) Dennis Brack / IPN/Aurora Photos; 441 (cr) Robert Llewellyn/SuperStock; 441 (tl) Randy Wells/Stone/Getty Images; 442 Art Resource, NY; 444 Ken Biggs /Stone/ Getty Images; 444 (b) Archivo Iconografico, S.A./Corbis; 445 Künstler Enterprises; 446 Library of Congress, Washington D.C., USA/Bridgeman Art Library; 446 (inset) The Granger Collection, New York; 447 Collection of The New York Historical Society, accession number 1867.304; 448 Christie's Images/Bridgeman Art Library; 448 Joseph Sohm; ChromoSohm Inc/Corbis; 449 Geoffrey Clements/Corbis; 449 The Granger Collection, New York; 451 Künstler Enterprises; 451 Independence National Historical Park; 451 Art Resource, NY; 458 Winterthur Museum, Garden & Library; 459 (l) Dennis Brack/Stock Photo; 459 (r) Collection, The Supreme Court Historical Society, photographed by Steve Petteway; 459 (tc) Joseph Sohm; Visions of America/Corbis; 460 Bettmann/Corbis; 462 Bettmann/Corbis; 463 Craig Aurness/Corbis; 463 Jonathan Hodson/Robert Harding Picture Library Ltd/Alamy Images; 464 Social History Division, Smithsonian Institution, National Museum of American History; 466 Pentagram Design, Inc., San Francisco; 466 (b) New-York Historical Society, New York, USA/ Bridgeman Art Library; 469 (inset) Bridgeman Art Library; 469 (tr) PhotoDisc; 470 Corbis; 471 John Pritchett; 472 Pentagram Design, Inc., San Francisco; 472 Hulton Archive/ Getty Images; 473 Pentagram Design, Inc., San Francisco; 473 The Granger Collection, New York; 473 Library of Congress, Prints & Photographs Division, WWI Posters, [LC-USZC4-6262]; 474 The Granger Collection, New York; 475 AP/Wide World Photos; 476 (bl) Hulton Archive/Getty Images; 476 (tl) Christie's Images/Bridgeman Art Library; 476 (tr) The Granger Collection, New York; 477 (bc) Wally McNamee/Corbis; 477 (bl) Jason Laure/The Image Works, Inc.; 477 (br) Ron Sachs/Consolidated News Photos/Corbis; 477 (tc) The Granger Collection, New York; 477 (tl) Picture History; 477 (tr) Bettmann/Corbis; 478 (tl) AP/Wide World Photos; 478 (tr) AP/ Wide World Photos; 479 Time Life Pictures/ Getty Images; 480 Paul Fusco/Magnum Photos; 481 George Ballis/Take Stock; 482 New-York Historical Society, New York, USA/Bridgeman Art Library; 483 Hulton Archive/Getty Images; 483 The Granger Collection, New York; 483 Jonathan Hodson/ Robert Harding Picture Library Ltd/Alamy Images; 484 Getty Images Editorial; 485 (br) John McGrail Photography; 485 (c) John McGrail Photography; 485 (tr) Courtesy of the National Constitution Center

UNIT 6

Opener 488-489 The Granger Collection, New York; 490 History Museum Mexico City/Dagli Orti/Art Archive; 490 Bettmann/Corbis; 494 Hulton Archive/Getty Images; 495 SuperStock; 500 Albright-Knox Art Gallery/ Corbis; 501 Christopher Wood Gallery, London, UK/Bridgeman Art Library; 502 Boone's First View of Kentucky by William T. Ranney from the collection of Gilcrease Museum, Tulsa, Oklahoma; 503 North Wind Picture Archives; 506 Bridgeman Art Library; 508 The Granger Collection, New York; 509 (b) Courtesy of The Hubbard Museum of the American West, Ruidoso Downs, New Mexico, Photographer: Cheryl D. Knobel; 509 (t) Andre Jenny/Alamy Images; 513 Ohio Historical Society; 514 The Granger Collection, New York; 516 (bc) The Granger Collection, New York; 516 (bl) Painting "Lewis and Clark: The Departure from St. Charles, May 21, 1804" by Gary R. Lucy. Courtesy of the Gary R. Lucy Gallery, Inc. Washington, MO - www.garylucy.com; 516 (br) "Lewis and Clark at Three Forks" by E.S. Paxson, Oil on Canvas, 1912, Courtesy of the Montana Historical Society. Don Beatty photographer 10/1999; 516 (tc) Picture History; 516 (tl) Missouri Historical Society, St. Louis; 516 (tr) National Historical Park, Independence, Missouri, MO, USA/Bridgeman Art Library; 517 Corbis; 517 (bl) "Lewis and Clark Meeting the Indians at Ross' Hole" by Charles M. Russell, Oil on Canvas, 1912, Mural in State of Montana Capitol, Courtesy of the Montana Historical Society, Don Beatty photographer 10/1999; 517 (br) Henry Francis Dupont Winterthur Museum, Delaware, USA/Bridgeman Art Library; 517 (cl)

Smithsonian Institution, NNC, Jeff Tinsley; 517 (cr) Smithsonian Institution, NNC, Jeff Tinsley; 517 (tl) Künstler Enterprises; 517 (tr) Stanley Meltzoff; 518 Independence National Historical Park; 519 The Granger Collection, New York; 520 Private Collection/ Bridgeman Art Library; 522 (l) Photograph courtesy of the Royal Ontario Museum; 522 (r) The Field Museum, negative #A93851c; 523 Paramount Press; 524 Smithsonian American Art Museum, Washington, DC/Art Resource, NY; 527 The Granger Collection, New York; 528 (l) National Portrait Gallery, Smithsonian Institution/Art Resource, NY; 528 (r) Bettmann/Corbis; 529 John Slemp/Look South; 530 (b) Marilyn "Angel" Wynn/Nativestock.com; 530 (t) SuperStock; 531 John Slemp/Look South; 532 National Portrait Gallery, Smithsonian Institution/Art Resource, NY; 532 The Granger Collection, New York; 533 David Young-Wolff/PhotoEdit; 533 Ron Chapple/Taxi/Getty Images; 533 Walter Hodges/Corbis; 533 Bob Rowan; Progressive Image/Corbis; 534 The Granger Collection, New York; 535 SuperStock; 535 Künstler Enterprises; 536 Greg Ryan/Sally Beyer Photography; 540 Jedediah Smith in the Badlands, Harvey Dunn, The South Dakota Art Museum; 541 Brooklyn Museum of Art, New York, USA/Bridgeman Art Library; 541 (t) Greenwich Workshop Inc.; 542 National Frontier Trails Museum; 543 Private Collection /Bridgeman Art Library; 544 (l) Charles Mauzy/Corbis; 544 (r) John M. Roberts/Corbis; 545 Lowell Georgia/ Corbis; 546 Kennedy Galleries, New York, USA/Bridgeman Art Library; 546 The Granger Collection, New York; 548 Denver Public Library, Western History Collection, X-11929; 548 Courtesy of The Hubbard Museum of the American West, Rusidoso Downs, New Mexico, Photographer: Cheryl D. Knobel; 549 Courtesy of The Hubbard Museum of the American West, Rusidoso Downs, New Mexico, Photographer: Cheryl D. Knobel; 549 Centerfire-rigged Western stock saddle, JP Mason, Leather, metal, wood, circa 1860, Museum of the American West Collection, Autry National Center, Purchase made possible by the McBean Family Foundation; 549 High Desert Museum; 550 Tim Thompson/Corbis; 551 Call number 1963.002:1350--FR, Courtesy of The Bancroft Library University of California, Berkeley/Bancroft Library, University of California, Berkeley; 552 Texas State Library & Archives Commission; 552 (inset) Texas State Library & Archives Commission; 554 (c) Texas State Library & Archives Commission; 554 (inset) US Postal Service Licensing Group; 555 National History Museum Mexico City/Dagli Orti/Art Archive; 555 Dagli Orti/TravelSite; 556 Tate Gallery, London/Art Resource, NY; 557 Haworth Art Gallery, Accrington, Lancashire, UK/ Bridgeman Art Library; 558 Butler Institute of American Art, Youngstown, OH, USA/ Bridgeman Art Library; 560 (b) Chicago Historical Society, Chicago, USA/Bridgeman Art Library; 560 (t) Historical Art Prints; 561 (b) Private Collection/Bridgeman Art Library; 561 (l) Picture History; 561 (r) The Granger Collection, New York; 562 Dave G. Houser/Corbis; 564 Hulton Archive/Getty Images; 565 Dianne Arndt/SuperStock; 566 Larry Sheerin; 570 SuperStock; 572 Museum of the City of New York/Corbis; 573 National Portrait Gallery, Smithsonian Institution/Art Resource, NY; 574 (c) National Portrait Gallery, Smithsonian Institution/Art Resource, NY; 574 (t) Andre Jenny/Alamy Images; 575 The Granger Collection, New York; 576 SuperStock; 579 US Postal Service Licensing Group; 579 Brooklyn Museum of Art, New York, USA/Bridgeman Art Library; 579 Historical Art Prints; 580 Virginia Swartzendruber/End of the Oregon Trail Interpretive Center; 580 (inset) Keith Buckley/End of the Oregon Trail Interpretive Center; 581 (tc) Gary Poush/ZUMA/End of the Oregon Trail Interpretive Center; 581 (tl) David Jensen; 581 (tr) Charles Haire/ SCPhotos/Alamy Images; 582 Smithsonian Institution, NNC, Jeff Tinsley

REFERENCE

R1 Bettmann/Corbis; R2 The Granger Collection, New York; R3 Bettmann/ Corbis; R4 The Granger Collection, New York; R4 The Granger Collection, New York; R4 The Granger Collection, New York; R5 Bettmann/Corbis; R5 Corbis; R6 SuperStock; R7 Künstler Enterprises; R7 A & L Sinibaldi/Stone/Getty Images; R8 Library of Congress, Prints & Photographs Division, Detroit Publishing Company Collection, [LC-USZC4-1584]; R9 Bettmann/Corbis; R10 Gary Conner/Index Stock Imagery; R11 Picture History; R12 Bettmann/Corbis; R13 Bettmann/Corbis; R13 Culver Pictures; R14 AP/Wide World Photos; R15 Henny Ray Abrams/AFP/Getty Images; R15 Allan Tannenbaum/The Image Works, Inc.; R16 Digital image © 1996 CORBIS; Original image courtesy of NASA; R17 Chip Henderson/Index Stock Imagery; R17 David Young-Wolff/PhotoEdit

All other photos from Harcourt School Photo Library and Photographers: KenKinzie, April Riehm and Doug Dukane.

All maps created by MAPQUEST.COM.

California History–Social Science Standards and Analysis Skills

CALIFORNIA STANDARDS

Source for California Standards: California Department of Education

History–Social Science Content Standards

United States History and Geography: Making a New Nation

Students in grade five study the development of the nation up to 1850, with an emphasis on the people who were already here, when and from where others arrived, and why they came. Students learn about the colonial government founded on Judeo-Christian principles, the ideals of the Enlightenment, and the English traditions of self-government. They recognize that ours is a nation that has a constitution that derives its power from the people, that has gone through a revolution, that once sanctioned slavery, that experienced conflict over land with the original inhabitants, and that experienced a westward movement that took its people across the continent. Studying the cause, course, and consequences of the early explorations through the War for Independence and western expansion is central to students' fundamental understanding of how the principles of the American republic form the basis of a pluralistic society in which individual rights are secured.

5.1 Students describe the major pre-Columbian settlements, including the cliff dwellers and pueblo people of the desert Southwest, the American Indians of the Pacific Northwest, the nomadic nations of the Great Plains, and the woodland peoples east of the Mississippi River.

5.1.1 Describe how geography and climate influenced the way various nations lived and adjusted to the natural environment, including locations of villages, the distinct structures that they built, and how they obtained food, clothing, tools, and utensils.

5.1.2 Describe their varied customs and folklore traditions.

5.1.3 Explain their varied economies and systems of government.

(continued)

5.2 Students trace the routes of early explorers and describe the early explorations of the Americas.

5.2.1 Describe the entrepreneurial characteristics of early explorers (e.g., Christopher Columbus, Francisco Vásquez de Coronado) and the technological developments that made sea exploration by latitude and longitude possible (e.g., compass, sextant, astrolabe, seaworthy ships, chronometers, gunpowder).

5.2.2 Explain the aims, obstacles, and accomplishments of the explorers, sponsors, and leaders of key European expeditions and the reasons Europeans chose to explore and colonize the world (e.g., the Spanish Reconquista, the Protestant Reformation, the Counter Reformation).

5.2.3 Trace the routes of the major land explorers of the United States, the distances traveled by explorers, and the Atlantic trade routes that linked Africa, the West Indies, the British colonies, and Europe.

5.2.4 Locate on maps of North and South America land claimed by Spain, France, England, Portugal, the Netherlands, Sweden, and Russia.

5.3 Students describe the cooperation and conflict that existed among the American Indians and between the Indian nations and the new settlers.

5.3.1 Describe the competition among the English, French, Spanish, Dutch, and Indian nations for control of North America.

5.3.2 Describe the cooperation that existed between the colonists and Indians during the 1600s and 1700s (e.g., in agriculture, the fur trade, military alliances, treaties, cultural interchanges).

5.3.3 Examine the conflicts before the Revolutionary War (e.g., the Pequot and King Philip's Wars in New England, the Powhatan Wars in Virginia, the French and Indian War).

5.3.4 Discuss the role of broken treaties and massacres and the factors that led to the Indians' defeat, including the resistance of Indian nations to encroachments and assimilation (e.g., the story of the Trail of Tears).

5.3.5 Describe the internecine Indian conflicts, including the competing claims for control of lands (e.g., actions of the Iroquois, Huron, Lakota [Sioux]).

5.3.6 Explain the influence and achievements of significant leaders of the time (e.g., John Marshall, Andrew Jackson, Chief Tecumseh, Chief Logan, Chief John Ross, Sequoyah).

(continued)

5.4 Students understand the political, religious, social, and economic institutions that evolved in the colonial era.

5.4.1 Understand the influence of location and physical setting on the founding of the original 13 colonies, and identify on a map the locations of the colonies and of the American Indian nations already inhabiting these areas.

5.4.2 Identify the major individuals and groups responsible for the founding of the various colonies and the reasons for their founding (e.g., John Smith, Virginia; Roger Williams, Rhode Island; William Penn, Pennsylvania; Lord Baltimore, Maryland; William Bradford, Plymouth; John Winthrop, Massachusetts).

5.4.3 Describe the religious aspects of the earliest colonies (e.g., Puritanism in Massachusetts, Anglicanism in Virginia, Catholicism in Maryland, Quakerism in Pennsylvania).

5.4.4 Identify the significance and leaders of the First Great Awakening, which marked a shift in religious ideas, practices, and allegiances in the colonial period, the growth of religious toleration, and free exercise of religion.

5.4.5 Understand how the British colonial period created the basis for the development of political self-government and a free-market economic system and the differences between the British, Spanish, and French colonial systems.

5.4.6 Describe the introduction of slavery into America, the responses of slave families to their condition, the ongoing struggle between proponents and opponents of slavery, and the gradual institutionalization of slavery in the South.

5.4.7 Explain the early democratic ideas and practices that emerged during the colonial period, including the significance of representative assemblies and town meetings.

5.5 Students explain the causes of the American Revolution.

5.5.1 Understand how political, religious, and economic ideas and interests brought about the Revolution (e.g., resistance to imperial policy, the Stamp Act, the Townshend Acts, taxes on tea, Coercive Acts).

5.5.2 Know the significance of the first and second Continental Congresses and of the Committees of Correspondence.

5.5.3 Understand the people and events associated with the drafting and signing of the Declaration of Independence and the document's significance, including the key political concepts it embodies, the origins of those concepts, and its role in severing ties with Great Britain.

5.5.4 Describe the views, lives, and impact of key individuals during this period (e.g., King George III, Patrick Henry, Thomas Jefferson, George Washington, Benjamin Franklin, John Adams).

(continued)

5.6 Students understand the course and consequences of the American Revolution.

5.6.1 Identify and map the major military battles, campaigns, and turning points of the Revolutionary War, the roles of the American and British leaders, and the Indian leaders' alliances on both sides.

5.6.2 Describe the contributions of France and other nations and of individuals to the outcome of the Revolution (e.g., Benjamin Franklin's negotiations with the French, the French navy, the Treaty of Paris, The Netherlands, Russia, the Marquis Marie Joseph de Lafayette, Tadeusz Kósciuszko, Baron Friedrich Wilhelm von Steuben).

5.6.3 Identify the different roles women played during the Revolution (e.g., Abigail Adams, Martha Washington, Molly Pitcher, Phillis Wheatley, Mercy Otis Warren).

5.6.4 Understand the personal impact and economic hardship of the war on families, problems of financing the war, wartime inflation, and laws against hoarding goods and materials and profiteering.

5.6.5 Explain how state constitutions that were established after 1776 embodied the ideals of the American Revolution and helped serve as models for the U.S. Constitution.

5.6.6 Demonstrate knowledge of the significance of land policies developed under the Continental Congress (e.g., sale of western lands, the Northwest Ordinance of 1787) and those policies' impact on American Indians' land.

5.6.7 Understand how the ideals set forth in the Declaration of Independence changed the way people viewed slavery.

(continued)

5.7 Students describe the people and events associated with the development of the U.S. Constitution and analyze the Constitution's significance as the foundation of the American republic.

5.7.1 List the shortcomings of the Articles of Confederation as set forth by their critics.

5.7.2 Explain the significance of the new Constitution of 1787, including the struggles over its ratification and the reasons for the addition of the Bill of Rights.

5.7.3 Understand the fundamental principles of American constitutional democracy, including how the government derives its power from the people and the primacy of individual liberty.

5.7.4 Understand how the Constitution is designed to secure our liberty by both empowering and limiting central government and compare the powers granted to citizens, Congress, the president, and the Supreme Court with those reserved to the states.

5.7.5 Discuss the meaning of the American creed that calls on citizens to safeguard the liberty of individual Americans within a unified nation, to respect the rule of law, and to preserve the Constitution.

5.7.6 Know the songs that express American ideals (e.g., "America the Beautiful," "The Star Spangled Banner").

(continued)

5.8 Students trace the colonization, immigration, and settlement patterns of the American people from 1789 to the mid-1800s, with emphasis on the role of economic incentives, effects of the physical and political geography, and transportation systems.

5.8.1 Discuss the waves of immigrants from Europe between 1789 and 1850 and their modes of transportation into the Ohio and Mississippi Valleys and through the Cumberland Gap (e.g., overland wagons, canals, flatboats, steamboats).

5.8.2 Name the states and territories that existed in 1850 and identify their locations and major geographical features (e.g., mountain ranges, principal rivers, dominant plant regions).

5.8.3 Demonstrate knowledge of the explorations of the trans-Mississippi West following the Louisiana Purchase (e.g., Meriwether Lewis and William Clark, Zebulon Pike, John Fremont).

5.8.4 Discuss the experiences of settlers on the overland trails to the West (e.g., location of the routes; purpose of the journeys; the influence of the terrain, rivers, vegetation, and climate; life in the territories at the end of these trails).

5.8.5 Describe the continued migration of Mexican settlers into Mexican territories of the West and Southwest.

5.8.6 Relate how and when California, Texas, Oregon, and other western lands became part of the United States, including the significance of the Texas War for Independence and the Mexican-American War.

5.9 Students know the location of the current 50 states and the names of their capitals.

Kindergarten Through Grade Five

History–Social Science Content Standards

Historical and Social Sciences Analysis Skills

The intellectual skills noted below are to be learned through, and applied to, the content standards for kindergarten through grade five. They are to be assessed *only in conjunction with* the content standards in kindergarten through grade five.

In addition to the standards for kindergarten through grade five, students demonstrate the following intellectual, reasoning, reflection, and research skills:

Chronological and Spatial Thinking

1. Students place key events and people of the historical era they are studying in a chronological sequence and within a spatial context; they interpret time lines.
2. Students correctly apply terms related to time, including *past, present, future, decade, century,* and *generation.*
3. Students explain how the present is connected to the past, identifying both similarities and differences between the two, and how some things change over time and some things stay the same.
4. Students use map and globe skills to determine the absolute locations of places and interpret information available through a map's or globe's legend, scale, and symbolic representations.
5. Students judge the significance of the relative location of a place (e.g., proximity to a harbor, on trade routes) and analyze how relative advantages or disadvantages can change over time.

(continued)

Research, Evidence, and Point of View

1. Students differentiate between primary and secondary sources.
2. Students pose relevant questions about events they encounter in historical documents, eyewitness accounts, oral histories, letters, diaries, artifacts, photographs, maps, artworks, and architecture.
3. Students distinguish fact from fiction by comparing documentary sources on historical figures and events with fictionalized characters and events.

Historical Interpretation

1. Students summarize the key events of the era they are studying and explain the historical contexts of those events.
2. Students identify the human and physical characteristics of the places they are studying and explain how those features form the unique character of those places.
3. Students identify and interpret the multiple causes and effects of historical events.
4. Students conduct cost-benefit analyses of historical and current events.

Big Sur, California